SIDONIUS

II

420

SIDONIUS

POEMS AND LETTERS

WITH AN ENGLISH TRANSLATION BY

W. B. ANDERSON †

FORMERLY HULME PROFESSOR OF LATIN IN THE UNIVERSITY OF MANCHESTER

IN TWO VOLUMES

II

LETTERS, BOOKS III–IX

CAMBRIDGE, MASSACHUSETTS
HARVARD UNIVERSITY PRESS

LONDON
WILLIAM HEINEMANN LTD

MCMLXXXIV

American ISBN 0–674–99462–0
British ISBN 0 434 99420 0

First printed 1965
Reprinted 1984

Printed in Great Britain

CONTENTS

INTRODUCTION

Many people will be surprised to see that this second volume of the works of Sidonius, now first appearing in the Loeb series twenty-nine years after the publication of the first in 1936 has, like the first, the authorship of Professor W. B. Anderson, who died in 1959. During the latter part of his life he was working steadily on this his final task—the translation of Books III to IX of Sidonius' letters. He let us have long ago Book III of these complete, except notes on the subject-matter and on the Latin text, which I added after his death. Books IV to IX still remained in doubt. As the final years came upon him he grew more and more self-distrustful and more and more loath, so it seemed, to produce a complete volume which might be inferior. At last he told me that the translation was nearly finished, but that much was yet to be done. The last time I saw him in his rooms at St. John's College, Cambridge, I nearly had some of his material for books IV–IX in my hands; but he felt he could not give it to me; and, as I found later, he was justified in his gentle refusal.

After Anderson's death I secured, through the kindness of the authorities at St. John's College and of Dr. A. McDonald of Clare College, all the manuscript of Anderson's work on this second volume of Sidonius. On receiving the manuscript (some parts

of which had been revised by Anderson, but of which the greater part was in pencil, full of tentative corrections and alternative phrases, roughly written—sometimes scribbled—as a first draft with marginal queries and reminders), I handed it over to Professor W. H. Semple, who himself had worked on Sidonius and whose help in the preparation of Volume I Anderson had generously acknowledged in his Preface to that volume. Professor Semple, by the permission of the University of Manchester, had the secretarial assistance of Miss Joan Sutcliffe, who, having been Anderson's secretary in his Manchester days, had the skill to decipher his handwriting and was able to make a typed copy of his work with all its corrections, alternatives, and notes. This copy Professor Semple redacted to a firm translation, testing every line against the Latin, critically selecting the most suitable from among Anderson's variant renderings, and here and there (with the permission of the Editors) shaping the tentative English phrasing into a more formal style such as Anderson, we believe, would have finally approved; and sometimes, but rarely (as is indicated in our footnotes) it was necessary to recast a passage, or to provide a translation for a passage entirely omitted. But it should be affirmed that in the main the work is Anderson's own—a second example of his magisterial scholarship in this field. The completed draft of the translation Professor Semple handed over to us for the addition of such *apparatus criticus* and such historical and explanatory notes as would make this a true companion volume to the first. The Editors would therefore wish to acknowledge the generous help which, both

in the redaction of the translation and in the scrutiny of the proofs, Anderson's old Department of Latin in the University of Manchester and, above all, Professor Semple himself, have given *pietatis causa.* The translation, after the time when I received it from Professor Semple, and with his approval, was in some places further changed by me and in a few by my colleague Professor L. A. Post.

There remained the tasks of adding to the translation footnotes (for Anderson had provided very few) and of preparing a Latin text with critical notes. A large number of English footnotes has now been added, and also a Latin text which is based on that of Luetjohann and that of Mohr but has no claim to be better than either's. For the text here presented and for the critical notes on this text I am wholly responsible; on pages 609 ff. will be found some Additional Notes on the text which should not be overlooked by critics and other scholars because it may be that a few suggestions made in them deserve a more prominent place in the book, while others might be justly refuted. Of the English footnotes and parts of footnotes, those to which *A.* is appended are by Anderson; those to which *W.H.S.* are appended are by Semple; all others, whether signed *E.H.W.* or unsigned, are by me. I acknowledge with thanks a number of improvements in fact and substance by my son B. H. Warmington, Reader in Ancient History in the University of Bristol, and several corrections by H. Huxley, Reader in Latin in the University of Manchester. In these footnotes I have included some of Anderson's musings; they contain a number of his last thoughts and comments, and

give hints of the difficulties which beset any interpreter of Sidonius' strange style.

To the details of the life and times of Sidonius, and of the Sidonian tradition and scholarship, as outlined already by Anderson in the first volume, should now be added especially the following:

Loyen, A. *Sidoine Apollinaire.* Tome I. Poèmes. Paris: Les Belles Lettres, 1960 (Budé).

Loyen, A. *Recherches historiques sur les Panégyriques de Sidoine Apollinaire.* Paris, 1942.

Loyen, A. *Sidoine Apollinaire et l'esprit précieux en Gaule aux derniers jours de l'empire.* Paris, 1943.

Haarhoff, T. J. *Schools of Gaul.* Johannesburg, 1958.

Rutherford, H. *Sidonius Apollinaris. L'homme politique, l'écrivain, l'évêque* . . . Thèse Clermont-Ferrand, 1938.

Chadwick, Nora. *Poetry and Letters in Early Christian Gaul.* Bowes and Bowes, 1955.

Jones, A. H. M. *The Later Roman Empire.* Three volumes. Oxford, 1964.

Stroheker, K. F. *Der senatorische Adel im spätantiken Gallien.* Tübingen, 1948.

A detailed survey of the transmission of Sidonius' published work so far as it can be deduced from the extant MSS. was not given in our Volume I; nor can it be provided here. But to the short account given by Anderson in his introduction to that Volume I add the following. It has long been agreed among scholars that, of the many MSS. of all or part of

Sidonius' work, less than fifty are of any serious importance; and that we need hardly go outside the codices *LMTCFP* (see Volume I of Sidonius in the Loeb series, pp. lxviii–lxix) to establish a " Sidonian " text. But I have fulfilled Anderson's intention to continue taking account of the readings in the Codex Remensis known as *R* (which may once have contained all Sidonius' works but is now available for the Epistulae only and was not used by Luetjohann or by Mohr) in the light of Malcolm Burke's useful study of it and of the other chief MSS. (*De Apollinaris Sidonii Codice Nondum Tractato*, Munich, 1911).[1] I have also noted readings in codd. *N* and *V*. Burke's tentative " stemma codicum " of the Epistulae (see his p. 17) may be accepted (instead of Leo's on p. XLI of Luetjohann's edition of Sidonius in *Monumenta Germaniae Historica, Auct. Antiquiss. Tom. VIII*)[2]; according to it, cod. *L* and cod. *N* are connected with each other in near ancestry; so it seems are *R* and *V*; so are *MTCFP*. Apparently the source of all extant MSS. recording the Epistulae was a lost MS. whose defects were partly remedied from another lost MS. by ancestors of codd. such as *MTCFP*. For the Carmina we have to rely on five MSS. only—*MTCFP*.

[1] Users of Burke's dissertation should beware of some serious misprints in it, particularly on its p. 6, where III. 39 should be III. 8. 3 fin., and at the top of p. 11, where, in lines four and five, IV should be IX.

[2] Anderson, on p. lxvii of the first volume of the Loeb Sidonius, refers to the " stemma " of Burke and the first " stemma " of Leo, but by a lapse of memory treats these two " stemmata " as if they applied to the Carmina as well as to the Epistulae.

Leo (*op. cit.*, p. XLIII) gives for the Carmina a separate "stemma codicum" which we may accept. According to it, all these manuscripts come ultimately from a lost archetype; but *M* is derived from a lost intermediary (which contained the Epistulae also) better than the lost intermediaries from which *TCFP* are derived. Our material for Sidonius' published work as a whole can reasonably be traced back to two main sources: (i) a damaged MS. containing the Epistulae only; and (ii) a MS. containing the Carmina and also probably the Epistles; but the whole, it is agreed, comes ultimately from one lost archetype only. Of "Sidonian" MSS. in Great Britain some are of no importance; and even such as contain all Sidonius' work—Codex Regius 4. B. IV in the British Museum and the very closely related Codex Bodleianus Rawl. G. 45 at Oxford [1]—do not repay scrutiny. But one of the British MSS. is in a wholly different class of value. Therefore I have examined cod. *L*—the Codex Laudianus lat. 104 in the Bodleian Library—with special reference to some doubtful places in the text. It does not contain the Carmina, but for Sidonius' Epistulae it is reasonably claimed to be the best MS.; yet, though neatly written, it betrays a "common" Latin speaker rather than a "cultured" or learned one. The writing in what survives of Book IX of the Epistulae is a little different from that in the earlier books, but the same man, it seems to me, wrote the whole codex. I feel that he was approaching old age, and

[1] Codex Bodleianus Digby B.N.6, now called MS Digby 61, also once had all Sidonius' works, but is mutilated.

that some sclerosis or hardening of the lenses of his eyes made him keep them close to his " copy " and to his own handwriting, so as to get clear images; but that now and again he held his head higher for a few moments and thus caused some blurring of his vision and so caused also some of the wrong writing which he did not notice and revise. It may be also that his speed, though usually level, was fairly fast. The final part of the MS. does not exist, and the surviving part ends with the word *levis* (in *Ep.* IX. 7. 3) [1] in the course of a sentence, at the end of the bottom line of leaf now numbered 102. The last leaf, however, of the codex as we have it is leaf now numbered 103, containing *Ep.* VIII. 12. 5 *bicoloribus*—VIII. 13. 4 *aperuerit.* This misplaced leaf 103 should come between leaves now numbered and placed 96 and 97.

Of the nine codices *LNRVMTCFP*, only *TCFP* have all the Carmina; *M* has only the first eight; *LNRV* lack all of them. In the Epistulae the following are the most important omissions and gaps.[2] I. 1 and 2: absent from *V*. 1. 7. 5 *hanc*—I. 7. 7 *curandam*: absent from *R*. III. 3. 7 and 8: absent from

[1] I very much doubt whether it is right to believe (with *e.g.* Leo *op. cit.*, p. XXXIII) that this abrupt ending of *L* indicates the abrupt ending of the MS. from which the writer of *L* made his copy. His writing indicates clearly that he continued on another leaf. His source may well have been damaged at its own end; but surely one or more leaves are now missing from the end of *L* itself.

[2] On omissions that appear to be intentional see especially Mommsen in Luetjohann's edition of Sidonius (*Monumenta* etc. as cited above) page XXV; on causes of some other omissions see Burke *op. cit.* pp. 19 ff.

LNVRT. III. 5 and 6 and 7: absent from *T*. IV. 24. 2 *verum et*—IV. 25. 1 *cupientem*: absent from *R*. VI. 5 and 6 and 7: absent from *N*. VI. 12. 2 *terseris*—end of letter: absent from *LNVRT* (from *R* from *verecundia quam* onwards). VII. 1 and 2 and 3 and 4: absent from *LNVRT*. VII. 5. 1–2 as far as (*sacro*)*sanctam*: absent from *LNVRT*. VII. 6 and 7: absent from *LNVRTP*. VII. 9. 9 *everberat*—VII. 9. 18 (*consilio*)*siore*: absent from *R*. VII. 18. 4 *hic licebat*—end of letter: absent from *LNVT*. VIII. 2: absent from *LNVRT*. VIII. 4. 2 *Narbonensibus* onwards and all succeeding letters (*i.e.* to IX. 16): absent from *R*. VIII. 12. 8 *confligant* onwards and all succeeding letters: absent from *V*. VIII. 14 except the end: absent from *N*. IX. 1: absent from *LNT*. IX. 4 and 5 and part of 6: absent from *N*. IX. 7 and all succeeding letters: absent from *NT*. IX. 7. 3 *ac modis* onwards and all succeeding letters: absent from *L*.

Further study of the manuscripts and of the language of Sidonius may well lead to improvements in the Latin text of Sidonius' work where it is now admittedly corrupt or is later found to be so. But the common urge to emend should normally confine itself to suggestions; and some people will feel that some of the emendations of modern scholars which I have admitted into the present text ought to have remained among the suggestions and that a conservative critic is the wisest unless he is very expert indeed. Be that as it may, it is right to say that Sidonius is in need of explanation rather than emendation. It is our hope that this volume, which is a memorial of W. B. Anderson, has made a con-

tribution to both needs. This Introduction was finished and signed on the fifth anniversary of Anderson's death.

E. H. Warmington

Birkbeck College (University of London), Malet Street, London W.C.1

9th December 1964

LETTERS OF GAIUS SOLLIUS APOLLINARIS SIDONIUS

BOOKS III–IX

GAI SOLLII APOLLINARIS SIDONII EPISTVLARVM

LIBER TERTIVS

I

SIDONIVS AVITO SVO SALVTEM

1. Multis quidem vinculis caritatis ab ineunte pueritia quicquid venimus in iuventutem gratiae sese mutuae cura nexuerat, primum quia matribus nostris summa sanguinis iuncti necessitudo, dein quod ipsi isdem temporibus nati magistris usi, artibus instituti lusibus otiati, principibus evecti stipendiis perfuncti sumus; et, quod est ad amicitias ampliandas his validius efficaciusque, in singulis quibusque personis vel expetendis aequaliter vel cavendis iudicii parilitate certavimus. 2. propter

* Published, it seems, separately. The first letter of it was written about A.D. 471 after Sidonius was made bishop (see p. 4, n. 2). Other letters in it fall within the years 461–474. The book contains allusions to the sieges of Clermont during 471–474 by the Visigoths, to whom all Auvergne was ceded in 475. In 475 and 476 Sidonius was in exile and confinement; in 476 he went to Bordeaux, returning to Clermont during the same year (see pp. 441 ff.). Not before 477 could he have had

LETTERS OF GAIUS SOLLIUS APOLLINARIS SIDONIUS

BOOK III *

I

SIDONIUS TO HIS DEAR AVITUS, GREETING

1. Right from our earliest boyhood to our present stage of manhood our earnest desire for mutual regard had bound itself with many chains of affection: first, because our mothers were united by the closest tie of kindred blood; then because we were born in the same times, studied under the same teachers, were trained in the same accomplishments, amused ourselves with the same sports, received advancement under the same emperors and passed through the same state service; added to all this was a force which is even more powerful and effective in strengthening friendships—I mean that in seeking no less than in avoiding intimacy with such and such individuals our judgments always coincided. 2. For

inducement or opportunity to publish the book. Cf. C. Stevens, *Sidonius Apollinaris*, 145 ff.; 170; 197 ff. Avitus of the first letter was a kinsman it seems of the Emperor Eparchius Avitus and of Sidonius, that emperor's son-in-law. In *Carm.* XXIV. 75–79 Sidonius refers to the recipient of this letter as "our Avitus," and as "friend."

quae omnia (praetereo[1] conscientiam, quae interius tibi longe praestantior eminentiorque) multum voluntates nostras copulaverat decursarum forinsecus actionum multitudo.[2] sed, quod fatendum est, diu erectis utrimque amoris machinis ipse culmina pretiosa posuisti ecclesiam Arverni municipioli, cui praepositus, etsi immerito, videor, peropportuna oblatione locupletando; cuius possessioni plurimum contulisti Cuticiacensis praedii suburbanitate, non minus nostrae professionis fraternitatem loci proximitate dignatus ditare quam reditu. 3. et licet sororiae hereditatis duo consortes esse videamini, exemplo tamen fidei tuae superstes germana commota est ad boni operis imitationem. itaque tibi caelitus iure redhibetur tui facti meritum, alieni incitamentum. quo fit ut reperiare dignissimus quem divinitas inusitato successionum[3] genere sublimet; quae tamen nec diu distulit religiosam devotionem centuplicatis opulentare muneribus quaeque, ut confidimus, nihilo segnius caelestia largietur, cum terrena

[1] praetereo *Anderson*: praeter.
[2] multitudo *L*: similitudo.
[3] successuum *LNT*.

---

[1] So Anderson, following the more logical reading *multitudo* of the good MS codex Laudianus. But other MSS have *similitudo*, similarity; and we have *similitudo* in the same kind of sentiment at *Ep*. V. 9. 1.

[2] The people Arverni lived in Auvergne, but this name Arverni was also given to their capital, formerly called Augustonemetum, the modern Clermont-Ferrand. Sidonius was enthroned here as Bishop of the Arverni not earlier than 469 nor later than 472. Cf. Mommsen, in *Monumenta Germaniae*

all these reasons (I say nothing of the sense of right, which your heart possesses in a far more excellent and outstanding degree) the large number[1] of public activities discharged by us knitted our sympathies very closely together. But (as I must admit) although the masonry of love had long been erected on both sides, it was you who set a costly coping upon it by enriching with your most timely donation the church of the little town of the Arverni[2] over which I, though unworthy, am now the reputed head. To the property of this church you have made a great contribution by your gift of the farm of Cuticiacum so near to the city; indeed the possession with which you have seen fit to enrich the brotherhood of our profession is valuable for its proximity no less than for the revenue which it gives. 3. And though both of you are formally partners in the inheritance from your deceased sister, yet you have set the example of devotion by which your surviving sister has been stirred to imitate the good work. Therefore heaven is justly bestowing a recompense for your generosity and also for the stimulus you have given to the generosity of another, and so it comes about that you are found most worthy to be exalted by the divine power through an unusual form of inheritance; that power has not waited long to enrich your pious devotion by rewarding you an hundredfold, and (as we trust) will as promptly bestow on you heavenly blessings, when it has

Historica. Auct. Antiquiss. Tom. VIII. p. xlviii; L. Schmidt, *Geschichte der deutschen Stämme*, 264; O. M. Dalton, *The Letters of Sidonius*, Vol. I, p. xxxiv; Stevens, *Sid. Apoll.*, 113 ff.

iam solverit. Nicetiana namque, si nescis, hereditas Cuticiaci supernum pretium fuit. 4. quod restat, exposcimus ut sicut ecclesiae nostrae ita etiam civitatis aeque tibi sit cura communis, quae cum olim, tum debebit ex hoc praecipue tempore ad tuum patrocinium vel ob tuum patrimonium pertinere. quod cuius meriti esse possit, quippe si vestra crebro illud praesentia invisat, vel Gothis credite, qui saepenumero etiam Septimaniam suam fastidiunt vel refundunt, modo invidiosi huius anguli etiam desolata proprietate potiantur. 5. sed fas est praesule deo vobis inter eos et rempublicam mediis animo quietiora concipere,[1] quia, etsi illi veterum finium limitibus effractis omni vel virtute vel mole possessionis turbidae metas in Rhodanum Ligerimque proterminant, vestra tamen auctoritas pro dignitate sententiae sic partem utramque moderabitur ut et nostra discat quid debeat negare cum petitur et poscere adversa desinat cum negatur. vale.

[1] repetere *Par.* 2782.

---

[1] Flavius Nicetius, an eminent Arvernian; see VIII. 6, 2 ff.

[2] The district along the coast from the Pyrenees to the Rhône, including such important places as Narbo, Nemausus, and Tolosa. Its usual name had been Narbonensis Prima.

completed the payment of earthly benefits. For, let me tell you, your inheritance from Nicetius [1] was heaven's reward for your gift of Cuticiacum. 4. To conclude, we entreat of you to extend your protection to our community equally with our church; for now, not for the first time, but more than ever before, it will rightfully be under your patronage, if only because you have given it of your patrimony. What the value of that patrimony may be, at least if your presence deigns to pay it frequent visits, you may learn even from the Goths, for they often feel constrained to despise or renounce their own Septimania [2] for the prospect of gaining possession of this coveted corner, even though they should first lay it waste. 5. But it is proper that you, who stand between them and the Empire, should under God's guidance, devise more peaceful measures; for though they have broken through the frontier of their ancient possessions and are advancing the borders of their violent appropriation towards the Rhône and the Loire [3] with all the valour—or brute force—which they can command, your authoritative voice will exercise restraint upon both sides by virtue of the prestige attaching to your word, with the result that our side will learn what to refuse when asked, and our opponents will cease to demand when they get a refusal. Farewell.

[3] This seems to refer to Gothic incursions in the neighbourhood of Arles in A.D. 471. Avitus may have been commissioned to negotiate with Euric at this time. If so, he failed to effect a settlement. An army under Anthemius marched against Euric and was totally defeated. See Stevens, pp. 149 f., 204. For Euric see p. 90.

II

SIDONIVS CONSTANTIO SVO SALVTEM

1. Salutat populus Arvernus, cuius parva tuguria magnus hospes implesti, non ambitiosus comitatu sed ambiendus adfectu. deus bone, quod gaudium fuit laboriosis cum tu sanctum pedem semirutis moenibus intulisti! quam tu ab omni ordine sexu aetate stipatissimus ambiebare! quae salsi erga singulos libra sermonis! quam te blandum pueri, comem iuvenes, gravem senes metiebantur! quas tu lacrimas ut parens omnium super aedes incendio prorutas et domicilia semiusta fudisti! quantum doluisti campos sepultos ossibus insepultis! quae tua deinceps exhortatio, quae reparationem suadentis [1] animositas! 2. his adicitur quod, cum inveneris civitatem non minus civica simultate quam barbarica incursione vacuatam, pacem omnibus suadens caritatem illis, illos patriae reddidisti. quibus tuo monitu non minus in unum consilium quam in unum oppidum revertentibus muri tibi debent plebem

[1] suadens *F*.

* The probable date of this letter is A.D. 473 or 474. Constantius was a priest of Lyon. Cf. *Ep*. I. 1; VII. 18; VIII. 16; II. 10.3; IX. 16.1

[1] See the preceding letter, n. 2 on p. 4.

II

SIDONIUS TO HIS FRIEND CONSTANTIUS,* GREETING

1. The community of the Arverni [1] greet you, the mighty guest, who have filled their humble cottages with your presence, not seeking to amaze by your retinue, but worthy of being sought after through your kindliness.[2] Merciful God, what a joy it was to the harassed folk when you set your sacred foot within our half-demolished walls! What dense crowds surrounded you of every class, sex and age! How nicely you adjusted your piquant remarks to suit the individuals you addressed! How winning the children considered you, how courteous the young people, how impressive their elders! What tears you shed, as if you were the father of us all, over buildings levelled by fire and houses half-burnt![3] How you lamented the fields buried under the bones of the unburied! And then how animating was your encouragement, what a great spirit you showed in urging them to rebuild! 2. It is your further merit that, finding the city made desolate no less by civic dissension than by barbarian assault, you pressed reconciliation upon all, and so restored kind feeling to the people and the people to the service of their city. It was at your admonition that they returned not only to a united town but also to a united policy, and to you the walls owe the

[2] We have *ambiendus* . . . *ambitiosus* in VII. 9.22 also.

[3] In all probability this refers to buildings outside the walls damaged or destroyed by the Visigoths.

reductam, plebs reducta concordiam. quocirca satis te toti suum, satis se toti tuos aestimant; et, quae gloria tua maxima est, minime falluntur. 3. obversatur etenim per dies mentibus singulorum quod persona aetate gravis infirmitate fragilis, nobilitate sublimis religione venerabilis solius dilectionis obtentu abrupisti tot repagula, tot obiectas veniendi difficultates, itinerum videlicet longitudinem brevitatem dierum, nivium copiam penuriam pabulorum, latitudines solitudinum angustias mansionum, viarum voragines aut umore imbrium putres aut frigorum siccitate tribulosas, ad hoc aut aggeres saxis asperos aut fluvios gelu lubricos aut colles ascensu salebrosos aut valles lapsuum adsiduitate derasas;[1] per quae omnia incommoda, quia non privatum commodum requirebas, amorem publicum rettulisti. 4. quod restat, deum precamur ut aevi metis secundum vota promotis bonorum amicitias indefessim expetas capias referas sequaturque te adfectio quam relinquis, et initiatae per te ubicumque gratiae longum tibi redhibeantur quam fundamenta tam culmina. vale.

[1] taediosas *Wilamowitz*: *fort.* ruderatas *Luetjohann*: desperatas *coni. Warmington*: *cf.* Additional Notes, p. 609.

return of their people, to you the returned people their harmony. And so one and all feel that you are theirs, and they are yours: and it is your crowning glory that they are not mistaken. 3. For day after day there is a picture before the mind of each, how you, a personage weighed down by years and frail through ill-health but exhalted in birth and venerable for your piety, with no pretext but that of affection broke through all the obstacles and all the hindrances in the way of your coming, I mean the length of the stages and the shortness of the days, the superabundance of snow and the scarcity of provisions, the wide expanse of the solitudes and the cramped space of the rest-houses; sloughs in the road, here rotten with soaking rain, there made jagged by dry frost; besides these, the rough stones of the causeways and the slippery ice of the streams, rugged hills to climb and valleys scoured by continual landslides; through all which discomforts, as you sought no private advantage, you won the love of a people. 4. To conclude, we pray God that the limits of your life may be advanced in accordance with your hopes, and that you may without interruption seek, win, and carry away with you the friendly feelings of good men, and that the affection which you are leaving behind you may attend you hereafter, and that not only the foundations but the completed edifice of that harmony which you have instituted in this or that part of the land may for many years bring you a due recompense. Farewell.

III

SIDONIVS ECDICIO SVO SALVTEM

1. Si quando, nunc maxume Arvernis meis desideraris, quibus dilectio tui immane dominatur, et quidem multiplicibus ex causis: primum quod summas in adfectu partes iure sibi usurpat terra quae genuit, dein quod saeculo tuo solus ferme mortalium es qui patriae non minus desiderii nasciturus quam gaudii natus feceris; astipulantur assertis materni quondam puerperii tempora, quae proficiente conceptu concordantibus civium votis numerabantur. 2. omitto illa communia quidem, sed quae non mediocria caritatis incitamenta sunt, istius tibi reptatas caespitis glaebas. praetereo quod haec primum gramina incessu, flumina natatu, venatu nemora fregisti. omitto quod hic primum tibi pila pyrgus, accipiter canis, equus arcus ludo fuere. mitto istic ob gratiam pueritiae tuae undique gentium confluxisse studia litterarum tuaeque personae quondam debitum quod sermonis Celtici squamam depositura nobilitas nunc oratorio stilo, nunc etiam Camenalibus modis imbuebatur. 3. illud in te adfectum principaliter universitatis accendit, quod, quos olim Latinos fieri ex-

* Son of the emperor Avitus and brother of Sidonius' wife Papianilla. Cf. *Ep.* II. 1; II. 2.15; V. 16.1; *Carm.* XX; and introduction to Vol. I of the Loeb Sidonius, p. xxix. During the sieges of Clermont by the Visigoths (Stevens, 130 ff., 197 ff.–202), he had forced a way into the city, probably in A.D. 471.

III

SIDONIUS TO HIS DEAR ECDICIUS,* GREETING

1. Now, if ever, you are wanted by my Arvernians, who have an overmastering love for you, and this for manifold reasons: first, because the land which has begotten one rightly claims the chief place in one's affections; secondly, because in your generation you are almost the only man who has given his native town as much longing in the prospect of his birth as delight in its occurrence. This statement is borne out by what happened when, as your natal day approached, the passage of time was anxiously counted amid the unanimous prayers of the citizens. 2. I say nothing of the commonplace fact (though such a thing is no slight incentive to affection) that this is the land on whose sward you made your first ventures in crawling. I refrain from pleading that here you first broke through the grass by walking, the streams by swimming, the woods by hunting. I do not remind you that here you began to amuse yourself with ball and dice-box, hawk and hound, horse and bow; I make no mention of the congregation of learning assembled from all parts of the world for the benefit of your youthful years, and that at one time it was due to you personally that the leading families, in their efforts to throw off the scurf of Celtic speech, were initiated now into oratorical style and now again into the measures of the Muses. 3. What chiefly kindles the devotion of the whole community to you is that after first requiring them to become Latins you

egeras, barbaros deinceps esse vetuisti. non enim potest umquam civicis pectoribus elabi, quem te quantumque nuper omnis aetas ordo sexus e semirutis murorum aggeribus conspicabantur, cum interiectis aequoribus in adversum perambulatis et vix duodeviginti equitum sodalitate comitatus aliquot milia Gothorum non minus die quam campo medio, quod difficile sit posteritas creditura, transisti. 4. ad nominis tui rumorem personaeque conspectum exercitum exercitatissimum stupor obruit ita ut prae admiratione nescirent duces partis inimicae quam se multi quamque te pauci comitarentur. subducta est tota protinus acies in supercilium collis abrupti, quae cum prius applicata esset oppugnationi, te viso non est explicata congressui. interea tu caesis quibusque optimis, quos novissimos agmini [1] non ignavia sed audacia fecerat, nullis tuorum certamine ex tanto desideratis solus planitie quam patentissima potiebare, cum tibi non daret tot pugna socios quot solet mensa convivas. 5. hinc iam per otium in urbem reduci quid tibi obviam processerit officiorum plausuum, fletuum gaudiorum, magis temptant vota conicere quam verba reserare. siquidem cernere

[1] agminis *coni. Gustafsson.*

---

[1] Of Arverni = Augustonemetum (Clermont-Ferrand).
[2] Ten, says Gregory of Tours, *Hist. Franc.* II. 16 (24).

next prevented them from becoming barbarians. For never can the hearts of our citizens cease to cherish the memory of the noble and great man they beheld in you, as every age and class and both sexes watched you from the ruined ramparts [1] not long ago, when you traversed with no backward look the level ground that intervened, and with a following of barely eighteen [2] mounted comrades you made your way through several thousands of Goths not merely in the middle of the day, but in the middle of an open plain—an achievement such as posterity will hardly credit. 4. At the mere mention of your name and sight of your person a well-seasoned army was so utterly astounded that the enemy generals in their amazement could not realise how many were their followers and how few were yours. The whole army was at once withdrawn to the brow of a precipitous hill, and, though previously employed in a storming assault, was not deployed for an encounter after sighting you. Meanwhile, after slaying their best men, who were in the rear of the march owing to their courage, not owing to their cowardice, you, without suffering the loss of a single one of your company in this formidable conflict, were left in sole possession of an exceedingly wide stretch of plain; and yet in that battle you did not have as many comrades as your table generally has guests. 5. Next you proceeded to make your way back in leisurely fashion to the town. What a procession went out to meet you—what homage and plaudits, what tears and rejoicings! It was a scene which thought can more readily essay to imagine than words to describe. The crowded halls of your spacious palace presented

erat refertis capacissimae domus atriis illam ipsam felicissimam stipati reditus tui ovationem, dum alii osculis pulverem tuum rapiunt, alii sanguine ac spumis pinguia frena suscipiunt, alii sellarum equestrium madefacta sudoribus fulcra resupinant, alii de concavo tibi cassidis exituro flexilium lamminarum vincla diffibulant, alii explicandis ocrearum nexibus implicantur, alii hebetatorum caede gladiorum latera dentata pernumerant, alii caesim atque punctim foraminatos circulos loricarum digitis livescentibus metiuntur. 6. hic licet multi complexibus tuorum tripudiantes adhaerescerent, in te maximus tamen laetitiae popularis impetus congerebatur; tandemque in turbam inermem quidem veneras sed de qua te nec armatus evolveres; ferebasque nimirum eleganter ineptias gratulantum et, dum inruentum tumultuoso diriperis amplexu, eo condicionis accesseras piissimus publici amoris interpres ut necesse esset illi uberiorem referre te gratiam qui tibi liberiorem fecisset iniuriam. 7. taceo deinceps collegisse te privatis viribus publici exercitus speciem parvis extrinsecus maiorum opibus adiutum et infreniores [1] hostium ante discursus castigatis cohercuisse populatibus. taceo

[1] infreniores *Mohr*, infrenes *Buecheler*: inferiores.

---

[1] The date of this exploit seems to be A.D. 471.

the same spectacle of a return acclaimed by an encircling multitude. Some kissed away the dust which covered you, others caught the bridle that was thick with blood and foam; some turned back the pommels of the horses' saddles, which were bathed in sweat, others, when you wished to free your head from the skull-piece of the helmet, unclasped the bands of pliant steel; some entangled themselves in disentangling the fastenings of your greaves; some counted the dents on the edges of swords blunted with slaughter; others by forcing in their envious fingers measured the holes made by blade and point amid the rings of the cuirasses. 6. Then, though many, as they danced for joy, hugged your followers in a close embrace, still the main impact of the popular exultation was concentrated upon you. True, you had at last come into the midst of an unarmed crowd, but, armed though you were, it was a crowd from which you could not escape. To be sure, you bore the stupidities of your welcomers with a good grace, and although you were being torn in pieces by the riotous embrace of the throng that swooped upon you, your loyal heart had recognised the universal affection beneath it all, and you had brought yourself to such a frame of mind that you felt bound to make the most cordial acknowledgment to the man who did you the most outrageous violence. 7. I will not tell how you next collected with your private means a sort of public army,[1] with only small help from outside, furnished by great men, and how you punished the enemy's pillagings and put a stop to his promiscuous forays, which had formerly been quite unchecked. I do not recount how by frequent

te aliquot superventibus cuneos mactasse turmales e numero tuorum vix binis ternisve post proelium desideratis et tantum calamitatis adversae parti[1] inopinatis certaminibus inflictum ut occulere caesorum numerositatem consilio deformiore meditarentur. siquidem quos humari nox succincta prohibuerat decervicatis liquere cadaveribus, tamquam minoris indicii foret quam villis[2] agnosci crinitum dimisisse truncatum. 8. qui postquam luce revoluta intellexerunt furtum ruinae suae crudeli vilitate patuisse, tum demum palam officiis exsequialibus occupabantur, non magis cladem fraude quam fraudem festinatione celantes; sic tamen quod nec ossa tumultuarii caespitis mole tumulabant, quibus nec elutis vestimenta nec vestitis sepulchra tribuebant, iuste sic mortuis talia iusta solventes. iacebant corpora undique locorum plaustris convecta rorantibus, quae, quoniam perculsis indesinenter incumberes, raptim succensis conclusa domiciliis culminum superlabentum rogalibus fragmentis funerabantur. 9. sed quid ego istaec iusto plusculum garrio, qui laborum tuorum non ex asse historiam texere sed pro parte memoriam facere praesumpsi,

[1] parti *Mohr*: partis.

[2] quem non velis *Engelbrecht*: quem nolles *Luetjohann*: quam villis *codd. cf.* Additional Notes, p. 609.

surprises you annihilated phalanxes of cavalry, without suffering the loss of more than two or three of your men on each occasion; or how you inflicted so much damage upon the opposing side by your unexpected attacks that they designed a rather hideous ruse to disguise the number of the slain; that is to say, they decapitated the bodies of all the men whose burial was prevented by the shortness of the night, and left them thus, imagining that less would be revealed if one abandoned a man in a headless state than if he were to be recognized by the tufts of hair on his head! 8. It was only when daylight returned and they realised that their attempt to disguise their disaster had actually been made plain by their savage baseness, that they began to concern themselves openly with the offices of burial, trying now to hide their deception by hurry, just as they had tried to hide their losses by deception; yet this they did in such fashion that they did not even erect over the remains any mass of hastily piled earth, nor did they wash the bodies and then clothe them and consign them thus clothed to tombs, very properly according such casual dues to men killed in such a way. The bodies lay where they had been conveyed from all quarters on dripping waggons, and, since you never slackened in your pursuit of the routed fugitives, these corpses were hastily enclosed in various houses, to which fire was set, and so they got their obsequies, with fragments of collapsing roofs to form their pyre. 9. But why this rather excessive chatter about these things, when I had no presumptuous idea of composing a complete history of your achievements, but only meant to

quo magis crederes votis tuorum, quorum exspectationi aegrescenti nulla salubrius ociusque quam tui adventus remedia medicabuntur? igitur, si quid nostratium precatibus adquiescis, actutum in patriam receptui canere festina et adsiduitatem tuam periculosae regum familiaritati celer exime, quorum consuetudinem expertissimus [1] quisque flammarum naturae bene comparat, quae sicut paululum a se remota inluminant, ita satis sibi admota comburunt. vale.

IV

SIDONIVS FELICI SVO SALVTEM

1. Gozolas natione Iudaeus, cliens culminis tui, cuius mihi quoque esset persona cordi, si non esset secta despectui, defert litteras meas, quas granditer anxius exaravi. oppidum siquidem nostrum quasi quandam sui limitis obicem circumfusarum nobis gentium arma terrificant. sic aemulorum sibi in medio positi lacrimabilis praeda populorum, suspecti Burgundionibus, proximi Gothis, nec impugnantum

[1] expertissimus *Leo*: spectatissimus.

---

[1] This was probably written in A.D. 475. Ecdicius was made Patrician and *magister militum* by the Emperor Iulius Nepos in 474 but recalled to Italy and dismissed in 475. See W. Ensslin, *Klio*, XXIV (1931) pp. 495–496.

* Magnus Felix (son of the Magnus of I. 11.10 and *Carm.* 23.455) of Narbonne, a school-fellow of Sidonius and who became Praetorian Prefect of Gaul. Cf. *Ep.* II. 3; III. 7;

recall them in some measure, in order to convince you more deeply of the desires of your friends, whose hearts are sick with waiting for you and cannot get any remedy which will heal them so quickly and effectively as your arrival? So, if you consent to the petitions of your townsmen, hasten at once to sound a retreat back to your native town, and be quick to withdraw your duteous attendance from the dangerous intimacy of princes;[1] for the most experienced observers well compare their friendship to the behaviour of flames, which illuminate what is a little way off, but consume that which comes within their reach. Farewell.

IV

SIDONIUS TO HIS FRIEND FELIX,* GREETING

1. Gozolas,[2] a Jew by nationality and a dependent of your Excellency—a man whom I too should like as a person, if I did not despise his religious faith—brings you a letter from me, which I have penned in great anxiety; for the armed bands of the tribes that surround us are terrifying our town, which they regard as a sort of barrier restricting their frontiers. So we are set in the midst of two rival peoples and are become the pitiable prey of both; suspected by the Burgundians, and next neighbours of the Goths, we are spared neither the fury of our invaders nor

IV. 5; IV. 10; *Carm.* 9; 24, 91. Stevens, 196–197. Sidonius dedicated his poems to him.

[2] Cf. *Ep.* IV. 5.1.

ira, nec propugnantum caremus invidia. 2. sed istinc alias. interea, si vel penes vos recta sunt, bene est. neque enim huiusmodi pectore sumus, ut, licet apertis ipsi poenis propter criminum occulta plectamur, non agi prospere vel ubicumque velimus. nam certum est non minus vitiorum quam hostium esse captivum, qui non etiam inter mala tempora bona vota servaverit. vale.

V

SIDONIVS HYPATIO SVO SALVTEM

1. Si vir spectabilis morumque vestrorum suspector admiratorque Donidius solam rationem domesticae utilitatis habuisset, satis abundeque sufficeret fides vestra commodis suis, etsi nullus intercessor accederet. sed amore meo ductus est, ut, quod ipse per se impetraverat, me faceret postulare. itaque nunc honori vestro hic quoque cumulus accrescit, quod duo efficimur debitores, cum tamen unus e nobis beneficium consequatur. 2. Eborolacensis praedii etiam ante barbaros desolatam medietatem, quae domus patriciae iura modo respicit, suffragio vestro

[1] The invaders were the Visigoths, the "protectors" were the Burgundians who were jealous of the Visigoths.

* Nothing further is known of Hypatius.

[2] See II. 9; VI. 5. For *spectabilis* and other honorific epithets, see A. H. M. Jones, *The Later Roman Empire*, Vol.

the malignity of our protectors.[1] 2. But this subject I will continue another day. Meanwhile, if things go well at least with you, I rejoice: for we are not of the spirit that does not welcome prosperity in any part of the world, although we ourselves are being visited with glaring penalties for obscure offences. Indeed it is certain that he who in times of distress does not maintain his friendly wishes for others is the prisoner of his failings as much as of his enemies. Farewell.

V

SIDONIUS TO HIS FRIEND HYPATIUS,* GREETING

1. If the eminent Donidius,[2] an ardent admirer of your character, had considered nothing but his private advantage, your sense of honour would have been enough and more than enough to make his interests secure without any additional pressure from an intermediary. But he has been led by his love for me to make me ask as a favour what he would certainly have secured by himself. And so to crown your prestige you have the two of us becoming your debtors, though it is only one of us who wins the favour. 2. A moiety of the estate of Eborolacum,[3] a part which was left waste even before the barbarians came, and which now acknowledges a patrician house as its owners, he desires with your

I, pp. 143, 161, 282, 378; II. 528 ff., 542, 551–2, 641; III. 151–153.

[3] Ébreuil on the Sioule, near Gannat.

iuri[1] suo optat adiungi. neque ad hanc nundinationem stimulo cupiditatis sed respectu avitae recordationis adducitur. siquidem fundi ipsius[2] integritas familiae suae dominium usque in obitum vitrici nuper vita decedentis aspexit; nunc autem vir alieni non appetens, sui parcus possessionis antiquae a se alienatae non tam damno angitur quam pudore; quam ut redimere conetur non avaritiae vitio sed verecundiae necessitate compellitur. 3. tribuere dignare votis suis, precibus meis, moribus tuis, ut ad soliditatem ruris istius te patrocinante perveniat, cui rem parentum sibique non solum notam verum etiam inter lactantis infantiae rudimenta reptatam sicut recepisse parum fructuosum, sic non emeruisse nimis videtur ignavum. ego vero tantum obstringar indultis ac si meae proficiat peculiariter proprietati, quicquid meus aetate frater professione filius, loco civis fide amicus acceperit. vale.

[1] ruri *coni. Gustafsson.*
[2] istius *Luetjohann.*

assistance to have added to his own domain. He is not incited to this trafficking by the spur of greed, but by his cherished recollections of his ancestors. In fact the whole of the estate saw subjection to the lordship of his family till the recent death of his step-father; but now Donidius, who is no coveter of other men's property but a thrifty manager of his own, is hurt not so much by the loss of an old family possession, now alienated from him, as by a feeling of shame; and in attempting to regain it he is impelled not by the vice of avarice but by the irresistible power of self-respect. 3. Deign to satisfy his desires, my prayers, and your own disposition by enabling him by your advocacy to arrive at the complete possession of that estate; it was his parents' property, and he not only knows it well but it is the spot where, in his babyhood, he made his first efforts at crawling; so he feels that although to have got it back will mean little profit for him, not to have worked for that end would show a poor spirit. I shall be as much indebted to you for this favour as if my own private estate reaped the profit of any benefit received by this man, who is my brother in years, my son[1] by religious profession, a fellow-citizen by domicile, and a friend by his loyalty. Farewell.

[1] He means that his bishopric enables him to regard Donidius as a son.

VI

SIDONIVS EVTROPIO SVO SALVTEM

1. Si veteris commilitii, si deinceps innovatae per dies gratiae bene in praesentiarum fides vestra reminiscitur, profecto intellegitis ut vos ad dignitatum sic nos ad desideriorum culmina ascendere. ita namque fascibus vestris gratamur omnes, ut erectam per illos non magis vestram domum quam nostram amicitiam censeamus. testis est ille tractatus in quo exhortationis meae non minimum incitamenta valuerunt. 2. quibus vix potuistis adduci ut praefecturam philosophiae iungeretis, cum vos consectanei vestri Plotini dogmatibus inhaerentes ad profundum intempestivae quietis otium Platonicorum palaestra rapuisset, cuius disciplinae tunc fore adstruxi liberam professionem, cum nil familiae debuisses.[1] porro autem desidiae vicinior putabatur contemptus ille militiae, ad quam iactitant lividi bonarum partium viros non posse potius quam nolle conscendere. 3. igitur, quod loco primore fieri par

[1] debuisses *LRPNM*: debuisset *CFM*[2]*N*[1]: *om. hanc ep. T.*

---

* Not the Bishop of Orange of *Ep.* VI. 6. See I. 6, which is the "homily" referred to in § 1. This letter congratulates Eutropius on his Praetorian Prefecture of Gaul in succession *c.* 470 to Magnus Felix of letter 4, above.

[1] The expression *in praesentiarum,* a contraction of *in*

VI

SIDONIUS TO HIS FRIEND EUTROPIUS,* GREETING

1. If your true heart has at the present moment [1] a faithful recollection of our companionship in the public service in old days and of our constant renewal of friendly relations since then, you certainly understand that as you rise to the heights of official distinction I rise to the summit of my desire. For we all rejoice with you in your new elevation with the feeling that your family and our friendship are alike advanced. As evidence there is that homily of mine with its rousing exhortation, which has had a splendid effect. 2. Yet even these appeals were hardly able to induce you to combine the charge of a province with your philosophical studies, for you were absorbed in the dogmas of your master Plotinus,[2] and the school of the Platonists had swept you towards the profound inactivity of an unseasonable quietism. I showed that the liberty to profess such a doctrine would only come when you no longer owed a debt to your family. And further, your contempt for the public service was looked upon as being rather akin to indolence, for our jealous detractors are fond of saying that men of the sound party lack the strength rather than the desire to reach these posts. 3. So then, as it is right to do at the outset, we give

praesentia rerum, occurs several times in Sidonius in the sense " at the present time."

[2] Famous Neo-Platonist philosopher (A.D. 204–270) whose philosophical system is known from his extant treatises.

est, agimus gratias uberes Christo, qui statum celsitudinis tuae ut hactenus parentum nobilitate decorabat, ita iam nunc titulorum parilitate fastigat; simul et animorum spebus erectis fas est de cetero sperare meliora. certe creber provincialium sermo est annum bonum de magnis non tam fructibus quam potestatibus existimandum. qua de re vestrum est, domine maior, exspectationem nostram competentibus dispositionibus munerari. nam memor originis tuae nobilium sibi persuasit universitas, quamdiu nos Sabini familia rexerit, Sabiniani familiam non timendam. vale.

VII

SIDONIVS FELICI SVO SALVTEM

1. Longum a litteris temperatis. igitur utrique nostrum mos suus agitur: ego garrio, vos tacetis. unde etiam, vir ad reliqua fidei officia insignis, genus reor esse virtutis tanto te otio non posse lassari. ecquid numquamne [1] respectu movebere familiaritatis antiquae, ut tandem a continuandi [2] silentii proposito pedem referas? aut [3] nescis quia

[1] numquamne *LMC*: nūquam ne* (*litt. erasa*) P^1: nūquam (ne *inducto*) *F*: numquam nec *Luetjohann*.
[2] continuati *MCFP*: *om. hanc ep. T*.
[3] an *coni. Gustafsson*.

---

[1] *domine maior* seems to occur in Sidonius only. See Vol. I (Loeb) pp. 330–331, n.
[2] Sabinus was evidently a well known ancestor of Eutropius. But the allusion in Sabinianus is unknown. A Sabinianus was *magister militum per Illyricum* in the 470s.

abundant thanks to Christ, for He had hitherto glorified your Eminence's condition by the exalted rank of your ancestors, and now He is crowning it with a career of like distinction for yourself. Moreover, with our hearts' hopes thus uplifted it is reasonable to hope for better times ahead. Certainly it is an everyday saying of provincials that a good year should be judged by the greatness not of its harvests but of the governing powers. And so, my honoured lord,[1] it is yours to reward our expectations by a fitting administration. For the whole body of our nobility, remembering the race from which you are sprung, is convinced that so long as the family of Sabinus provides our governors, we need not fear the family of Sabinianus.[2] Farewell.

VII

SIDONIUS TO HIS FRIEND FELIX,* GREETING

1. For a long time you have refrained from writing. Each of us then observes his own practice: I chatter, you keep silence. And so, as you are conspicuously diligent in the performance of every other obligation that a sense of duty imposes, I really think that your tireless endurance of that long inactivity must be a kind of virtue. Will you never be moved by regard for our old intimacy to shift from your resolution of perpetual silence? Or do you not know that to give no answer to a chatterer

* See letter 4 of this book. The present letter was written towards the end of A.D. 474.

garrulo non respondere convicium est? tu retices vel bybliothecarum medius vel togarum et a me officium paupertini sermonis exspectas, cui scribendi, si bene perspicis, magis est facilitas quam facultas. 2. certe vel metus noster materiam stilo tuo faciat, mementoque viatorum manus gravare chartis, quatinus amicorum cura relevetur, et indicare festina, si quam praevio deo quaestor Licinianus trepidationi mutuae ianuam securitatis aperuerit. persona siquidem est, ut perhibent, magna exspectatione maior adventu, relatu sublimis inspectione sublimior et ob omnia felicitatis naturaeque dona monstrabilis. 3. summa censura, par comitas et prudentia fidesque misso mittentique conveniens; nihil adfectatum simulatumque, ponderique sermonum vera potius severitas quam severitatis imitatio; et nec, ut plurimi, qui cum credita diffidenter allegant, volunt videri egisse se [1] cautius, sed neque ex illo, ut ferunt, numero qui secreta dirigentium principum venditantes ambiunt a barbaris bene agi cum legato potius quam cum legatione. 4. hunc nobis morum viri tenorem secundus rumor invexit. mandate perniciter, si vero dicta conquadrant, ut tantisper a pervigili statione respirent quos a murali-

[1] se *secl. Luetjohann, fortasse recte.*

---

[1] He was *quaestor sacri palatii* and was sent by the Emperor Iulius Nepos (A.D. 474–5) to investigate and settle the difficulties of the Arvernians with their Visigothic neighbours. He brought with him the patent of the Patriciate for Ecdicius (V. 16. 1). His mission had little success.

is to revile him? You, deep in your library or immersed in civil business, you never write me a line: but from me you expect the service of a letter, a jejune letter—from me who (a perceptive critic will note) have a facility, not a faculty, for composition. 2. At least let our anxieties, if nothing else, provide material for your pen; take care to load the arms of travellers with despatches, so that the cares of your friends may be lightened, and do not delay to inform us whether under God's guidance Licinianus[1] the quaestor has opened any door of safety to our joint alarm. People say that he is a person who inspires large expectations and exceeds them all when he appears, who is exalted in repute but rises still higher on acquaintance, a man remarkable for every endowment of fortune and of nature. 3. He is very strict, but no less courteous and wise, and he shows a conscientiousness which befits the emissary as much as the master who sends him. There is no affectation or pretence about him, and his weighty deliverances show genuine rectitude not a mere imitation of it. He is not like most people, who deliver with an air of hesitation the message with which they are charged and expect to be considered to have acted cautiously; still less, I am told, is he of the number of those who traffic in the secrets of the princes who instruct them and who seek to secure from the barbarians favourable treatment for the envoy rather than for his mission. 4. This is the general trend of the man's character which favourable report has conveyed to us. Write promptly if what is said about him squares with the truth, that our guards may get some little respite

bus excubiis non dies ninguidus, non nox inlunis et turbida receptui canere persuadent; quia, etsi barbarus in hiberna concedat, mage differunt quam relinquant[1] semel radicatam corda formidinem. palpate nos prosperis, quia nostra non tam procul est a vobis causa quam patria. vale.

VIII

SIDONIVS EVCHERIO SVO SALVTEM

1. Veneror antiquos, non tamen ita ut qui aequaevorum[2] meorum virtutes aut merita postponam. neque si Romana respublica in haec miseriarum extrema defluxit, ut studiosos sui numquam remuneretur, non idcirco Brutos Torquatosque non pariunt saecula mea. "quorsum istaec?" inquis. de te mihi ad te sermo est, vir efficacissime, cui debet respublica quod supra dictis solutum laudat historia. 2. quapropter ignari rerum temeraria

[1] relinquent *F*: relinquunt *Luetjohann*.

[2] ut qui aequaevorum *cdd.*: non tamen, ita ut quidam, aequaevorum *Geisler*: ut utique aequaevorum *Leo*: ut coaequaevorum *Wouweren*.

---

[1] The Visigoths, besieging Clermont on and off.

* Cf. VII. 9.18—not St. Eucherius, Bishop of Lyon, of *Ep*. IV. 3.7. The present Eucherius was a *vir inlustris* (VII. 9. 18; A. H. M. Jones as cited at *Ep*. III. 5.1). There is no doubt that he was the Eucherius who after Euric had gained control of Auvergne was wrongly put to death by the governor Count Victorius the pro-Gothic Roman. Chaix, II. 74; Duchesne, *Fastes Épisc*. II. 117.

[2] This Brutus is L. Iunius Brutus who according to a dubious Roman tradition played a leading part in the ex-

from their persistent watch; for at present neither snowy days nor moonless and stormy nights persuade them to beat any retreat from their posts on the walls, because, even if the barbarian[1] retires to winter quarters, the heart only suspends and would not throw off a terror which has once struck deep its roots. Soothe us then with good tidings, for our cause is not so remote from you as our town. Farewell.

VIII

SIDONIUS TO HIS FRIEND EUCHERIUS,* GREETING

1. I reverence the ancients, but not so much as to underrate by comparison the qualities or the good services of my contemporaries. Even though the Roman commonwealth has sunk to such an extremity of helplessness that it no longer rewards those who are devoted to it, it does not follow that my times never give birth to a Brutus or a Torquatus.[2] "What are you driving at?" you ask me. I am speaking to you about yourself, you marvel of efficiency, for the state owes you the recognition which history praises it for having paid to the above-named persons. 2. So let those who do not understand the facts

pulsion of the Tarquins and the foundation of the Roman republic dated by tradition in 509 B.C.; not M. Iunius Brutus, one of the "liberators" of Rome by the murder of Julius Caesar in 44 B.C. Torquatus would be T. Manlius Torquatus chosen dictator twice (353, 349 B.C.) and consul thrice (347, 344, 340 B.C.); champion of Rome against the Gauls of those days and against the Latins and Campanians.

iudicia suspendant nec perseverent satis aut suspicere praeteritos aut despicere praesentes; quandoquidem facile clarescit rempublicam morari beneficia vos mereri. quamquam mirandum granditer non sit, natione foederatorum [1] non solum inciviliter Romanas vires administrante verum etiam fundamentaliter eruente, si nobilium virorum militariumque et supra vel spem nostrae vel opinionem partis adversae bellicosorum non tam defuerint [2] facta quam praemia. vale.

IX

SIDONIVS RIOTHAMO SVO SALVTEM

1. Servatur nostri consuetudo sermonis; namque miscemus cum salutatione querimoniam, non omnino huic rei studentes, ut stilus noster sit officiosus in titulis, asper in paginis, sed quod ea semper eveniunt de quibus loci mei aut ordinis hominem constat

[1] f(a)eneratorum *MCFP*.
[2] defuerint *MCFP*: defuerunt.

[1] Rome was forced to admit foreigners into Roman territory as *foederati*, who received lands from Roman landowners (see Vol. I of the Loeb Sidonius, page x, n. 2; A. H. M. Jones, *The Later Roman Empire*, II, 611–612). Thus of the German Franks who dwelt between the Main and the North Sea, Salian Franks became *foederati* after the middle of the fourth century A.D., between the Meuse and the Scheldt. In A.D. 413 Burgundians of the Upper Main who had crossed the Rhine were allowed as *foederati* to live in the province of Upper Germany; later, Goths were allowed as *foederati* to settle in

suspend hasty judgments, and not persist unduly in looking up to men of the past or looking down on those of the present; for it is clear as daylight that though the commonwealth defers recognition, you deserve it. However, it is no great wonder, at a time when a horde of Federates [1] is not only controlling the resources of Rome in a tyrannous spirit but even destroying them at their foundations, that men of noble birth and military experience, who show fighting qualities which surpass both our hopes and our opponents' calculations, have failed not so much in their services as in the attainment of rewards for them. Farewell.

IX

SIDONIUS TO HIS FRIEND RIOTHAMUS,* GREETING

1. Here is a letter in my usual style, for I combine complaint with greeting, not with an express intention of making my pen respectful in its superscription but harsh in the letter itself, but because things are always happening about which it is obviously impossible for a man of my rank and cloth to speak without incurring unpleasantness or to be silent without

Gaul and then, not later than A.D. 439, established the independent Visigothic kingdom. Cf. Semple *Qu. Exeg.* 17–19.

* Riothamus was king of Aremorica—see note 1 on p. 36. He helped in resisting the Visigoths, but was defeated at Bourg-de-Déols near Châteauroux and driven from his kingdom by Euric, King of the Visigoths about A.D. 469. Riothamus took refuge with the Burgundians and Euric became master of Tours, Bourges and much of Aquitanica Prima.

inconciliari, si loquatur, peccare, si taceat. sed et ipsi sarcinam vestri pudoris inspicimus, cuius haec semper verecundia fuit, ut pro culpis erubesceretis alienis. 2. gerulus epistularum humilis obscurus despicabilisque etiam usque ad damnum innocentis ignaviae mancipia sua Britannis clam sollicitantibus abducta deplorat. incertum mihi est an sit certa causatio; sed si inter coram positos aequanimiter obiecta discingitis,[1] arbitror hunc laboriosum posse probare quod obicit, si tamen inter argutos armatos tumultuosos, virtute numero contubernio contumaces poterit ex aequo et bono solus inermis, abiectus rusticus, peregrinus pauper audiri. vale.

X

SIDONIVS TETRADIO SVO SALVTEM

1. Plurimum laudis iuvenes nostri moribus suis applicant quotiens de negotiorum[2] meritis ambigentes ad peritorum consilia decurrunt, sicuti nunc vir clarissimus Theodorus, domi quidem nobilis, sed modestissimae conversationis opinione generosior, qui per litteras meas ad tuas litteras, id est ad

[1] discingetis *Leo*.
[2] negotiorum suor̄ *T*.

---

[1] The inhabitants of Aremorica, between the Seine and the Loire, came to be called Britanni during Sidonius' lifetime owing to the settlement there of many S. Britons fleeing from the Saxons. Those mentioned in this letter were presumably followers of Riothamus.

* Of Arles; see *Carm.* XXIV. 81.

[2] See Vol. I. p. 400, n. 2. A. H. M. Jones as cited at III. 5.1.

incurring guilt. However, I am a direct witness of the conscientiousness which weighs on you so heavily, and which has always been of such delicacy as to make you blush for the wrongdoing of others. 2. The bearer of this letter, who is humble and obscure, and so unassertive that he might even be taxed with harmless indolence, complains that his slaves have been enticed from him by underhand persuasions of certain Bretons.[1] I cannot say whether his complaint is just: but if you bring the opponents face to face and impartially unravel their contentions, I fancy that this poor fellow is likely to make good his plaint, that is, if amid a crowd of noisy, armed, and disorderly men who are emboldened at once by their courage, their number, and their comradeship, there is any possibility for a solitary unarmed man, a humble rustic, a stranger of small means, to gain a fair and equitable hearing. Farewell.

X

SIDONIUS TO HIS FRIEND TETRADIUS,* GREETING

1. Our young men reflect great credit on their character when, being uncertain how they stand in certain matters of business, they have recourse to the counsels of the experienced. So it is at the present moment with Theodorus, a man of the class of Honourable,[2] who is a nobleman by birth, but also has the still higher rank derived from the reputation of a well-disciplined life. With my letter to introduce him, he is now betaking himself, with laudable

meracissimum scientiae fontem laudabili aviditate proficiscitur, non modo reperturus illic ipse quod discat sed et forsitan relaturus inde quod doceat. 2. cui contra potentes factiososque, si vestra peritia non abundanter opitularetur, prudentia consulta sufficeret. respondete, obsecramus, nisi vobis tamen utriusque nostrum sociae preces oneri fastidiove reputabuntur, iudicio suo, testimonio meo et substantiam causamque supplicis fluctuantem medicabilis responsi salubritate fulcite. vale.

XI

SIDONIVS SIMPLICIO SVO SALVTEM

1. Etsi desiderium nostrum sinisteritas tanta comitatur ut etiam nunc nostris invidearis obtutibus, non idcirco is es, virorum optime, de cuius nos moribus lateant celsa memoratu: ita cuncti nostrates idemque summates viri optimarum te exactissimarumque partium praestantissimum patremfamilias consono praeconio prosequuntur. 2. adstipulatur huic de te sententiae bonorum vel sic electus gener vel educta sic filia; in quorum copula tam felicem tibi controversiam vota pepererunt ut ambigas utrum

* Of Vaison, apparently a kinsman of Sidonius. Cf. V. 4; IV. 4 and 7 and 12; VII. 4.

eagerness, to your lettered erudition, that is, to the purest possible fount of knowledge, in the hope not only of finding there something for himself to learn but also perhaps of carrying away something to teach others. 2. Even if your own experience did not supply abundant means of helping him to confront men of powerful position and busy intriguers, your discreet wisdom would amply suffice for this purpose. Do, I pray you (unless our united petitions seem to you a burden and an annoyance), make a fitting response to his discrimination in your favour and to my testimony, and sustain the drooping estate and cause of your petitioner by the wholesomeness of a curative reply. Farewell.

XI

SIDONIUS TO HIS KINSMAN SIMPLICIUS,* GREETING

1. Although such ill luck dogs my longing for your presence that my eyes are still grudged a sight of you, that, most excellent of men, does not mean that I have missed the superlative accounts of such a character as yours; so zealously do all the leaders of our land acclaim you in chorus as a paragon among fathers of the best and most particular class. 2. This opinion that good men hold of you is confirmed both by your choice of a son-in-law and by your bringing-up of your daughter: indeed the good wishes called forth by their union have raised an enviable problem for you, and you cannot decide whether you have achieved the greater success in your selection or in

iudicio an institutione superaveris. sed tamen hinc vel maxume, parentes ambo venerabiles, este securi: idcirco ceteros vincitis, quod vos filii transierunt. igitur dona venia litteras primas, quas ut necdum mittere desidia fuerat, ita vereor ne sit misisse garrulitas. carebit sane nostrum naevo loquacitatis officium si exemplo recursantis alloquii impudentiam paginae praesentis absolveris. vale.

XII

SIDONIVS SECVNDO SVO SALVTEM

1. Avi mei, proavi tui tumulum hesterno (pro dolor!) die paene manus profana temeraverat; sed deus adfuit, ne nefas tantum perpetraretur. campus autem ipse dudum refertus tam bustualibus favillis quam cadaveribus nullam iam diu scrobem recipiebat; sed tamen [1] tellus, humatis quae superducitur, redierat in pristinam distenta planitiem pondere nivali seu diuturno imbrium fluxu sidentibus acervis: quae fuit causa ut locum auderent tamquam vacantem corporum baiuli rastris funebribus impiare. 2. quid plura? iam niger caespes ex viridi, iam supra anti-

[1] sed iam *Luetjohann*.

* Secundus is not mentioned elsewhere. See the first note on § 5 of this letter.

[1] Apollinaris, Praetorian Prefect of Gaul under Constantine III in 408. He was apparently buried in the cemetery by the church built at Lyon by Patiens (see *Ep.* II. 10.2 ff.; IX. 3.5) and later named church of St Justus (cf. *Ep.* V. 17. 3).

your training. But of one thing above all you may rest assured, right worthy parents both: the point in which you excel all others is that your children have surpassed you. Be so good then as to pardon my writing first, for though delaying to send the letter would have implied neglect, yet I fear that to have sent it may amount to garrulity. But my friendly attention will be cleared of the blemish of loquacity if you acquit the present sheet of impertinence by sending me a sample of correspondence in return. Farewell.

XII

SIDONIUS TO HIS DEAR SECUNDUS,* GREETING

1. Yesterday, alas! a profane hand almost violated the tomb of him who was my grandfather [1] and your great-grandfather; but God helped us, and would not allow this great wickedness to be committed. The field of burial itself had for a long time been so filled up both with ashes from the pyres and with bodies that there was no more room for digging; but the earth which it is customary to pile upon the buried had spread out until the surface resumed its original flatness, the various heaps having gradually sunk down owing to the weight of snow and a long exposure to downpours of rain. And this was the reason that some coffin-bearers dared to desecrate the ground with grave-diggers' tools, imagining it to be free of bodies. 2. Well, I will cut my story short: the surface had changed

quum sepulchrum glaebae recentes, cum forte pergens urbem ad Arvernam publicum scelus e supercilio vicini collis aspexi meque equo effuso tam per aequata quam per abrupta proripiens et morae exiguae sic quoque impatiens, antequam pervenirem, facinus audax praevio clamore compescui. dum dubitant in crimine reperti dilaberentur an starent et superveni (confiteor errorem), supplicia captorum differre non potui, sed supra senis nostri ipsum opertorium torsi latrones, quantum sufficere posset superstitum curae, mortuorum securitati. 3. ceterum nostro quod sacerdoti nil reservavi, meae causae suaeque personae praescius in commune consului, ne vel haec iusto clementius vindicaretur vel illa iusto severius vindicaret. cui cum tamen totum ordinem rei ut satisfaciens ex itinere mandassem, vir sanctus et iustus iracundiae meae dedit gloriam, cum nil amplius ego venia postularem, pronuntians more maiorum reos tantae temeritatis iure caesos videri. 4. sed ne quid in posterum casibus liceat, quos ab exemplo vitare debemus, posco ut actutum me quoque absente tua cura sed

---

[1] See Ep. III. 1. n. on § 2.

[2] The meaning seems to be that he gave them their torture (the penalty which they had legally incurred) in the form of a flogging. See § 3.

[3] The bishop was perhaps Patiens, Bishop of Lyon.

from green to black, and fresh clods were already covering the ancient burial-place, when I, happening to be on my way to the Arvernian capital,[1] saw this offence against the community from the brow of a neighbouring hill. I gave the reins to my horse and galloped over level and steep ground alike, and even so was impatient at the slight delay in getting there; I therefore, before I reached the spot, stopped the wicked proceeding by sending a shout ahead of me. Whilst the offenders, thus caught in the act, were hesitating whether to slip away or hold their ground, I arrived on the scene. I could not persuade myself (I confess my indiscretion) to delay the punishment of my prisoners: so these robbers were tortured[2] over the very coffin of our ancestor, severely enough to satisfy the piety of the survivors and to secure peaceful rest to the dead. 3. But in not reserving any part of the case for our bishop's[3] decision, I had in view the claims both of my own cause and of his public character, and I acted in the interest of both: otherwise there might have been shown too much mercy to satisfy the first or too much severity to befit the second. Nevertheless, I sent him a full report of the incident whilst still on my journey, in the tone of one ready to make reparation; and he, being a holy and just man, awarded praise to my indignation when I only asked forgiveness, declaring that men guilty of such carelessness seemed to him rightly punished in accordance with the customs of our ancestors. 4. However, to leave no room for mischances in future (and after this warning we are bound to prevent them), I request you, without delay and without

meo sumptu resurgat in molem sparsa congeries, quam levigata pagina tegat. ego venerabili Gaudentio reliqui pretium lapidis operisque mercedem. carmen hoc sane, quod consequetur, nocte proxima feci, non expolitum, credo, quod viae non parum intentus. 5. quod peto ut tabulae, quantulumcumque est, celeriter indatur; sed vide ut vitium non faciat in marmore lapidicida; quod factum sive ab industria seu per incuriam mihi magis quam quadratario lividus lector adscribet. ego vero, si pio studio rogata curaveris, sic agam gratias quasi nil tibi quoque laudis aut gloriae accedat, quem patruo tuo remoto solida praesentis officii sollicitudo mansisset pro gradu seminis.

Serum post patruos patremque carmen
haud indignus avo nepos dicavi,
ne fors tempore postumo, viator,
ignorans reverentiam sepulti
tellurem tereres inaggeratam.
praefectus iacet hic Apollinaris,
post praetoria recta Galliarum
maerentis patriae sinu receptus,
consultissimus utilissimusque

[1] Cf. Ep. I. 4; I. 3.2.

[2] Secundus was perhaps really a grand-nephew of Sidonius' father, and therefore a first cousin once removed of Sidonius. Cf. Mommsen in *Monumenta Germaniae Historica. Auct. Antiquiss.* Tom. VIII, xlvii, xlix.

[3] The term *militia* was loosely used in Sidonius' time (A. H. M. Jones, *The Later Roman Empire*, I. 377–8, 507; II. 566). But here it might mean in fact military service in contrast with *forum* in the sense of non-military service.

even awaiting my return, to see that the material which has been scattered should be built up again, under your supervision but at my expense, ready to be covered by a smooth slab of stone. I have left in the hands of the venerable Gaudentius [1] money to pay both for the stone and for wages. The verse-inscription, which will be appended, I composed last night, perhaps a not very polished piece, as I was too much occupied with my journey. 5. But, for what it is worth, I should like you to have it promptly cut on the slab: and see that the mason makes no blunders on the marble: because if such a thing is done, whether from perversity or from carelessness, the malignant reader is sure to put it down to me rather than to the engraver. If, however, you attend to my request with pious care, I shall thank you as warmly as if you also did not gain some praise and glory by the act; for if I, your uncle,[2] had passed away, the entire responsibility for this duteous deed would have rested with you in virtue of your degree of relationship.

"This tardy legend I, a grandson, have with good right, now that my father and uncles are no more, dedicated to my grandsire, lest in after-time thou, wayfarer, knowing not that a tomb claims thy reverence, shouldst tread upon the unmounded earth. Here lies the prefect Apollinaris, received into the bosom of his mourning country after righteous governance of Gaul; a most wise and beneficent worker in the fields of the farm, the state,[3] and the forum, and likewise (perilous

ruris militiae forique cultor,
exemploque aliis periculoso
liber sub dominantibus tyrannis.
haec sed maxima dignitas probatur,
quod frontem cruce, membra fonte purgans
primus de numero patrum suorum
sacris sacrilegis renuntiavit.
hoc primum est decus, haec superba virtus,
spe praecedere quos honore iungas,
quique hic sunt titulis pares parentes,
hos illic meritis supervenire.

6. Novi quidem auctoris nostri non respondere doctrinae epitaphii qualitatem, sed anima perita musicas non refutat inferias. tibi quoque non decet [1] tardum videri quod heres tertius quartusque dependimus, cum tot annorum gyro voluto magnum Alexandrum parentasse manibus Achillis et Iulium Caesarem Hectori ut suo iusta solvisse didicerimus. vale.

XIII

SIDONIVS APOLLINARI SVO SALVTEM

1. Unice probo gaudeo admiror, quod castitatis adfectu contubernia fugis impudicorum, praesertim

[1] debet *T*.

---

[1] Or perhaps "holy water."

[2] In 334 B.C. Alexander the Great, on his way to overthrow the Persian power, visited the site of Troy and sacrificed to the

example for others to follow) a free man under the tyranny of despots. But of all his honours this is acclaimed the greatest, that he cleansed his brow with the cross, his body with the waters of baptism,[1] and was the first of his line to renounce pagan worship. 'Tis a crowning glory, a proud merit, for a man to surpass in hope his peers in rank and beyond the grave to excel in merits his fathers who are in this world his equals in their roll of dignities."

6. I am aware that the quality of this epitaph does not match the learning of our ancestor, but the soul of the cultured does not scorn a funeral offering from the Muses. Nor must you think this a belated tribute because we who pay it are in the third and fourth degrees of succession from him; for we have been taught that a long cycle of years passed before the great Alexander made his offering to the shades of Achilles or Julius Caesar performed funeral rites to Hector as one of his line.[2] Farewell.

XIII

SIDONIUS TO HIS DEAR APOLLINARIS,* GREETING

1. I feel the utmost satisfaction, joy, and admiration, inasmuch as your love of purity causes you to shun the society of lewd men, and especially of

shade of the Greek hero Achilles as Julius Caesar did three centuries later to that of the Trojan hero Hector.

* This show-piece probably does not allude to an actually existing person. The Apollinaris to whom it is addressed is the writer's son. Cf. V. 11.3; IX. 1.5.

quibus nihil pensi, nihil sancti est in appetendis garriendisque turpitudinibus quique, quod verbis inverecundis aurium publicarum reverentiam incestant, granditer sibi videntur facetiari. cuius vilitatis esse signiferum Gnathonem patriae nostrae vel maxumum intellege. 2. est enim hic gurges de sutoribus fabularum, de concinnatoribus criminum, de sinistrarum opinionum duplicatoribus, loquax ipse nec dicax ridiculusque nec laetus arrogansque nec constans curiosusque nec perspicax atque indecenter adfectato lepore plus rusticus; tempora praesentia colens, praeterita carpens, futura fastidiens; beneficii, si rogaturus est, importunus petendi derogator negati, aemulator accepti callidus reformandi, querulus flagitati garrulus restituti; at si rogandus, simulator parati dissimulator petiti, venditator [1] praestiti publicator occulti, calumniator morati infitiator soluti; 3. osor ieiuniorum, sectator epularum; laudabilem proferens non de bene vivente sed de bene pascente sententiam; inter haec tamen ipse avarissimus quemque non pascit tam panis bonus quam panis alienus, hoc solum comedens domi,

[1] venditator *coni. Mohr*: venditor.

---

[1] The "parasite" or sponger in Terence's extant *Eunuchus* which appeared first in 161 B.C. For *signifer* Anderson put "ringleader"; but the word seems rather to mean "forerunner," "original example."

those who let no consideration and no reverence restrain them as they pursue foul deeds and chatter about them, and who fancy that it is the height of wit to pollute the modest ears of the community with immodest language. Of this low behaviour, let me tell you, Gnatho[1] is the prime example in our country. 2. For he is a very cesspool fed by the concocters of gossip, the inventors of scandal, and the magnifiers of sinister imputations; he is a chatterer without wit, a buffoon without humour, assertive but not consistent, inquisitive but not discerning, and all the more awkward for his unseemly affectation of elegance. He is a devotee of the present, a carper at the past, and a scorner of the future. If he has occasion to ask a favour, he is a shameless beggar; if it is refused he belittles it, if it is granted he would do better; he is cunning in amending the terms, grumbles when repayment is demanded, and when he makes restitution talks a great deal about it. If, on the other hand, he is the person to be asked, he is good at ignoring the request and also at pretending he has supplied the need; he is wont to advertise any favour that he bestows, to make secret transactions public, to revile the slow payer and deny the receipt of payment. 3. He detests fasts but frequents feasts; he sounds the praises not of the man who lives well but of him who entertains well; and all the time he is a downright miser and one who lives not so much on good bread as on other men's bread; all that he eats in his own house is what he has sent there first, out of the dishes seized by him amidst a tempest of buffets. However, I must not entirely

si quid e raptis inter alaparum procellas praemisit obsoniis. sed nec est sane praedicabilis viri in totum silenda[1] frugalitas: ieiunat quotiens non vocatur; sed sic quoque levitate parasitica, si invitetur, excusans; si vitetur, explorans; si excludatur, exprobrans; si admittatur, exsultans; si verberetur, exspectans. 4. cum discubuerit, fertur actutum, si tarde comedat, in rapinas; si cito saturetur, in lacrimas; si sitiat, in querellas; si inebrietur, in vomitus[2]; si fatiget, in contumelias; si fatigetur, in furias; faeculentiae omnino par cloacali, quae quo plus commota, plus faetida est. ita vivens paucis voluptati, nullis amori, omnibus risui; vesicarum ruptor fractorque ferularum, bibendi avidus, avidior detrahendi, rabido pariter ore spirans caenum, spumans vinum, loquens venenum facit ambigi putidior, temulentior an facinorosior existimetur. 5. sed dicis: "animi probra vultu[3] colorat et deprecatur ineptiam[4] mentis qualitas corporis; elegans videlicet homo pervenustusque cuiusque sit spectabilis persona visentibus." enimvero illa[5] sordidior est atque deformior cadavere rogali quod facibus admotis semicombustum moxque sidente strue torrium devolutum reddere pyrae iam fasti-

[1] silendi *Luetjohann.*
[2] vomitus *edd.*: vomitum *edit. Wouweren.*: vomicas.
[3] vultus *Luetjohann.*
[4] ineptiam *NL*: ineptias.
[5] ille *Luetjohann.*

fail to mention the frugality of this truly praiseworthy gentleman. He fasts when he has received no invitation; but even so, when he gets an invitation he will show the characteristic waywardness of the parasite by making some demur. If he is avoided, he searches for an opening; if he is shut out, he becomes abusive; if he is let in, he is jubilant; if he is beaten, he bides his time. 4. When he has taken his place, if the meal is served late he straightway raids the viands; if he gets his fill quickly he bursts into tears; he breaks into protests if he is thirsty, into vomiting if he gets tipsy, into insults if he is bantering another, into frenzy if he himself is bantered. In short, he is just like the filth of a sewer, which stinks the more, the more you stir it. So he lives, giving pleasure to few, loved by none, laughed at by all, a man on whom bladders are burst [1] and birches broken, greedy of drinking and still more greedy of detraction, with a madman's mouth that breathes out filth and foams with wine and talks poison all at once. Thus he makes it a moot point whether he is to be reckoned most remarkable for stinking manners or drunkenness or roguery. 5. But you suggest: "He puts a gloss on the vileness of his disposition by his handsome face, and the style of his personal appearance makes excuse for the deficiency of his intelligence; in fact he is a man of elegance and winsome grace, and his person is such as to attract the admiring gaze of the onlooker." No: the fact is that it is fouler and uglier than a corpse on the pyre after the torches have been applied, when it is half-burnt and the pile of faggots collapses and it

[1] Cf. Seneca, *Nat. Quaest.*, II, 27.

diosus pollinctor exhorret. praeter hoc lumina gerit idem lumine carentia, quae Stygiae vice paludis volvunt lacrimas per tenebras. 6. gerit et aures immanitate barrinas, quarum fistulam biforem pellis ulcerosa circumvenit saxeis nodis et tofosis umore verrucis per marginem curvum protuberantibus. portat et nasum, qui cum sit amplus in foraminibus et strictus in spina, sic patescit horrori quod angustatur olfactui. praetendit os etiam labris plumbeum rictu ferinum, gingivis purulentum dentibus buxeum, quod spurcat frequenter exhalatus e concavo molarium computrescentum mephiticus odor, quem supercumulat esculenta ructatio de dapibus hesternis et redundantum sentina cenarum. 7. promit et frontem, quae foedissimo gestu cutem plicat supercilia distendit. nutrit et barbam, quae iam senectute canescens fit tamen morbo nigra Sullano. tota denique est misero facies ita pallida veluti per horas umbris maestificata larvalibus. taceo reliquam sui molem vinctam podagra pinguedine solutam. taceo cerebrum crebra vibice peraratum, quod parum amplius tegi constat capillis quam cicatricibus. taceo pro brevitate cervicis occipiti supinato scapularum adhaerere confinia. 8. taceo quia decidit honor umeris, decor bracchiis, robur lacertis. taceo chira-

[1] The *pollinctores* anointed and perfumed the dead and took casts of their faces for making portraits.

[2] So-called phthiriasis, probably venereal disease, though its existence in Europe of ancient times is not certain. Sulla, who made himself "dictator" at Rome, died in 78 B.C.

rolls down, nauseating even the undertaker's man,[1] so that he shrinks from replacing it. Besides this he has eyes devoid of light, which, like the pool of Styx, roll their tears onward through darkness. 6. Also he has ears elephantine in their vastness; the two apertures are encircled by ulcerated skin, and stony knots and warts oozing with pus project along the exterior curves. Also he carries a nose that is large in its openings and constricted at its bridge, gaping wide enough to give you the creeps, yet too narrow for the sense of smell. He displays a mouth with leaden lips and the ravening jaws of a wild beast, with festering gums and yellow teeth; it is frequently befouled by a mephitic stench exhaled from the hollow seat of decaying grinders; and this stench is reinforced by meaty belching from yesterday's feast and the sewage of suppers that keep coming back upon him. 7. He also shows a forehead which has a most disgusting trick of wrinkling the skin and stretching the eyebrows. He likewise grows a beard, which is already whitening with old age and yet blackening with Sulla's disease.[2] Again, the whole face of the wretch is as pale as if it were harassed every hour by disembodied shades. I say nothing of the rest of his heavy bulk, which is constricted by gout and relaxed by obesity. I say nothing of his scalp, which is ploughed by numerous weals and is beyond doubt covered as much by scars as by hairs. I will not mention that his neck is so short that the edges of the shoulder-blades cling to the back of his head when it is thrown back. 8. I pass over the fact that his shoulders have no comeliness, his arms no grace, his biceps no strength. I say

gricas manus unctis cataplasmatum pannis tamquam caestibus involutas. taceo quod alarum specubus hircosis atque acescentibus latera captiva vallatus nares circumsedentum ventilata duplicis Ampsancti peste funestat. taceo fractas pondere arvinae iacere mammas quasque foedum esset in pectore virili vel prominere, has ut ubera materna cecidisse. taceo ventris inflexi pendulos casses parti genitalium, quia debili, bis pudendae turpibus rugis turpius praebere velamen. 9. iam quid hic tergum spinamque commemorem? de cuius licet internodiorum fomitibus erumpens arcam [1] pectoris texat curvatura costarum, tota nihilominus haec ossium [2] ramosa compago sub uno velut exundantis abdominis pelago latet. taceo lumborum corpulentiam cluniumque, cui crassitudini comparata censetur alvus exilis. taceo femur aridum ac pandum, genua vasta poplites delicatos, crura cornea vitreos talos, parvos digitos pedes grandes. cumque distortis horreat ita liniamentis perque multiplicem pestilentiam exsanguis semivivusque nec portatus sedeat [3] nec sustentatus incedat, verbis tamen est ille quam membris exsecrabilior. 10. nam quamquam pruritu laborat sermonis inhonesti, tamen

[1] arcam *C*: aream.
[2] ossuum *MTV*, *fortasse recte*.
[3] sedeat *Luetjohann*: sentiat (senciat *C*).

nothing of his gouty hands, which are wrapped in oily rags of plasters, suggesting a boxer's thongs. I say nothing of the goatish, fetid caverns of the armpits, which imprison his sides with their ramparts, so that he mortifies his neighbour's nostrils by spreading abroad the plague of a double Ampsanctus.[1] I do not mention that his breasts are flaccid and depressed by a weight of fat, and hang down like a mother's paps, though for a man's breast even to protrude at all would have been disgusting enough. I say nothing of his belly curving in pendulous folds, its wrinkles, ugly in themselves, making a still uglier cover for genitals rendered doubly shameful by their impotence. 9. Why go on to mention his back and his spine? Though the curvature of his ribs, bursting from their starting-points in the joints of the vertebrae, forms the fabric of the chest, still all this branch-like structure of bones is hidden, so to speak, beneath one great sea of overflowing abdomen. I say nothing of the corpulence of his loins and buttocks, the thickness of which makes his paunch seem meagre by comparison. I say nothing of his thighs, withered and twisted, his huge knees and limp houghs, his horny legs and his brittle ankles, his large feet and his tiny toes. And though he is such a hideous mass of misshapen features, though he is bloodless and half-dead with manifold disease, and though he can neither sit when carried nor walk when supported, still he is more detestable for his language than for his limbs. 10. For although he suffers from an itching for depraved talk, still he is

[1] Le Mofete in the centre of Italy; a valley having a cave known for its unpleasant fumes (Virgil, *Aen.*, VII. 563–571).

patronorum est praecipue cavendus arcanis, quorum est laudator in prosperis, delator in dubiis; et [1] si ad occulta familiarium publicanda temporis ratio sollicitet, mox per hunc Spartacum quaecumque sunt clausa franguntur quaeque obserata reserantur; ita quod, quas domorum nequiverit machinis apertae simultatis impetere, cuniculis clandestinae proditionis impugnat. hoc fabricatu Daedalus noster amicitiarum culmen aedificat, qui sicut sodalibus velut Theseus inter secunda sociatur, sic ab his postmodum velut Proteus inter adversa dilabitur. 11. igitur ex voto meo feceris si talium sodalitati ne congressu quidem primore sociere, maxume illorum quorum sermonibus prostitutis ac theatralibus nullas habenas, nulla praemittit repagula pudor. nam quibus citra honestatis nitorem iactitabundis loquacis faece petulantiae lingua polluitur infrenis, his conscientia quoque sordidatissima est. denique facilius obtingit ut quispiam seria loquens vivat obscene, quam valeat ostendi qui pariter exsistat improbus dictis et probus moribus. vale.

[1] et *Luetjohann*: at.

---

[1] A Thracian slave who escaped from a gladiators' training-school at Capua in Italy and became a heroic leader of an army of runaway slaves 73–71 B.C.

[2] The mythical Greek architect and sculptor, not the real sculptor of the fourth century B.C.

most dangerous when taken into the confidence of his patrons, being a flatterer in prosperity and a tell-tale in time of jeopardy; and if circumstances incite him to spread abroad the secrets of his intimates, all bars are broken down and all bolts unbolted by this Spartacus;[1] nay, if he fails to batter any families by the engines of open enmity, he will assail them with the mines of secret treachery. Such is the architecture with which our Daedalus[2] builds the lofty eminences of his friendships; in prosperity he draws as close as Theseus[3] to his companions, then in adversity he slips away from them like a Proteus.[4] 11. So you will act as I desire if you do not get mixed up with such company even by way of slight acquaintance, especially with those on whose abandoned low-comedy talk shame imposes neither rein nor bar. Those braggarts who shine not with the sheen of virtue but whose unbridled tongue is defiled with the filth of babbling indecency are as foul in their inmost hearts as in their speech. For after all it would be easier to find a man who talks piously and lives immorally than to point to one who is at the same time wicked in language and good in character. Farewell.

[3] The famous traditional hero and ruler of prehistoric Attica and Athens. He was renowned for true friendship.

[4] Mythical Greek prophet who could be consulted only when held fast but could turn into anything at will unless held relentlessly.

XIV

SIDONIVS PLACIDO SVO SALVTEM

1. Quamquam te tua tenet Gratianopolis, comperi tamen hospitum veterum fido relatu quod meas nugas sive confectas opere prosario seu poetarum stilo cantilenosas plus voluminum lectione dignere repositorum. gaudeo hoc ipso, quod recognovi chartulis occupari nostris otium tuum; sed probe intellego quod moribus tuis hanc voluptatem non operis effectus excudit sed auctoris adfectus, ideoque plus debeo, quia gloriae punctum, quod dictioni negares, das amicitiae. 2. de ceteris vero studii nostri derogatoribus quid ex asse pronuntiem, necdum deliberavi. nam qui maxume doctus sibi videtur, dictionem sanam et insanam ferme appetitu pari revolvit, non amplius concupiscens erecta quae laudet quam despecta quae rideat. atque in hunc modum scientia pompa proprietas linguae Latinae iudiciis otiosorum maximo spretui est, quorum scurrilitati neglegentia comes hoc volens tantum legere, quod carpat, sic non utitur litteris quod abutitur. vale.

---

* Nothing further is known of Placidus.

[1] Grenoble.

[2] Publication of Sidonius' poems had been completed in A.D. 469; the first two books of the letters were published after A.D. 476.

XIV

SIDONIUS TO HIS FRIEND PLACIDUS,* GREETING

1. Although you are still detained in your beloved Gratianopolis,[1] I have ascertained by the trustworthy report of old friends that you are kind enough to esteem my poor writings (whether fashioned in prose or warbling in poetic style) more highly than the reading of the rolls that are stored in your cases. This itself is a delight to me, to have learnt that my sheets occupy your leisure hours; but I quite realise that it is not the effectiveness of the work but affection for the author that produces such an enjoyment in a nature like yours; and so I am all the more in your debt, because you grant to friendship an award of distinction which you would be bound to refuse to the composition in itself. 2. But as to the complete answer which I must give to the other sort, who depreciate my literary work,[2] I have not yet made up my mind. For the man who considers himself the best critic generally studies sound and unsound composition with equal interest, being no more greedy for lofty utterances to praise than for contemptible ones to ridicule. In this way technique, grandeur, and propriety in the use of the Latin language are particularly underrated by the armchair critics, who, with an insensibility which goes hand in hand with scurrility, and wishing to read only what they may criticize, cannot, by their very abuse of literature, be making a proper use of it. Farewell.

LIBER QVARTVS

I

SIDONIVS PROBO SVO SALVTEM

1. Soror mihi quae uxor tibi: hinc inter nos summa et principalis necessitudo, et ea quidem patruelis, non germana fraternitas, quae plerumque se purius fortius meracius amat. nam facultatum inter germanos prius lite sopita iam qui nascuntur ex fratribus nihil invicem controversantur, et hinc saepe caritas in patruelibus maior, quia desistit simultas a divisione nec cessat affectus a semine. secundus nobis animorum nexus accessit de studiorum parilitate, quia idem sentimus culpamus laudamus in litteris et aeque nobis quaelibet dictio placet improbaturque. 2. quamquam mihi nimis arrogo iudicium meum conferens tuo. quis enim iuvenum nesciat seniorumque te mihi magistrum fuisse proprium, cum videremur habere communem, et si quid heroicus arduum comicus lepidum, lyricus cantilenosum orator decla-

---

* Probus was elder brother of Sidonius' schoolfellow Magnus Felix. See *Carm.* IX. 332; XXIV. 91–94; Felix: cf. *Ep.* II. 3; III. 4; III. 7; IV. 5; IV. 10.

[1] Eulalia (*Carm.* XXIV. 95–98). Here *soror* "sister" means cousin.

BOOK IV

I

SIDONIUS TO HIS COUSIN PROBUS,* GREETING

1. Your wife [1] is my cousin; hence comes the greatest and chiefest bond between us—not, be it noted, a brotherly tie but that cousinly relationship in which the affection is often purer, stronger, and more unalloyed; for when brothers' disputes about property have been set at rest, their children no longer have any quarrel with one another, and there is often greater love between cousins just because the enmity arising from the division of the inheritance dies out while the attachment due to kinship shows no diminution. A second bond between our hearts has come from the affinity of our intellectual interests, for we have the same taste in literary matters, praising or blaming the same things, and we are always at one in our approval or disapproval of any particular form of diction. 2. It is true that I am presumptuous in comparing my judgment with yours. Everyone, young or old, must know that you were my special teacher, although we appeared to have a common master, and that it was you who revealed to each and all of your school-fellows (except to such as lacked talent or failed to use their opportunities) the achievements of writers in many fields—the lofty utterance of the epic poet, the wit of the comedian, the tunefulness of the lyric poet, the

matorium,[1] historicus verum satiricus figuratum, grammaticus regulare panegyrista plausibile, sophista serium epigrammatista [2] lascivum, commentator lucidum iurisconsultus obscurum multifariam condiderunt, id te omnifariam singulis, nisi cui ingenium sibique quis defuit, tradidisse? deus bone! quam sibi hinc patres nostri gloriabantur, [3] cum viderunt sub ope Christi te docere posse, me discere, et non solum te facere quod posses sed et velle quod faceres ideoque te bonum non minus quam peritum pronuntiari! 3. et vere intra Eusebianos lares talium te quaedam moneta susceperat disciplinarum, cuius philosophica incude formatus nunc varias nobis rerum sermonumque rationes ipso etiam qui docuerat probante pandebas, nunc ut Platon discipulus iam prope potior sub Socrate, sic iam tu sub Eusebio nostro inter Aristotelicas categorias artifex dialecticus atticissabas, cum ille adhuc aetatulam nostram mobilem teneram crudam modo castigatoria severitate decoqueret, modo mandatorum salubritate condiret. 4. at qualium, deus bone, quamque pretiosorum, quae si quis deportaret philosophaturus aut ad paludicolas Sygambros aut ad Caucasigenas

[1] orator declamatorium *Leo:* o. minaturum *coni. Warmington* (*coll. Ep.* VII. 9. 1 oratoriae minae): oratorq; maturum.
[2] epigrammatista *Luetjohann*: epigrammista.
[3] gloriabantur *codd.*: gratulabantur *Luetjohann.*

---

[1] A teacher of philosophy at Lyon.
[2] The Sygambri were originally a strong German tribe along the east bank of the Rhine between the Sieg and the Lippe;

orator's rhetoric, the historian's truth, the satirist's artful malice, the grammarian's observance of rules, the panegyrist's rousing utterance, the sophist's gravity, the epigrammatist's sportiveness, the commentator's lucidity, the jurist's abstruseness. Gracious heaven! How proud our fathers were to see that with Christ's help you had the power to teach and I to learn, and that you not only did what you could but took pleasure in what you did, so that you were declared to be no less kind-hearted than you were accomplished! 3. And truly you had found in Eusebius's [1] house a kind of mint of such studies; shaped on its philosophic anvil you used sometimes to expound to us the various principles involved in subjects and discourses in such a way that the very master who had taught you approved; at other times, just as Plato under Socrates was already almost superior to his teacher, so you under our teacher Eusebius already showed yourself a real Athenian, a past master of dialectic, versed in the Aristotelian categories, while Eusebius was still tempering our unstable, feeble, raw immaturity with stern rebuke or seasoning it with wholesome precepts. 4. And, gracious heaven! what precepts they were, and how precious! if any budding missionary philosopher were to convey them to the Sygambrian [2] marsh-dwellers or to the Caucasian Alans [3] or to the

they were ultimately settled by the Romans in Gaul between the Rhine and the lower Meuse. W. Schultze, *Deutsche Gesch.*, II. 38.

[3] Iranian nomads who spread into south Russia and later made incursions into the Asiatic and Danubian regions of the Roman empire.

Alanos aut ad equimulgas Gelonos, bestialium rigidarumque nationum corda cornea fibraeque glaciales procul dubio emollirentur egelidarentur neque illorum ferociam stoliditatemque, quae secundum beluas ineptit brutescit accenditur, rideremus contemneremus pertimesceremus. 5. igitur quia nos ut affinitas, ita studia iunxerunt, precor, quoquo loci es, amicitiae iura inconcussa custodias longumque tibi etsi sede absumus, adsimus affectu: cuius intemeratae partes, quantum spectat ad vos, a nobis [1] in aevum, si quod est vitae reliquum, perennabuntur. vale.

II

CLAVDIANVS SIDONIO PAPAE SALVTEM

1. Si possibile factu esset, ut te, dominum meum, vel aliquotiens aliquantulum convenirem, non undeunde quarumpiam personarum aut voluntates aut necessitates anquirerem,[2] quae [3] in rem debiti mei usui mihi esse possent. quippe revisionis potestas

[1] ad vos, a nobis *Luetjohann*: ad nos (*om.* a nobis) *F*: a nobis (*om.* ad nos) *LMTCP*; ad nos, vobis *coni. Mohr.*

[2] inquirerem *MTCFP*.

[3] quae *LRN*: sed quae *MTCFPN*[1].

---

[1] Of Ukraine, associated by Greek and Roman writers with the Budini in south and central Russia but not later defined as any distinct people.

[2] With hesitation I retain, with Anderson, Luetjohann's reading. But *cuius* (sc. *amicitiae*) . . . *partes quantum spectat, a nobis in aevum . . . perennabuntur* may well be right.

mare-milking Gelonians,[1] the horny hearts and icy vitals of those brutish hardened peoples would assuredly be softened and thawed, and we should no longer deride, despise, and fear that dull ferocity of theirs, senseless and stupid and inflammable like that of wild beasts. 5. Well, then, since our studies no less than our kinship have united us, I beseech you, wherever you may be, to keep the claims of friendship unshaken, and although our dwelling-places are far removed, let our affection draw us close to one another. As far as you are concerned,[2] the obligations of this friendship shall ever be preserved by me inviolate through all the span of life that remains to me. Farewell.

II

CLAUDIANUS * TO BISHOP SIDONIUS, GREETING

1. If it were possible, my Lord, for me to meet you just occasionally and for a short time, I should not have to search in all quarters for some persons whose inclinations or necessities might be of use to me in paying the debt [3] I owe you. The fact is that the possibility of seeing you again is barred to me in

* This letter is the only one in the collection of Sidonius' letters which was not written by Sidonius himself.

Claudianus Mamertus was a priest of Vienna (modern Vienne), where his brother Saint Mamertus (for whom see also *Ep.* VII. 1) was bishop. He dedicated to Sidonius his work in three books *De statu animae* (see § 2 below). Cf. *Ep.* IV. 3; IV. 11. 1; V. 2. 1.; Vol. I of Sidonius (Loeb) p. xxxiii. For Sidonius' election to be Bishop of Clermont, see *Ep.* III. 1. 2.

[3] By carrying a letter to his friend.

multis modis et miseris perinde causis intercluditur. enimvero scribendi facultas aut raro idonea suppetit aut nec suppetit. istaec eadem remissibilia sint necne, tute iudicaveris. 2. porro autem vero, quod saepenumero scriptis vestris alii inpertiuntur, qui id ipsum nec ambiunt quam egomet forsan nec merentur amplius, non arbitror amicitiae legibus inpune committi. illud etiamnum dolenter faxo tacitum, quod libellos illos, quos tuo nomine nobilitari non abnuis, nullo umquam inpertivisti rescripto. sed vacuum forte non suppetit, quod tute modicum magnae admodum impendas amicitiae. 3. ecquo tumet occupatu umquam uspiamve implicabere, quin illud in aliorum commoda revergat? cum precatu deum placas, eundem non modo amicis sed ignotis quoque concilias. cum scripturarum caelestium mysteria rimaris, quo te studiosius imbuis, eo doctrinam ceteris copiosius infundis. cum tuas opes in usus inopum prodigis, tibi quidem maxume, sed aliis quoque consultum facis. proinde nihil videlicet, profecto nihil est tam infecundum actionum tuarum omnium, quod tibi uni soli tantum et non aliis quoque multis tecum uberem fructum ferat. 4. nulla igitur cuiusquam praepedimenti occasio praetendi vel falso potest, cur egomet specialis atque intumus [tuus] [1] nihil ab speciali meo fructi feram, a quo ignoti quoque multum capiant plurimi. sed, uti ego autumo, iuxta

[1] tuus *vulg.*: *om. codd.*

many ways, and by deplorable circumstances as well. As for writing, seldom or never do I get a reasonable chance of doing any. It is for you to judge whether or not these facts really excuse me. 2. At the same time, others who do not perhaps solicit or deserve the privileges more than I do, are often favoured with letters from you, and in my opinion this is an offence, and no venial offence, against the laws of friendship. Another grievance, which I shall likewise ruefully refrain from airing, is that you have never favoured with a word of acknowledgment those little books, to which you graciously lend the lustre of your name. But it may be that you cannot spare a few moments for the claims of a very great friendship. 3. I doubt if you will ever anywhere involve yourself in any occupation without making your efforts redound to other people's advantage. When you seek God's mercy in prayer, you beseech His grace not only for your friends but also for those unknown to you. When you search the mysteries of the heavenly scriptures, the more diligently you steep yourself in them, the more plentifully do you shower instruction on others. When you lavish your wealth for the needs of the poor, you do indeed benefit yourself most of all, but others share the benefit. So clearly there is nothing, no nothing, in all your actions so unproductive as to yield rich fruit to yourself alone and not to many others beside. 4. Consequently, it is impossible to allege, or even pretend, that there is any impediment to debar me, a special and intimate friend, from getting some profit from my own special friend, from whom even many total strangers get a great deal. But methinks you are

formam euangelici largitoris quod non das amico esurienti dabis improbo pulsatori. porro si etiamnum solito [1] obdurueris, faxim egomet quod tete paenitebit, quoniam, si peccabis [2] ultra reticendo, ego protinus ulciscar scribendo. porro enim ambiguo caret tam te puniendum scripto meo, quam punior egomet silentio tuo. vale.

III

SIDONIVS CLAVDIANO SVO SALVTEM

1. Committi, domine maior, in necessitudinis iura pronuntias, cur quod ad salve tibi debitum spectat a stilo et pugillaribus diu temperem quodque deinceps nullas viantum volas mea papyrus oneraverit, quae vos cultu sedulae sospitatis [3] impertiat. praeter aequum ista coniectas, si reare mortalium quempiam, cui tamen sermocinari Latialiter cordi est, non pavere, cum in examen aurium tuarum quippe scriptus adducitur; tuarum, inquam, aurium, quarum peritiae, si me decursorum ad hoc aevi temporum praerogativa non obruat, nec Frontonianae

[1] silentio *Leo*.
[2] peccabis *LT*: peccaris *P*: peccatis *MCFR*.
[3] sodalitatis *coni. Luetjohann*.

---

[1] Luke xi. 5–8.
* See the preceding letter.
[2] Marcus Cornelius Fronto (*c.* A.D. 100–170), orator,

modelling yourself upon the bountiful giver in the gospel,[1] and you will give to the importunate knocker at your door what you will not give to a hungry friend. So if you still prove unrelenting as before, I must needs do a thing that will make you think better of it, for if you carry your sinful silence any further, I will immediately take my revenge by writing myself. There is no doubt whatever that a letter from me will be as great a punishment to you as your silence is to me. Farewell.

III

SIDONIUS TO HIS FRIEND CLAUDIANUS,* GREETING

1. My honoured lord, you declare that I am offending against the laws of friendship. Your grievance is about the words of greeting which I owe you; you charge me with having long been chary with my tablets and stylus, and complain that I have not in my turn loaded the hands of travellers with papyrus destined to bring you the tribute of assiduous salutation. You misconceive the facts if you imagine that there is any man, at least anyone with a real regard for Latin expression, who is not alarmed when he is submitted, and in written form too, to the judgment of your ears—of your ears, I repeat, with whose skill, if the privileged position of the generations before our time did not overawe me, I should not rank even the abundant flow of Fronto's [2] impressive utterance

rhetorician, advocate, and teacher, some of whose writings survive.

gravitatis, aut ponderis Apuleiani fulmen aequiperem, cui Varrones, vel Atacinus vel Reatinus,[1] Plinii, vel avunculus vel Secundus, compositi in praesentiarum rusticabuntur. 2. adstipulatur iudicio meo volumen illud, quod tute super statu animae rerum verborumque scientia divitissimus propalavisti. in quo dum ad meum nomen prooemiaris, hoc munus potissimum cepi, ut meae fama personae, quam operae pretium non erat librorum suorum titulis inclarescere, tuorum beneficio perpetuaretur. at quod, deus magne, quantumque opus illud est, materia clausum declamatione conspicuum, propositione obstructum disputatione reseratum, et quamquam propter hamata syllogismorum puncta tribulosum, vernantis tamen eloquii flore mollitum! 3. nova ibi verba, quia vetusta, quibusque conlatus merito etiam antiquarum litterarum stilus antiquaretur; quodque pretiosius, tota illa dictio sic caesuratim succincta, quod profluens; quam rebus amplam strictamque sententiis sentias plus docere

[1] Reatinus *Leo*: terentius (terrentinus *FCP*).

---

[1] Lucius Apuleius of Madaura in Numidia in Africa was born *c.* A.D. 125; he was a philosopher and rhetorician whose most famous extant work is the romance *The Metamorphoses* or *On The Golden Ass*.

[2] Publius Terentius Varro, *c.* 82–36 B.C., a poet born near the river Atax (Aude), whose works are lost; and the learned Marcus Terentius Varro (116–27 B.C.) of Reate in Italy, whose *De Re Rustica* and (in part) *De Lingua Latina* have survived. I accept (as Anderson did), but with hesitation, Leo's reading *Reatinus* for *Terentius*. The MSS. suggest that the lost archetype had *Terentius*; and if this is right, Sidonius would mean " the Varros, he of the Atax and *the* Terentius," thus stressing the renowned scholar.

and of Apuleius's [1] weighty words; yes, when compared with you the Varros, he of the Atax and he of Reate [2] and both Plinies, the uncle and Secundus,[3] must needs become rustics for the time being. 2. This judgment of mine is confirmed by the book you have published on the nature of the soul, the work of a man with a rich command both of words and of matter. You preface the work with a dedication to me, and so I have got a gift of supreme value, inasmuch as my personal reputation, which the merits of my own books could not have raised to a renown worth my pains, is, thanks to your books, assured for all time. And, great heaven! what a work, what a grand work it is!—abstruse in matter but clear in exposition, beset with obstacles in the introductory presentation but opened up in the discussion, roughened and furrowed by the barbed points of the syllogisms, and yet made soft to the tread by a flowery carpet of lush eloquence. 3. There one finds words which are new because they are old—indeed the language even of antique literature would justly fall from favour by comparison with it. A more valuable merit is that all that diction flows freely, though broken up into short groups of words; and with the abundance of matter and the conciseness of phrase, it seems to teach more than it expresses.

[3] "The Second"—word play by Sidonius; both the elder and the younger Pliny had the additional name Secundus. The former is regularly called *avunculus* by his nephew. Sidonius does not seem to have read him. C. Plinius Secundus, whose great *Naturalis Historia* survives, died in A.D. 79; and his nephew Publius Caecilius Secundus = C. Plinius Caecilius Secundus, of whom we have besides the famous letters a panegyric on the Emperor Trajan, lived from *c.* A.D. 61 to A.D. 113.

quam dicere. denique et quondam, nec iniuria, haec principalis facundia computabatur, cui paucis multa cohibenti curae fuit causam potius implere quam paginam. 4. at vero in libris tuis iam illud quale est, quod et teneritudinem quamquam [1] continuata maturitas admittit interseritque tempestivam censura dulcedinem, ut lectoris intentionem per eventilata disciplinarum philosophiae membra lassatam repente voluptuosis excessibus quasi quibusdam pelagi sui portibus foveat? o liber multifariam pollens, o eloquium non exilis sed subtilis ingenii, quod nec per scaturrigines hyperbolicas intumescit nec per tapinomata depressa tenuatur! 5. ad hoc unica singularisque doctrina et in diversarum rerum assertione monstrabilis, cui moris est de singulis artibus cum singulis artificibus philosophari, quaeque, si fors exigit, tenere non abnuit cum Orpheo plectrum cum Aesculapio baculum, cum Archimede radium cum Euphrate horoscopium,[2] cum Perdice circinum cum Vitruvio perpendiculum quaeque numquam investigare destiterit cum Thalete tempora, cum Atlante sidera, cum Zeto [3] pondera, cum Chrysippo numeros, cum Euclide mensuras. 6. ad extremum nemo saeculo meo quae voluit affirmare sic valuit. si-

[1] quaquam *L*: quampiam *Wilamowitz*.
[2] horoscopum *L*: horoscopium *rell*.
[3] Zeto *fortasse corrigendum*.

---

[1] Orpheus: mythical lyre-player; Aesculapius = Asclepius: god of the medical art; Archimedes: mathematician c. 287–212 B.C.; Euphrates: Stoic philosopher and orator of the time of the Emperor Hadrian (A.D. 117–138); Perdix or the like: mythical nephew (?) of Daedalus; Vitruvius: M. Vitruvius Pollio, architectural writer, who flourished in the

Nay, even in olden days it was considered, and with good reason, that the supreme eloquence was that which said much in few words, aiming at a full treatment rather than a full page. 4. But besides this, what a merit it is in your books that, although they show maturity all through, yet there are touches of tenderness, and your strictures are interspersed with well-timed winsomeness, so that the reader's strained concentration, exhausted with a minute examination of the various divisions of philosophical teaching, is suddenly refreshed by charming digressions, which are like havens in his troubled sea! O book of manifold power! O utterance of a mind not thin but fine, which is neither swollen with hyperbolical spouting nor emaciated by mean and trivial words. 5. In addition, we find here a learning peerless and unique, able to hold its own with distinction in many fields, a learning that is wont to reason about the several arts with their several masters, not declining, if need be, to hold the quill with Orpheus, the staff with Aesculapius, the rod with Archimedes, the horoscope with Euphrates, the compasses with Perdix, the plummet with Vitruvius; a learning that has never ceased to investigate times with Thales, stars with Atlas, weights with Zethus, numbers with Chrysippus, and measures with Euclid.[1] 6. Lastly, no one in my age has shown the ability of my friend to establish points which he wished to

time of the Emperor Augustus 30 B.C.–A.D. 14; Thales of Miletus, 640–546 B.C., to whom were attributed a number of astronomical discoveries; Atlas: mythical; Zethus: mythical; Chrysippus: Stoic philosopher *c.* 280–206 B.C.; Euclid: born 323 B.C.

quidem dum sese adversus eum, quem contra loquitur, exertat, morum ac studiorum linguae utriusque symbolam iure sibi vindicat. sentit ut Pythagoras dividit ut Socrates, explicat ut Platon implicat ut Aristoteles, ut Aeschines blanditur ut Demosthenes irascitur, vernat ut Hortensius aestuat ut Cathegus, incitat ut Curio moratur ut Fabius, simulat ut Crassus dissimulat ut Caesar, suadet ut Cato dissuadet ut Appius persuadet ut Tullius. 7. iam si ad sacrosanctos patres pro comparatione veniatur instruit ut Hieronymus destruit ut Lactantius adstruit ut Augustinus, attollitur ut Hilarius summittitur ut Iohannes, ut Basilius corripit ut Gregorius consolatur, ut Orosius affluit ut Rufinus stringitur, ut Eusebius narrat ut Eucherius sollicitat, ut Paulinus provocat ut Ambrosius perseverat. 8. iam vero de hymno tuo si percontere quid sentiam, commaticus est

---

[1] Pythagoras: philosopher, sixth century B.C.; Socrates: *c.* 470–399 B.C.; Plato: 427–347 B.C.; Aristotle: 384–322 B.C.; Aeschines: orator of Athens, 389–314 B.C. Demosthenes: orator of Athens 384(3?)–322 B.C.; Q. Hortensius: Roman orator, born 114 B.C.; Cethegus: probably M. Cornelius Cethegus who died in 196 B.C.; Curio: not, probably, the C. Scribonius Curio who until his death in 49 B.C. supported Julius Caesar (murdered in 44 B.C.) but rather his father the orator who died in 53 B.C.; Fabius: Q. Fabius Maximus, the famous "delaying" general against Hannibal during Rome's second war (218–202 B.C.) with Carthage; Crassus: the orator Lucius Licinius Crassus, 140–91 B.C.; or perhaps M. Licinius Crassus the financier and politician 105 (or earlier)–53 B.C.

[2] Caesar: 100–44 B.C.; Cato: M. Porcius Cato 95–46 B.C.; Appius: Appius Claudius Caecus who in old age persuaded the Romans to reject terms offered by Pyrrhus after the battle of Heraclea in B.C. 280; Cicero: 106–43 B.C.

[3] Jerome: *c.* A.D. 335–420; Lactantius: mid-third century–

prove; for when proceeding to refute an opponent he claims with good right the joint resources of his character and of his acquaintance with Greek and Latin lore. He makes judgments like Pythagoras, distinguishes like Socrates, unfolds like Plato, and enfolds like Aristotle; he cajoles like Aeschines and storms like Demosthenes, luxuriates like Hortensius, and seethes like Cethegus; incites like Curio, holds back like Fabius, simulates like Crassus[1] and dissimulates like Caesar, advises like Cato, dissuades like Appius, and persuades like Cicero.[2] 7. If we now turn to the hallowed Fathers for purposes of comparison, he is instructive like Jerome, destructive like Lactantius, constructive like Augustine; he exalts his tone like Hilary and subdues it like John; he rebukes like Basil and comforts like Gregory; he is diffuse like Orosius and compressed like Rufinus; he narrates like Eusebius, urges like Eucherius, challenges like Paulinus and perseveres like Ambrose.[3] 8. Again, if you ask me what I think of your hymn—abundant in matter but with ample pauses, de-

c. A.D. 327; Augustine: A.D. 354–430; Hilary: Pictaviensis, made Bishop of his native Poitiers c. A.D. 350; died in 368; John: perhaps Chrysostom (A.D. c. 345–407); Basil: Bishop of Caesarea in Cappadocia; lived A.D. 329–379; Gregory: Bishop of Nazianzos A.D. 329–390; Orosius: Paulus Orosius of Tarragona, of the late fourth and early fifth century; Rufinus: possibly Turannius (Turranius) or Toranus c. A.D. 345–410; Eusebius: of Caesarea, ecclesiastical historian, c. A.D. 264–c. 340; Eucherius: Saint Eucher, a monk of Lérins who became Bishop of Lyon; lived in the late fourth century and early fifth century to c. 450; Paulinus: perhaps the Paulinus of *Ep.* VIII. 11. 2; or Meropius Pontius Anicius Paulinus, Bishop of Nola in the early fifth century; born c. A.D. 353; Ambrose: probably the Saint, c. A.D. 340–397.

copiosus, dulcis elatus, et quoslibet lyricos dithyrambos amoenitate poetica et historica veritate supereminet. idque tuum in illo peculiare, quod servatis metrorum pedibus pedum syllabis syllabarumque naturis intra spatii sui terminum verba ditia versus pauper includit nec artati carminis brevitas longitudinem phalerati sermonis eliminat; ita tibi facile factu est minutis trochaeis minutioribusque pyrrhichiis non solum molossicas anapaesticasque ternarias sed epitritorum etiam paeonumque quaternatas [1] supervenire iuncturas. 9. excrescit amplitudo proloquii angustias regulares et tamquam parvo auro grandis gemma vix capitur emicatque ut equi potentis animositas, cui frementi, si inter tesqua vel confraga frenorum lege teneatur, intellegis non tam cursum deesse quam campum. quid multis? arbitro me in utroque genere dicendi nec Athenae sic Atticae nec Musae sic musicae iudicabuntur, si modo mihi vel censendi copiam desidia longior non ademit. nam dum inpactae professionis obtentu novum scribendi morem gradatim appeto et veterem saltuatim dedisco, de bono oratore nil amplius habeo quam quod malus poeta esse plus coepi. 10. proin, quaeso, delicti huius mihi gratiam facias, quod

[1] quaternas *MTCFPRVN*: quaternatas *L*: quaternarias *coni. Malcolm Burke.*

---

[1] If we write – for a long syllable, ⏑ for a short one, then: trochee: – ⏑; pyrrhic: ⏑ ⏑; molossus: – – –; anapaest:

lightful but elevated, it combines the charm of a poet with the veracity of a historian to a degree not found in any lyrical dithyramb you care to name. Moreover, it has a merit all your own, in that while the feet appropriate to the metre, the syllables appropriate to the feet, and the character appropriate to the syllables are kept throughout, yet within its allotted space a meagre line is made to hold rich words, and the brevity of your restricted verse does not preclude the amplitude of majestic speech, so easy is it for you to make tiny trochees and tinier pyrrhics surpass combinations not only of trisyllabic molossi and anapaests but even of quadrisyllabic epitrites and paeons.[1] 9. The breadth of your utterance transcends the narrow limits imposed by rules; like a large gem, it is barely contained in its small gold setting; it flashes out like the mettle of a powerful horse, which chafes if held in by the law of the bit amid wild and broken country, and obviously lacks not speed but space. To cut a long story short, it seems to me that in both kinds of composition Athens will be judged less Attic and the Muses less musical than you—unless indeed a rather long inactivity has deprived me of my critical faculty; for by reason of the sacred calling which has been thrust upon me I am gradually essaying a new mode of composition and quickly unlearning the old one, and as a result there is nothing of the good prose-writer in me except that I have begun to be more decidedly a bad poet. 10. So, I pray you, be indulgent to this my shortcoming, that remembering

◡ ◡ –; epitrite: ◡ – – – or – ◡ – – or – – ◡ – or – – – ◡; paeon: – ◡ ◡ ◡ or ◡ – ◡ ◡ or ◡ ◡ – ◡ or ◡ ◡ ◡ –.

aliquantisper mei meminens arentem venulam rarius flumini tuo misceo. tuam tubam totus qua patet [1] orbis iure venerabitur, quam constat geminata felicitate cecinisse, quando nec aemulum repperit nec aequalem, cum pridem aures et ora populorum me etiam circumferente pervagaretur. nobis autem grandis audacia, si vel apud municipales et cathedrarios oratores aut forenses rabulas garriamus, qui etiam cum perorant, salva pace potiorum, turba numerosior illitteratissimis litteris vacant. nam te, cui, seu liberum seu ligatum placeat alternare sermonem, intonare ambifariam suppetit, pauci, quos aequus amavit, imitabuntur. vale.

IV

SIDONIVS SIMPLICIO ET APOLLINARI SVIS SALVTEM

1. Eccum vel tandem adest promissio mea, expectatio vestra, Faustinus, pater familias domi nobilis et inter maxima patriae iam mihi sibique communis ornamenta numerandus. hic meus frater natalium parilitate, amicus animorum similitudine; saepe

[1] patuit *LMCFP*: patuerit *Wilamowitz*.

---

[1] Virgil, *Aen.* VI. 129: pauci, quos aequus amavit|Iuppiter.
* For Sidonius' kinsmen Simplicius and Apollinaris see *Carm.* XXIV. 85, n.; *Ep.* III. 11; IV. 6 and 12, V. 3 and 4 and 6; VII. 4.

what I am I have for some time past only rarely mingled my parched rill with your stream. As for your own clarion, it shall be justly revered throughout the length and breadth of the world. All agree that it has sounded its strains with two-fold success, in that it found neither an equal nor a rival, after passing through the ears and lips of all peoples, with me also helping to spread its fame. For me, on the other hand, it would be colossal effrontery to deliver my chatter even before provincial or academic orators or before the brawling pettifoggers of the forum, men who even when they actually plead in the courts (if I may say it without offence to the superior few), in most cases occupy themselves with a very unliterary kind of letters. But as for you, who, whether you choose to turn to prose or to verse, have the power in either case to utter resounding tones, only "a few, favoured and loved,"[1] will be able to imitate you. Farewell.

IV

SIDONIUS TO HIS KINSMEN SIMPLICIUS AND APOLLINARIS,* GREETING

1. Behold! At long last the subject of my promise, the object of your expectation, is with you, Faustinus,[2] father of a family, scion of a noble house, a man to be reckoned among the greatest adornments of that homeland, which is now mine as well as his. He is my brother by the equality of our birth, my friend by the likeness of our minds. Many a time

[2] A priest. See letter 6, 1 of this Book.

cum hoc seria, saepe etiam ioca miscui; cumque abhinc retro iuvenes eramus, in pila in tesseris, saltibus cursu, venatu natatu sancta semper ambobus, quia manente caritate, contentio. mihi quidem maior hic natu, tantum tamen, ut eum non tam honorari necesse esset quam delectaret imitari; simul et ipse hinc amplius capiebatur, quod se diligi magis quam quasi coli intellegebat. sed provectu aetatis et [1] militia clericali, cum esset amabilis prius, coepit modo esse venerabilis. 2. per hunc salutem dico, videre vos sub ope Christi quam maturissime, si per statum publicum liceat, cupiens. quocirca, nisi desiderium meum videtur onerosum, remeante praefato fiam locorum vestrorum et temporum gnarus. stat sententia eluctari oppositas privatarum occupationum difficultates et conplectendis pectoribus vestris quamlibet longum officium deputare, si tamen, quod etiam nunc veremur, non vis maior disposita confundat. 3. quae vos quoque non perindignum est cum fratre Faustino, prout tempora monent, tractatu communicato deliberare. quem ego quia diligo, tamquam qui me diligat misi: si respondet iudicio meo, gratias ago; porro autem cum vir bonus ab omnibus censeatur, non est homo peior, si non est optimus. valete.

[1] et *LN*: ex.

have I shared jest and earnest with him, and in the bygone days of our youth we contended in ball-games and dicing, jumping and running, hunting and swimming, with no guile in our rivalry, for our love never faltered. True, he was older than I, but only so much as to make me glad to imitate him without the necessity of treating him with deference; at the same time he on his part found it all the more charming to feel that he was loved rather than made a sort of idol. But with advancing years and holy orders he who was lovable before has now begun to be venerable. 2. Through him I send you my greeting, while intending with Christ's help to see you at the earliest possible moment, should the public situation allow. Accordingly, unless my desire seems troublesome, when the aforesaid visitor is returning let me know about your part of the country and how things stand. It is my fixed intention to struggle clear of the confronting difficulties of my private occupations, and to devote a visit, no matter of what length, to the pleasure of clasping you to my heart, at least if some greater force should not—as even now I fear may happen—upset my arrangements. 3. It would not be much amiss for you to consider these plans according to the signs of the times, taking joint counsel with brother Faustinus. I have sent him as one who loves me, for I love him; if he answers to my opinion of him, I give thanks, and anyhow, since all rate him as a good man, he cannot be of less than average quality,[1] even if he is not of the highest excellence. Farewell.

[1] Semple, *Quaest. Exeg.*, 23.

V

SIDONIVS FELICI SVO SALVTEM

1. Iterat portitorem salutationis iteratio: Gozolas vester, deus tribuat ut noster, apicum meorum secundo gerulus efficitur. igitur verecundiam utrique eximite communem; nam si etiamnum silere meditemini, omnes et me cui et illum per quem scribere debebas[1] indignum arbitrabuntur. 2. de temporum statu iam nihil ut prius consulo, ne sit moribus tuis oneri, si adversa significes, cum prospera non sequantur. nam cum te non deceat falsa mandare atque item desint[2] votiva memoratu, fugio quicquid illud mali est per bonorum indicia cognoscere. vale.

VI

SIDONIVS APOLLINARI SVO SALVTEM

1. Per Faustinum antistitem non minus mihi veteris contubernii sodalitate quam novae pro-

[1] debebas *L*: debeas *R*: debeatis.

[2] desint *MTCPR*: desinit *F*[1]: cum sint *L*: *lacunam stat. Luetjohann post* item, *et* ⟨ancipitia⟩ *vel* ⟨ambigua⟩ (*vel sim.*) cum sint *coni.*

---

* Magnus Felix of Narbonne. See *Ep.* II. 3; III. 4; III. 7; IV. 5 and 10; *Carm.* IX and XXIV. 91.

[1] A Jew. Cf. *Ep.* III. 4. 1. Or put it thus: "Your

V

SIDONIUS TO HIS DEAR FELIX,* GREETING

1. Once more a greeting and once more the same bearer! Your Gozolas [1] (and God grant he may be mine also) is for the second time made my letter-carrier; therefore save him and me from a common sense of humiliation, for if you still mean to be silent, everyone will think that both I to whom and he through whom you ought to have written are unworthy persons. About the present state of affairs I no longer ask your opinion as I did before, lest it trouble your conscience if you presage ill and good times do not follow; for since it is not right for you to send a false message, and since there is no news such as one would like to tell, I am loth to learn of the evil, whatever it may be, through the reports of good men. Farewell.

VI

SIDONIUS TO HIS KINSMAN APOLLINARIS,* GREETING

1. Through the priest Faustinus,[2] a man to whom I am closely attached no less by the bonds of our

man Gozolas (and God grant I may say *our* man Gozolas) . . ."; perhaps Sidonius hopes that Gozolas may be converted —that he may be one with us in faith.

* See *Ep.* IV. 4. The present letter was apparently written in the winter of A.D. 471–2.

[2] See above, letter 4 of this Book.

fessionis communione devinctum verbo quaepiam cavenda mandaveram: dicto paruisse vos gaudeo. siquidem prudentibus cordacitus insitum est vitare fortuita, sicut itidem absurdum, si coeptis audacibus adversetur eventus, consurgere in querimonias et inconsultarum dispositionum culpabiles exitus ad infamanda casuum incerta convertere. 2. "quorsum istaec?" ais. fateor me nimis veritum, ne tempore timoris publici non timeres [1] et solidae domus ad hoc aevi inconcussa securitas ad tempestuosos hostium incursus pro intempestiva devotione trepidaret inchoaretque apud animorum matronalium teneritudinem sollemnitas expetita vilescere: [2] quamquam in pectoribus earundem ita sibi sit genuina sanctitas peculiare metata domicilium, ut, si quid secus viantibus accidisset, laetaturae fuerint quoddam se pro martyre tolerasse martyrium. ast ego, cui maiorem diffidentiam minor innocentia facit, super hoc ambiguo sententiae cautiori libentius adhaeresco nec difficulter applicor etiam tuta metuentibus. 3. proinde factum bene est, quod anceps iter salubriter distulistis neque intra iactum tantae aleae status tantae familiae fuit. et licet inchoata via potuerit prosperari, ego tamen huiusmodi consilio

[1] timeretis *F*.
[2] expetita ⟨valescere, itineris difficultas despecta⟩ vilescere *Luetjohann*: *v. Mohr in praef.* xxiii.

old comradeship than by the association of my new calling, I sent you a verbal warning to beware of certain things. I am glad that you have heeded my words; for it is a rooted principle of the wise to avoid blind hazards, and in the same way it is absurd, when a foolhardy attempt turns out badly, to burst into complaints and make the discreditable results of ill-considered plans an excuse for blaspheming the uncertainties of chance. 2. "What means all this?" you ask. Well, I confess I was terribly afraid that in a time of general fear you might fear nothing, that the security of your solid house, unshaken up to the present, might, because of your untimely devotion, tremble in face of the enemy's stormy assaults, and that the solemn ceremony which was the object of your journey might begin to lose its merit in the eyes of your tender-hearted women-folk—although their innate piety has so thoroughly established a home for itself in their hearts that if something untoward had happened to the people on pilgrimage, they would have rejoiced to think that they had in a manner suffered martyrdom on account of the martyr.[1] But I, who am less innocent and therefore more apprehensive than they, prefer to cling to the more cautious view of the present uncertain situation, and I readily side with those who fear even what is safe. 3. So it is a good thing that you have wisely put off your pilgrimage and not exposed the fortunes of so great a family to so great a risk. And even though your journey, if you had started on it, might have ended prosperously, I for

[1] Probably Saint Julian of Auvergne. His shrine was at Brivas (Brioude).

album calculum minime apponam, cuius temeritas absolvi nequit nisi beneficio felicitatis. dabit quidem talia vota divinitas dignis successibus promoveri licebitque adhuc horumce terrorum sub pacis amoenitate meminisse; sed praesentia faciunt cautos quos videbunt futura securos. 4. interim ad praesens apicum oblator damna sibi quaepiam per Genesium vestrum inflicta suspirat. si perspicis a vero non discrepare querimoniam, tribue, quaeso, convincenti reformationem, peregrino celeritatem. si vero calumniam plectibili sufflammat invidia, in eo iam praecessit vindicta pulsati, quod procax petitor sumptu et itinere confectus temere propositae litis exsudat incommoda, atque hoc in maximo hiemis accentu summisque cumulis nivium crustisque glacierum; quod tempus, quantum ad sectatores litium spectat, breve quidem saepe est audientiae sed diuturnum semper iniuriae. vale.

VII

SIDONIVS SIMPLICIO SVO SALVTEM

1. Solet dicere " currentem mones " qui rogatur, ut faciat quod facturus fuerat etiam non rogatus.

[1] The Thracians were accustomed to commemorate happy events with white stones, unhappy ones with black. But Sidonius alludes rather to an old Greek and Roman custom of using, in voting, a white stone for agreement (or for acquittal), and a black one for disagreement (or for condemnation).

[2] So Anderson. But probably " often means a short hearing but always a prolonged grievance ".

* Cf. *Ep.* IV. 4 and 12; V. 4; III. 11; VII. 4, 4.

my part should by no means mark with a white stone[1] a project whose rashness cannot be justified except by a favourable stroke of luck. No doubt the Divine Power will by and by allow such desires as yours to be carried out with the success which they deserve, and we shall yet be permitted to call to mind the terrors of today amid smiling scenes of peace, but the present imposes caution upon those whom the future will see freed from anxiety. 4. Meanwhile there is a question of the moment to be dealt with: the bearer of this letter bemoans some losses inflicted on him by your Genesius. If you find that his complaint is not at variance with the truth, grant redress, I pray you, to a just claimant and an expeditious settlement to a poor stranger. But if he is stirring up a false charge with culpable enmity, the vengeance of the person he is bothering has already arrived ahead of time; for my man, a shameless plaintiff, worn out with travel and expense, is toiling and sweating through the hardships of a rashly instituted suit—and that in the severest part of winter, amid great piles of snow and cakes of ice, at a season which, as far as litigants are concerned, is often indeed too short for a hearing but is always too long for a grievance.[2] Farewell.

VII

SIDONIUS TO HIS KINSMAN SIMPLICIUS,* GREETING

1. " You urge the runner to run " is a common rejoinder by one who is asked to do something that

percontere forsitan, quo spectet ista praemitti. baiulus apicum sedulo precatur, ut ad vos a me litteras ferat, cuius a nobis itinere comperto id ipsum erat utique, si tacuisset, orandus; namque hoc officium vester potius amor quam geruli respectus elicuit. ceterum hic ipse beneficium se computat meruisse, qui praestitit, quamquam identidem quod poposcit acceperit, sed quae nobis amicitiarum iura minime agnoscens. 2. unde quamquam absens facile coniecto, quo repente stupore ferietur, cum intuitu nostri dignanter admissus intellexerit se paginam meam magis otiose flagitasse quam tradere. videre mihi videor, ut homini non usque ad invidiam perfaceto nova erunt omnia, cum invitabitur peregrinus ad domicilium, trepidus ad conloquium, rusticus ad laetitiam, pauper ad mensam, et cum apud crudos caeparumque crapulis esculentos hic agat vulgus, illic ea comitate retractabitur [1] ac si inter Apicios epulones et Byzantinos chironomuntas hucusque ructaverit. 3. attamen qualis ipse quantusque est,[2] percopiose me officii votivi compotem fecit. sed

[1] tractabitur C^2.

[2] quantusque ⟨cumque⟩ est *coni. Luetjohann.*

---

[1] So *A*. Perhaps rather: "his demand that I should write this my page of introduction for him was more superfluous than his delivery of it." See § 1.

[2] One of these gourmets lived in the time of Sulla *c.* 100 B.C.; a second in the time of the Emperor Augustus 30 B.C.–A.D. 14; and a third in that of the Emperor Trajan, early in the second century after Christ.

[3] So Anderson. But possibly "plays the vulgarian."

he would have done even without being asked. You may perhaps inquire what is the point of this foreword. The bearer of this letter earnestly begs me to let him take a note from me to you, although I should inevitably have besought him to do that very thing, even if he had said nothing about it, as soon as I discovered what way he was going; for it is my love for you rather than deference to the courier that has elicited this message. But he reckons that the credit of the favour he has conferred belongs to himself, although he got what he insistently asked for without realising at all how strong are the claims of our friendship. 2. Hence, although I cannot be there to see, I can easily imagine the bewilderment which will suddenly strike him when he is graciously admitted out of regard for me, and finds that he is not so much the due deliverer of my letter as the man who superfluously demanded it.[1] I picture to myself how novel everything will be to this fellow, who is scarcely an enviable paragon of gentility, when you bid the stranger welcome to your home, the nervous messenger to a talk with you, the bumpkin to your gaiety, the poor man to your table, and when a man who is here the ringleader [3] in a dyspeptic mob that gorges itself in a surfeit of onions, there finds himself treated with as much courtesy as if he had hitherto made himself sick in the company of gormandising Apicii [2] and of posturing [4] carvers from Byzantium. 3. But whatever his character or importance, he has enabled me to discharge my incumbent duty to the

[4] χειρονομῶ "wield the hands," "gesticulate." The wealthy employed master-carvers to serve them—see Petronius, *Satyr.* 16; Juvenal, V. 120 ff.

quamquam huiuscemodi saepe personae despicabiles ferme sunt, in sodalibus tamen per litteras excolendis dispendii multum caritas sustinet, si ab usu frequentioris alloquii portitorum vilitate revocetur. vale.

VIII

SIDONIVS EVODIO SVO SALVTEM

1. Cum tabellarius mihi litteras tuas reddidit, quae te Tolosam rege mandante mox profecturum certis amicis confitebantur, nos quoque ex oppido longe remotum rus petebamus. me quidem mane primo remoratum [1] vix e tenaci caterva prosecutorum paginae tuae occasio excussit, ut satisfacere mandato saltim viator, saltim eques possem. 2. ceterum diluculo familia praecesserat ad duodeviginti milia passuum fixura tentorium, quo quidem loci sarcinulis relaxandis multa succedunt conducibilia, fons gelidus in colle nemoroso, subditus ager herbis abundans, fluvius ante oculos avibus ac pisce multo refertus, praeter haec iunctam habens ripae domum novam vetus amicus, cuius inmensae humanitati nec si adquiescas nec si recuses modum ponas. 3. igitur huc nostris antecedentibus, cum tui causa substitissemus, quo puer ocius vel e capite vici remit-

[1] moratum *LRV*.

---

* Not otherwise known.

[1] Euric, King (from A.D. 466 to 485) of the Visigoths in succession to his brother Theoderic II whom he murdered in 466. See A. H. M. Jones, *The Later Roman Empire*, I. 239, 242 ff.; II. 965; Vol. I of Sidonius (Loeb) xxvii ff.

[2] So Anderson; but *saltim. . . . saltim* may mean "either. . . or."

full. And after all, although persons of that sort are generally insignificant creatures, yet in the matter of paying regard to our friends by letters affection loses much if it is deterred from indulging in more frequent correspondence by the lowliness of the bearers. Farewell.

VIII

SIDONIUS TO HIS FRIEND EUODIUS,* GREETING

1. When the courier gave me your letter, which confessed to your tried friends that you were soon going to start for Tolosa at the bidding of the king,[1] we also were leaving the town for a distant place in the country. I myself was delayed in early morning, but a crowd of friends who had come to speed my departure so clung to me that the excuse of your letter could scarcely shake me free of them so as to let me satisfy your demand even on my way—and on horseback too.[2] 2. My servants had gone on ahead of me at the first streak of dawn, intending to pitch their tent eighteen miles on, in a place with great advantages for breaking the journey, a cool spring on a wooded slope, with rich grass-land down below, a river abounding in birds and fishes before their eyes, and, besides that, an old friend with a new house close to the bank, a man to whose immeasurable kindness you could set no bounds, whether you accepted or declined it. 3. And so, while my folks preceded me to that place, I halted on your account, in order that the messenger might be sent back the sooner, starting his journey at least on the outskirts

teretur, iam duae secundae facile processerant, iam sol adultus roscidae noctis umorem radio crescente sorbuerat: aestus ac sitis invalescebant atque[1] in profunda serenitate contra calorem sola quae tegeret nebula de pulvere; tum longinquitas viae per virens aequor campi patentis exposita visentibus, quippe ob hoc ipsum sero pransuris, ingemebatur; nam viaturos etsi nondum terebat labore, iam tamen expectatione terrebat. 4. quae cuncta praemissa, domine frater, huc tendunt, ut tibi probem neque animo vacasse me multum neque corpore neque tempore, cum[2] postulatis obtemperavi. ilicet, ut ad epistulae vestrae tenorem iam revertamur, post verba, quae primum salve ferebant, hoc poposcisti, ut epigramma transmitterem duodecim versibus terminatum, quod posset aptari conchae capaci, quae per[3] ansarum latus utrumque in extimum gyri a rota fundi senis cavatur striaturis. 5. quarum puto destinas vel ventribus pandis singulos versus vel curvis meliore consilio, si id magis deceat, capitibus inscribere; istoque cultu expolitam reginae Ragnahildae disponis offerre, votis nimirum tuis pariter atque actibus patrocinium invictum praeparaturus. famulor iniunctis quomodocumque, non ut volebam; sed tuae culpae primus ignosce, qui spatii plus praestitisti argentario quam poetae, cum procul dubio non te lateret intra officinam litteratorum

[1] eratque *Luetjohann.* [2] cum *Leo*: quo.
[3] praeter *coni. Luetjohann.*

[1] "Two second hours." Cf. *Carm.* XXIII. 489 *horam alteram secundam* "another second hour," where Anderson suspects a pun in *secundam* ("favourable"). But there is no pun in the letter here. [2] In religion only.

[3] Ragnahild or Ragnhild, Euric's Queen.

of the village. The fourth [1] hour was now well on its way, the sun was up and with increasing warmth had absorbed the dewy moisture of the night; heat and thirst were growing more intense, and in the boundless brightness the only cloud to give protection against the weather was one of dust. Moreover, the long road running through a green expanse of open plain and fully visible to the eye of the beholder made us groan, knowing as we did that it meant a late lunch for us; for although, with our journey still before us, it was not yet wearing us with toil, it was already worrying us with the prospect. 4. All this preamble, my honoured brother,[2] is aimed at convincing you that I had scant freedom of mind or body and little time at my disposal when I complied with your demand. Well, then, to return to the substance of your letter, after the words which began by bidding me greeting, you asked me to send you a little poem, limited to twelve lines, suitable for inscribing on a capacious shell-shaped basin, in which the side where each handle is placed is traversed by six fluted grooves, winding from the round base to the end of their sinuous course. 5. I suppose you intend to inscribe a line in each of their arched bellies or, better still, on each of their curving ridges, and you plan to offer the basin, thus embellished, to Queen Ragnahilda,[3] in the hope, no doubt, of securing beforehand an invincible support alike for your ambitions and for your actions. I obey your injunctions as best I can, not, however, in the way I wanted; but you must be the first to forgive what is really your fault, for you have granted less time to the poet than to the silversmith, although you were certainly well aware that in the literary

carminis si quid incus metrica produxerit non minus forti et asprata lima poliri.[1] sed ista vel similia quorsum? ecce iam canta.[2]

Pistrigero quae concha vehit Tritone Cytheren
hac sibi conlata cedere non dubitet.
poscimus, inclina paulisper culmen erile
et munus parvum magna patrona cape
Euodiumque libens non aspernare clientem,
quem faciens grandem tu quoque maior eris.
sic tibi, cui rex est genitor, socer atque maritus,
gnatus rex quoque sit cum patre postque patrem.
felices lymphae, clausae quae luce metalli
ora tamen dominae lucidiora fovent!
nam cum dignatur regina hinc tinguere vultus,
candor in argentum mittitur e facie.

si tantum amore nostro teneris, ut scribere has nugas non erubescas, occule auctorem, de tua rectius parte securus. namque in foro tali sive Athenaeo plus charta vestra quam nostra scriptura laudabitur. vale.

[1] formari *F*.
[2] canto *coni. Luetjohann*: cantilena *aut* cantatio *coni. Warmington*.

---

[1] In Greek mythology, the goddess Aphrodite after her birth from sea-foam was brought to land first on the island Cythera (now Cerigo), about 8 miles from Cape Malea in S. Greece, and her worship was established there. Hence

workshop any poem that has been beaten out on the metrical anvil requires a file no less strong and rough than the artificer's to finish it off. But what is the point of all this sort of talk? Here! Start your poem!

"The shell that carries Cythere[1] on the back of fishy-tailed Triton would not hesitate to yield place if compared with this one. Incline for a moment, I pray thee, thy sovereign majesty, accept as a great protectress this small gift, and be pleased not to spurn Euodius as thy vassal, whom making great thou shalt thyself be greater. So mayest thou, with father and husband and husband's father all kings, see likewise thy son a king with his father and after him. Happy the water which, enclosed in the radiant metal, refreshes the still more radiant countenance of its mistress! For when the Queen deigns to moisten her face from this basin a gleam is shed upon the silver from her visage."

If you are so attached to me that you do not blush to inscribe this trifle, conceal its authorship. You have better reason to feel easy in your mind about your own contribution; in that sort of forum or Athenaeum[2] your writing-material will get more praise than my writing. Farewell.

[1] Cythere = Aphrodite (Venus). Triton was a mythical personification of roaring waters.

[2] Any place or buildings, dedicated to Athena, where writers read or recited their works; such as the Athenaeum at Rome which the Emperor Hadrian established near the Forum *c.* A.D. 135, and that at Constantinople established about 425 by Theodosius II, Emperor of the East A.D. 408–450. Sidonius here means that in the barbaric court the silver basin will be more valued than the poem inscribed on it.

IX

SIDONIVS INDVSTRIO SVO SALVTEM

1. Interveni proxime Vettio[1] inlustri viro et actiones eius cotidianas penitissime et veluti ex otio inspexi. quas quoniam dignas cognitu inveni, non indignas relatu existimavi. primore loco, quod iure ceteris laudibus anteponemus, servat inlaesam domino domus par pudicitiam; servi utiles: rustici morigeri, urbani amici oboedientes patronoque contenti; mensa non minus pascens hospitem quam clientem; humanitas grandis grandiorque sobrietas. 2. illa leviora, quod ipse, quem loquimur, in equis canibus accipitribus instituendis spectandis circumferendis nulli secundus; summus nitor in vestibus, cultus in cingulis, splendor in phaleris; pomposus incessus, animus serius (iste publicam fidem, ille privatam asserit dignitatem); remissio non vitians, correptio non cruentans, et severitas eius temperamenti, quae non sit taetra sed tetrica. 3. inter haec sacrorum voluminum lectio frequens, per quam inter edendum saepius sumit animae cibum; psalmos crebro lectitat,

[1] Vettio *L*: vectio.

---

* Not otherwise known.

[1] Cf. *Ep.* IV. 13. He lived near Chantelle-la-Vieille in

IX

SIDONIUS TO HIS FRIEND INDUSTRIUS,* GREETING

1. The other day I came into contact with the Illustrious Vettius,[1] and I examined his daily actions most thoroughly and, so to speak, at my leisure. As I found them worth knowing, so I have deemed them worth relating. First and foremost—for it is with good reason that I shall put this merit before all the others—his home, like its master, preserves an untarnished purity. His slaves are efficient; those in the country are ready helpers, while his town servants are friendly, obedient, and contented with their patron. His table is as open to the guest as to the retainer; his kindness is great, but greater is his sobriety. 2. A less important fact is that this man of whom I am speaking is second to none in training horses, in judging dogs, and in carrying hawks about. There is the utmost elegance in his dress, refinement in his girdles, splendour in his trappings. His gait is dignified, his disposition serious; the former wins for him public confidence, the latter private respect. He is lenient without spoiling, he chides without wounding, and his strictness is so nicely tempered as to be austere but not abhorrent. 3. Moreover, he is a frequent reader of the sacred books, by which means on many occasions he absorbs food for the soul while at meals. He often reads the Psalms and still oftener chants

Allier. Only cd. *L* gives his name as Vettius, the other MSS having it as Vectius, maybe rightly.

crebrius cantat; novoque genere vivendi monachum complet non sub palliolo sed sub paludamento; ferarum carnibus abstinet, cursibus adquiescit; itaque occulte delicateque religiosus venatu utitur nec utitur venatione. 4 filiam unicam parvam post obitum uxoris relictam solacio caelibatus alit avita teneritudine, materna diligentia, paterna benignitate; erga familiam suam nec in proferendo alloquio minax nec in admittendo consilio spernax nec in reatu investigando persequax; subiectorum statum condicionemque non dominio sed iudicio regit; putes eum propriam domum non possidere sed potius administrare. 5. qua industria viri ac temperantia inspecta ad reliquorum quoque censui pertinere informationem, si vel summotenus vita ceteris talis publicaretur, ad quam sequendam praeter habitum, quo interim praesenti saeculo imponitur, omnes nostra professionis homines utilissime incitarentur, quia, quod pace ordinis mei dixerim, si tantum bona singula in singulis erunt, plus ego admiror sacerdotalem virum quam sacerdotem. vale.

---

[1] The *pallium*, worn by monks and philosophers.
[2] The *paludamentum*, a soldier's cloak, usually a general's.

them, and by his novel manner of life he acts the monk, though wearing not the habit [1] of an order but the habiliment [2] of a general. He abstains from game, but countenances the chase, and so, with his hidden and fastidious religiousness, he enjoys the hunt but not the hunted.[3] 4. He has an only daughter, left in early childhood to comfort his loneliness on the death of his wife. Her he brings up with a grandparent's tenderness, a mother's care, and a father's kindliness. Towards his household he is not threatening in his manner of address, contemptuous in his reception of suggestions, or vindictive in his investigation of wrong-doing; he regulates the lot and condition of his subordinates with discretion, not with a high hand; you could think he was not the owner of his own house but the steward in charge of it. 5. After examining this man's assiduity and moderation, I thought it would be conducive to the instruction of everyone else if such a life were proclaimed to the skies for everyone, in order that all men of my profession might, to their great benefit, be incited to follow it, not contenting themselves with the mere garb of a cleric, which sometimes serves to impose upon the present generation; for—be it said with all respect to my order—if each individual man must have just one single merit, I feel bound to admire a priest-like man more than a man in the priesthood. Farewell.

[3] Anderson's "attends the meet but shuns the meat" perpetrates a pun much worse than Sidonius' simpler word-play with *venatus* and *venatio*.

X

SIDONIVS FELICI SVO SALVTEM

1. Erumpo in salutationem licet seram, domine meus, annis ipse iam multis insalutatus, frequentiam veteris officii servare non audens, postquam me soli patrii finibus eliminatum peregrinationis adversa fregerunt. quapropter vos quoque ignoscere decet erubescentibus, siquidem convenit humiliatos humilia sectari neque cum illis parem familiaritatis tenere constantiam, quibus forte sit improbum plus amoris quam reverentiae impendere. propter hoc denique iam diu taceo vosque tacuisse, cum filius meus Heliodorus huc venit, magis toleranter quam libenter accepi. 2. sed dicere solebas, quamquam fatigans, quod meam quasi facundiam vererere. excusatio istaec, etiamsi fuisset vera, transierat, quia post terminatum libellum, qui [1] parum cultior est, reliquas denuo litteras usuali, licet accuratus mihi melior non sit, sermone contexo; non enim tanti est poliri formulas editione carituras. ceterum si caritatis tuae

[1] Cf. Additional Notes, p. 609.

---

* This letter to Magnus Felix was written after the Goths had occupied Auvergne (in A.D. 475) and, as the opening words show, long after the composition of *Ep.* 5 of this book which Felix had not answered. The arrival of Heliodorus had recently raised vain hopes that he might be the bearer of a letter from Felix to Sidonius. For Felix, see *Ep.* III. 4.

[1] That is, spiritual son; Sidonius speaks as a bishop. Nothing further is known of this Heliodorus.—*A*.

X

SIDONIUS TO HIS FRIEND FELIX,* GREETING

1. My lord, I am breaking out into a message of greeting, a late one indeed, but for many years I have not had a word from you, and I had not the courage to keep up my once frequent correspondence when I was ousted from my native soil and broken with the hardships of a sojourn in an alien land. In these circumstances it behoves you on your part to excuse my shamefaced reticence, for it is fitting that the humbled should have humble aspirations and not keep up the old constant intimacy with those on whom it would now perhaps be wrong to bestow more affection than veneration. For this reason, then, I have long kept silence, and when my son [1] Heliodorus came here, I bore with more patience than willingness my disappointment on finding that you likewise had been silent. 2. It is true that you used to say, though in a bantering way, that you were overawed by my eloquence (if one may so call it). This excuse, even if it had ever been true, had now ceased to hold good, for after finishing my little book,[2] which has some slight pretension to polish, I am making a change and compiling my remaining letters in ordinary speech (although in my case elaborate embellishment might be no improvement); for it is not worth while to polish phrases which will never be published. But if you once more direct your

[2] The *libellus* may be a published edition of Book III or possibly of Books I–III.

morem pristino colloquiorum cursui reddis, et nos vetustae loquacitatis orbitas recurremus, praeter haec avide praevio Christo, sicubi locorum[1] fueritis, modo redux patronus indulgeat, advolaturi, ut rebus amicitia vegetetur, quae verbis infrequentata torpuerat. vale.

XI

SIDONIVS PETREIO SVO SALVTEM

1. Angit me nimis damnum saeculi mei nuper erepto avunculo tuo Claudiano oculis nostris, ambigo an quempiam deinceps parem conspicaturis. vir siquidem fuit providus prudens, doctus eloquens, acer et hominum aevi loci populi sui ingeniosissimus quique indesinenter salva religione philosopharetur; et licet crinem barbamque non pasceret, pallium et clavam nunc inrideret, nunc etiam execraretur, a collegio tamen conplatonicorum solo habitu ac fide dissociabatur. 2. deus bone, quid erat illud, quotiens ad eum sola[2] consultationis gratia conveniebamus!

[1] sicubi locorum *MTCFPR*: sicubiculorum *L*: sicubi *** culorum *Luetjohann*: Christo sic, ubi locorum *Mohr*.
[2] *om.* sola *F*: *seclud. Luetjohann*: *fortasse* solitae.

---

[1] Probably Victorius, a Catholic Gallo-Roman in the service of the Visigoths, appointed Count of Auvergne by Euric; Cf. *Ep.* VII. 17. 1; Gregory of Tours, *Hist. Franc.*, II, 15(20); *de Gloria Martyrum*, 44; *Vit. Patr.*, 3. 1. Vol. I of Sidonius (Loeb) p. xlviii.

* Not otherwise known.

habitual affection into the old channels of correspondence, I also will once more traverse the tracks of my old garrulousness and, more than that, wherever you may be, I will with Christ's guidance eagerly fly thither, should my overlord [1] allow it on his return, and thus I will revive by action the friendship which has languished through dearth of words. Farewell.

XI

SIDONIUS TO HIS FRIEND PETREIUS,* GREETING

1. I am deeply grieved at the loss which my generation has sustained by the removal of your uncle [2] Claudianus from our eyes, which will scarcely, methinks, see his like again. He was a man both provident and prudent, learned, eloquent, ardent, the most talented among men of his time, his country, and of his people, and one who ceaselessly devoted himself to philosophy without detriment to religion—indeed, although he did not let his hair and beard grow long, and although he sometimes ridiculed, sometimes even execrated the philosopher's cloak and cudgel,[3] it was only in his dress and in his religion that he parted company with the Platonic brotherhood. 2. Gracious heaven! What an experience it was when we gathered to him for the sole purpose of holding discussions! How he would

[2] In fact his great-uncle, Claudianus Mamertus. See *Ep.* IV. 2.

[3] The *pallium* and the *clava* marked the philosopher. Cf. *Ep.* IV. 9. 3; IX. 9. 14; *Carm.* XV. 197.

quam ille omnibus statim[1] totum non dubitans, non fastidiens aperiebat, voluptuosissimum reputans, si forte oborta quarumpiam quaestionum insolubilitate labyrinthica scientiae suae thesauri eventilarentur. iam si frequentes consederamus, officium audiendi omnibus,[2] uni solum quem forsitan elegissemus deputans ius loquendi, viritim vicissimque, non tumultuatim nec sine schematis cuiuspiam gestu artificioso doctrinae suae opes erogaturus. 3. dein quaecumque dixisset protinus reluctantium syllogismorum contrarietatibus excipiebamus; sed repellebat omnium nostrum temerarias oppositiones: itaque nihil non perpensum probatumque recipiebatur. hinc etiam illi apud nos maxima reverentia fuit, quod non satis ferebat aegre pigram in quibuspiam sequacitatem. haec apud eum culpa veniabilis erat; quo fiebat esset ut nobis patientia eiusdem sine imitatione laudabilis. quis[3] enim virum super abditis consuleret invitus, a cuius disputationis communione ne idiotarum quidem imperitorumque sciscitatio repudiabatur?[4] 4. haec pauca de studiis. ceterum cetera quis competenti praeconio extollat, quod condicionis humanae per omnia memor clericos opere sermone populares, exhortatione maerentes destitutos solacio, captivos pretio ieiunos cibo nudos operimento consolabatur? pariter et super his plura

[1] statū *M*: ū *corr. in* ī *M*,[1] *eras. M*.[2]
[2] omnibus ⟨iniungebat⟩ *Luetjohann*.
[3] quisve *L*.
[4] repudiabatur *L*: repudiaretur.

straightway expound everything to us all without hesitation and without arrogance, deeming it a great delight if some questions presented a labyrinthine intricacy which required him to ransack the treasure-houses of his wisdom! Again, if there was a large assembly of us, he would assign to all but one the function of listeners and to one man, perhaps chosen by ourselves, the duty of speaking, his object being to dispense the wealth of his teaching to us individually and in turn, not in hasty disorder or with neglect of some artistic manipulation which forms a rhetorical figure. 3. Thereupon we would immediately encounter all his observations with a battery of opposing syllogisms, but he always routed his opponents' rash objections; the upshot was that no idea was accepted without being thoroughly weighed and tested. Another thing which made us respect him most deeply was that he showed little trace of annoyance at the slow apprehension of certain pupils, this was a fault that in his opinion was pardonable: hence, for us, tolerance of the same fault seemed admirable and beyond the reach of imitation. Who indeed could have felt reluctant to consult on obscure problems a man who did not debar even amateurish and ignorant questioners from participation in his discussion? 4. So much in brief about his learned pursuits. As for his other excellences, who could extol them with adequate laudation, showing how he was in all things mindful of the lot of humanity, aiding the clergy by his work, the laity by his discourse, the mourner by his exhortation, the destitute by his help, the prisoners with ransom, the hungry with food, the naked with clothing?

replicare superforaneum statuo. nam merita sua, quibus divitem conscientiam censu pauperatus locupletavit, spe futurae retributionis celare plus studuit. 5. * * *[1] episcopum fratrem maiorem natu affectuosissime observans, quem diligebat ut filium, cum tamquam patrem veneraretur. sed et ille suspiciebat hunc granditer, habens in eo consiliarium in iudiciis vicarium in ecclesiis, procuratorem in negotiis vilicum in praediis, tabularium in tributis in lectionibus comitem, in expositionibus interpretem in itineribus contubernalem. sic utrique ab alterutro usque ad invidiam exempli mutua fide germanitatis officia restituebantur. 6. sed quid dolorem nostrum moderaturi causis potius doloris fomenta sufficimus? ergo, ut dicere institueramus, huic iam, ut est illud Maronianum, cineri ingrato id est gratiam non relaturo neniam condidimus tristem luctuosamque propemodum laboriose, quia faceret dictandi desuetudo difficultatem, nisi quod animum natura desidiosissimum dolor fletu gravidus accendit. eius hoc carmen est:[2]

germani decus et dolor Mamerti,
mirantum unica pompa episcoporum,
hoc dat[3] caespite membra Claudianus,

[1] *lacunam stat. Leo.*
[2] eius hoc carmen est *secludere malit Gustafsson.*
[3] condit *coni. Gustafsson.*

---

[1] *Aen.* VI. 213.
[2] As elsewhere in Sidonius, *dictare* means to compose, write,

Since Anderson left no translation of the rest of this letter, W. H. Semple completed it as follows: To reveal more than this to the same effect I count as unnecessary. As with his learning, so with these virtues —I deem it superfluous to enlarge upon them: for the good deeds with which, though poor in worldly estate, he richly endowed his conscience, he was the more concerned to conceal in the hope of reward hereafter. 5. His elder brother, the bishop, he held in most affectionate regard, loving him as a son and respecting him as a father. The brother, too, regarded him with the highest esteem, having in him a counsellor in his court, a deputy in his churches, an agent in his business, a factor on his estates, an accountant in his revenues, an associate in his reading, an interpreter in his exegesis, and a companion in his travels. So each repaid to the other the services of brotherhood in mutual good faith, setting an example which might well inspire envy. 6. But why, hoping to calm my grief, do I go on supplying fuel to the flame of it? So, then, as I had started to say at first, I have composed this sad and mournful dirge, in honour, as Virgil's phrase [1] has it, of the unthankful ashes (that is to say, the dead who can show no gratitude): the work has been in a sense laborious, for my disuse of composition [2] was making it a difficult task, except that my natural indolence was quickened by my tear-burdened grief. This is his epitaph:

Under this mound rests the body of Claudianus.
He was the pride and sorrow of his brother Mamertus,
And the unique boast of admiring bishops.

triplex bybliotheca quo magistro,
Romana, Attica, Christiana, fulsit;
quam totam monachus virente in aevo
secreta bibit institutione,
orator, dialecticus, poeta,
tractator, geometra, musicusque,
doctus solvere vincla quaestionum
et verbi gladio secare sectas,
si quae catholicam fidem lacessunt.
psalmorum hic modulator et phonascus
ante altaria fratre gratulante
instructas docuit sonare classes.
hic sollemnibus annuis paravit
quae quo tempore lecta convenirent.
antistes fuit ordine in secundo,
fratrem fasce levans episcopali.
nam de pontificis tenore summi
ille insignia sumpsit, hic laborem.
at tu, quisque doles, amice lector,
de tanto quasi nil viro supersit,
udis parce genis rigare marmor:
mens et gloria non queunt humari.

7. Ecce quod carmen, cum primum affui, super unanimi fratris ossa conscripsi. namque tunc afui, cum funerarentur;[1] nec ob hoc tamen perdidi in totum desideratissimam flendi occasionem. nam

[1] funerarentur *L*: funeraretur.

Under his teaching three literatures were illumined,
Latin, Greek, and Christian:
All of them as a monk in his prime
He absorbed in his unobtrusive studies.
He was prose-writer, philosopher, poet, preacher,
geometer, and musician:
skilled in disentangling knotty problems,
and with the sword of the word to hew down
the sectaries [1]
who assail the Catholic faith.
Precentor and choirmaster,
He taught well-trained companies to chant before
the altar,
winning his brother's admiration.
For the yearly festivals he selected readings
suitable to each season.
He was a priest of the second order,
who eased the load his brother carried as bishop,
for from the routine of a bishop's life
the brother took the honours, he did the work.
But thou, whoe'er thou art, friendly reader, who dost
grieve to think that of a man so great nothing
now remains,
Forbear to wet this monument with flowing tears:
His mind and glory can never descend to the grave.

7. There you have the poem which, as soon as I arrived, I inscribed over the remains of a much-beloved brother. I was away at the time when they were interred; but I did not on that account altogether lose the much desired opportunity of mourn-

[1] In the Latin, Sidonius makes word-play by *secare sectas* "to split the split." "dissect the sects."

dum forte meditarer, lacrimis habenas anima parturiente laxavi fecique ad epitaphium quod alii fecerunt ad sepulchrum. haec ergo scripsimus tibi, ne forsitan arbitrarere solam nos colere vivorum sodalitatem reique tuo iudicio essemus, nisi amicorum vita carentum semper aeque ut incolumium reminisceremur. namque et ex hoc, quod vix reservatur imaginaria fides vel superstitibus, non praeter aequum opinabere, si perpaucos esse conicias, qui mortuos ament. vale.

XII

SIDONIVS SIMPLICIO ET APOLLINARI SVIS SALVTEM

1. Deus bone, quantum naufragioso pelago conformis est motus animorum, quippe cum nuntiorum turbinibus adversis quasi propria tempestate confunditur![1] nuper ego filiusque communis Terentianae Hecyrae sales ruminabamus; studenti assidebam naturae meminens et professionis oblitus quoque absolutius rhythmos comicos incitata docilitate sequeretur, ipse etiam fabulam similis argumenti id est Epitrepontem Menandri in manibus habebam. 2. legebamus pariter laudabamus iocabamurque et, quae vota communia sunt, illum lectio, me ille

[1] confundimur *Luetjohann qui et* confunduntur *coni.*

---

* See *Ep.* IV. 4.

[1] Much of this play "The Arbitrants" has been recovered (See F. G. Allinson, *Menander*, Loeb Class. Libr. pp. 2 ff.) though most of the work of Menander is lost. He lived from 342 to 291 B.C.

ing for him; for while I was conning over my poem, my soul welled up within me and I gave free rein to my weeping; in presence of the epitaph I broke down as others had done at the tomb. Well, then, I have written you this letter, lest you should perhaps think that it is only the living whose companionship I cherish: else I might be at fault in your judgment, if I did not always keep in mind my departed friends equally with those who survive. For since nowadays there is kept scarcely a shadow of loyalty towards even living friends, you will not be far out in supposing that they are very few in number who love the dead. Farewell.

XII

SIDONIUS TO HIS FRIENDS SIMPLICIUS AND APOLLINARIS,* GREETING

1. Gracious heaven! How the stirring of our minds resembles a ship-wrecking sea, for it is thrown into confusion by adverse squalls of news as if by a self-engendered storm! The other day I and the son to all of us were browsing on the wit of Terence's *Mother-in-Law*. I was seated beside him as he studied, following my natural inclination and forgetful of my sacred calling, and in order to spur his receptive mind and enable him to follow the comic measures more perfectly, I had in my own hands a play of similar content, the *Epitrepontes*[1] of Menander. 2. We were reading, praising, and jesting together, and, such are the desires we all share, he was charmed with the reading, and I with him,

capiebat, cum repente puer familiaris adstitit vultuosus. cui nos: "quid ita?" et ille: "lectorem," inquit, "Constantem nomine pro foribus vidi a dominis Simplicio et Apollinare redeuntem; dedit quidem litteras quas acceperat sed perdidit quas recepit." 3. quibus agnitis serenitas laetitiae meae confestim nubilo superducti maeroris insorduit tantamque mihi bilem nuntii huiusce contrarietas excitavit, ut per plurimos dies illum ipsum hermam stolidissimum venire ante oculos meos inexoratus arcuerim, laturus aegre, si mihi apices aut quoscumque aut quorumcumque non redderet, taceam vestros, qui mihi, dum recti compos animus durat, minime frequentes maxime desiderabiles iudicabuntur. 4. at postquam nostra sensim temporis intervallo ira defremuit, percontor admissum,[1] num verbo quippiam praeterea detulisset. respondit ipse, quamquam esset trepidus et sternax et prae reatu balbutiret ore, caecutiret intuitu, totum quo instrui, quo delectari valerem, paginis quae intercidissent fuisse mandatum. quocirca recurrite ad pugillares, replicate membranas et scripta rescribite. tamdiu enim aequanimiter admitto, ut desiderio meo sinister eventus officiat, donec ad vos nostro sermone perveniat ad nos vestrum non pervenisse sermonem. valete.

[1] admissum *LN*[1]: *om. rell.*

when suddenly a domestic stood before us with a wry face. "Why that look on your face?" we said. He answered "I have seen, at the door, the reader called Constans, who has come back from my Lords Simplicius and Apollinaris. He duly delivered to them the letters he had received from you but he has lost the one he received from them in reply." 3. When I learned this, my sunny joy was instantly overcast by a dark cloud of grief, and the unconscionable conduct of this messenger kindled in me such a raging fury that for several days I inexorably forbade that senseless blockhead to present himself to my sight, for I should have been indignant if he had failed to deliver to me any letters from any persons whatsoever, to say nothing of yours, which, so long as I retain a sense of the fitness of things, will always seem to me as supremely desirable as they are lamentably infrequent. 4. But when my anger had gradually abated in course of time, I received him and asked if he had brought some verbal message in addition. Unnerved though he was, and, grovelling, with tongue stammering and vision blurred through the sense of his guilt, he answered, that the words from which I might have derived such instruction and delight had been wholly committed to the pages which had disappeared on the way. So please rush back to your tablets, fold the sheets, and rewrite what you wrote; for I can bear calmly the thwarting of my desire by this unlucky accident only until such time as it comes to your knowledge through my words that your words have not come to me. Farewell.

XIII

SIDONIVS VETTIO[1] SVO SALVTEM

1. Nuper rogatu Germanici spectabilis viri Cantillensem ecclesiam inspexi. est ipse loco sitorum[2] facile primus quique post tergum cum iam duodecim lustra transmittat, cotidie tamen habitu cultuque conspicuo non iuvenescit solum sed quodammodo repuerascit. enimvero vestis adstricta, tensus coturnus, crinis in rotae specimen accisus barba intra rugarum latebras mersis ad cutem secta forcipibus. 2. ad hoc et munere superno membrorum solida coniunctio, integer visus, amplus in celeri gressus incessu, incorruptae lactea dentium compage gingivae. non illi stomachus nauseat, non vena flammatur, non cor incutitur, non pulmo suspirat, non riget lumbus, non iecur turget, non mollescit manus, non spina curvatur, sed praeditus sanitate iuvenali solam sibi vindicat de senectute reverentiam. 3. propter quae beneficia peculiaria dei, quoniam vobis iura amicitiae grandia vigent, quippe vicinis, obsecro ac moneo, ut consilio tuo, cui sequendo per conscientiam magnam maximam tribuis auctoritatem, non multum fidat ambiguis nec nimis nimiae credat

[1] Vettio] *cp. Ep.* IV. 9. 1: Vectio (*om. inscript. L*).
[2] positorum *malit Gustafsson.*

---

* See *Ep.* IV. 9. 1.
[1] Chantelle-la-Vieille, rather than Chantelle-la-Châtel, in Allier.

XIII

SIDONIUS TO HIS FRIEND VETTIUS,* GREETING

1. The other day I inspected the church at Cantiliae[1] on the invitation of the honourable Germanicus. He is easily the leading personage of the place. Although he has some sixty years behind him, yet in his dress and get-up which one cannot fail to notice, he not merely grows youthful every day but virtually becomes a boy again. His garments are close-fitting, his boots tightly fastened, his hair is cut in a wheel-like fashion, his beard is close-clipped to the skin with scissors pressed into the hollows of the wrinkles. 2. Moreover, by the favour of heaven his limbs are firmly knit, his sight is unimpaired, he walks quickly with long strides, and his gums are perfectly sound, with an array of milk-white teeth. His stomach does not get upset, his veins are never inflamed, his heart has no spasms, his lungs do not pant, his loins are not hardened, his liver is not swollen, his hands do not grow flabby, his spine is not curved; on the contrary, he is endowed with the healthiness of a young man, and the only attribute of old age he can claim is reverence. 3. In view of these peculiar bounties from God, since you and he being neighbours have strong bonds of friendship, I beseech and admonish you to give him your advice (for by your great conscientiousness you greatly influence one to follow your advice); urge him not to put much faith in uncertainties or trust excessively to his excessive health, but now at last to embrace

incolumitati, sed tandem professione religionis arrepta viribus potius resurgentis innocentiae convalescat, faciat se vetustus annis meritis novum. 4. et quoniam nemo ferme est, qui plectibilibus careat occultis, ipse super his, quae clam commissa reminiscitur, palam fusa satisfactione solvatur. nam sacerdotis pater filiusque pontificis, nisi sanctus est, rubo similis efficitur, quem de rosis natum rosasque parientem et genitis gignentibusque floribus medium pungentibus comparanda peccatis dumorum vallat asperitas. vale.

XIV

SIDONIVS POLEMIO SVO SALVTEM

1. Gaius Tacitus unus e maioribus tuis, Ulpianorum temporum consularis, sub verbis cuiuspiam Germanici ducis in historia sua rettulit dicens: "cum Vespasiano mihi vetus amicitia; et, dum privatus esset, amici vocabamur." "quo respicit," ais, "ista praefari"? ut scilicet memineris eo tempore, quo personam publicam portas, gratiae te privatae memorem semper esse oportere. biennium prope clauditur, quod te praefectum praetorio Galliarum

* See *Carm.* XIV. He was Praetorian Prefect of Gaul (the last ever to be appointed) for two years. Chaix, I. 347; II. 254. C. Stevens *Sid. Apoll.* 197. Date: about 471–472.

[1] Ulpius was the family-name of Trajan, Emperor A.D. 98–117.

the profession of religion and to choose rather to grow strong with the strength of reviving innocence, and now that he is old in years to make himself a new man by virtues. 4. And as there is scarcely anyone who is free from hidden faults that merit punishment, let him gain absolution by giving open and widespread satisfaction for the secret sins which he remembers. For the father of a priest and the son of a bishop, if he is not holy, becomes like a briar which, being sprung from roses and producing roses, and placed between the flowers it has produced and those which produced it, is enclosed by prickly thorns as are bushes symbolising the sins which prick the soul. Farewell.

XIV

SIDONIUS TO HIS FRIEND POLEMIUS,* GREETING

1. Gaius Tacitus, one of your ancestors, a man of consular rank in the time of Trajan,[1] records in his history the following words as uttered by a German commander:[2] "I have a long-standing friendship with Vespasian, and while he was an ordinary citizen we were called friends." "What," you ask, "is the object of this preamble?" It is to make you remember that you ought, when wearing an official dignity, to be ever mindful of your private friendship. For almost two whole years I have rejoiced to see you praetorian prefect of Gaul—not because of your

[2] The Batavian chief Claudius Civilis, referring to Vespasian, Emperor A.D. 69–79. Tacitus, *Hist.* V. 26.

non nova vestra dignatione sed nostro affectu adhuc vetere gaudemus, qui, si Romanarum rerum sineret adversitas, aegre toleraremus, nisi singulae personae, non dicam provinciae, variis per te beneficiis amplificarentur. 2. et nunc, cum id, quod possibilitas tua non habet, verecundia non petatur,[1] dicas velim, qualiter futurus fueris humanus in factis, qui perduras avarus in verbis. nam tuorum peritiae comparatus non solum Cornelios oratores sed Ausonios quoque poetas vincere potes. si te hactenus philosophantem [2] nova subito ob iurisdictionem gloria capit: et nos aliquod nomenque decusque gessimus. 3. at si videtur humilitas nostrae professionis habenda contemptui, quia Christo res humanas vitasque medicaturo putrium conscientiarum ultro [3] squalens ulcus aperimus, quod in nostri ordinis viris, etsi adhuc aliquid de neglegentia fetet, iam tamen nihil de superbia tumet, noveris volo non, ut est apud praesulem fori, sic esse apud iudicem mundi. namque ut is, qui propria vobis non tacuerit flagitia, damnatur, ita nobiscum qui eadem deo fuerit confessus absolvitur. unde liquido patet incongrue a partibus

[1] petat *Leo*.
[2] philosophante *L*.
[3] cultro *MTCFPN*¹.

---

[1] The family-name of the historian Tacitus was Cornelius. Ausonius was a poet and rhetorician of Bordeaux, *c.* A.D. 310–395, a considerable number of whose writings survives.

new rank but because of our old friendship; and if the unpropitious state of Rome's fortunes gave scope for such things, I should be distressed if each individual, let alone each province, were not enriched by various favours from your hands. 2. And as things are, at a time when shame forbids our asking for what is beyond your power, I should like you to tell me how you would have been liberal with your deeds, when you are so persistently stingy with your words; for if comparison is made between your skill and that of your ancestors you will win the palm not only from prose writers like Tacitus but from poets like Ausonius.[1] If, thanks to your office, a new pride is suddenly getting hold of you who have hitherto been philosophically inclined —well, "I too have borne high title and dignity."[2] 3. But if the lowliness of our profession seems to you worthy of disdain because we clerics take it upon ourselves to reveal the unsightly wounds of mouldering guilt to Christ who offers his healing touch to human concerns and human lives (and in men of our profession those wounds may still fester a little from neglect, but they are completely cured of the swelling of pride), I would have you know that before the judge of all the earth it is not as before the judge of an earthly court. With you the man who openly acknowledges his crimes is condemned, but with us the man who confesses them to God has absolution. Hence it is clear as daylight that it is incongruous for your set to

[2] Virgil, *Aen.* II. 89. This does not mean, as some have thought, that Sidonius was ever Praetorian Prefect of Gaul.

vestris nimis reum pronuntiari cuius causa plus spectat tribunal alienum. 4. quapropter imminentem querellam nostri doloris nequaquam valebis ulterius effundere,[1] quia, succedentibus prosperis sive obliviscare seu neglegas gratiam antiquam, iuxta est acerbum. proinde si futura magni pensitas, scribe clerico, si praesentia, scribe collegae; et hanc in te ipse virtutem, si naturalis est, excole, si minus, ut insiticiam appone, qua sodales vetustos numquam pro consequentum novitate fastidias. porro autem videbere sic amicis uti quasi floribus, tamdiu gratis, donec recentibus. vale.

XV

SIDONIVS ELAPHIO SVO SALVTEM

1. Epulum multiplex et capacissima lectisternia para: plurimis viis, pluribus turbis (ita bonorum contubernio sedit [2]) ad te venitur, quippe postquam omnibus tempus futurae dedicationis inclaruit. nam baptisterium, quod olim fabricabamini, scribitis posse iam consecrari. ad quae festa vos voti nos ministerii, officii multos fidei totos causa sollicitat; siquidem res est grandis exempli eo tempore a vobis nova

[1] refundere *Wilamowitz*: effugere *Leo*.
[2] sedet *C*.

* Not otherwise known.

pronounce a strong verdict of guilty on one whose case more properly belongs to the tribunal of another. 4. And so you will certainly not be able any more to shake off the imminent complaint of my resentment, because, whether with the access of prosperity one forgets or neglects an old attachment, the one is as grievous as the other. Accordingly, if you attach importance to the future life, write to your cleric; if you value things present, write to your colleague; and if this virtue is innate in you, develop it; if not, graft it into your nature—I mean the virtue which will keep you from ever scorning old comrades for the novelty of later ones: otherwise you will seem to treat your friends like flowers, which are pleasing just as long as they are fresh. Farewell.

XV

SIDONIUS TO HIS FRIEND ELAPHIUS,* GREETING

1. Prepare a copious banquet and a huge spread of couches; people are coming to you by very many ways and in crowds more numerous still (so the brotherhood of your good friends has resolved), now that the time of the coming dedication has been published to all: for you write that the baptistery, which you had long been building, is now ready for consecration. To this festival you are urged by reason of your vow, I by reason of my episcopal office, many by the claims of duty and all by the faith that they hold; for it is a signal phenomenon that you should be building new church-roofs at a

ecclesiarum culmina strui, quo vix alius auderet vetusta sarcire. 2. quod restat, optamus, ut deo nostro per uberes annos, sicut vota redditis, ita reddenda voveatis, idque non solum religione celata, sed et conversione manifesta; mitigatoque temporum statu tam desiderio meo Christus indulgeat quam Rutenorum, ut possitis et pro illis offerre sacrificia, qui iam pro vobis offertis altaria. 3. de cetero, quamquam et[1] extremus autumnus iam diem breviat et viatorum sollicitas aures foliis toto nemore labentibus crepulo fragore circumstrepit inque castellum, ad quod invitas, utpote Alpinis rupibus cinctum, sub vicinitate brumali difficilius escenditur,[2] nos tamen deo praevio per tuorum montium latera confragosa venientes nec subiectas cautes nec superiectas nives expavescemus, quamvis iugorum profunda declivitas aggere cocleatim fracto saepe redeunda sit, quia, et si nulla sollemnitas, tu satis dignus es, ut est Tullianum illud, propter quem Thespiae visantur. vale.

[1] et *seclud. Luetjohann.*
[2] ascenditur *MTCFP.*

---

[1] Of old Segodunum, Rodez in Rouergue, which Sidonius visited on duty. This would probably be in A.D. 469; in 470 the Visigoths were in occupation there.

time when scarcely any other person would dare even to repair old ones. 2. For the future, I pray that, even as you are now paying vows to our God, so you will afterwards make fresh vows to be paid throughout fruitful years, and that, too, as the outcome not only of secret worship but of open conversion; I pray also that with the advent of better times Christ may indulge the desire which I share with the Ruteni,[1] that you, who are now offering an altar for your own soul's sake, may be able also to offer sacrifice on their behalf. 3. Well, although the latter end of autumn is already shortening the day and makes a crackling rustle round the anxious ears of travellers as the leaves fall from every tree; and though it is less easy on the verge of winter to climb up to the castle to which you invite me (beset as it is by Alpine crags), yet with God's guidance I will traverse the broken sides of your mountains, undaunted by the spiky rocks yawning below or the snow hanging above, aye, undaunted although the road with its spiral bends may often force me to retraverse the deep hill-slopes. For even if there were no solemnity in prospect, you are a sufficient reason why, as Cicero says, Thespiae [2] should be visited. Farewell.

[2] Cicero, *In Verr.*, II. 4. 2, sect. 4. It was a common saying that people would visit Thespiae only to admire the "Eros" of Praxiteles of the latter part of the fourth century B.C. and later.

XVI

SIDONIVS RVRICIO SVO SALVTEM

1. Accepi per Paterninum paginam vestram, quae plus mellis an salis habeat incertum est. ceterum eloquii copiam hanc praefert, hos olet flores, ut bene appareat non vos manifesta modo verum furtiva quoque lectione proficere. quamquam et hoc furtum quod deprecaris exemplati libelli non venia tam debeat respicere quam gloria. quid tu enim facias absque virtute, qui nec ipsa peccata sine laude committis? 2. ego vero quicquid impositum est fraudis mihi, utpote absenti, libens audio principalique pro munere amplector, quod[1] quodammodo damnum indemne toleravi. neque enim quod tuo accessit usui, decessit hoc nostrae proprietati aut ad incrementa scientiae vestrae per detrimenta venistis alienae. quin potius ipse[2] iure abhinc uberi praeconio non carebis,[3] qui magis igneo ingenio naturam decenter ignis imitatus es[4] de quo si quid demere velis, remanet totus totusque transfertur. unde iam parce trepidare deque moribus amici plusculum recto secus credere. namque in hoc facto nos magis vulnus polluit culpae, si feriat ictus invidiae. vale.

[1] quod *LR*: qui.
[2] ⟨is⟩ ipse *Luetjohann*.
[3] carebit *Luetjohann*.
[4] est *Luetjohann*.

* Belonging to a senatorial family. When he married Iberia in A.D. 470 Sidonius wrote an Epithalamium (*Carm.* X and XI). Ruricius became Bishop of Limoges in 484. He was author of two books of letters which are extant. See also Sidonius' letters *Ep.* V. 15; VIII. 10; B. Krusch in Luetjohann's edition of Sidonius, *Monumenta Germaniae Historica*, Auct. Antiquiss. Tom. VIII, pp. LXII ff. and 299 ff.

XVI

SIDONIUS TO HIS FRIEND RURICIUS,* GREETING

1. I have received your letter by the hand of Paterninus. One could not say whether it has more of honeyed sweetness or of the salt of wit; anyhow, it displays such fertility of utterance, and such fragrant flowers of style that you are clearly profiting not only from open but stealthy reading. Yet even this "theft," for which you apologise, of a book which you have copied out, must needs be matter for pride rather than for pardon; for how could you do anything wrong when even your faults are not without merit? 2. For my part I am quite pleased to hear of the little trick played on me in my absence, and I welcome as a splendid gift the fact that I have, so to speak, sustained a loss which is no loss. For that which has gone to serve your use has not gone from my ownership, nor have you acquired an increase of your technical skill through the diminution of another's. On the contrary, you will henceforth with good right enjoy ample applause in that with your flaming genius you have fittingly chosen to imitate the character of fire; for one may seek to take from a fire, but the fire that is left and the fire that is removed are each a complete fire. So don't be alarmed, and don't cherish a rather unfair opinion of your friend's character; for in the present case the wound of guilt might more truly be said to taint me, if I felt a stab of envy. Farewell.

XVII

SIDONIVS ARBOGASTI[1] SVO SALVTEM

1. Eminentius amicus tuus, domine maior, obtulit mihi quas ipse dictasti litteras litteratas et gratiae trifariam renidentis[2] cultu refertas. quarum utique virtutum caritas prima est, quae te coegit in nobis vel peregrinis vel iam latere cupientibus humilia dignari; tum verecundia, cuius instinctu dum inmerito trepidas, merito praedicaris; tertia urbanitas, qua te ineptire facetissime allegas et Quirinalis impletus fonte facundiae potor Mosellae Tiberim ructas, sic barbarorum familiaris, quod tamen nescius barbarismorum, par ducibus antiquis lingua manuque, sed quorum dextera solebat non stilum minus tractare quam gladium. 2. quocirca sermonis pompa Romani, si qua adhuc uspiam est, Belgicis olim sive Rhenanis abolita terris in te resedit, quo vel incolumi vel perorante, etsi apud limitem [ipsum][3]

[1] Arbogasti *Mommsen*: arvogasti *aut* arvogasto *codd. pler.* (*om. inscript. L*).
[2] renitentis *FM*².
[3] ipsum *om. LR*: eū (*sc.* eum) *TF*.

* Count, that is, governor of Trèves; he was a good Christian, according to Auspicius, Bishop of Toul (Migne, *Patr. Lat.*, LXI. p. 1006). It may have been he who became Bishop of Chartres in A.D. 473 or 474. Cf. *Hist. Litt. de la France . . . par les Religieux de S. Maur*, II. 478, 548; L. S. de Tillemont, *Mémoires* etc. XVI. 250 etc. Son of Arigius, he was ap-

XVII

SIDONIUS TO HIS FRIEND ARBOGASTES,* GREETING

1. My honoured Lord, your friend Eminentius has handed me a letter written by your own hand, a really literary letter, replete with the grace of a three-fold charm. The first of its merits is certainly the affection which prompted such condescension to my lowly condition, for if not a stranger I am in these days a man who courts obscurity; the second virtue is your modesty, which while causing you unmerited nervousness wins for you well-merited praise; in the third place comes your urbanity which leads you to make a most amusing profession of clumsiness when as a matter of fact you have drunk deep from the spring of Roman eloquence and, dwelling by the Moselle, you speak the true Latin of the Tiber:[1] you are intimate with the barbarians but are innocent of barbarisms, and are equal in tongue, as also in strength of arm, to the leaders of old, I mean those who were wont to handle the pen no less than the sword. 2. Thus the splendour of the Roman speech, if it still exists anywhere, has survived in you, though it has long been wiped out from the Belgian and Rhenic lands: with you and your eloquence surviving, even though Roman law has ceased at our

parently descended from that Arbogast who, a barbarian in the Roman army, first became famous late in the fourth century. He is called a Frank by several authorities. The proper spelling of his name seems to be Arbogastes.

[1] *Lit.* "you who drink the waters of the Moselle give forth a Tiber-stream of eloquence."—*A.*

Latina iura ceciderunt, verba non titubant. quapropter alternum salve rependens granditer laetor saltim in inlustri pectore tuo vanescentium litterarum remansisse vestigia, quae si frequenti lectione continuas, experiere per dies, quanto antecellunt beluis homines, tanto anteferri rusticis institutos. 3. de paginis sane quod spiritalibus vis ut aliquid interpres improbus garriam, iustius haec postulantur[1] a sacerdotibus loco propinquis aetate grandaevis, fide claris opere vulgatis, ore promptis memoria tenacibus, omni denique meritorum sublimium dote potioribus. namque ut antistitem civitatis vestrae relinquam, consummatissimum virum cunctarumque virtutum conscientia et fama iuxta beatum, multo opportunius de quibuscumque quaestionibus tibi interrogantur[2] incliti Galliarum patres et protomystae, nec satis positus in longinquo Lupus nec parum in proximo Auspicius, quorum doctrinae abundanti eventilandae nec consultatio tua sufficit. proinde quod super hac precum parte non parui, benignus quidem sed et iustus ignosce, quia si vos imperitiam fugere par est, me quoque decet vitare iactantiam. vale.

bu
[1] postulantur *M*[1].

bu
[2] interrogabuntur *P*: interrogantur *M*[1].

border,[1] the Roman speech does not falter. For this reason, as I reciprocate your greeting, I rejoice greatly that at any rate in your illustrious breast there have remained traces of our vanishing culture. If you extend these by constant reading you will discover for yourself as each day passes that the educated are no less superior to the unlettered than men are to beasts. 3. With regard to your wish that I (and a presumptuous babbler I would be!) should attempt an exegesis of Holy Writ, I assure you that such requests would more reasonably be addressed to priests who are not only near you in residence but old in years, renowned for their faith and famed for their works, ready in speech and tenacious in memory, in short, superior in all the graces of supreme worth. For to say nothing of your own people's bishop, a paragon of a man, blessed with a character that knows every virtue and with a reputation to correspond, it would be much more fitting for you to consult, on any problems whatsoever, those illustrious fathers and leading hierophants of Gaul, the not too distant Lupus [2] and the not insufficiently near Auspicius,[3] men whose learning is so abundant that not even your questioning could sift it to the bottom. So you must be kind and at the same time reasonable, and forgive my refusal to satisfy this part of your petition; for if it is right for you to flee from ignorance, it is also right for me to avoid pretentiousness. Farewell.

[1] Apparently the frontier between the shrunken Empire and the Franks rather than the Visigoths and Burgundians.

[2] Saint Lupus, Bishop of Troyes. See *Ep.* VI. 1, first note.

[3] Learned Bishop of Toul. Cf. *Ep.* VII. 11 (10).

XVIII

SIDONIVS LVCONTIO SVO SALVTEM

1. Obliviscceris quod rogaris eque contrario, si quid iniungas, ex asse meministi. repetere perlongum est de cito reditu quae tu tuique promiseritis mihi meisque, quorum omnium non sunt vel minima completa. quin potius, cum fugam a nobis machinaremini, quo reversuros ad sacrum pascha vos putaremus, nullae graves sarcinae ad praedium ex oppido ductae, nulla serraca, nulla esseda subvehendis oneribus adtrahebantur. 2. utque de matronalium partium nil querar fraude, quas cum expeditis tulistis impedimentis, tuque fraterque communis Volusianus vix singulorum clientum puerorumque comitatu ambiebamini; per quod sollicitudinem prosequentum vana mox recurrendi spe fefellistis; certe frater Volusianus, qui forte pergens in praedia Baiocassina totamque [1] provinciam Lugdunensem secundam pervagaturus,[2] expectationem nostram specie brevioris itineris elusit. 3. et nunc ipse sic multis contra fidem diebus otiabundus ais tibi si quas postea luserim metro nugas mitti

[1] totamque *codd.*: totam *Luetjohann*: qui *post* Volusianus *secludere voluit Leo.*
[2] pervagaturus *codd.*: pervagatur *Luetjohann.*

---

* Or perhaps Lucentius. Not otherwise known, however.
[1] See *Ep.* VII. 17. He was not a real brother.
[2] *forte* ? "in reality"; "as a matter of fact."—*A.*

XVIII

SIDONIUS TO HIS FRIEND LUCONTIUS,* GREETING

1. You forget what you are asked to do, and on the other hand, you never fail to remember all your own demands. It would be quite tedious to recount all the assurances of a speedy return which you and your family showered on me and mine: and yet not a particle of them has been fulfilled—far from it. When you were arranging to run away from us you intended to make us think you would be back by Holy Easter; and so no heavy baggage was transported from town to your estate; no carriages, no wagons for carting luggage followed in your train. 2. I refrain from complaining about the trickery of the ladies whom you carried off with only the slightest modicum of luggage, but you and Volusianus,[1] whom we both own as a brother, had scarcely one client and one servant to escort you, and thus you beguiled the disquietude of those who saw you off by holding out the vain hope that you would hurry back to them. Certainly our brother Volusianus did so, for he cheated our hope and expectation with the pretence of a shorter trip when really[2] proceeding to his property at Baiocassium[3] and therefore likely to traverse the whole province of Lugdunensis Secunda. 3. And now you yourself, after thus taking your ease for many days in defiance of your promise, say that I must send you any metrical trifles with which I may have toyed since you left.

[3] In Bessin.

oportere. annuo iniunctis, quia dignus es, ut talia legas; nam carmen ipsum, quod nunc e manibus elabitur, tam rusticanum est tamque impolitum, ut me non illud ad villam sed potius e villa mittere putes. 4. basilicam sancti pontificis confessorisque Martini Perpetuus episcopus, dignissimus tanto praedecessore successor, multum priori [1] quae fuit hactenus capaciorem novavit. magnum est, ut ferunt, opus nominandumque quod in honorem talis viri factum talis vir fecisse debuerit. huius me parietibus inscribere supradictus sacerdos hoc epigramma compellit, quod recensebis, ut est in his, quaecumque deposcit, privilegio caritatis imperiosissimus. 5. atque utinam molis illius pompam sive donaria nihil huius obsequii turpet oblatio; quod secus fore plurimum timeo, nisi forsitan inter omnia venusta sic epigrammatis istius foeditas placeat, ut niger naevus candido in corpore, qui quidem solet sic facere risum quod accipere suffragium. sed quid hinc amplius? pone fistulas ipse pastorias et elegiae nostrae, quia pede claudicat, manum porrige.

Martini corpus totis venerabile terris,
  in quo post vitae tempora vivit honor,

[1] priore *C*: priori.

---

[1] See *Ep.* VII. 9; sixth in succession, it seems, after Saint Martin as Bishop of Tours A.D. 458–488; see line 7 of the *carmen* below. But Gregory of Tours, in *Hist. Franc.* XI. 31 refers to Perpetuus as sixth after Saint Gatien, and, in *Hist. Franc.* II. 14, as fifth after Saint Martin. In the period A.D. 466–472 he rebuilt the church erected by Saint Brice

I yield to your behest because you deserve to read such trash, for the poem which is now being allowed to pass into circulation is so boorish and inelegant that you might well think I was sending it not to, but from, a rustic abode. 4. Bishop Perpetuus,[1] worthy successor of such a great predecessor, has rebuilt the church of the saintly pontiff and confessor, Martin, and has extended it far beyond its former area. It is a great and notable piece of work, they say, a worthy tribute from such a man to such a man. Well, the said cleric (who uses love's prerogative to be most insistent in any demands he makes) presses me to inscribe on the walls of the church the following poem which you will now judge for yourself. 5. I would fain hope that this dutiful contribution will not disfigure the majesty of that great edifice or the offerings which it contains; but I greatly fear the worst—unless perhaps amid all that beauty the ugliness of this poem find some favour like a black mole on a fair body which, though causing a smile, generally wins approval. But why say any more on the subject? Lay down your shepherd's pipe and stretch forth a helping hand to my elegy[2] with its limping[3] foot:

"In this place Martin's body, throughout the world revered, whose honour still lives after life's

round the remains of Saint Martin. *Ut ferunt* indicates that Sidonius had not seen it.

[2] Included in a collection of inscriptions copied from those in the church of St. Martin at Tours (a collection made it seems before A.D. 558 when the first of two disastrous fires occurred) is this poem of Sidonius. MSS of this collection have in line 11 of the text of Sidonius *in spatiis edis*.

[3] Because one line has six feet, the other five.

texerat hic primum plebeio machina cultu,
  quae confessori non erat aequa suo.
nec desistebat cives onerare pudore
  gloria magna viri, gratia parva loci;
antistes sed qui numeratur sextus ab ipso
  longam Perpetuus sustulit invidiam,
internum removens modici penetrale sacelli
  amplaque tecta levans exteriore domo;
creveruntque simul valido tribuente patrono
  in spatiis aedes,[1] conditor in meritis,
quae Salamoniaco potis est confligere templo,
  septima quae mundo fabrica mira fuit.
nam gemmis auro argento si splenduit illud,
  istud transgreditur cuncta metalla fide.
livor, abi, mordax absolvanturque priores,
  nil novet aut addat garrula posteritas;
dumque venit Christus, populos qui suscitet omnes,
  perpetuo durent culmina Perpetui.

6. Obtulimus, ut cernis, quod cantilenae recentis obvium manui fuit; sed nec hoc minus, si moras nectis, astra quatiemus, versibus quoque satirographis, si res exegerit, usuri, quos huic carmini lenitate adaequandos falso putabis. namque efficacius citius ardentius natura mortalium culpat aliqua quam laudet. vale.

[1] aedes *codd. pler.*: aedis.

---

[1] The church had to be rebuilt again by Gregory of Tours (A.D. 538–594), whose description of it finds confirmation

end, was first covered by an edifice of mean style, ill-befitting its patron-confessor; and shame lay ever heavy upon the people that the glory of the man should be so great, the beauty of the place so small. But Perpetuus the prelate sixth in order after him took away this age-long reproach: he removed the inner shrine that formed the modest chapel and raised a lordly pile by building outside and over it; and so by the favour of its mighty patron the church has grown in size, the builder in merit, and well might it vie with Solomon's temple which was the world's seventh wonder; that sanctuary gleamed with gold and silver and precious stones, but this one surpasses all metals with the gleam of faith. Get thee gone, biting envy! May our forefathers be absolved, and may babbling posterity neither alter nor add anything; and until Christ comes to rouse all peoples from the dead, may the edifice of Perpetuus perpetually endure.[1] "

6. I have passed on to you, as you see, the only bit of my recent doggerel that I had ready to hand; but that will not keep me from shaking the welkin if you persist in tarrying; and, should the case require it, I will even resort to satire, and you will be wrong if you think my satiric verses will match this poem in mildness. For human nature is more powerful, more ready, and more fiery in censure than in praise. Farewell.

through modern excavations on this site. Chaix, I. pp. 328–329. Gregory of Tours, *Hist. Franc.*, II. 14; IV. 20; X. 31.

XIX

SIDONIVS FLORENTINO SVO SALVTEM

1. Et moras nostras et silentium accusas. utrumque purgabile est; namque et venimus et scribimus. vale.

XX

SIDONIVS DOMNICIO[1] SVO SALVTEM

1. Tu, cui frequenter arma et armatos[2] inspicere iucundum est, quam voluptatem, putamus, mente conceperas,[3] si Sigismerem regium iuvenem ritu atque cultu gentilicio ornatum, utpote sponsum seu petitorem, praetorium soceri expetere vidisses! illum equus quidem phaleris comptus, immo equi radiantibus gemmis onusti antecedebant vel etiam subsequebantur, cum tamen magis hoc ibi decorum conspiciebatur,[4] quod cursoribus[5] suis sive pedisequis pedes et ipse medius incessit, flammeus cocco rutilus auro lacteus serico, tum cultui tanto coma rubore[6] cute concolor. 2. regulorum autem sociorumque

[1] Domnicio *C*: Domnitio (*om. inscript. L*). *Cf. Ep.* V. 17. 6.

[2] arma et armatos *LNTR*²: arma et armatum et armatos *VCFP*¹*N*¹: arma et armatum et animatos *MP* (*add. s.l.* vel armatos *M*¹*P*¹). arma et armatum [et armatos] *Burke recte?* v. Additional Notes p. 610.

[3] conceperas *LR*: conciperes.

[4] inspiciebatur *MTCFP*.

[5] praecursoribus *F*.

[6] ore *Wilamowitz*: tuore *coni. Luetjohann. v. Mohr XXV.*

XIX

SIDONIUS TO HIS FRIEND FLORENTINUS,* GREETING

You blame both my delay and my silence. Both these charges can be refuted: for I am coming and I am now writing. Farewell.

XX

SIDONIUS TO HIS FRIEND DOMNICIUS,† GREETING

1. You who are so fond of looking at arms and armed men, what delight, methinks, you would have felt if you had seen the young prince Sigismer,[1] decked out in the garb and fashion of his nation, as the chosen lover or as suitor paying a visit to the palace of his lady's father! Before him went a horse gaily caparisoned: other horses [2] laden with flashing jewels preceded or followed him. But the most gracious sight in the procession was the prince himself marching on foot amid his runners and footmen, clad in gleaming scarlet, ruddy gold, and pure-white silk, while his fair hair, glowing cheeks, and white skin matched the colours of such bright dress. 2. The

* Not otherwise known.

† Not otherwise known, except in *Ep.* V. 17. 6.

[1] Perhaps a Frank, or a Burgundian.

[2] This is the only mention of horses in this letter. Resist any temptation to read, in section 2, *equorum pedes primi* (the forefeet of the horses), because *pero* is a soldier's boot, and the effect might be comic.

comitantum forma et in pace terribilis; quorum pedes primi perone saetoso talos adusque vinciebantur; genua crura suraeque sine tegmine; praeter hoc vestis alta stricta versicolor vix appropinquans poplitibus exertis; manicae sola brachiorum principia velantes; viridantia saga limbis marginata puniceis; penduli ex umero gladii balteis supercurrentibus strinxerant clausa bullatis latera rhenonibus. 3. eo quo comebantur ornatu muniebantur; lanceis uncatis securibusque missibilibus [1] dextrae refertae clipeis laevam partem adumbrantibus, quorum lux in orbibus nivea, fulva in umbonibus ita censum prodebat ut studium. cuncta prorsus huiusmodi, ut in actione thalamorum non appareret minor Martis pompa quam Veneris. sed quid haec pluribus? spectaculo tali sola praesentia tua defuit. nam cum viderem quae tibi pulchra sunt non te [2] videre, ipsam eo tempore desiderii tui inpatientiam desideravi. vale.

XXI

SIDONIVS APRO SVO SALVTEM

1. Est quidem princeps in genere monstrando partis paternae praerogativa, sed tamen multum est,

[1] missilibus *VR*. [2] te non *TC*.

---

[1] Or perhaps "companions," "friends," "comrades."—*A*. *From this point onwards the notes and ponderings of Anderson on his own translation, on the Latin text, and on the subject-matter, become more copious. Of these we include the more relevant.*

[2] *alta = altata*; *Carm.* V. 244.—*A*.

[3] Perhaps "belts" rather than "coats," made out of skins of reindeer.

princelings and allies [1] who escorted him presented an aspect terrifying even in peacetime. Their feet from toe to ankle were laced in hairy shoes; knees, shins, and calves were uncovered: above this was a tight-fitting many-coloured garment, drawn up high,[2] and hardly descending to their bare houghs, the sleeves covering only the upper part of the arm. They wore green mantles with crimson borders. Their swords suspended from the shoulders by overrunning baldrics pressed against sides girded with studded deer-skins.[3] 3. This equipment adorned and armed them at the same time. Barbed lances and missile axes filled their right hands; and their left sides were protected by shields, the gleam of which, golden on the central bosses and silvery white round the rims, betrayed at once the wearers' wealth and ruling passion. The total effect was such that this bridal drama displayed a pageant of Mars no less than of Venus. But why say more about it? The fine show lacked only one thing—your presence. For when I saw that you were not seeing the sights your eye delights in, at that moment I wanted not to feel the want of you. Farewell.

XXI

SIDONIUS TO HIS FRIEND APER,* GREETING

1. In any statement of one's genealogy the father's side takes the place of honour;[4] nevertheless, we

* An Aeduan. Cf. *Ep.* V. 14.
[4] Or "a privileged position."—*A.*

quod debemus et matribus. non enim a nobis aliquid exilius fas honorari quod pondera illarum quam quod istorum semina sumus. sed originis nostrae definiendae materia vel ratio sit penes physicos: nos, unde haec ipsa praemisimus, persequamur. 2. Haeduus pater tibi, mater Arverna est. primis Haeduis deberis, ergo non solis, vel propter illud exemplum nostri Maronis, quo teste Pallas, sic habitus Arcas quod pariter et Samnis, in Mezentium movere potuisset ut peregrinus arma Etruscorum, ni mixtus matre Sabella partem quoque patriae inde traxisset. ecce habes magnum maximo auctore documentum, quod patriae pars computanda sit et regio materna, nisi poetas et cum ab historia non recedunt mentiri existimabis. 3. igitur Arverni si portionem tui saltim vicissim iure sibi vindicant, patienter admitte querimoniam desiderantum, qui tibi per unius oris officium non unius pectoris profudere secretum. quos palam et coram dicere puta: " quid in te mali tantum, ingrate, commisimus, ut per tot annos quondam humum altricem nunc velut hosticum solum fugias? hic incunabula tua fovimus; hic vagientis infantiae lactantia membra formavimus; hic civicarum baiulabare pondus ulnarum. 4. hinc avus

---

[1] The Aeduans dwelt in Autun, Châlon, Mâcon, and Nevers.

[2] *Aen.* VIII. 510, *ni mixtus matre Sabella|hinc partem patriae traheret.* Sidonius misquotes. He must intend *inde* to mean *ex Samnio.*—*A.*

[3] The Etruscans needed a foreign leader, whereas Pallas was an Italian on his mother's side.

[4] Cf. Pliny, *Ep.*, VI. 21. 6.

owe a great deal to our mothers as well; for it is not right that some slighter honour should be given to the truth that we were our mothers' burden than to the fact that we are our fathers' seed. But let us leave to scientists the exact theoretic treatment of our origin; and let me go on to the theme which actually suggested this preamble. 2. Your father is an Aeduan,[1] your mother an Arvernian. Thus you owe your existence primarily to the Aeduans, but not solely to them: for this we have the authority of our own Virgil,[2] who testifies that Pallas, who was reckoned an Arcadian indeed but also in equal measure a Samnite, could have led the armed might of the Etruscans against Mezentius "had he not been of mixed race because of his Sabellian mother, so that from her land also he drew part of his nativity."[3] Here you have grand evidence from the grandest authority to show that a mother's country must also be counted part of one's fatherland—unless you choose to think that poets lie even when they stick to sober history.[4] 3. So if your Arvernians are justified in claiming, in their turn, at least a part of you, listen patiently to their longing plaint, for they have availed themselves of one mouth to pour forth the secret thoughts of many hearts. You must imagine them saying openly to your face: "What great wrong have we done you, ungrateful man, that for so many years you should have shunned the land that once nurtured you, shunned it as if it were enemy territory? Here we fostered your infancy, here when you were a wailing baby we shaped your tender limbs, here you were carried in the arms of your fellow countrymen. 4. From this land came

Fronto, blandus tibi sibi severus, qui exemplo esse potuisset his, quos habemus nos in exemplo; hinc avia Auspicia, quae tibi post tuae matris orbato[1] decessum dependit una curam duarum. sed et matertera tua hinc, et hinc[2] fuit sanctior sanctis Frontina virginibus, quam verebatur mater pater venerabatur, summae abstinentiae puella, summi rigoris, ac fide ingenti[3] sic deum timens, ut ab hominibus metueretur. hic te imbuendum liberalibus disciplinis grammatici rhetorisque studia florentia monitu certante foverunt, unde tu non tam mediocriter institutus existi, ut tibi liceat Arvernos vel propter litteras non amare. 5. taceo territorii peculiarem iucunditatem; taceo illud aequor agrorum, in quo sine periculo quaestuosae fluctuant in segetibus undae, quod industrius quisque quo plus frequentat, hoc minus naufragat; viatoribus molle, fructuosum aratoribus, venatoribus voluptuosum; quod montium cingunt dorsa pascuis latera vinetis, terrena villis saxosa castellis, opaca lustris aperta culturis, concava fontibus abrupta fluminibus; quod denique huiusmodi est, ut semel visum advenis multis patriae oblivionem saepe persuadeat. 6. taceo civitatem

[1] orbato *Luetjohann*: orbata.

[2] *seclud.* et *Luetjohann*: hinc *secludendum putat Anderson, prob. Semple.*

[3] fide ingenti *Luetjohann*: fidei ingenti *R*: fide indigenti *L*: fidei ingentis *rell.*

---

[1] This Fronto is not otherwise known for certain.

[2] Reading *orbato* with Luetjohann. *Orbata* will mean "who in her loneliness after your mother's death."—*A.*

[3] nuns.

your grandfather Fronto,[1] gentle with you, austere with himself, one who could have been an example to those whom we take for an example; hence also sprang your grandmother Auspicia, who when you were left an orphan [2] by your mother's death bestowed on you a double portion of maternal care. Yes, and from the same land came your aunt Frontina, holier than the holy virgins,[3] revered by her mother, venerated by her father, a lady remarkable for the self-denial and austerity of her life, who in the immensity of her faith was so filled with the fear of God that she filled all men with awe. Here eminent schools of grammar and rhetoric nurtured you, each in eager rivalry as they sought to ground you in the liberal arts: and from this schooling you issued into the world with no such ordinary training that you can justly refuse to love the Arvernians, particularly on the score of education. 5. I pass over the particular charm of the countryside; I say nothing of the arable lands stretching like a sea in which waves that bring profit without danger surge and sway in the corn, and in which the industrious man has the less chance of shipwreck the oftener he goes there. It is a region soft to the feet of the traveller, fruitful to the tiller, delightful to the hunter; the ridges of the mountains surround it with pasture, their sides with vineyards, the earthy parts with country-houses, the rocky parts with fortresses, the shady woods with coverts, the open parts with cultivation, the hollows with springs, and the steep slopes with streams; in short, such is the place that, when but once seen, it often induces many visitors to forget their own native land. 6. I

ipsam tui semper sic amantissimam, ut soli[1] nobilium contubernio praeferre nil debeas, cui tu manu iniecta feliciter raptus inserebare; sicque omnes praesentiae vestrae voluptas, quod tamen nullum satias cepit. iam quid istic de re familiari tua dicam, cuius hic status est, ut tuam expensam hoc sit facilius toleratura, quo crebrius? nam dominus agricola, si larem hic foveat, sic facit sumptum quod auget et[2] reditum." haec unus tibi omnium civium, certe bonorum, voto petitu vice garrio; qui cum tanto honore te poscant, tanto amore desiderent, intellegi datur gaudii plus te, dum tribuis quod rogaris, assecuturum. vale.

XXII

SIDONIVS LEONI·SVO SALVTEM

1. Vir magnificus Hesperius, gemma amicorum litterarumque, nuper urbe cum rediit e Tolosatium, praecipere te dixit, ut epistularum curam iam terminatis libris earum converteremus ad stilum historiae. reverentia summa, summo et[3] affectu talem atque tantam sententiam amplector; idoneum quippe pronuntias ad opera maiora quem mediocria

[1] soli *MFP* (i *in ras. P*[2]): solo *LTC*: sedulo *Luetjohann.*
[2] et *om. T.*
[3] summo studio et *F.*

* A Catholic of Narbonne, minister to King Euric of the Visigoths. He was a learned orator, jurist, philosopher and poet. See *Carm.* IX. 314; XXIII. 446 ff.; *Ep.* VIII. 3; IX. 13, first *carm.* 20; and IX. 15, *carm.* 19–20.

[1] See *Ep.* II. 10. He taught a son of Ruricius (see above, p. 124), who wrote three of his extant letters to him.

pass over the city itself, which is always so affectionately disposed to you, that (to take only one instance) the company of noble friends, into which you were ushered by hands that claimed you as their happy spoil, deserves the foremost place in your regard; and your presence was always a delight such as never even palled on anyone. And why should I say anything here about your property, which is so constituted that the oftener you make any outlay the more easily it can stand it? For the proprietor who farms his land, if he makes his home here, actually increases his income by spending his money." This talk comes to you from my mouth alone, but it is uttered by the desire and at the request and on the behalf of all the citizens, at any rate of all the worthy citizens. As they call for you with such respect and long for you with such love, you can well understand that you will gain greater joy for yourself by granting their request. Farewell.

XXII

SIDONIUS TO HIS FRIEND LEO,* GREETING

1. The honourable Hesperius,[1] jewel of friends and star of letters, on returning not long ago from Toulouse, reported that you enjoined me to turn my thoughts to the composition of history when my books of letters were completed. I welcome with the utmost respect and affection an opinion of such tenor and of such authority; for when you think I should desert humbler tasks, you declare me suited

putas deserere debere. sed, quod fatendum est, facilius audeo huiusmodi suspicere iudicium quam suscipere consilium. 2. res quidem digna quam tu iuberes sed non minus digna quam faceres. namque et antiquitus, cum Gaius Cornelius Gaio Secundo paria suasisset, ipse postmodum quod iniunxit arripuit, idque ab exemplo nunc melius [1] aggredieris,[2] quia et ego Plinio ut discipulus assurgo et tu vetusto genere narrandi iure Cornelium antevenis, qui saeculo nostro si revivisceret teque qualis in litteris et quantus habeare conspicaretur, modo verius Tacitus esset. 3. itaque tu molem thematis missi [3] recte capessis, cui praeter eloquentiam singularem scientiae ingentis magna opportunitas. cotidie namque per potentissimi consilia regis totius sollicitus orbis pariter [eius] [4] negotia et iura, foedera et bella, loca spatia merita cognoscis. unde quis iustius sese ad ista succinxerit, quam ille, quem constat gentium motus legationum varietates, facta ducum pacta regnantum, tota denique publicarum rerum secreta didicisse, quique praestanti positus in culmine non necesse

1 me melius *NMTCFP*: melius *L*.
2 aggredieris *Wilamowitz*: aggrederis.
3 *fortasse* iussi.
4 eius *LMCFP*: *om. codd. nonnulli.*

---

1 See Pliny (the younger), *Ep.* V. 8, written not to Tacitus but to Titinius Capito.

2 Omit *me*. Read with Wilamowitz *aggredieris*. But see the present tense used in *capessis* § 3 *init.*; *audeo* (not *ausim*) in § 1 is somewhat similar.—*A*.

3 Sidonius makes word-play, *tacitus* of course meaning "silent." Cf. *Carm.* II. 192; XXIII. 154.

4 Euric.

for greater ones. But I must confess that I can more easily bring myself to give respect to such a judgment than to give effect to your advice. 2. The undertaking was indeed a worthy one for you to suggest, but it was equally worthy for you to perform yourself. For even in the old days Gaius Cornelius (Tacitus), after giving similar advice to Gaius Secundus (Pliny),[1] himself appropriated later the task he had imposed: and, according to this precedent, you will even more fitly attempt it,[2] seeing that to Pliny I yield homage as a pupil, whereas in the old historical style you rightly take precedence of Tacitus, so that if he could come to life again in our day and see the greatness of your distinction in literature, he would now be "Tacitus"[3] in a more real sense. 3. Thus it is right that you should take on yourself the burden of the theme you have given out, being blessed not only with an unrivalled power of expression but also great facilities for acquiring immense information. For every day in the councils of a most powerful king[4] you meticulously gather information about the whole world's affairs[5] and rights, treaties and wars, localities, distances, and merits alike. So who with better right could gird himself for this task than the man who by common consent has acquainted himself with the movements of nations, the diversities of embassies, the deeds of leaders, the compacts of sovereigns, in short all the secrets of governments, and who being placed in a position of the greatest eminence is not under the

[5] *totius orbis* probably not to be taken with *sollicitus*. Is *eius* then genuine?—*A*. I think *eius* should be omitted, as *sollicitus* certainly goes with *cognoscis*.—*W.H.S.*

habet vel supprimere verum vel concinnare mendacium? 4. at nostra longe condicio dispar, quibus dolori peregrinatio nova nec usui lectio vetus, tum [1] religio professioni est, humilitas appetitui, mediocritas obscuritati, nec in praesentibus rei tantum, quantum in futuris spei locatum, postremo languor impedimento iamque vel sero propter hunc ipsum desidia cordi; aequaeva certe iam super studiis nulla laus curae, sed ne postuma quidem. 5. praecipue gloriam nobis parvam ab historia petere [2] fixum, quia per homines clericalis officii temerarie nostra iactanter aliena, praeterita infructuose praesentia semiplene, turpiter falsa periculose vera dicuntur. est enim huiusmodi thema [vel opus],[3] in quo bonorum si facias mentionem, modica gratia paratur, si notabilium, maxuma offensa. sic se illi [4] protinus dictioni color odorque satiricus admiscet. ilicet: scriptio historica videtur ordine a nostro multum abhorrere, cuius inchoatio invidia, continuatio labor, finis est odium. 6. sed tunc ista

[1] vetus tum *LN*: vetust— *R*: vetusta tum *TCFPN*[1]: vetusta tū *M*[1].

[2] praeterire *coni. Anderson vel* parum *pro* parvam.

[3] *seclud. Wilamowitz.*

[4] ille *MTCFP*.

---

[1] He means "it would have been better if I had been inclined to inactivity sooner," *i.e.* (i) I should not then have brought all this trouble upon me, or (ii) I should not have written so much poor stuff.—*A.*

[2] *praecipue . . . fixum.* These words (which no one

necessity either of suppressing the truth or of inventing a lie? 4. But my situation is very different. My new sojourn in foreign parts is painful, my old reading profitless to me; again, religion is my profession, humility my ambition, and my insignificance wraps me in obscurity; and I find less reality in the present than hope in the future; lastly, ill-health hampers me, and already (or perhaps I should say "too late")[1] this in itself inclines me to inactivity: at any rate contemporary praise for my literary efforts no longer interests me, nor does posthumous praise either. 5. But the chief reason why I am firmly resolved to seek but small glory from historical writing is this[2]—for men of the clerical profession it is foolhardy to record our own affairs and arrogant to record those of the outside world: our account of things past is profitless, that of things present is only half-complete; and while it is shameful to utter falsehoods, it is dangerous to tell the truth; for it is an undertaking in which any reference to the good brings but scant favour, and any allusion to the infamous[3] brings great offence:[4] so inevitably[5] does the colour and flavour of satire pervade that kind of composition. Well, then, historical writing seems very ill suited to our cloth: enmity dogs its beginning, toil its continuation, hatred its conclusion. 6.

hitherto has made a serious attempt to translate) mean: "If I ever attempt anything in the way of historical writing, I am resolved that it will be on a very humble scale." *Praecipue* goes with the *quia* clause.—*A*.

[3] Not "notables" or "notabilities."—*A*.

[4] Cf. Pliny, *Ep*. V. 8. 12, fin. *graves offensae, levis gratia*.

[5] *protinus*. "all through"? "from the outset"? The atter is better. See *Ep*. IV. 23. 3.—*A*.

proveniunt, clericis si aliquid dictetur auctoribus; qui colubrinis oblatratorum molaribus fixi, si quid simpliciter edamus, insani, si quid exacte, praesumptiosi vocamur. at si tu ipse, cui datum est saltibus gloriae proterere posse [1] cervices vituperonum seu supercurrere, materiae istius libens provinciam sortiare, nemo te celsius scripserit, nemo et antiquius, etiamsi placeat recentia loqui; quandoquidem sermonum copia impletus ante, nunc rerum, non reliquisti, cur venenato morsu secere. atque ideo te in posterum consuli utilitas, audiri voluptas, legi auctoritas erit. vale.

XXIII

SIDONIVS PROCVLO SVO SALVTEM

1. Filius tuus, immo communis ad me cucurrit, qui te relicto deliquisse se maeret, obrutus paenitendi pudore transfugii. igitur audito culpae tenore corripui latitabundum verbis amaris vultu minaci et mea quidem voce sed vice tua dignum abdicatione

[1] posse *om. T.*

---

* Not the Proculus of *Ep.* IX. 2. 1, but a Ligurian poet, compared in *Ep.* IX, *carm.* 44 ff. to Homer and Virgil. Ennodius, in *Carm.* I. 3, Vogel, p. 202, equates him with Pindar.

[1] The traditional punishment for the murder of a near relation (*parricidium*) was to sew the culprit in a sack along with a dog, a cock, serpents, and later also an ape, and to fling them into the sea or into a river. In places where this could not be done, the condemned might be burnt alive or flung to the beasts.—*A*.

But it is only when we clerics take up our pens that these consequences follow—the viper's teeth of snarling critics fasten upon us, and if we express ourselves with frankness we are called mad, and if with scrupulous care, presumptuous. On the other hand, if you to whom has been given the power to trample upon or run over the necks of fault-finders with glory's triumphant leaps, if you (I say) should of your free will take this subject-matter as your province it will be found that no one ever wrote more sublimely or indeed with more of the good old style, even though you should choose recent history as your theme; for with your present wealth of information added to the wealth of expression previously acquired, you have left no excuse for any poisoned tooth to tear you; and so in days to come it will be a benefit to consult you, a pleasure to listen to you, and an assurance of the truth to read you. Farewell.

XXIII

SIDONIUS TO HIS FRIEND PROCULUS,* GREETING

1. Your son—I ought rather to say our son—has fled to me; he grieves that he went astray by straying from you, and he is plunged in shame at the thought of his regrettable desertion. Accordingly, after hearing a general account of his offence, I rebuked the skulking fugitive with bitter words and threatening looks; and although it was my lips that spoke, they spoke for you when I shouted that he was worthy of disinheritance, the cross, the sack,[1]

cruce culleo clamans ceterisque suppliciis parricidalibus. ad haec ille confusus inrubuit, nil impudenti excusatione deprecatus errorem, sed ad cuncta convictum cum redarguerem, verecundiae iunxit comites lacrimas ita profluas ubertimque manantes, ut secuturae correctioni fidem fecerint. 2. rogo ergo sis clemens in se severo et deum sequens non habeas te iudice reum se profitente damnabilem; quem si inaudita genera poenarum iubeas inexoratus excipere, non potest amplius per te dolore quam per se pudore torqueri. libera metu desperationem suam, libera confidentiam meam et, pietatis paternae necessitatem si bene interpretor, te quoque absolve, qui conficeris occulto, quod filius publico maerore conficitur. cui fecisse me constat plurimum iniuriae, si tu tamen vel parum feceris, quam certe, ut spero, non facies, nisi scopulis durior duras aut adamantibus rigidior perseveras insecabilibus. 3. ergo si de moribus tuis deque amicitiis iuste meliora praesumo, excusato propitius indulge, quem reconcilians fore fidelem constanter in posterum spondeo, quoque velociter culpa soluto ego beneficio ligor, magnopere deposcens, non ut ignoscas modo verum ut et pro-

---

[1] By encouraging him to go back and seek forgiveness.—*A*.

[2] "Show yourself harder than the hardest rocks"; "harden your heart to a more than rocklike hardness."—*A*.

and the other punishments of parricides. At this he blushed in his confusion but made no attempt to extenuate his fault by shameless excuses; on the contrary, as I convicted him on every point and brought his guilt home to him, he reinforced his contrition with gushing floods of tears that gave assurance of his future amendment. 2. I therefore beg you to be lenient with one who is so severe with himself; follow the divine example and do not by your judgment pronounce guilty one who by his own confession has condemned himself. Even if you should be inexorable and order him to undergo unexampled forms of punishment, the pain inflicted by you cannot torture him more than the shame with which he tortures himself. Deliver from anxiety both his despairing heart and my trust in you; and (if I rightly understand the ties of a father's love) bring relief to yourself also, racked as you are by hidden grief for the unconcealed grief that racks your son. If, in spite of my appeal, you find you have not caused him enough hurt, it is quite clear that I have done him a very great hurt; [1] but surely, I trust, you will not do any more—unless your heart is hardened beyond the hardness of rocks [2] and unless you continue more rigid than impervious diamonds. 3. So if I am right in taking the more favourable view of your character and of your friendship, show a kindly lenience towards him for whom I have pleaded. In commending him to your forgiveness I guarantee that he will be unswervingly true to you in the future. If you absolve him promptly of his guilt you thereby bind me by your kindness, for I earnestly entreat you not merely to pardon him but to pardon him instantly,

tinus, et revertentem non domo solum sed et pectore admittas. deus magne, quam laetus orietur tibi dies, mihi nuntius, animus illi, cum paternis pedibus affusus ex illo ore laeso, ore terribili, dum convicium expectat,[1] osculum exceperit! vale.

XXIV

General remarks

This letter bears every sign of having been very much elaborated for publication. There are several things that do not ring true, apart from the elaborate playing with words. (Let us hope that the sacrifice of decency to verbal play in § 2 init. *was not actually sent to a man whose father was* in extremis.) *Obviously* [1] *Turpio was dead at the supposed time of writing. Thus the heirs would get a year's grace. But surely the original letter was sent off at once along with that of Maximus [at one time in the Palatine civil service (see note on § 1), later a cleric], while the life of Turpio still hung in the balance (at least, as far as they knew). The last part of the letter implies that the death had already occurred—but recently, as the settlement of the estate and other arrangements consequent upon death were not quite completed. Then in the same part of the letter Turnus is urged to secure the payment of the debt immediately (protinus) and threatened with the withdrawal of Maximus' kind offer if he does not do so. And he is asked to pay at least the amount of the principal, although all the interest had been remitted.*

This is not all. Surely Maximus, the zealous priest, did not say that in forgoing the interest as his clerical office required (§ 6, 'mei officii ratio'; but Dalton [Vol. II. p. 234]

[1] dum convicium expectat *LR*[2]: convicium expectā (*om.* dum) *R*[1]: convicium expectans *vel sim.* (*om.* dum) *alii.*

---

[1] But see page 157.

and on his return to receive him into your heart as well as into your home. Heaven bless us! How joyous will dawn that day for you, how gladsome the news for me, how blithe the lad's heart will be when he flings himself at his father's feet, and from those aggrieved lips, those lips he so dreads, he receives not the reproaches he expects but a kiss! Farewell.

XXIV

on Ep. IV. 24

takes this differently), he was acting out of love for the sons of Turpio or that such a remission was a special indulgence which he was not compelled to give (§ 6, "superpositam medietatem . . . indulgeam"). The fact is that this letter is a show-piece without consistency or plausibility.

We are not told why the bailiffs had come down upon Turpio. Presumably not on the instructions of Maximus. Had his agent acted without his knowledge? And what really was the attitude of Maximus to usury? He had only recently taken holy orders, which strictly forbade him to practise usury, and he may not have had time to bring his financial dealings into harmony with his obligations. But Sidonius does not indicate either that Maximus had any intention of doing so or (except for 'mei officii ratio', see above) that either he or Sidonius considered the exaction of interest wrong in a priest. It is thus impossible to draw from this highly coloured jumble any confident inference about the attitude of Maximus. What we may infer with comparative safety was that, in spite of the prohibition, usury among the clergy was not unknown and that Sidonius, when he wrote the letter, did not entirely condemn it.—A.

W. H. Semple adds: There is nothing that interests Sidonius so much as the change in a man's principles and manner of life when he ceases to be a layman and becomes a cleric. These letters are full of comments on his own change of outlook and behaviour once he had been ordained: for example,

his abandonment of secular poetry as a frivolity unfitting in a churchman. And so in this letter (which I grant to be elaborated and worked up for publication) he wishes to point the difference between the attitude of Maximus, in regard to a normal business transaction, before and after his ordination as priest. Before, he said "business is business." After, he adjusted his whole behaviour to a rule of Christian discipline and charity, so that when he once realised the plight of Turpio and his family he at once remitted the interest and only asked for the return of the loan. Sidonius complicates the issue by introducing the third person, Turnus, the son of Turpio, to

XXIV

SIDONIVS TVRNO SVO SALVTEM

1. Bene nomini, bene negotio tuo congruit Mantuani illud:

Turne, quod optanti divum promittere nemo
auderet, volvenda dies en attulit ultro.

pecuniam pater tuus Turpio, vir tribunicius, mutuam pridem, si recordaris, a Maximo Palatino postulavit

* Not otherwise known.

[1] Virgil, in the *Aeneid*, IX. 6 ff.

[2] Turpio did not need to be told that his father had been a tribune; the absurdly unnecessary addition of *vir tribunicius* is due to Sidonius' itch for antithesis; he wants something to contrast with *Palatino.—A.* But *tribunicius* is simply honorific.

[3] *Palatino.* The name "Palatine" (from *palatium*, palace) was used of offices, belonging to the departments of the imperial civil service, which were centred at Rome under the direct control of the emperor; and in which the service was

whom he gives a lot of solemn advice about the need for prompt repayment of what is now a straight loan.—W.H.S.

Anderson was clearly upset by this letter; and Semple's remarks are wise. I believe that a letter such as this was indeed sent (with Maximus') to Turnus before Turpio died, though he was near death. Anderson says "Obviously Turpio was dead at the supposed time of writing." Is this true? Even the opening of § 2 does not prove it; §§ 7 and 8 appear to me to present Sidonius' present advice to Turnus, and Sidonius' suggestions as to how Turnus might argue on the assumption that Turpio does die very soon.—E.H.W.

XXIV

SIDONIUS TO HIS FRIEND TURNUS,* GREETING

1. The saying of the Mantuan [1] aptly fits both your name and your business:

"See, Turnus! what no God, howe'er besought
Dare promise thee, time's course hath brought
unbidden."

Your father, the ex-tribune [2] Turpio, long ago, as you may remember, asked for and obtained a loan from Maximus of the Palatine [3] civil service. He did

sometimes called *militia palatina*, where *militia* had no necessary reference to military duties. Cf. *Ep.* I. 3. 1, where Palatine and really military "masterships" are contrasted. So in a civil sense the Palatini were officials of the *comitatus*, the central government. In *Carm.* V. 307, however, there is a reference to Palatini who were indeed military, being guards stationed in various parts of Italy under the command of the *magister utriusque militiae* "Master of both services" infantry and cavalry at the same time. The term Palatini could be applied to any members of the field army.

impetravitque, nil quidem loco fiduciae pignorisque vel argenti sequestrans vel obligans praediorum; sed, ut chirographo facto docetur, cauta centesima est faeneratori, quae per bilustre producta tempus modum sortis ad duplum adduxit. 2. sed cum pater tuus morti propinquae morbo incumbente succumberet atque ob hoc ipsum publica auctoritas male valentem patremfamilias violentius ad reformandum debitum artaret nec sustineri valeret improbitas executorum, proficiscenti mihi Tolosam iam desperatus litteris imperavit, ut me rogante creditor vester modicas saltim largiretur indutias. precibus orantis citus annui, quia cum Maximo mihi non notitiae solum verum et hospitii vetera iura. igitur ad amicum libens ex itinere perrexi, quamquam villa non paucis aggere a publico milibus abesset. 3. ut veni, occurrit mihi ipse, quem noveram anterius corpore erectum gressu expeditum, voce liberum facie liberalem, multum ab antiquo dissimilis incessu. habitus viro, gradus pudor, color sermo religiosus,

---

[1] In the case of *fiducia*, property was transferred to the ownership of the creditor as security for the debt; in the case of *pignus* it passed into his "possession," *i.e.* he held it but did not own it. These words may denote either the contract made between the two parties or the property so transferred. *Sequestrare* properly means "to deposit in trust with a third party," but in the present context that limited meaning is improbable.—*A.* [who then gives another rendering:] "He did not deposit any silver plate as fiduciary security or as pledge, nor did he mortgage any of his landed property."—*A.*

[2] per annum. The Latin says "one per cent" (per month).

[3] Really more than double.—*A.*

[4] A closer translation, getting something of Sidonius' word-play which here so disgusted Anderson, would be: "But

not have to make over any of his silver plate by way of mortgage or pledge nor to give a lien on any of his landed property;[1] but, as the bond given under his hand shows, interest at the rate of twelve per cent[2] was guaranteed to the lender; this interest has gone on accumulating for ten years and has thus increased the debt to double the amount of the principal.[3] 2. But when your father was sinking under a weight of illness and death seemed imminent,[4] and when for that very reason the authority of the law was the more stringently pressing the ailing paterfamilias to discharge his debt and the effrontery of the bailiffs[5] could not be withstood, he was driven to desperation and wrote to me as I was setting out for Toulouse, adjuring me to intercede and obtain from your creditor at least a short period of grace. I readily acceded to the suppliant's request, as I had with Maximus old ties not only of acquaintance but of hospitality. So in the course of my journey I willingly went to see my friend, although his country-house was several miles from the high-road. 3. When I arrived he came himself to meet me, but the man who (as I had known him) had been erect in stature, brisk in step, bluff in voice, and beaming in countenance, now carried himself in anything but his old style: his dress, his step, his modest air, his colour and his talk, all had a religious suggestion; moreover,

when your father, with illness lying upon him, was lying under death which was close to him."

[5] *Executor.* An officer who carried out the decision of a civil court of justice; otherwise *intercessor.* Cf. *Cod. Iust.* XVIII. 16 (17). 7 *executores a quocunque iudice dati ad exigenda debita ea quae civiliter poscuntur.*—*A.*

tum coma brevis barba prolixa, tripodes sellae, Cilicum vela foribus appensa, lectus nil habens plumae, mensa nil purpurae, humanitas ipsa sic benigna quod frugi, nec ita carnibus abundans ut leguminibus; certe, si quid in cibis unctius, non sibi sed hospitibus indulgens. 4. cum surgeremus, clam percontor adstantes, quod genus vitae de tribus arripuisset ordinibus, monachum ageret an clericum paenitentemve.[1] dixerunt nuper impacto sacerdotio fungi, quo recusantem factiose ligasset civicus amor. luce revoluta, dum pueri clientesque capiendis animalibus occuparentur, secretae conlocutionis peto copiam. praestat: amplector nil opinantem gratularique me primum pro sui status apice confirmo, tum consequentes misceo preces. 5. Turpionis nostri rogata profero, allego necessitates, extrema deploro, quae duriora maerentibus amicis hinc viderentur, quod faenore ligatus corpore solveretur: meminisset ergo professionis novae, sodalitatis antiquae, exactorumque circumlatrantum barbaram instantiam indultis tantisper indutiis moderaretur; et, si decessisset aeger, tribueret heredibus annui luctus tempus immune; si, quod optarem, pristinam Turpio salutem recuperasset, indulgeret exhausto

[1] paenitentemve *Leo*: penitentemne *vel sim.*

---

[1] *Cilicum vela* (Cf. *Ep.* II. 9. 8) were cloths or rugs made of goats' hair and named from the Cilicians in Asia Minor.

[2] Those who had risen from the couches round the table and could at this point be spoken to privately (*clam*) about their host's peculiarities.

his hair was short, his beard long, three-legged stools served as seats, his door-ways had hangings of hair-cloth,[1] his couch was devoid of down, his table of purple, and even his hospitality, though kindly, was frugal, with a greater abundance of vegetable than of meat—at least, if there was ever anything more dainty on the menu, he was making a concession to the guests, not to himself. 4. As we rose from the table, I quietly asked those standing near [2] me which way of life from among the three orders he had suddenly adopted—was he monk or clergyman or penitent? They said he was filling the office of priest which had lately been thrust upon him; for his affectionate fellow-citizens had cunningly involved him in it in spite of his protests. Next morning, while slaves and dependants were busy catching the sumpter animals, I begged for the favour of a private interview, which he granted. To his surprise, embracing him, I first affirmed the pleasure I felt at his honourable advancement: then I introduced my petitions as follows. 5. I brought forward the request of our friend Turpio, pleaded his hard circumstances, and lamented his desperate illness, which I said, seemed to his sad friends all the harder because he was being loosed from the body while bound by debt. "Therefore," I continued, "bethink you of your new profession and of your old comradeship and, by allowing him some measure of postponement, check the savage importunity of the bailiffs who noisily ring him round: and should the invalid die, exempt the heirs until the end of their year of mourning; if on the other hand, as I earnestly hope, Turpio should recover his health, let the exhausted

per otium facultatem convalescendi. 6. adhuc rogabam, cum repente vir caritatis flere granditer coepit non moram debiti sed periculum debitoris; frenatoque singultu: "absit a me," inquit, "ut haec reposcam clericus ab aegro, quae vix petissem miles a sospite. sed et liberos eius ita diligo, ut etiam si quid adversum cesserit amico, nil sum ab his amplius postulaturus quam mei officii ratio permittit. quapropter scribe sollicitis (quoque plus credant litteris tuis, meas iunge), quisquis ille fuerit languoris eventus, quem tamen fratri prosperum optamus, quod et annuum solutioni spatium prorogabo et superpositam medietatem, quae per usurae nomen accrevit, indulgeam, sola simpli restitutione contentus." 7. egi ad haec gratias deo maximas, hospiti magnas, qui sic amaret tam suam famam quam conscientiam, confirmans amicum praemittere sibi quod dimitteret vobis, atque hinc superna regna mercari, quod beneficia terrena non venderet. ergo quod restat enitere, ut auctore te protinus saltim commodata summa solvatur, sic ut ingentes nihilominus gratias agas etiam nomine illorum, qui tibi germanitate coniuncti fors per aetatem sapere non possunt, quid muneris consequantur. 8. non est cur dicere incipias: "habeo consortes necdum celebrata

[1] Strange to find *indulgeam* as a future! [There are other examples in Sidonius.] *superpositam medietatem*: *i.e.* the interest due which was now half the total debt (cf. § 1, *fin.*).—*A.*

[2] In renouncing earthly treasure he was laying up treasure in heaven.—*A.*

[3] That is, refusing to charge interest on the loan.

man have the chance of regaining his strength in peace." 6. I was continuing my entreaties, when suddenly this man of charity burst into a flood of tears, not for the default in the payment of the debt but for the critical state of the debtor. Stifling a sob, he said: "Far be it from me to demand as a cleric from a sick man that restitution which as a government official I should hardly have claimed from a man in health. And, what is more, I love his sons so dearly that, even if anything untoward should happen to my friend, I will not claim from them more than the law of my office sanctions. So write to the anxious family, and to gain additional credence for your letter add one from me, to the effect that, whatever be the issue of the malady (and indeed I pray that it may turn out well for my brother), I will not only extend the time of payment for a year but remit the added moiety [1] which has accrued by way of interest, contenting myself with the sole restoration of the principal." 7. At this I gave chief thanks to God and also no small thanks to my host for so cherishing both his good name and his conscience. I declared that my friend was consigning in advance to himself [2] all that he was resigning for you and that in refusing to sell earthly kindnesses [3] he was buying a place in the kingdom of heaven. So it remains for you to use every effort to secure by your insistence the prompt payment of at least the sum lent, and at the same time you must not fail to express boundless thanks in the name, too, of those brothers or sisters of yours who are not perhaps of an age to realise what a bounty they are obtaining. 8. You must not begin to object: "I have co-heirs; the formal division

divisio est; avarius me constat esse tractatum quam coheredes; frater ac soror sub annis adhuc tutelaribus agunt; sorori necdum maritus, fratri necdum curator, curatori necdum satisdator inventus est." quod quidem totum creditoribus bene, sed malis dicitur; at cum habet talis persona contractum, quae velit medium relaxare, cum totum possit exigere, si moram patitur, quicquid propter misericordiam concesserat pie, iuste reposcit propter iniuriam. vale.

XXV

SIDONIVS DOMNVLO SVO SALVTEM

1. Nequeo differre, quin grandis communione te gaudii festinus inpertiam, nimirum nosse cupientem, quid pater noster in Christo pariter et pontifex Patiens Cabillonum profectus more religionis, more constantiae suae fecerit. cum venisset in oppidum suprascriptum provincialium sacerdotum praevio partim, partim comitante collegio, scilicet ut municipio summus aliquis antistes ordinaretur, cuius

---

[1] Is *curator* here in its proper legal sense (guardian of one between puberty and twenty-five years of age, etc.) or = *tutor* (cf. *sub annis adhuc tutelaribus*)?—*A*.

* Philosopher, poet, and churchman. Cf. *Ep.* IX. 13. 4; IX. 15, in *carm.* 38.

[2] Saint Patiens was a rich and generous man, Archbishop of Lyon before A.D. 470. Cf. *Ep.* VI. 12; II. 10. 2; III. 12. 3. Gregory of Tours, *Hist. Franc.* II. 24; Duchesne, *Fastes Épisc.* II. 163; Sidonius, *Ep.* V. 17. 3, note.

of the property has not yet been made; it is well known that I have been treated more stingily than the other heirs; I have a brother and sister still in their minority; no husband has yet been found for my sister, no curator [1] for my brother, no guarantor for the curator." All this may quite well be said to creditors, I mean to *evil* creditors; but when you are under a contract with a person of such a nature that he is willing to remit half the debt when he could exact the whole, then, if you keep him waiting, he might justly claim back because of this ill usage all that he had charitably remitted out of compassion. Farewell.

XXV

SIDONIUS TO HIS FRIEND DOMNULUS,* GREETING

1. I cannot refrain from hastening to make you a sharer in a great joy; for of course you want to know what Patiens,[2] our father in Christ and our bishop, did with characteristic piety and firmness after setting out for Cabillonum.[3] When he arrived at the aforesaid town he was partly preceded and partly escorted by the priests associated with him in the province.[4] Their purpose, you must know, was the ordination of a man as chief priest of that community,

[3] Châlon-sur-Saône. For elections to bishoprics cf. Stevens *Sid. Apoll.*, pp. 122–129; Nora Chadwick, *Poetry and Letters in Early Christian Gaul*, 290–292 (reading Châlon-sur-Saône for Châlons).

[4] Is *collegio* here technical? Is *provincialium* here political or ecclesiastical?—*A*. Cf. *Ep*. VI. 1. 3.

ecclesiae disciplina nutabat, postquam iunior episcopus Paulus discesserat decesseratque, exceperunt pontificale concilium variae voluntates oppidanorum, nec non et illa quae bonum publicum semper evertunt studia privata; 2. quae quidam triumviratus accenderat conpetitorum, quorum hic antiquam natalium praerogativam reliqua destitutus morum dote ructabat, hic per fragores parasiticos culinarum suffragio comparatos Apicianis plausibus ingerebatur, hic, apice votivo si potiretur, tacita pactione promiserat ecclesiastica plosoribus suis praedae praedia fore. 3. quod ubi viderunt sanctus Patiens et sanctus Euphronius, qui rigorem firmitatemque sententiae sanioris praeter odium gratiamque primi tenebant, consilio cum coepiscopis prius clam communicato quam palam prodito strepituque despecto turbae furentis iunctis [1] repente manibus arreptum nihilque tum minus quam quae agebantur optantem suspicantemque sanctum Iohannem, virum honestate humanitate mansuetudine insignem. 4. (lector hic

[1] iunctis *LN*: iuntis *R*: iactis *TCFPNM*[1]: iectis *M*.

---

[1] Bishop of Châlon. Not the Paulus of *Ep*. I. 9. 1, nor the Paulus of II. 7. 2.

[2] *Apicianis plausibus*—applause worthy of an Apicius (see above, *Ep*. IV. 7. 2). Dalton may be right in seeing here a play on the words *apice* and *Apicianis* as in *praedae* and *praedia* (Dalton Vol. II, pp. 234–235).

[3] Euphronius was Bishop of Autun (Augustodunum of the Aedui). See *Ep*. VII. 8; IX. 2. He died very old—about the year A.D. 476. Duchesne, *Fastes Épisc*. II. 117.

where church-discipline had been shaky ever since the junior bishop Paulus [1] departed from the place and from the world. The episcopal council was received by the townsmen with a conflict of wills and some of those personal interests which are always subversive of the public weal. 2. These discussions had been kindled by a triumvirate of rival candidates, of whom one kept prating about the prior claim of his ancient lineage although bankrupt on the moral side; the second, having secured the noisy approval of parasites with the help of his kitchens, was pressing his pretensions amid gourmets' [2] plaudits; the third had undertaken in secret bargaining that, if he won the coveted dignity, the church lands should be the plunder of his partisans. When this came to the notice of those two holy men, Patiens and Euphronius,[3] they were foremost in maintaining a strict and steadfast adherence to the sounder course, unaffected by enmity or favour: communicating their plan in private to their fellow-bishops before making it public, they then, with total contempt for the clamour of the raging crowd, suddenly seized with hands clasped in his a man who at that moment had not the slightest inkling about, or desire for, the action that was being taken. He was the saintly John,[4] a man eminent for his virtue, his kindliness, and his gentleness. 4. He had first been a Reader [5] and, as such,

[4] Who was now made Bishop of Châlon. Duchesne, *op. cit.*, II. 192.

[5] *Lector*, in Greek ἀναγνώστης. From the time of Tertullian (Tertull. *De Praescr.* 41) he belonged to one of the minor orders in the Church and read the scriptures from a *pulpitum* or *tribunal ecclesiae*.

primum, sic minister altaris, idque ab infantia, post laborum temporumque processu archidiaconus, in quo seu gradu seu ministerio multum retentus propter industriam diu dignitate non potuit augeri, ne potestate posset absolvi): attamen hunc iam secundi ordinis sacerdotem dissonas inter partium voces, quae differebant laudare non ambientem sed nec audebant culpare laudabilem, stupentibus factiosis erubescentibus malis, acclamantibus bonis reclamantibus nullis collegam sibi consecravere. 5. nunc ergo Iurensia si te remittunt iam monasteria, in quae libenter solitus escendere[1] iam caelestibus supernisque praeludis habitaculis, gaudere te par est de communium patrum vel patronorum seu sic sentiente concordia seu sic concordante sententia. illius quoque nomine exulta, quem creaverunt Euphronius testimonio, manu Patiens, ambo iudicio, in quo fecit Euphronius quod conveniret non senectutis modo suae verum etiam dignitatis longaevitati, fecit et Patiens, vir quamlibet magnis par tamen laudibus, quod satis decuit facere personam, quae caput est civitati nostrae per sacerdotium, provinciae vero per civitatem. vale.

[1] ascendere *MTCFP*.

---

[1] Perhaps rather: he could not be promoted in rank lest he might possibly be parted from his present authority (*sc.* as archdeacon which he used so well).

a servant of the altar, as indeed he had been from infancy; then with the passing of laborious years he had become an archdeacon. In this grade or ministry he had been kept for a long time, for because of his efficiency he could not be promoted in rank for fear of loosing him from an office of such importance.[1] However, this priest of a second rank they have now consecrated as their colleague—amid the discordant voices of factions, slow to praise one who was no place-seeker, although not daring to find fault with one so praiseworthy; and thus the schemers were dumbfounded, the wicked blushed, the good shouted approval, and none shouted disapproval. 5. Well, then, if by this time you are now being released by the monasteries of Jura to which you so often gladly climb, there to have a foretaste of the heavenly mansions above, it is fitting that you should rejoice over a harmony of such sentiment, or a sentiment of such harmony, on the part of our common fathers or patrons. Exult also for the sake of him whom they appointed, Euphronius by his testimony, Patiens by the laying on of hands, and both together by their good judgment. Herein Euphronius acted as beseemed not only his advanced years but also his long-held dignity; and Patiens, a man for whom no praise could be too high, did what entirely befitted a person who by virtue of his sacred office is the leading man of our city and because of our city's precedence the first man of our province.[2] Farewell.

[2] *I.e.* the importance of Lugdunum makes its first citizen also the first man in the whole province.—*A*.

LIBER QVINTVS

I

SIDONIVS PETRONIO SVO SALVTEM

1. Audio, quod lectitandis epistulis meis voluptuosam patientiam inpendas. magnum hoc est et litterarum viro convenientissimum, cum studiis ipse maxumis polleas, ea in aliis etiam minima complecti. sed ex hoc ipso consummatissima tibi gloria reponderatur; nam satis eminet meritis ingenii proprii qui fuerit fautor alieni. 2. commendo Vindicium necessarium meum, virum religiosum et leviticae dignitati, quam nuper indeptus est, accommodatissimum. cui meis e pugillaribus transferre quae iusseras non vacans proquam provincia [1] fuit, hic vobis aliquid neniarum munusculi vice detuli; [2] quamquam, quae tua sanctitas, semper grandia litteras nostras praemia putes. 3. interea necessitatem praefati

[1] perquam provincia (-tia) *codd.* (provintiam *T*): qui meis . . . proquam provincia *Gustafsson*: cui . . . non vacans (*vel* vacans animus) per suam (*vel* nescio quam) provinciam *coni. Luetjohann*: perquam praecinctus (*vel etiam* procinctus) fuit *aut* fui *coni. Warmington.*

[2] detuli *Mohr*: detulit.

---

* A man of Arles learned in law and letters. It was he who persuaded Sidonius to publish book VIII of the Letters—See *Ep.* VIII. 1; II. 5; I. 7. 4; VIII. 16. 1.

[1] A deacon of Auvergne; cf. VII. 4. 1.

BOOK V

I

SIDONIUS TO HIS FRIEND PETRONIUS,* GREETING

1. I hear that you devote pleasurable pains to the reading of my letters. It is a noble trait, and highly becoming in a man of letters, that one who himself excels in literary labours of the greatest importance should welcome even the humblest efforts in others. But this very thing brings you consummate glory as your recompense; for the man who shows favour to another's talent brings the qualities of his own into special prominence. 2. I commend to you my good friend Vindicius,[1] a religious man eminently fitted for the dignity of deacon which he has recently gained. Not having any time to copy for him from my tablets the writing you asked for, as was my duty,[2] I have here consigned some doggerel to you as a humble gift—although, in your goodness of heart, you always think a letter from me a great prize. 3. Incidentally, I bring to your notice the

[2] "as was my duty," *i.e.* to give to Vindicius for conveyance to Petronius. The reading *proquam* (Gustafsson) for *perquam* is very uncertain.—*A*. We might perhaps read *praecinctus* (or even *procinctus*) for *provincia*, and also read *qui* with Gustafsson but keep *perquam* and *detulit* of the MSS: (Vindicius) "who, not having any time—he has been in a very great hurry" (literally "very girt up")—"to copy from my tablets the writing which you had asked for, has here brought to you some doggerel as a humble gift."

portitoris insinuo, quem traxit isto negotii oborti bipertita condicio. siquidem hac definitione perrexit, ut aut ineat litem aut adeat hereditatem. nam patrueli paterno caelibi intestatoque defuncto per agnationis praerogativam succedere parat, nisi tamen coeptis factiosa vis obviet. contra quas tamen cunctas difficultates solus post opem Christi supplici tuo sufficis, cuius confido quod, si meruerit persona gratiam, consequetur causa victoriam. vale.

II

SIDONIVS NYMPHIDIO SVO SALVTEM

1. Librum de statu animae tribus voluminibus inlustrem Mamertus Claudianus peritissimus Christianorum philosophus et quorumlibet primus eruditorum totis sectatae[1] philosophiae membris artibus partibusque comere et excolere curavit, novem quas vocant Musas disciplinas aperiens esse, non feminas. namque in paginis eius vigilax lector inveniet veriora nomina Camenarum, quae propriam de se sibi pariunt nuncupationem. illic enim et grammatica dividit et oratoria declamat et arithmetica numerat et geometrica metitur et musica ponderat et dia-

[1] secretae *coni. Luetjohann*: *Sed vide* VII. 9. 9 sectatae anachoreseos.

---

* Grandfather it seems of Polemius (*Ep.* IV. 14); possibly the Nymphidius of *Carm.* XV. 200.

[1] See *Ep.* IV. 2, first note. [2] The Muses.

[3] So Anderson translates *ponderat*; perhaps rather "meditates"; or "balances" as Dalton renders it; literally "weighs," poises. See Additional Notes, p. 611.

plight of the aforesaid bearer, who has been brought to your neighbourhood by a piece of business which has cropped up, presenting a double possibility; for he has proceeded on his way with the express intention either to enter suit or to enter upon his inheritance. He had a cousin on his father's side who died unmarried and intestate, and he is taking steps to succeed him by right of agnate kinship, at least unless some crafty influence should thwart his purpose. But next to Christ's help, yours and yours alone has the power to sustain your suppliant in the face of all these difficulties, and I feel sure that, if his personality should win your favour, his cause will gain the victory. Farewell.

II

SIDONIUS TO HIS FRIEND NYMPHIDIUS,* GREETING

1. Mamertus Claudianus,[1] the most expert philosopher among the Christians and the first of all savants Christian or otherwise, has taken pains to deck and embellish the three volumes of his notable work " On the nature of the soul " with all the members, joints, and parts of the philosophy he affects, making it clear that the nine so-called Muses are branches of learning, not females. In his pages the vigilant reader will find the truer names of the Camenae,[2] who themselves bring forth the appellations appropriate to them: for in that work grammar classifies, rhetoric declaims, arithmetic numbers, geometry measures, music modulates,[3] dialectic

lectica disputat et astrologia[1] praenoscit et architectonica struit et metrica modulatur. 2. huius lectionis novitate laetatus excitatusque maturitate raptim recensendam transferendamque, ut videras, petisti, ut petieras, impetrasti sub sponsione citae redhibitionis. nec me falli nec te fallere decet. tempus est commodata restitui, quia liber ipse, si placuit, debuit exhibere satietatem, si displicuit, debuit movere fastidium. tu autem, quicquid illud est, fidem tuam celeriter absolve, ne si repetitum libellum serius reddere paras, membranas potius videaris amare quam literas. vale.

III

SIDONIVS APOLLINARI SVO SALVTEM

1. Par erat quidem garrulitatem nostram silentii vestri talione frenari. sed quoniam perfecta dilectio non tam debet recolere, quid officiorum solvat, quam meminisse, quid debeat, etiam nunc laxatis verecundiae habenis obsequium alloquii impudentis iteramus. cuius improbitas vel hinc maxime dinoscitur, quod tacetis. ergone quid tempore hostilitatis

[1] astrologica *Engelbrecht*.

---

* See *Ep.* IV. 4, first note.

[1] *tacetis* . . . *ageretis* . . . *dissimulastis*, etc. It is not quite certain that all the 2nd person plurals are really singular in meaning.—*A*.

discusses, astronomy foretells, architecture builds, and metric regulates. 2. You were delighted with the novelty of this work and stimulated by its ripe perfection: so you had no sooner seen the book than you asked for it that you might hurriedly go through it and copy it, and you had no sooner asked than you obtained it under a promise to return it speedily. It is not seemly that I should be deceived or that you should deceive me. It is time to restore the loan, because the book itself, if approved, ought by now to have afforded you ample satisfaction, and if not approved it ought to have aroused disgust. But however that may be, do discharge your promise quickly, for if you intend to wait longer before returning the wanted book, you are in danger of being thought to be fonder of parchment than of literature. Farewell.

III

SIDONIUS TO HIS KINSMAN APOLLINARIS,* GREETING

1. It was right that my loquacity should be checked by the revenge of silence on your part; but since perfect affection should not so much reflect upon the duty it discharges as remember the duty it still owes, I have even in the present circumstances loosened the reins of modesty to send you once more the homage of a shameless letter. The very fact that you [1] choose to be silent is the supreme evidence of my effrontery in so doing. Well, my brother, have I not deserved to be told how things are going with you

ageretis, frater, nosse non merui? dissimulastis trepido pro vobis amico vel securitatem prodere vel timorem? 2. quid est aliud, si requirenti tuas supprimas [1] actiones, quam suspicari eum, qui tui sollicitus existat, aut certe non gavisurum compertis prosperis aut tristem, si diversa cesserint, non futurum? facessat haec a bonis moribus impietatis opinio et a candore suo vera caritas naevum tam miserae suspicionis eliminet. namque, ut Crispus vester affirmat, idem velle atque idem nolle, ea demum firma amicitia est. 3. interea si vel vos valetis, bene est. ego autem, infelicis conscientiae mole depressus, vi febrium nuper extremum salutis accessi, utpote cui indignissimo tantae professionis pondus impactum est, qui miser, ante compulsus docere quam discere et ante praesumens bonum praedicare quam facere, tamquam sterilis arbor, cum non habeam opera pro pomis, spargo verba pro foliis. 4. quod restat, orate, ut operae pretium sit, quod ab inferna propemodum sede remeavimus, ne, si in praeteritis criminibus manserimus, incipiat ad animae potius mortem pertinere quod vivimus. ecce quod agimus indicamus; ecce adhuc, quid agatis, inquirimus. fit a nostra parte quod pium est, vos deinceps facite quod videtur. illud sane

[1] supprimis *MCFPRN*[1].

---

[1] Sallust, *Catiline*, 20. 4. "To be for or against the same things," "to have all wishes and aversions in common."—*A.* The *cognomen* of Sallust (86–34 B.C.) was Crispus.

in the time of hostilities? Have you avoided revealing your confidence or your fear, as the case may be, to a friend who is alarmed on your behalf? 2. If you hide your doings from an enquiring friend, does not this imply a suspicion on your part that he who shows concern for you will certainly not rejoice if he hears good news, or will not be sad if the opposite has befallen you? Chase such a notion of disloyalty from your noble disposition, and let true friendship banish from its immaculate beauty the disfigurement of such a wretched suspicion. As your favourite Crispus [1] declares, to have the same inclinations and the same aversions, that is what firm friendship means. 3. Meanwhile, if *you* are well, I rejoice; but as for me, besides being oppressed by the load of an unhappy conscience, I have lately been brought almost to death's door by the ravages of fever, as might well happen to one on whose totally unworthy shoulders has been thrust the burden of such a high calling; and in my wretched plight, compelled to teach before learning, and presuming to preach goodness before doing it, I am like a sort of barren tree—not having works as fruit, I scatter words as leaves. 4. For the rest, pray that my return almost from the gates of death may not prove to be in vain: for it is to be feared that, if I persist in the sins of the past, my preservation may bring not life but death to my soul. Take note that I am disclosing my doings to you; take note also that I am still seeking to learn your doings. On my side affection's duty is being discharged; you in your turn must do what seems good to you. One thing at least you must believe as if it were graven on bronze like Attic

velut Atticas [1] leges ita aeri [2] credite incisum, nos sub ope Christi numquam admissuros amoris terminum, cuius studuimus fundare principium. vale.

IV

SIDONIVS SIMPLICIO SVO SALVTEM

1. Quod non recepi scripta qui miseram, imputo amicitiae, sed deputo plus pudori. nam, nisi praeter aequum autumo, ut salutatio mihi debita dissimularetur, non illud contumacia sed verecundia fuit. at si ulterius paginae garrienti forem claudis, pessulum opponis, quieti quidem tuae non invitus indulgeo, sed non procul a te reos meos inventurum me esse denuntio. 2. nam totam silentii vestri invidiam verti non iniurium est ad superbiam filiorum, qui se diligi sentientes quoddam patiuntur de nostra sedulitate fastidium. quos monere pro

[1] antiquas *coni. Lips, Gustafsson.*
[2] ita aeri *Geisler*: in aere *Luetjohann*: ita aere (*vel* ere).

---

[1] There is no evidence that Attic laws were inscribed on bronze. It has been suggested that Attic laws were transported to Rome and may then have been set up on bronze tablets. At some stage perhaps *āticas* was found and miscopied as *atticas* rather than *antiquas*.

* See *Ep.* IV. 4, first note. On this letter see Semple, *Quaest. Exeg.*, 29–33. His interpretation seems to be reasonable.

laws:[1] Christ helping me, I will never acquiesce in the ending of a friendship the beginning of which I have striven so earnestly to establish. Farewell.

IV

SIDONIUS TO HIS KINSMAN SIMPLICIUS,* GREETING

1. The fact that I received no reply to the letter I sent you seems to me a discredit to your friendship, but I credit it rather to your feeling of shame; for, unless I am unfair, your failure to send me the greeting you owed was due to embarrassment, not to arrogance. But if you go on shutting and bolting the door upon my chattering page, I am indeed quite willing to make every concession to your peace and quiet, but at the same time I give notice that I will find my culprits not far from you. 2. For it is fair enough that all the dislike I feel for your silence should be directed against the uppishness of your children,[2] who being well aware of my affection for them experience a sort of disdain as the result of my constant attentions. It will be your duty, in view of your paternal authority, to warn them that they

[2] "children" rather than "sons." There was a daughter, if this is the Simplicius of *Ep.* III. 11. I disagree in more than one point with Semple's interpretation of this letter in his *Quaest. Exeg.* 29. I think this is certainly (as he says) a "familiar letter"; and I don't for a moment believe (with Dalton) that *pudori* and *verecundiae* here mean "shame" or the like (*praeter aequum* implies that *verecundia* here has the idea of shame for some shortcoming).—*A.* On this, *W.H.S.* gracefully says *Salve magne parens*. . . .

patria auctoritate debebitis, ut contractae apud nos offensae amaritudinem politis affatibus dulcare non desinant. vale.

V

SIDONIVS SYAGRIO SVO SALVTEM

1. Cum sis consulis pronepos idque per virilem successionem (quamquam id ad causam subiciendam minus attinet), cum sis igitur e semine poetae, cui procul dubio statuas dederant litterae, si trabeae non dedissent (quod etiam nunc auctoris culta versibus verba testantur), a quo studia posterorum ne parum quidem, quippe in hac parte, degeneraverunt, immane narratu est, quantum stupeam sermonis te Germanici notitiam tanta facilitate rapuisse. 2. atqui pueritiam tuam competenter scholis liberalibus memini imbutam et saepenumero acriter eloquenterque declamasse coram oratore satis habeo compertum. atque haec cum ita sint, velim dicas, unde subito hauserunt pectora tua euphoniam gentis alienae, ut modo mihi post ferulas lectionis Maronianae postque desudatam varicosi Arpinatis opu-

---

* Cf. *Ep.* VIII. 8. Great-grandson of Flavius Afranius Syagrius of Lyon (for whom see *Ep.* I. 7. 4; V. 17. 4; *Carm.* XXIV. 36). Some scholars wrongly think that this *Ep.* V. 5 at any rate and possibly VIII. 8 also were written to another Syagrius, son of Aegidius of Soissons, defeated there by Clovis, King of the Salian Franks, in A.D. 486. See K. Stroheker, *Der senatorische Adel im spätantiken Gallien*, no. 369.

[1] *trabeae*, robes of state.

must never cease to sweeten with elegant letters the bitter taste of the grievance I have against them. Farewell.

V

SIDONIUS TO HIS FRIEND SYAGRIUS,* GREETING

1. You are the great-grandson of a consul, and in the male line too—although that has little to do with the case before us; I say, then, you are descended from a poet, to whom his literary glory would have brought statues had not his magisterial glories [1] done so, as even to this day this author's words enshrined in verse bear witness; and the culture of his successors has not declined one whit from his standard, particularly in this respect.[2] I am therefore inexpressibly amazed that you have quickly acquired a knowledge of the German tongue with such ease. 2. And yet I remember that your boyhood had a good schooling in liberal studies and I know for certain that you often declaimed with spirit and eloquence before your professor of oratory. This being so, I should like you to tell me how you have managed to absorb so swiftly into your inner being the exact sounds of an alien race, so that now after reading Virgil under the schoolmaster's cane and toiling and working through the rich fluency of the varicose man [3]

[2] *in hac parte, i.e.* in poetry? or in literature?—*A.*

[3] Cicero, presumed to be varicose merely because he was always standing in public as he made his speeches. Cf. Quintilian, XI. 3. 143; Macrobius, *Saturn.*, II. 3.

entiam loquacitatemque quasi de harilao[1] vetere novus falco[2] prorumpas? 3. aestimari minime potest, quanto mihi ceterisque sit risui, quotiens audio, quod te praesente formidet linguae suae facere barbarus barbarismum. adstupet tibi epistulas interpretanti curva Germanorum senectus et negotiis mutuis arbitrum te disceptatoremque desumit. novus Burgundionum Solon in legibus disserendis, novus Amphion in citharis, sed trichordibus, temperandis, amaris frequentaris, expeteris oblectas, eligeris adhiberis, decernis audiris. et quamquam aeque corporibus ac sensu rigidi sint indolatilesque, amplectuntur in te pariter et discunt sermonem patrium, cor Latinum. 4. restat hoc unum, vir facetissime, ut nihilo segnius, vel cum vacabit, aliquid lectioni operis[3] impendas custodiasque hoc, prout es elegantissimus, temperamentum, ut ista tibi lingua teneatur, ne ridearis, illa exerceatur, ut rideas. vale.

[1] harilao *LT*: arilao *R*[2] *in marg.*: hilario *MCFP*: ilario *R*: Syagrio *Colvius ex ms. Claromontanensi*: haliaeëto *sive* haliaëto *coni. Warmington*: aviario *coni. Burke.*

[2] Franco *Colvius ex ms. Claromontanensi.*

[3] operae *Luetjohann.*

---

[1] This word is uncertain; so is the reading. I have conjectured *haliaeëto* or *haliaëto* "sea-eagle" so that the whole phrase may express rejuvenation. But *harilao* may be sound and may be a Teutonic or German word (like names beginning Chari-, for example Chariobaudus or Hariobaudus of *Ep.* VII. 16) and may be connected with falconry; or it may mean eyrie, a nest of a bird of prey, as *A.* takes it.

from Arpinum you burst forth before my eyes like a young falcon from an old nest.[1] 3. You have no idea what amusement it gives me, and others too, when I hear that in your presence the barbarian is afraid to perpetrate a barbarism in his own language. The bent elders of the Germans are astounded at you when you translate letters, and they adopt you as umpire and arbitrator in their mutual dealings. A new Solon [2] of the Burgundians in discussing the laws, a new Amphion in attuning the lyre—a three-stringed [3] lyre, it is true—you are loved, your company is sought, you are much visited, you delight, you are picked out, you are invited,[4] you decide issues and are listened to. And although these people are stiff and uncouth [5] in body and mind alike, they welcome in you, and learn from you, their native speech combined with Roman wisdom. 4. Only one thing remains, most clever of men: continue with undiminished zeal, even in your hours of ease, to devote some attention to reading; and, like the man of refinement that you are, observe a just balance between the two languages: retain your grasp of Latin, lest you be laughed at, and practise the other, in order to have the laugh of them. Farewell.

[2] An allusion to the famous Solon of Athens, whose reforms there took place in 594–3 B.C.

[3] Amphion was, in Greek mythology, able to move stones even to build themselves into a wall when he played his lyre. Three-stringed implies very simple and uncomplicated. Cf. Plutarch, *de mus.* 18. 2.

[4] Or "summoned to give counsel."—*A.*

[5] So *A.* The meaning is rather not capable of being shaped or improved.

VI

SIDONIVS APOLLINARI SVO SALVTEM

1. Cum primum aestas decessit autumno et Arvernorum timor potuit aliquantisper ratione temporis temperari, Viennam veni, ubi Thaumastum, germanum tuum, quem pro iure vel sanguinis vel aetatis reverenda [1] familiaritate complector, maestissimum inveni. qui quamquam recenti caelibatu granditer afficiebatur, pro te tamen parum minus anxius erat: timebat enim verebaturque, ne quam tibi calumniam turbo barbaricus aut militaris concinnaret improbitas. 2. namque confirmat magistro militum Chilperico, victoriosissimo viro, relatu venenato quorumpiam sceleratorum fuisse secreto insusurratum tuo praecipue machinatu oppidum Vasionense partibus novi principis applicari. si quid hinc tibi tuisque suspicionis incutitur, raptim doce recursu familiarium paginarum, ne vobis sollici-

[1] reverendae *malit Mohr*.

---

* See *Ep.* IV. 4, first note. This letter was written about September, A.D. 474.

[1] See *Carm.* XXIV. 85 and note there; and letter 7 of this book.

[2] *reverenda* must here be used for *veneranti*. Mohr suggests *reverendae* to go with *aetatis*—which is very plausible.—*A.*

[3] or: "that a whisper based on the poisonous report of some villains has secretly reached the ears of Chilperic, to the effect that . . . ."—*A.*

[4] This Chilperic or Hilperic (not Childeric I, King of the

VI

SIDONIUS TO HIS KINSMAN APOLLINARIS,* GREETING

1. As soon as summer gave place to autumn and the Arvernians, in view of the season, were able to abate their fear for a time, I went to Vienne, visiting your brother Thaumastus,[1] whom I cherish with a respectful [2] friendship, in virtue of our kinship and our ages. I found him plunged in grief. Although he was greatly distressed by the recent loss of his wife, he was little less concerned on your behalf, for he was full of fear and apprehension lest the riotous barbarians or unscrupulous soldiers should trump up a false accusation against you. 2. He declares that some villains have secretly whispered [3] into the ears of that most victorious leader Chilperic,[4] the Master of the Soldiers, a poisonous tale to the effect that the town of Vaison was attaching itself to the party of the new Emperor [5] chiefly owing to your scheming. If any suspicion from that quarter is being cast on you and yours,[6] make haste to let me know by a friendly note in return, lest the timely help of my

Salian Franks) was King of the Burgundians, father of Clotilda, Clovis' queen. See n. on V. 7. 1.

[5] Iulius Nepos, emperor in A.D. 474–475, not recognised by Chilperic, who represented Glycerius, emperor in A.D. 473. Some Gallo-Romans, friends of Chilperic, apparently accused Apollinaris of having favoured an attempt to drive the Burgundians from Vaison and to hold the town for Nepos.

[6] One would expect *suspicionem incutere* to mean "put a suspicion into one's head." Does it mean that here? *I.e.* "If any suspicion is being forced upon you and yours."—*A.*

tudinis aut praesentiae meae opportunitas pereat. curae mihi peculiariter erit, si quid tamen cavendum existimabis, ut te faciat aut gratia impetrata securum aut explorata iracundia cautiorem. vale.

VII

SIDONIVS THAVMASTO SVO SALVTEM

1. Indagavimus tandem, qui apud tetrarcham nostrum germani tui et e diverso partium novi principis amicitias criminarentur, si tamen fidam sodalium sagacitatem clandestina delatorum non fefellere vestigia. hi nimirum sunt, ut idem coram positus audisti, quos se iamdudum perpeti inter clementiores barbaros Gallia gemit. hi sunt, quos timent etiam qui timentur. hi sunt, quos haec

---

[1] *Tamen* implies the sense: "If in spite of all I can do to scotch this suspicion, you still think that danger is imminent . . ."—*W.H.S.*

* See V. 6. 1 and *Carm.* XXIV. 85 and note there.

[2] A tetrarch had control over a tetrarchy, in strict language one-quarter of any region. In the imperial times of Rome the word tetrarch meant a dependent prince; or a ruler of part only of a kingdom; or ruler of a very small territory. The tetrarch in this letter may be the Burgundian King Chilperic of the preceding letter; but tetrarch would apply better after his death to his nephew Chilperic II, who shared the kingship with his three brothers, Gundobad, Gundomar, and Godegesil, and himself ruled at Vienne. If, however, Sidonius does indeed allude to the first Chilperic, the title "tetrarch" is hardly meant seriously. L. Schmidt, *Gesch. der deutschen Stämme*, I. 376, 380.

solicitude or of my presence be lost to you. If you really [1] form the opinion that there is danger ahead, I will make it my special care to ensure either that a grant of pardon shall make you feel safe, or that a full investigation of the anger you have incurred shall make you more cautious. Farewell.

VII

SIDONIUS TO HIS FRIEND THAUMASTUS,* GREETING

1. At last we have found out who brought before our tetrarch [2] the allegation of friendship between your brother, on the one side, and the party of the new Emperor,[3] on the other—unless indeed the stealthy tracks of the informers have misled the trusty shrewdness of our comrades. These informers, of course, as you have also heard said in your presence,[4] are the men whom Gaul, much to her sorrow, has long endured among barbarians who are milder than they.[5] These are the men whom even they fear who are themselves feared. These are the men

[3] Iulius Nepos, emperor in 474–475.

[4] *Coram positus* means "while you were actually in the presence (of someone)." *A.* had other renderings: "heard from my lips" and "heard on the spot."

[5] Probably the point is that the culprits were Gallo-Roman self-seekers. If this is not right, then the meaning must be that the other "barbarians" are milder than they. Dalton's translation will scarcely do.—*A.* The point is that the German barbarians were bad enough, but these Gallo-Romans were worse. Dalton seems to me to give the general sense adequately in his rather free translation.—*W.H.S.*

peculiariter provincia manet,[1] inferre calumnias deferre personas, afferre minas auferre substantias. 2. hi sunt, quorum laudari audis in otio occupationes in pace praedas, inter arma fugas inter vina victorias. hi sunt, qui causas morantur adhibiti impediunt praetermissi, fastidiunt admoniti obliviscuntur locupletati. hi sunt, qui emunt lites vendunt intercessiones, deputant arbitros iudicanda dictant dictata convellunt, attrahunt litigaturos protrahunt audiendos, trahunt addictos retrahunt transigentes. hi sunt, quos si petas etiam nullo adversante beneficium, piget promittere pudet negare paenitet praestitisse. 3. hi sunt, quorum comparationi digitum tollerent Narcissus Asiaticus, Massa Marcellus, Carus Parthenius, Licinus et Pallas. hi sunt, qui invident tunicatis otia stipendia paludatis, viatica veraedariis [2] mercatoribus nundinas, munuscula lega-

[1] maeret *coni. Baret*: meret *T*: manet *rell.*

[2] veraedariis *L*: veredariis.

---

[1] *Manet* seems odd. What about *maeret*? (*meret T*). If *manet* is correct it must govern *quos inferre*, etc., as a noun clause, *i.e.* whom it is the lot of this province to see levelling accusations, etc.? But this construction seems unparalleled and unlikely.—*A*. I think Anderson boggles because he takes *provincia* in the sense of "province"; but Sidonius often uses it in the sense of "duty" or "function," and I am sure that this is its sense here. We have made the change in the translation.—*W.H.S.*

[2] All these were powerful freedmen in imperial affairs, Narcissus under the Emperor Claudius (A.D. 41–54), Asiaticus under Vitellius (July–Dec. A.D. 69), Massa, Marcellus, and Carus under Nero (A.D. 54–68), Parthenius under Domitian (A.D. 81–96), Licinus under Augustus (30 B.C.–A.D. 14), and Pallas under Claudius and Nero.

whose peculiar function it is [1] to level false accusations, to denounce individuals, to launch threats, and to lift property. 2. These are the men whom you hear praising their activities in times of rest, their plundering in times of peace, their decamping from the battlefield, and their victories in their cups. These are the men who spin out law cases when summoned as witnesses, obstruct them when not summoned, show contempt when notified of the case, and forget all about it when they have had their fee. They are the men who buy up lawsuits, sell intercessions, assign arbitrators, dictate judgments, tear up the decisions made, entice prospective litigants, put off cases that are due for hearing, drag off the condemned, and drag back those who are completing their business. They are the men who when asked to do a kindness even when no one objects, hate to promise it, are ashamed to refuse it, and are sorry when they have granted it. 3. They are the men before whom Narcissus and Asiaticus, Massa and Marcellus, Carus and Parthenius, Licinus and Pallas [2] would have held up their hands in despair.[3] These are the men who grudge to men retired from civil life their leisure, to the military men [4] their pay, to post-boys their perquisites, to merchants their

[3] *digitum tollere,* "lift up a finger." This gesture could signify polite recognition of superiority, or admission of defeat, as shown in ancient works of art. K. Sittl, *Die Gebärden der Griechen und Römer* s.v. "Zeigefinger"; E. N. Gardiner, *Athletics of the Ancient World,* 173, 180, pp. 199, 203.

[4] *Tunicati,* dressed in tunic only when the *toga* of working hours had been put aside and one could relax in less formal dress. Cf. Pliny, *Ep.* V. 6. 45; Juvenal, III. 171–172. *Paludati,* dressed in military cloak.

tis portoria quadruplatoribus, praedia provincialibus flamonia municipibus, arcariis pondera mensuras allectis salaria tabulariis, dispositiones numerariis praetorianis sportulas, civitatibus indutias vectigalia publicanis, reverentiam clericis originem nobilibus, consessum prioribus congressum aequalibus, cinctis iura discinctis privilegia, scholas instituendis mercedes instituentibus litteras institutis. 4. hi sunt, qui novis opibus ebrii, ut et minima cognoscas, per utendi intemperantiam produnt imperitiam possidendi; nam libenter incedunt armati ad epulas, albati ad exsequias, pelliti ad ecclesias, pullati ad nuptias, castorinati ad litanias. nullum illis genus hominum ordinum temporum cordi est. in foro Scythae, in cubiculo viperae, in convivio scurrae, in exactionibus Harpyiae, in conlocutionibus statuae, in quaestionibus bestiae, in tractatibus cocleae, in contractibus trapezitae; ad intellegendum saxei, ad iudicandum lignei, ad suscensendum flammei, ad ignoscendum ferrei, ad amicitias pardi, ad facetias ursi, ad fallendum vulpes, ad superbiendum tauri, ad consumendum minotauri. 5. spes firmas in rerum motibus habent, dubia tempora certius amant, et ignavia pariter conscientiaque trepidantes, cum sint

---

[1] Does *provincialibus* here mean "country-dwellers"?—*A*.

[2] Possibly Dalton (Vol. II, p. 57) has the right idea: "superiors their seats in council, equals equality."—*A*.

markets, to ambassadors their douceurs, to the customs officers their dues, to the provincials [1] their farms, to the men of the country-towns their priesthoods, to the public treasurers their weights, to the receivers their measures, to the registrars their salaries, to the cashiers their settlements, to the praetorians their gratuities, to cities the deferment of their taxes, to tax-farmers their revenues, to the clergy their reverence, to the nobility their lineage, to superiors their privilege of sitting together, to equals the right of social intercourse,[2] to magistrates their rights, to unofficial persons their privileges, to prospective learners their schools, to teachers their salaries, to the educated their culture. 4. These are the men who (if I am to tell you even their smallest offences) are intoxicated with unaccustomed wealth and by their intemperate use of it reveal how small is their experience of possession; for they like to march in armour to feasts, in white to funerals, in furs to church, in mourning to weddings, in beaver fur to prayers. No man, order, or occasion of any kind pleases them. In the forum they are Scythians, in a room they are vipers, at a dinner party they are buffoons, in their exactions harpies, in conversations statues, in investigations brute beasts, in discussions snails, in contracts usurers; in intelligence they are like stones, in judgment wooden, fiery in anger, unforgiving as iron, in their friendship they are panthers, in their witticisms bears, in their deceitfulness foxes, in their arrogance bulls, in their voracity minotaurs. 5. They have firm hopes in unsettlement, they cherish troubled times with special confidence; nervous alike from cowardice and from a bad

in praetoriis leones, in castris lepores, timent foedera, ne discutiantur, bella, ne pugnent. quorum si nares afflaverit uspiam robiginosi aura marsupii, confestim videbis illic et oculos Argi et manus Briarei et Sphingarum ungues et periuria Laomedontis et Ulixis argutias et Sinonis fallacias et fidem Polymestoris et pietatem Pygmalionis adhiberi. 6. his moribus obruunt virum non minus bonitate quam potestate praestantem. sed quid faciat unus, undique venenato vallatus interprete? quid, inquam, faciat, cui natura cum bonis, vita cum malis est? ad quorum consilia Phalaris cruentior Mida cupidior, Ancus iactantior Tarquinius superbior, Tiberius callidior Gaius periculosior, Claudius socordior Nero impurior, Galba avarior Otho audacior, Vitellius sumptuosior Domitianus truculentior redderetur. 7. sane, quod principaliter medetur afflic-

---

[1] Everything seems to indicate that the subject of *discutiantur* is like that of *pugnent*, *i.e.* "they," the men. The idea of the context is thus better: they thrive in disturbed times. *Discutio* must then mean "examine," "bring to book." If *foedera* were the subject *discutiantur* would mean "be put an end to," "dissolved," "quashed."—*A*. Or "brought to nought," "frustrated, pulled to pieces."

[2] In Greek story Argos Panoptes ("All-seeing") had one hundred eyes and Briareus one hundred arms; Sphinxes were provided with claws of lions or of vultures; Laomedon, King of Troy, broke his word to the gods Poseidon and Apollo, and again to Heracles; Odysseus (Ulysses) was renowned for his cunning; Sinon betrayed the Trojans in the stratagem of the wooden horse; and Polymestor grossly betrayed the trust put in him by Priam, King of Troy, so that *fidem* and *pietatem* are ironical. Pygmalion here is Dido's brother who slew her husband Sychaeus, and is not the Pygmalion who loved the ivory statue which he had made.

conscience, they are lions in the palace and hares in the camp, fearing treaties lest they be brought to book and wars lest they have to fight.[1] If the whiff of a musty purse reaches their nostrils from any quarter you will at once see them employ there the eyes of Argus, the hands of Briareus, the claws of Sphinxes, the perjuries of Laomedon, the wiles of Ulysses, the deceits of Sinon, the good faith of Polymestor and the brotherly love of Pygmalion.[2] 6. Such are the morals with which they are trying to overwhelm a man eminent no less for his goodness than for his position of authority. But what can one man do, hemmed in on all sides by experts in poisoned misrepresentation? What, I repeat, can a man do when his nature sides with the good but his daily life is among the wicked—among men whose influence would make Phalaris more bloodthirsty, Midas more greedy,[3] Ancus more boastful, Tarquin more overbearing,[4] Tiberius more crafty, Gaius more dangerous, Claudius more stupid, Nero more vile, Galba more grasping, Otho more reckless, Vitellius more extravagant, Domitian more ferocious?[5] 7. It is

[3] Phalaris was the (allegedly) brutal tyrant (unconstitutional ruler) of the Greek city Acragas in Sicily *c.* 570–554 B.C.; Midas was ruler of Phrygia in Asia Minor.

[4] Ancus Marcius and Tarquinius Superbus (the Proud) were traditional and probably real kings of ancient Rome; the behaviour of Tarquinius led to the establishment of the Roman republic in 510–509 B.C. or later.

[5] Roman emperors: Tiberius A.D. 14–37; Gaius 37–41; Claudius 41–54; Nero 54–68; Galba 68–Jan. 69; Otho Jan.–April (?) 69; Vitellius (Jan.) July–Dec. 69; (Vespasian 69–79 and Titus 79–81 are not mentioned by Sidonius here); Domitian 81–96.

tis, temperat Lucumonem nostrum Tanaquil sua et aures mariti virosa susurronum faece completas opportunitate salsi sermonis eruderat. cuius studio [factum [1]] scire vos par est nihil interim quieti fratrum communium apud animum communis patroni iuniorum Cibyratarum venena nocuisse neque quicquam deo propitiante nocitura, si modo, quamdiu praesens potestas Lugdunensem Germaniam regit, nostrum suumque Germanicum praesens Agrippina moderetur. vale.

VIII

SIDONIVS SECVNDINO SVO SALVTEM

1. Diu quidem est, quod te hexametris familiarius inservientem stupentes praedicantesque lectitabamus. erat siquidem materia iucunda, seu nupti-

[1] factum *seclud. Sirmond*: ⟨o⟩ factum! *coni. Warmington.*

---

[1] Lucumo was Tarquinius Priscus (the Elder), a traditional king of ancient Rome. His queen Tanaquil was said to have ruled his household. Here Sidonius likens Chilperic to this Tarquin and his queen to Tanaquil.

[2] *factum* might be construed, I suppose, but it is curiously superfluous. With *ut* etc. it would, of course, have been quite natural.—*A.*

[3] The reference is to the brothers Tlepolemos and Hieron from Cibyra in Phrygia, who helped the Roman Gaius Verres when he plundered his province Sicily in 73–70 B.C. Cicero, *in Verrem*, IV. 4. 30–33, 37.

[4] A half-jocular term.—*A.* Sidonius alludes to the domination of the Burgundians.

[5] Sidonius here likens Chilperic to Germanicus Caesar the

true—and this is the chief comfort in our distress—that our Lucumo is restrained by his Tanaquil,[1] who by the timely intervention of wholesome talk clears her husband's ears of the poisonous filth which the whisperers have instilled. You ought to know that it is thanks to her interest [2] that so far the venom of our modern Cibyrates [3] has not so worked on the mind of our common patron as to imperil the security of our common brothers in the least degree, and with God's blessing it never will do so, provided that, so long as the present ruler governs Lyonese Germany,[4] the present Agrippina governs our and her Germanicus.[5] Farewell.

VIII

SIDONIUS TO HIS FRIEND SECUNDINUS,* GREETING

1. It is quite a long time since we used to read with marvelling acclamation the hexameters on which you lavished such expert devotion; their matter was equally delightful whether you portrayed

elder, nephew of the emperor Tiberius (A.D. 14–37). He was engaged in campaigns against the Germans, especially A.D. 13–16, and is represented in our records as a fine man. Chilperic's queen is compared with Agrippina the elder, Germanicus' admired wife, who was with him on the Rhine and again in the East, and is represented as something like the ideal Roman matron.

* Of Lyon. Mentioned also in *Ep.* II. 10. 3. He was a poet, and, with Constantius the priest who suggested to Sidonius that Sidonius might publish letters, and with Sidonius himself, shared in writing metrical inscriptions for the church at Lyon built by Archbishop Patiens.

ales tibi thalamorum faces sive perfossae regiis ictibus ferae describerentur. sed triplicibus trochaeis nuper in metrum hendecasyllabum compaginatis nihil, ne tuo quidem iudicio, simile fecisti. 2. deus bone, quid illic inesse fellis [1] leporis piperataeque facundiae minime tacitus inspexi! nisi quod ferventis fulmen ingenii et eloquii salsa libertas plus personis forte quam causis impediebantur; ut mihi non figuratius Constantini domum vitamque videatur vel pupugisse versu gemello consul Ablabius [2] vel momordisse disticho tali clam Palatinis foribus appenso:

Saturni aurea saecla quis requirat?
sunt haec gemmea, sed Neroniana.

quia scilicet praedictus Augustus isdem fere temporibus extinxerat coniugem Faustam calore balnei, filium Crispum frigore veneni. 3. tu tamen nihilo segnius operam saltim facetis satirarum coloribus intrepidus impende. nam tua scripta nostrorum

[1] fellis *LT*: mellis *CFPT*[2]*M*[2].
[2] Ablabius *Wilamowitz*: ablavius.

---

[1] See also *Carm.* XXIII. 25–26 and *Ep.* II. 10. 3. The three trochees come in the later part of each line, as in the two lines written in this letter by Sidonius: *sāeclă quīs rĕquīrăt* and *sēd Nĕrōnĭānă.* The last syllable of any line could in practice be long or short.

[2] *Praefectus praetorio* from 326 to 337, and consul in A.D. 331. Constantine was fond of him, but he was exiled by Constantius and later murdered.

[3] "a couple of verses." Semple, *Quaest. Exeg.*, 34–35 would

a torchlit bridal procession or wild beasts transfixed by royal weapons. But even in your opinion you have never before produced anything to match your recent success in welding the triple trochees [1] into the hendecasyllabic metre. 2. Gracious heaven! What a combination of gall and grace and pungent well-spiced eloquence I found there to call forth my loud admiration! It is true, perhaps, that the lightning of your glowing genius and the witty frankness of your utterance tended to take less liberty with persons than with abuses: indeed it seems to me that no greater power of satiric suggestion was shown by the consul Ablabius [2] when in a couple of verses [3] he stabbed at the life and family of Constantine and put his tooth [4] into them with this distich posted up secretly on the door of the palace!

> Who would now want the golden age of Saturn?
> Ours is a diamond age—of Nero's pattern.

He wrote this, of course, because the aforesaid Augustus had almost simultaneously got rid of his wife Fausta with a hot bath and his son Crispus [5] with cold poison. 3. But you must not abate your efforts; you must cultivate fearlessly at any rate the witty effects of satire; for your writings will find rich

translate "in a line the twin of yours," that is, a hendecasyllabic line.

[4] "stabbed" or, if you like, "bit."—*A.*

[5] Son of Constantine (the title Augustus was given to all emperors) by Minervina. He was poisoned by Constantine after he was accused by Constantine's wife Fausta; who herself was put to death by suffocation in the steam of a hot bath when Crispus was found to be innocent.

vitiis proficientibus tyrannopolitarum[1] locupletabuntur. non enim tam mediocriter intumescunt quos nostra iudicia saeculi[2] culpa[3] fortunatos putant, ut de nominibus ipsorum quandoque reminiscendis sit posteritas laboratura: namque improborum probra aeque ut praeconia bonorum inmortalia manent. vale.

IX

SIDONIVS AQVILINO SVO SALVTEM

1. In meo aere duco, vir omnium virtutum capacissime, si dignum tu quoque putas, ut quantas habemus amicitiarum causas, tantas habeamus ipsi amicitias. avitum est quod reposco; testes mihi in praesentiarum avi nostri super hoc negotio Apollinaris et Rusticus advocabuntur, quos laudabili familiaritate

[1] tyrannopolitarum *LMRN*: tyrannopolitanorum *vel sim. rell.*
[2] saecula *MTCFP*.
[3] culpa *Leo*: loco *coni. Warmington*: loca.

---

[1] Perhaps the reading *tyrannopolitanorum* is right (with a glance at *constantinopolitanorum*?).—*A*. Sirmond was probably right in seeing an allusion to the Burgundians here. If that is so, Sidonius means not the earlier Chilperic (see above, V. 6. 2 and 7. 1) but Chilperic's nephew Gundobad, who ruled at Lyon and, after being exiled by his brother Chilperic II and Gundomar (Godomar), regained Lyon and killed Chilperic II and his queen and his children.

[2] [See Additional Notes, p. 611.] I think I have got near to the sense if the reading is right; in the phrase *saeculi culpa* the word *culpa* is an emendation. The meaning, if I am right,

material in the flourishing vices of our tyrant-governed [1] citizens. For the men whom our judgment, thanks to the perversity of this age, ranks as fortune's favourites are swollen with no such ordinary conceit that posterity will some day find it hard to remember their names; for the infamies of the wicked are no less immortal than the praises of the good.[2] Farewell.

IX

SIDONIUS TO HIS FRIEND AQUILINUS,* GREETING

1. Dear master of all the virtues, I consider it an asset (if you also approve) that our friendship should be as strong as our reasons for friendship. The privilege I claim is an inherited one; on the present occasion I will call as witnesses in my suit our grandfathers Apollinaris [3] and Rusticus,[4] whom the similarity of their literary pursuits and their dignities,

is "The names of the wicked today will not be so utterly forgotten in future ages that your satires about them will fall flat." But *laborare de*: should it not mean "be troubled, concerned, solicitous about"? Could *intumescunt* mean "are increasing in number"?—*A.* No: I am sure that *intumescunt* here means "to be swollen with self-importance."—*W.H.S.*

* Not otherwise known.

[3] Sidonius' grandfather Apollinaris was Praetorian Prefect of Gaul in A.D. 408 under the usurper Constantine III (see p. 40.) Cf. *Ep.* III. 12. See next page.

[4] This Rusticus was Aquilinus' grandfather Decimus Rusticus, Praetorian Prefect of Gaul in A.D. 409 under Constantine III. Not long afterwards he was killed by generals of the Emperor Honorius. Gregory of Tours, *Hist. Franc.* II. 9.

coniunxerat litterarum dignitatum, periculorum conscientiarum similitudo, cum in Constantino inconstantiam, in Iovino facilitatem, in Gerontio perfidiam, singula in singulis, omnia in Dardano crimina simul execrarentur. 2. aetate, quae media, patres nostri sub uno contubernio, vixdum a pueritia in totam adulescentiam evecti, principi Honorio tribuni notariique militavere tanta caritate peregrinantes, ut inter eos minima fuerit causa concordiae, quod filii amicorum commemorabantur.[1] in principatu Valentiniani imperatoris unus Galliarum praefuit parti, alter soliditati; sed ita se quodam modo tituli amborum compensatione fraterna ponderaverunt, ut prior fuerit fascium tempore[2] qui erat posterior dignitate. 3. ventum ad nos id est ventum est ad nepotes, quos nil decuerit plus cavere, quam ne parentum antiquorumque nostrorum per nos forte videatur antiquata dilectio. ad hoc in similem familiaritatem praeter hereditariam praerogativam multifaria opportunitate compellimur; aetas utrius-

[1] commerebantur *coni. Anderson.*
[2] tempore *LMTF*: tenore.

---

[1] Flavius Claudius Constantinus, usurper in Britain, Gaul, and Spain A.D. 407–411 during the reign of Honorius. It was in Britain that his friends proclaimed him emperor.

[2] Gallo-Roman noble proclaimed Emperor by the Burgundian King Gundahar in 411; suppressed by Athaulf in 413 in the interests of Honorius.

[3] Commander under Constantine in Spain, he revolted and raised Maximus to imperial power, drove Constans (son of Constantine) from Spain and killed him. He besieged Constantine in Arles without success, fled, and met his death in 411.

[4] Praetorian Prefect of Gaul under the Emperor Honorius A.D. 409–410.

their dangers and their consciences had joined to one another in an attachment that did them honour; for they both abhorred in Constantine [1] his fickleness, in Jovinus [2] his pliability, in Gerontius [3] his faithlessness, in each his particular vice, but in Dardanus [4] all the vices together. 2. In the generation between them and us our fathers, when they had scarcely emerged into full manhood, shared the same quarters, serving the Emperor Honorius [5] as tribunes and secretaries; and in this sojourn abroad they lived on such affectionate terms that the least cause of their camaraderie was that they were talked [6] of as the sons of friends. In the reign of Valentinian [7] one of them governed part, the other the whole, of Gaul; but the honours of both were balanced in such a nicety of brotherly equipoise that the one who was second in status was first in the date of appointment. 3. Now it is the turn of us, the third generation, and it behoves us above all things to ensure that the affectionate friendship of our parents and of the ancients of our line should not by any chance seem to have been scrapped by us.[8] Moreover, we are urged to cherish a like intimacy not only by our hereditary privilege but by many fortunate coincidences: our

[5] A.D. 393–423. The office of *tribunus et notarius* was a single civil one in the emperor's service—"confidential secretary." A. H. M. Jones, *The Later Roman Empire*. II. 574, 572. Sidonius' father may have had the name Apollinaris. See also *Ep.* VIII. 6. 5.

[6] Or accept Anderson's *commerebantur* in the sense "they served together."

[7] Valentinian III, emperor A.D. 425–455.

[8] The word-play may perhaps be rendered "of our dead ancients . . . to have become a dead letter through our fault."—*A*.

que[1] non minus iuncta quam patria; unus nos exercuit ludus, magister instituit; una nos laetitia dissolvit, severitas cohercuit, disciplina formavit. 4. de cetero, si deus annuit, in annis iam senectutis initia pulsantibus, simus, nisi respuis, animae duae, animus unus, imbuamusque liberos invicem diligentes[2] idem velle nolle, refugere sectari. hoc patrum vero iam supra vota, si per Rusticum Apollinaremque proavorum praedicabilium tam reformentur corda quam nomina. vale.

X

SIDONIVS SAPAVDO SVO SALVTEM

1. Si quid omnino Pragmatius illustris, hoc inter reliquas animi virtutes optime facit, quod amore studiorum te singulariter amat, in quo solo vel maxume animum advertit veteris peritiae diligentiaeque resedisse vestigia. equidem non iniuria tibi fautor est; nam debetur ab eo percopiosus litteris honor. 2. hunc olim perorantem et rhetorica sedilia plausibili oratione frangentem socer

[1] utriusque *MTCFP*: utrique.
[2] diligenter *Wilamowitz*.

---

[1] Son of Aquilinus.
[2] Son of Sidonius.
* A rhetor of Vienne. In the latter part of this letter I found Anderson's translation so clearly awaiting revision that, using some of his words and phrases, I have reset the sentence-structure so as to bring out more effectively (I think) the purport of Sidonius' meaning.—*W.H.S.*
[3] Not the bishop of *Ep.* VI. 2. The *viri illustres* were the

ages are no less near to one another than our birthplaces; the same school drilled us, the same master taught us, the same joys cheered us, the same strictness checked us, the same training moulded us. 4. For the future, if God so wills, now that we are on the threshold of old age, let us (unless you refuse) be two souls with a single mind, and let us teach our children to live in mutual affection desiring or rejecting, seeking or avoiding the same things. It would indeed surpass the dearest wishes of their fathers if Rusticus [1] and Apollinaris [2] were to reproduce the hearts as well as the names of their illustrious great-grandfathers! Farewell.

X

SIDONIUS TO HIS FRIEND SAPAUDUS,* GREETING

1. If among the qualities of heart and head which distinguish the illustrious Pragmatius [3] anything stands out as specially praiseworthy, it is that his love of letters inspires him with a unique love of you, for he sees that in you alone, and in the highest degree, there still abide some traces of the ancient skill and care. His enthusiasm for you as a man of letters is certainly not without cause; for he owes to letters a very full acknowledgment. 2. Long ago, when he was practising declamation [4] and bringing down the house

highest in rank in the senatorial order, *spectabiles* coming below them, and *clarissimi* below these. A. H. M. Jones, *The Later Roman Empire*, as cited in note on *Ep.* III. 5. 1.

[4] *perorantem*: "pleading a case" or "practising as advocate or pleader"?—*A*.

eloquens ultro in familiam patriciam adscivit, licet illi ad hoc, ut sileam de genere vel censu, aetas venustas pudor patrocinarentur. sed, ut comperi, erubescebat iam etiam[1] tunc vir serius et formae dote placuisse, quippe cui merito ingenii suffecisset adamari. et vere[2] optimus quisque morum praestantius pulchritudine placet; porro autem praetervolantia corporis decoramenta currentis aevi profectu defectuque labascunt. hunc quoque manente sententia Galliis post praefectus Priscus Valerianus consiliis suis tribunalibusque sociavit, iudicium antiquum perseverantissime tenens, ut cui scientiae obtentu iunxerat subolem, iungeret et dignitatem. 3. tua vero tam clara, tam spectabilis dictio est, ut illi divisio Palaemonis gravitas Gallionis, abundantia Delphidii Agroecii disciplina, fortitudo Alcimi Adelphii teneritudo, rigor Magni dulcedo Victorii non modo non superiora sed vix aequiperabilia scribant. sane ne videar tibi sub hoc quasi

[1] etiam *LMTFP*: *om. alii.* [2] vere *cdd. pler.*: vero.

---

[1] Priscus Valerianus, Praetorian Prefect of Gaul; see below and *Carm.* VIII.

[2] Or "had been quite content."—*A.*

[3] *I.e.* he was made one of his *consilium.*—*A.*

[4] Quintus Remmius Palaemon was author of a lost work on grammar during the reigns of Tiberius and Claudius A.D. 14–54. But there was also a Palaemon living in the reign of Hadrian A.D. 117–138. The Gallio here mentioned would not be Iunius Gallio, rhetorician and friend of Lucius (Marcus?) Seneca the elder (*c.* 54 B.C.–A.D. 39), but that Marcus Annaeus Novatus who was adopted by this Gallio (and so became L. Iunius Gallio) and was the son of Annaeus Seneca the elder

with his much-applauded oratory, his eloquent father-in-law[1] was so carried away that he admitted him into his patrician family—although it is true that the young man's age, good looks, and modesty, not to mention his lineage and his means, helped to further this consummation. But I am informed that, even at that early stage, he was serious-minded enough to blush at the thought that his physical appearance had commended him, for he would have been quite content[2] to be loved for his intellectual worth. And indeed the best people are always appreciated far more for their beauty of character; moreover, the fugitive charms of the body wilt with the advance and decline of the rushing years. Later, when made Prefect of Gaul, Priscus Valerianus, his opinion still unchanged, associated his son-in-law with his deliberations[3] and his tribunal, holding steadfastly to his old estimate of him, with the result that the man to whom he had married his daughter out of regard for his learning was now joined as partner in his dignity. 3. But your style is so clear and so distinguished that one can scarcely put on a level with it (let alone on a higher level) the product of Palaemon's analysis, of Gallio's dignity, of the copiousness of Delphidius, the system of Agroecius, the strength of Alcimus, the delicacy of Adelphius, the hardness of Magnus, or the sweetness of Victorius.[4] Lest I be thought to

and brother of Lucius Annaeus Seneca the younger, the statesman and philosopher, *c.* 3 B.C.–A.D. 65. Delphidius and Agroecius (not the Bishop of Sens of *Ep.* VII. 5) are mentioned by Ausonius (*c.* A.D. 310–395). Jerome (*c.* 340–420) mentions Magnus as an orator of fame. Alcimus and this Victorius are otherwise unknown.

hyperbolico rhetorum catalogo blanditus quippiam gratificatusque, solam tibi acrimoniam Quintiliani pompamque [1] Palladii comparari non ambigo [2] sed potius adquiesco. 4. quapropter si quis post vos Latiae favet eruditioni, huic amicitiae gratias agit et sodalitati vestrae, si quid hominis habet, tertius optat adhiberi. quamquam, quod est gravius, non sit satis ambitus iste fastidium vobis excitaturus, quia pauci studia nunc honorant, simul et naturali vitio fixum est radicatumque pectoribus humanis, ut qui non intellegunt artes non mirentur artifices. vale.

XI

SIDONIVS POTENTINO SVO SALVTEM

1. Multum te amamus; et quidem huiusce dilectionis non est erroneus aut fortuitus affectus. namque ut sodalis tibi devinctior fierem, iudicavi. est enim consuetudinis meae, ut eligam ante, post

[1] pompamque *LR*[2]*N*: pompam.
[2] ambigo *MTCFP*: ambio.

---

[1] Quintilian lived from *c.* A.D. 40 to *c.* A.D. 118. There was a rhetorician Palladius of Methone in the early part of the fourth century A.C., but the one here mentioned may be the author (lived *c.* A.D. 367–*c.* 430) of the *Lausiac History* and other works; he may be the Palladius who became Bishop of Helenopolis *c.* A.D. 400; or one of the famous family of the Palladii of Auvergne—see *Ep.* VII. 9. 24 and note there.

have flattered you at all or curried favour by this seemingly hyperbolical catalogue of professors, I declare that you are comparable only to the pungency of Quintilian and the splendour of Palladius [1]—and this is a comparison I do not doubt, I yield it silent acquiescence.[2] 4. Thus anyone who, following in your steps, shows a partiality for Latin learning thanks this friendship for it and, if he has any human feeling in him, longs to be co-opted into your fraternity as a third member. However (and this is a pity), such a wish and longing is not likely to cause you any great [3] annoyance, for nowadays there are but few who hold literature in honour. Besides, owing to a natural defect, it is fixed and rooted in the human breast that failure to understand the art means failure to esteem the artist. Farewell.

XI

SIDONIUS TO HIS FRIEND POTENTINUS,* GREETING

1. I am your devoted friend: what is more, there is nothing wayward or haphazard in this attachment: it was my deliberate choice to form the closest ties with you, for it is my custom to make selection pre-

[2] *Ambigo, adquiesco.* Are these legal expressions? Sidonius acquiesces in the verdict (or contention), but that does not mean that he really agrees with it—*i.e.* he would not rank even Quintilian or Palladius with Sapaudus; but should it be contended that in the qualities named they are worthy to be compared with Sapaudus, he is prepared to let it pass.—*A.*

[3] *satis*: practically = *nimis* here.—*A.*

* Not otherwise known.

diligam. quaenam,[1] inquis, in me tibi probanda placuere? 2. dicam libenter et breviter, quorum unum fieri gratia, alterum charta conpellit. veneror in actionibus tuis, quod multa bono cuique imitabilia geris. colis ut qui sollertissime; aedificas ut qui dispositissime; venaris ut qui efficacissime; pascis ut qui exactissime; iocaris ut qui facetissime; iudicas ut qui aequissime; suades ut qui sincerissime; commoveris ut qui tardissime; placaris ut qui celerrime; redamas ut qui fidelissime. 3. haec omnia exempla vivendi iam hinc ab annis puberibus meus Apollinaris si sequitur, gaudeo; certe ut sequatur, admoneo. in quo docendo instituendoque, modo sub ope Christi disposita succedant, plurimum laetor maximam me formulam vitae de moribus tuis mutuaturum. vale.

XII

SIDONIVS CALMINIO SVO SALVTEM

1. Quod rarius ad vos a nobis pagina meat, non nostra superbia sed aliena impotentia facit. neque super his quicquam planius quaeras, quippe cum

[1] et quaenam = ecquaenam *T*.

---

[1] *pascis* may mean "feed the *familia* (slaves)."—*A*.
[2] Son of Sidonius.

cede affection. "Pray what merits," you ask, "did you find in me to please you?" 2. I will tell you willingly and briefly; my fondness for you makes me willing, considerations of space make me brief. In your various activities I note with admiration the many examples that your conduct sets before all good men. You cultivate your land with the greatest skill, you build on the most methodical plan, you hunt in the most successful way, you entertain[1] to perfection, your jests are triumphs of wit, your judgments are absolutely fair, your advice as sound as could be; no one could be more slow to anger, more quick to relent, or more faithful in returning affection. 3. If my Apollinaris,[2] even in these budding years of manhood, is following all those examples of the way to live, I rejoice; certainly I urge him to follow them. It is a great joy to me to think that in teaching and training him (if only with Christ's help my plans turn out well) I shall borrow from your conduct the finest pattern of life for him. Farewell.

XII

SIDONIUS TO HIS FRIEND CALMINIUS,* GREETING

1. If a line from me comes to you all too seldom, it is not superciliousness in me but the violence in others that is to blame. You must not ask me to be more explicit on this subject; you feel the same fear as

* Son of the Eucherius of *Ep.* III. 8 and VII. 9. 18 (not of Eucherius, Bishop of Lyon, *Ep.* IV. 3. 7); he was forced by Euric to fight against his country Auvergne.

silentii huius necessitatem par apud vos metus interpretetur. hoc solum tamen libere gemo, quod turbine dissidentium partium segreges facti mutuo minime fruimur aspectu, neque umquam patriae sollicitis offerris obtutibus, nisi forsitan cum ad arbitrium terroris alieni vos loricae, nos propugnacula tegunt. ubi ipse in hoc solum captivus adduceris, ut pharetras sagittis vacuare, lacrimis oculos implere cogaris, nobis quoque non recusantibus, quod tua satis aliud moliuntur vota quam iacula. 2. sed quia interdum etsi non per foederum veritatem, saltim per indutiarum imaginem quaedam spei nostrae libertatis fenestra resplendet, impense flagito, uti nos, cum maxime potes, affatu paginae frequentis impertias, sciens tibi in animis obsessorum civium illam manere gratiam, quae obliviscatur obsidentis invidiam. vale.

---

[1] *A.* took, with hesitation, *solum* here to be *sōlum*, "only," not *sŏlum*, soil, land; and wondered whether *ubi* means *quo* = *huc* "hither." He translates "when you imprison yourself here, the effect on you is merely to constrain you to . . ." On which *W.H.S.* remarks: I think this is wrong. See n. 3 below.

[2] *sciens* may refer either to *flagito* or to *impertias.*—*A.* I think the latter.—*W.H.S.* The mention of truce and treaty does not serve to date this letter, but the year A.D. 474 seems probable.

[3] *A. adds the following postscript*: I am puzzled by the

we do, and it will explain the necessity for this silence on my part. The only thing I openly bewail is that, severed as we are by the tumult of contending parties, we scarcely ever enjoy the sight of one another, and you never present yourself to the anxious gaze of your fellow-townsman, except perhaps when at the dictate of a menacing foreign power you have donned your armour and we are covered by our fortifications. On such occasions you are brought to this land,[1] a virtual prisoner, that you may be forced to empty your quiver of its arrows and fill your eyes with tears; but there is no protest from us, who realise that your prayers are aimed at something very different from your missiles. 2. But because for the moment we have, not indeed the reality of a treaty, but at least the ghost of a truce, admitting a glimpse of freedom to brighten our hopes, I earnestly beseech you, now that the opportunity exists, to favour us with many a missive sheet; for be assured [2] that in the hearts of the besieged citizens there is reserved for you such an affection as will obliterate any odium you incur as a besieger.[3] Farewell.

middle part of the letter, *neque umquam . . . iacula.* "At such times you are led as a prisoner to this soil (*sŏlum*) being compelled to empty your quiver of its arrows and fill your eyes with tears, and we do not protest, for . . ." Thus Calminius must have been compelled to fight against Auvergne in the Visigoth ranks (an unusual thing). But I am still uneasy about *ubi*: "in which circumstances," *i.e.* at such times. But what is the authority for such a usage? *On which W.H.S.* remarks: I am quite sure that Anderson's postscript gives the right sense, and I have therefore incorporated it in the main translation.

XIII

SIDONIVS PANNYCHIO SVO SALVTEM

1. Seronatum Tolosa nosti redire? si nondum, et credo quod nondum, vel per haec disce. iam Clausetiam pergit Euanthius iamque contractas operas cogit eruderare, si quid forte deiectu caducae frondis agger insorduit. certe si quid voraginosum est, ipse humo advecta scrobibus oppletis trepidus exaequat, utpote beluam suam de valle Tarnis ducaliter antecessurus, musculis similis inter saxosa vel brevia ballaenarum corpulentiam praegubernantibus. 2. at ille sic ira celer, quod piger mole, ceu draco e specu vix evolutus iam metu exanguibus Gabalitanis e proximo infertur; quos singulos sparsos inoppidatos nunc inauditis indictionum generibus exhaurit, nunc flexuosa calumniarum fraude circumretit, ne tum quidem domum laboriosos redire permittens, cum tributum annuum datavere. 3.

---

* Cf. *Ep.* VII. 9. 18. Not otherwise known.

[1] This man was not the governor of Aquitanica Prima, but *Vicarius Septem Provinciarum* (for which see Sidonius, Vol. I, Loeb, p. 347 n.) *c.* A.D. 469; K. Stroheker, *Der senatorische Adel im spätantiken Gallien*, no. 352. He supported the Visigoths, was arraigned for various misdeeds, sent to Rome, and sentenced to death. Cf. *Ep.* II. 1. 1; VII. 7. 2; L. Schmidt, *Gesch. der deutschen Stämme*, I. 261; Chaix, I. 377.

[2] Some official of public works.

XIII

SIDONIUS TO HIS FRIEND PANNYCHIUS,* GREETING

1. Do you know that Seronatus [1] is on his way back from Toulouse? If you don't yet know (and I suppose you don't), then know it hereby. Evanthius [2] is already hurrying to Clausetia [3] and is making gangs of workmen clean up the road wherever it happens to show an untidy mess of fallen foliage: certainly wherever it is pitted he himself brings up earth, fills up the chasms, and nervously levels it off, for he means to precede his beast [4] from the Tarn-valley as a guide, like the pilot-fish that go in front to steer the whales' corpulence among the reefs and shallows. 2. But Seronatus is as quick in temper as he is lumbering in bulk; the Gabelitans[5] are already pale with terror as from close quarters he bears down upon them like a snake only just uncoiling from its den; scattered individuals in a sparsely populated country, not in a compact township, he sometimes drains them dry with unheard-of kinds of imposts or again ensnares them in the tortuous guile of false accusations; and not even when they have paid him an annual tribute,[6] does he allow the poor wretches to return home. 3. This, too, is a certain

[3] A place probably between Clermont and Toulouse.

[4] The "beast" is Seronatus.

[5] Of Javols near Mende; an Aquitanian people of the north-western slopes of the Cevennes. Cf. *Ep.* VII. 6. 7.

[6] The property-tax (realty) was generally paid in three instalments, 1 Sept., 1 Jan., 1 May.—*A.*

signum et hoc certum est imminentis adventus, quod catervatim, quo se cumque converterit, vincti trahuntur vincula trahentes; quorum dolore laetatur, pascitur fame, praecipue pulchrum arbitratus ante turpare quam punire damnandos; crinem viris nutrit, mulieribus incidit; e quibus tamen si rara quosdam venia respexerit, hos venalitas solvit, vanitas illos, nullos misericordia. sed explicandae bestiae tali nec oratorum princeps Marcus Arpinas nec poetarum Publius Mantuanus sufficere possunt. 4. proinde quia dicitur haec ipsa pernicies appropinquare, cuius proditionibus deus obviet, praeveni morbum providentiae salubritate contraque lites iurgiosorum, si quae moventur, pactionibus consule, contra tributa securitatibus, ne malus homo rebus bonorum vel quod noceat vel quod praestet inveniat. in summa, de Seronato vis accipere quid sentiam? ceteri affligi per suprascriptum damno verentur; mihi latronis et beneficia suspecta sunt. vale.

---

[1] Cicero.
[2] Virgil.

sign of his imminent arrival that wherever he turns hordes of chained prisoners are dragged along dragging their chains; he delights in their suffering, he feasts his heart on their hunger. He thinks it particularly splendid to disfigure before punishment his victims due for conviction; he makes the men grow their hair long and he cuts short the hair of the women. If on rare occasions any of them should obtain pardon their release is due in some cases to his venality, in others to ostentation, in none to compassion. But neither Marcus [1] of Arpinum, prince of orators, nor Publius [2] of Mantua, prince of poets, would be equal to the task of describing such a monster. 4. And so, as that very plague (whose betrayals may God prevent!) is said to be approaching, forestall the disease by wholesome foresight, contrive to obviate the lawsuits of the quarrelsome, if any such are being instituted, by agreements, contrive to obviate demands for tribute by official receipts, so that this evil man may find no scope either for injuring or assisting the fortunes of good men. In short, will you listen to my opinion of Seronatus? Others are afraid of suffering damage at the aforesaid's hands; but to me even the favours of a robber are suspect. Farewell.

XIV

SIDONIVS APRO SVO SALVTEM

1. Calentes[1] nunc te Baiae et scabris cavernatim ructata pumicibus aqua sulpuris atque iecorosis ac phthisiscentibus languidis medicabilis piscina delectat? an fortasse montana sedes circum castella et in eligenda sede perfugii quandam pateris ex munitionum frequentia difficultatem? quicquid illud est, quod vel otio vel negotio vacas, in urbem tamen, nisi fallimur, rogationum contemplatione revocabere. 2. quarum nobis sollemnitatem primus Mamertus pater et pontifex reverentissimo[2] exemplo, utilissimo experimento invenit instituit invexit. erant quidem prius, quod salva fidei pace sit dictum,

[1] calentes *Savaron ut ex codd.*: caientes *aut sim.*
[2] reverendissimo *Luetjohann.*

---

* An Aeduan. Cf. *Ep.* IV. 21. Not otherwise known.

[1] For Baiae (famous resort called Baia today, on the coast in Campania, Italy, having warm sulphur-springs) as a generic term for a spa, compare *Carm.* XXIII. 13. Sidonius may mean the place called Aquae Calidae (" Warm Waters ") in the Peutinger Table, usually identified with the modern Vichy. A. de Valois, *Not. Gall.* 47. Michel Bertrand (quoted by Grégoire and Collombet) would identify both Aquae Calidae and Calentes Baiae with the site on the Mont d'Or, near Clermont, where the remnants of baths have been discovered. Savaron and Sirmond suggest Chaudesaigues in the south-east of Auvergne. These suggestions do not exhaust the possibilities. *calentes* certainly refers to the hot thermal springs. The name Aquae Calidae was given to several watering places.

[2] In Virgil, *Aen.* V. 440, the idea is of a besieger surrounding

XIV

SIDONIUS TO HIS FRIEND APER,* GREETING

1. Are you enjoying your warm Baiae [1] and the sulphurous water forced out from the hollows in the rough porous rock and the bathing-pool so health-giving to liverish and consumptive invalids? Or do you perchance lodge among mountain fastnesses? [2] and do you find some difficulty in choosing your place of retreat owing to the multitude of such fortifications? No matter how you are spending your time, whether in business or in idleness, you will, if I mistake not, be drawn back to the city [3] by the prospect of the Rogations.[4] 2. The solemn observance of these was first initiated, and introduced to us by the father and pontiff Mamertus, who thereby set an example worthy of all reverence and launched a most salutary venture. Before this the public prayers (with all respect to the faith, be it said) were irregular,

the stronghold(s). But *circum* seems to be used differently by Sidonius—"from stronghold to stronghold." Apparently he means a round of visits to friends in fortified dwellings like the "Burgus" of Pontius Leontius (*Carm.* XXII). Probably there were many such in those troublous times, not least in Auvergne.—*A*.

[3] Clermont-Ferrand (Augustonemetum).

[4] Solemn prayers in procession in time of danger, first instituted by Bishop Mamertus at Vienne, and instituted also by Sidonius at Clermont during irruptions and siege by the Visigoths. Cf. *Ep.* VII. 1.2.6; Gregory of Tours, *Hist. Franc.* II. 34; Caesarius of Arles, *Homilies*, 30. Stevens, *Sid. Apoll.*, 152, 202–3; he fixes the date of Sidonius' introduction of rogations early in A.D. 473.

vagae tepentes infrequentesque utque sic dixerim oscitabundae supplicationes, quae saepe interpellantum prandiorum obicibus hebetabantur, maxime aut imbres aut serenitatem deprecaturae; ad quas, ut nil amplius dicam, figulo pariter atque hortuloni non oportuit convenire. 3. in his autem, quas suprafatus summus sacerdos nobis et protulit pariter et contulit, ieiunatur oratur, psallitur fletur. ad haec te festa cervicum humiliatarum et sternacium civium suspiriosa contubernia peto; et, si spiritalem animum tuum bene metior, modo citius venies, quando non ad epulas sed ad lacrimas evocaris. vale.

XV

SIDONIVS RVRICIO SVO SALVTEM

1. Officii sermone praefato bybliopolam nostrum [1] non gratiose sed iudicialiter expertus insinuo, cuius ut fidem in pectore, sic in opere celeritatem circa dominum te [2] mihi sibique communem satis abunde probavi. librum igitur hic ipse deportat heptateuchi, scriptum velocitate summa, summo nitore, quamquam et a nobis relectum et retractatum. defert

[1] nostrum *LRTN*: vestrum.
[2] te *seclud. Luetjohann.*

[1] A strange episcopal joke. The potter would pray for dry weather, the gardener for rain. The construction is odd. As Savaron says, the acc. *figulum* and *hortulonem* might have been expected.—*A.* Perhaps *non* (which could arise from (*h*)*ortulano* of some MSS) should be deleted. In any case Sidonius is making fun.

lukewarm, sparsely attended, and, so to speak, full of yawns; their purpose was frequently obscured by the disturbing interruptions for meals, and they tended to become for the most part petitions for rain or for fine weather; indeed, to put it mildly, the potter and the gardener [1] ought not to have attended them together. 3. But in these Rogations, which the aforesaid chief priest has both made known to us and made over to us, there are prayer and fasting, psalmody and lamentation. I beg your presence at this festival of humbly bowed heads, this fellowship of sighing suppliants; and if I am a true judge of your spiritual leanings you will come all the more promptly now that you are summoned not to a feast but to tears. Farewell.

XV

SIDONIUS TO HIS FRIEND RURICIUS,* GREETING

1. First I present my duty to you: next I introduce to you my bookseller, not as a call upon your friendship but because I have tried him with judicial impartiality and have abundantly proved both the honesty of his heart and the speed of his work where it concerns you, who can command his service and mine too. So he is bringing you by his own hand a copy of the heptateuch,[2] written by him with great speed and great elegance, but also read over and revised by myself. He is bringing you a volume of

* See *Ep.* IV. 16, first note, and VIII. 10.

[2] The first seven books of the Old Testament.

volumen et prophetarum, licet me absente decursum, sua tamen cura manuque de supervacuis sententiis eruderatum, nec semper illo contra legente, qui promiserat operam suam; credo, quia infirmitas fuerit impedimento, quominus pollicita compleret. 2. restat, ut exhortatio vestra seu sponsio famulum sic vel studentem placere vel meritum gratia competenti remuneretur; quae utique pro tali labore si solvitur, incipiet ad vestram respicere mercedem. sed cum hoc ego de sola gratia precer, vos quid mereatur aspicite quem constat affectum domini magis ambire quam praemium. vale.

XVI

SIDONIVS PAPIANILLAE SVAE SALVTEM

1. Ravenna veniens quaestor Licinianus, cum primum tetigit Alpe transmissa Galliae solum, litteras adventus sui praevias misit, quibus indicat esse se gerulum codicillorum, quorum in adventu

[1] The position of *et* seems to indicate that *volumen* has the same sense as *librum* above.—A.

[2] Anderson translates this passage: "Should this (favour) at least be paid to him in return for his toil, he will begin to have hopes of doing business with you." And he adds: "I think this must be the meaning." *W.H.S.* says: "I cannot see that Anderson's rendering makes sense in the context, and I have ventured to change his translation so as to approximate to my note on the passage in *Quaest. Exeg.*, 36–37."

[3] *dominus* is here used simply as a title of respect.

* Wife of Sidonius, daughter of Avitus (not him of *Ep.* III. 1) whom Sidonius married before Avitus was declared Emperor

the prophets [1] as well: it was entirely written in my absence, but he has cleared it diligently and by his own hand of all interpolations: the man who had promised his services as a reader for purposes of collation was not always available; I suppose it was illness that prevented him from keeping his word. 2. It now remains that some encouragement or some promise on your part should recompense with an adequate mark of favour a servant who both strives to please you and has deserved so well of you. If this favour is paid in keeping with the excellent services he has rendered it will soon redound to your own profit.[2] I am pleading now only in respect of the mark of favour: but you must consider what he *deserves*—this man of yours who undoubtedly seeks the affection of his master [3] more than any reward. Farewell.

XVI

SIDONIUS TO HIS DEAR PAPIANILLA,* GREETING

1. On his way from Ravenna the quaestor Licinianus,[4] as soon as he had crossed the Alps and touched the soil of Gaul, sent a letter ahead of him. In it he reports that he is the bearer of letters patent, with the arrival of which this honour of the patriciate comes

in July A.D. 455. For Ecdicius her brother cf. *Ep.* II. 1, III. 3, and II. 2. 15. This letter was probably written at Sidonius' family-town Lyon where his mother, daughters, and sisters were, to Papianilla when she was elsewhere.

[4] Cf. *Ep.* III. 7. 2.

fratri etiam tuo Ecdicio, cuius aeque titulis ac meis gaudes, honor patricius accedit, celerrime, si cogites eius aetatem, si merita, tardissime. namque ille iam pridem suffragium dignitatis ineundae non solvit in lance sed in acie, aerariumque publicum ipse privatus non pecuniis sed manubiis locupletavit. 2. hoc tamen sancte Iulius Nepos, armis pariter summus Augustus ac moribus, quod decessoris Anthemii fidem fratris tui sudoribus obligatam, quo citior,[1] hoc laudabilior absolvit; siquidem iste complevit, quod ille saepissime pollicebatur. quo fit, ut deinceps pro republica optimus quisque possit ac debeat, si quid cuipiam virium est, quia securus, hinc avidus impendere, quandoquidem mortuo quoque imperatore laborantum devotioni quicquid spoponderit princeps, semper redhibet principatus. 3. interea tu, si affectum tuum bene colligo, hisce compertis magnum solacium inter adversa maxima capis nec animum tuum a tramite communium gaudiorum vicinae quoque obsidionis terror exorbitat. novi enim probe ne meo quidem te, quem ex lege

[1] citior *Luetjohann*: citerior.

---

[1] *etiam, i.e.* to Ecdicius as well, for Sidonius himself was a patrician.

[2] *lanx*, a dish, was a word used also for each pan of a balance. Sidonius alludes to the practice of using one's money in order to get honours or favour. In A.D. 471 Ecdicius raised a force at his own expense and defeated Gothic predators in Auvergne several times. Cf. Jordanes, *Get.*, xlv, 240; Sidonius, *Ep.* III. 3. 7; Stevens, pp. 199 ff.

[3] The sense is: in spite of the change of emperors, the great services of Ecdicius have been remembered and rewarded. —*W.H.S.*

also [1] to your brother Ecdicius, in whose distinctions you take as much delight as in mine. It is very quick promotion, if you consider his age, very slow if you consider his deserts; for he has long been making payment for his advancement to this dignity not on the gold-scales [2] but in the battlefield, and as a free-lance soldier he has enriched the Treasury not with money but with the spoils of war. 2. But [3] Iulius Nepos, an Emperor [4] supreme alike in arms and in goodness, has shown a high sense of duty in fulfilling, with a promptitude [5] which redounds all the more to his credit, the pledge with which his predecessor Anthemius [6] bound himself to reward your brother's exertions; what the other repeatedly promised he has actually brought to pass. The upshot of this is that in each succeeding era the best citizens can and ought to expend their utmost powers with an eagerness based on perfect confidence, seeing that even after the death of an Emperor any reward that that prince has promised to his devoted servants is always duly paid by the principate. 3. Meanwhile, if I rightly judge your affection, this news is bringing you great comfort in the midst of very great misfortunes, and even the menace of a siege so near cannot divert your heart from the path of our common rejoicings; for I am well aware that even *my* advancement, which you have a legal right to share, did not give you as much pleasure as this, because, while you are a good wife, you are a particularly good sister.

[4] A.D. 474–475.

[5] Luetjohann seems right in proposing *citior*.

[6] Emperor of the West (nominated by Leo I of the East) A.D. 467–472. See *Carm.* II.

participas, sic honore laetatam, quia, licet sis uxor bona, soror optima es. qua de re propitio deo[1] Christo ampliatos prosapiae tuae titulos ego festinus gratatoriis apicibus inscripsi, pariter absolvens sollicitudinem tuam, fratris pudorem; quem nil de propria dignitate indicaturum, si verecundum forte nescires, nec sic impium iudicares. 4. ego vero non tantum insignibus vestris, quae tu hactenus quanto liberius, tanto inpatientius praestolabare (quamquam his quoque granditer), quantum concordia fruor; quam parem nostris suisque liberis in posterum exopto, votis[2] in commune deposcens, ut sicut nos utramque familiam nostram praefectoriam nancti etiam patriciam divino favore reddidimus, ita ipsi quam suscipiunt patriciam faciant consularem. 5. Roscia salutat, cura communis; quae in aviae amitarumque indulgentissimo sinu, quod raro nepotibus contingit alendis,[3] et cum severitate

[1] deo *om. T.*
[2] totis *L,* "*fortasse recte*" *Luetjohann.*
[3] alendis *Wilamowitz*: alienis.

---

[1] The affection between Ecdicius, on the one hand, and Sidonius (with Papianilla), on the other?—*A.*

[2] As Avitus, the father of Papianilla and of Ecdicius, had been emperor and *consul*, I don't quite see the point of Sidonius' remark. Is the word *nos* = *ego*? And does *utramque familiam nostram* mean " my father's family and my mother's family "? This seems unlikely. Surely *nos* means *ego et Ecdicius.*—*A.* Sidonius' grandfather and his father had both

Hence I have lost no time in writing a letter of congratulation honouring the distinction which has, with the blessing of Christ our God, been added to your family honours. In doing so I have at the same time relieved both your anxiety and your brother's modesty—although even if you did not know how modest he is, you would not think it unbrotherly on his part to shrink from announcing his own dignity. 4. But for my part, much as I rejoice in the honour to your family, to which you yourself have all the time been looking forward with equal frankness and impatience, I rejoice still more in our mutual affection.[1] I fervently hope that there will be a like feeling in days to come between our children and his, and I earnestly pray for both households alike that, just as we found our families praefectorian and by the favour of Heaven made them also patrician, so they in their turn, starting with a patrician family, may make it a consular one.[2] 5. Roscia,[3] our common anxiety, sends her greetings. She is being nurtured in the indulgent arms of her grandmother and also of her aunts—a rare advantage in the bringing up of grandchildren; at the same time she is treated with

been Praetorian Prefect of Gaul, and in A.D. 468 Sidonius himself was *Praefectus Urbi* (that is, of Rome—he was it seems never Prefect of Gaul), and was given the title of patrician.

[3] She was a daughter of Sidonius and Papianilla. Alcima (Gregory of Tours, *Hist. Franc.* III. 2 and 12; *de Gloria Martyrum*, 64—Sidonius nowhere mentions her name) and Severiana (*Ep.* II. 12. 2) were apparently two others. See Introd. to Sidonius Vol. I (Loeb), xxxvi. It is rash to conclude, as even Stevens does (*Sid. Apoll.* 84–85), from Sid. *Carm.* XVII. 3, that two of Sidonius' children were twins.

nutritur. qua tamen tenerum non infirmatur aevum sed informatur ingenium. vale.

XVII

SIDONIVS ERIPHIO SVO SALVTEM

1. Es, Eriphi meus, ipse qui semper numquamque te tantum venatio civitas ager avocat, ut non obiter litterarum voluptate teneare; fitque eo studio, ut nec nostra fastidias, qui tibi, ut scribis, Musas olemus. quae sententia tamen large probatur vero carere, quamque [1] et [2] apparet aut ex ioco venire, si laetus es, aut ex amore, si serius. ceterum a iusto longe resultat, cum mihi assignas [3] quae vix Maroni vix [4] aut Homero competenter accommodarentur. 2. haec relinquamus idque, unde causa, sermocinemur. dirigi ad te praecipis versus, quos viri amplissimi, soceri tui, precibus indulsi; qui contubernio mixtus aequalium vivit moribus ad iubendum obsequendumque iuxta paratis. sed quia scire desideras et locum et causam, quo facilius intellegas rem perexiguam, tibi potius vitio verte, quod loquacior erit opere praefatio. 3. conveneramus ad sancti Iusti sepul-

[1] quamque *L*: quāq *P*: quamquam *TC*: quanquam *MF*: namque *coni. Luetjohann.*

[2] *om. Wilamowitz.*

[3] assignat *T*.

[4] vix *seclud. Luetjohann.*

strictness, although it is the strictness that does not strain the tender age, but trains the mind. Farewell.

XVII

SIDONIUS TO HIS FRIEND ERIPHIUS,* GREETING

1. My dear Eriphius, you are the same as ever, and never does the chase, the city, or the country so distract you that you do not occasionally succumb to the charm of literature; and your enthusiasm is such that you do not disdain even my productions, for you write that I seem to you to be redolent of the Muses. This opinion is abundantly proved to have no truth in it; clearly it is uttered in jest if you are in a merry mood, or from affection if you are serious. But it is a wild departure from reasonableness when you ascribe to me qualities which could scarcely with propriety be attributed to Virgil or Homer. 2. Let us drop this chat and talk about the matter that gave rise to it. You bid me send you the verses which I conceded to the entreaties of that distinguished man, your father-in-law, whose conduct in the society of his fellows shows an equal readiness to command and to obey. But as you are eager to know both the scene and the occasion in order to facilitate your understanding of a most insignificant trifle, you must blame yourself rather than me if the preamble is more wordy than the actual composition. 3. We had gathered to-

* Of Lyon, son-in-law of Philomathius [thus Wilamowitz for the MSS' Filimati(us)] of *Ep.* I. 3.

chrum (sed tibi infirmitas impedimento,[1] ne tunc adesses); processio fuerat antelucana, sollemnitas anniversaria, populus ingens sexu ex utroque, quem capacissima basilica non caperet quamlibet cincta diffusis cryptoporticibus. cultu peracto vigiliarum, quas alternante mulcedine monachi clericique psalmicines concelebraverant, quisque in diversa secessimus, non procul tamen, utpote ad tertiam praesto futuri, cum sacerdotibus res divina facienda; 4. de loci sane turbarumque compressu deque numerosis luminibus inlatis nimis anheli; simul et aestati nox adhuc proxima tecto [2] clausos vapore torruerat, etsi iam primo frigore tamen autumnalis Aurorae detepescebat. itaque cum passim varia ordinum corpora dispergerentur, placuit ad conditorium Syagrii consulis civium primis una coire, quod nec impleto iactu sagittae separabatur. hic pars sub umbra palmitis adulti, quam stipitibus altatis cancellatimque pendentibus pampinus superducta texuerat, pars caespite in viridi sed floribus odoro consederamus. 5. verba erant dulcia iocosa fatigatoria;

[1] impedimento fuit *F*.
[2] tecto *Luetjohann*: tacito. *Fortasse* tetro *aut* tacite.

---

[1] The church built at Lyon by Patiens, Archbishop of Lyon, before A.D. 470 (see *Ep.* II. 10. 2) in honour of Saint

gether at the tomb[1] of St. Justus (you, however, were prevented by illness from being there); the annual solemnity of the procession before daylight was over. There was an enormous congregation of both sexes, too great for the very spacious church to contain, even with the expanse of covered porticoes which surrounded it. After the Vigils, which monks and clerics had celebrated with alternate strains of sweet psalmody, we all withdrew in various directions, but not far, as we wanted to be at hand for tierce when the priests should celebrate the Mass. 4. Owing to the cramped space, the pressure of the crowd, and the numerous lights which had been brought in, we were absolutely gasping for breath; moreover, imprisoned as we were under the roof, we were broiled by the heat of what was still almost a summer night, although just beginning to be touched with the coolness of an autumn dawn. So when groups of various classes were dispersing in different directions, the leading citizens resolved to go in a body to the tomb of Syagrius,[2] which was not quite a full bowshot away. Here some of us sat down under the shadow of a full-grown vine whose overarching foliage made a shady canopy formed by tall stems that drooped over in an interlaced pattern; others of us sat down on the green turf, which was also fragrant with flowers. 5. Conversation ensued,

Justus, Bishop of Lyon, who died *c.* 390. For Patiens see also the second footnote to *Ep.* IV. 25.

[2] Afranius Syagrius of Lyon, *magister officiorum* in A.D. 379, Praetorian Prefect of Gaul 380–382, consul 381. See *Ep.* VII. 12. 1 and note there. Cf. *Ep.* I. 7. 4; *Carm.* XXIV. 36. For his great-grandson see *Ep.* V. 5; VIII. 8.

praeterea, quod beatissimum, nulla mentio de potestatibus aut de tributis, nullus sermo qui proderetur, nulla persona quae proderet.[1] fabulam certe referre dignam relatu dignisque sententiis quisque potuisset: audiebatur ambitiosissime; nec erat idcirco non distincta narratio, quia laetitia permixta. inter haec otio diu[2] marcidis aliquid agere visum. 6. mox bipertitis, erat ut aetas, acclamationibus efflagitata profertur his pila, his tabula. sphaerae primus ego signifer fui, quae mihi, ut nosti, non minus libro comes habetur. altera ex parte frater meus Domnicius,[3] homo gratiae summae, summi leporis, tesseras ceperat quatiebatque, quo velut classico ad pyrgum vocabat aleatores. nos cum caterva scholasticorum lusimus abunde, quantum[4] membra torpore statarii laboris hebetata cursu salubri vegetarentur. 7. hic vir inlustris Philomatius, ut est illud Mantuani poetae,

> ausus et ipse manu iuvenum temptare
> laborem,

sphaeristarum se turmalibus constanter immiscuit. pulchre enim hoc fecerat, sed cum adhuc essent

[1] proderet nulla persona quae proderetur *MTCFP*.
[2] diutino *coni. Luetjohann*.
[3] Domnitius *C*: Domitius *F*: *Cf. Ep.* IV. 20.
[4] in quantum *coni. Luetjohann*.

---

[1] In fact a friend. Cf. *Ep.* IV. 20.

pleasant, jesting, bantering, and a specially happy feature in it was that there was no mention of officials or of taxes, no talk that invited betrayal, no informer to betray it; certainly everyone could have told freely any story worth relating and worthy in its sentiments. The audience listened in a spirit of eager rivalry; and the story-telling, though tinged with hilarity, was not on that account formless. By and by, having for some time felt sluggish for want of exertion, we resolved to do something energetic. 6. Thereupon we raised a two-fold clamour demanding according to our ages either ball or gaming-board, and these were soon forthcoming. I was the leading champion of the ball; for, as you know, ball no less than book is my constant companion. On the other hand, our most charming and delightful brother,[1] Domnicius, had seized the dice and was busy shaking them, as a sort of trumpet-call summoning the players to the battle of the box.[2] We on our part played with a troop of students, indeed played hard until our limbs deadened by inactive sedentary work could be reinvigorated by the healthful exercise. 7. Here the Illustrious Philomathius [3] resolutely plunged into the ranks of the ball-players.

"Daring, even he, to essay vigorously the toil of youths," as the Mantuan poet has it.[4] He had been a fine player, but that was when still quite young.

[2] There is a play on words; *pyrgus* (Lat. *turricula*) is a battlemented tower or a gaming-box of that shape.—*A*. We might translate it here "battlement of the box."

[3] All the MSS have Filimatius as also in the superscription of *Ep*. I. 3.

[4] Virgil, Aen., V. 499.

anni minores. qui cum frequenter de loco stantum medii currentis impulsu summoveretur, nunc quoque acceptus in aream tam pilae coram praetervolantis quam superiectae nec intercideret[1] tramitem nec caveret ac[2] per catastropham saepe pronatus aegre de ruinoso flexu se recolligeret, primus ludi ab accentu sese removit suspiriosus extis incalescentibus. namque et iecusculi fibra tumente pungebant exercitatum crebri dolores. 8. destiti protinus et ipse, facturus communione cessandi rem caritatis, ne vere-

[1] interciperet *coni. Anderson.*

[2] ac *Luetjohann*: hinc *Wilamowitz*: huc *L*: ad hoc *alii*: caveret ⟨et⟩ ad hoc per *L. A. Post.*

---

[1] The whole passage describing the ball-game is difficult, but there is no excuse for the mishandling of it in Smith's *Dictionary of Antiquities*. According to R. W. Moore in *Greece and Rome*, I (1932), 118 f., a game rather like this one is played today. His note is tantalisingly brief, but I suppose he means the game which many of us used to play in a simple and crude form—standing in a ring with one player in the middle, who tries to intercept and secure the ball as it is thrown from one player to another. In the game described by Sidonius with his usual pretentious obscurity the players apparently formed up in a circle or a double row, with one man (the *medius currens*, "runner in the middle," "inside runner") in the centre of the ring or play-space (*area*). A ball was passed from one to another of the players, and the inside man tried to intercept the passes and, presumably, to secure the ball. When he succeeded in doing so either the thrower or the man for whom the pass was intended would change places with the *medius currens* (see *Ep.* II. 9. 4). A good deal of jostling and horse-play was evidently allowed. The meaning of *catastropha* is a problem. The interpretation in the *Dictionary of Antiquities* is surely impossible—at least for Sidonius. I think *catastropha* ("overturning", "upsetting") was a technical term, applied to a diving tackle by which the *medius currens* tried to upset the man who had caught, or was trying to catch, the ball. He would make his

Now [1] he was repeatedly pushed by the inside runner from his place in the standing circle, then again, being brought inside the ring,[2] he failed alike to cut across [3] or to dodge the path of the ball on its course, as it flew close to his face or was flung over his head; and he would often bend low in a flying tackle and then scarcely manage to recover from his staggering swerve. So he was the first to retire from the stress and strain of the game, puffing and blowing in a state of internal inflammation: indeed, his poor swollen liver was sending frequent stabs of pain through his overtaxed body. 8. I also left off immediately, wishing by this joint withdrawal to do a friendly act and prevent my wearied brother from

dive, flinging himself forward almost doubled up (*pronatus*: cf. *duplicabantur*, II. 9. 4); and if he is too late he has to check himself suddenly and go for the player to whom the ball has now been thrown. This twisting and turning in different directions, in which the player would be very apt to lose his balance, is here suitably indicated by *ruinoso flexu* (*ruinoso*, "tending to cause a bad fall").—*A*. The game was it seems a form of harpastum (Greek ἁρπάζω, seize), "hand-ball." L. A. Post suggests that it is usually the tackled person who suffers most, not the tackler; that *catastropha* is simply an "upset" or an "overturn"; and that the man missed a catch and fell on his face in a falling twist (*ruinoso flexu*) or twisting fall. Post's reading *caveret* ⟨*et*⟩ *ad hoc* may well be right: "and when this happened" or "and besides this." For the rest of the clause "*per catastropham . . . recolligeret*" he suggests something like the following: "he was often, by being overturned, brought down on his face (*pronatus*) and was scarcely able to recover from his contorted collapse." But note that *Ep.* II. 9. 4 shows *catastropha* to be a special Greek word used in Roman ball-play.

[2] *I.e.* being made *medius currens* in his turn.—*A*.

[3] The sense "cut off" or "cut short" is rather surprising, and I feel fairly sure that Sidonius wrote *interciperet*.—*A*.

cundiam lassitudo fraterna pateretur. ergo, ut resedimus,[1] [et][2] illum mox aquam ad faciem petere sudor admonuit: exhibita poscenti est, pariter et linteum villis onustum, quod pridiana squama politum casu sub ipsis aediculae valvis bipatentibus de ianitoris erecto trochleatim fune nutabat. 9. quo dum per otium genas siccat: "vellem," inquit, "ad pannum similis officii aliquod tetrastichon mihi scribi iuberes." "fiat," inquam. "sed quod meum," dixit,[3] "et nomen metro teneret." respondi possibilia factu quae poposcisset. ait[4] et ipse: "dicta ergo." tunc ego arridens: "ilico scias Musas moveri, si choro ipsarum non absque arbitris vacem." respondit ille violenter et perurbane, ut est natura vir flammeus quidamque facundiae fons inexhaustus: "vide, domine Solli, ne magis Apollo forte moveatur, quod suas alumnas solus ad secreta sollicitas." iam potes nosse, quem plausum sententia tam repentina, tam lepida commoverit. 10. nec plus moratus mox suo scriba, qui pugillarem iuxta tenebat, ad me vocato subditum sic epigramma composui:

[1] resedimus *MCFPR*²: sedemus *L*: sedimus *T*.
[2] et *seclud. Luetjohann.*
[3] inqut (*i.e.* inquit) *T*.
[4] *seclud.* ait *Luetjohann.*

---

[1] The point of this little poem—the point, such as it is—seems to be that the towel thirsts for the wet from Philomathius' distinguished face. *bibulum vellus* in *Ep.* IX. 13. 5,

feeling humiliation. Well, when we had sat down, the pouring sweat next prompted him to ask for water to bathe his face. It was brought at his request, along with a thick shaggy towel which, as it so happened, had been washed from the previous day's grime and was swinging on a rope belonging to the porter which had been hoisted with a pulley close to the double doors of the lodge. 9. While he was drying his cheeks with it in leisurely fashion he remarked: "I wish you would command to be written for me a quartet of verses in honour of this cloth that has done me such a service." "Very well," said I. "But," he added, "I want it to get my name into the metre." I answered that what he demanded might be done. "Go on then and dictate," he said. I replied with a smile: "You must know straight away that the Muses are sure to be annoyed if I devote myself to their company in the presence of witnesses." Whereupon he answered vehemently and most wittily, being naturally fiery and at the same time a sort of inexhaustible fountain of eloquence: "Take care, my lord Sollius, lest Apollo be still more annoyed with you for tempting his wards to a secret interview all alone." You can realise without being told what applause was aroused by this sally at once so unpremeditated and so neat. 10. Without further delay, I next called to my side his secretary, who had his writing tablet ready to hand, and without more ado composed the following epigram:[1]

carm. 19 is different.—*A.* Anderson attempted to translate the poem into verse; but I have felt it better to substitute prose.—*W.H.S.*

Mane novo seu cum ferventia balnea poscunt
seu cum venatu frons calefacta madet,
hoc foveat pulcher faciem Filimatius udam,
migret ut in bibulum vellus ab ore liquor.

Epiphanius noster vix suprascripta peraraverat, et nuntiatum est hora monente progredi episcopum de receptorio, nosque surreximus. 11. da postulatae tu veniam cantilenae. illud autem ambo, quod maius est quodque me nuper in quendam dies bonos male ferentem parabolice seu figurate dictare iussistis quodque expeditum cras dirigetur, clam recensete; et, si placet, edentes fovete; si displicet, delentes ignoscitote. vale.

XVIII

SIDONIVS ATTALO SVO SALVTEM

1. Haeduae civitati te praesidere coepisse libens atque cum gaudio accepi. laetitiae causa quadripertita est: prima, quod amicus; secunda, quod iustus es; tertia, quod severus; quarta, quod proximus. quo fit, ut nostris nostrorumque con-

[1] This Epiphanius is not otherwise known.

* Not otherwise known unless he was the Count of Autun, an ancestor of Gregory of Tours (Greg., *Hist. Franc.* III. 15).

[2] Autun, provided that *civitas* means city here.

[3] *contractibus*. With *nostris* it perhaps means simply "personal relationships," "intimate associations." With

"At dawn, or when the steaming bath invites him, or when his forehead is hot and damp from the chase, with this towel let handsome Philomatius comfort his streaming face, so that all the moisture flows into the absorbent fleece."

Scarcely had our good friend Epiphanius[1] the secretary written the above lines when it was announced that the bishop, at the beckoning of the appointed hour, was proceeding from his lodging, and so we arose. 11. You must treat with indulgence this doggerel you insisted on having. But there is the more important work which you bade me write in allegorical or ironical style against a certain person who bore ill his days of good fortune. It will be finished and despatched to you tomorrow. You must both assess it in private and, if satisfied with it, publish and support it, if dissatisfied, destroy and forgive it. Farewell.

XVIII

SIDONIUS TO HIS FRIEND ATTALUS,* GREETING

I learned with pleasure and delight that you had assumed charge of the Aeduan city.[2] I have four reasons for rejoicing: first, because you are my friend; second, because you are just; third, because you are incorruptible; fourth, because you are so near to us. It follows that you are bound and able and willing to further effectively our mutual dealings[3]

nostrorum it will mean "business dealings" or "deals" in the American sense.—*A.*

tractibus plurimum[1] velis debeas possis opitulari. igitur amplectens in familiari vetusto novum ius potestatis indeptae materiam beneficiis tuis iam diu quaero. quibus me tantum fidere agnosce, ut, etsi non invenio quae poscam, quaesiturus mihi videaris ipse quae tribuas. vale.

XIX

SIDONIVS PVDENTI SVO SALVTEM

1. Nutricis meae filiam filius tuae rapuit: facinus indignum quodque nos vosque inimicasset, nisi protinus scissem te nescisse faciendum. sed conscientiae tuae purgatione praelata[2] petere dignaris culpae calentis impunitatem. sub condicione concedo: si stupratorem pro domino iam patronus originali solvas inquilinatu. 2. mulier autem illa iam libera est; quae tum demum videbitur non ludibrio addicta sed assumpta coniugio, si reus noster, pro quo precaris, mox cliens factus e tributario plebeiam potius incipiat habere personam quam colonariam. nam meam haec sola seu compositio

[1] plurimum *LRNT*: primum.
[2] praefata *coni. Luetjohann.*

---

* Not otherwise known.

[1] *Inquilinus*—in classical law the tenant of a house or dwelling not his own property. In late Roman times the term seems frequently to denote a landless labourer or cottager on a large estate; in practice his status differed little from that of a *colonus* (*Cod. Just.* XI, 48, 13) and in this letter the terms are synonymous. *Coloni* were tenant farmers on a large estate, many of whom, since the time of Diocletian, were tied to the soil though in strict law free men; the condition of such

and those of our peoples. Welcoming therefore the new power which has come to my old friend from the post he has obtained, I have spent a long time devising some claim on your kind offices. You may be sure that I rely on them so implicitly that, although I cannot find anything to ask for, I believe you will of your own accord devise favours to confer upon me. Farewell.

XIX

SIDONIUS TO HIS FRIEND PUDENS,* GREETING

1. The son of your nurse has run off with the daughter of mine—a scandalous thing, which would have estranged you and me had I not known that you knew nothing of the deed being done. But after some words disclaiming complicity you think fit to beg that this flagrant offence go unpunished. I consent on one condition—that you release the ravisher from his hereditary position of *inquilinus*, becoming his patron instead of his master.[1] 2. The woman is already free. The only thing that will cause her to be regarded as taken in lawful marriage, not made over as a plaything, will be that our culprit, on whose behalf you plead, should promptly be made a client instead of a tributory payer and so begin to have the standing of a plebeian rather than of a *colonus*. For nothing

coloni was hereditary, and when estates were sold, they passed, together with the land they were farming, to new *domini*. The term *originalis* here used of the status of an *inquilinus* is regularly used also of *coloni* denoting their bondage to the land by virtue of their *origo*. The meaning of *tributarius* is some-

seu satisfactio vel[1] mediocriter contumeliam emendat; qui tuis votis atque amicitiis hoc adquiesco, si laxat libertas maritum, ne constringat poena raptorem. vale.

XX

SIDONIVS PASTORI SVO SALVTEM

1. Quod die hesterno tractatui civitatis in concilio defuisti, ex industria factum pars melior accepit, quae suspicata est id te cavere, ne tuis umeris onus futurae legationis imponeretur. gratulor tibi, quod istis moribus vivis, ut necesse habeas electionem tui timere; laudo efficaciam, suspicio prudentiam, prosequor laude felicitatem; opto denique aequalia his, quos aequaliter amo. 2. multi frequenter, quos

[1] vel non *CFPM*[1]*T*[2]: *om.* vel *LRMNT*.

---

what obscure, but seems to denote a *colonus* (or *inquilinus*) for whose taxes the landlord was responsible, which seems to be the case here. Sidonius asks that the *inquilinus* should now be made a free tenant farmer who, however humble his status —*plebeia persona*—would be distinguished by, among other things, liability for his own taxes. From the woman's point of view, the change in the man's status would mean that their children would be free, whereas children of tied *coloni* and *inquilini* were bound by their father's *origo* even though the mother was free. Justinian later decided children in the latter category should also be free (*Cod. Just.* XI, 48, 24). The maintenance of the hereditary colonate was the Government's answer to a chronic shortage of agricultural labour which seriously affected the imperial revenue, since most of this derived directly or indirectly from the produce of the land. It was also in the interests of the landowning class to which

short of this arrangement or amends can in any degree set right this insult to me: and I am content to make this concession to your prayers and to our friendship —that, if the conferring of freedom releases the husband, no punishment shall fetter the ravisher. Farewell.

XX

SIDONIUS TO HIS FRIEND PASTOR,* GREETING

1. Your failure to be present at yesterday's debate in the city council [1] was considered by the better sort to be intentional. They suspected that you wished to avoid having the burden of the coming embassy placed upon your shoulders. I congratulate you on living your life in such a spirit that you are constrained to fear your own election; I praise your efficiency, I look up to your wisdom, I pay honour to your good fortune; indeed, I pray that the like gifts may be possessed by all for whom I have a like affection. 2. Many men, urged by an accursed passion

* Not otherwise known.

[1] Probably the *Curia* of Lyon.

Sidonius and his friends belonged, since they needed tenants who would not move away. The rights of landowners over their tied *coloni* progressively increased, but in spite of this, free peasants sometimes voluntarily adopted the status for protection in these troubled times. In contrast, it was no doubt rare for a landlord to give up one of his *coloni*. See A. H. M. Jones, *The Later Roman Empire*, Vol. II, pp. 795–803 and Vol. III, pp. 256–260.

execrabilis popularitas agit, civium maximos manu prensant deque consessu publico abducunt ac sequestratis oscula impingunt, operam suam spondent, sed non petiti; utque videantur in negotii communis assertionem [1] legari, evectionem refundunt ipsosque sumptus ultro recusant et ab ambitu clam rogant singulos, ut ab omnibus palam rogentur. 3. sic quoque, cum fatigatio gratuita possit libenter admitti, libentius tamen [2] atque amabilius [3] verecundi leguntur, idque cum expensa; tantum impudentia sese ingerentum ponderis habet, etiam fasci cum tributario nomine ipsorum nil superfunditur. proinde quamquam non te fefellit, quid boni quique meditarentur, redde te tamen exspectantium votis expetentumque caritatem proba, qui iam probasti pudorem. quod defuisti primum, modestiae adscribitur; ad ignaviam respicit secunda dilatio. 4. praeterea tibi Arelatem [4] profecturo est venerabilis in itinere mater fratres amantes redamantisque patriae solum, ad quod et praeter occasionem voluptuose venitur; tum domus propria, cuius

[1] assertionem *Luetjohann*: assertione.
[2] etiam *F*.
[3] avidius *coni. Luetjohann frustra.*
[4] arelate *L*.

---

[1] The tenses in this sentence are odd; a rather extreme instance of present for future.—*A*.

for popularity, constantly grasp [1] the leading citizens by the hand, draw them aside from a public meeting, and having thus got them by themselves press kisses upon them, and promise services for which no one asked them. To create the impression that their election as ambassadors would mean a firm championship of public interests, they are ready to forgo the privilege of the Imperial post and actually to decline the ordinary expenses.[2] Thus their intriguing spirit makes them sue individuals in private, in order that they may be publicly invited by all. 3. But even so, though exertions that cost nothing may be readily acceptable, yet modest men are chosen more willingly and more pleasurably even though their election entails expenditure—so obnoxious is the shamelessness [3] of pushing self-seekers, even when nothing has to be added to the burden of taxation on their account. So although you must have known the thoughts in the minds of the better sort, surrender yourself now to their expectant prayers and prove the affection of the friends who invite you, having already given proof of your modesty. Your failing them at first is attributed to diffidence, but to put them off a second time must savour of a poor spirit. 4. Besides this, your departure for Arles opens up the prospect of visiting on the way your venerable mother, your loving brothers and the soil of your native place, which loves and is loved by you, a delight to visit even when there is no special occasion for it; there is also your own house, where it is well

[2] *Evectio*, the right to use the *cursus publicus* (official rapid transport) without paying.

[3] Or: "such is the overpowering effect of . . . ."—*A*.

actorem, vineam messem olivetum, tectum quoque ipsum, vel dum praeterveharis, inspicere res commodi est. quapropter, missus a nobis, et tibi pervenis; namque erit talis viae tuae causaeque nostrae condicio, ni fallor, atque opportunitas, ut pro beneficio civitati posse imputare quandocumque [1] videaris, quod tuos videris. vale.

XXI

SIDONIVS SACERDOTI ET IVSTINO SVIS SALVTEM

1. Victorius patruus vester, vir, ut egregius, sic undecumque doctissimus, cum cetera potenter, tum potentissime condidit versus. mihi quoque semper a parvo cura Musarum; nunc vos parenti venitis heredes, quam iure, tam merito: ilicet ego poetae proximus fio professione, vos semine. ergo iustissimum est, ut diem functo [2] sic quisque nostrum succedat, ut iungitur. ideoque patrimonia tenete, date carmina. valete.

[1] quandoque *T*.
[2] diem fincto *LN*: die functo (defuncto *F*): die finito *V* (*add*. vel functo *V*[1]).

---

* These men were brothers—*Carm*., XXIV, 26 ff.
[1] *date carmina*: ?" Produce verses." For this meaning of dare, v. *Thes. Lingu. Lat.* s.v. *do*, 1666; or " Let me have the poetry." *Date* in this sense gives a good antithesis for *tenete*,

worth while to inspect, even in passing, the overseer, the vineyard, the cornfields, the olive-plantation, and the building itself. Hence, although sent by us, you serve yourself in going there; for if I am not mistaken, the opportune coincidence by which our business makes you travel that way will be so felicitous that in the issue you will seem to be able to call the city your debtor for your having seen your people. Farewell.

XXI

SIDONIUS TO HIS FRIENDS SACERDOS AND JUSTINUS,* GREETING

Victorius, your paternal uncle, a most distinguished man and learned in every respect, showed mastery in everything but particularly in poetical composition. I also from boyhood have constantly cultivated the Muses; but now you come forth as heirs of your kinsman's house, by legal right and no less by merit. So then I am akin to a poet by profession, you by blood; accordingly, it is entirely right that each of us should succeed the departed according to the nature of his connection; so do you keep the property for yourselves, and hand over the verses to me.[1] Farewell.

but the meaning is somewhat pointless. Still, I think it is probably right, the idea being not " leave poetry to me," but " let me inherit your uncle's poetic talent."—*A*. I am so sure that this latter interpretation is correct that I have embodied it in the translation.—*W.H.S.*

LIBER SEXTVS

I

SIDONIVS DOMINO PAPAE LVPO SALVTEM

1. Benedicitur[1] spiritus sanctus et pater dei omnipotentis, quod tu, pater patrum et episcopus episcoporum et alter saeculi tui Iacobus, de quadam specula caritatis nec de inferiore Hierusalem tota ecclesiae dei nostri membra superinspicis, dignus qui omnes consoleris infirmos quique merito ab omnibus consularis. et quid nunc ego dignum dignationi huic, putris et fetida reatu terra, respondeam? 2. colloquii salutaris tui et indigentiam patiens et timorem recordatione vitae plectibilis adducor, ut clamem tibi quod dixit domino tuus ille collega: exi a me, quia homo peccator sum, domine. sed si

[1] benedictus *codd. pler.*

* All the letters in this book are addressed to bishops; this shows intentional grouping by Sidonius. Saint Lupus was born at Toul. In A.D. 426 or A.D. 427 he became Bishop of Troyes, which he induced the Hun Attila to spare in A.D. 451. An extant letter of congratulation by him to Sidonius when Sidonius became Bishop of Clermont (see p. 4) may be a forgery. He died in A.D. 479. See also *Ep.* VI. 4 and 9; IX. 11; VII. 13. 1; VIII. 14. 2 and 15. 1; also IV. 17. 3 (not VIII. 11); *Carm.* XVI. 111. Stevens, 206.

BOOK VI

I

SIDONIUS TO THE LORD BISHOP LUPUS,* GREETING

1. Blessed is [1] the Holy Spirit and the Father of omnipotent God, in that you, father of fathers and bishop of bishops,[2] the James of your age,[3] oversee from your watch-tower of love and your no whit inferior Jerusalem all the branches of the church of our God; a man right worthy to comfort the sick and to be consulted by all. And now what adequate reply am I to make to this condescension of yours, I who am but earth crumbling and fetid with guilt? 2. Feeling the need of salutary converse with you and yet awed by the prospect, I am constrained by the memory of my unworthy life to cry out to you in the words addressed to our Lord by that great colleague [4] of yours: "Depart from me, for I am a sinful man, O Lord." [5] But if this awe I have of you is not modi-

[1] Note the variant reading *benedictus*. The translation of the indicative here must be "blessed is," surely not "blessed be."—*A*.

[2] Lupus was at the time the venerated doyen of Gallic bishops.—*A*. See also next note.

[3] *alter* better left untranslated, I think.—*A*. James (Jacob), called brother of Jesus Christ, came to be known as "bishop" (Clem. Alex. ap. Euseb., *Hist. Eccl.* II. 1) and even "bishop of bishops" (Clem. Rom., *Hom.*, superscription).

[4] Peter.

[5] Luke V. 8.

iste timor non temperetur affectu, vereor, ne Gerasenorum destituar exemplo et discedas a finibus meis. quin potius illud, quod mihi conducibilius est, conleprosi mei te proposita condicione constringam, ut aiam tibi: si vis, potes me mundare. qua ille sententia non plus de Christo quid peteret prodidit, quam quid crederet publicavit. 3. ergone cum sis procul ambiguo primus omnium toto, qua patet, orbe pontificum, cum praerogativae subiciatur, cum censurae tuae adtremat etiam turba collegii, cum in gravitatis vestrae comparationem ipsa etiam grandaevorum corda puerascant, cum post desudatas militiae Lirinensis excubias et in apostolica sede novem iam decursa quinquennia utriusque sanctorum ordinis quendam te conclamatissimum primipilarem spiritalia castra venerentur, tu nihilominus hastatorum antesignanorumque paulisper contubernio sequestratus ultimos calones tuos lixasque non despicis et ad extimos trahariorum, qui per insipientiam suam adhuc ad carnis sarcinas sedent, crucis diu portatae vexilla circumfers ac manum linguae porrigis in conscientia vulneratis? 4. nosti, ut apparet, ex adversa acie sauciatos, dux veterane, colligere et

---

[1] Matth. VIII. 28–34; Mark, V. 1–20; Luke, VIII. 26–39. In all three gospels the readings of MSS record Gerasenes, Gergesenes, and Gadarenes. Gerasenes seems right in Mark and Luke, Gadarenes in Matthew.

[2] Does he mean the conditional clause in the quotation, *i.e. si vis*? But perhaps *condicio* here = *optio*.—*A*.

[3] Luke V. 12.

[4] *A*. seemed puzzled by this sentence. The sense is: when the bishops are subordinate to Lupus, how much more the ordinary clergy and such a one as himself who has just ceased to be a layman.—*W.H.S.* For *collegium*, cf. *Ep.* IV, 25. 1.

fied by my affection for you, I fear that I may be abandoned like the Gerasenes[1] and that you may depart from my borders. Let me rather do what befits me better, and constrain you by putting before you the condition[2] uttered by my fellow-leper, saying to you: "If thou wilt, thou canst make me clean."[3] In that sentence he proclaimed what he believed of Christ as fully as he revealed what he sought from Him. 3. You are, beyond all doubt,[4] the first of all bishops everywhere in the world; members even of your provincial college bow to your pre-eminence and tremble before your censure; and your commanding prestige makes the minds even of the old seem childish by comparison. After keeping the laborious watches in the holy warfare at Lérins[5] and after serving forty-five years in an apostolic see, you are venerated by the spiritual camps of both saintly orders[6] as, so to speak, their most famous captain. Is it possible, then, in spite of all this greatness, that you separate yourself for a while from the company of the front-rank fighters and standard-bearers and do not scorn your lowliest batmen and sutlers? Is it possible that to the meanest of the sledge-men, who in their foolishness still sit attached to the burdens of the flesh, is it possible that to these you carry the flag of the Cross you have borne for so long, and that to those wounded in their conscience you extend by your words a hand of help? 4. It is clear, veteran leader, that you know how to gather the

[5] Île de St. Honorat, one of two islands (Îles de Lérins) near Cannes. Cf. *Ep.* VII. 13. 3; VIII. 14. 2; IX. 3. 4; *Carm.* XVI. 104 ff.

[6] He means "secular and regular (monastic) clergy."

peritissimus tubicen ad Christum a peccatis receptui canere; et euangelici pastoris exemplo non amplius laetaris, si permaneant sani, quam si non remaneant desperati. te ergo, norma morum, te, columna virtutum, te, si blandiri reis licet, vera, quia sancta, dulcedo, despicatissimi vermis ulcera digitis exhortationis contrectare non piguit; tibi avaritiae non fuit pascere monitis animam fragilitate ieiunam et de apotheca dilectionis altissimae sectandae nobis humilitatis propinare mensuram. 5. sed ora, ut quandoque resipiscam, quantum [1] meas deprimat oneris impositi massa cervices.[2] facinorum continuatione miser eo necessitatis accessi, ut is pro peccato populi nunc orare compellar, pro quo populus innocentum vix debet impetrare si supplicet. nam quis bene medelam aeger impertiat? quis febriens arroganti tactu pulsum distinguat incolumem? quis desertor scientiam rei militaris iure laudaverit? quis esculentus abstemium competenter arguerit? indignissimus mortalium necesse habeo dicere quod facere detrecto, et ad mea ipse verba damnabilis, cum non impleam quae moneo,[3] idem in me meam [4]

[1] c̃H (*ut videtur*) (*i.e.* cum enim) *T*.
[2] cervices ⟨vides⟩ *coni. Mommsen*.
[3] cum non impleam que moneo *LR*: cum imperem que non impleo.
[4] meam *om. MTCFP*: in meam *RV*: in me — *N*[1].

---

[1] Is *populus* here used in the special sense of "the laity"? —*A*.
[2] Or: "I could be condemned in face of my own words" (Dalton).

wounded from the opposing army and like a highly consummate trumpeter you are adept in sounding the signal for retreat from sin to Christ. And following the example of the shepherd in the Gospels, you feel as much pleasure over those who cease to be in desperate plight as over those who remain unscathed. Therefore you, the model of conduct, you, the pillar of virtues, you (if a sinner may use the language of flattery), the fount of that true sweetness that comes from holiness, did not scorn to touch with the healing fingers of exhortation the sores of a most despicable worm; you did not grudge to feed with admonitions a soul starving through its weakness, and to lavish upon me from the store-house of your most deep affection a draught of the humility that I must needs follow. 5. But pray that sooner or later I may come to my senses and realise how my shoulders sag under the weight of the massive burden put upon me. By my never-ceasing iniquities I am brought to such a wretched pass that I am now forced to offer prayer for the sin of my people [1]—I who am so unworthy that, even if a sinless people prayed for me, they could scarcely expect to be heard. For how could a sick man be a fit healer? How could a fever-stricken sufferer by his presumptuous touch ever recognise a healthy pulse? What right has a deserter to praise military science? What glutton has any right to take the abstemious to task? I, the most unworthy of mortals, am under the necessity of preaching what I refuse to practise; I am condemned out of my own mouth,[2] in failing to fulfil my own admonitions, and I am every day compelled to pronounce my verdict against myself. 6. But if you,

cotidie cogor dictare sententiam. 6. sed si tu inter me et illum, cui concrucifigeris, dominum nostrum pro scelerum meorum populo, iunior mage quam minor Moyses, intercessor assistas,[1] non ulterius descendemus in infernum viventes nec per carnalium vitiorum incentiva flammati ad altare domini ignem diutius accendemus alienum; quia quamquam nos utpote reos gloriae libra non respicit, satis tamen superque gaudebimus, si precatu tuo levare valeamus interioris hominis nostri etsi non integrum ad remunerationem, certe vel cicatricatum pectus ad veniam. memor nostri esse dignare, domine papa.

II

SIDONIVS DOMINO PAPAE PRAGMATIO SALVTEM

1. Venerabilis Eutropia matrona, quod ad nos spectat, singularis exempli, quae parsimonia et humanitate certantibus non minus se ieiuniis quam cibis pauperes pascit et in Christi cultu pervigil sola in se compellit peccata dormire, maeroribus orbitatis

[1] existas *coni. Luetjohann.*

---

[1] Anderson queries his own rendering of his sentence; and I think his dissatisfaction arose from the fact that he had not seen the forced contrast and antithesis between *integrum* and *cicatricatum*, the former meaning "intact," "undamaged," "unscathed," and the latter "wounded," "scarred," "hacked." I have ventured, therefore, to introduce my own translation from *satis tamen superque gaudebimus* to the end of the sentence. The whole of this letter is so hyperbolically

a later rather than a lesser Moses, stand as intercessor for my multitude of sins between me and Him, our Lord, with whom you are crucified, then I shall no more descend alive into the pit; no longer aflame with the lure of fleshly vices shall I kindle strange flame at the altar of the Lord; for although a sinner like me can claim no recompense of glory, it will be for me joy abundant, joy superabundant, if through your prayers I am able to raise up my spiritual being,[1] presenting not indeed a heart unscathed in the fight now to receive its reward, but a heart battered and scarred to receive its pardon. Deign to hold me in remembrance, my Lord Bishop.

II

SIDONIUS TO THE LORD BISHOP PRAGMATIUS,* GREETING

The venerable matron Eutropia is a lady whom I for my part regard [2] as a shining example. She is one in whom abstemiousness and kindliness are equally matched; she feeds herself with fastings no less than she feeds the poor with food; she is unslumbering in Christ's service; sin is the only thing in her that is forced to sleep. Now the burden of a law-suit has been added to the sorrows of widowhood,

overwritten that I am sure Sidonius was more concerned with his style than with his sin.—*W.H.S.*

* Not the Pragmatius of *Ep.* V. 10. 1, 2. It is not known what his see was.

[2] This Eutropia is unknown otherwise unless she was the one included by the Romans among sainted widows celebrated on the 15th of September.

necessitate litis adiecta in remedium mali duplicis perfectionem vestrae consolationis expetere festinat, gratanter habitura, sive istud tibi peregrinatio brevis seu longum computetur officium. 2. igitur praefata venerabilis fratris mei nunc iam presbyteri Agrippini, ne iniuriosum sit dixisse nequitiis, certe fatigatur argutiis; qui abutens inbecillitate matronae non desistit spiritalis animae serenitatem saecularium versutiarum flatibus turbidare; cui filii nec post multo nepotis amissi duae pariter plagae recentes ad diuturni viduvii vulnus adduntur. 3. temptavimus inter utrumque componere, nos maxume, quibus in eos novum ius professio vetustumque faciebant amicitiae, aliqua censentes, suadentes quaepiam, plurima supplicantes; quodque miremini, in omnem concordiae statum promptius a feminea parte descensum [1] est. et quamquam se altius profuturum [2] filiae paterna iactaret praerogativa, nurui tamen magis placuit munificentiae socrualis oblatio. 4. iurgium interim semisopitum vestris modo sinibus infertur. pacificate certantes, et pontificalis auctoritate censurae suspectis sibi partibus indicite gratiam, dicite veritatem. sancta enim Eutropia, si quid

[1] descensum *Luetjohann*: discensum *L*: discessum.
[2] profuturam *coni. Mohr.*

---

[1] Not his real brother.
[2] The son of Eutropia had married the daughter of Agrippinus: the son had died, and the young widow preferred to remain with her mother-in-law, whose generous treatment of her Sidonius stresses.

and she is hurrying to seek the supreme benefit of your comfort as a cure for her double affliction; she will be highly gratified whether you reckon her business as likely to involve merely a brief absence from home or a prolonged waiting on your pleasure. 2. Well, the aforesaid lady is being worried by sharp practices (I don't want to be abusive and call them villainies) on the part of my reverend brother [1] Agrippinus, now a presbyter. Taking advantage of her unprotected weakness, he never ceases from troubling the serenity of that spiritual soul with blasts of worldly subtleties, although by the loss of her son and a little later of her grandson a double blow has recently been added to the wound of her long widowhood. 3. I tried to mediate between the two, as I was specially entitled to do, seeing that my profession gave me a new and my friendship an old claim upon them; I expressed opinions on this and that and gave various advice together with many entreaties. You will be surprised, but it was the woman who showed the greater readiness to accede to every basis of agreement; and although the girl's father claimed that his privileged position [2] would enable him to benefit his daughter more effectively,[3] she preferred the liberal offer made by her mother-in-law. 4. This quarrel, half allayed for the time being, is now being confided to your care. Appease the disputants, and by the authority of your episcopal judgment enjoin conciliation on the two parties that now view each other with distrust, and declare the truth. For the saintly Eutropia (if you put any trust in my assurance)

[3] A very unusual if not unique use of *altius*.—*A*.

vadimonio meo creditis, victoriam computat, si vel post damna non litiget. unde et suspicor vobis unam pronuntiandam domum discordiosam, licet inveniatis utramque discordem. memor nostri esse dignare, domine para.

III

SIDONIVS DOMINO PAPAE LEONTIO SALVTEM

1. Etsi nullis hortatibus [1] primordia nostrae professionis animatis neque sitim ignorantiae hactenus saecularis ullo supernae rigatis imbre doctrinae, non ego tamen tantum mei meminens non sum, ut a meis ⟨ac tuis⟩ [2] praesumam partibus aequali officiorum lance certandum. nam cum nostra mediocritas aetate vitae, tempore dignitatis, privilegio loci, laude scientiae, dono conscientiae vestrae facile vincatur, nullum meremur, si par expectamus alloquium. 2. igitur non incusantes silentium vestrum sed loquacitatem nostram potius excusare nitentes

[1] hortationibus *F*.
[2] ⟨ac tuis⟩ *vel* ⟨et tuis⟩ *vel* ⟨tuisque⟩ *coni. Anderson.*

---

[1] Another of these troublesome present indicatives.—*A*.

* Not Pontius Leontius of *Ep.* VIII. 11, *carm.* 33 and VIII. 12. 5, but a Bishop of Arles and friend of Pope Hilarus. The bishop helped to arrange a peace with Euric. *Ep.* VII. 6. 10. In the fifth century, bishops of Arles claimed and partly exercised metropolitan rights over a large area; hence probably the expression "your exceptional standing" in § 1.

[2] Read *meis ac tuis* (or *meis et tuis* or *meis tuisque*).—*A*. In view of this suggested change in the text, I am not sure that Anderson caught the exact sense in § 1 of *ut a meis praesumam*

will count[1] it a victory if she is saved from litigation even at the expense of financial loss. This being so, I suspect you will pronounce only one of the two families to be disputatious, although you find both of them disputing. Deign to hold me in remembrance, my Lord Bishop.

III

SIDONIUS TO THE LORD BISHOP LEONTIUS,* GREETING

1. Although so far I have received from you no word of exhortation to inspire me in my new profession, no shower of heavenly teaching to water the drought of my worldly ignorance, yet I do not so forget myself as to expect an equally balanced competition in attentions from your side and from mine;[2] for my poor insignificance pales easily before the ripeness of your years, the seniority of your office, your exceptional standing, the eminence of your knowledge and your gift of self-knowledge; and so, if I expect your letters to keep pace with mine, I do not deserve to receive a single one. 2. Thus I am not blaming your silence but rather endeavouring to

partibus aequali officiorum lance certandum. Sidonius has been complaining that Bishop Leontius did not write him a letter on the occasion of his appointment to the See of Auvergne. "But," says Sidonius, "I am not so conceited as to return tit for tat, and to repay your nothing with a like nothing. If I expected an answer from you for every letter of mine, such presumption would deserve *no* letter from you *ever*. So in this letter I am not blaming you for ignoring me, I am only trying to give a reason why I do now write—and the reason is this recommendation of the letter-carrier."—*W.H.S.*

commendamus apicum portitorem, cuius si peregrinationem prompto favore foveatis, grandis actionibus illius portus securitatis aperitur. negotium huic testamentarium est. latent eum propriarum merita chartarum: togatorum illic perorantum peritiam consulere perrexit, pro victoria computaturus, si se intellexerit iure superari, modo ne sibi suisque desidiae vitio perperam cavisse culpetur. hunc eatenus commendare praesumo, ut, si eum instruere dignanter advocatio consulta fastidit, auctoritas coronae tuae dissimulantibus studeat excudere responsi celeritatem. memor nostri esse dignare, domine papa.

IV

SIDONIVS DOMINO PAPAE LVPO SALVTEM

1. Praeter officium, quod incomparabiliter eminenti apostolatui tuo sine fine debetur, etsi absque intermissione solvatur, commendo supplicum baiulorum pro nova necessitudine vetustam necessitatem,[1] qui in Arvernam regionem longum iter, his quippe

[1] necessitudine (necessitate N^1)· vetustam necessitudinem N: necessitate vetustam necessitudinem $TCFPM^1$.

---

[1] *corona*, the clerical "crown," the tonsure. The word could be used even for a priest himself. Cf. *Ep.* VII. 8. 1.

* See the first note on *Ep.* VI. 1. On the present letter cf. Stevens, *Sid. Apoll.*, 118 ff.

[2] I think Mohr's reading is right. *necessitudine*, *i.e.* the close relationship between Lupus and Sidonius; either they had only recently become friends or Sidonius' recent election to a bishopric had brought him into closer relations with

excuse my talkativeness when I commend to you the bearer of this letter. Should you support with ready favour his visit to a far country, a great haven of security will be opened to his pleas. His case concerns a will. He is not clear about the merits of his own documents and he has gone to seek skilled advice from the advocates who practise there. He will count it as good as winning the case if he finds that he is lawfully the loser; only, he does not want to be accused of having failed through indolence to guard the interests of himself and his family. I take it upon me to recommend him to this extent that, in case the counsel he calls in should disdain to favour him with instructions, the influence of your tonsure[1] may exert itself to force a quick response from those negligent gentlemen. Deign to hold me in remembrance, my Lord Bishop.

IV

SIDONIUS TO THE LORD BISHOP LUPUS,* GREETING

1. Besides presenting my humble duty (a debt due in a supreme degree to your apostolic eminence, a debt which, though paid ceaselessly, is still owed in perpetuity), I commend to you, in virtue of our new relationship,[2] an old trouble of the suppliant bearers of this letter. Having travelled to the Arvernian country, a long journey in such days as these,[3] they

Lupus than he had known before.—*A*. There is word-play with *necessitudo* and *necessitas*.

[3] For *quippe* cf. *Ep*. V. 5. 1.

temporibus, emensi casso labore venerunt. namque unam feminam de affectibus suis, quam forte Vargorum (hoc enim nomine indigenas latrunculos nuncupant) superventus abstraxerat, isto deductam ante aliquot annos isticque distractam cum non falso indicio comperissent, certis quidem signis sed non recentibus inquisivere vestigiis. 2. atque obiter haec eadem laboriosa, priusquam hi adessent, in negotiatoris nostri domo dominioque palam sane venumdata defungitur, quodam Prudente (hoc viro nomen), quem nunc Tricassibus degere fama divulgat, ignotorum nobis hominum collaudante contractum;[1] cuius subscriptio intra formulam nundinarum tamquam idonei adstipulatoris ostenditur. auctoritas personae, opportunitas praesentiae tuae inter coram positos facile valebit, si dignabitur, seriem totius indagare violentiae, quae, quod gravius est, eo facinoris accessit, quantum portitorum datur nosse memoratu, ut etiam in illo latrocinio quendam de numero viantum constet extinctum. 3. sed quia iudicii vestri medicinam expetunt civilitatemque, qui negotium criminale parturiunt, vestrarum, si bene metior, partium pariter et morum est, aliqua

[1] colludente contractui *coni. Anderson, ut videtur.*

---

[1] A Teutonic word meaning outlaw or exile.
[2] In his translation Anderson put " one of our business men." In the margin he wrote " my agent," which I have adopted as preferable.—*W.H.S.*

got no profit for their pains. They had discovered from reliable information that a kinswoman, who had been abducted in a raid of Vargi[1] (for so they call the local brigands), had been brought here a number of years ago and sold on the spot; and so they have been searching for her, following up certain clues which are certain enough though not fresh. 2. Meanwhile before their arrival this same unfortunate woman died in the house and in the ownership of my agent.[2] She had indeed been sold quite openly: the transaction (the parties to which are strangers to me) was recommended[3] by a certain Prudens (such is the man's name) who, according to current report, is now living at Troyes; his signature in the capacity of a good and sufficient co-promiser[4] appears in the sales-register of the market. If you will deign to meet the parties face to face, you with your personal prestige and the advantage of your actual presence will have no difficulty in worming from them the whole story of this outrage, which has an even more serious side; for, as far as one can discover from the evidence of the bearers, the affair went to such atrocious lengths that one of the travellers on the road is actually known to have lost his life in the course of the kidnapping. 3. But because the persons who are contemplating a criminal charge now desire the remedy of your civil judgment it will, if I am not mistaken, be in keeping both with your duty and your character to relieve the distress of the one party and the danger of the other by compound-

[3] ? *colludente contractui*? so *A*. seems to conjecture.

[4] An *adstipulator* was an accessory promiser in the form of transaction called *stipulatio*—Gaius, III. 100–112.

indemni compositione istorum dolori, illorum periculo subvenire et quodam salubris sententiae temperamento hanc partem minus afflictam, illam minus ream et utramque plus facere securam; ne iurgii status, ut sese fert temporis locique qualitas,[1] talem descendat[2] ad terminum, quale coepit habere principium. memor nostri esse dignare, domine papa.

V

SIDONIVS DOMINO PAPAE THEOPLASTO SALVTEM

1. Causam meam nesciens agit qui ad vos a me litteras portat; nam, dum votivi mihi fit gerulus opportunus officii, beneficium praestat, quod se arbitratur accipere, sicuti nunc venerabilis Donidius dignus inter spectatissimos quosque numerari. cuius clientem puerosque commendo, profectos seu in patroni necessitate seu in domini. laborem

[1] qualitas *Gustafsson* (Cf. *Ep.* VIII. 11. 6 temporis loci qualitate): civilitas.

[2] descendat *mut. in* discedat M^1: discendat *L*: discedat *TCFP*.

---

[1] *Compositio*, which often means "arrangement," "accommodation" of a dispute, is also used for medical mixture or compound. Both meanings are blended here: that the medical idea is present is shown by *medicina* and *temperamento*; medical metaphors in this sort of context occur

ing[1] some innocuous remedy and to administer a decision wholesomely tempered, as it were, so as to make the one side less distressed, the other less guilty, and both more easy in their minds, lest this quarrel, as is the natural tendency in this quarter and in these times, should in the end develop a character such as now at the beginning it threatens to assume. Deign to hold me in remembrance, my Lord Bishop.

V

SIDONIUS TO THE LORD BISHOP THEOPLASTUS,* GREETING

He who carries a letter from me to you pleads my cause without knowing it; for in becoming the opportune bearer of a homage I longed to pay, he is really conferring a kindness while imagining that he is receiving it. So it is now with the venerable Donidius,[2] a man worthy to be numbered among the most sterling of mankind.[3] I commend to you his client and slaves, who have left home on the urgent business of patron or master.[4] Support the labour

elsewhere in Sidonius, cf. *Ep.* V. 19. 2; V. 13. 4; III. 3. 9; III. 10. 2 fin.

* Perhaps Bishop of Geneva (Duchesne, *Fastes Épiscopaux*, I. 227).

[2] Cf. *Ep.* II. 9; III. 5.

[3] Perhaps with a side-reference to Donidius' title of *spectabilis.*—*A.* See above, p. 22.

[4] Donidius was "patron" of his client and "master" of his slaves. From the previous sentence one might have assumed that Donidius himself was the bearer of the letter; as it is, the language is very far-fetched, especially *beneficium . . . accipere.*—*A.*

peregrinantum qua potestis ope humanitate intercessione tutamini; ac, si in aliquo amicus ipse per imperitiam novitatemque publicae conversationis videbitur minus efficax, vos hoc potius aspicite, quid absentis causa, non quid praesentis persona mereatur. memor nostri esse dignare, domine papa.

VI

SIDONIVS DOMINO PAPAE EVTROPIO SALVTEM

1. Postquam foedifragam gentem redisse in sedes suas comperi neque quicquam viantibus insidiarum parare, nefas credidi ulterius officiorum[1] differre sermonem, ne vester affectus quandam vitio meo duceret ut gladius inpolitus de curae raritate robiginem. unde misso in hoc solum negotii gerulo litterarum, quam vobis sit corpusculi status in solido quamve ex animi sententia res agantur, sollicitus inquiro, sperans, ne semel mihi amor vester indultus aut interiecti itineris longitudine aut absentiae com-

[1] officiosum *coni. Luetjohann.*

---

[1] Does Sidonius intend a jest? The *vir spectabilis* is scarcely likely to have been so inexperienced, but he may have disliked business. *Ep.* III. 5 has a kinship. There again Donidius uses Sidonius to persuade another person to use his influence to secure another's help for him.—*A.*

* Not the Eutropius of I. 6 and III. 6, but Bishop of Orange. Duchesne, I. 265.

[2] The Visigoths. When he was younger Sidonius had

of these travellers with all the help, the sympathy, and the intervention you can give; and if my friend himself shall seem to you rather lacking in practical ability owing to his inexperience and unfamiliarity with the ways of the busy world,[1] consider the merits of the absent Donidius' cause rather than the demerits of his representative's personality. Deign to hold me in remembrance, my Lord Bishop.

VI

SIDONIUS TO THE LORD BISHOP EUTROPIUS,* GREETING

1. When I heard that the race of treaty-breakers [2] had returned to their homes and were no longer setting ambushes for travellers I felt it would be outrageous to defer longer the payment of my respects, anxious as I was that your affection should not through any fault of mine become like an unburnished sword, gathering rust, so to speak, through want of regular attention. Accordingly, I have sent the bearer of my letter on this sole errand, and I now anxiously enquire how well your bodily health is maintained and how far your fortunes answer to your wishes; and I hope that the love you have once bestowed on me may not be impaired either by the long distance that separates us or by the long time that has passed

adhered to pro-Gothic policy, and as a Visigothic subject had to be careful; but he did not like barbarians (cf. *Ep.* VII. 14. 10, for example); and when relations were bad the Visigoths were to him unreliable as they were to others (Ammianus Marcellinus XXII. 7). Cf. Stevens, 48, 49, 66, 167.

munis diuturnitate tenuetur, quia bonitas conditoris habitationem potius hominum quam caritatem finalibus claudit angustiis. 2. restat, ut vestra beatitudo conpunctorii salubritate sermonis avidam nostrae ignorantiae pascat esuriem. est enim tibi nimis usui, ut exhortationibus tuis interioris hominis maciem saepenumero mysticus adeps et spiritalis arvina distendat. memor nostri esse dignare, domine papa.

VII

SIDONIVS DOMINO PAPAE FONTEIO SALVTEM

1. Si aliquid ad inchoandam gratiam compendii posteris tribuit necessitudo praemissa seniorum, ego quoque ad apostolatus tui notitiam pleniorem cum praerogativa domesticae familiaritatis accedo. nam sic te familiae meae validissimum in Christo semper patronum fuisse reminiscor, ut amicitias tuas non tam expetendas mihi quam repetendas putem. his adicitur, quod indignissimo mihi impositum sacerdotalis nomen officii confugere me ad precum vestrarum praesidia compellit, ut adhuc ulcerosae conscientiae nimis hiulca vulnera vestro saltim cicatricentur oratu. 2. quapropter me meosque commendans et excusans litteras seriores granditer obsecro, ut

[1] Something like the above must be the meaning I suppose; but one is tempted to read *nimis in usu* " it is quite habitual." —*A*.

since we met; for the Creator's goodness, though it sets men's dwelling-places within narrow bounds, imposes no such limits on their love. 2. It now remains for your Beatitude to feed the greedy hunger of my starving ignorance with a wholesome meal of stimulating discourse; for it is to your truest advantage [1] that your exhortations should often cause a mystic fat and spiritual lard to fill out the leanness of the inner man. Deign to hold me in remembrance, my Lord Bishop.

VII

SIDONIUS TO THE LORD BISHOP FONTEIUS,* GREETING

1. If a preliminary reference to the ties of intimacy subsisting among their elders is some help to the younger generation in making friendships, I, too, in seeking a fuller acquaintance with your Lordship, may urge the claims of an intimate family friendship; for I remember that you have always been by Christ's grace a most powerful patron of my family, and so I feel that your friendship need not so much be sought as resought by me. Besides this, the eminence of the priestly office laid upon my most unworthy shoulders compels me to resort to the protection of your prayers, that the still widely gaping wounds of my conscience may form healing scars through your supplications, even if all else should fail. 2. For this reason I commend myself and my people to you, and, with an apology for this rather belated letter, I

* Cf. *Ep.* VII. 4. Bishop of Vaison. Duchesne, I. 262.

intercessione consueta, cuius viribus immane polletis, clericalis tirocinii in nobis reptantia rudimenta tueamini, ut, si quid dignabitur de morum pravitate nostrorum immutabilis dei mutare clementia, totum id suffragiorum vestrorum patrocinio debeamus. memor nostri esse dignare, domine papa.

VIII

SIDONIVS DOMINO PAPAE GRAECO SALVTEM

1. Apicum oblator pauperem vitam sola mercandi actione sustentat; non illi est opificium quaestui, militia commodo, cultura compendio; ⟨ob⟩[1] hoc ipsum, quod mercennariis prosecutionibus et locaticia fatigatione cognoscitur, fama quidem sua sed facultas crescit aliena. sed tamen quoniam illi fides magna est, etsi parva substantia, quotiens cum pecuniis quorumpiam catapli recentis nundinas adit, creditoribus bene credulis sola deponit morum experimenta pro pignore. 2. inter dictandum mihi ista suggesta sunt, nec ob hoc dubito audita fidenter asserere, quia non parum mihi intumos agunt[2] quibus est ipse satis intumus. huius igitur teneram frontem, dura

[1] ob *add. Luetjohann.*
[2] intumi suggerunt *Mommsen.*

* Cf. *Ep.* VII. 2 and 7 and 10 (11); IX. 4. Bishop of Marseille; appointed by Iulius Nepos, emperor in 474–475,

earnestly beseech you to protect the immature efforts of my clerical beginnings by your wonted intercession, whose strength gives you enormous power. Should the mercy of the never-changing God deign to change aught in the depravity of my ways, I would fain owe it all to your protecting help! Deign to hold me in remembrance, my Lord Bishop.

VIII

SIDONIUS TO THE LORD BISHOP GRAECUS,* GREETING

1. The bearer [1] of this letter wins a poor livelihood solely by acting as a purchasing-agent; no craft brings him gain, no public service brings him pay, no farm-work a profit. The very fact that he is known for his paid attendances and hired exertions means increasing repute for him, no doubt, but increasing wealth only for others. Yet for all the smallness of his means his name stands high, and whenever the cargo of a recently arrived merchantman [2] comes into the market and he goes to the sale with other people's money he deposits with these creditors, who do well to credit him, no security except his tried honesty. 2. This fact was put before me as I wrote, but I do not hesitate on that account to guarantee the report with full confidence, for those with whom he is very intimate are on quite intimate terms with me. So I com-

with three others to negotiate with Euric. See *Ep.* VII. 6. 10 f.

[1] Amantius. See *Ep.* VII. 7, second note.

[2] For cataplus see *Ep.* VII. 7. 1 and note there.

rudimenta commendo; et, quia nomen eiusdem lectorum nuper albus accepit, agnoscitis profecturo civi me epistulam, clerico debuisse formatam; quem propediem non iniuria reor mercatorem splendidum fore, si hinc ad vestra obsequia festinans frigoribus fontium civicorum sapientiae fontem meracioris [1] anteferat. memor nostri esse dignare, domine papa.

IX

SIDONIVS DOMINO PAPAE LVPO SALVTEM

1. Vir iam honestus Gallus, quia iussus ad coniugem redire non distulit, litterarum mearum obsequium, vestrarum reportat effectum. cui cum pagina, quam miseratis, reseraretur, actutum compunctus ingemuit destinatamque non ad me epistulam sed in se sententiam iudicavit. itaque confestim iter in patriam spopondit adornavit arripuit. quem

[1] sapientiae fontem meracioris *Housman*: saepe fontem meri caloris vestri *coni. Mohr*: caloris tui *Leo*: *alii alia*: saepe fontem *codd.* mercatoris *MFPR*: mercatoribus *LCN* (medicatoris N^1): medi(i tui)atoris *T*.

---

[1] In his MS Anderson had underlined as doubtful the translation of *teneram frontem, dura rudimenta.* Personally I would prefer some such rendering as "I commend to you this man who looks so young and has had such a hard schooling."—*W.H.S.* "After hard schooling, no hardened character."—L. A. Post.

[2] A letter given by bishop to priest or clerk to admit him to

mend to you this man with all his air of rawness and his untutored roughness.[1] As the register of Readers has lately received his name, you can understand that, besides owing a letter to a fellow-citizen at the start of his journey, I also owed a canonical letter [2] to one who is a cleric. I think, and with good reason, that he will shortly show himself a brilliant man of business if he hurries hence to pay duty to you, preferring a fount of purer [3] wisdom to the chilly waters of his native springs. Deign to hold me in remembrance, my Lord Bishop.

IX

SIDONIUS TO THE LORD BISHOP LUPUS,* GREETING

1. Gallus, who has now established his character by immediately complying with your order to return to his wife, takes back in this letter my dutiful respects, and takes back in himself the effectual result of your letter. When the letter you had sent was opened he was straightway seized with contrition, and groaned, taking it not as a letter addressed to me but as a sentence pronounced against himself; and he immediately promised, prepared, and welcomed with open arms a journey to his native soil. The very

sacraments and so on when travelling abroad. Even a bishop had to get one for himself from a superior.

[3] Anderson was surely right in accepting Housman's emendation in *Classical Review*, XIV, 54 *sapientiae fontem meracioris*. Housman compares *ad meracissimum scientiae fontem* in *Ep.* III. 10. 1.

* See the first footnote to *Ep.* VI. 1.

nos propter hanc ipsam paenitudinis celeritatem non increpative sed consolatorie potius compellare curavimus, quia vicinaretur innocentiae festinata correctio. 2. neque enim quisquam etiam sibi bene conscius plus facere praesumpsit, si quis tamen vestrae correptionis orbitam non reliquit, quippe cum ea ipsa, quae legimus, parcentis verba censurae maxuma [1] emendationis incitamenta sint.[2] nam quid potest esse castigationis huiusce tenore pretiosius, in qua forte peccato animus aeger repperit intrinsecus remedium, cum non valeret extrinsecus invenire convicium? 3. quod superest, obsecramus, ut crebra oratione, per quam vitiis omnibus immane dominamini, nos quoque, sicut euangelicos magos remeasse manifestum est, vel iam nunc per aliam viam morum in beatorum patriam redire faciatis. paene omiseram, quod minime praetereundum fuit: agite gratias Innocentio, spectabili viro, qui, ut praeceperatis, naviter morem gessit iniunctis. memor nostri esse dignare, domine papa.

[1] maxuma *Mohr*: maxumae *aut* maximae.
[2] sint *LRN*: sunt *MTFPVN*[1].

---

[1] Anderson bracketed his translation from *neque enim quisquam* to *incitamenta sint*, and wrote in the margin "this can't be right: what does it mean?" I have ventured to

swiftness of his repentance constrained us to address him in comforting rather than reproachful tones, because such a speedy amendment seemed next door to innocence. 2.[1] For no man, not even one with a perfect conscience, has ever presumed to do more than give a kindly reproof (provided always that the offender has not passed beyond the range of your rebuke), since those very words of sparing censure which I read out to him are the most powerful incentives to reform.[1] What can be more precious than the wording of this reprimand, by virtue of which the sin-sick soul found within itself a remedy inasmuch as it could not find harsh words without?[2] 3. I close by beseeching you to offer frequently on my behalf those supplications by which you so mightily master all sins, that even as the Wise Men in the Gospel manifestly returned home by a different way,[3] so you may cause me from now on to return by a different path of conduct to the home of the blessed. I had almost omitted a matter which ought on no account to have been passed over! Give my thanks to the eminent Innocentius, who diligently attended to my injunctions in accordance with your instructions. Deign to hold me in remembrance, my Lord Bishop.[4]

alter his translation somewhat so as to bring out that which I think must be the meaning.—*W.H.S.*

[2] Sidonius seems to mean harsh words of other people which might help to bring remedy to a sick soul.

[3] Matthew II. 12.

[4] Anderson added a footnote for the end of this letter: "This translation requires revision, esp. § 2." I have given it a certain amount of revision.—*W.H.S.*

X

SIDONIVS DOMINO PAPAE CENSORIO SALVTEM

1. Gerulum litterarum levitici ordinis honestat officium. hic cum familia sua depraedationis Gothicae turbinem vitans in territorium vestrum delatus est ipso, ut sic dixerim, pondere fugae; ubi in re ecclesiae, cui sanctitas tua praesidet, parvam sementem semiconfecto caespiti advena ieiunus iniecit, cuius ex solido colligendae fieri sibi copiam exorat. 2. quem si domesticis fidei deputata humanitate foveatis, id est, ut debitum glaebae canonem non petatur, tantum lucelli praestitum sibi computat (peregrini hominis ut census, sic animus angustus), ac si in patrio solo rusticaretur. huic si legitimam, ut mos est, solutionem perexiguae segetis indulgeas, tamquam opipare viaticatus cum gratiarum actione remeabit. per quem si me stilo solitae dignationis impertias, mihi fraternitatique istic sitae pagina tua veluti polo lapsa reputabitur. memor nostri esse dignare, domine papa.

---

* Bishop of Auxerre.

X

SIDONIUS TO THE LORD BISHOP CENSORIUS,* GREETING

1. The bearer of this letter holds the honourable office of deacon. He with his family, seeking an escape from the whirlwind of Gothic depredation,[1] was carried into your territory by the very impetus of his flight, so to speak. There on some farm land, belonging to a church over which your Holiness is set, this starving newcomer made a small sowing of seed on some half-tilled soil; and he earnestly pleads to be allowed to garner the whole crop. 2. If you cherish him with the kindness due to "them who are of the household of the faith," I mean by waiving the rent due from the glebe, then he, a stranger whose outlook is as limited as his means, will consider that little acquisition as good as the profits of farming his native soil. Should you, as is your custom, let him off the statutory payment due for his exceedingly small bit of land, he will regard himself as liberally equipped with travelling expenses and will return with words of gratitude on his lips. If by his hand you make me the happy recipient of a characteristically gracious message your letter will be regarded here by the brethren one and all as a blessing dropped straight from heaven. Deign to hold me in remembrance, my Lord Bishop.

[1] This might refer to any of the years A.D. 471–474 or early 475. Cf. VI. 12. 5; III. 3. 7.

XI

SIDONIVS DOMINO PAPAE ELEVTHERIO SALVTEM

1. Iudaeum praesens charta commendat, non quod mihi placeat error, per quem pereunt involuti, sed quia neminem ipsorum nos decet ex asse damnabilem pronuntiare, dum vivit; in spe enim adhuc absolutionis est cui suppetit posse converti. 2. quae sit vero negotii sui series, ipse rectius praesentanea coram narratione patefaciet. nam prudentiae satis obviat epistulari formulae debitam concinnitatem plurifario sermone porrigere. sane quia secundum vel negotia vel iudicia terrena solent huiuscemodi homines honestas habere causas, tu quoque potes huius laboriosi, etsi impugnas perfidiam, propugnare personam. memor nostri esse dignare, domine papa.

XII

SIDONIVS DOMINO PAPAE PATIENTI SALVTEM

1. Aliquis aliquem, ego illum praecipue puto suo vivere bono, qui vivit alieno quique fidelium calamitates indigentiamque miseratus facit in terris opera

---

* Not otherwise known.

[1] Not Gozolas of *Ep.* III. 4. 1; IV. 5. 1.

[2] Probably a law-suit.—*A.*

[3] I wonder if Sidonius knew the meaning of *concinnitas*.—*A.*

[4] *I.e.* Christian bishop though you are.—*A.*

[5] Note *perfidia* = false belief, heresy.—*A.* It is taken in

XI

SIDONIUS TO THE LORD BISHOP ELEUTHERIUS,* GREETING

1. The present note commends to you a Jew,[1] not because I favour a false belief through which all who are involved in it are lost, but because it is not seemly to pronounce any of those persons entirely beyond redemption, so long as life remains to him; for one who still has a chance of conversion still has a prospect of absolution. 2. It is best that he should tell you with his own lips in a personal interview the whole story of his trouble;[2] for it is unwise to swell with discursive talk the trim compactness[3] proper to the epistolary style: after all, from the standpoint of earthly business and jurisdiction people of this sort commonly have quite good cases; so even you[4] may well defend this unfortunate man's person while attacking his persuasion.[5] Deign to hold me in remembrance, my Lord Bishop.

XII

SIDONIUS TO THE LORD BISHOP PATIENS,† GREETING

Opinions differ, but I think that he most truly lives for his own good who lives for the good of others and who, by taking pity on the misfortunes and the destitution of the faithful, does on earth the work of

this sense by Souter in his *Glossary of Later Latin* (published in 1949).—*W.H.S.*

† See the second note on *Ep.* IV. 25.

caelorum. "quorsum istaec?"[1] inquis. te ista[2] sententia quam maxume, papa beatissime, petit, cui non sufficit illis tantum necessitatibus opem ferre, quas noveris, quique usque in extimos terminos Galliarum caritatis indage porrecta prius soles indigentum respicere causas quam inspicere personas. 2. nullius obest tenuitati debilitatique, si te expetere non possit. nam praevenis manibus illum, qui non valuerit ad te pedibus pervenire. transit in alienas provincias vigilantia tua et in hoc curae tuae latitudo diffunditur, ut longe positorum consoletur angustias; et hinc fit,[3] ut, quia crebro te non minus absentum verecundia quam praesentum querimonia movet, saepe terseris eorum lacrimas, quorum oculos non vidisti. 3. omitto illa, quae cotidie propter defectionem[4] civium pauperatorum inrequietis toleras excubiis precibus expensis. omitto te tali semper agere temperamento, sic semper humanum, sic abstemium iudicari, ut constet indesinenter regem praesentem prandia tua, reginam laudare ieiunia. omitto tanto te cultu ecclesiam tibi creditam convenustare, ut dubitet inspector, meliusne nova opera consurgant an vetusta reparentur. 4. omitto per te plurimis locis basilicarum fundamenta consurgere, ornamenta duplicari; cumque multa in statu fidei

[1] istaec *L*: ista *C*: ista haec. [2] ista *om. codd. pler.*
[3] fit *Wouweren*: fuit. [4] refectionem *coni. Mohr.*

[1] Chilperic the earlier, King of the Burgundians, who had been allowed under King Gundieuc (Gundioc) to occupy Lyon, probably soon after A.D. 461.

heaven. "What are you driving at?" you ask me. This pronouncement is aimed in a very special degree at you, most blessed of bishops, who are not content merely to ease the necessities known to you at first hand, but are wont to spead the net of your charity to the uttermost bounds of Gaul, and to look to the claims of the needy before you have looked at their persons. 2. It is no disadvantage to the poor and the afflicted if they cannot seek you out; your outstretched hand forestalls the sufferer whose feet have not been able to reach you. Your watchfulness crosses over into provinces other than your own, and the broad sweep of your benevolence ranges so far afield as to relieve the distress of those in distant parts. And so, since you are frequently moved as much by thoughtful consideration for the absent as by the plaints of those at your door, you have often wiped away the tears of people whose eyes you have never seen. 3. I say nothing of the unceasing watchfulness, prayer, and expenditure—burdens imposed upon you daily by the distress of your impoverished townsmen. I say nothing of the sense of proportion which guides all your actions, of your blending of geniality and asceticism which is so generally acknowledged that the present king,[1] as everyone knows, unceasingly praises your feasts, and the queen your fasts. Other things, too, I pass over—that you beautify the church committed to you with such taste that he who views it cannot decide whether the new buildings or the restorations of the old are to be preferred; 4. that in many places, thanks to you, the foundations of churches are rising or that their embellishments are being doubled; that many things in the establish-

tuis dispositionibus augeantur, solum haereticorum numerum minui, teque quodam venatu apostolico feras Fotinianorum mentes spiritualium praedicationum cassibus implicare, atque a tuo barbaros iam sequaces, quotiens convincuntur verbo, non exire vestigio, donec eos a profundo gurgite erroris felicissimus animarum piscator extraxeris. 5. et horum aliqua tamen cum reliquis forsitan communicanda collegis; illud autem deberi tibi quodam, ut iurisconsulti dicunt, praecipui titulo nec tuus poterit ire pudor infitias, quod post Gothicam depopulationem, post segetes incendio absumptas peculiari sumptu inopiae communi per desolatas Gallias gratuita frumenta misisti, cum tabescentibus fame populis nimium contulisses, si commercio fuisset species ista, non muneri.[1] vidimus angustas tuis frugibus vias; vidimus per Araris et Rhodani ripas non unum, quod unus impleveras, horreum. 6. fabularum cedant figmenta gentilium et ille quasi in caelum relatus pro reperta spicarum novitate Triptolemus, quem Graecia sua, caementariis pictoribus significibusque [2] illustris, sacravit templis formavit statuis effigiavit imaginibus. illum dubia fama concinnat [3]

[1] muneri *Luetjohann*: munere.

[2] significibus *M*. §§ *3–9 non habent LNVRT*.

[3] concinnat *Luetjohann*: cantitat *coni. Mohr*: conciliat *codd.* (conciliet *F*).

---

[1] Heretics who during the fourth century followed the beliefs (similar to the Arians') of Photinus, Bishop of Sirmium in Hungary.

ment of the faith are increased by your measures, but nothing is diminished except the number of heretics; and that, engaging in an apostolic huntsman's chase as it were, you entangle the wild minds of the Photinians [1] in the mesh of spiritual preaching, and the barbarians, already inclined to follow whenever they are convicted by your word, do not leave your tracks until you, a most successful fisher of souls, pull them out of the deep waters of error. 5. It may indeed be true that your colleagues must share in the credit for some of these things; but there is one glory which, with all your modesty, you must acknowledge to be due to you "by special title," as the lawyers say. When the crops had been consumed by fire you sent free supplies of corn through all the devastated Gallic lands at your private expense to relieve the public destitution, although you would have conferred an ample boon upon the starving population if that commodity had been offered for sale, not as a gift. We have seen the roads jammed with your grain-traffic, we have seen along the banks of the Saône and the Rhône many a barn which your hand alone had filled. 6. Now the inventions of pagan fable must yield pride of place, with their Triptolemus [2] supposedly consigned to Heaven, for discovering the unfamiliar corn-ear, for which reason his land of Greece, famous for its builders, painters, and statuaries, has hallowed him with temples, moulded him in statues, and depicted him in portraits. A doubtful tradition makes him a rover among the still

[2] In Greek mythology the inventor of agriculture. He was a chief object of cult in the Eleusinian mysteries (see note 4 on p. 282).

per rudes adhuc et Dodonigenas populos duabus vagum navibus, quibus poetae deinceps formam draconum deputaverunt, ignotam circumtulisse sementem. tu, ut de mediterranea taceam largitate, victum civitatibus Tyrrheni maris erogaturus granariis tuis duo potius flumina quam duo navigia complesti. 7. sed si forte Achaicis Eleusinae superstitionis exemplis tamquam non idoneis religiosus laudatus offenditur, seposita mystici intellectus reverentia venerabilis patriarchae Ioseph historialem diligentiam comparemus, qui contra sterilitatem septem uberes annos insecuturam facile providit remedium, quod praevidit. secundum tamen moralem sententiam nihil iudicio meo minor est qui in superveniente simili necessitate non divinat et subvenit. 8. quapropter, etsi ad integrum conicere non possum, quantas tibi gratias Arelatenses[1] Reienses,[2] Avenniocus Arausionensis quoque et Albensis, Valentinaeque nec non et Tricastinae urbis possessor exsolvat, quia difficile est eorum ex asse vota metiri, quibus noveris alimoniam sine asse col-

[1] Arelatensis *Luetjohann*. V. Additional Notes, p. 611.

[2] Reienses *Mohr*: Regensis *Luetjohann*: regensens *codd.* (regenses *F*).

---

[1] "Natives of Dodona" in Epirus at Dramisos where an oracle of Zeus was centred in an old sacred oak of the kind called Valonia oak (*Quercus aegilops*) bearing edible acorns.

[2] That part of the Mediterranean Sea which is west of Italy.

[3] See the end of § 5.

[4] Eleusis was a district of ancient Attica in Greece and was

barbarous and acorn-fed[1] people with two ships, to which the poets in course of time attributed the form of serpents, wherewith he circulated the unknown seed. You (never to speak of your generosity in your midland bishopric), in order to supply food from your granaries for the cities on the Tuscan Sea,[2] filled, not two ships, but rather two rivers.[3] 7. But it may be that a minister of religion finds it offensive to be praised by means of Greek analogies derived from the idolatry of Eleusis,[4] which he regards as inappropriate; therefore, leaving out of account the special sanctity of his mystic understanding,[5] I would fain bring into comparison the solicitude (considered as a historical fact) of the venerable patriarch Joseph, who because he had prevision easily made provision against the dearth that was to follow the seven years of plenty: and indeed after all, from the moral point of view, a man seems in my judgment no whit inferior who, without the power to foresee, comes to the rescue in just such an emergency. 8. Accordingly, although I can only partially guess the amount of grateful recognition paid to you by the people of Arles and Riez, your man of Avignon, Orange, Viviers, residents of the cities Valence and Trois-Châteaux,[6] because it is difficult to estimate to the last farthing the benedictions of those on whom (as one knows) sustenance has been lavished without a

the chief centre of worship of Demeter and Persephone and of the famous sacred "mysteries" celebrated in their honour.

[5] A reference to Joseph's power of interpreting dreams.—*A.*

[6] Saint-Paul-Trois-Châteaux, in Drome. So d'Anville. But it may be rightly sited at Aouste-en-Diois. Anderson put Troyes, which was Tricasses.

latam, Arverni tamen oppidi ego nomine uberes perquam gratias ago, cui ut succurrere meditarere, non te communio provinciae, non proximitas civitatis, non opportunitas fluvii, non oblatio pretii adduxit. 9. itaque ingentes per me referunt grates quibus obtigit per panis tui abundantiam ad sui sufficientiam pervenire. igitur si mandati officii munia satis videor implesse, ex legato nuntius ero. ilicet scias volo: per omnem fertur Aquitaniam gloria tua; amaris laudaris, desideraris excoleris, omnium pectoribus, omnium votis. inter haec temporum mala bonus sacerdos, bonus pater, bonus annus es quibus operae pretium fuit fieri famem suam periculo, si aliter esse non poterat tua largitas experimento. memor nostri esse dignare, domine papa.

---

[1] Clermont-Ferrand. In Latin *ex asse* means "to the whole amount," "wholly," but in the next clause of Sidonius *as* is the piece of money.

farthing to pay, in the name of the Arvernian capital[1] at least I offer you limitless thanks. In this case thought of succouring was not prompted by community of province, by nearness of city to city, by the convenience of a river, or by an offer of payments. 9. And so through my agency measureless thanks are conveyed to you by those who have had the good fortune, through an abundant supply of your bread, to gain a sufficient supply of their own. So if you think I have adequately discharged the mission entrusted to me I shall now become a news-bearer instead of an envoy. Be it known to you, then, that your glory is noised abroad through all Aquitania; you are loved and praised, and longed for and honoured in the hearts and prayers of all. In these bad times you are to them a good priest, a good father, a good harvest;[2] it was worth their while to be brought into peril of starvation, if in no other way they could have experience of your bountifulness. Deign to hold me in remembrance, my Lord Bishop.

[2] Lit. "a good year." Cf. *Ep.* III. 6. 3, where Sidonius says that a daily saying of provincials is that a good year should be judged so not because of its good harvest but because of its good officials.

LIBER SEPTIMVS

I

SIDONIVS DOMINO PAPAE MAMERTO SALVTEM

1. Rumor est Gothos in Romanum solum castra movisse: huic semper irruptioni nos miseri Arverni ianua sumus. namque odiis inimicorum hinc peculiaria fomenta subministramus, quia, quod necdum terminos suos ab Oceano in Rhodanum Ligeris alveo limitaverunt, solam sub ope Christi moram de nostra tantum obice patiuntur. circumiectarum vero spatia tractumque regionum iam pridem regni minacis importuna devoravit impressio. 2. sed animositati nostrae tam temerariae tamque periculosae non nos aut ambustam murorum faciem [1] aut putrem sudium cratem aut propugnacula vigilum trita pectoribus confidimus opitulatura; solo tantum [2] invectarum te auctore rogationum palpamur auxilio, quibus inchoandis instituendisque populus Arvernus,

[1] maceriem *Leo*.
[2] tantum *Mohr*: iam *Luetjohann*: tamen.

* Bishop of Vienna (Vienne). See *Ep.* IV. 11. 6; V. 14. 2. He was elder brother of Claudianus Mamertus, for whom see *Ep.* IV. 2 and 3; IV. 11. 1; V. 2. 1. The first eleven letters of this book are addressed to bishops. The present letter

BOOK VII

I

SIDONIUS TO THE LORD BISHOP MAMERTUS,* GREETING

1. There is a rumour that the Goths have moved their camp into Roman soil;[1] we luckless Arvernians are always the gateway to such incursions, for we kindle our enemies' hatred in a special degree; the reason is, that their failure so far to make the channel of the Loire[2] the boundary of their territories between the Atlantic and the Rhône is due, with Christ's help, solely to the barrier which we interpose. As for the surrounding country, its whole length and breadth has long since been swallowed up by the insatiate aggression of that threatening power. 2. But we have little confidence that our reckless and dangerous courage will be supported by our hideously charred walls, our palisades of rotting stakes, our battlements worn by the breasts of many a sentinel; our only comfort is in the aid of the Rogations[3] which we introduced on your advice. In the inception and establishment of these the Arvernian people, with a fervour equal to yours, though not with equal

alludes to incursions of the Visigoths in A.D. 471 and 472 and siege in 473.

[1] In A.D. 473 not only were Arles and Marseille taken by the Visigoths but also a general of Euric pushed his way into Italy.

[2] Cf. W. H. Semple, *Quaest. Exeg.*, 38.

[3] See *Ep.* V. 14. 1, note.

etsi non effectu pari, affectu certe non impari coepit initiari, et ob hoc circumfusis necdum dat terga terroribus. 3. non enim latet nostram sciscitationem, ⟨quod⟩ [1] primis temporibus harumce supplicationum institutarum civitas caelitus tibi credita per cuiusque modi [2] prodigiorum terriculamenta vacuabatur. name modo scaenae [3] moenium publicorum crebris terrae motibus concutiebantur; nunc ignes saepe [4] flammati caducas culminum cristas superiecto favillarum monte tumulabant; nunc stupenda foro cubilia collocabat audacium pavenda mansuetudo cervorum: cum tu inter ista discessu primorum populariumque statu urbis exinanito ad nova celer veterum Ninivitarum exempla decurristi, ne divinae admonitioni tua quoque desperatio conviciaretur. 4. et vere iam de deo tu minime poteras absque peccato post virtutum experimenta diffidere. nam cum vice quadam civitas conflagrare coepisset, fides tua in illo ardore plus caluit; et cum in conspectu pavidae plebis obiectu solo corporis tui ignis recussus in tergum fugitivis flexibus sinuaretur, miraculo terribili novo invisitato [5] affuit flammae cedere per reverentiam, cui sentire defuit per naturam. 5. igitur primum nostri ordinis viris et

[1] quod *add. Luetjohann.*

[2] cuiusque modi *Luetjohann*: cuiuseemodi *MFP*: huiuscemodi *C*. *Om. hanc ep. LNVRT.*

[3] pinnae *coni. Mommsen non bene.*

[4] sepe *codd.*: sulpure *Luetjohann*: saeve (*vix* sebo?) *coni. Warmington.*

[5] invisitato *Haupt*: inusitato.

efficacy, have started their initiation: and it is because of these rogations that they are not yet retreating from the terrors that encircle them. 3. Our enquiries have not failed to discover that at the time when these supplications were first instituted the city entrusted to you by heaven was being emptied of its people by alarms caused by all kinds of prodigies. At one time the public buildings would be shaken by a series of earthquakes; at another fires would be repeatedly kindled and bury falling roof-tops under an incumbent mountain of ashes; again, numbers of deer alarmingly bold in their tameness would spread consternation by making their lairs in the very market-place. When amid these terrors the city-strength was being depleted by the flight of citizens both high and low, you promptly resorted to a new version of the historic procedure at Nineveh,[1] that you at least might not bring reproach on the divine warning by giving way to despair. 4. And in truth you of all men could not, without sinning, have distrusted God after the experience you had had of his mighty works:[2] for on one occasion, when a blaze had started in the city, your faith burned stronger amid the conflagration; in full view of the panic-stricken populace the mere interposition of your body beat off the fire, causing it to curl backward in retreating curves, and so, by a startling miracle never known or seen before, the flame which by nature was devoid of any understanding was from awe of you given power to recede. 5. So first of all for members of our order,

[1] Jonah, III. 5 ff.

[2] Is *virtutes* used technically of divine power or blessings? See Semple, *Quaest. Exeg.* 39.—*A*.

his paucis indicis ieiunia interdicis flagitia, supplicia praedicis remedia promittis; exponis omnibus nec poenam longinquam esse nec veniam; doces denuntiatae solitudinis minas orationum frequentia esse amoliendas; mones assiduitatem furentis incendii aqua potius oculorum quam fluminum posse restingui; mones minacem terrae motuum conflictationem fidei stabilitate firmandam. 6. cuius confestim sequax humilis turba consilii maioribus quoque suis fuit incitamento, quos cum non piguisset fugere, redire non puduit. qua devotione placatus inspector pectorum deus fecit esse obsecrationem vestram vobis saluti, ceteris imitationi, utrisque praesidio. denique illic deinceps non fuere vel damna calamitati vel ostenta formidini. quae omnia sciens populus iste Viennensibus tuis et accidisse prius et non accessisse posterius vestigia tam sacrosanctae informationis amplectitur, sedulo petens, ut conscientiae tuae beatitudo mittat orationum suarum suffragia quibus exempla transmisit. 7. et quia tibi soli concessa est, post avorum memoriam vel confessorem Ambrosium duorum martyrum repertorem, in partibus orbis occidui martyris

---

[1] Or "men of our order and they were but few" (the others having fled).—*A*.

[2] "an example for imitation to all the rest" (apart from the citizens of Vienne).

[3] *conscientiae tuae beatitudo*: hard to translate; abstract noun with genitive attached in the sense of a personal noun with an adjective, as often in Sidonius (also an allusion to the title *beatitudo vestra* or *tua*). For the Rogations, see above, § 2.

few indeed in number,[1] you proclaimed fasts, proscribed sins, prescribed supplications, and promised remedies; you declared to all that neither punishment nor forgiveness was far off; you taught them that the menace of the threatened destruction was to be averted by frequency of prayer; you warned them that the incessant raging of fire could be quenched rather by the water of tears than by the water of rivers, and that the appalling shock of earthquakes could be arrested by firmness of faith. 6. The instant readiness of the humbler people to follow this advice spurred on their superiors likewise, who, although they had not scrupled to run away, were not ashamed to return. Appeased by this piety, God, who searches the heart, caused your supplication to be a deliverance to you, an example to all others,[2] and a protection to both. So thenceforth losses were no calamity and portents no terror in that city. This people of Clermont, knowing that these calamities all came upon your people of Vienne before your intervention and have not come near them since, eagerly follow the lead of your hallowed instruction, diligently entreating that one so blessedly supreme in spirituality may grant the support of his prayers to those to whom he has now sent copies of the Rogations.[3] 7. Moreover, you have been granted a privilege unique in the western world within the memory of our grandfathers, or in other words, since the time of the Confessor Ambrose,[4] discoverer [5]

[4] The Saint, c. A.D. 337–397. Not the Ambrosius of IX. 6.

[5] Saint Ambrose discovered the remains of Saint Gervasius and Saint Protasius. Dalton, Vol. II, 241–242.

Ferreoli solida translatio adiecto nostri capite Iuliani, quod istinc turbulento quondam persecutori manus rettulit cruenta carnificis, non iniurium est, quod pro compensatione deposcimus, ut nobis inde veniat pars patrocinii, quia vobis hinc rediit pars patroni. memor nostri esse dignare, domine papa.

II

SIDONIVS DOMINO PAPAE GRAECO SALVTEM

1. Oneras, consummatissime pontificum, verecundiam meam, multifaria laude cumulando si quid stilo rusticante peraravero. atque utinam reatu careat, quod apicum primore congressu quamquam circumscriptus veritati resultantia tamen et diversa conexui; ignorantiae siquidem meae callidus viator imposuit. nam dum solum mercatoris praetendit officium, litteras meas ad formatae vicem, scilicet ut lector, elicuit, sed quas aliquam gratiarum actionem continere decuisset. namque, ut post comperi, plus

[1] This martyr (not Tonantius Ferreolus of *Ep.* VII. 12; I. 7. 4; II. 9. 1 nor his son of *Ep.* IX. 13 and 15) is not otherwise known. There was a shrine of Saint Julianus in Auvergne at Brivas (Brioude on the Allier)—Gregory of Tours, *Hist. Franc.* II. 11. Not the bishop Julianus of *Ep.* IX. 5.

* Bishop of Marseille. See *Ep.* VI. 8; VII. 7 and 10(11); IX. 4; VII. 6. 10.

[2] Notice the word-play, although *perarare,* "plough

of two martyrs: for you have translated the complete body of Ferreolus [1] together with the head of our Julianus, which in bygone days the bloody hand of the executioner brought away to the brutal persecutor. So what we claim as compensation is not unfair—that a portion of patronage should come to us from Vienne, seeing that a portion of our patron saint has returned from here to you. Deign to hold me in remembrance, my Lord Bishop.

II

SIDONIUS TO THE LORD BISHOP GRAECUS,* GREETING

1. Most consummate of pontiffs, you overwhelm my modesty with a load of manifold praise every time that I scribble anything with my clownish pen.[2] I only wish I could establish my innocence in one matter: it is true that I had been taken in by false pretences, but the fact remains that the first time I corresponded with you I spun [3] a tale utterly at variance with the truth. A wily traveller [4] imposed upon my ignorance; ostensibly a mere trader, he succeeded, on the plea of being a Reader, in extracting from me a letter in the canonical form,[5] a letter, however, which ought properly to have contained some expression of thanks. For, as I afterwards

through," in itself may be used for "to write" without ulterior meaning.—*A.*

[3] *conexui* perhaps "appended." See *Ep.* VI. 8. 2 *init.*, which seems to show that this is so.—*A.*

[4] Amantius who often carried letters between Sidonius and Graecus—*Ep.* VII. 7. 1; IX. 4; VI. 8.

[5] See above, p. 270, n. 2.

Massiliensium benignitate provectus est,[1] quam status sui seu per censum seu per familiam forma pateretur. 2. quae tamen ut gesta sunt si quispiam dignus relator evolveret, fierent iucunda memoratu. sed quoniam iubetis ipsi,[2] ut aliquid vobis a me laetum copiosumque pagina ferat, date veniam, si hanc ipsam tabellarii nostri hospitalitatem comicis salibus comparandam salva vestrarum aurium severitate perstringamus, ne secundo insinuatum non [3] nunc primum nosse videamur. simul et, si moris est regularum [4] ut ex materia omni usurpentur principia dicendi, cur hic quoque quodcumque mihi sermocinaturo materia longius quaeratur expetaturque, nisi ut sermoni nostro sit ipse pro causa, cui erit noster sermo pro sarcina? 3. Arverni huic patria; parentes natalibus non superbis sed absolutis, et sicut nihil illustre iactantes, ita nihil servile metuentes, contenti censu modico sed eodem vel sufficiente vel libero; militia illis in clericali potius quam in Palatino decursa comitatu. pater istius granditer

[1] provectus est (*vel* profecit) *coni. Mohr*: profectus est.
[2] ipsi *Luetjohann*: ipse.
[3] non *CFP*: ñ** *M*[1]: nos *Leo*: *om. hanc Ep. LNVRT*.
[4] rabularum *coni. Semple*: regularumque *Warmington*: cf. *Ep.* II. 9. 5 *in usum regulamque*: saecularium *coni. Mohr.*

---

[1] Anderson accepts the reading *provectus est* (Mohr, *praef.*, xxxii).

[2] More literally " my object is not to appear as if this is not the first time that I really know."

[3] Does it refer to illustrations in grammar taken from various sources, " the established rules "? But see Semple *Quaest. Exeg.* 40 on this passage, though I don't like his emendation *rabularum*. I am not sure what *principia dicendi* means here.—*A*. I think it means " that they may reserve liberty to draw the opening paragraphs of their composition

discovered, the kindness of the people of Massilia advanced [1] him further than could be justified by his standing in respect of wealth or of birth. 2. If the real story of these doings were unfolded by a worthy narrator it would make a pleasant tale; but as you yourself demand that my letter should bring you something both cheerful and lengthy, forgive me if, with all respect to your grave ears, I sketch this same reception accorded to our mail-carrier, a reception which will bear comparison with the jests of comedy. I hope thus to convince you that I do not want to look as if introducing a man for the second time and not now knowing him for the first.[2] Besides, if the established rules [3] allow a composition to start from any sort of material, why in the preparation of a casual screed should I go out of my way in seeking and searching for material instead of making the subject of my screed Amantius himself, whose luggage will be this screed of mine? 3. He is a native of Auvergne; his parents' origin, though not imposing, is irreproachable: boasting no grandeur and fearing no servile degradation, they are content with a modest fortune—modest but adequate and unencumbered.[4] Their public office has been in the service of the Church rather than of the State.[5] His father is immensely frugal and niggardly towards his

from the world at large", and if such liberty is accorded to writers and speakers in general, if they may go anywhere for their beginning, why may I not take the adventure of my letter-carrier Amantius for my subject in this epistle?—*W.H.S.*

[4] *libero*: the word might mean "more than sufficient," "comfortable," "ample," "abundant."—*A.*

[5] Palatine = imperial civil service. See note on *Ep.* IV. 24. 1. For *militia* see p. 44.

frugi et liberis parum liberalis quique per nimiam parsimoniam iuveni filio plus prodesse quam placere maluerit. quo relicto tunc puer iste vos petiit nimis expeditus, quod erat maximum conatibus primis impedimentum; nihil est enim viatico levi gravius. 4. attamen primus illi in vestra moenia satis secundus introitus. sancti Eustachii, qui vobis decessit, actutum dicto factoque gemina benedictio; hospitium brevi quaesitum, iam Eustachii cura facile inventum, celeriter aditum, civiliter locatum. iam primum crebro occursu [1] excolere vicinos, identidem ab his ipse haud aspernanter resalutari. agere cum singulis, prout aetatis ratio permitteret: grandaevos obsequiis, aequaevos officiis obligare. 5. pudicitiam prae ceteris sobrietatemque sectari, quod tam laudandum in iuventute quam rarum. summatibus deinceps et tunc comiti civitatis non minus opportunis quam frequentibus excubiis agnosci innotescere familiarescere, sicque eius in dies sedulitas maiorum sodalitatibus promoveri; fovere boni quique certatim, votis omnes plurimi consiliis, privati donis cincti [2] beneficiis adiuvare; perque haec spes opesque istius raptim saltuatimque cumulari. 6. forte accidit, ut deversorio, cui ipse

[1] occursu *Mohr*: accursu.
[2] cuncti *CFPM*[2].

---

[1] Word-play again—*primus* . . . *satis secundus*.
[2] As Bishop of Marseille.

children, and as his son grew up by excess of parsimony he chose to give him more profit than pleasure. Thereupon the son had left his father and had betaken himself to your town. He carried small equipment—a great burden to his first efforts, for there is no heavier handicap than a light scrip. 4. Nevertheless, good luck seconded his first entry into your city.[1] At the outset he received the double blessing of your predecessor [2] Saint Eustachius in word and deed; a lodging was soon sought and then through the efforts of Eustachius easily found; he speedily presented himself and it was courteously let to him. Now he began to pay attentions to his neighbours in frequent visits,[3] and his greetings were constantly returned in the most affable way. His converse with individuals was regulated by a consideration of their years; he attached the older generation to him by marks of respect, his own generation by personal services. He was conspicuously devoted to chastity and sobriety; this in early manhood is as laudable as it is rare. By watchfulness as well timed as it was frequent, he came to be recognised, then known, then admitted to intimacy by the magnates one after another and then by the Count of the city, and so his assiduity gained him promotion to higher and higher circles every day: the best people vied in cherishing him; all supported him with their good wishes, many by their counsels, private persons by their gifts, officials by their favours; and thus his hopes and his resources increased by leaps and bounds. 6. It chanced that near the lodging where he had taken up

[3] *occursu* Mohr for *accursu* of the MSS. Probably right. It (and *resalutari*) seem to refer to actual visits.—*A*.

successerat, quaedam femina non minus censu quam moribus idonea vicinaretur, cuius filia infantiae iam temporibus emensis necdum tamen nubilibus annis appropinquabat. huic hic blandus (siquidem ea aetas infantulae, ut adhuc decenter) nunc quaedam frivola, nunc ludo apta virgineo scruta donabat; quibus isti parum grandibus causis plurimum virgunculae animus copulabatur. 7. anni obiter thalamo pares: quid morer multis? adulescens, solus tenuis peregrinus, filius familias et e patria patre non solum non volente verum et ignorante discedens, puellam non inferiorem natalibus, facultatibus superiorem, medio episcopo, quia lector, solacio comitis, quia cliens, socru non inspiciente substantiam, sponsa non despiciente personam, uxorem petit, impetrat, ducit. conscribuntur tabulae nuptiales; et si qua est istic municipioli nostri suburbanitas, matrimonialibus illic inserta documentis mimica largitate recitatur. 8. peracta circumscriptione legitima et fraude sollemni levat divitem coniugem pauper adamatus et diligenter quae ad socerum[1] pertinuerant rimatis convasatisque, non parvo etiam corollario facilitatem credulitatemque munificentiae socrualis[2] emungens receptui in patriam cecinit praestigiator invictus. quo profecto mater puellae pro hyperbolicis instrumentis coepit actionem

[1] socrum *C*. [2] socralis *MP*.

---

[1] *filius familias*: cf. *Ep.* VII. 9. 21.
[2] *comes* and *cliens*; the count is *patronus*.

residence there lived a certain lady as attractive in character as in income, whose daughter though past childhood was still a good way short of the marriageable age. He used to pet the child (her tender years still allowed this to be done without impropriety), and he would give her from time to time some trifles or some frippery suitable for a girl's amusement: and for these slender reasons her girlish heart became strongly attached to him. 7. Time passed, and the marriageable age arrived. Not to make a long story of it, this young man, alone and of modest resources, a stranger, a minor [1] who left his native place not only without the consent but without the knowledge of his father, sought, won, and married a girl of not inferior birth and of superior fortune, with the mediation of the bishop, because he was a Reader, and the sympathy of the Count, because he was a client; [2] for the mother did not look into his means any more than the girl looked down upon his person. The marriage settlements are written out, and any and every estate in the vicinity of our little town here was entered in the matrimonial documents and read out with theatrical grandeur. 8. When this legal chicanery and solemn fraud had been completed the penniless inamorato carries off his rich wife; and having carefully investigated and collected the property which had belonged to his father-in-law, and taking advantage of his generous mother-in-law's good nature and credulity to extract a considerable bounty into the bargain, then, and only then, did this swindler beat a retreat to his native soil undefeated. After his departure the girl's mother was minded, in view of this grossly fabricated agreement, to institute an action

repetundarum velle proponere et tunc demum de mancipiorum sponsaliciae donationis paucitate maerere, quando iam de nepotum numerositate gaudebat. ad hanc placandam noster Hippolytus perrexerat, cum litteras meas prius obtulit. 9. habetis historiam iuvenis eximii, fabulam [1] Miletiae [2] vel Atticae parem. simul et ignoscite praeter aequum epistularem formulam porrigenti, quam ob hoc stilo morante produxi, ut non tamquam ignotum reciperetis quem civem beneficiis reddidistis. pariter et natura comparatum est, ut quibus impendimus studium praestemus affectum. vos vero Eustachium pontificem tunc ex asse digno herede [3] decessisse monstrabitis, si ut propinquis testamenti, sic clientibus patrocinii legata solvatis. 10. ecce parui et oboedientis officium garrulitate complevi, licet qui indocto negotium prolixitatis iniungit, aegre ferre

[1] fabulae *malit Luetjohann.*

[2] Miletiae *Mommsen*: Milesiae *Savaron*: militie *F*: miliciȩ *MCP.*

[3] heredi *coni. Anderson.*

---

[1] The man who resisted the sexual love of his step-mother in Euripides' famous play *Hippolytus*. Cf. Semple, *Quaest. Exeg.* 41.

[2] Hippolytus (see the preceding note) was renowned in Greek mythology and as a character in Athenian (Attic) tragedy. The much later *Milesian Tales* of Aristeides of Miletus, *c.* 100 B.C., translated into Latin by Cornelius Sisenna, is a lost work noted for its erotic character. Indeed, " Milesiae (Fabulae) " at Rome became a title for erotic tales in general.

for restitution; but it was late to begin grieving over the meagreness of the bridegroom's contribution of assets when she was rejoicing at the now increasing number of her grandchildren. It was to appease the old lady that our Hippolytus [1] had made his journey on the occasion when he presented my former letter. 9. So here you have the story of this splendid young man, a tale fit to match any that Miletus or Athens [2] has produced. At the same time you must pardon me for exceeding the recognised bounds of a letter, which I have made long by letting my dawdling pen wander on to ensure that you should not receive as a stranger a man whom you have made a fellow-townsman by your kindnesses; moreover, nature has so ordered it that we bestow our affection on those in whom we take an active interest. You on your part will show that Bishop Eustachius has left to fill his place an entirely worthy heir [3] if you pay to his dependants their legacy of patronage just as you pay to his relatives the bequests in his will. 10. You see, I have done as you ordered, discharging my duty of obedience by my garrulity: I must add, however, that a man who imposes on a mere amateur the obligation of prolixity has no right to be annoyed if

[3] I incline to read *heredi*; cf. § 4 *qui vobis decessit*. I wonder if *ex asse* means simply "entirely" here. I don't think so.—*A*. Anderson was inclined to take *ex asse* with *herede* or *heredi* and in the sense of "in whole," "entirely." If a man was heir to all of another's property, he was *heres ex asse*. But Graecus was not *heres ex asse*—he was executor and paid legacies to others. It appears then that Sidonius means Graecus will be an heir wholly worthy even if he is not heir in whole. The expression *ex asse* with an epithet occurs elsewhere in Sidonius.

non debeat, si non tam eloquentes epistulas recipit quam loquaces. memor nostri esse dignare, domine papa.

III

SIDONIVS DOMINO PAPAE MEGETHIO SALVTEM

1. Diu multumque deliberavi, quamquam mihi animus affectu[1] studioque[2] parendi sollicitaretur,[3] an destinarem, sicuti iniungis, contestatiunculas, quas ipse dictavi. vicit ad ultimum sententia, quae tibi obsequendum definiebat. igitur petita transmisi: et quid modo dicemus? grandisne haec oboedientia? puto, grandis est; grandior impudentia tamen. hac enim fronte possemus fluminibus aquas, silvis ligna transmittere; hac [enim][4] temeritate Apellen peniculo, caelo Phidian,[5] malleo Polyclitum muneraremur.[6] 2. dabis ergo veniam praesumptioni, papa sancte facunde venerabilis, quae

[1] animus affectu *Luetjohann*: animi affectus *coni. Mohr*: animo affectus. *Om. hanc ep. LNVRT.*

[2] studio quoque *coni. Mohr.*

[3] sollicitarentur *P.*

[4] enim *seclud. Luetjohann*: igitur *C.*

[5] fidian *MCFP. Om. hanc. ep. LNRT.*

[6] venneraremur *CP*: emularemur *F.*

---

[1] Anderson's final note on this letter is: "This whole letter requires revision, etc., especially the second half." We have to

he receives a letter which is loquacious rather than eloquent. Deign to hold me in remembrance, my Lord Bishop.[1]

III

SIDONIUS TO THE LORD BISHOP MEGETHIUS,* GREETING

Although my mind was urged on by affection and by eagerness to comply with your wish, I considered long and seriously whether I ought to obey your injunction and send you the little discourses[2] I have composed. In the end the view that your wish must be respected prevailed, so I have sent them as you requested. Well, what shall we say now? Is this a fine example of obedience? I suppose so, but it is a still finer example of shamelessness. With effrontery of this sort one might send water to the rivers or timber to the forest; with rashness of this sort one might present Apelles with a brush, Phidias with a chisel, or Polyclitus with a mallet.[3] 2. So, holy eloquent and venerable bishop, you must forgive my presumption

some extent acted on the hint in reviewing Anderson's translation.

* This Megethius (who is not the Megethius of *Ep.* VIII. 14. 8) is not otherwise known.

[2] *Contestationes* were prefaces for the Mass. But here according to Grégoire and Collombet they may be actual Masses composed by Sidonius.

[3] Apelles the most famous of Greek painters, living in the later half of the fourth century B.C.; Phidias the great Greek sculptor of the fifth century B.C.; and his famous contemporary Polyclitus the elder, also a famous sculptor.

doctissimo examini tuo naturali garrulitate deblaterat. habet consuetudo nostra pro ritu, ut etsi pauca edit, multa conscribat, veluti est canibus innatum, ut, etsi non latrant, tamen hirriant. memor nostri esse dignare, domine papa.

IV

SIDONIVS DOMINO PAPAE FONTEIO SALVTEM

1. Insinuare quoscumque iam paveo, quia commendatis nos damus verba, vos munera; tamquam non principalitas sit censenda beneficii, quod a me peccatore digressis sanctae communionis portio patet. testis horum est Vindicius noster, qui segnius domum pro munificentiae vestrae fasce remeavit, quoquo loco est, constanter affirmans, cum sitis opinione magni, gradu maximi, non tamen esse vos amplius dignitate quam dignatione laudandos. 2. praedicat melleas sanctas et floridas, quae procedunt de temperata communione, blanditias; nec tamen ex hoc quicquam pontificali deperire personae, quod sacerdotii fastigium non frangitis comitate, sed flectitis. quibus agnitis sic inardesco, ut tum me sim felicissimum iudicaturus, cum mihi coram posito sub divina ope contigerit tam securum de deo suo pectus licet praesumptiosis, artis tamen fovere

---

* Bishop of Vaison. Cf. *Ep.* VI. 7.

[1] See *Ep.* V. 1. 2.

in submitting to your expert judgment the babbling utterance of an inborn garrulity. It is a custom religiously observed by me to write much but publish little, just as it is an inborn habit with dogs to growl even if they do not bark. Deign to hold me in remembrance, my Lord Bishop.

IV

SIDONIUS TO THE LORD BISHOP FONTEIUS,* GREETING

I am now afraid of introducing people to you, because to any I commend to you I give mere words but you give them gifts—as if it were not to be thought a supreme kindness that to those who depart from me a sinner a share in the converse of a saint is freely offered. This is attested by the case of our friend Vindicius,[1] who returned home the more slowly because of the load of your bounty, and who, wherever he may be, resolutely affirms that, great as you are in reputation and very great in rank, you are as much to be praised for your condescension as for your lofty position. 2. He lauds the gracious words, so sweet, so holy, so elegant, that flow from your well-regulated geniality; and he adds that, with all this, you do not suffer any loss of pontifical consequence, for by your affability you do not break your priestly eminence—you unbend it. And now, having learnt all this, I am so fired with eagerness that I shall deem myself at the height of felicity when, with God's help, I come into your presence and am privileged to clasp in a close, albeit presumptuous, embrace a breast

complexibus. 3. accipite confitentem: suspicio quidem nimis severos et imbecillitatis meae conscius aequanimiter fero asperos mihi; sed, quod fatendum est, hisce moribus facilius humilitate submittimur quam familiaritate sociamur.[1] in summa, viderit, qua conscientiae dote turgescat, qui se ambientibus rigidum reddit; ego tamen morum illius aemulator esse praeelegerim,[2] qui etiam longe positorum incitare in se affectat affectum. 4. illud quoque mihi inter maxima granditer cordi est, quod apostolatus vestri patrocinium copiosum verissimis dominis animae meae, Simplicio et Apollinari, intermina intercessione conferre vos comperi. si verum est, rogo, ut non habeat vestra caritas finem; si falsum est, peto, ut non differat habere principium. praeterea commendo gerulum litterarum, cui istic, id est in Vasionensi oppido,[3] quiddam necessitatis exortum sanari vestrae auctoritatis reverentiaeque [4] pondere potest. memor nostri esse dignare, domine papa.

[1] sociamur (e *suprascr.*) M^1: sotiemur *F*: sociamur *CP*: *om. hanc epist.* *LNVRT*.
[2] praeelegerim *vulgo*: plegerim, *i.e.* perlegerim.
[3] id . . . oppido *fortasse secludenda.*
[4] reverentiaeque *Luetjohann*: reverendae *coni.* *Mohr*: reverentiae.

---

[1] See *Ep.* IV. 4, first note.

that is so wholly at peace with its God. 3. Hear a confession: I do indeed respect excessively strict persons and, conscious as I am of my own weakness, I feel no resentment at all when they are severe with me: still, I must admit that I am more ready to bow in humility before such characters than be linked with them in intimacy. In short, the man who shows himself stern to his near associates must judge how far his superior attitude is justified by the merits of his inner life: for myself, I should prefer to imitate the character of one who aspires to win the affection even of those in distant places. 4. Another item in the tale of your great merits gives me the greatest satisfaction; I have heard that through your constant intercession you bestow in abundance the blessing of your apostolic protection upon those two veritable possessors of my heart, both Simplicius and Apollinaris.[1] If this is true, I beseech you that your benevolence may never have an end: if it is not true, I beg that it lose no time in making a beginning. Further, I commend to you the bearer of this letter; a bit of trouble has arisen for him over there [2]—in your town of Vaison, I mean; it can be set right by the weight of your influence and sanctity. Deign to hold me in remembrance, my Lord Bishop.

[2] Mohr suggests that *in Vasoniensi oppido* is a gloss, as the man to whom the letter is addressed would not need to be told that *istic* means "at Vaison." But Sidonius, like his contemporaries, constantly uses *istic* in the sense of "here." In the present passage it is used in its classical sense "where you are"; so Sidonius guards against a serious misunderstanding by adding *in Vasoniensi oppido*.—*A*.

V

SIDONIVS DOMINO PAPAE AGROECIO SALVTEM

1. Biturigas decreto civium petitus adveni: causa fuit evocationis titubans ecclesiae status, quae nuper summo viduata pontifice utriusque professionis ordinibus ambiendi sacerdotii quoddam classicum cecinit. fremit populus per studia divisus; pauci alteros, multi sese non offerunt solum sed inferunt. si aliquid pro virili portione secundum deum consulas veritatemque, omnia occurrunt levia varia fucata, et (quid dicam?) sola est illic simplex impudentia. 2. et nisi me immerito queri iudicaretis, dicere auderem tam praecipitis animi esse plerosque tamque periculosi, ut sacrosanctam sedem dignitatemque affectare pretio oblato non reformident, remque iam dudum in nundinam mitti auctionemque potuisse, si quam paratus invenitur emptor, venditor tam desperatus inveniretur. proin quaeso, ut officii mei novitatem pudorem necessitatem exspecta-

---

* See also *Ep.* VII. 9. 6. He was Bishop of Sens. Sidonius went to Bourges apparently in A.D. 470. Cf. also Stevens, 127–129. Not the Agroecius of *Ep.* V. 10. 3.

[1] This probably means "clerical and lay," as would appear from *Ep.* VII. 9. 14 and 16.

[2] I think *sacerdotium* here refers to the office of bishop, not to "the office of the priest"—which latter would imply that

V

SIDONIUS TO THE LORD BISHOP AGROECIUS,* GREETING

1. I have arrived at Bourges, being called upon by a decree of the people: the reason for their appeal was the tottering condition of the church, which having recently lost its supreme pontiff, has, so to speak, sounded a bugle-note to the ranks of both professions [1] to begin canvassing for the sacred office.[2] The population, split into different factions, buzzes with excited talk; candidates are being put forward, or say rather thrust forward, in a few cases by others, in many cases by themselves. If one forms any judgment, following, as far as man can, the way of God and of truth, one is met with nothing but frivolous, inconsistent, and specious pleas, and in fact—how shall I put it?—there is no simplicity there but simple shamelessness. 2. Indeed, were it not that you would think my complaint unfounded, I should dare to say that a great many of them are in such a reckless and dangerous temper that they would not shrink from offering bribes to secure the sacred see and the position that goes with it, and the prize might before now have been put up for auction in the open market if there had existed as conscienceless a seller as there does exist a willing buyer. So I beg that your longed-for arrival may arm [3] me with your companionship and sustain me with your help

there was a scramble among lay candidates to be ordained! —*A*.

[3] Or: "enrich," "honour," "equip."—*A*.

tissimi[1] adventus tui ornes contubernio, tuteris auxilio. 3. nec te, quamquam Senoniae caput es, inter haec dubia subtraxeris intentionibus medendis Aquitanorum, quia minimum refert, quod nobis est in habitatione divisa provincia, quando in religione causa coniungitur. his accedit, quod de urbibus Aquitanicae primae solum oppidum Arvernum Romanorum[2] reliquum partibus bella fecerunt. quapropter in constituendo praefatae civitatis antistite provincialium collegarum deficimur numero, nisi metropolitanorum reficiamur assensu. 4. de cetero quod ad honoris vestri spectat praerogativam, nullus a me hactenus nominatus, nullus adhibitus, nullus electus est; omnia censurae tuae salva inlibata solida servantur. tantum hoc meum duco, vestras invitare personas expectare voluntates laudare sententias,

[1] exspectatissimi *Luetjohann*: spectatissimi.
[2] romanis *MCFPR*.

---

[1] So called, after Aquitanica was divided, because this part contained the capital Bourges (Avaricum, later Biturigae). Its Bishop was the metropolitan of Aquitanica Prima and primate of the two Aquitanicas.

[2] Clermont-Ferrand (Augustonemetum). One gathers from this passage that Clermont was the only town in Aquitanica Prima not occupied by the Goths. If so, then Bourges was so occupied. [The other sees were those at Albigenses (Albi), Cadurci (Cahors), Gabali (Javols), Lemovices (Limoges), Ruteni (Rouergue), Vellavi (St. Paulien).—*E.H.W.*] Why were not the other Bishops of Aquitaine free to come to the election if Bourges was allowed to proceed with its election? Doubtless this was owing to the policy of Euric, the Gothic king. As for the last words of § 4, it is obvious that, if a sufficient number of other bishops of the same province was not

in this duty of mine, in which, as a novice, I am diffident and embarrassed. 3. And although you are the ruler of Senonia, do not in this unquiet situation refrain from setting right the purposes of the Aquitanians, for it matters little that our province is geographically separated from yours, since in the sphere of religion our cause is united. Moreover, of all the cities of Aquitanica Prima[1] the wars have left only the capital[2] of the Arverni on the side of the Romans; hence in appointing a prelate for the aforementioned country, we are weak in the number of provincial colleagues unless we are confirmed by the consent of the metropolitans. 4. It only remains to say, in respect of the precedence belonging to your rank, that so far no one has been nominated, summoned, or elected by me; everything is being reserved—untouched, unimpaired, and entire—for your judgment. The only part I claim for myself is to invite your personal attendance, to await your will, to applaud your decision, and, when anyone[3]

available for the purposes of an election, others might be invited from neighbouring provinces. Agroecius, to whom this letter is addressed, was actually metropolitan of Senonia (Lugdunensis IV), but we must not infer from Sidonius that the deficiency in local bishops had to be made up by metropolitans from outside. I scarcely think that *vestras personas* of § 4 is a real plural: it is rather a grandiose reference to Agroecius alone. Or does *metropolitanorum assensu* at the end of § 3 imply that provincial bishops must get the permission of their metropolitan to visit another province or take part in an election there? It goes without saying that the repressive measures taken by Euric in the case of some dioceses were not taken in Bourges.—*A*. See note on § 6 of the next letter.

[3] *quisque* = *quisquis* = *quicumque* = *quilibet*?—*A*. Yes.

et[1] cum in locum statumque pontificis quisque sufficitur, ut a vobis praeceptum, a me procedat obsequium. 5. sed si, quod tamen arbitror minime fore, precibus meis apud vos malesuadus obstiterit interpres, poteritis praesentiam vestram potius excusare quam culpam; sicut e diverso, si venitis, ostenditis, quia terminus potuerit poni vestrae quidem regioni, sed non potuerit caritati. memor nostri esse dignare, domine papa.

VI

SIDONIVS DOMINO PAPAE BASILIO SALVTEM

1. Sunt nobis munere dei novo nostrorum temporum exemplo amicitiarum vetera iura, diuque est quod invicem diligimus ex aequo. porro autem, quod ad communem conscientiam pertinet, tu patronus: quamquam hoc ipsum praesumptiose arroganterque loquar;[2] namque iniquitas mea tanta est, ut mederi de lapsuum eius assiduitate vix etiam tuae supplicationis efficacia queat. 2. igitur,

[1] et *seclud. Wilamowitz.*
[2] loquar arroganterque *M*: *om. hanc epist. LNVRTP.*

---

* Not Caecina Basilius of *Ep.* I. 9. 2, but the Bishop of Aix, who was one of the four bishops appointed by the Emperor Iulius Nepos to negotiate with Euric. See § 10 below and

is being elected into the position and standing of a bishop, to see to it that the instructions come from you and obedience from me. 5. But if it should happen (although I do not in the least believe it will) that some evil counsellor's false representations to you should thwart my entreaties, then you will find it easier to offer excuses for not coming than to escape blame for defaulting, just as, conversely, if you do come, you thereby show that limits may have been set to your sphere of jurisdiction, but none to your charity. Deign to hold me in remembrance, my Lord Bishop.

VI

SIDONIUS TO THE LORD BISHOP BASILIUS,* GREETING

1. By the bounty of God we enjoy the privileges of a long-standing friendship in a manner new to these times; yes, for many a year we have loved one another on terms of equality. But, as far as concerns our inner spiritual life, the relationship is different: here you are the patron and I the client—though it would be presumptuous and arrogant to say even this, for my iniquity is so great that even the potency of your supplications can scarcely cure it, owing to its constant relapses.[1] 2. So, because your position as

Gregory of Tours, *Hist. Franc.* II. 25, who refers to this letter.

[1] I think *de* is causal here; at least I do not know any other instance of *mederi de* "to cure of," "to heal of," "to recover (a patient) from."—*A.*

quia mihi es tam patrocinio quam dilectione bis dominus, pariter et quod memini probe, quo polleas igne sensuum, fonte verborum, qui viderim Modaharium, civem Gothum, haereseos Arianae iacula vibrantem quo tu spiritualium testimoniorum mucrone confoderis, servata ceterorum tam reverentia quam pace pontificum non iniuria tibi defleo, qualiter ecclesiasticas caulas istius aetatis [1] lupus, qui peccatis pereuntium saginatur animarum, clandestino morsu necdum intellecti dentis arrodat. 3. namque hostis antiquus, quo facilius insultet balatibus ovium destitutarum, dormitantum prius incipit cervicibus imminere pastorum. neque ego ita mei meminens non sum, ut nequaquam me hunc esse reminiscar, quem longis adhuc abluenda fletibus conscientia premat; cuius stercora tamen sub ope Christi quandoque mysticis orationum tuarum rastris euderabuntur. sed quoniam supereminet privati reatus verecundiam publica salus, non verebor, etsi carpat zelum in me fidei sinister interpres, sub vanitatis invidia causam prodere veritatis. 4. Evarix, rex Gothorum, quod limitem regni sui rupto dissolutoque foedere antiquo vel tutatur armorum iure vel pro-

[1] aetatis *coni. Mohr*: haereseos *Wilamowitz*: aevi is *aut* aevi *aut* aedis *coni. Warmington*: aeris (ae^ta^tis M^1). Cf. Additional Notes, p. 612.

---

[1] A Visigoth otherwise unknown.

[2] "Some perverse impugner of my good faith"; or "some perverse interpreter of the faith," where perverse = Arian. —*A*. Or: "zeal for the faith by some malign critic."

patron and as friend makes you doubly my master, and also because I remember well the power of your glowing thoughts and flowing words (for I saw how, when Modaharius [1] the Goth launched his darts of Arian heresy, you transfixed him with the sword of spiritual testimony)—for these reasons, without offence or slight to the other bishops, I feel justified in sadly reporting to you how the wolf that battens on the sins of perishing souls is preying on the sheep-folds of the church in this age, biting by stealth and as yet unnoticed. 3. For the old Enemy, in order the more easily to pounce upon the bleating undefended sheep, is first threatening the necks of the sleeping shepherds. I am not indeed so forgetful of myself as not to remember that I am a man oppressed by a guilty conscience that still requires long weeping to make it clean (though I hope that, with Christ's help, the dung of my soul will some day be cleared away by the mystic rake of your prayers); nevertheless, as the public welfare must override the shameful sense of one's personal guilt, I will disregard any aspersions cast upon my zeal by some malign critic of my good faith,[2] and under the evil eye of vanity I shall not fear to proclaim the cause of truth.[3] 4. Euric, King of the Goths,[4] having broken and shattered the old treaty, is "defending," in other words, extending the boundaries of his kingdom by the arbitrament of the sword, and in

[3] *prodere* = betray. This infinitive with *non verebor*, does it mean "*non prodam*"? Or does the word mean publish? —*A*. I have taken it in the second sense which I think is required by the context here.—*W.H.S.*

[4] See page 90.

movet, nec nobis peccatoribus hic accusare nec vobis sanctis hic discutere permissum est. quin potius, si requiras, ordinis res est, ut et dives hic purpura byssoque veletur et Lazarus hic ulceribus et paupertate feriatur; ordinis res est, ut, dum in hac allegorica versamur Aegypto, Pharao incedat cum diademate, Israelita cum cophino; ordinis res est, ut, dum in hac figuratae Babylonis fornace decoquimur, nos cum Ieremia spiritalem Ierusalem suspiriosis plangamus ululatibus et Assur fastu regio tonans sanctorum sancta proculcet. 5. quibus ego praesentum futurarumque beatitudinum vicissitudinibus inspectis communia patientius incommoda fero; primum, quod mihi quae merear introspicienti, quaecumque adversa provenerint, leviora reputabuntur; dein quod certum scio maximum esse remedium interioris hominis, si in hac area mundi variis passionum flagellis trituretur exterior. 6. sed, quod fatendum est, praefatum regem Gothorum, quamquam sit ob virium merita terribilis, non tam Romanis moenibus quam legibus

---

[1] Anderson questioned the meaning of *hic*. *Hic* is shown by the whole sense of the context here to mean "in this present world."—*W.H.S.*

[2] Luke, XVI. 19 ff.

[3] The *cophinus* of Juvenal III. 14 and VI. 542 was apparently a basket stuffed with hay (and other wrappings?) in which food for the Sabbath (on which the Jewish law prohibited the use of fire) was kept warm. But this does not seem to suit the present passage; the context suggests that *cophinus* here betokens something menial or degrading. Dung-basket or the like?—*A*. I think that, since the degrading slavery of the Hebrews in Egypt is referred to, the *cophinus* here must mean "work-basket" or "hod" for the carrying of building material for Pharaoh's edifices. This seems proved by the words of Psalm LXXX (*Eng. 81*), verse 7 (*Eng. 6*), where the

this situation [1] it is equally impossible for a sinner like myself to lodge a complaint or for a saint like you to investigate the case: on the contrary, if you ask me, it is the regular thing for the rich man here [1] to be clothed in purple and fine linen and for Lazarus [2] to be smitten with sores and poverty; it is the regular thing that while (allegorically speaking) we dwell in this land of Egypt, Pharaoh should walk abroad bearing his diadem, and the Israelite carrying his work-basket;[3] it is the regular thing that, while (in a figure of speech) we are scorched in this Babylonian furnace,[4] we should (like Jeremiah) lament for the spiritual Jerusalem with sighs and groans,[5] and that the Assyrian thundering in his royal pride should trample the Holy of Holies underfoot. 5. When I consider these alternations of present and future joys [6] I bear more patiently our common afflictions; for, in the first place, a scrutiny of my own deserts will surely make any misfortunes which befall me seem less heavy; and, in the second place, I know for a certainty that the most effective cure for the inner man is for the outer man to be flailed by divers sufferings on the threshing-floor of the present world. 6. But I must confess that, although the said King of the Goths is justly feared for his armed might, I dread less his designs against our Roman city-walls

Psalmist refers to the liberation from Egypt: *divertit ab oneribus dorsum eius; manus eius in cophino servierunt.*—*W.H.S.*

[4] Daniel III. 20 ff.

[5] Lamentations I. 1 ff.

[6] *I.e.* cases like those mentioned in the previous paragraph, where the afflicted in their turn were blessed while the proud were brought low.—*A.*

Christianis insidiaturum pavesco. tantum, ut ferunt, ori, tantum pectori suo catholici mentio nominis acet, ut ambigas ampliusne suae gentis an suae sectae teneat principatum. ad hoc armis potens acer animis alacer annis hunc solum patitur errorem, quod putat sibi tractatuum consiliorumque successum tribui pro religione legitima, quem potius assequitur pro felicitate terrena. 7. propter quod discite cito catholici status valetudinem occultam, ut apertam festinetis adhibere medicinam. Burdigala, Petrogorii, Ruteni, Lemovices, Gabalitani, Helusani, Vasates, Convenae, Auscenses, multoque iam maior numerus civitatum summis sacerdotibus ipsorum morte truncatus nec ullis deinceps episcopis in defunctorum officia suffectis, per quos utique minorum ordinum ministeria subrogabantur, latum spiritalis ruinae limitem traxit. quam fere constat sic per singulos dies morientum patrum proficere defectu, ut non solum quoslibet haereticos praesentum verum etiam haeresiarchas priorum temporum potuerit inflectere: ita populos excessu pontificum orbatos tristis intercisae fidei desperatio premit. 8. nulla

---

[1] Euric was a bigoted Arian, and appears if no worse to have at least banished some bishops (see below) and forbidden the election of new ones to succeed these and any who died. In spite of what Sidonius says in this letter and the evidence of Gregory of Tours and others, real persecution by Euric is doubtful. G. Yvers, "Euric Roi des Wisigoths" in *Ét. d' Hist. du Moyen Âge dédiées à Gabriel Monod*, 42–46.

[2] Saint-Bertrand-de-Comminges.

[3] The meaning is not clear. Is *civitatum* distinguished from

than against our Christian laws. So repugnant, they say, is the mention of the word "catholic" to his mouth and his heart that one doubts whether he is more the ruler of his nation or of his sect.[1] Moreover, with all his military might, his ardent spirit, and his youthful energy, he labours under one delusion: he imagines that the success of his dealings and plans comes from the genuine orthodoxy of his religion, whereas it would be truer to say that he achieves it by earthly good-fortune. 7. This being so, let me tell you briefly the secret malady of the body catholic, in order that you may quickly administer an open remedy. Bordeaux, Périgueux, Rodez, Limoges, Javols, Eauze, Bazas, Saint-Bertrand,[2] Auch, and a far greater number of other cities [3] have now, by the death of the incumbents, lost their bishops, and no bishops have been appointed to succeed the departed—the men, of course, by whom new presentations to the cures of the minor orders were made; and in consequence, a wide tract of spiritual devastation has been created: it is generally agreed that, so increasingly extensive is this ruin becoming because of the daily decrease in the ranks of priests through death, that it might appal not only any heretics of the present but also arch-heretics of past days: to such an extent are the peoples, left desolate by the death of their bishops, sunk in a gloomy despair at the disruption of their faith. 8. In the desolate dioceses

the places just mentioned? Is *maior* = *maximus*? (But would not this require *maior pars*?) Anyhow, there is surely some exaggeration. Were so many bishops put to death by Euric? Could so many sees have lapsed by Euric's ban on appointing successors?—*A*.

in desolatis cura dioecesibus [1] [parochiisque].[2] videas in ecclesiis aut putres culminum lapsus aut valvarum cardinibus avulsis basilicarum aditus hispidorum veprium fruticibus obstructos. ipsa, pro dolor, videas armenta non modo semipatentibus iacere vestibulis sed etiam herbosa viridantium altarium latera depasci. sed iam nec per rusticas solum solitudo parochias: ipsa insuper urbanarum ecclesiarum conventicula rarescunt. 9. quid enim fidelibus solacii superest, quando clericalis non modo disciplina verum etiam memoria perit? equidem cum clericus quisque defungitur, si benedictione succidua non accipiat dignitatis heredem, in illa ecclesia sacerdotium moritur, non sacerdos. atque ita quid spei restare pronunties, ubi facit terminus hominis finem religionis? altius inspicite spiritalium damna membrorum: profecto intellegetis, quanti subrepti sunt [3] episcopi, tantorum vobis populorum fidem periclitaturam. taceo vestros Crocum Simpliciumque collegas, quos cathedris sibi traditis eliminatos similis

[1] diocesibus *MCF*.
[2] parochiisque (*vulgo*: parrochiis *MCF*) *delet Leo*.
[3] subrepti sunt *Luetjohann*: sub r & e p̄ mitis *C*: sub**** p̄ munt' *M*[2]: surripiuntur *F*: quantis fueritis privati episcopis *Wilamowitz*.

---

[1] The meaning is not very clear.—*A*.
[2] Anderson was again doubtful here. I think that the subject of *accipiat* is *clericus*, the dying incumbent, who by his blessing *admits* the heir or successor to the cure. Here as elsewhere *succiduus* is for *succidaneus* = *successivus, continuus*: "if he does not get a successor to his office by an unbroken episcopal benediction," "through the carrying on of the episcopal blessing," *i.e.* if the bishopric has lapsed and so

[and parishes] there is no one to exercise oversight; you can see in the churches roofs crumbling and falling or door-hinges torn away, and the entrances to the basilicas blocked by thickets of rough briers; sadder still, one can see cattle not only lying in the vestibules half-open to the sky but actually cropping the sides of grass-grown altars. And now it is not only in the country parishes that solitude reigns; to crown all, the congregation even in the city churches is becoming sparser. 9. What comfort is left to the faithful when not only the teaching of the clergy but even the memory of them perishes?[1] If, when one of the clergy dies, he does not admit an heir to his office by handing on his benediction,[2] then assuredly it is the priesthood that dies in that church, not the priest. And what hope would you say remains when the end of a man's life implies the end of religion? Examine more deeply these losses of spiritual members, and you will certainly realise that with each removal of a bishop[3] you will have the faith of a people[4] put in jeopardy. I need scarcely mention your colleagues, Crocus and Simplicius,[5] ousted from the thrones to which they had succeeded and suffering different tortures from a

there is no bishop to give his blessing to a new incumbent.—*W.H.S.*

[3] The reading is very uncertain.

[4] *Populorum* in the ecclesiastical sense "flocks." So probably in § 7, *fin.*

[5] Crocus was Bishop of Nîmes, if Sirmond's opinion is right. But the only man of this name recorded elsewhere lived in the seventh century (Duchesne, *Fastes Épisc.* I. 313). The see of this Simplicius is likewise unknown; he was neither of the other men named Simplicius occurring in Sidonius' letters.

exilii cruciat poena dissimilis. namque unus ipsorum dolet se non videre quo redeat; alter se dolet videre quo non redit. 10. tu sacratissimorum pontificum, Leontii Fausti Graeci, urbe ordine caritate medius inveniris; per vos mala foederum currunt, per vos regni utriusque pacta condicionesque portantur. agite, quatenus haec sit amicitiae [1] concordia [2] principalis,[3] ut episcopali ordinatione permissa populos Galliarum, quos limes Gothicae sortis incluserit, teneamus ex fide, etsi non tenemus ex foedere. memor nostri esse dignare, domine papa.

[1] amicitiae *Luetjohann*: amicitia.

[2] concordia *codd.*: concordia ⟨condicio⟩ *vel* ⟨condicio⟩ concordia *vel* amicitiae et concordiae ⟨condicio⟩ *coni. Anderson.*

[3] principali *Mommsen.*

---

[1] The one had been banished far away, the other could still view his old diocese.—*A.*

[2] When in A.D. 475 Euric, in control of Provence, offered to exchange it for Auvergne, two missions were sent to him; but it is not quite certain which one came first. It seems that the Emperor Iulius Nepos first sent Epiphanius (not him of Sidonius, *Ep.* V. 17. 10), Bishop of Pavia, to discuss terms (Ennodius, *Vita Epiph.* 81 ff.—he does not mention the four other bishops here named by Sidonius). Apparently Epiphanius (who is not mentioned by Sidonius) accepted Euric's chief proposal but left further discussions and the drafting of a treaty to Basilius, the recipient of this letter, and the three other Gallic bishops here mentioned by Sidonius. Leontius (*Ep.* VI. 3) was Bishop of Arles, Faustus (born in Britain? Abbot of Lérins for many years—*Ep.* IX. 3 and 9) Bishop of Riez, Graecus (*Ep.* VI. 8; VII. 2 and 7 and 10(11); IX. 4) Bishop of Marseille. It is not certain that Sidonius knew the full details of the agreement made. For different views see

similar exile; for one of them laments [1] that he does not see the place to which he would fain return, the other that he sees the place to which he cannot return. 10. You are surrounded by those most holy pontiffs, Leontius, Faustus, and Graecus; [2] you have a middle [3] place among them in the location of your city and in seniority, and you are the centre of their loving circle; you four are the channels through which the unfortunate treaties flow; through your hands pass the compacts and stipulations of both realms.[4] Work, therefore, that this may be the chief article of the peace [5]—that episcopal ordination being permitted we may hold according to the faith, though we cannot hold according to the treaty, those peoples of Gaul who are enclosed within the bounds of the Gothic domain.[6] Deign to hold me in remembrance, my Lord Bishop.

Stevens, 158–160, 198–199, 207 ff.; L. Schmidt, *Geschichte d. deutschen Stämme*, 265.

[3] *caritate medius* "intermediate as regards affection," *i.e.* an intermediary in the brotherly love that passes between them.—*A.*

[4] Probably the Visigoths and the Romans are meant in this context, not the Burgundians. In the *Carmina* Sidonius uses *regnum* of the Empire. Cf. pp. 360, 510, 519.

[5] Anderson makes several suggestions here to emend the text. I think Luetjohann's emendation gives reasonable sense: "make it your aim that this should be the main agreement of peace—namely, that episcopal ordination should be permitted etc." The *quatenus* clause is used by Sidonius like an *ut* clause depending on *agite*, and the *ut* clause, which follows, more explicitly defines the *quatenus* clause.—*W.H.S.*

[6] We cannot be sure to what extent the final result of the negotiations—the cession in A.D. 475 of all Auvergne to Euric—must be attributed to Epiphanius and to what extent it was the fault of the other four bishops. See the next letter.

VII

SIDONIVS DOMINO PAPAE GRAECO SALVTEM

1. Ecce iterum Amantius, nugigerulus noster, Massiliam suam repetit, aliquid, ut moris est, de manubiis civitatis domum reportaturus, si tamen . . . aut [1] cataplus arriserit. per quem iaculariter plura garrirem, si pariter unus idemque valeret animus exercere laeta et tristia sustinere. siquidem nostri hic nunc est infelicis anguli status, cuius, ut fama confirmat ⟨misera⟩ minus [2] fuit sub bello quam sub pace condicio. 2. facta est servitus nostra pretium securitatis alienae. Arvernorum, pro dolor,

[1] aut *om. F*, *expunxit* M^1: *om. hanc Ep. LNTVRP*: tamen ⟨sors⟩ aut *coni. Semple*: tamen ante *coni.* Gustafsson: trāmen *coni. Warmington.* Cf. Additional Notes, p. 613.

[2] ⟨misera⟩ minus *Mohr*: minus ⟨tristis⟩ *Luetjohann*: minus *CM*: min^{or} M^1: melior *F*: mitior *aut* mollior *coni. Warmington.*

---

* See the preceding letter, § 10 and *Ep.* VI. 8, first note.

[1] Letter-carrier between Sidonius and Graecus. See *Ep.* VII. 2 and VII. 10. 1; IX. 4. 1; VI. 8. 1.

[2] Anderson had translated *Massiliam suam repetit* thus: "is on his way back to his native Massilia," forgetting that Amantius is the same person whom in VII. 2. 3 he had introduced to the same Bishop Graecus in the words "*Arverni huic patria.*" So the passage really means: "Amantius is returning again (on one of his journeys as a merchant) to his favourite market, Marseille." The next clause "*aliquid, ut moris est, . . . reportaturus*" refers jestingly to Amantius' last successful raid on the Massilienses, set out in VII. 2, when *circumscriptione legitima* he gained a wife and a considerable

VII

SIDONIUS TO THE LORD BISHOP GRAECUS,* GREETING

1. Here is Amantius[1] again, the bearer of my trifles; he is returning again to his well-loved Massilia in order to carry home, as usual, his pickings from the city's spoils—at least if the . . . or the incoming ships should favour him.[2] I should be sending through him a further instalment of jocular chatter, if one and the same mind could simultaneously indulge in hilarity and endure sorrows. For such is now the condition of our unhappy corner that, as report declares, its plight was less miserable in war than it is now in peace. 2. Our freedom has been bartered for the security of others, the freedom of the Arvernians (O the pity of it!)

fortune. *Cataplus*: From Ausonius, *Ordo Urbium Nobilium*, XIII, 18–21:

> *te maris Eoi merces et Hiberica ditant*
> *aequora, te classes Libyci Siculique profundi*:
> *et quidquid vario per flumina, per freta cursu*
> *advehitur, toto tibi navigat orbe cataplus*;

and from Martial XII. 74. 1, *dum tibi Niliacus portat crystalla cataplus*, it seems clear that *cataplus* means the arrival of merchant ships, by sea or by river, at a port; and so Amantius goes down from Auvergne on a business trip to Marseille, hoping again to have a profitable venture—"if," says Sidonius, "the incoming merchant fleets happen to favour him." He is a buyer at the port of Marseille, acting as agent for persons in Auvergne, as Sidonius says in VI. 8. 1, *cum pecuniis quorumpiam catapli recentis nundinas adit*. I am not sure what should fill the lacuna marked by Luetjohann; perhaps *sors* either in the sense of "luck" or of "capital money."—*W.H.S.* See Additional Notes, p. 613.

servitus, qui, si prisca replicarentur, audebant se quondam fratres Latio dicere et sanguine ab Iliaco populos computare. si recentia memorabuntur, hi sunt, qui viribus propriis hostium publicorum arma remorati sunt; cui saepe populo Gothus non fuit clauso intra moenia formidini, cum vicissim ipse fieret oppugnatoribus positis intra castra terrori. hi sunt, qui sibi adversus vicinorum aciem tam duces fuere quam milites; de quorum tamen sorte certaminum si quid prosperum cessit, vos secunda solata sunt, si quid contrarium, illos adversa fregerunt. illi amore rei publicae Seronatum barbaris provincias propinantem non timuerunt legibus tradere, quem convictum deinceps res publica vix praesumpsit occidere. 3. hoccine meruerunt inopia flamma, ferrum pestilentia, pingues caedibus gladii et macri ieiuniis proeliatores? propter huius tam [1] inclitae pacis expectationem avulsas muralibus rimis herbas in cibum traximus, crebro per ignorantiam venenatis graminibus infecti, quae indiscretis foliis sucisque

[1] tam *Luetjohann*: tamen.

[1] For this claim see also *Ep.* II. 2. 19. The (Latin) Romans made a similar claim. For the present passage see Lucan, *Phars.* I. 427 ff.: *Arvernique ausi Latio se fingere fratres| sanguine ab Iliaco populi. A.* is doubtful whether in Sidonius here *Latio* goes with *fratres* or with *dicere.* He also suggests " confusion with the Aedui (Caes. *B.G.* I. 31. 3) " and points out that in Lucan *populi* may mean " communities." Through-

who, if ancient story be recalled, dared once to call themselves "brothers to Latium" and counted themselves "a people sprung from Trojan blood."[1] If recent events be brought to mind these are the men who by their unaided strength checked the arms of the common enemy; these are the people who many a time, though besieged within their walls, felt no fear of the Goth, but in their turn struck terror into their assailants even when these were in their own camp: these are the men who, in facing the enemy host at their gates, were their own leaders as well as soldiers, and yet when their arms had any success their triumph benefited you, whereas if they were worsted it was only they who were crushed by the blow. It was they who, out of love for the State, feared not to hand over Seronatus[2] to the law when he was lavishing whole provinces on the barbarians; and the State in its turn scarcely had the courage to put him to death after his conviction. 3. Is this our due reward for enduring want and fire and sword and pestilence, for swords fed fat with gore and warriors emaciated with hunger? Was it for the prospect of this famous peace[3] that we ripped the herbage from the cracks in our walls and took it away for food, and that in our ignorance we were often poisoned by noxious grasses, which, being green, with nothing to distinguish their leaves or sap, were often plucked by a hand that starvation

out this letter Sidonius is thinking specially of the city Clermont-Ferrand.

[2] See V. 13, second note.

[3] Ironical, of course. Auvergne was ceded to the Visigoths in A.D. 475. See above, pp. 322–323.

viridantia saepe manus fame concolor legit? pro his tot tantisque devotionis experimentis nostri,[1] quantum audio, facta iactura est? 4. pudeat vos, precamur, huius foederis, nec utilis nec decori. per vos legationes meant; vobis primum pax quamquam principe absente non solum tractata reseratur, verum etiam tractanda committitur. veniabilis sit, quaesumus, apud aures vestras veritatis asperitas, cui convicii invidiam dolor eripit. parum in commune consulitis; et, cum in concilium convenitis, non tam curae est[2] publicis mederi periculis quam privatis studere fortunis; quod utique saepe diuque facientes iam non primi comprovincialium coepistis esse, sed ultimi. 5. at quousque istae poterunt durare praestigiae? non enim diutius ipsi maiores nostri hoc nomine gloriabuntur, qui minores incipiunt non habere. quapropter vel consilio, quo potestis, statum concordiae tam turpis incidite. adhuc, si necesse est, obsideri, adhuc pugnare, adhuc esurire delectat. si vero tradimur, qui non potuimus viribus

[1] nostri *vulgo*: nostris.
[2] est *om. MC.*

---

[1] "proofs of devotion"—is this the meaning of *experimentis*?—*A.* Yes; cf. VI. 8. 1 about Amantius: *creditoribus bene credulis sola deponit morum experimenta pro pignore*; the only security he deposits is the evidence, the tested experience, of his character.—*W.H.S.*

[2] *A.* takes *vos* as a real plural, but thinks *vestras aures* refers to one person only.

[3] Sidonius is suggesting that this group of four bishops has

had made as green as they? Is it for these many signal proofs of our devotion [1] that (as I am informed) we have now been jettisoned? 4. We pray that you and your colleagues [2] may feel ashamed of this fruitless and unseemly treaty. You are the channel through which embassies come and go; to you first of all, even though the Emperor is absent,[3] peace is not only reported when negotiated, but entrusted to be negotiated. Pray do not let the harsh truth grate unpardonably on your ears—the fact of our grief removes from our words the odium of mere abuse. You are not acting for the common weal; and when you come together into the council [4] you are less concerned to relieve public dangers than to advance personal interests; and, having done this at all hazards for a long time and many times, you are now beginning to be not first, but last, among the members of your province.[4] 5. How long will this jugglery be able to continue? Soon our ancestors will no longer glory in the name of ancestor when they are ceasing to have descendants. Cut short at least by counsel, in which you have the power, this present state of disgraceful concord. If necessary, it will be a joy to us still to endure siege, still to fight, still to starve. But if we are surrendered, we who could not be taken by force, it is undeniably you who devised

plenipotentiary authority to decide and to take action. For the task of these bishops see the preceding letter *Ep.* VII. 6. 10, and notes there.

[4] *concilium . . . comprovincialium.* What is the meaning of these two words? *Concilium* may be the Concilium Septem Provinciarum (for which see Vol. I of the Loeb Sidonius, p. 347 n.); or is it the assembly or synod of the bishops in the provinces?—*A*.

obtineri, invenisse vos certum est quid barbarum suaderetis [1] ignavi. 6. sed cur dolori nimio frena laxamus? quin potius ignoscite afflictis nec imputate maerentibus. namque alia regio tradita servitium sperat, Arverna supplicium. sane si medicari nostris ultimis non valetis, saltem hoc efficite prece sedula, ut sanguis vivat, quorum est moritura libertas; parate exulibus terram, capiendis redemptionem, viaticum peregrinaturis. si murus noster aperitur hostibus, non sit clausus vester hospitibus. memor nostri esse dignare, domine papa.

VIII

SIDONIVS DOMINO PAPAE EVPHRONIO SALVTEM

1. Quandoquidem me clericalis officii vincula ligant, felicissimum mediocritatis meae statum pronuntiarem, si nobis haberentur quam territoria vicina tam moenia. de minimis videlicet rebus coronam tuam maximisque consulerem, fieretque

[1] adiuvaretis *Mommsen.*

---

[1] "It is certain that you have discovered what a barbarous thing you with your cowardice recommended." I doubt if this is right. If it is, then *iam* before *invenisse* seems a likely conjecture. But what of the tense of *suaderetis*? I don't like Mommsen's *adiuvaretis*.—*A*. I agree with Anderson's doubts. I am sure that Sidonius is trying to pin the blame of the betrayal on Graecus and his colleagues of the peace-commission. "You were responsible," he says. "There

the barbarous expedient which in your cowardice you recommended.[1] 6. But why do I give free rein to my excessive grief? Nay, pardon the afflicted and do not blame the mourner; for any other surrendered region expects servitude, but Auvergne is faced with torture. If you cannot save us in our extremity, at least secure by unceasing prayer that the blood of those whose liberty is doomed may still survive; provide land for the exiles, ransom for the captives-to-be, and aid for the refugees on their way. If our walls are opened to admit our foes, let not yours be closed to exclude your friends. Deign to hold me in remembrance, my Lord Bishop.

VIII

SIDONIUS TO THE LORD BISHOP EUPHRONIUS,* GREETING

1. Since the bonds of my clerical office tie me to the spot, I should regard the position of my unworthy self as extraordinarily happy, if our cities were as near to one another as our dioceses.[2] I should then, of course, consult your reverence [3] on things both great and small, and the course of my

can be no doubt but that you thought up, excogitated, the barbarous formula which as cowardly appeasers you could recommend for a settlement."—*W.H.S.*

* Bishop of Autun (Augustodunum of the Aedui). See also *Ep*. IX. 2; IV. 25. 3 and note there.

[2] The land of the Aedui bordered on that of the Arverni, but there was considerable distance between the capitals (seats of the bishops) Autun and Clermont.

[3] *corona* was the tonsure. See *Ep*. VI. 3. 2.

actionum mearum quasi cuiuspiam fluvii placidus [1] cursus atque inoffensus, si e tractatu [2] tuo veluti ex saluberrimo fonte manaret. procul dubio tunc ille non esset aut spumosus per iactantiam aut turbidus per superbiam aut caenosus per conscientiam aut praeceps per iuventutem. quin potius in illo squalidum si quid ac putre sorderet, totum id admixta consilii tui vena dilueret. 2. sed quoniam huiuscemodi votis spatia sunt longa interposita praepedimento, sedulo precor, ut consulentem de scrupulo incursae ambiguitatis expedias et, quia Simplicium, spectabilem virum, episcopum sibi flagitat populus Biturix ordinari, quid super tanto debeam negotio facere, decernas. huius es namque vel erga me dignationis vel erga reliquos auctoritatis, ut si quid fieri voles (voles autem quicquid aequissimum est), non suadere tam debeas quam iubere. 3. de quo tamen Simplicio scitote narrari plurima bona, atque ea quidem a plurimis bonis. quae testimonia mihi prima fronte conloquii non satis grata, quia satis gratiosa, iudicabantur. at postquam aemulos eius nihil vidi amplius quam silere, atque eos maxume, qui fidem fovent Arianorum, neque

[1] placidus *LRN*: placidissimus *MTCFP*.
[2] e tractatu *LMCP*: retractatu *T*.

---

[1] The sense is "the dilemma in which I have become involved."—*A*.
[2] A title, as elsewhere.

actions, springing as it would from the health-giving source of your converse, would be like the placid and unbroken flow of a river. Certainly it would not be frothy through conceit or turbid through haughtiness or muddy through a bad conscience or rash through youth; on the contrary, any nasty rotting filth in it would be wholly washed away by the mingling stream of your counsel. 2. But as the great distance separating us prevents such longed-for bliss, I earnestly pray you to enlighten me now when I put before you a thorny problem which has confronted me.[1] The people of Bourges demand that the eminent [2] Simplicius [3] be ordained as their bishop. Pray decide what I ought to do about this serious business; for you enjoy such prestige with me and such authority with others that whatever you want to be done (and you will always want what is fairest), you ought not so much to recommend as to command. 3. But about this Simplicius, let me tell you that a great many good things are related, and by a great many good men. At the outset of the conference these testimonies seemed to me not quite acceptable because rather too partial; [4] but when I found that his opponents, and in particular the adherents of the Arian faith, contented themselves with silence, and that no lawful dis-

[3] This Simplicius (Cf. *Ep.* VII. 9. 16 and 25) was son of Eulogius and son-in-law of Palladius who were bishops of Bourges. Chaix II. 20.

[4] The translation given here has roughly the right meaning but it is not ideal. Dalton's "favour and favouritism" is good, but he omits *conloquii*. Perhaps thus: "my first impression at the conference was that these testimonies were rather too partial to be pleasing."—*A*.

quippiam nominato, licet necdum nostrae professionis, inlicitum opponi, animum adverti exactissimum virum posse censeri, de quo civis malus loqui, bonus tacere non posset. 4. sed cur ego istaec[1] ineptus adieci, tamquam darem consilium qui poposci? quin potius omnia ex vestro nutu arbitrio litterisque disponentur sacerdotibus, popularibus manifestabuntur. neque enim ita desipimus in totum, ut evocandum te primum, si venire possibile est, deinde, si quid sequius,[2] certe consulendum decerneremus, nisi in omnibus obsecuturi. memor nostri esse dignare, domine papa.

IX

SIDONIVS DOMINO PAPAE PERPETVO SALVTEM

1. Desiderio spiritalium lectionum, quarum[3] tibi tam per authenticos quam per disputatores bybliotheca fidei catholicae[4] perfamiliaris est, etiam illa, quae maxume[5] tuarum scilicet aurium minime digna

[1] istaec *Mohr*: ista haec.
[2] sequius *LR*: secus *MTCFP*.
[3] quoniam *coni. Anderson*.
[4] fidei catholicae *aut delere aut ante* bybliotheca *ponere malit Luetjohann*.
[5] maxumam *Wouweren*.

---

[1] It is just possible that *nominato* = *praefato*, "the aforesaid" although I scarcely think so.—*A*.

* Bishop of Tours. Cf. *Ep*. IV. 18. 4.

[2] *fidei catholicae*: this is scarcely intelligible where it stands. Luetjohann reasonably suggests that it be either omitted or

qualification was alleged against the nominee,[1] though he is not yet a member of our profession, I saw that the man, about whom bad citizens could not say a word and good citizens could not keep silence, might justly be regarded as of supreme excellence. 4. But why have I stupidly added these remarks, as if after asking for advice I were now giving it? On the contrary, all instructions to be given to priests and communicated to the laity shall follow your nod and pleasure and the tenor of your letter. I am not so wholly senseless as to decide that you should in the first instance be invited here if you are able to come, and failing that should by all means be consulted, if I had not intended to obey you in all things. Deign to hold me in remembrance, my Lord Bishop.

IX

SIDONIUS TO THE LORD BISHOP PERPETUUS,* GREETING

1. In your zeal for spiritual reading (and you are familiar with the whole library of Catholic [2] reading, whether composed by the scriptural writers or by the expositors) you wish to acquaint yourself with even those productions which are obviously quite unworthy to hold the discriminating attention of such a

placed immediately after *disputatores*. Or should we read *quoniam* for *quarum*?—*A*. I think that, if *quarum* is retained, it must depend on *authenticos* and *disputatores*; and then *fidei catholicae* will depend on *bybliotheca* which is its natural concordance.—*W.H.S.*

sunt occupare censuram, noscere cupis; siquidem iniungis, ut orationem, quam[1] videor[2] ad plebem Biturigis in ecclesia sermocinatus, tibi dirigam; cui non rhetorica partitio, non oratoriae minae,[3] non grammaticales figurae congruentem decorem disciplinamque suppeditaverunt. 2. neque enim illic, ut exacte perorantibus mos est, aut pondera historica aut poetica schemata scintillasve controversalium clausularum libuit aptari. nam cum me partium seditiones studia varietates in diversa raptarent, sic dictandi mihi materiam suggerebat iniuria, quod tempus occupatio subtrahebat. etenim tanta erat turba competitorum, ut cathedrae unius numerosissimos candidatos nec duo recipere scamna potuissent. omnes placebant sibi, omnes omnibus displicebant. 3. neque [enim][4] valuissemus aliquid in commune consulere, nisi iudicii sui faciens plebs lenita iacturam sacerdotali se potius iudicio subdidisset, presbyterorum sane paucis angulatim fringultientibus, porro autem palam ne mussitantibus quidem, quia plerique non minus suum quam reliquos ordines pertimescebant. igitur, dum publice totos singuli

[1] quam *MTCFP*: qua.
[2] fateor *aut* confiteor *coni. Warmington.*
[3] machinae *coni. Mohr. Sed v. Quint. IX. 2. 102–103.*
[4] enim *seclud. Luetjohann.*

---

[1] *maxume*: surely *maxume* supported by the MSS is right, both in itself and because of the Sidonian antithesis with *minime.—A.*

[2] *quam videor . . . sermocinatus*: what is *videor*? Is it = "*mihi videor*"? rather *tibi videor*, "I am supposed." Cf. VII. 17. 4, *praepositus illis quidem videtur sanctus Auxanius.* And what force has *sermocinatus?—A.* Possibly *fateor* or *confiteor* for *videor*. See Additional Notes, p. 613.

critic as yourself;[1] for you ask me to send you the oration which I am reputed to have delivered[2] in the church to the people of Bourges. But it was a homily which had none of the harmonious grace and artifice contributed by rhetorical partition, oratorical shocks, and grammatical figures.[3] 2. I did not choose, after the fashion of finished orators, to build into it the weightiness of history, or the devices of poetry, or the sparkling finishes of quasi-forensic declamations;[4] for since the dissensions, passions, and diversities of parties tore me this way and that, my sense of grievance did indeed supply matter for my pen, but, on the other hand, my busy existence stole away my time. There was indeed such a crowd of competitors that two whole rows of seats could not have accommodated those numerous candidates for one throne. Each one of them was as well pleased with himself as he was displeased with everyone else. 3. We should not have managed to take any common counsel if the mass of the people had not calmed down and, sacrificing their own judgment, submitted themselves to priestly judgment; it is true that a few of the presbyters twittered in holes and corners, but they did not make even the slightest murmur in public, because most of them were as much afraid of their own order as of the other orders; thus, as each individual in public fought shy of all the others, it

[3] or: verbal novelties.—*W.H.S.*

[4] *pondera historica, poetica schemata, controversalium clausularum*: See Semple, *Quaest. Exeg.*, pp. 41–43. I think *clausulae* here refers, not to the rhythmical cadences of individual sentences, but to the conclusion of individual passages and, of course, to the finish of the speech as a whole; "climaxes" might do as a translation.—*A.*

cavent, factum est, ut omnes non aspernanter audirent quod deinceps ambienter exponerent.[1] 4. itaque paginam sume subditis voluminibus adiunctam, quam duabus vigiliis unius noctis aestivae Christo teste dictatam plurimum vereor ne ipsi amplius lectioni, quae hoc de se probat, quam mihi credas. memor nostri esse dignare, domine papa.

CONTIO

5. Refert historia saecularis, dilectissimi, quendam philosophorum discipulis advenientibus prius tacendi patientiam quam loquendi monstrasse doctrinam et sic incipientes quosque inter disputantium consectaneorum cathedras mutum sustinuisse quinquennium, ut etiam celeriora quorumpiam ingenia non liceret ante laudari quam deceret agnosci. ita fiebat, ut eosdem post longam taciturnitatem locutos quisque audire coeperat, non taceret[2] quia, donec scientiam natura combiberit, non maior est gloria dixisse quod noveris quam siluisse quod nescias. 6. at nunc mediocritatem meam manet longe diversa condicio, cui per suspiriosas voragines et flagitiorum volutabra gradienti professionis huiusce

[1] exponerent *TC*: expeterent *LMFP*: expenderent (*vix* exprimerent?) *coni. Anderson.*
[2] tacere placeret *Mommsen.*

---

[1] *exponerent* or *expeterent.* "to speed abroad in a form which would reflect credit on themselves," "to make known with an eye on their own credit." The verb *exprimerent* is scarcely satisfying. What of *expenderent*?—*A*. He reads *exponerent* with some MSS.

came about that all gave a respectful welcome to a proposal which in their turn they could eagerly explain to others.[1] 4. Receive, therefore, the sheet appended to the accompanying roll.[2] It was composed, as Christ is my witness, in no longer than two watches of a single summer night—although I greatly fear that you will believe this less from my assertion than from the actual contents, which make the fact self-evident. Deign to remember me, my Lord Bishop.

ADDRESS

5. Dearly beloved, secular history relates of one[3] of the philosophers that when pupils came to him he taught them the lesson of patient silence before he taught them the lore of speaking, and that all the novices endured five years of dumbness among the chairs where their fellow-disciples sat at their discussions, so that even the quicker minds were not allowed to gain a word of praise before it was proper for them to be recognised. The regular result was that, when these pupils spoke after their long silence, no man when he first heard them could fail to say that until the mind of man has absorbed knowledge, it is quite as great a glory to be mute where you don't know as to be vocal where you do know. 6. But in the present case a very different situation confronts my unworthy self, for the responsibilities of this sacred calling were thrust upon me while I strayed

[2] *subditis voluminibus*: The *volumina* contained, I supposed, a detailed account of the election and of its attendant circumstances.—*A*.

[3] Pythagoras, sixth century B.C.

pondus impactum est; et prius quam ulli bonorum reddam discentis obsequium, cogor debere ceteris docentis officium. adicitur huic inpossibilitati pondus pudoris, quod mihi peculiariter paginae decretalis oblatu pontificis eligendi mandastis arbitrium coram sacrosancto et pontificatu maximo dignissimo papa; qui cum sit suae provinciae caput, sit etiam mihi usu institutione, facundia privilegio, tempore aetate praestantior, ego deque coramque metropolitano verba facturus, et provincialis et iunior, pariter fero imperiti verecundiam, procacis invidiam. 7. sed quoniam vestro sic libitum errori, ut ipse prudentia carens prudentem vobis, in cuiusque personam bona multa concurrant, sub ope Christi episcopum exquiram, noveritis huiusmodi assensu multum me honoris, plus oneris excipere. primore loco grandem publicae opinionis sarcinam penditote, quod iniunxistis incipienti consummata iudicia atque ab hoc rectum consilii tramitem postulatis,[1] in quo recolitis adhuc nuper erratum. igitur quia vobis id fuit cordi, obsecro, ut quales nos fide creditis, tales intercessione faciatis atque dignemini humilitatem no-

[1] postulastis *coni. Anderson.*

---

[1] *paginae decretalis*: if (as seems most probable) this here refers to the *decretum* in *Ep.* VII. 5. 1, then it seems that *coram . . . papa* must be taken with *eligendi*. A slight change of order in the translation would make this right; but there is something rather odd about it.—*A*.

[2] *papa*: generally supposed to be Agroecius, Bishop of Sens (see *Ep.* 5 of this Book).

[3] *suae provinciae caput*: cf. *Ep.* VII. 5. 3, *Senoniae caput es.*

[4] *huiusmodi assensu*: "the cordial acceptance of the proposal," or Sidonius' acceptance of it?—*A*.

amid the lamentable gulfs and sloughs of iniquity; and before rendering to any righteous man the allegiance of a learner, I am perforce called upon to discharge for others the duty of an instructor. Besides the impossibility of such a task, a feeling of shame oppresses me, because to me, to me of all men, you have entrusted, by the presentation of your official mandate,[1] the right of choosing your bishop, and that, too, in the presence of a hallowed prelate[2] who is well worthy of the chief pontificate. Not only is he head of his province[3] but he is superior to me in experience and training, in eloquence and endowments, in length of office and of years; and so, proposing as I do to speak about a metropolitan in the presence of a metropolitan, I, a provincial bishop and a younger man, feel at once the diffidence of ignorance and the stigma of presumption. 7. But since you have been so misguided as to desire that I, who am void of wisdom, should with Christ's help seek out for you as your bishop a wise man uniting in his person many virtues, I want you to know that your united decision[4] is for me very honourable but still more onerous. Consider above all the heavy weight of public opinion under which you labour, since you have called upon a beginner to deliver perfect judgments, and you ask[5] to be guided along the straight path of wisdom by one whose recent straying still remains in your memory. Well, seeing that this has been your pleasure, I beg that by your supplications you may make me the man that in your trusting faith you believe me to be, and that you may see

[5] *postulatis*: or perhaps *postulastis*?—*A*.

stram orationibus potius in caelum ferre quam plausibus. 8. primum tamen nosse vos par est, in quas me obloquiorum Scyllas et in quos linguarum, sed humanarum, latratus quorundam vos infamare conantum turbo coniecerit. est enim haec quaedam vis malis moribus, ut innocentiam multitudinis devenustent scelera paucorum, cum tamen e diverso bonorum raritas flagitia multorum nequeat excusare virtutibus communicatis. 9. si quempiam nominavero monachorum, quamvis illum, Paulis Antoniis, Hilarionibus Macariis conferendum, sectatae anachoreseos praerogativa comitetur, aures ilico meas incondito tumultu circumstrepitas[1] ignobilium pumilionum murmur everberat conquerentum: "hic qui nominatur," inquiunt, "non episcopi, sed potius abbatis complet officium et intercedere magis pro animabus apud caelestem quam pro corporibus apud terrenum iudicem potest." sed quis non exacerbescat, cum videat sordidari virtutum sinceritatem criminatione vitiorum? 10. si eligimus humilem, vocatur abiectus: si proferimus erectum, superbire censetur; si minus institutum, propter imperitiam

[1] circumstrepitans *Leo*.

---

[1] *par . . . quas . . . Scyllas . . . linguarum . . . humanarum latratus quorundam . . . infamare.* The Latin here if spoken produces a sort of barking—a deliberate effect by Sidonius.

[2] What Sidonius means is: a wicked and unscrupulous minority taints and infects the reputation of a wholesome majority, but the process doesn't work in reverse: a saintly minority can't, as it were, socialise its own virtues and spread them over the wicked majority.—*W.H.S.*

fit to raise me to the skies, humble as I am, by prayers rather than by plaudits. 8. But first, it is right that you should know among what Scyllas of obloquy, among what a din of barking tongues—human ones in this case [1]—I have been flung by the storm which certain persons have raised in their efforts to discredit you. There is indeed a sort of active principle in wickedness the effect of which is that the crimes of the few besmirch the innocence of the many, while on the other hand a sprinkling of good people cannot by sharing their virtues [2] extenuate the iniquities of the many. 9. If I nominate a monk, even though he be worthy of comparison with a Paulus, an Antonius, a Hilarion, or a Macarius,[3] even though he possess the special claim of having followed the life of an anchorite, my ears will straightway be assailed by the noise of ignoble pygmies raising a confused uproar on every side. "This nominee," they will protest, "discharges the office not of a bishop but rather of an abbot; he is better qualified to intercede with the heavenly Judge for our souls than with an earthly judge for our bodies." But who could help being exasperated when he finds the flawlessness of virtues sullied by the allegation of faults? 10. If we choose a humble man he is termed [4] spiritless, if we bring forward a self-reliant man he is deemed arrogant; if a man of small education, he is thought a laughing-stock because of his

[3] These were monks—see *Carm.* XVI. 100–101, where (100) two Macarii are mentioned.

[4] Perhaps the English translation should be put in the future tense, "will be called." And so in the following sentences. —*A.*

creditur inridendus: si aliquatenus doctum, propter scientiam clamatur inflatus; si severum, tamquam crudelis horretur: si indulgentem, facilitate culpatur; si simplicem, despicitur ut brutus: si acrem, vitatur ut calidus;[1] si diligentem, superstitiosus decernitur: si remissum, neglegens iudicatur; si sollertem, cupidus: si quietum, pronuntiatur ignavus; si abstemium producimus, avarus accipitur: si eum qui prandendo pascat, edacitatis impetitur: si eum qui pascendo ieiunet, vanitatis arguitur. 11. libertatem pro improbitate condemnant: verecundiam pro rusticitate fastidiunt; rigidos ob austeritatem non habent caros: blandi apud eos communione vilescunt. ac sic, utrolibet genere vivatur, semper hic tamen bonarum partium mores pungentibus linguis maledicorum veluti bicipitibus hamis inuncabuntur. inter haec monasterialibus disciplinis aegre subditur vel popularium cervicositas vel licentia clericorum. 12. si clericum dixero, sequentes aemulantur, derogant antecedentes. nam ita ex his pauci, quod reliquorum pace sit dictum, solam clericatus diuturnitatem pro meritis autumant calculandam, ut nos in antistite consecrando non utilitatem velint eligere sed aetatem, tamquam diu potius quam bene vivere debeat accipi ad summum sacerdotium adipiscendum

[1] calidus *Anderson*: callidus.

---

[1] I conjecture *calidus* for *callidus*. If *callidus* is right, then *acer* surely must mean " clever "; but although *acre ingenium* has this sense, could *acer homo* mean a clever man?—*A*.

ignorance, but if a man of some learning, he is declared conceited on account of his knowledge; if strict, he is abhorred as cruel, if indulgent, he is blamed for laxity; if guileless, he is scorned as stupid; if energetic, he is avoided as a hot-head;[1] if he is careful, he is regarded as finicking; if placid, he is considered negligent; if resourceful, he is thought self-seeking; if quiet, he is declared to be listless; if we present an abstemious person, he is made out to be greedy; if the kind of man who enjoys food and hospitably entertains, he is taxed with gluttony; if he hospitably entertains but himself fasts, he is charged with ostentation. 11. Outspokenness is condemned as effrontery and reserve scorned as rusticity; the strict are disliked for their austerity, and the genial are belittled for their good-fellowship. Thus whether a man's way of life tends in this direction or in that, he will always[2] on such an occasion be caught by the two-barbed hook of slanderers' tongues intent on stabbing the characters of the good. In these circumstances the laity in their obstinacy and the clergy in their unruliness will alike object to being under monastic control. 12. If I nominate a cleric, his inferiors will be jealous of him and his superiors will disparage him: for a few of these—if the others will allow me to say so—maintain that only length of service and not merits should be taken into consideration, and so they would have us, in instituting a bishop, choose not usefulness but age, as if a long life rather than a good life should be accepted as replacing the prestige and lustre and

[2] *semper hic tamen*: that troublesome Sidonian "hic" again!—*A*.

pro omnium gratiarum privilegio decoramento lenocinamento. et ita quipiam, in ministrando segnes in obloquendo celeres, in tractatibus otiosi in seditionibus occupati, in caritate infirmi in factione robusti, in aemulationum conservatione stabiles in sententiarum assertione nutantes, nituntur regere ecclesiam, quos iam regi necesse erit[1] per senectam. 13. sed nec diutius placet propter paucorum ambitus multorum notare personas: hoc solum astruo, quod, cum nullum proferam nuncupatim, ille confitetur repulsam, qui profitetur offensam. sane id liberius dico, de multitudine circumstantium multos episcopales esse, sed totos episcopos esse non posse; et, cum singuli diversorum charismatum proprietate potiantur, sufficere omnes sibi, omnibus neminem. 14. si militarem dixero forte personam, protinus in haec verba consurgitur: "Sidonius ad clericatum quia de saeculari professione translatus est, ideo sibi assumere metropolitanum de religiosa congregatione dissimulat; natalibus turget, dignitatum fastigatur insignibus, contemnit pauperes Christi." 15. quapropter in praesentiarum solvam quam non tam bonorum caritati quam maledicorum suspicioni

[1] erit *LT*: est *MCFP*. §§ 9 (everberat. . . .)—18 (. . . consilio [siore) *non habet R*.

---

[1] *ille confitetur repulsam qui profitetur offensam*: *i.e.* I suppose anyone who declares himself offended by my remarks, thereby shows himself to be one of those whom I have just criticised and, by implication, eliminated from the contest, put out of the running.—*A*.

charm of all the graces as a qualification for the highest priesthood. So it is that some individuals, slow in their ministry but quick in detraction, idle in preaching but busy in dissension, weak in love but strong in faction, steady in maintaining jealousies but vacillating in expressions of opinion, strive to direct the Church although they are so old that presently they themselves will need direction. 13. But I do not want any longer to brand the characters of many because of the machinations of a few; but this one thing I do affirm—that, although I mention no names, anyone who professes himself aggrieved by my words, thereby confesses himself a rejected candidate.[1] I do indeed say rather frankly that in the multitude standing around me, there are many men of episcopal quality, but they cannot all be bishops; and possessing as they do their special portions of the diverse spiritual graces, they all satisfy their own requirements, but none satisfies the requirements of everybody. 14. If I nominate a member of the Government service,[2] all will rise to their feet saying: "Because Sidonius was transferred to the ranks of the clergy from a secular profession, he is reluctant to take as colleague a metropolitan from the ranks of the clergy: he is swollen with pride of birth; he is uplifted by the insignia of his dignities; he looks down on the poor of Christ." 15. I will therefore in the present circumstances duly give a guarantee which is laid upon me by the suspicion of slanderers more than by the affection of the

[2] *militarem . . . personam*: "a member of the Government service"—this seems to be the meaning of *militarem* here.—*A*. For *militia*, see p. 44.

debeo fidem (vivit[1] Spiritus Sanctus, omnipotens Deus noster, qui Petri voce damnavit in Simone mago cur opinaretur gratiam benedictionis pretio sese posse mercari) me in eo, quem vobis opportunum censui, nec pecuniae favere nec gratiae, sed statu satis superque trutinato personae temporis, provinciae civitatis, virum, cuius in consequentibus raptim vita replicabitur, competentissimum credidisse. 16. benedictus Simplicius, hactenus vestri iamque abhinc nostri, modo per vos deus annuat, habendus ordinis comes, ita utrique parti vel actu vel professione respondet, ut et respublica in eo quod admiretur et ecclesia possit invenire quod diligat. 17. si natalibus servanda reverentia est, quia et hos non omittendos euangelista monstravit (nam Lucas laudationem Iohannis aggressus praestantissimum computavit, quod de sacerdotali stirpe veniebat, et nobilitatem vitae praedicaturus prius tamen extulit familiae dignitatem): parentes ipsius aut cathedris aut tribunalibus praesederunt. inlustris in utraque conversatione prosapia aut episcopis floruit[2] aut praefectis: ita semper huiusce maioribus aut humanum aut divinum dictare ius usui fuit.

[1] vivit *codd.*: novit *Leo*: iuvet *Wilamowitz*: ut vivit *coni. Anderson.*

[2] floruit *LMTCP*: claruit *FP*².

---

[1] *vivit Spiritus Sanctus*: Anderson sees merit in Leo's suggestion of *novit* for the *vivit* of the MSS. He also thinks it possible to keep the parenthesis as marked in Mohr's text but with the reading *ut vivit*—" as the Holy Spirit lives."

[2] Acts VIII. 18–24.

[3] *benedictus Simplicius*: cf. *Ep.* VII. 8. 2–3.

good: (the Holy Spirit liveth,[1] our God omnipotent, who by the lips of Peter condemned the error of Simon the sorcerer in thinking that he could buy with money the grace of benediction):[2] my guarantee is this—that in the case of the one whom I have judged suitable for you I am not biased by money or favour, but that after weighing with due and more than due care the nature of the person, the times, the province, and the city, I was convinced that the man whose life will be hurriedly recalled in the words that follow was the most competent of all. 16. The blessed Simplicius,[3] up till now a member of your order, but henceforth to be reckoned a member of ours, if God grants it through your assent, is so fitted for both spheres by his conduct and by his profession, that the state is able to find in him something to admire and the church something to love. 17. If respect is to be paid to birth, since the evangelist has shown that even this must not pass unmentioned (for Luke[4] in beginning his eulogy of John counted it a signal distinction that he came of priestly stock, and though his theme was to be the nobility of John's life, he nevertheless first extolled the rank of his family), his fathers[5] presided over sees or courts: his race has been illustrious in both walks of life, with a galaxy of bishops and prefects; thus it has always been the custom[6] of his ancestors to enunciate the law either of God or of man. 18. If we take a

[4] Luke I. 5–17.

[5] *parentes*: is *parentes* here = French "parents," and Italian "parenti"?—*A.*

[6] *usui fuit*: this must surely (in this context) mean "has been the custom."—*A.*

18. si vero personam suam tractatu [1] consiliosiore pensemus, invenimus eam tenere istic inter spectabiles principem [2] locum. sed dicitis iure [3] Eucherium et Pannychium inlustres haberi superiores: quod hactenus eos esto putatos, sed praesentem iam modo ad causam illi ex canone non requiruntur, qui ambo ad secundas nuptias transierunt. si annos ipsius computemus, habet efficaciam de iuventute, de senectute consilium. si litteras vel ingenium conferamus, certat natura doctrinae. 19. si humanitas requirenda est, civi clerico peregrino, minimo maximoque, etiam supra sufficientiam offertur, et suum saepius panem ille potius, qui non erat redditurus, agnovit. si necessitas arripiendae legationis incubuit, non ille semel pro hac civitate stetit vel ante pellitos reges vel ante principes purpuratos. si ambigitur quo magistro rudimentis fidei fuerit imbutus: ut proverbialiter loquar, domi habuit unde disceret. 20. postremo iste est ille,

[1] trutina *coni. Anderson.*
[2] principes *MTCFP.*
[3] iure *Mommsen*: viros *T*: vero *C*: viro *rell.*: isti viro *coni. Anderson*: spectabili viro *Wilamowitz.*

---

[1] *tractatu*: I can't help thinking that Sidonius may have written *trutina*, not *tractatu*—" if we weigh his *persona* in more prudent scales," *i.e.* if we judge it by a criterion more cogent than his family distinctions. If my rendering of the text is correct, " the more prudent line " is more prudent than the urging of his family distinctions.—*A.*

[2] Eucherius: *Ep.* III. 8; Pannychius: V. 13.

[3] *dicitis iure*: so Mommsen. But the evidence for *viro* is

more prudent line [1] and assess his own individual standing we find that he occupies a leading place among the Eminents. But you say that Eucherius and Pannychius,[2] having the title "Illustrious," are rightly [3] considered superior to him. I grant that they have been so considered hitherto; but for the present purpose they are not wanted, according to the canon, for they have both married a second time. If we consider his years, he has the energy of youth and the wisdom of age.[4] If we compare his culture and his talent, we find that his natural ability rivals his learning. 19. If it is a question of human kindness he is at the service of citizen, cleric, and alien, the least as well as the greatest, even giving more than a sufficiency, and often it was rather the man from whom no repayment could be expected that acknowledged his gift of sustenance. Time and again, when the necessity of undertaking an urgent embassy was laid upon him, he stood as spokesman of this city before skin-clad monarchs or purple-clad princes.[5] If the question is asked, under what teacher he was initiated into the rudiments of the faith, let me answer in the proverbial words, "He had at home one from whom he could learn." [6] 20. Finally, dear friends, this is the man to whom, when

strong. Wilamowitz, reading *spectabili viro*, thinks *s.* was a contraction for *spectabilis*; then the omission of this *s.* after *dicitis* would be a simple haplography. Or could we suggest *isti viro*?—*A.* The *illustres* held the highest rank in the senatorial order.

[4] *de senectute consilium*: was Simplicius middle-aged?—*A.*

[5] *ante principes purpuratos*: Anderson thought these might include consuls; but that can hardly be so.

[6] Terence, *Adelphi* 413.

carissimi, cui in tenebris ergastularibus constituto multipliciter obserata barbarici carceris divinitus claustra patuerunt. istum, ut audivimus, tam socero quam patre postpositis ad sacerdotium duci oportere vociferabamini; quo quidem tempore plurimum laudis domum rettulit, quando honorari parentum maluit dignitate quam propria. 21. paene transieram, quod praeteriri non oportuerat. sub Moyse quondam, sicut psalmographus ait, "in diebus antiquis," ut tabernaculi foederis forma consurgeret, totus Israel in eremo ante Beselehelis pedes oblaticii symbolam coacervavit impendii. Salomon deinceps, ut templum aedificaret in Solymis, solidas populi vires in opere concussit, quamvis Palaestinorum

---

[1] *in tenebris ergastularibus*: this seems to be literal, not figurative—a Gothic prison is presumably meant.—*A.* *Ergastula* were prisons in which were housed slaves (and, under the empire, convicts) chosen or condemned to do hard labour. At night always, and sometimes while working by day, they were chained.

[2] *tam socero quam patre postpositis*: "this is the man whom you rated above his father and his father-in-law when you kept shouting that he ought to be appointed to the priesthood: but on that occasion he brought home with him glory beyond measure since he . . ."—*A.* Simplicius' father was Eulogius, and his father-in-law was Palladius.

[3] *parentum . . . dignitate*: Is *parentum* a generalising plural? If it is true that the father and father-in-law of Simplicius preceded him as bishops [of Bourges], then the plural is a real one.—*A.* Chaix, II. 20.

[4] Only these three words should be attributed to the Psalms; the rest belong to the book of Exodus. See next note.

[5] Exodus XXXVI. 1 sqq. Dutripon's *Concordantia Bibliorum Sacrorum* gives thirty-two instances of *tabernaculum foederis* in the Book of Numbers alone.—*W.H.S.* The tabernacle is also called a number of times *tabernaculum*

he was confined in a dark dungeon,[1] the much-bolted doors of a barbarian prison were opened by the hand of God. This is the man, as I have heard, whose claims you rated above those of his father and his father-in-law [2] when you cried out that he ought to be instituted into the priesthood; but on that occasion, he came home loaded with praise, since he chose to be honoured by his parents' advancement [3] rather than by his own. 21. I had almost passed over a matter that it would have been wrong to pass by. Under Moses, "in ancient days," [4] as the psalmist has it, in order that the structure of the tabernacle of the covenant might rise and take shape,[5] all Israel in the wilderness laid at the feet of Bezaliel their several contributions of material freely offered. Next Solomon, wishing to construct the temple in Jerusalem, shattered the entire strength of the people in the building of it,[6] and that, too, although the captured wealth of the Palestinians and the tributary

testimonii. Numbers XVII. 7 and XVII. 10; II Chron. XXIV. 6; Acts VII, 44.

[6] What is the meaning of *concussit*? Whipped up? ransacked? taxed to the uttermost? strained? The words which follow seem to show that *vires* here means "resources," "means," in money or kind, not physical strength. But however we take it, it does not tally with the narrative in I Kings; and, incidentally, the Queen of Sheba arrived after the temple was finished! (cf. II Chron. VIII. 9). I don't know any evidence either in I Kings or II Chronicles that Israelites were employed in the work of building the temple. Solomon employed the aliens living in the land of Israel; also, of course, Hiram's Tyrians. If *vires* refers to physical labour, the reference is (or ought to be) to these. If it refers to resources in money or kind one can only say that Scripture seems to give no foundation for it.—*A*.

captivas opes et circumiectorum regum tributarias functiones australis reginae Sabaitis gazae cumulaverit. hic vobis ecclesiam iuvenis miles, tenuis solus, adhuc filius familias et iam pater extruxit, nec illum a proposita[1] devotione suspendit vel tenacitas senum vel intuitus parvulorum, et tamen fuit morum factura quae taceret; 22. vir est namque, ni fallor, totius popularitatis alienus; gratiam non captat omnium sed bonorum, non indiscreta familiaritate vilescens sed examinata sodalitate pretiosus et a[2] bono viratu aemulis suis magis prodesse cupiens quam placere, severis patribus comparandus, qui iuvenum filiorum non tam cogitant vota quam commoda; in adversis constans in dubiis fidus in prosperis modestus, in habitu simplex in sermone communis, in contubernio aequalis in consilio praecellens; amicitias probatas enixe expetit, constanter retinet, perenniter servat; inimicitias indictas honeste exercet, tarde credit, celeriter deponit; maxime ambiendus, quia minime ambitiosus, non studet suscipere sacerdotium, sed mereri. 23. dicit aliquis: "unde tibi de illo tam cito tanta conperta sunt?" cui respondeo: prius Bituriges noveram quam Biturigas. multos in itinere multos

[1] propositi *T recte*? [2] a *LRTN*: *om. MCFP.*

---

[1] *filius familias*: cf. *Ep.* VII. 2. 7.
[2] *intuitus parvulorum*: is this "the sight of his little ones" or "the thought of," "regard for"?

dues of the surrounding kings were swollen by the treasure brought from the south by the Queen of Sheba. But this man, a young government-servant, poor and unaided, still a minor [1] but already a father, built you a church, not allowing either the parsimony of the old people or consideration [2] for his little ones to interfere with the sacred task he had set before him. With all this, his moral make-up was such as to keep silent about himself; 22. for he is a man, if I am not mistaken, wholly incapable of self-advertisement. He abhors all hunting for popular favour; he seeks the goodwill, not of all men, but only of the best; he does not make himself cheap by indiscriminate familiarity but enhances his value by carefully choosing his associates, and his upright manliness makes him more anxious to benefit his rivals than to please them, so that he may be compared to those strict fathers who consider the best interests of their young children rather than the satisfaction of their desires. He is constant in times of adversity, faithful in times of uncertainty, moderate in prosperity; simple in dress, genial in converse, an equal among his comrades, pre-eminent as a counsellor; well-proven friendships he strenuously pursues, staunchly maintains, and guards to the end; a quarrel declared against him he conducts honourably, ever slow to credit it and quick to lay it down. A man to be desired in the highest degree because he desires so little for himself, he seeks not to assume the priesthood but to deserve it. 23. Here someone asks, " Where did you get all that information about him in such a short time? " I answer him thus: I knew Biturigans before I knew their city. I have

in commilitio, multos in contractu multos in tractatu, multos in sua multos in nostra peregrinatione cognoscimus. plurima notitiae dantur et ex opinione compendia, quia non tam parvos terminos posuit famae natura quam patriae. quocirca si urbium status non tam murorum ambitu quam civium claritate taxandus est, non modo primum qui essetis, sed ubi essetis agnovi. 24. uxor illi de Palladiorum stirpe descendit, qui aut litterarum aut altarium cathedras cum sui ordinis laude tenuerunt. sane quia persona matronae verecundam succinctamque sui exigit mentionem, constanter adstruxerim respondere illam feminam sacerdotiis utriusque familiae, vel ubi educta crevit vel ubi electa migravit. filios ambo bene et prudenter instituunt, quibus comparatus pater inde felicior incipit esse, quia vincitur. 25. et quia sententiam parvitatis meae in hac electione valituram esse iurastis, siquidem non est validius dicere sacramenta quam scribere, in nomine patris et filii et spiritus sancti Simplicius est, quem provinciae nostrae metropolitanum, civitati

---

[1] A number of more or less distinguished men with the name Palladius are recorded. But Sidonius refers to a Gallo-Roman family of "landed gentry" who lived in Auvergne in the fifth (and fourth?) and sixth centuries. The rhetor Palladius of Sidonius *Ep.* V. 10. 3 may well have belonged to the family, as did at least two bishops of Bourges during the times of Sidonius, and several very renowned men recorded as living in the sixth century.

[2] *altarium cathedras*: could this be used of priests in general?—*A*.

made the acquaintance of many on the road, in the comradeship of the public service, in the course of contracts or negotiations, or in their or my travels in distant parts. One may also get much in outline from current common opinion, for nature has not set such narrow bounds to reputation as to one's homeland. So if the standing of a city is to be judged not so much by the circumference of its walls as by the eminence of its citizens, I learned at the outset not only what you were like but where you stood. 24. This man's wife is descended from the illustrious stock of the Palladii,[1] who have held professorial chairs or episcopal thrones [2] with credit to their order.[3] And since the personality of that lady demands a brief and respectful mention, I would unhesitatingly affirm that her character befits the priesthoods held by both her families, the one in which she was reared and grew up, and the one into which she passed as a chosen bride. They train their two sons well and prudently; compare them with their father and you will find that he is beginning to have the crowning happiness of being surpassed by them. 25. Well, since you have sworn that the verdict of my humble self shall hold good in this election (for an oath spoken has no less validity than a written one), in the name of the Father, the Son, and the Holy Ghost, Simplicius is the man whom I declare worthy to become Metropolitan of our province [4]

[3] *cum sui ordinis laude*: *i.e.* clergy or laity as the case may be. For this use of *ordo*, cf. § 16 supra: probably episcopal. —*A*.

[4] *provinciae nostrae metropolitanum*: the Bishop of Bourges was apparently Metropolitan of Aquitanica Prima.—*A*.

vestrae summum sacerdotem fieri debere pronuntio. vos autem de viro, quo[1] loquimur, si novam sententiam meam sequimini, secundum vestram veterem consonate.

X (XI)

SIDONIVS DOMINO PAPAE GRAECO SALVTEM

1. Invideo felicitati consuetudinarii portitoris, a quo contigit[2] saepius vos videri. sed quid de Amantio loquar, cum ipsas quoque litteras meas aemuler, quae sacrosanctis reserabuntur digitis, inspicientur obtutibus? et ego istic inter semiustas muri fragilis clausus angustias belli terrore contigui desiderio de vobis meo nequaquam satisfacere permittor. atque utinam haec esset Arvernae forma vel causa regionis, ut minus excusabiles excusaremur.[3] 2. sed, quod est durius, per iniustitiae nostrae merita conficitur, ut excusatio nobis iusta non desit. quocirca salutatione praefata, sicut mos poscit officii, magno opere deposco, ut interim remittatis occursionis debitum

[1] quem *Luetjohann, non bene.*
[2] contingit *MCFP.*
[3] excusaremur *MTCFP*: iudicaremur *LV.*

[1] *novam sententiam meam . . . vestram veterem*; this odd *novus—vetus* business obscures the meaning. The *vetus sententia* is, I think, the decision of the people to put the election in the hands of Sidonius.—*A.*

* Note that Epistles 10 and 11 of this book and in this

and chief priest of your city. As for you, if you accept my new judgment concerning him of whom I speak, then in accordance with your old judgment [1] shout your approval all together.

X (XI) *

SIDONIUS TO THE LORD BISHOP GRAECUS,[2] GREETING

1. I envy the good fortune of my usual letter-carrier, who has had the privilege of seeing you frequently. But why speak of Amantius,[3] the letter-carrier, when I am jealous even of my letters, which will be opened by your blessed fingers and examined by your blessed eyes? And I, personally, shut in here within the half-burnt confines of a fragile wall, am totally debarred by the menace of a war close at hand from satisfying my longing for you. I only wish that the shape and condition of Auvergne were such as to give me less excuse for excusing myself. 2. The worst of it is that, because of my sinfulness,[4] I have no lack of a just excuse. So after the greeting which ordinary courtesy demands, I earnestly enjoin you to remit for the moment my debt of a personal visit, even though I pay you nothing but

edition are, in Luetjohann's, interchanged. Only cod. *C* has them in Luetjohann's order, other MSS having them as here.

[2] Bishop of Marseille. See *Ep.* VI. 8.

[3] See *Ep.* VI. 8; VII. 2 and 7; IX. 4.

[4] *I.e.* the afflictions of Auvergne, which prevent me from going to see you, are a just punishment for my unrighteousness. *nostrae* must be "my" here, although the sin of the whole people is blamed elsewhere.—*A*.

vel verba solventi. nam si commeandi libertas pace revocetur, illud magis verebor, ne assiduitas praesentiae meae sit potius futura fastidio. memor nostri esse dignare, domine papa.

XI (X)

SIDONIVS DOMINO PAPAE AVSPICIO SALVTEM

1. Si ratio temporum regionumque pateretur, non per sola officia verborum amicitias semel initas excolere curarem. sed quoniam fraternae quietis voto satis obstrepit conflictantium procella regnorum, saltim inter discretos separatosque litterarii consuetudo sermonis iure retinebitur, quae iam pridem caritatis obtentu merito inducta veteribus annuit [1] exemplis. superest, ut sollicito veneratori culpam rarae occursionis indulgeas, qui [2] quo minus assidue conspectus tui sacrosancta contemplatione potiatur, nunc periculum de vicinis timet, nunc invidiam de

[1] annuit *MTCFP*: anuit *L*: ac novis vivit *Anderson qui et* eminuit *vel* nunc vivit *coni.*: annititur *coni. Warmington.*
[2] qui *Anderson*: quae.

---

* See the first note of the preceding letter.
[1] Learned Bishop of Toul. Cf. *Ep.* IV. 17. 3.
[2] Probably the Visigoths and the Burgundians. See pp. 323, 510, 519.
[3] *annuit: anuit* of MS. *L* is surely wrong even though adopted by Luetjohann. Perhaps *ac novis vivit* or *eminuit*, or *nunc vivit*?—*A*. I would keep *annuit* and translate something

words; for should peace restore freedom to come and go, my fear will rather be that my constant presence may prove more boring than welcome. Deign to hold me in remembrance, my Lord Bishop.

XI (X) *

SIDONIUS TO THE LORD BISHOP AUSPICIUS,[1] GREETING

If the times and the places in which we live allowed it I should be taking good care to cultivate our friendship, once begun, not merely by the courtesy of correspondence; but since the tempest of battling kingdoms [2] breaks noisily upon our desire for quiet brotherly communion, this custom of epistolary converse will rightly be maintained, at least between parties sundered and removed from one another; it was deservedly introduced long ago for reasons of friendship and is in agreement [3] with old examples. It remains for you to pardon your anxious worshipper for the fault of visiting you so rarely; for, as an obstacle to his often enjoying the hallowed sight of you face to face, he [4] has the fear now of danger from his neighbours, now of enmity from his patrons.[5]

like this—"which we have long since initiated, and rightly, on the score of our affection for each other, and which is in such harmony with the classical examples of friendship."—*W.H.S.*

[4] *quae quo minus assidue*, etc.: surely not *quae*, but *qui*. I wonder how editors take *quae*. As far as I can see, it is practically impossible.—*A.* I agree.—*W.H.S.*

[5] *invidiam de patronis*: Savaron says the *vicini* are the Goths and the *patroni* the Burgundians—probably right.

patronis. sed de his ista: haec etiam[1] multa sunt. 2. interim Petrum, tribunicium virum, portitorem nostri sermonis, insinuo, qui id ipsum sedulo exposcit, quique quid negotii ferat praesentaneo conpendiosius potest intimare memoratu. cui, precor, quod in vobis opis est, intuitu paginae praesentis accedat, manente respectu nihilominus aequitatis, contra quam nec magis familiarium causas commendare consuevi. memor nostri esse dignare, domine papa.

XII

SIDONIVS FERREOLO SVO SALVTEM

1. Si amicitiae nostrae potius affinitatisque quam personae tuae tempus ordinem statum cogitaremus, iure vobis in hoc opere, quantulumcumque est, primae titulorum rubricae, prima sermonum officia

[1] istaec: et iam *Mohr*: istaec etiam *L*: ista haec etiam *MTCFP*.

---

[1] *tribunicium virum*: he had been *tribunus et notarius*. See note on *Ep*. I. 3. 2. (in vol. i. of Loeb Sidonius) for explanation and references.

* Not the Ferreolus of *Ep*. VII. 1. 7, nor the Tonantius of *Ep*. IX. 13 and IX. 15, but the latter's father Tonantius Ferreolus (cf. *Ep*. I. 7. 4; II. 9. 1; *Carm*. XXIV. 34–36) a Gallo-Roman related to Sidonius through Sidonius' wife Papianilla. Ferreolus' maternal grandfather was Flavius Afranius Syagrius (*Ep*. I. 7. 4; V. 17. 4; cf. V. 5. 1; VIII. 8. 3). Ferreolus was Praetorian Prefect of Gaul in A.D. 451, and helped to secure co-operation between Romans and Visigoths, and saved Arles when Thorismund besieged it (see below). To his son is addressed *Ep*. IX. 13.

[2] The gist, says *W.H.S.*, is: "Had I written from the point

So much for that; I have already dwelt rather too long on it. 2. Meanwhile I introduce to you Petrus, a man of tribunician rank,[1] the bearer of this letter, who earnestly desires the introduction, and who can indicate to you more succinctly by word of mouth the nature of his business. I pray you, from regard for this letter, to grant him all the help in your power, subject always to a proper respect for justice, for it is not my habit to oppose justice in urging the causes even of my more intimate friends. Deign to hold me in remembrance, my Lord Bishop.

XII

SIDONIUS TO FERREOLUS,* GREETING

1. Had [2] I considered the chronology, history, and standing of our friendship and kinship rather than your personal career,[3] rank, and status, the first red-letter title and the first epistolary greeting in this work [4] of mine, however unimportant, would justly

of view of a friend and kinsman, my letter to you would have had the first place in the book, and it would have descanted on your glories and those of your ancestors. But I have put the letters to clerics first, for the most humble ecclesiastic must rank above the most distinguished layman." A. does not altogether agree with Semple [*Quaest. Exeg.*, 43–46]—but admits that he is the only one to make sense and attend to the Latin.

[3] *personae tuae tempus etc.*: the meaning of *tempus, etc.* cannot be the same when applied to *amicitiae* and *affinitatis* as when applied to *persona*. The meaning of *tempus* is obscure in either case. It may possibly mean "circumstances."—*A.*

[4] *in hoc opere*: *i.e.* the first letter of Bk. VII or of Bks. VI–VII. No evidence in this first paragraph to support the statement that Ferreolus took orders.—*A.*

dedicarentur. isset per avitas tibi stilus noster curules, patricias nihilominus infulas enumeraturus; non tacuisset triplices praefecturas et Syagrio tuo pro totiens mutatis praeconibus praeconia non negasset; patrem inde patruosque minime silendos percucurrisset. 2. et quamlibet posset triumphalibus adoreis familiae tuae defetigari, non tamen eatenus explicandis antiquorum stemmatibus exinaniretur, ut ob hoc ad narrandam gloriam tuam fieret obtusior; qui, si etiam in scribendis maiorum tuorum virtutibus fuisset hebetatus, tuis denuo meritis cacuminaretur.[1] sed salutationem tibi publicam destinaturus non quid fuisses, sed quid nunc potius esses consideravit. 3. praetermisit Gallias tibi administratas tunc, cum maxume incolumes erant. praetermisit Attilam Rheni hostem, Thorismodum Rhodani hospitem,

[1] cacuminaretur *L*: acuminaretur.

---

[1] The triple prefecture of Syagrius [for whom see *Ep.* V. 17. 4, note], was one continuous term, in that his prefecture of 380 was extended to three years (380–382). He was consul also in 381. Cf. Stroheker, no. 368.

[2] For *praeco*, cf. *Ep.* I. 3. 2 and *Carm.* 7. 467. It is scarcely conceivable that a prefect whose term of office was extended employed a new *praeco* as a matter of course.—*A.*

[3] *adorea* (*sc. donatio*), a gift concerned with *ador*, wheat, as a primitive reward for valour.

[4] *tunc, cum maxime*: or it could be taken *tunc cum maxime*, "just when," "precisely when," "at the very time when she was unscathed."

[5] Flavius Aëtius. For his great career see Vol. I of Sidonius, Loeb, pp. xiii–xx. He defeated Attila on the Mauriac Plains

have been dedicated to you. My pen would have traced the curule offices of your ancestors, nor would it have failed to enumerate their patrician insignia; it would not have been silent about the three prefectures,[1] and it would not have refused a tribute of praise to your Syagrius for his frequent change of heralds.[2] Then it would have treated in detail your father and your uncles who are personages never to be passed in silence. 2. And although it might well have been worn out by all the triumphal honours [3] of your family, it would not therefore have been so exhausted by unfolding your genealogy as to become numbly apathetic to a record of your own glory; for even if it had been dulled in describing the virtues of your ancestors, it would have been sharpened afresh by your merits. But in preparing to address to you a public salutation it has considered not what you have been but what you are. 3. Thus it has passed over your administration of Gaul in her days [4] of greatest security, nor has it told how it was solely through your salutary arrangements that you coped with the needs of Aëtius,[5] the liberator of the Loire, and stood up against[6] Attila the pest of the Rhine, and

in a great battle in which Aëtius' ally Theoderic I of the Visigoths was killed. Aëtius was murdered by Valentinian III.

[6] *tolerasse*: *tolerasse* has a double meaning, but both meanings seem a little odd. With *te* omitted or *tua* substituted, the sentence would be clearer: *Aëtium* as subject; *Attilam* and *Thorismodum* the objects.—*A.* Attila, King of the Huns A.C. 433–453, ruled during about twenty years over lands stretching from the Caspian Sea to the Rhine. But *hostis* (" public enemy," with word-play on *hospes* " guest ") alludes specially to his crossing of the Rhine in A.D. 451 and devastation of Belgic Gaul. The Visigoths sided with Rome.

Aetium Ligeris liberatorem sola te dispositionum salubritate tolerasse, propterque prudentiam tantam providentiamque currum tuum provinciales cum plausuum maximo accentu spontaneis subisse cervicibus, quia sic habenas Galliarum moderarere, ut possessor exhaustus tributario iugo relevaretur. praetermisit regem Gothiae ferocissimum inflexum affatu tuo melleo gravi, arguto inusitato, et[1] ab Arelatensium portis quem Aetius non potuisset proelio te prandio removisse. 4. haec omnia praetermisit, sperans congruentius tuum salve pontificum quam senatorum iam nominibus adiungi; censuitque iustius fieri, si inter perfectos Christi quam si inter praefectos Valentiniani constituerere. neque te sacerdotibus potius admixtum vitio vertat malignus interpres; nam grandis ordinum ignorantia tenet hinc aliquid derogaturos, quia, sicuti cum epulum festivitas publica facit, prior est in prima mensa conviva postremus ei, qui primus fuerit in secunda, sic absque conflictatione praestantior secundum bonorum sententiam computatur honorato maximo[2] minimus[3] religiosus. ora pro nobis.

[1] et *om. P, erasit M*[1].
[2] maximo *LN*: maxime.
[3] minimus *Luetjohann*: minus *LMCFPR*: quisque *T*.

---

[1] King of the Visigoths A.D. 451–453; son of Theoderic I and brother of Theoderic II who assassinated him in 453.

Thorismund[1] the guest of the Rhône, nor how in recognition of your great wisdom and foresight the provincials[2] amid a chorus of loud applause spontaneously lifted your car shoulder-high, because you wielded the reins of Gaul in a way that brought relief to the property-owner, exhausted as he was under the yoke of taxation. Nor has my pen told how the fierce king of the Gothic lands was influenced to abandon his purpose by your appeal at once mellifluous and solemn, subtle and novel, and how by means of a banquet you removed from the gates of Arles one whom Aëtius had been unable to remove by war. 4. All this my pen has passed over, confident that a greeting to you could now be more fittingly appended to a list of bishops than senators and deeming it more proper for you to be placed among the perfected saints of Christ than among the prefects of Valentinian.[3] And let no malicious interpreter misconstrue it as a fault on my part that you are classed with priests. A great ignorance of the two orders possesses those who would disparage this profession. When a public festival provides a banquet the last guest at the first table ranks before the first guest at the second table; so beyond question, according to the view of the best men, the humblest ecclesiastic ranks above the most exalted secular dignitary. Pray for us.

Thorismund withdrew resistance to Attila and favoured the former policy of Visigothic expansion. See also introductory note to this letter.

[2] *provinciales.* Is it "the men of the provinces"?—*A*.

[3] Valentinianus III, emperor A.D. 425–455.

XIII

SIDONIVS SVLPICIO SVO SALVTEM

1. Himerius antistes, filius tuus, notus mihi hactenus parum vultu, satis opinione, quae quidem in bonam partem porrigebatur, Lugdunum nuper a Tricassibus venit, quo loci mihi raptim ac breviter inspectus sanctum episcopum Lupum, facile principem pontificum Gallicanorum, suae tam professionis magistrum quam dignitatis auctorem, morum nobis imitatione restituit. 2. deus bone, quae viro censura cum venustate, si quid vel[1] deliberet forte vel suadeat! abundat animi sale, cum consulitur, melle, cum consulit. summa homini cura de litteris, sed maxime religiosis, in quibus eum magis occupat medulla sensuum quam spuma verborum. tota illi

[1] vel *LRN*: *om. MTCFP.*

---

* Sulpicius is otherwise unknown.

[1] *antistes*: certainly not bishop, which is the usual but not universal meaning of the word in Sidonius. Sirmond is inclined to think that he was an abbot (cf. the application of the word to the monk Abraham in *Ep.* 17. 1, of this book).—*A.* We also have *antistes ordine in secundo* applied to the priest Claudianus Mamertus (See *Ep.* IV. 11, *carm.* 18), and *antistes* to Riochatus in *Ep.* IX. 9. 6. Here also we may conclude that Himerius was a priest not yet of episcopal rank.

[2] *in bonam partem porrigebatur*: possibly "which was spreading among the better sort of people."—*A.* I am rather doubtful about Anderson's translation both in the text above and in this note. Sidonius has just said that so far he has known Himerius "*parum vultu, satis opinione,*" "very little

XIII

SIDONIUS TO HIS FRIEND SULPICIUS,* GREETING

Your son, the priest[1] Himerius, hitherto known to me all too little by sight but amply by reputation, which was indeed widespread and excellent,[2] recently arrived at Lyon from Troyes, where[3] I had a brief and hasty view of him and found that he recalled to my mind the saintly bishop Lupus,[4] easily the first of our Gallic pontiffs, who had trained[5] him for his profession and instituted him in his office; for your son's character was modelled on that great exemplar. 2. Gracious heaven! What judgment and also what charm he shows at any time in deliberating and advising. When he is consulted he is full of piquant mother-wit, when he consults he is full of honeyed sweetness. He cares much for literature, but chiefly for religious literature, in which he is more concerned with the pith of the sense than with the froth of the words. The incentive, quickener, and

personally, but quite well by reputation." Now, *opinio* is a colourless neutral word, so Sidonius hastens to strengthen it by adding the clause, "*quae quidem in bonam partem porrigebatur*"; "by reputation, which however was entirely good in its tendency."—*W.H.S.*

[3] *quo loci*: I suppose this refers to Lugdunum.—*A.* But then in a later note Anderson adds: "Surely the brief and hasty inspection was made at Troyes, and the remainder of the letter gives the result of the writer's much more thorough inspection at Lyons. Both Latin and sense favour this view."

[4] See *Ep.* VI. 1, first note.

[5] *dignitatis auctorem*: presumably Lupus had ordained him to the priest's office or instituted him into his abbacy.—*A.*

actionum suarum intentio celeritas mora Christus est. quodque mirere vel laudes, nihil otiosum facit, cum nihil faciat non quietum. 3. ieiuniis delectatur, edulibus[1] adquiescit; illis adhaeret propter consuetudinem crucis, istis flectitur propter gratiam caritatis: summo utrumque moderamine, quia comprimit, quotiens prandere statuit, gulam, quotiens abstinere, iactantiam. officia multiplicat propria, vitat aliena; cumque ipsi vicissim deceat occurri, gratius habet, si sibi mutuus honos debeatur mage quam rependatur. 4. in convivio itinere consessu inferioribus cedit; quo fit, ut se illi voluptuosius turba postponat superiorum. sermonem maximo temperamento cum conloquente dispensat, in quo non patitur ullam aut verecundiam externus aut familiaris iniuriam, aut credulus invidiam aut curiosus repulsam aut suspiciosus nequitiam, aut peritus calumniam aut imperitus infamiam. simplicitatem columbae in ecclesia servat, in foro serpentis astutiam; bonis prudens, malis cautus, neutris callidus iudicatur. 5. quid plura? totum te nobis ille iam reddidit; totam tuam temperantiam religionem, libertatem verecundiam et illam delicatae

[1] edulibus *LT*: eduliis.

---

[1] *tota illi actionum suarum intentio etc.*: "the sole aim (incentive) of all his actions, the sole force that quickens or checks them."—*A.*

[2] *nihil faciat non quietum*: for *quietus* cf. VII. 9. 10 *fin.*,

moderator of all his actions is Christ alone.[1] A thing worthy of wonder or praise is that he never does anything otiose—though tranquillity marks his every action.[2] 3. He rejoices in fasts,[3] but permits himself to take part in feasts: he clings to the former owing to the custom of the cross, and is attracted by the latter owing to the grace of bonhomie; but in both he exercises the utmost moderation, for whenever he decides to feast he restrains his appetite, and when he decides to fast he avoids ostentation. He multiplies his own acts of courtesy but is reluctant to accept those of others: when etiquette requires his kindness to be returned, he likes it better if this reciprocal attention remains a debt owed than a debt repaid. 4. At table, on the road, and in conference he gives place to his inferiors; the consequence is that his superiors find special pleasure in yielding precedence to him. In conversation he shares the talk with his interlocutor in the justest proportion; thus the stranger feels no embarrassment, the friend no injustice, the credulous no jealousy, the inquisitive no rebuff; the suspicious man senses no mischievous intent, the well-informed no chicanery, the ignorant no humiliation. In the church he preserves the harmlessness of the dove, in courts the wisdom of the serpent. To the good he seems discreet, to the bad cautious, to neither crafty. 5. In a word—he has now presented to us the complete image of yourself; he has made a delightfully realistic copy of all your moderation, your piety, frankness, and modesty,

"placid, without fuss."—*A*. There is word-play with *otiosum*, *quietum*.

[3] *ieiuniis etc.*: cf. VII. 9. 10 fin.

mentis pudicissimam teneritudinem iucunda similitudine exscripsit. quapropter quantum volueris deinceps frui secreto, indulgere secessui, licebit indulgeas; quandoquidem nos in fratre meo Himerio avum nomine, patrem facie, utrumque prudentia iam tenemus. vale.

XIV

SIDONIVS PHILAGRIO SVO SALVTEM

1. Proxime inter summates viros (erat et frequens ordo) vestri mentio fuit. omnes de te boni in commune senserunt omnia bona, cum tamen singuli quique varia virtutum genera dixissent. sane cum sibi quipiam de praesentia tua, quasi te magis nossent, praeter aequum gloriarentur, incandui, quippe cum dici non aequanimiter admitterem virum omnium litterarum vicinantibus rusticis quam institutis fieri remotioribus notiorem. 2. processit in ulteriora contentio; et cum aliqui super hoc errore pervicaciter controversarentur (idiotarum siquidem est, sicut facile convinci, ita difficile compesci), con-

---

[1] *in fratre meo*: *frater* in the sense of "fellow-cleric."

* See note on *Carm.* VII. 156, p. 130 of Vol. I of the Loeb Sidonius, where it is denied that the Philagrius mentioned

and that nicely sensitive refinement of a fastidious mind: and so, however much you may choose in future to enjoy seclusion and give yourself up to country life, you may do so to the full, for in my brother[1] Himerius I now have one with the name of his grandfather, the aspect of his father, and the wisdom of both. Farewell.

XIV

SIDONIUS TO HIS FRIEND PHILAGRIUS,* GREETING

The other day, in a gathering of leading men (a well attended meeting of our order[2] it was, too), your name came up. All the best people with one accord expressed the best possible opinion of you, though each individually mentioned various aspects of your excellence. When some actually plumed themselves unduly on their proximity to you as if they knew you particularly well I flared up, for I could not calmly admit the statement that such a consummate man of letters was better known to his rustic neighbours than to men of learning who lived farther away. 2. The argument extended itself still further; and as some stubbornly disputed about this false notion (for the trouble about the uninstructed is that, though it is easy to refute them, it is difficult to quell them), I stoutly maintained that, if a merely

there is the same as the one mentioned here.—*A.* See also *Carm.* XXIV. 93; *Ep.* II. 3. 1.

[2] *frequens ordo*: the *ordo senatorius.*

stanter asserui, si eloquentibus amicis numquam agnitio contemplativa proveniat, esse asperum utcumque, tolerabile tamen, quia praevaleant ingenia sua, coram quibus imperitia civica peregrinatur, ad remotarum desideria provinciarum stilo adminiculante porrigere; per quem saepenumero absentum dumtaxat institutorum tantus colligitur affectus, quantus nec praesentanea sedulitate conficitur. igitur, si ita est, desistant calumniari communis absentiae necessitatem vultuum mage quam morum praedicatores. 3. equidem si humana substantia rectius mole quam mente censenda est, plurimum ignoro, quid secundum corpulentiam per spatia quamvis porrecta finalem in homine miremur, quo nihil aeque miserum destitutumque nascendi condicio produxit. quippe cum praebeat tamquam ab adverso bovi pilus, apro saeta, volucri pluma vestitum (quibus insuper, ut vim vel inferant vel repellant,

[1] *A.* put " speculative " and remarked: a knowledge of one another derived only from theory or imagination, not from personal acquaintance. *agnitio contemplativa* is probably a translation of ἐπιστήμη θεωρητική. But *contemplativa* as from *contemplor* may be in the physical sense of " gaze at "; in that case, *proveniat* = takes place. But the Thesaurus does not support this. If *contemplativa* has its ordinary meaning, then *provenio* must mean " succeed," not " come to pass." —*A.* But when one reads this letter down to the end of the second sentence in § 7, one is forced to believe that by *agnitio contemplativa* is meant visual acquaintance; *proveniat* might indeed mean " be of use," " be a success "; but in this letter seems to imply simply " occurs ".

visual[1] acquaintance between friends who have the gift of words can never be complete success, it was indeed a hard misfortune in any circumstances, but it may be rendered tolerable[2] by the fact that, with the help of the pen, such men are able to extend to eager recipients in distant provinces the thoughts of their minds, in the presence of which their ignorant compatriots are like strangers in a strange land. Through the medium of the pen there is often formed between people separated by wide distances—at any rate between people of education—such a great affection as even assiduous personal attentions cannot produce. If this is the case, then, let those men who make a song about faces rather than value character cease to put a false construction on unavoidable mutual separation. 3. Really, if the human make-up is to be assessed in terms of matter, not of mind, I for my part quite fail to see what we are to admire in man beyond his bodily bulk (and this, though it may cover a considerable space is nevertheless subject to limits). Indeed, no creature has been brought forth more miserable and helpless than man by the lot of its birth. As if in direct contrast,[3] we find clothing supplied to the ox by its hair, to the wild boar by its bristles, to the bird by its plumage; moreover, they have natural weapons for attack or defence in their horns, tusks, and claws. On the other hand, one would

[2] *asperum, utcumque tolerabile tamen*: so Mohr punctuates, but I feel sure that *asperum utcumque, tolerabile tamen*, is the correct punctuation.—*A*. And so it is translated.

[3] *tamquam ab adverso*: perhaps it may also be rendered "almost at the other extreme," "almost in direct contrast," "as if in direct opposition."—*A*.

cornu dens unguis arma genuina sunt), membra vero nostra in hunc mundum sola censeas eiecta, non edita; cumque gignendis[1] artubus animalium ceterorum multifario natura praesidio quasi quaedam sinu patente mater occurrat, humana tantum corpora effudit, quorum inbecillitati quodammodo novercaretur. 4. nam[2] illud, sicuti ego censeo, qui animum tuum membris duco potiorem, non habet aequalitatem, quod statum nostrum supra pecudes veri falsique nescias ratiocinatio animae intellectualis evexit; cuius si tantisper summoveant dignitatem isti, qui amicos ludificabundi non tam iudicialiter quam ocular iter intuentur, dicant velim in hominis forma quid satis praestans, quid spectabile putent. 5. proceritatemne? quasi non haec saepe congruentius trabibus aptetur. an fortitudinem? quae valentior in leoninae cervicis toris regnat. an decorem liniamentorum? quem crebro melius infigit[3] et argilla simulacris et cera picturis. an velocitatem? quae competentius canibus adscribitur. an vigilantiam? cui certat et noctua. an vocem? cui non cesserit asinus claritate. an industriam?

[1] gignendis *MTCFPRN*: signendis *L*: fingendis *Luetjohann*.
[2] unum *coni. Mohr*.
[3] infingit *coni. Luetjohann*.

[1] *nam illud*: *nam* seems = "but" here. Mohr suggests *unum*, but I don't know how he took the rest of the sentence. If the translation of *non habet aequalitatem* is right, *illud*

think that our limbs, and our limbs alone, had not been brought into this world, but cast out upon it; and while in giving birth to the limbs of other animals nature assists them with manifold protection like a mother with open arms, human bodies are the only ones she has just cast forth to accord them in their weakness a stepmother's treatment. 4. But,[1] as I hold, who consider your soul more precious than your body, all that is of minor importance, because the reasoning faculty of an understanding mind has raised us above the beasts of the field, who do not know true from false. If the importance of this reasoning power is, even for a moment,[2] suppressed by these mockers whose view of their friends is derived, not from reasoned judgment, but from the outward eye, I should like them to state what they think specially outstanding and remarkable in the human frame. 5. Its height? As if this word would not often be more fittingly used of beams! Its strength?[3] As if there was not more of this in the muscles of a lion's neck! Its graceful lines? Why, clay often puts these more successfully into images or wax into pictures. Its swiftness? That is more properly ascribed to dogs. Its wakefulness? Even an owl could hold its own there. Its voice? Why even an ass would not yield to it in loudness. Its

refers to what he has been saying about the bodily disadvantages of the human race. One would like to make *illud* look forward to the *quod* clause. We might take it so only if *non habet aequalitatem* might mean "is on a different level." The general meaning would not be much altered.—*A*.

[2] *tantisper*. I have taken it in the "deictic" sense.—*A*.

[3] *fortitudinem*: this must here mean "strength" not "courage."

cui pro suo modulo comparari nec formica formidat. 6. sed forsitan praeferunt vim videndi: tamquam non sit eminentior visus aquilarum. praeferunt audiendi efficaciam: tamquam sus hispidus non antistet auditu. praeferunt odorandi subtilitatem: tamquam non praecedat vultur olfactu. praeferunt gustandi discretionem: tamquam non plurimum hinc nos [1] cedamus [2] et simio. quid de tactu loquar, quinto sensu corporis nostri? quem sibi indifferenter tam philosophus quam vermiculus usurpant. taceo hic de appetitibus inlecebrosis, quos in coitu motui beluino carnis humanae voluptas inclinata communicat. 7. ecce quam miseriam praeferunt excoluntque qui mihi, quod eis solo sis obtutu notior, turgidi insultant. ast ego illum semper Philagrium video, cuius si tacentis viderem faciem, Philagrium non viderem. unde illud simile vulgatum est, quod ait quidam in causa dispari sententia pari: "filium Marci Ciceronis populus Romanus non agnoscebat loquentem." conclamata sunt namque [3] iudicio universali scientiae dignitas virtus praerogativa, cuius ad maximum culmen meritorum gradibus ascenditur. 8. primum etiam bestiale corpus, si iam

[1] nos *T*: nosse. *Vide infra.*
[2] nos secedamus *vel potius* nos decedamus *coni. Warmington.*
[3] sunt namque *codd.*: sancitaque *Wilamowitz.*

---

[1] *praeferunt*: *praefero* often = "laud" in late Latin.—*A*. I suppose this is an extention of the sense "give preference to."—*W.H.S.*

[2] *decedamus* is a suggested reading here; *decedere* regularly took the dative; the same may have been true of *secedere*, from which verb *secedamus* likewise is a possible reading here—"withdraw far from this position in favour of the ape."

industry? Here even the ant, in proportion to her size, does not fear comparison. 6. But perhaps they laud[1] its power of vision. As if the vision of eagles were not more remarkable! Or its power of hearing. As if the bristly boar did not hear better! Or its fine sense of smell. As if the vulture were not superior in keenness of scent! Or its discriminating sense of taste. As if we were not far inferior[2] in this even to the ape! Why say anything of touch, the fifth of our bodily senses, which is enjoyed alike by the philosopher and the smallest worm? I say nothing here of those ensnaring appetites which man's carnal pleasure, when it has surrendered to desire, causes to indulge, during sexual union, in an orgasm which is shared with that of beasts. 7. Now you see what a wretched state of affairs is lauded and glorified by those who arrogantly insult me because you are better known to them by sight alone. I, on the other hand, always see before me a different Philagrius, a Philagrius whose face if I saw without getting a word from him, I should not be seeing the true Philagrius. There is a well-known saying[3] of this sort, uttered by a certain man in different circumstances but with the same meaning: "The Roman people did not recognise[4] the son of Marcus Cicero when he spoke." For the judgment of the whole world has always acclaimed the dignity, the worth, and the pre-eminence of knowledge, the highest peak of which is reached by the ladder of merit. 8. In the first place, the body even of a lower

[3] Its source is not known.

[4] Because he had not his father's eloquence and was not otherwise noteworthy.

forte formatum est, dignitate transcendit materiam informem; deinde formato praeponitur corpus animatum; tertio praecedit animam pecudis animus humanus, quia, sicut inferior est caro vitae, sic vita rationi, cuius assequendae substantiam nostram compotem deus artifex, ferinam vero impotem fecit; ita tamen, quod in statu mentis humanae pollet bipertita condicio. nam sicut animae humanitus licet ratiocinantes, hebetes tamen pigrioresque prudentum acutarumque calcantur ingenio, ita si quae sunt, quae sola naturali sapientia vigent, hae peritarum se meritis superveniri facile concedunt. 9. quorum ego graduum differentiam observans illum Philagrium cordis oculo semper inspicio, cui me animus potentialiter notum morum similitudine facit. nam licet bonis omnibus placeas, nemo te plus valuit intrinsecus intueri quam qui forinsecus affectat imitari. sane qualiter studiorum tuorum consectaneus fiam, consequa paginae parte reserabitur. 10. amas, ut comperi, quietos; ego et ignavos. barbaros vitas, quia mali putentur; ego, etiamsi boni. lectioni adhibes diligentiam; ego quoque in illa parum mihi patior nocere desidiam. comples ipse [1] personam religiosi; ego vel imaginem. aliena non appetis; ego etiam refero ad quaestum, si propria non perdam. delectaris contuberniis erudi-

[1] ipse *L*: *om. rell.*

---

[1] As *diligentia* is here opposed to *desidia*, one is tempted to think that it means " diligence."—*A*.

[2] *religiosi*: I suppose *religiosus* has its technical meaning here.—*A*.

animal, if already formed, transcends in dignity mere formless matter. In the second place, a body possessed of life ranks higher than one with nothing but form. Thirdly, the mind of man takes precedence of the vital force of a beast, because, just as flesh is inferior to life, so is life inferior to reason, which God the creator has made our substance capable of attaining, but that of wild animals incapable, though with this reservation, that a double law controls the standing of the human intellect; for just as some minds, though they reason in human fashion, are dull and rather sluggish and so are overtrodden by the ability of minds which are both wise and clever, so those which derive their strength only from natural wisdom readily admit that they are eclipsed by the superior merits of highly trained intelligences. 9. Keeping in view these different grades, I always scrutinise Philagrius with the inner eye, seeing a man to whom my mind makes me potentially known through the likeness of our characters; for though you please all good men, no one has been better able to view you inwardly than he who seeks to imitate you outwardly. Certainly the next part of my letter will reveal how I am becoming a follower of your pursuits. 10. You love quiet people, I find; I love even the lethargic. You shun barbarians because they are reputed bad; I shun them even if they are good. You devote great attention [1] to reading: I, too, do not permit indolence to damage me there. You fill the rôle of an ecclesiastic; [2] I represent at least the shadow of one. You do not covet the possessions of others; I count it gain if I do not lose my own. You delight in

torum; ego turbam quamlibet magnam litterariae artis expertem maxumam solitudinem appello. 11. diceris esse laetissimus; ego quoque lacrimas omnes perire definio, quas quisque profuderit, nisi quotiens deo supplicat. humanissimus esse narraris; nostram quoque mensulam nullus, ut specum Polyphemi, hospes exhorruit. summa clementia tibi in famulos esse perhibetur; nec ego torqueor, si mei, quotiens peccaverint, non totiens torqueantur. 12. ieiunandum alternis putas? non piget sequi. prandendum? non pudet praevenire. de cetero, si vos a me videri Christi munere datur, ita gaudeam tamquam cui de te nec minora subtracta sint. porro autem quae sint in te maiora iam satis novi. propter quae fieri facilius potest, ut et si quandoque faciem tuam coram positus inspexero, aliqua de te recens mihi laetitia potius quam sententia accedat. vale.

XV

SIDONIVS SALONIO SVO SALVTEM

1. Quotiens Viennam venio, emptum maximo velim, ut te fratremque communem colonum civitatis

---

[1] *gaudeam* = *gaudebo*: present subjunctive for future indicative as elsewhere in Sidonius.

[2] *porro autem* seems to mean "on the other hand" or "on the contrary."—*A*.

* This seems to be a mild rebuke to two rich clerics (brothers) who gave most of their time to their broad acres and neglected their duties in the city.

gatherings of the learned; to me, any assembly, however large, which is devoid of literary talent seems a complete wilderness. 11. You are said to be a most cheerful man; I also reckon as wasted every tear a man sheds unless when he is praying to God. You are reported to be most philanthropic; so too my humble board has never been shunned by any stranger as though it were the cave of Polyphemus. You are credited with the utmost forbearance towards your servants; well, it is not torture to me if my servants are not tortured when they misbehave. 12. Do you favour fasting day and day about? I do not mind following you. Or do you favour feasting? I am not ashamed to outstrip you there. Finally, if by Christ's grace I ever have the privilege of seeing you I shall rejoice[1] as one from whom not even your minor qualities have been withheld; of your more important characteristics, on the other hand,[2] I have already an ample knowledge; and it is because of this deeper acquaintance that, if ever I shall see you face to face, I shall perhaps get some fresh pleasure from the encounter, but certainly not a new opinion of you. Farewell.

XV *

SIDONIUS TO HIS FRIEND SALONIUS,[3] GREETING

1. Every time I visit Vienne, I would give a great deal to find that your town residence saw more of you

[3] Not otherwise known.

habitatio plus haberet, qui mihi non amore solum verum etiam professione sociamini. sed et ille imputationem meam praetextu frequentatae suburbanitatis eludit, per quam efficitur, ut nobis nec praesens ipse nec reus sit, et tu habes quo te interim excuses, quod te diu possidet vix recepta possessio.

2 quicquid illud est, iam venite, hac deinceps condicione discessum impetraturi, ut aut vicissim redeatis aut † serius.[1] nam quamlibet ruri positi strenuos impleatis agricolas, tum vere propriam terram fecundabitis, si ecclesiam, quam plurimum colitis, plus colatis. vale.

[1] serius *codd.*: sertius *aut* consertius *coni. L. A. Post*: saepius *coni. Mohr*: *et* simitu (*aut* simitur) *et* secus *et* serius ocius *coni. Anderson*: rarius *coni. Semple.*

---

[1] The translation takes colonus in the sense of "inhabitant" or "inmate"; but the word might be applied to the inhabitant of a colony, and I suppose Vienne was a colony. On the other hand, *frater communis* has been used in a previous letter in the sense "yours and mine." Cf. IV. 18. 2, *tuque fraterque communis Volusianus*; IV. 12, 1, *ego filiusque communis*; IV. 23. 1, *filius tuus, immo communis.* Yet it is hard to see how we are to take *colonum* if we take *fratrem* and *communem* together. Lastly, *colonum* might just mean "farmer."—*A.* I think this last suggestion is the correct one, "your brother who like you is a farmer."—*W.H.S.*

[2] Anderson made several efforts to correct *serius.* I would myself suggest *rarius*—"please come to the city and visit me" says Sidonius to the two agricultural brothers: "when you do visit me, I won't let you go back to the country except on one condition, that either you go back singly and by turns, or

and of its fellow-tenant,[1] your brother, linked as you both are to me not only by affection but also by profession. But your brother dodges my reproach by the pretext of being constantly on his suburban farm, which results in his being never at home for me and at the same time in his being exempt from blame; and you on your part have for the time being the excuse that a landed possession, which you have barely succeeded in recovering, has long possessed your attention. 2. However that may be, come at once, and you will then in due time receive permission to leave, on condition that you come back, either turn and turn about, or both together after a longer interval.[2] For however much you station yourselves in the country and play the active farmer, you will not really be fructifying your own proper soil unless you cultivate [3] more the field which you adorn most, the church. Farewell.

that you go back *rarius*, at less frequent intervals."—*W.H.S.* I think this gets a right contrast—between *discessus* a departure from city to country, and *redire* as expressing return to the city; and thus Sidonius means that, once they have come to town, he will approve of their departure again only if they agree to come back to town yet again, either each in turn or both acting together. In any case, *serius* will hide a word meaning the opposite of *vicissim* "each in turn." Sidonius may have written *simul*, but I had proposed a word which does not occur elsewhere—*sertius* ("more jointly," "with more co-operation"), as if from *serte*, on the analogy of *conserte* which does occur. L. A. Post has had the same idea, and suggests either *sertius* or *consertius* at this point. This solution seems to have occurred to him before it did to me. —*E.H.W.*

[3] *colatis*: I don't think that *colatis* = *incolatis* as Grégoire and Collombet think. Sidonius is playing on the different meanings of *colo*.—*A.*

XVI

SIDONIVS CHARIOBAVDO[1] ABBATI SALVTEM

1. Facis, unice in Christo patrone, rem tui pariter et amoris et moris, quod peregrini curas amici litteris mitigas consolatoriis. atque utinam mei semper sic recorderis, ut sollicitudines ipsas angore [2] succiduo concatenatas, qui exhortator attenuas, intercessor incidas! 2. de cetero, libertos tuos causis quas iniunxeras expeditis reverti puto, quos ita strenue constat rem peregisse, ut nec eguerint adiuvari. per quos nocturnalem cucullum, quo membra confecta ieiuniis inter orandum cubandumque dignanter tegare, transmisi, quamquam non opportune species villosa mittatur hieme finita iamque temporibus aestatis appropinquantibus. vale.

[1] CHARIOBALDO *T*.
[2] languore *coni. Semple*: anguore *MTFP*: angore.

* Not otherwise known. I think this letter was written in Sidonius' term of exile after the cession of Auvergne to the Goths in A.D. 475; and I am not sure that in § 1 we should not read *languore* for *angore*, when we compare IV. 22. 4 *languor impedimento iamque vel sero propter hunc ipsum desidia cordi;*

XVI

SIDONIUS TO THE ABBOT CHARIOBAUDUS,* GREETING

1. It is just like your loving heart and custom, my matchless patron in Christ,[1] to assuage the worries of your friend in another land by a letter of consolation. I only wish that you might always so remember me as to sever by your intercession, as you alleviate by your exhortation, even this chain of anxieties which is one continuous torture to me. 2. For the rest, I believe that your freedmen are on their way back, having despatched the business you had charged them with. It is clear that they transacted their business with such diligence that they did not even require a helping hand. I have sent you by them a cowl for night wear in the hope that you will use it between your prayers and your lying-down, to cover your limbs, wasted as they are by fastings—although woollen material[2] is not a very suitable present now that winter is over and summertime approaches. Farewell.

and V. 3. 3 *infelicis conscientiae mole depressus, vi febrium nuper extremum salutis accessi*: the evidence seems to indicate that his exile had caused him extreme depression (*sollicitudine*) linked with physical weakness and illness (*languore succiduo concatenatas*).—*W.H.S.* For Sidonius in exile, see below, and Stevens, *Sid. Apoll.*, 162 ff.

[1] For the phrase, see also *Ep.* IV. 25. 1; VI. 7. 1.

[2] In the mercantile sense, "goods," "commodities."—*A.*

XVII

SIDONIVS VOLVSIANO FRATRI SALVTEM

1. Iubes me, domine frater, lege amicitiae, quam nefas laedi, iam diu desides digitos incudibus officinae veteris imponere et sancto Abrahae diem functo neniam sepulchralem luctuosis carminibus inscribere. celeriter iniunctis obsecundabo, cum tua tractus auctoritate, tum principaliter amplissimi viri Victorii comitis devotione praeventus, quem iure saeculari patronum, iure ecclesiastico filium excolo ut cliens, ut pater diligo; qui satis docuit, quae sibi aut qualis erga famulos Christi cura ferveret, cum torum circa decumbentis antistitis, non dignitatem minus quam membra curvatus ac supra vultum propinqua morte pallentem dolore concolor factus, quid viro vellet lacrimis indicibus ostenderet. 2. et quia sibi maximas humandi funeris partes ipse praeripuit, totum apparatum[1] supercurrentis impendii

[1] apparatum *Sirmond*: apparatu.

* Not a real brother but a close friend (cf. *Ep.* IV. 18. 2), probably the one who was later Bishop of Tours in succession to Perpetuus (*Ep.* VII. 9).

[1] *luctuosis carminibus inscribere.* I am not happy about this phrase. I think it means " write an epitaph to be put among the other epitaphs." Cf. *Ep.* II. 10. 3 for loose use of *inscribo* (inscribe on = inscribe for placing on).—*A.* I regard *luctuosis carminibus* as an abl. of attendant circumstances, meaning simply " to write a funeral dirge in mournful

XVII

SIDONIUS TO HIS BROTHER VOLUSIANUS,* GREETING

1. You bid me, my lord and brother, by the law of friendship, which it would be infamous to violate, to apply my fingers so long inactive to the anvils of my old workshop and to write a sepulchral lament [1] for that holy man, the deceased Abraham,[2] to be included among the mournful inscriptions. I will make haste to obey your injunction, influenced partly by your authority, but principally following the lead which the great Count Victorius [3] has given by his devotion, a man whom I honour as my patron by worldly law and as my son by the law of the Church. He amply proved the reality and the quality of his earnest solicitude for the servants of Christ when at the bed of the dying abbot he bent not only his dignity but his limbs; and stooping, sympathetically pallid, over that face already marked with the pallor of approaching death he shewed by the telltale tears how he felt towards the man. 2. And since he has taken upon himself the main responsibility for the obsequies, making complete provision of

strains." There is no need to press the meaning of *inscribere.* —*W.H.S.*

[2] Saint Abraham of Mesopotamia in Persian territory from which he was expelled for his Christianity—see below and Gregory of Tours, *Vitae Patrum*, 3; *Hist. Franc.* II. 21. He died in A.D. 477. In 1804 his relics were taken to the church of St. Eutropius (who lived in the third century) at Saintes.. Chaix, II. 224.

[3] Cf. *Ep.* IV. 10. 2 and note there.

quod funerando sacerdoti competeret impertiens, saltim ad obsequium quae remanserunt verba conferimus, nihil aliud exaraturi stili scalpentis impressu quam testimonium mutuae dilectionis. ceterum viri mores gesta virtutes indignissime meorum vilitate dictorum ponderabuntur.

Abraham sanctis merito sociande patronis,
  quos tibi collegas dicere non trepidem:
nam sic praecedunt, ut mox tamen ipse sequare;
  dat partem regni portio martyrii:
natus ad Euphraten, pro Christo ergastula passus
  et quinquennali vincula laxa fame,
elapsus regi truculento Susidis orae
  occiduum properas solus ad usque solum.
sed confessorem virtutum signa sequuntur
  spiritibusque malis fers, fugitive, fugam.
quaque venis, Lemurum se clamat cedere turba:
  daemonas ire iubes exul in exilium.
expeteris cunctis, nec te capit ambitus ullus;
  est tibi delatus plus onerosus honor.
Romuleos refugis Byzantinosque fragores
  atque sagittifero moenia fracta Tito.

---

[1] Anderson's translation has been altered to fit Sirmond's reading. But we could keep *apparatu* and translate: "affording, by provision of the very high cost, all that befitted the funeral of a priest." Having already used the word *impendii*, Sidonius goes on to use *impertiens* instead of the usual *impendens*.

[2] I take it that this means that Abraham's sufferings, in the Persian persecution, were a partial martyrdom, so that he shares in the glory and the heavenly reward of the martyrs. —*A*.

[3] For *ergastula* see page 352, note 1.

the overmounting cost[1] which befits the funeral of a priest, I gave as my tribute what at least is left to me—words, and the impress of my scratching style shall inscribe nothing but a testimony to our mutual love. Apart from that, my poor words will utterly fail to give the true measure of the man's character, achievement, and virtues.

" Abraham, worthy to be joined to the company of patron saints, whom I should not be afraid to call thy colleagues (for they take precedence only in the sense that thou followest close behind), thy portion of martyrdom givest thee a part in the Kingdom[2] of Heaven. Born by the Euphrates, thou didst suffer the dungeon[3] for Christ's sake and the chains that grew loose about thee through five years of hunger. Escaping[4] from the savage King[5] of Susa's realm, thou didst fare alone all the way to the western land. But signs of his virtues accompanied this wandering confessor, and thou, a fugitive thyself, didst put to flight the evil spirits. Wherever thou didst pass, the horde of fiends[6] shouted their surrender, and thou, an exile, didst bid the demons go into exile. Thou art sought out by all, yet no self-seeking takes hold on thee; a more onerous kind of honour has been bestowed on thee. Thou didst shun the din of Rome and Byzantium and the walls[7] broken by Titus with

[4] With an angel's help, according to Gregory of Tours, *Vitae Patrum* 3.

[5] Yezdegerd II of the Sassanids (successors in Iran of the Parthians after A.D. 225), A.D. 438–457, whose persecution began apparently in 446. Susa was the capital city.

[6] What is the meaning of *Lemures* here?—*A*. Lemures were ghosts, especially of the dead.

[7] Of Jerusalem, taken by Titus in A.D. 70.

murus Alexandri te non tenet Antiochique;
spernis Elisseae Byrsica tecta domus.
rura paludicolae temnis populosa Ravennae
et quae lanigero de sue nomen habent.
angulus iste placet paupertinusque recessus
et casa, cui culmo culmina pressa forent.
aedificas hic ipse deo venerabile templum,
ipse dei templum corpore facte prius.
finiti cursus istic vitaeque viaeque:
sudori superest dupla corona tuo.
iam te circumstant paradisi milia sacri;
Abraham iam te conperegrinus habet;
iam patriam ingrederis, sed de qua decidit Adam;
iam potes ad fontem fluminis ire tui.

3. Ecce, ut iniunxeras, quae restant sepulto iusta persolvimus; sed, si vicissim caritatis imperiis fratres amicos commilitones obsequi decet, ad vicem, quaeso, tu quoque quibus emines institutis discipulos eius aggredere solari fluctuantemque regulam

[1] Sidonius probably alludes to the exploit of Titus during the capture of Jerusalem, when he killed twelve foes with twelve arrow-hits: Suetonius, *Titus*, 5; Eutropius, VII. 21; cf. Josephus. *B.J.*, V. 6. 5.

[2] Alexandria, founded in 332 B.C.

[3] Antioch, founded by Seleucus in 300 B.C.

[4] The citadel of Carthage. Elissa was another name for Dido.

[5] Mediolanum (that is, Milan, not the other Mediolan(i)um = Saintes), so-called because there was found (so it was said) in its centre (in *medio*) a woolly boar (*sus lanea*).—Isidore, *Orig.*, XV. 1. Cf. Claudian X. 183 and Gesner's note.

his bowmen.[1] Neither Alexander's [2] nor Antiochus' [3] city held thee, and thou didst scorn the dwellings of Byrsa,[4] Dido's home. Thou didst despise the thronged territory of Ravenna amid the marshes and the region that takes its name from a fleecy boar.[5] Thy choice was this nook, to be thy poor retreat, with a hut whose roof is thatched with straw. Here thou didst thyself build to God a hallowed temple, thou who hadst first made thy body a temple for God. In this place ended the course both of thy wayfaring and of thy life; there remains for thee a double crown [6] to reward thy toil. Now the teeming thousands in holy Paradise stand around thee; now Abraham,[7] a pilgrim like thyself, has thee with him; now thou dost enter thy native land (but the one from which Adam fell); now thou art able to advance to the fountain-head of thine own river." [8]

3. You see, I have paid, as you had ordered me, the remaining dues to the buried abbot; but if it becomes men who are brothers, friends, and fellow-soldiers [9] to take turn about in obeying the commands which affection lays upon them, do you in your turn, I pray you, try to help his disciples by instilling those principles in which you excel, and

[6] That is, *abbatis et confessoris*, apparently.

[7] The Biblical patriarch.

[8] On the basis of Genesis II, the Euphrates, near which St. Abraham was born, was considered to have its source in the Garden of Eden. Sidonius speaks as if the heavenly Paradise were planned like the earthly one. It was from the heavenly Paradise that Adam fell—that is apparently the significance of *sed de qua decidit Adam*.—*A*.

[9] In the religious sense. So also St. Paul, *To the Philipp.*, 2. 25; *To Philemon*, 2.

fratrum destitutorum secundum statuta Lirinensium patrum vel Grinincensium festinus informa; cuius disciplinae si qui rebelles, ipse castiga; si qui sequaces, ipse conlauda. 4. praepositus illis quidem videtur sanctus Auxanius, qui vir, ut nosti, plusculum iusto et corpore infirmus et verecundus ingenio eoque parendi quam imperandi promptior exigit te rogari, ut tuo ipse sub magisterio monasterii magister accedat et, si quis illum de iunioribus spreverit tamquam imperitum vel pusillanimem, per te unum sentiat utrumque non impune contemni. quid multa? vis ut paucis quid velim agnoscas? quaeso, ut abbas sit frater Auxanius supra congregationem, tu vero et supra abbatem. vale.

XVIII

SIDONIVS CONSTANTIO SVO SALVTEM

1. A te principium, tibi desinet. nam petitum misimus opus raptim electis [1] exemplaribus, quae

[1] electis *LTN*: relectis *rell. recte?*

---

[1] In the monastic sense, of course.—*A.*

[2] On the Rhône near Vienne. For Lérins see 249. The community established by Abraham near Clermont became the monastery of St. Cyrgues.

[3] Cf. *Ep.* I. 7. 6 (if he is the same). He became abbot after Abraham.

* Letter 17 of Book VII was meant by Sidonius to be the last that he would publish. But the other letters had stirred up so much interest, and so much desire in people to be represented in any published series, that more were added by Sidonius. Stevens, *Sid. Apoll.*, 168 ff.

make haste to fashion the faltering rule[1] of the desolate brethren according to the ordinances of the fathers of Lérins or Grigny,[2] rebuking in person any who rebel against that discipline and praising those who conform. 4. That good man Auxanius[3] has ostensibly become their head, but, as you know, he is physically rather frail and, being naturally shy, he is more ready to obey than to command; so he urges that you should be invited to the place, in order that he may himself be under your direction when he assumes the direction of the monastery, and that, in case any of the junior brethren should scorn him as being inexperienced or timid, you, acting alone, should make the offender feel that neither of you can be slighted with impunity. Why labour the point? Do you wish me to tell you in a word what I want? I ask that brother Auxanius as abbot may be over the congregation, but that you should be over the abbot. Farewell.

XVIII *

SIDONIUS TO HIS FRIEND CONSTANTIUS,[4] GREETING

1. "With thee begun, with thee 'twill end"[5] I send you the work you sought, having hastily selected

[4] See *Ep.* I. 1; III. 2; VIII. 16; II. 10. 3; IX. 16. 1.
[5] From Virgil, *Ecl.* 8. 11. *tibi* = to thee, *i.e.* in thine honour.—*A.* It was Constantius who had originally asked Sidonius to publish his more polished letters; and the first letter of Book I is a dedicatory letter of Sidonius to Constantius.

ob hoc in manus pauca venerunt, quia mihi nil de libelli huiusce conscriptione meditanti hactenus incustodita nequeunt inveniri. sane ista pauca, quae quidem et levia sunt, celeriter absolvi, quamquam incitatus semel animus necdum scripturire desineret, servans hoc sedulo genus temperamenti, ut epistularum [non][1] produceretur textus, si numerus breviaretur. 2. pariter et censui librum, quem lector delicatissimus desiderares, et satis habilem nec parum excusabilem fore, si, quoniam te sensuum structurarumque levitas poterat offendere, membranarum certe fascibus minus onerarere. commendo igitur varios iudicio tuo nostri pectoris motus, minime ignarus, quod ita mens pateat in libro velut vultus in speculo. dictavi enim quaepiam hortando, laudando plurima et aliqua suadendo, maerendo pauca iocandoque nonnulla. 3. et si me uspiam lectitavisti in aliquos concitatiorem, scias volo Christi dextera opitulante numquam me

[1] epistularum non *F*: epistularum ñ *s.l.* *M*[1]: ⟨tum⟩ epistularum produceretur *coni. Anderson.*

---

[1] Or, "had hitherto been neglected."—*A.*

[2] *A.* was doubtful. I always take *temperamentum* as indicating a certain compensating balance; and here Sidonius, in apologising for the relative fewness of the published letters, says that he tries to balance the small total number of the collection by adding to the length of individual letters—the more so as he finds his old zest for composition revives as soon as his mind gets working on the material. This excellent sense is afforded by Mohr's text, which omits the *non* before *produceretur*.—*W.H.S.*

[3] *et si me uspiam lectitavisti*: "if here and there in your reading of me," "if anywhere in your reading." I am not quite happy about *uspiam lectitavisti*. Is the frequentative

certain copies; only a small number came to hand, because I had no thought of compiling a little volume of this sort and so a number of pieces which so far had not been carefully kept [1] cannot now be discovered. As a matter of fact, the present specimens, being few in number and indeed of little importance, have been quickly finished off—although, when once my mind had been set to work I found the urge to write as strong as ever; and I studiously kept to this compromise [2] that the text of my letters should be extended if their number was reduced. 2. At the same time I thought that the book which you, most fastidious of readers, desired, would be reasonably convenient to handle and not quite inexcusable if (in view of the fact that you might well be offended by its flimsiness of sense and structure), you were at least not burdened with great sheaves of paper. So I commend to your judgment the varied feelings of my heart, being well aware that the mind is as fully exposed in a book as the face in a mirror. I have written some exhortations, a great deal of praise, a certain amount of advice, a few laments, and a good number of jests. 3. And if in your reading you have anywhere [3] found me rather vehemently roused against some persons, I would have you know that with the help of Christ's right hand I will never

form used without notion of repetition? I doubt if my translation will do (and does it square with the facts?)—*A.* I don't think there is any need to make heavy weather of this clause. Sidonius merely says that, wherever in the letters he is found to be too choleric and outspoken, he has a good explanation or excuse: for he can't abide a mealy-mouthed servile person, and he claims the right to speak his mind without suppression of any genuine feeling.—*W.H.S.*

toleraturum animi servitutem, compertissimum tenens bipertitam super his moribus hominum esse censuram. nam ut timidi me temerarium, ita constantes liberum appellant. inter quae ipse decerno satis illius iacere personam, cuius necesse est latere sententiam. 4. ad propositum redeo. interea tu, si quid a lectionis sacrae continuatione respiras, his licebit neniis avocere. nec faciet materia ut immensa fastidium, quia cum singulae causae singulis ferme epistulis finiantur, cito cognitis in quae oculum intenderis ante legere cessabis quam lecturire desistas. vale.

LIBER OCTAVVS

I

SIDONIVS PETRONIO SVO SALVTEM

1. Tu quidem pulchre (mos hic tuus, et persevera), vir omnium bonorum, qui uspiam degunt, laude dignissime, quod amicorum gloriae, sicubi locus, lenocinaris. hinc est quod etiam scrinia Arverna petis eventilari, cui sufficere suspicabamur,

---

[1] Anderson at the end of his translation of this Letter wrote "11. Sept. 1945. Grace à Dieu."—a sentiment which we can feelingly echo.

tolerate servility of spirit, although I am very well aware that men have two opinions about this attitude; for the timid call me reckless and the stout-hearted call me outspoken. As between these two views my judgment is that he whose opinion must needs lie hidden is an abject character. 4. Now I return to my theme. If you ever allow yourself a respite from your continual reading of sacred literature, you may in that interval be diverted by these trivialities. The matter will not weary you by seeming interminably long, for as a rule each letter deals only with one matter, and so you will quickly get the hang of any bit on which you cast your eye, and you will leave off reading before you lose the desire to read.[1] Farewell.

BOOK VIII *

I

SIDONIUS TO HIS FRIEND PETRONIUS,[2] GREETING

1. You certainly act nobly (it is your custom: stick to it), most worthy of the praise of all good men living anywhere, in that you seek to further the reputation of your friends at every opportunity. Hence it is that you desire even my Arvernian book-cases to be ransacked, although I had a feeling that you were

* See remark at the head of VII. 18.

[2] See *Ep.* V. 1, first note.

si quid superiore vulgatu protulissemus. itaque morem geremus iniunctis, actionem tamen stili eatenus prorogaturi, ut epistularum seriem nimirum a primordio voluminis inchoatarum in extimo fine parvi adhuc numeri summa protendat, opus videlicet explicitum quodam quasi marginis sui limbo coronatura. 2. sed plus cavendum est, ne sera propter iam propalati augmenta voluminis in aliquos forsitan incidamus vituperones, quorum fugere linguas cote livoris naturalitus acuminatas ne Demosthenis quidem Ciceronisque sententiae artifices et eloquia fabra potuere, quorum anterior orator[1] Demaden, citerior Antonium toleravere derogatores; qui lividi[2] cum fuerint malitiae clarae, dictionis obscurae, tamen ad notitiam posterorum per odia virtutum decucurrerunt. 3. sed quia hortaris, repetitis laxemus vela turbinibus et qui veluti maria transmisimus, hoc quasi stagnum pernavigemus. nam satis habeo deliberatum, sicut adhibendam in

[1] orator *MTCPR*: orat' (*i.e.* oratus) *L*: *om*. *F*.
[2] lividi *an secludendum sit quaerit Luetjohann.*

---

[1] *ut epistularum . . . protendat*: the sentence is complicated by Sidonius' propensity to word-play and antithesis: but one thing seems to me certain—*inchoatarum* means "imperfect."—*A*.

[2] *voluminis*: the word both here and in § 2 evidently means "work," no matter how many books it consisted of. The question is—does it here refer to the whole of Books I–VII, or to a lesser part of the collection? Surely the former.—*A*.

[3] 384 or 383–322 B.C.

[4] 106–43 B.C.

[5] He was an unscrupulous Athenian orator, leader of the

content with what I had brought to light in my earlier publication. So I shall comply with your command, but I mean to continue the activity of my pen only so far as to extend my series of letters (imperfect [1] as they are, no doubt, from the first page [2] onwards) by the addition of a quite small number at the extreme end—just enough, I mean, to embellish the already completed work with a sort of marginal fringe. 2. But a danger to be particularly heeded is that these supplements to an already published collection may perhaps cause us to fall foul of some fault-finders. Even the masterly thoughts and finished eloquence of Demosthenes [3] and Cicero [4] could not escape the tongues of such people, tongues sharpened by nature on the whetstone of jealousy; the first had to suffer the detractions of Demades,[5] the latter of Antonius,[6] and these spiteful persons, though their ill-nature was as clear as their diction was obscure, have nevertheless passed into the cognisance of posterity simply through their hatred of merit. 3. But since you urge it, let me loosen my sails once more to the stormy winds, and after traversing oceans, as it were, let me cross this mere pond: for I am firmly convinced that it is as necessary

pro-Macedonian party and a bitter enemy of Demosthenes. No doubt he carped at Demosthenes as an orator, but I don't know of any recorded saying of his on this head, unless that recorded in Plutarch, *Demosthenes* XI *ad fin.*—" Demades exclaimed, 'Demosthenes teach me! Will a sow teach Athena?'" is to be so classed. He left no writings (Cic. *Brut.* 36; Quintil. XII. 10. 49), but a number of trenchant sayings of his have come down to us.

[6] Marcus Antonius against whom Cicero delivered the "Philippic" orations that led to Cicero's destruction in 43 B.C.

conscriptione diligentiam, ita tenendam in editione constantiam. demum vero medium nihil est: namque aut minimum ex hisce metuendum est aut per omnia omnino conticescendum. vale.

II

SIDONIVS IOHANNI SVO SALVTEM

1. Credidi me, vir peritissime, nefas in studia committere, si distulissem prosequi laudibus quod aboleri tu litteras distulisti, quarum quodammodo iam sepultarum suscitator fautor assertor concelebraris, teque per Gallias uno magistro sub hac tempestate bellorum Latina tenuerunt ora portum, cum pertulerint arma naufragium. 2. debent igitur vel aequaevi vel posteri nostri universatim ferventibus votis alterum te ut Demosthenen, alterum ut Tullium nunc statuis, si liceat, consecrare, nunc imaginibus, qui te docente formati institutique iam sinu in medio sic gentis invictae, quod tamen alienae, natalium[1] vetustorum signa retinebunt: nam iam

[1] alienae natalium *Luetjohann*: aliena (alienae M^1) talium *MC*: alienae talium *FP*. *Om. hanc ep. LNVRT*.

[1] *constantiam*: Birt (apud Kraemer, *Res Libraria*, p. 35) sees in *constantiam* a punning reference to Constantius, who had suggested the original publication of the Letters. [For such a word-play see *Ep*. V. 9. 1, in Constantino inconstantiam]. But I find this hard to believe.—*A*.

* Apparently not the Johannes of *Ep*. II. 5. 1; certainly not the Bishop of Châlon, *Ep*. IV. 25. 3.

to keep a stout heart [1] in publishing as it is to take pains in writing. In short, there is no middle course; we must either refuse to fear such critics or be silent altogether in all circumstances. Farewell.

II

SIDONIUS TO HIS FRIEND JOHANNES,* GREETING

1. It seemed to me, my paragon of scholars, that it would be an outrage against learning if I delayed the tribute of praise due to you for delaying the extinction of literary culture, for you are acclaimed as its reviver, promoter, and champion when it lay more or less buried, and through the length and breadth of Gaul you stand alone as the teacher who amid the storms of war has enabled Latin speech to gain a haven of refuge, although Latin arms have suffered shipwreck. 2. Therefore contemporaries and posterity alike should universally, amid a chorus of fervent vows, consecrate you as a second Demosthenes or a second Cicero, now with statues (if so allowed), now with portraits; for they have been so moulded and trained by your teaching that, though now in the very midst of an unconquerable and alien race,[2] they will preserve the signs of their ancient

[2] *sic gentis invictae quod tamen alienae*: the suggestion in the clause seems to be—" they were formerly under the aegis of an incomparable race, the Romans: they are still under an unconquerable race, but that race is no longer Roman." —*A*. As so often in Sidonius, *sic . . . quod* has exactly the sense of the classical *ita . . . ut* in contrasting phrases. *W.H.S.*

remotis gradibus dignitatum, per quas solebat ultimo a quoque summus quisque discerni, solum erit posthac nobilitatis indicium litteras nosse. 3. nos vero ceteros supra doctrinae tuae beneficia constringunt, quibus aliquid scribere assuetis quodque venturi legere possint elaborantibus saltim de tua schola seu magisterio competens lectorum turba proveniet. vale.

III

SIDONIVS LEONI SVO SALVTEM

1. Apollonii Pythagorici vitam, non ut Nicomachus senior e Philostrati sed ut Tascius Victorianus e Nicomachi schedio exscripsit, quia ius-

---

[1] *nobilitatis indicium nosse*: perhaps intentionally ambiguous.—*A*. Sidonius' statement is most significant.

[2] *constringere*. I think it must amount to *obstringere* here. —*A*.

[3] *schola seu magisterio*: "from the school and education which you provide"—*W.H.S.*

* See *Ep.* IV. 22, first note.

[4] Apollonius of Tyana (born about 4 B.C.) was a wandering neo-Pythagorean philosopher.—*A*. The *Life* is one of the extant works of Philostratus of the first half of the third century after Christ.

[5] *exscribo* means "to copy, transcribe." This is also the common meaning of *transfero*, and the corresponding noun, *translatio*, here means "transcription." Mommsen misunder-

birthright; for now that the old degrees of official rank are swept away, those degrees by which the highest in the land used to be distinguished from the lowest, the only token of nobility will henceforth be a knowledge of letters.[1] 3. But the benefits derived from your teaching especially claim[2] gratitude from me above all others—me who practise authorship and endeavour to produce something that posterity can read; for at least from your schoolroom or from your lessons[3] there will always emerge a qualified crowd of readers. Farewell.

III

SIDONIUS TO HIS FRIEND LEO,* GREETING

1. I have sent, at your command, the "Life of Apollonius[4] the Pythagorean," not as the elder Nicomachus copied[5] it from the manuscript[6] of Philostratus but as Tascius Victorianus copied it

stands the passage and thinks that Nicomachus translated the Life of Apollonius by Philostratus, and that Victorianus corrected this copy. Apart from other considerations, this view spoils the point of *Opica* (= *barbara* as opposed to Greek). Sidonius says that his copy has been done so hastily that the Greek no longer looks like Greek.—*A*. But Mommsen may well have been right about Nicomachus having translated the Life.

[6] Sidonius must be using *schedium* in the sense of *scheda* (or rather *scida*), a pure Latin word which late Greek borrowed. *Schedium* (neuter of *schedius*, *σχέδιος*) is borrowed from the Greek and is used of an improvised poem. It is conceivable that Sidonius used it in the sense of a rather hastily written (*inconditum et inelaboratum*) manuscript.—*A*.

seras, misi; quam, dum parere[1] festino, celeriter eiecit in tumultuarium exemplar turbida et praeceps et Opica translatio. neque mihi rem credito diuturnius elaboratam vitio vertas: nam dum me tenuit inclusum mora moenium Livianorum, cuius incommodi finem post opem Christi tibi debeo, non valebat curis animus aeger saltim saltuatim tradenda percurrere, nunc per nocturna suspiria, nunc per diurna officia distractus.[2] 2. ad hoc, et cum me defetigatum ab excubiis ad devorsorium crepusculascens hora revocaverat, vix dabatur luminibus inflexis parvula quies; nam fragor ilico, quem movebant vicinantes impluvio cubiculi mei duae quaepiam Getides anus, quibus nil umquam litigiosius bibacius vomacius erit. sane, cum primum reduci aliquid otii fuit, inpolitum hunc semicrudumque et, ut aiunt, tamquam musteum librum plus desiderii tui quam officii mei memor obtuli. 3. quocirca sepone tantisper Pythicas lauros Hippocrenenque et illos carminum modos tibi uni tantum penitissime familiares, qui tamen doctis, ut es ipse,

[1] parare *L.*
[2] distractus *MTCFP*: destrictus *L*: districtus *Luetjohann.*

---

[1] Virius Nicomachus Flavianus: pagan statesman and literary man, *c.* A.D. 334–394; Tascius: a later editor of texts.
[2] Opici = Osci, a primitive folk of Campania in Italy.
[3] Or Liviana; near Carcassonne; perhaps Capendu. Here Sidonius after arrest by Euric's order was confined for about a year during 475–476. Stevens, *Sid. Apoll.*, 162 ff.
[4] *musteum* [from *mustum*, new, unfermented wine]: the adjective is borrowed from Pliny, *Epist.* 8. 21. 6.—*A.*

from that of Nicomachus.[1] In my haste to obey your wish, I hurriedly flung the work into a haphazard copy, making a wild precipitate barbarian[2] transcription. And you must not blame me for taking longer over the work than was expected. So long as arrest within the walls of Livia[3] kept me a prisoner (and it is to your help, after Christ's, that I owe the ending of that burden), my heart was sick with anxieties and harassed by sighs at night and by obligations during the day, so that it was unable, even with occasional spurts, to get quickly through the work I had to consign to you. 2. To make matters worse, when the approach of the twilight hour had recalled me from my post of duty to my living-quarters, my drooping eyelids scarcely got a wink of sleep; for a din would immediately arise from the two old Gothic women near the skylight of my bedroom, the most quarrelsome, drunken, vomiting creatures the world will ever see. Certainly, in offering you this inelegant, half-raw, and, as the saying is, newly-vinted book[4] at my first spare moment after getting home again, I have paid more regard to your desire than to my own duty.[5] 3. So lay aside for a moment Apollo's bays and Hippocrene[6] and all those poetic measures of which you alone are uniquely the master—though it is true that

[5] The meaning is that his duty was to improve the copy before sending it to Leo; but, in view of Leo's desire to have it, he sent it just as it was. *I.e.* in view of your desire for it I have sent the copy just as I wrote it, although my duty demanded that I should revise and improve it.—*A.*

[6] "Horse-fountain," sacred to the Muses and Apollo, on Mount Helicon; the story told was that it was started by the stamping of Bellerophon's winged horse Pegasus.

personis non tam fonte quam fronte sudantur. suspende perorandi illud quoque celeberrimum flumen, quod non solum gentilicium sed domesticum tibi quodque in tuum pectus per succiduas aetates ab atavo Frontone transfunditur. sepone pauxillulum conclamatissimas declamationes, quas oris regii vice conficis, quibus ipse rex inclitus modo corda terrificat gentium transmarinarum, modo de superiore cum barbaris ad Vachalin trementibus

---

[1] *qui tamen doctis etc.*: This clause is an afterthought harking back to the mention of Hippocrene, the Muses' spring: it is prompted both by the desire to make a bad pun (*fonte, fronte*) and by the desire to pay a compliment to Leo's poetry. The epithet *doctus* (in *Carm.* XXIII. 446 Leo is described as *doctiloquus*) as applied to a poet by Sidonius and by many others before him connotes a skilfully acquired mastery of the technique and machinery of poetry. Leo would no doubt appreciate such a description; but unfortunately Sidonius, with his itch for antithesis and word-play, has unconsciously suggested that inspiration (implied by *fonte*) was not very conspicuous in his friend's poetry. Perhaps his blundering words were meant to affirm that Leo's wonderful brain need not go to any mythical fountain for inspiration—his poetry is "all out of his own head."—*A.* Yes, I agree. Sidonius has invited Leo to forget for a moment Hippocrene; but then he realises that, in addressing this very scholarly man, he is attributing to inspiration, to poetic μανία, what in fact is due to Leo's own intellectual creativeness. So Leo's poetry is the result of a conscious intellectual effort, not the effect of involuntary possession by the Muse.—*W.H.S.*

[2] More literally: "are sweated not so much out of that spring as from their own brow."

[3] *ab atavo Frontone*: Fronto (not he of *Ep.* IV. 21. 4) was famous for his oratory: see VIII. 10. 3 and IV. 14. 2.

[4] Probably the Vandals; Euric had extended his rule over most of Spain and thus approached the Vandals in N. Africa; maybe Saxons also are alluded to.

[5] *de superiore*: *Sc.* Hispania or Germania, according to

in the case of scholarly persons[1] such as yourself, these poetic measures are the product not so much of Delphic inspiration as of intellectual effort.[2] Suspend too that renowned flow of oratory which belongs not only to your clan but to your family, and which often flowing on through successive generations from your own ancestor Fronto[3] now discharges itself into your breast. Put aside for an instant those much-acclaimed declamations which you compose as the royal spokesman, and through which the famous King himself terrifies the hearts of nations far across the sea,[4] or from his commanding eminence[5] makes after his victory a complicated treaty with the barbarians[6]

Savaron: hence Grégoire and Collombet, "au sujet de l'Espagne supérieure." But why should King Euric conclude a treaty with those extremely northern Germans on the subject of Spain? Is there a play on *de superiore victor* = "victorious over a superior"?—*A.* I think *de superiore* simply means "haughtily," "condescendingly," "disdainfully."—*W.H.S.*

[6] The Franks. These were a number of German tribes between the Main and the North Sea, the "Ripuarians" living by the Rhine, the "Salians" by the sea. Defeated by the emperor Julian (after A.D. 355) they were confirmed in their earlier occupation of Toxandria (between Meuse and Scheldt) as *foederati* of the Romans, serving in the Roman army. Early in the fifth century the Salians became independent tribes each under its own king. One of these kings, Chlodio or Chlogio, about A.D. 431 invaded more Roman territory, was defeated by Aëtius, but remained master of much of northern Gaul. Franks aided Rome again when Aëtius defeated Attila the Hun in Mauriac in 451. Between c. 456 and 481 a new king Childeric was now friendly now hostile to Rome. His successor Clovis conquered all Gaul except Burgundian territory and Provence, defeating the Roman Syagrius at Soissons in 486 or 487. In the next century the Merovingian house became supreme over all Gaul. L. Schmidt, *Gesch. d. deutschen Stämme*, II. 433 ff.

foedus victor innodat, modo per promotae limitem sortis[1] ut populos sub armis, sic frenat arma sub legibus. 4. exuere utcumque continuatissimis curis et otium tuum molibus aulicis motibusque furare. historiam flagitatam tunc recognosces opportune competenterque, si cum Tyaneo nostro nunc ad Caucasum Indumque, nunc ad Aethiopum gymnosophistas Indorumque bracmanas totus lectioni vacans et ipse quodammodo peregrinere. 5. lege virum fidei catholicae pace praefata in plurimis similem tui, id est a divitibus ambitum nec divitias ambientem; cupidum scientiae continentem pecuniae; inter epulas abstemium, inter purpuratos linteatum, inter alabastra censorium; concretum hispidum hirsutum in medio nationum delibutarum atque inter satrapas regum tiaratorum murrhatos pumicatos malobathratos venerabili squalore pretiosum; cumque proprio nihil esui aut indutui de pecude conferret, regnis ob hoc, quae pererravit, non tam suspicioni, quam [fuisse][2] suspectui; et a fortuna regum sibi in omnibus obsecundante illa tantum beneficia poscentem, quae mage sit suetus oblata praestare quam sumere. 6. quid multis? si vera metimur aestimamusque, fors fuat an philosophi vitae scriptor aequalis maiorum temporibus

[1] promotam limite sortem *coni. Anderson.*
[2] fuisse *secludit Luetjohann.*

---

[1] *per promotae limitem sortis*: this is odd: one would expect *per promotam limite sortem* or the like.—*A.*

[2] Apollonius. See § 1.

[3] "Naked professors," a name given by the ancient Greeks to those Hindu philosophers who looked on clothing and even

trembling on the banks of the Waal, or having restrained people by arms now restrains arms by laws through the whole extent of his enlarged domains.[1] 4. Divest yourself somehow of your never-ending cares and steal respite of your own from the burdens and commotions of the court. You will not study advantageously and adequately the tale you have requisitioned unless you give undivided attention to the reading of it and, so to speak, travel in person along with our man [2] of Tyana, now to the Caucasus or the Indus, now to the gymnosophists [3] of Aethiopia and the Brahmins of India. 5. Read of a man who—be it said with all due deference to the Catholic faith—was in most respects like you, that is, sought after by the rich but not seeking riches for himself; greedy for knowledge but chary of money-making; abstemious in feasts, clad in plain linen amid the purple-robed, severe as a censor amid luxurious perfumes; unkempt, hairy, and bristly in the midst of scented foreigners, and treasured for dignified squalor among the myrrh-scented, pumice-rubbed, cinnamon-soaked satraps of tiara'd kings; more respected than suspected in the Eastern kingdoms he traversed because he derived no article of food or clothing from an animal; and asking from the royal resources which were placed fully at his disposal only such boons as he was accustomed to accept for bestowal on others, not for retention by himself. 6. I need say no more. If we weigh and reckon the truth of the matter, it comes to this: it may be questioned whether the philosopher's life has found a narrator on a level

food as hindrances to thinking. There was a popular confusion of East Africa (Ethiopia) with India.

accesserit, certe par saeculo meo per te lector obvenit. vale.

IV

SIDONIVS CONSENTIO SVO SALVTEM

1. Umquamne nos dei nutu, domine maior, una videbit ille ager tuus Octavianus, nec tuus tantum quantum amicorum? qui civitati fluvio mari proximus hospites epulis, te pascit hospitibus, praeter haec oculis intuentum situ decorus, primore loco, quod domicilium parietibus attollitur ad concinentiam scilicet architectonicam fabre locatis; tum sacrario porticibus ac thermis conspicabilibus late coruscans; ad hoc agris aquisque, vinetis atque olivetis, vestibulo campo colle amoenissimus; iam super penum vel supellectilem copiosam thesauris bibliothecalibus large refertus, ubi ipse dum non minus stilo quam vomeri incumbis, difficile discernitur domini plusne sit cultum rus an ingenium. 2. igitur hic tu, quantum recordor, citos iambos, elegos acutos ac rotundatos hendecasyllabos et

---

* Son of the Consentius of Narbonne—IX. 15. 1 (*carm.* 22 ff.). To this younger Consentius is addressed *Carm.* XXIII. He was a poet in both Latin and Greek and was a trusted friend of the Emperors Valentinian III and Avitus.

[1] *Octavianus*: The explanation of this title is unknown.

[2] The city is Narbonne, the river is the Aude (Atax).

[3] Or perhaps translate, "the house rises high and the walls are of course skilfully arranged so as to produce an architectural harmony."—*A*.

[4] Or: "remarkable," "notable".

[5] *plusne sit cultum rus an ingenium*: cf. *Ep.* I. 6. 3, *non minus est tuorum natalium viro personam suam excolere quam*

with the writers of our ancestors' time; but unquestionably this generation of mine has found in you a reader to match the subject. Farewell.

IV

SIDONIUS TO HIS FRIEND CONSENTIUS,* GREETING

My honoured lord, will that Octavian [1] property of yours ever, by God's good pleasure, see us united? It is indeed not so much your property as the property of your friends. Close to the city, the river,[2] and the sea, it feeds your guests with feasts and you with guests; moreover, its lay-out charms the eye of the beholder. In the first place the house rises high, with walls [3] skilfully arranged so as to produce an undoubted architectural symmetry. Again, it sends forth a gleam far and wide from the chapel, the colonnades and the baths, which are all conspicuous.[4] In addition, its fields and springs, vineyards and olive-groves, its entrance-court, its park, its hill present a most lovely view. Then, besides a well-stocked larder and abundant furniture, it is liberally filled with stores of books, amid which you expend as much energy on the pen as you give to the ploughshare, so that it is hard to decide whether the owner's land or his mind [5] has been the better cultivated. 2. Here then, as I remember, you produced with busy toil (and one could not say whether the rapidity of your composition or the

villam; and Pliny, *Ep.* IV. 6. 2, *nec agrum . . . sed ipsum me studiis excolo.*

cetera carmina musicos flores thymumque redolentia, nunc [1] Narbonensibus cantitanda, nunc Biterrensibus, ambigendum celerius an pulchrius elucubrasti, apud aequaevos gratiam tuam, famam apud posteros ampliaturus; certe mihi, quotiens tui versus a meditationis incude tamquam adhuc calidi deferebantur, sic videbatur, qui, etsi non bene scribo, bene iudico. 3. sed, quod fatendum est, talibus studiis anterior aetas iuste vacabat seu, quod est verius, occupabatur; modo tempus est seria legi, seria scribi deque perpetua vita potius quam memoria cogitari nimiumque meminisse nostra post mortem non opuscula sed opera pensanda. 4. quae quidem ad praesens non ita loquor, quasi tu non utraque laudanda conficias aut, si adhuc durat in sermone laetitia, non custodiatur in actione censura, sed ut qui Christo favente clam sanctus es, iam palam religiosa [2] venerandus [3] iugo salubri colla pariter et

[1] *Post* nunc *deficit R.*
[2] religiose *MP*: religione *coni. Anderson*: religiosus *coni. Semple.*
[3] veneranda *coni. Semple.*

---

[1] *citos iambos*: Horace, *Odes* I. 16. 24, speaks of *celeres iambos* = hasty or impetuous iambics. In *Ars Poetica* 251–252 Horace calls the *iambus* a *pes citus.*

[2] *in sermone laetitia*: does *sermone* here mean "conversation" or "writings" or both?—*A.*

[3] *religiosa venerandus iugo salubri etc.*: lit. "subjecting a religious neck and heart alike to a salutary yoke." This is the least absurd translation I can think of. Did Sidonius write either text as given in the MSS? They vary between *religiosa* and *religiose.* Perhaps *religiose* would be a little less offensive: "earning veneration in a religious way." But both readings offend. *religione,* to be taken closely with *venerandus,* would be much simpler and less shocking. Or

beauty of it was the more remarkable) swiftly moving[1] iambics, clever elegiacs, and shapely hendecasyllables, and your other verses all fragrant with the Muses' thyme and flowers, to be eagerly sung, now by the people of Narbonne, now by those of Béziers. By these poems you were bound to win more and more acceptance from your contemporaries and increased fame with posterity; at least, so it seemed to me whenever your verses were delivered to me still hot, as it were, from the composer's anvil —and I am a good judge, though not a good writer. 3. But I must make an avowal. My earlier life quite properly spared time or, more correctly, devoted all its energy to such pursuits; but now it is time for serious reading and serious writing; one should think about life eternal rather than posthumous renown, and never forget that after death it will be our deeds, not our screeds, that will be weighed in the balance. 4. I mention this on the present occasion not with any idea of implying that you do not meritoriously perform both, or that, if there still remains in your words a merry gaiety,[2] there is not maintained in your conduct a strict discretion; no, my aim is that you, who by Christ's grace are pious in private, should come into the open and earn veneration by subjecting neck and heart alike to the salutary yoke[3] of religion, your tongue

has *religiosa* come into the text as a gloss?—*A*. I have long thought that a solution might be to read: *iam palam religiosus veneranda*, etc., where *palam religiosus* would contrast well with the previous *clam sanctus*: this would mean: "becoming now an open, confessed believer, submit your respected head and heart to the salutary yoke of the Church."—*W.H.S.*

corda subdare invigiletque caelestibus lingua praeconiis, anima sententiis, dextra donariis: praecipue tamen dextra donariis, quia quicquid ecclesiis spargis, tibi colligis; ad cuius exercitia virtutis illud vel principaliter [1] te poterit accendere, quod inter opes quaslibet positi quae bona stultis falso vocantur, si quid largimur [2] nostrum, si quid habemus, alienum est. vale.

V

SIDONIVS FORTVNALI SVO SALVTEM

1. Ibis et tu in paginas nostras, amicitiae columen, Fortunalis, Hibericarum decus inlustre regionum; neque enim tibi familiaritas tam parva cum litteris, ut per has ipsas de te aliquid post te superesse non deceat. vivet ilicet, vivet in posterum nominis tui gloria. 2. nam si qua nostris qualitercumque gratia reverentia fides chartulis inest, sciat aetas volo postuma nihil tua fide firmius forma pulchrius,

[1] principaliter *MTCFP*: principale *L*.
[2] largimur *aut* largimus *coni. Anderson*: egemus *coni. Warmington*: agimus.

---

[1] The reading translated is *largimur* (or *largimus*?). Surely this gives the required sense and is probably right—*A*. But we might read *egemus* "what we lack is our own"; for *egere* with the accusative case cf. Plaut. *Men.* 121 *nec quicquam eges*; Publilius Syr. *Sententiae* 286 (ed. Friedrich, 1964, p. 53) *minimum eget*. In St Paul, Epist. to the Romans, III. 23, the Old Latin has *egent claritatem*, cod. Amiat. of the Vulgate having *egent gloriam*.
* Not otherwise known.
[2] Perhaps "by these letters."—*A*.

devoting itself to heavenly praises, your mind intent on heavenly thoughts, your right hand busy with heavenly offerings—especially your right hand with heavenly offerings, for whatever you scatter for the churches you gather for yourself. To the exercise of this virtue the following reflection could be your main incentive: though we are surrounded by never so much wealth (and wealth is falsely termed by the foolish a blessing), yet it is only what we give away that is our own;[1] whatever we hold, passes to our heirs. Farewell.

V

SIDONIUS TO HIS FRIEND FORTUNALIS,* GREETING

1. You also shall find a place in my pages, Fortunalis, pillar of friendship, bright glory of Spanish lands; for your familiarity with letters is not so small that it would be wrong for you to have some degree of immortality through this letter of mine.[2] So you see the glory of your name shall live on, yes it shall live for ages to come. 2. For if my poor sheets have, in whatever way, anything to bring them favour, respect, or credit,[3] I want future generations to know that there is nothing stronger than your faith,[4] nothing more handsome than your person,

[3] *gratia, reverentia, fides*: the translation above seems the likely meaning. But it might mean " if there is any goodwill, reverence, or honesty ": but this seems improbable.—*A*.

[4] *nihil tua fide firmius*: probably, but not certainly, in the religious sense of *fides*.—*A*.

sententia iustius patientia tolerantius, consilio gravius convivio laetius colloquio iucundius. illud quoque supra cetera agnoscet, praeconia laudibus tuis ex votorum contrarietate venisse. nam prope est, ut eminentius censeatur quod probaverunt te adversa constantem, quam si celarent secunda felicem. vale.

VI

SIDONIVS NAMATIO SVO SALVTEM

1. Gaium Caesarem dictatorem, quo ferunt nullum rem militarem ducalius administrasse, studia certatim dictandi lectitandique sibi mutuo vindicavere. et licet in persona unius eiusdemque tempore suo principis viri castrensis oratoriaeque scientiae cura certaverit ferme gloria aequipari, idem tamen numquam se satis duxit in utriusque artis arce compositum, priusquam vestri Arpinatis testimonio ceteris mortalibus anteferretur. 2. quod mihi quoque, si parva magnis componere licet, secundum modulum meum quamquam dissimillimo similiter

---

* I have made more alterations to the English phrasing of this letter than in any other of Anderson's translations so far. I am sure that, if he had lived to revise his first draft, he would have made it much better by the touch of his own incomparable *ultima manus.*—*W.H.S.*

[1] A Gallo-Roman naval officer of the Visigothic King Euric: he was stationed on the Atlantic coast to guard against pirates.

nothing juster than your judgment, more enduring than your patience, more weighty than your counsel, more cheerful than your company, more delightful than your conversation. And they will learn above all that your virtues have gained applause from the very negation of your aspirations: for it is an unavoidable conclusion that to have been tested and found steadfast in adversity is reckoned a higher glory than to be happy and obscure in prosperity. Farewell.

VI *

SIDONIUS TO HIS FRIEND NAMATIUS,[1] GREETING

1. Gaius Caesar the Dictator, whose conduct of military affairs is said to have shown a generalship never surpassed, was claimed for their own, with mutual rivalry, by the two literary disciplines of reading and composition. And although in the person of one and the same man, the leading man of his time, the studies of military and oratorical science strove to win almost equal glory, yet he never considered himself properly settled on the summit of both accomplishments until the testimony of your friend[2] from Arpinum pronounced[3] him superior to all other mortals. 2. If I may compare small things with great,[4] I myself, though entirely unlike him, have had a similar crowning glory in my small

[2] Cicero.

[3] Not it seems in any extant work of Cicero.

[4] Virgil, *Georgics*, IV. 176; *Ecl.* I. 23.

accessit. quae super cunctos te quam primum decuit agnoscere, quia tibi est tam gloria mea quam verecundia plurimum curae. Flavius Nicetius, vir ortu clarissimus, privilegio spectabilis, merito inlustris et hominum patriae nostrae prudentia peritiaque iuxta maxumus, praeconio, quantum comperi, immenso praesentis opusculi volumina extollit, insuper praedicans, quod plurimos iuvenum nec senum paucos vario genere dictandi militandique, quippe adhuc aevo viridis, ipse sim supergressus. 3. equidem, in quantum fieri praeter iactantiam potest, gaudeo de praestantissimi viri auctoritate, si certus est, amore, si fallitur: licet quis provocatus nunc ad facta maiorum non inertissimus, quis quoque ad verba non infantissimus erit? namque virtutes artium istarum saeculis potius priscis saeculorum rector ingenuit, quae per aetatem mundi iam senescentis lassatis veluti seminibus emedullatae parum aliquid hoc tempore in quibuscumque, atque id in paucis, mirandum ac memorabile ostentant. 4. huius tamen ego, etsi studiorum omnium caput est litterarumque, quia personam semper excolui, vereor sententiam supra quam veritas habet affectu ponderatiore prolatam. neque ob hoc infitias ierim me saepe luculentis eius actionibus adstitisse, quarum me, etsi reddere mutuum videor, vel ex

[1] Cf. *Ep.* III. 1. 3. Of Lyon. For the epithets here, see p. 22.

[2] I think the meaning must be "a varied record of authorship and public service."—*A.* I should prefer "the two distinct métiers of literature and public service." For the sentiment cf. *Carm.* II. 208–9, where the same contrast between the subject's youth and eminence is made.—*W.H.S.*

way. It was only right that the facts should as soon as possible be made known to you especially, since you take the deepest interest both in my success and in my modesty of bearing it. Flavius Nicetius,[1] a man by birth distinguished, by rank eminent, by desert illustrious, supreme among our countrymen in wisdom and experience alike, extols, I hear, with boundless eulogy the various books of the present little work, going so far as to declare that, though still in the prime of life, I have actually surpassed, in the two distinct métiers of literature and public service,[2] most of the younger generation and not a few of the veterans. 3. For my part, as far as is possible without vainglory, I rejoice at this renowned man's attestation if he is right, and at his affection if he is wrong. Yet who, if challenged in these days to match our forefathers' achievements, will not prove a sluggard, and who confronted with their words will not be like a speechless child? For it was in the men of bygone ages that the Ruler of all the ages preferred to implant the talents for such arts; but now, in an era when the world is growing old, these arts have lost the power of germinating, they are exhausted, they produce little that is remarkable or memorable in anyone, and even that only in a few. 4. But in the case of Nicetius, although he is the head and front of literary studies and culture, yet because I have always esteemed him personally I fear that he has let his affection sway the balance and carry his judgment beyond the limits of truth. But I am not on this account prepared to deny that I have often been present at brilliant speeches of his; and it is only right for me, even though seeming to repay a

parte cursimque fieri memorem fas est. 5. audivi eum adulescens atque adhuc nuper ex puero, cum pater meus praefectus praetorio Gallicanis tribunalibus praesideret, sub cuius videlicet magistratu consul Asturius [1] anni sui fores votivum trabeatus aperuerat. adhaerebam sellae curuli, etsi non latens per ordinem, certe non sedens per aetatem, mixtusque turmae censualium paenulatorum consuli proximis proximus [2] eram. itaque, ut primum brevi peracta, nec brevis, sportula datique fasti, acclamatum est ab omni Galliae coetu primoribus advocatorum, ut festivitate praeventa [3] horas antelucanas, qui [4] diem serum cum silentio praestolarentur, congrua emeritorum fascium laude honestarent. 6. Nicetium protinus circumspexere conspecti [5] qui non sensim singulatimque, sed tumultuatim petitus

[1] astyrius *L*: astirius (asterius *M²C*).

[2] consuli proximis proximus *Anderson*: consuli proxime proximus *MP* (proximis *M¹P¹*): consuli proximi (proxime *F²*) proximus *F*: consuli proxime proximis *C*: consulis proximae proximus *L*: proximae proximis consuli *T*: proxime consuli proximis *N. v. Mohr, praef. xxxv.*

[3] praeventa *Anderson*: praeventas.

[4] qui *TC*: que *FP*: quae *L*: quę *M* (ę *in ras.*).

[5] conspecti *codd.*: conspicati *Mommsen.*

---

[1] He was possibly called Apollinaris. Cf. *Ep.* V. 9. 2.

[2] Turcius Rufius Asturius (Astyrius, Asterius), consul with Protogenes in A.D. 449.

[3] The manuscripts give a variety of readings here—see the critical notes, and Additional Notes, p. 614.

[4] I would read *praeventa*, which I think is certain, and *qui* for *quae* or *que*, which I think most probable. Perhaps one should transfer the *qui*-clause: "demanding of the advocates

favour, to recall them at least in part and cursorily. 5. I heard him speak when I was a young man just recently emerged from boyhood. My father [1] was at that time president of the tribunals of the Gallic provinces as praetorian prefect, and of course it was during his tenure of office that the consul Asturius [2] had entered upon his year as wearer of the coveted consular robe. I was standing close to the curule chair (for though my age forbade me to be seated, my rank entitled me to some prominence); and so mingling with the crowd of cloaked census-officials I was next to those who were next to the consul.[3] Well, as soon as the largesse had been distributed (and it was quickly distributed though no small amount) and when the consular mementos had been presented, a shout went up from the whole Gallic assembly demanding of the chief advocates that those who were awaiting the afternoon in silence should anticipate the coming festivity [4] and grace the morning hours with fit eulogy of the most worthy consul.[5] 6. Immediately the men they looked at looked round [6] for Nicetius, and then called upon him, not gradually and singly, but in a general outburst of acclamation; whereupon he, in what I

that those who were awaiting the afternoon in silence should anticipate the coming festivity . . ."—*A.*

[5] I suppose *emeritorum* here means "well-earned" emblems of office or the like.—*A.* Roman custom precludes in this context the meaning "retired administration." Codd. *MTCFP* have *meritorum.*

[6] "The men they looked at looked round for Nicetius"; *conspecti* perhaps "with all eyes turned upon them" or "before the eyes of all." But more probably, I think, "those notables."—*A.*

et cunctim cum quodam prologo pudoris vultum modeste demissus inrubuit.[1] atque ob hoc illi maximum sophos non eloquentia prius quam verecundia dedit. dixit disposite graviter ardenter, magna acrimonia maiore facundia maxima disciplina, et illam Sarranis ebriam sucis inter crepitantia segmenta palmatam plus picta oratione, plus aurea convenustavit. 7. per ipsum fere tempus, ut decemviraliter loquar, lex de praescriptione tricennii fuerat proquiritata, cuius peremptoriis abolita rubricis lis omnis in sextum tracta quinquennium terminabatur. hanc intra Gallias ante nescitam primus, quem loquimur, orator indidit prosecutionibus edidit tribunalibus, prodidit partibus addidit titulis, frequente conventu raro sedente, paucis sententiis multis laudibus. 8. praeter ista per alias vices doctrinam illius, quo more citius homo discitur, inobservatus inspexi tunc, cum quae regit provincias fascibus Nicetiano regeretur praefectura consilio. quid multa? nil quod non meum vellem, nil quod non admirarer audivi. 9. propter quae omnia bona

[1] erubuit *C*.

---

[1] Of Theodosius II, which was enacted in Constantinople in A.D. 424; introduced into Gaul in 449. *Cod. Theod.* IV. 14.

[2] *I.e.* legal. The *decemviri stlitibus iudicandis*, "board of ten for judging disputes," were a very old judicial institution of ancient Rome.

[3] *prosecutionibus*. The word may be ablative.—*A*.

[4] This may refer to his praise of the law. Perhaps we

may call a prologue of modesty, bashfully lowered his eyes and blushed, with the result that his modesty won him a loud " bravo " before his eloquence did. The oration he then delivered was well ordered, dignified, and glowing, of great energy, greater fluency, and artistry greatest of all, and that consular robe of his, soaked in Tyrian dye, with palm leaves among the crackling fringes, was enhanced in its splendour by a speech more richly coloured and more golden still. 7. About the same time the law [1] about the thirty years' prescription had been promulgated (to use a decemviral [2] expression) whereby every law-suit that had been protracted for six quinquennia was by peremptory clauses annulled and terminated. This law, hitherto unknown in Gallic territory, our orator first introduced into legal proceedings,[3] published to the tribunals, expounded to contending parties, and placed upon the statute-book: and he did it in a crowded assembly where in their enthusiasm few of the audience remained seated and where the opinions expressed were few of criticism and much of praise.[4] 8. Besides these, there were other occasions in which I observed him unobserved—a quicker way of learning a man's quality—when the prefecture which controls the provinces by official authority was itself controlled by the counsel of Nicetius.[5] To put it shortly, I never heard a single word which I could not have wished uttered by myself, nor a single word that I did not admire. 9. It is because of all these qualities

might leave the ambiguity by saying " with many praises." —*A*.

[5] As *advocatus*, I suppose.—*A*.

in viro sita laetor ad puncta censoris omnium voce concelebrati. granditer enim sua in utramvis de me opinionem sententia valet; quae, si vera comperimus, tantum mihi est favens securitati, quantum fieret adversata formidini. de cetero fixum apud me stat constitutumque, prout rem ex asse cognovero, vel silentio lora [1] laxare vel stringere frena garritui. namque si supradicti confirmor assensu, Athenis loquacior, si minus, Amyclis ipsis taciturnior ero. 10. sed de sodali deque me satis dictum. tu nunc inter ista quid rerum? quas mihi ad vicem nosse non minus cordi. venaris, aedificas, rusticarisne? an horum aliquid unum? an singula vicissim? an pariter cuncta? [2] sed de Vitruvio sive Columella, seu alterutrum ambosve sectere, decentissime facis. potes enim utrumque more quo qui optimo, id est ut cultor aliquis e primis architectusque. 11. ceterum, ut tibi de venatoris officio quam minimum blandiaris, maxume iniungo. namque apros frustra in venabula vocas, quos canibus misericordissimis, quibus abundas, et quidem solus,[3] movere potius quam commovere consuesti. Esto,

[1] silentio me lora *MTCFPN*[1]: *om.* me *LN*.
[2] cuncta *T*: et cunctim *CM*[1] *in marg.*: et cuncta *aut sim.*
[3] et quidem solus *MTCFP*: etsi quidem solis *L*: et iis quidem solis *Mommsen*: etsi quietem solvis *coni. Leo*: et sic quidem Scoticis *coni. Warmington.*

---

[1] Virgil, *Aen.* X. 564. The town mentioned by Virgil as "silent" was Amyclae on the west coast of Italy, and the epithet was perhaps given to it because it was a colony of "laconic" Sparta; but other explanations were given; and in fact Sidonius may mean the other Amyclae in Greece.

residing in Nicetius that I rejoice in the approval of a censor who is himself acclaimed by the voice of all; for his verdict on me, whether it leans to one side or to the other, carries great weight; being (if I am informed aright) now favourable to me, it reassures me as much as, if adverse, it would alarm me. For the future, according to what I ascertain to be the whole of the matter, I am firmly resolved either to give silence a free rein or to put a strict curb on my garrulity. If I am encouraged by the approval of Nicetius I will be more garrulous than Athens; if not, I shall be even more silent than Amyclae.[1] 10. But I have said enough about my friend and about myself. What are you doing in these days? I am just as anxious to know this in my turn. Do you hunt? do you build? do you live the life of a countryman? Or do you do some one of these things, or each in turn or all together? As regards Vitruvius or Columella,[2] whether you are a devotee of one of them, or of both together, you are acting splendidly—for you are competent to follow each of them like one of their best disciples, I mean as an agriculturist or an architect of the first rank. 11. But as regards the hunter's business I do most strongly urge you not to flatter yourself unduly. It is no good your inviting the boars to face your spear, when it's your practice to hunt them with those most merciful hounds that you possess in plenty (and indeed you do it all alone[3]): you just set your quarry

[2] Vitruvius dedicated his extant work on architecture to the Emperor Augustus (he ruled 30 B.C.–A.D. 14); Iunius Columella wrote his extant work on agriculture before A.D. 70.

[3] On the text here, see Additional Notes, p. 614.

sit indulgentia dignum, quod reformidant catuli tui bestiis appropinquare terribilibus corpulentisque: illud ignoro quomodo excuses, quod capreas, pecus simum, pariter et dammas in fugam pronos iacentibus animis pectoribus erectis, passibus raris crebris latratibus prosequuntur. 12. quapropter de reliquo fructuosius retibus cassibusque scrupeas rupes atque opacandis habilia lustris plosor statarius nemora circumvenis ac, pudor si quis, temperas cursibus apertis [1] quatere campos et insidiari lepusculis Olarionensibus; quos nec est tanti, raro te insectante superandos, copulis palam ductis inquietari, nisi forsitan, dum tibi ac patri noster Apollinaris intervenit, rectius fiet ut exerceantur. 13. exceptis iocis fac sciam tandem, quid te, quid domum circa. sed ecce dum iam epistulam, quae diu garrit, claudere optarem, subitus a Santonis nuntius; cum quo dum tui obtentu aliquid horarum sermocinanter extrahimus, constanter asseveravit nuper vos classicum in classe cecinisse atque inter officia nunc nautae, modo militis litoribus Oceani curvis inerrare contra Saxonum pandos myoparones, quorum quot remiges

[1] apertos *coni. Luetjohann.*

---

[1] Their heads are not lowered to the scent.—*A.*

[2] I think *apertos* is right.—*A.* For *quaterent campos,* cf. Virgil, *Aen.* XI. 512–513.

[3] These Germans of Holstein were becoming powerful even *c.* A.D. 200 and later spread not only eastwards but also westwards into Gaul. For example in 286 or 287 they and the Franks infested the coasts of Aremorica and Belgica; in 371 they were defeated in northern Gaul by the Romans; at the beginning of the fifth century the northern coast of Gaul and

running, but never rouse him to a furious attack. Granted that it is forgivable in your little dogs to shrink from approaching huge fearsome beasts like boars; but I don't know how you can excuse their behaviour in the case of goats, those poor snub-nosed creatures, or timid skittish deer, whom they hunt head high [1] and spirits prone, and a maximum of barking to a minimum of speed. 12. So in future it will pay you better to surround with nets and toils the rugged crags and the woods so well suited to shroud the lairs of beasts, yourself applauding without stirring a foot; and if you have any sense of decency you will give up shaking the plains [2] with your free-ranging gallopings and lying in wait for the hares of Oléron; indeed, as they will rarely be caught when you are in pursuit, it is hardly worth while to disturb them by unleashing the packs in the open—unless perhaps when our friend Apollinaris drops in on you and your father, making it more fitting that they should be exercised. 13. Joking apart, let me know at last the news of yourself and family. But, lo and behold! when I was already hoping to close this letter, which has been chattering away for a long time, a messenger suddenly came from Saintes. I spent some hours with him in conversation about you, and he constantly affirmed that you had recently sounded the trump of war in the fleet and, in discharging the duties now of a sailor, now of a soldier, were roving the winding shores of Ocean to meet the curving sloops of the Saxons,[3] who give the

the south-east coast of Britain were called "Saxon shores" because of Saxon raids or even settlements; *c.* 450 Hengist and Horsa crossed to Britain.

videris, totidem te cernere putes archipiratas: ita simul omnes imperant parent, docent discunt latrocinari. unde nunc etiam ut quam plurimum caveas, causa successit maxuma monendi. 14. hostis est omni hoste truculentior. inprovisus aggreditur praevisus elabitur; spernit obiectos sternit incautos; si sequatur, intercipit, si fugiat, evadit. ad hoc exercent illos naufragia, non terrent. est eis quaedam cum discriminibus pelagi non notitia solum, sed familiaritas. nam quoniam ipsa si qua tempestas est huc [1] securos efficit occupandos, huc [1] prospici vetat occupaturos, in medio fluctuum scopulorumque confragosorum spe superventus laeti periclitantur. 15. praeterea, priusquam de continenti in patriam vela laxantes hostico mordaces anchoras vado vellant, mos est remeaturis decimum quemque captorum per aquales et cruciarias poenas plus ob hoc tristi quod superstitioso ritu necare superque collectam turbam periturorum mortis iniquitatem sortis aequitate dispergere. talibus se ligant [2] votis, victimis solvunt; et per huiusmodi non tam sacrificia purgati quam sacrilegia polluti religiosum putant caedis infaustae perpetratores de

[1] hinc *utroque loco* *FPM*[1]: hac *coni.* *Luetjohann.*
[2] se ligant *L*: eligunt *MTCFPV*[1]: eligant *VN*.

---

[1] " the shallow depths of enemy waters."—*A*.

impression that every oarsman you see in their crew is a pirate-captain—so universal is it for all of them simultaneously to issue orders and obey orders, to teach brigandage and to learn brigandage. Even now there has cropped up a very strong reason for warning you to be specially on your guard against danger from them. 14. That enemy surpasses all other enemies in brutality. He attacks unforeseen, and when foreseen he slips away; he despises those who bar his way, and he destroys those whom he catches unawares; if he pursues, he intercepts; if he flees, he escapes. Moreover, shipwreck, far from terrifying them, is their training. With the perils of the sea they are not merely acquainted—they are familiarly acquainted; for since a storm whenever it occurs lulls into security the object of their attack and prevents the coming attack from being observed by victims, they gladly endure dangers amid billows and jagged rocks, in the hope of achieving a surprise. 15. Moreover, when ready to unfurl their sails for the voyage home from the continent and to lift their gripping anchors from enemy waters,[1] they are accustomed on the eve of departure to kill one in ten of their prisoners by drowning or crucifixion, performing a rite which is all the more tragic for being due to superstition, and distributing to the collected band of doomed men the iniquity of death by the equity of the lot. Such are the obligations of their vows, and such the victims with which they pay their obligations. Polluting themselves by such sacrilege rather than purifying themselves by such sacrifices, the perpetrators of that unhallowed slaughter think it a religious duty to exact torture

capite captivo magis exigere tormenta quam pretia. 16. qua de re metuo multa, suspicor varia, quamquam me e contrario ingentia hortentur: primum quod victoris populi signa comitaris; dein quod in sapientes viros, quos inter iure censeris, minus annuo licere fortuitis; tertio, quod pro sodalibus fide iunctis, sede discretis frequenter incutiunt et tuta maerorem, quia promptius de actionibus longinquis ambigendisque sinistra quaeque metus augurat. 17. sed dicas non esse tantum forte curanda quae perhorresco. id quidem verum est; sed nec hoc falsum, quod his, quos amplius diligimus, plus timemus. unde nihilominus, precor, obortum tui causa sensibus nostris quam primum prospero relatu exime angorem. neque enim ex integro flecti umquam ad hoc possum, ut de peregrinantibus amicis, quippe quos bellicum [1] militarisque tessera terit, donec secunda cognosco, non adversa formidem. 18. Varronem logistoricum, sicut poposceras, et Eusebium chronographum misi, quorum si ad te lima pervenerit, si quid inter excubiales curas, utpote in castris, saltim sortito vacabis, poteris, postquam arma deterseris, ori quoque tuo loquendi robiginem summovere. vale.

[1] bellicum *L*: bellica.

---

[1] *ex integro = omnino.—A.*
[2] The *Libri Logistorici* of M. Terentius Varro (116–28 B.C.)

rather than ransom from a prisoner. 16. About this matter I have many fears and various apprehensions, although, on the other hand, there are important considerations that cheer me: first, you follow the standard of a victorious people; next, I incline to think that with provident men, among whom you are rightly classed, there is less opportunity for accidents to happen; thirdly, when one has friends united in loyalty but separated in domicile, events even that involve no danger often cause a feeling of concern and distress, because sinister forebodings about distant and indefinite occurrences are more readily prompted by fear. 17. But, you may say, the things I dread do not really warrant all this worry. That is true, but it is no less true that we fear most for those we most love; so I pray you none the less to send me good news as soon as possible and so remove the anxiety that fills my heart on your account; for until I get favourable tidings I can never quite[1] avoid a disposition to fear the worst about friends abroad, particularly those kept busy by the war-trumpet and orders of the day. 18. I send you Varro[2] logistoricus and Eusebius the chronographer, as you requested. I regard this literature as a kind of refining tool: if it reaches you safely—then, if being stationed in barracks[3] you secure (at least by lot) some leisure amid the duties of the watch, you will be able, after cleaning your weapons, to remove likewise from your lips their linguistic rust. Farewell.

are lost; but the chronographical work on the Bible (*Chronographia* and *Canones*) of Eusebius of Caesarea (*c.* A.D. 264–340) survives.

[3] *I.e.* not at sea.—*A*.

VII

SIDONIVS AVDACI SVO SALVTEM

1. Ubinam se nunc, velim dicas, gentium abscondunt qui saepe sibi de molibus facultatum congregatarum deque congestis iam nigrescentis argenti struibus blandiebantur? ubi etiam illorum praerogativa, qui contra indolem iuniorum sola occasione praecedentis aetatis intumescebant? ubi sunt illi, quorum affinitas nullo indicio maiore cognoscitur quam simultate? 2. nempe, cum primum bonis actibus locus et ad trutinam iudicii principalis appensa tandem non nummorum libra sed morum, remansere illi, qui superbissime opinabantur solo se censu esse censendos quique sic vitiis ut divitiis incubantes volunt vanitatis videri alienam surrexisse personam, cum nolint cupiditatis notari suam crevisse substantiam. in qua tamen detrahendi palaestra exercitati tamquam per oleum sic per infusa aemulationum venena macerantur. 3. Tu vero inter haec macte, qui praefecturae titulis ampliatus, licet hactenus e prosapia inlustri[1] computarere, pecu-

[1] inlustri *L*: illustri *T*: illustris.

---

* Castalius Innocentius Audax was *praefectus urbi* (at Rome) in A.D. 474 in the reign of Iulius Nepos, the "just Emperor." Cf. § 4, iuste sub iusto principe; cf. § 2 *init.*; and *Ep.* V. 16. 2 *init.*; Dessau 814; *C.I.L.* III. 6335.—*A.*

[1] Anderson took the Latin as meaning "solely on account of belonging to an earlier age." I am sure that the sense is "seniority," as may be seen from the general sense of *Ep.* VII. 9. 12, *ut nos in antistite consecrando non utilitatem velint eligere sed aetatem.*—*W.H.S.*

VII

SIDONIUS TO HIS FRIEND AUDAX,* GREETING

1. I wish you would tell me where in the world those people are now hiding who used so often to congratulate themselves on the masses of wealth they had assembled and on their accumulated piles of silver already tarnished with the blackness of age. Where, too, is the privileged position of those who, merely on the score of seniority,[1] proudly sought to suppress the spirit of the younger generation? Where are the men whose relationship is recognised by their quarrels more than by any other evidence? 2. To be sure, as soon as good actions got a fair field and the scales of the emperor's judgment at last began to weigh morals, not money, those individuals were left far behind who arrogantly claimed they should be assessed only by their income—men who gloat over their vices as over their riches and who would wish the rise of a different class of person to be regarded as presumption, though they would not wish the increase of their own property to be censured as greed. But, practised athletes in their arena of detraction, they steep themselves in the poison of their jealous rivalries (just as normal wrestlers do with oil), and it leaves them enervated and debilitated. 3. Meanwhile congratulations to you, for, although with your glorious prefectorian ancestry you had so far owed your reputation to your illustrious lineage, yet for yourself you did not shirk the most strenuous exertion to ensure that your

liariter nihilo segnius elaborasti, ut a te gloriosius posteri tui numerarentur. nil enim est illo per sententiam boni cuiusque generosius, quisquis ingenii corporis opum iunctam in hoc constans operam exercet, ut maioribus suis anteponatur. 4. quod superest, deum posco, ut te filii consequantur aut, quod [te][1] plus decet velle, transcendant et quicumque non sustinet[2] diligere provectum, medullitus aestuantes a semet ipso livoris proprii semper exigat poenas, cumque nullas in te habuerit umquam misericordiae causas, habeat invidiae; siquidem iuste sub iusto principe iacet qui, per se minimus et tantum per sua maxumus, animo exiguus vivit et patrimonio plurimus. vale.

VIII

SIDONIVS SYAGRIO SVO SALVTEM

1. Dic, Gallicanae flos iuventutis, quousque tandem ruralium operum negotiosus urbana fastidis? quamdiu attritas tesserarum quondam iactibus manus contra ius fasque sibi vindicant instrumenta cerealia? quousque tua te Taionnacus patriciae stir-

[1] te *L*: *om. rell.*
[2] sustinet *LN*: sustinet te *MCFP*: sustinent te *T*.

---

* This is the Syagrius to whom *Ep.* V. 5 is addressed. See the first note on that letter.

[1] *tua*—sc. *villa. Taionnacus*: the name of his estate, the location of which is unknown. Mommsen says "fortasse

descendants should gain enhanced glory from yourself. Truly, in the eyes of the most worthy judges there is nothing nobler than for a man unremittingly to combine mind, body, and estate in an effort to surpass his forefathers. 4. For the future, I pray God that your children may follow in your path or (a more fitting wish) may outstrip you; and anyone who cannot bear to love you in your onward progress, may he ever in the angry soul of him suffer self-inflicted seething tortures as punishment for his own jealousy; and never finding in you any grounds for pity, may he only find grounds for envy; for justly under a just emperor is he demoted who, unimportant in himself and important only for his possessions, lives his life small in mind though large in patrimony. Farewell.

VIII

SIDONIUS TO HIS FRIEND SYAGRIUS,* GREETING

1. Tell me, you brightest flower of our Gallo-Roman youth, how long, pray, are you going to busy yourself with rustic activities and disdain those of the town? How long will agricultural implements, in defiance of all law sacred and profane, claim for themselves those hands which once were worn with the casting of dice? How long is your estate of Taionnacus[1] going to exhaust you, a farmer of patrician

Suessionum (locus)." Sirmond suggests that it may refer to Taionnus which the "Tabula Itineraria" places in the land of the Aedui.

pis lassabit agricolam? quousque prati comantis exuvias hibernis novalibus non ut eques sed ut bubulcus abscondis? quousque pondus ligonis obtusi nec perfossis antibus ponis? 2. quid Serranorum aemulus et Camillorum cum regas stivam, dissimulas optare palmatam? parce tantum in nobilitatis invidiam rusticari. agrum si mediocriter colas, possides; si nimium, possideris. redde te patri, redde te patriae, redde te etiam fidelibus amicis, qui iure ponuntur inter affectus. aut si te tantum Cincinnati dictatoris vita delectat, duc ante Raciliam,[1] quae boves iungat. 3. neque dixerim sapienti viro rem domesticam non esse curandam, sed eo temperamento, quo [2] non solum quid habere sed quid debeat esse consideret. nam, si ceteris nobilium studiorum artibus repudiatis sola te propagandae rei familiaris urtica sollicitat, licet tu deductum nomen a trabeis atque eboratas curules et

[1] duc ante Raciliam *Sirmond*: ducanter aciliam *L*: duc*** erciliam *M*[2]: ducāt herciliam *T*: duc erciliam *CP*: dū erciliam *F* (duc *in marg.* *F*[1]).
[2] quo *L*: quod.

---

[1] *prati comantis exuvias*, etc.: I think this is just Sidonius' elaborate way of saying "sow in the winter the products of the summer cornfields."—*W.H.S.*

[2] Serranus: M. Atilius Regulus Serranus, who was sowing when his election to a consulship was reported to him in 257 B.C. Camillus: M. Furius Camillus, Roman statesman and soldier, who died in 365 B.C.

[3] as your father and your fatherland: I have ventured to

stock? How long, acting like a ploughman and not as a cavalier, will you continue burying in the winter tillage the spoils of the waving corn-land?[1] How long will you bring the weight of the blunt mattock to bear on vine-rows in a never-ending effort to dig them through? 2. Why guide the plough-handle in competition with Serranus and Camillus[2] and yet forgo all ambition for the consul's robe? Do not bring a slur on the nobility by staying so constantly in the country. Whoso cultivates a farm in moderation, owns it: whoso cultivates it to excess, is owned by it. Give yourself back to your father, to your fatherland, and also to your faithful friends, whom I hope I am justified in classing with such objects of affection[3]; or if the life of the dictator Cincinnatus[4] is so very attractive to you, first marry a Racilia[5] and let her yoke the oxen for you. 3. I would not indeed say that a wise man should fail to concern himself with his private affairs, but he should act on the even principle of considering not only what he should *have* but what he should *be*. If you reject all other forms of accomplishments that noblemen should cultivate, and if the sting to extend your property is the only emotion that stirs you, then you may look back on a name derived from consular robes, you may recall a series of curule seats and gilded travelling-chairs and purple

use here a translation long ago given me by A. E. Housman. —*W.H.S.*

[4] Lucius Quinctius Cincinnatus ("Curly-haired") was in 458 B.C. and again in 439 B.C. cultivating his small farm when called to be "dictator" in command of the whole State against its external foes.

[5] Wife of Cincinnatus.

gestatorias bratteatas et fastos recolas purpurissatos, is profecto inveniere, quem debeat sic industrium quod latentem non tam honorare censor quam censetor[1] onerare. vale.

IX

SIDONIVS LAMPRIDIO SVO SALVTEM

1. Cum primum Burdigalam veni, litteras mihi tabellarius tuus obtulit plenas nectaris florum margaritarum, quibus silentium meum culpas et aliquos versuum meorum versibus poscis, qui tibi solent per musicum palati concavum tinnientes voce variata quasi tibiis multiforatilibus effundi. sed hoc tu munificentia regia satis abutens iam securus post munera facis, quia forsitan satiricum illud de satirico non recordaris: Satur est cum dicit Horatius "euhoe." 2. quid multis? merito[2] me cantare ex otio iubes, quia te iam saltare delectat. quicquid illud est, pareo tamen, idque non modo non coactus verum etiam spontaliter facio; tantum tu utcumque moderere Catonianum superciliosae frontis arbi-

[1] censetor *Mohr*: censitor *Luetjohann*: cens& oronerare *L*: censens (censes) onerare.
[2] immerito *coni. Luetjohann dubitanter.*

---

* Cf. *Ep.* VIII. 11. 3; IX. 13. 2, *carm.* 21 and § 4; *Carm.* IX. 314; a poet and teacher of rhetoric at Bordeaux, who gained favour with Euric, King of the Visigoths. He was murdered by his own slaves.
[1] In A.D. 476.

mantles all recorded in the annals of the State, but nevertheless you will prove to be that obscure hard-working type who has less claim to be praised by the censor than to be preyed on by the tax-assessor. Farewell.

IX

SIDONIUS TO HIS FRIEND LAMPRIDIUS,* GREETING

1. As soon as I arrived at Bordeaux,[1] your courier handed me a letter full of nectar and flowers and pearls. In it you complain of my silence and demand some of my own verses, using verse to do so—and, in your case, verses are wont to ring through the musical concavity of the mouth and to come streaming forth in varied tones as from flutes of many holes. But you issue such a command, when you are in full enjoyment of the King's munificence: after his bounty to you, you are relieved of all care: and you fail, perhaps, to recall that remark of one satirist about another:

Well-fed is Horace when " Euhoe " he cries.[2]

2. To put it shortly, it is reasonable for you, from your position of ease, to bid me make music, since it pleases you now to be dancing. But however that may be, I obey you, and I do so not only without compulsion but of my own free will; only you must by all means control the Cato-like severity of a

[2] Juvenal, VII. 62; cf. Horace, *Odes* II. 19. Juvenal means that a man is best at poetry when he has fed well.

trium. nosti enim probe laetitiam poetarum, quorum sic ingenia maeroribus ut pisciculi retibus amiciuntur; et si quid asperum aut triste, non statim sese poetica teneritudo a vinculo incursi angoris elaqueat. necdum enim quicquam de hereditate socruali vel in usum tertiae sub pretio medietatis obtinui. 3. interim tu videris, quam tibi sit epigrammatis flagitati lemma placiturum; me tamen nequaquam sollicitudo permittit aliud nunc habere in actione, aliud in carmine. illud sane praeter iustitiam feceris, si in praesentiarum vicissim scripta quasi compares. ago laboriosum, agis ipse felicem; ago adhuc exulem, agis ipse iam civem: et ob hoc inaequalia cano, quia similia posco et paria non impetro. 4. quod si quopiam casu ineptias istas, quas inter animi supplicia conscripsimus, nutu indulgentiore susceperis, persuadebis mihi, quia cantuum similes fuerint olorinorum, quorum est modulatior clangor in poenis: similes etiam chordae lyricae violentius tensae, quae quo plus torta, plus musica est. ceterum si probari nequeunt versus

---

[1] Or "my third." According to Visigothic practice, a Visigoth had probably occupied two thirds of the estate. Dalton takes *medietas* as vaguely a portion instead of one half, and translates: "I am still unsuccessful in obtaining a decision about my mother-in-law's estate, even provisionally, though I have offered a third part as ransom." Mommsen believes that Sidonius has the usufruct of one-third provided that he buys one-half of the estate from the heirs, among whom he is not included. See Dalton's note in his Vol. II, p. 247; Stevens, *Sid. Apoll.*, 163–164. Sidonius' mother-in-law was the widow of the Emperor Avitus.

[2] For *epigramma* see Anderson's note on pp. lxvi and lxvii of Vol. I of Sidonius (Loeb).

[3] He had been confined to the fort called Livia near Car-

disdainful countenance. You well understand the happiness of poets: their spirits are immeshed by sorrows as fish by nets; if anything harsh or distressing occurs, the poetic sensibility does not readily free itself from the agonising entanglement. I have not yet obtained any part of my mother-in-law's estate—not even as much as the usufruct of a third[1] of it at the price of a half. 3. By this time you will have seen how far the theme of the little poem[2] you demand is likely to please you. As for me, my anxiety absolutely forbids me to make the content of my poetry different from the content of the life I lead. You will certainly act unjustly if you match on equal terms, so to speak, our respective writings composed on the present occasion. The parts we play are different; I am afflicted, you fortunate, I still an exile,[3] you are now a citizen;[4] and the reason why my verses are not on an equality with yours is just this—that I claim similar privileges but do not get the same treatment.[5] 4. But if by chance you do accept with a measure of indulgent approval these silly trifles of mine, written amid mental tortures, then you will convince me that they were like the songs of swans, whose cry is more tuneful in moments of agony, and like a lyre-string strung more forcibly than is wont, which is the more musical the more it is tensed. But if verses lacking ease and

cassonne (see above, p. 406) but was now, it seems, detained on parole by Euric in Bordeaux.

[4] Surely this means a Gothic citizen at the court of Euric in Bordeaux.—*A*.

[5] This indicates that Sidonius tried to obtain from Euric the same treatment as Lampridius received.

otii aut hilaritatis expertes, tu quoque in pagina, quam supter attexui, nil quod placeat invenies. 5. his adhuc adde, quod materiam, cui non auditor potius sed lector obtigerit, nihil absentis auctoris pronuntiatio iuvat. neque enim post opus missum superest quod poeta vel vocalissimus agat, quem distantia loci nec hoc facere permittit, quod solent chori pantomimorum, qui bono cantu male dictata commendant.

Quid Cirrham vel Hyantias Camenas,
quid doctos Heliconidum liquores,
scalptos alitis hinnientis ictu,
nunc in carmina commovere temptas,
nostrae o[1] Lampridius decus Thaliae,
et me scribere sic subinde cogis,
ac si Delphica Delio tulissem
instrumenta tuo novusque Apollo
cortinam tripodas, chelyn pharetras,
arcus grypas agam duplaeque frondis[2]
hinc bacas quatiam vel hinc corymbos?

[1] *secludit* o *Wilamowitz.*
[2] frondis *L, M*?: frontis.

---

[1] Thalia was the Muse who presided over comedy, which was composed in poetry.

[2] Cirrha, a town in Phocis in Greece, was sacred to Apollo. Here Parnassus also is meant, a mountain sacred to Apollo and the Muses.

[3] See next note, and *Carm.* IX. 283 ff.

[4] The range Mount Helicon in Boeotia in Greece was in Greek imagination the favourite haunt of the Muses. The

cheerfulness cannot be favourably received, then you will find nothing to please you in the sheet I have attached below. 5. Add to this the fact that matter which does not have the special advantage of being listened to, but is only read, is deprived of the help which the absent author's delivery might give; for once his work has been despatched, there is nothing more that even the most sweetly voiced poet can do: distance forbids him even to do what is commonly done by pantomimic choruses—make bad compositions acceptable by means of good singing.

"Lampridius, glory of our poesy,[1] why do you now try to stir to song Cirrha,[2] or the Boeotian Muses,[3] or the maids of Helicon at their inspired fountain dug by a stamp from the hoof of that neighing creature, the winged Pegasus?[4] Why do you suddenly[5] urge me to write, just as if I had carried the Delphic-holy implements for the Delian god[6] you worship, and as if I now were a new Apollo driving on my way the prophetic cauldron and tripod, the lyre, the quiver, the bow,[7] and the gryphons, and shaking here the twy-formed leafage with its berries, and there the

fountain was called Hippocrene ("horse-fountain"—see above, p. 407, n. 6.).

[5] Cf. line 37 where the word seems to mean "from time to time," "repeatedly." So perhaps here. See also *Ep.* VIII. 11, *carm.* 43.

[6] Apollo, whose famous oracle was at Delphi in Phocis; the island Delos where he was imagined to have been born was another renowned centre of his worship by the ancient Greeks.

[7] A lyre and a bow were usual attributes of Apollo; cauldron and tripod were connected with prophecy because Apollo's Pythian priestess at Delphi sat on a tripod when delivering any oracular reply. Sidonius could have added quite a list of animals.

tu iam, Tityre, rura post recepta
myrtos et platanona pervagatus
pulsas barbiton atque concinentes
ora et plectra tibi modos resultant,
chorda voce metro stupende psaltes:
nos istic positos semelque visos
bis iam menstrua luna conspicatur,
nec multum domino vacat vel ipsi,
dum responsa petit subactus orbis.
istic Saxona caerulum videmus
assuetum ante salo solum timere;
cuius verticis extimas per oras
non contenta suos tenere morsus
artat [1] lammina marginem comarum,
et sic crinibus ad cutem recisis
decrescit caput additurque vultus.
hic tonso occipiti, senex Sygamber,
postquam victus es, elicis retrorsum
cervicem ad veterem novos capillos.
hic glaucis Herulus genis vagatur,
imos Oceani colens recessus
algoso prope concolor profundo.

[1] artat *Mommsen*: altat.

---

[1] *bacas . . . corymbos . . .* In *Carm.* XXII. 68–73. Apollo's driving reins are of ivy and his *corymbi* obviously vines.—*A.* Is this right? In fact, in *carm.* XXII. 72 Anderson translates the word *corymbis* as ivy-berries; and we certainly have ivy in *Ep.* VIII. 11. 3, in *carm.* 6, in connection with Apollo. Other plants associated with Apollo were the palm (because he was supposed to be born under one on Delos island) and the bay, which was used for crowns at the Pythian games and in some sacrifices.

[2] A shepherd in Virgil's *Eclogues* (I. 1).

clustering vine.[1] You, my Tityrus,[2] with your land restored to you, range through the groves of myrtle and planes, and so you strike your lyre, and both words and plectrum make the echoes ring with harmonious melody, my minstrel friend—so marvellous with string and voice and measure. But as for me, here imprisoned am I, granted access (to the King)[3] but once, although two moons have now passed over me.[4] And indeed our lord and master, even he, has but little time to spare[5] while a conquered world makes suit to him.[6] Here in Bordeaux we see the blue-eyed Saxon afraid of the land, accustomed as he is to the sea; along the extreme edges of his pate the razor, refusing to restrain its bite, pushes back the frontier of his hair and, with the growth thus clipped to the skin, his head is reduced and his face enlarged. Here you, old Sygambrian,[7] who had shorn the back of your head after defeat, entice new hair to spread backward to your old neck.[8] Here wanders the Herulian[9] with his blue-grey eyes, who haunts the uttermost retreats of Ocean and is almost of one colour with its weedy

[3] Euric.

[4] In Bordeaux.

[5] "little time to spare even for himself"—so Purser. I don't think this is right. I think it means "even he, supreme lord though he is."—*A.*

[6] *responsa.* Perhaps "petitions for his (oracular) responses."—*A.* I don't think so: I prefer Anderson's translation in the text.—*W.H.S.*

[7] See *Ep.* IV. 1. 4. note.

[8] Anderson doubts his translation here, but Semple approves. Cf. *Carm.* V. 238–240.

[9] The Herulians were settled on the lower Rhine.

hic Burgundio septipes frequenter
flexo poplite supplicat quietem.
istis Ostrogothus viget patronis
vicinosque premens subinde Chunos,
his quod subditur, hinc superbit illis.
hinc, Romane, tibi petis salutem,
et contra Scythicae plagae catervas,
si quos Parrhasis ursa fert tumultus,
Eorice, tuae manus rogantur,
ut Martem validus per inquilinum
defendat tenuem Garumna Thybrim.
ipse hic Parthicus Arsaces precatur,
aulae Susidis ut tenere culmen
possit foedere sub stipendiali.
nam quod partibus arma Bosphoranis
grandi hinc surgere sentit apparatu,
maestam Persida iam sonum ad duelli

---

[1] *frequenter* may go with *flexo* " oft bends the knee and sues for peace."—*A*.

[2] Euric and his Visigoths, the Western Goths.

[3] The Eastern Goths, who came after A.D. 373 under the domination of the Huns. They did not recover independence until after the death of Attila in A.D. 453.

[4] Perhaps: " with the men of this place as his champions, the Ostrogoth flourishes and, crushing again and again his neighbours the Huns, he is enabled to lord it over those enemies by being subject to those friends."—*A*.

[5] Possibly an allusion to the kingship or domination of Italy by the barbarian (probably Scirian) Odoacer (Odovacar) from the region of the lower Danube *c.* 476–493 B.C. His supremacy marked the end of the Roman Empire in the West.

[6] Scythia was originally the steppe extending from the Carpathians to the Don. In the time of Sidonius the name was, it seems, still used for the Dobrudzha (Rumania); but

depths. Here the Burgundian seven-foot high oft[1] begs for peace on bended knee. Having these for patrons,[2] the Ostrogoth[3] crushes the Huns his neighbours, his proud spirit towards them is due to his humble obedience to his patrons.[4] From this source the Roman seeks salvation,[5] and against the hordes of the Scythian[6] clime, when the Arcadian Bear[7] brings forth commotion, it is your bands, Euric, that are called for, so that the Garonne, strong in its warlike settlers, may defend the dwindled Tiber. Here even the Parthian Arsaces[8] prays that he may be enabled to keep the towering palace of Susa under covenant of tribute; for perceiving that an armament with a vast muster of warlike might is surging up from here to take the side of Constantinople,[9] he thinks that Persia, depressed at the very sound of

at all times it meant vaguely all the regions north and north-east of the Black Sea.

[7] Parrhasia was a town in Arcadia in Greece. Arcadian Bear means the constellation of the Great Bear *i.e.* the North.

[8] A name used for a King, Perozes (Firoze), of the Sassanid dynasty who was fighting the White Huns. (Procopius, *De Bello Persico*, I. 4.)

[9] *partibus . . . Bosphoranis.* The phrase is undoubtedly *dativus commodi* and means "to support Constantinople." This is the culmination of Sidonius' flattering reference to King Euric's power; not only are the Visigoths, from their capital in Bordeaux, able to help Rome, but they are able to help the eastern side of the Empire against its most formidable enemy, the Parthian [Sassanid] kingdom. In a poem of exaggerated flattery it is not necessary to speak truth about fact and reality; it is merely necessary to utter acceptable hyperbole.—*W.H.S.* See Semple's note on this passage in his *Quaest. Exeg.*, pp. 48–49. This poem may well have moved Euric to be kind to Sidonius. Anyhow Sidonius returned to Clermont and his bishop's duties there in 476.

ripa Euphratide vix putat tuendam;
qui cognata licet sibi astra fingens
Phoebea tumeat propinquitate,
mortalem hic tamen implet obsecrando.
haec inter terimus moras inanes;
sed tu, Tityre, parce provocare;
nam non invideo magisque miror,
qui, dum nil mereor precesque frustra
impendo, Meliboeus esse coepi.

6. En carmen, quod recenseas otiabundus nostrumque sudorem ac pulverem spectans veluti iam coronatus auriga de podio. de reliquo non est quod suspiceris par me officii genus repetiturum, etiamsi delectere praesenti, nisi prius ipse destiterim vaticinari magis damna quam carmina. vale.

X

SIDONIVS RVRICIO SVO SALVTEM

1. Esse tibi usui pariter et cordi litteras granditer gaudeo. nam stilum vestrum quanta comitetur vel flamma sensuum vel unda sermonum, liberius assererem, nisi, dum me laudare non parum studes, laudari plurimum te vetares. et quamquam in epistula tua servet caritas dulcedinem, natura facundiam, peritia disciplinam, in sola materiae tamen electione pec-

---

[1] Sidonius is thinking of Meliboeus' words in Virgil, *Eclogues*, I. 11. Meliboeus had lost his lands in the country.

* See *Ep.* IV. 16, first note. The present letter may be a reply to an extant letter of Ruricius (Ruricius, *Ep.* I. 9).

[2] *nam* is common in this sense.

war, can scarcely be defended by the Euphrates' bank; and although he feigns himself related to the stars, and vaunts his kinship with Phoebus the Sun, here in Bordeaux he plays a mortal's part by making supplication. It is amid all this that I waste my days in fruitless waiting. Now, Tityrus, forbear to challenge me, for I feel no envy but rather wonder,—[1] I, an innocent sufferer lavishing my prayers in vain, and so almost on the way to become a Meliboeus."

6. There you have the poem for you to read as you take your ease, watching me struggle in the dust and sweat, while like a charioteer who has already won his crown you view the contest from the grandstand. For the future, there is no reason for you to suspect that I intend to repeat this kind of offering, however pleased you may be with the present one—certainly not until I have ceased dreaming of misfortunes rather than poems. Farewell.

X

SIDONIUS TO HIS FRIEND RURICIUS,* GREETING

1. I rejoice greatly that literary pursuits are both profitable and congenial to you, but [2] I should testify more freely to the glow of thought and the flow of language that accompany your writing, were it not that, while immensely anxious to praise me, you ban superlative praise for yourself. And really, although in your letter affection maintains constant charm, natural talent a flow of eloquence, and experience an unfailing correctness, the one respect in which you

casti, licet id ipsum praedicari possit in voto, quod videris errasse ⟨in⟩[1] iudicio. ingentes praeconiorum titulos moribus meis applicas; sed si pudoris nostri fecisses utcumque rationem, Symmachianum illud te cogitare par fuerat:[2] ut vera laus ornat, ita falsa castigat. 2. quo loci tamen si animum vestrum bene metior, super affectum, quem maximum ostendis, hoc tu et arte fecisti. nam moris est eloquentibus viris ingeniorum facultatem negotiorum probare difficultatibus et illic stilum peritum quasi quendam fecundi pectoris vomerem figere, ubi materiae sterilis argumentum velut arida caespitis macri glaeba ieiunat. scaturrit mundus similibus exemplis: medicus in desperatione, gubernator in tempestate cognoscitur; horum omnium famam praecedentia pericula extollunt, quae profecto delitescit, nisi ubi probetur invenerit. 3. sic et magnus orator si negotium aggrediatur angustum, tunc amplum plausibilius manifestat ingenium. Marcus Tullius in actionibus ceteris ceteros, pro

[1] in *add. Mohr.*
[2] fuerat *LTM*[1]: fuerit.

[1] Anderson's translation of this passage runs: "albeit in an expression of good wishes the matter in which your judgment seems to have erred might be a subject of praise," and he adds the marginal note: "I wonder if this is the meaning."—Personally I think the sense is otherwise: "you were clearly wrong in choosing me as the subject of your letter," says Sidonius; "this was an error of judgment; but you meant well, and therefore *in intention* your error of judgment is

have failed is choice of material—albeit the apparent error in judgment is something that can be commended in intention.[1] You apply to my character great screeds of eulogy; but if you had had any thought for my modesty it would have been right for you to consider the dictum of Symmachus: "True praise is an honour, false praise a rebuke." [2] 2. But in this matter (if I judge your mind correctly) quite apart from your affection, the strength of which you make abundantly plain, you acted from artistic motives as well. For eloquent men are accustomed to test the efficiency of their talent by difficult tasks: using their clever pen as the ploughshare of their fertile mind, they bring it to bear just where a subject consisting of sterile material grows starved on parched lean soil. The world is full of examples of this kind: the doctor shows his mettle in a desperate case, the helmsman in a storm. The fame of all such men is enhanced by the trials they have previously confronted; on the other hand, their fame is obscured if it has found no field to be tested in. 3. So also the great orator, if he tackles a troublesome business, displays his real talent more triumphantly. Marcus Tullius,[3] while in his other pleadings he surpassed all other speakers, in his defence of Aulus

commendable." I have altered the text of the translation accordingly.—*W.H.S.*

[2] Quintus Aurelius Symmachus (Cf. *Ep.* I. 1. 1; II. 10. 5; *Carm.* IX. 304), orator, who was consul in A.D. 391. Some of his speeches and nine books of his letters are extant, but the source of his statement here given by Sidonius is unknown.

[3] Cicero. A most admired speech of each orator is mentioned here. Cicero's extant speech *Pro Cluentio* was composed in 66 B.C.

Aulo Cluentio ipse se vicit. Marcus Fronto cum reliquis orationibus emineret, in Pelopem se sibi praetulit. Gaius Plinius pro Attia Viriola plus gloriae de centumvirali suggestu domum rettulit, quam cum Marco Ulpio incomparabili principi comparabilem panegyricum dixit. 4. sic et ipse fecisti, qui, dum vis exercere scientiam tuam, non veritus es fore tibi impedimento etiam conscientiam meam. quin potius supplicando meis medere languoribus neque per decipulum[1] male blandientis eloquii aegrotantis adhuc animae fragilitatem gloriae falsae pondere premas. sane cum tibi sermone pulchro vita sit pulchrior, plus mihi indulges, si mei causa orare potius velis quam perorare. vale.

XI

SIDONIVS LVPO SVO SALVTEM

1. Quid agunt Nitiobroges, quid Vesunnici tui, quibus de te sibi altrinsecus vindicando nascitur semper sancta contentio? unus te patrimonio populus, alter etiam matrimonio tenet; cumque hic

[1] decipulum *L*: decipulam.

---

[1] *c.* A.D. 100–170. The speech is not extant.

[2] The younger, *c.* A.D. 61–*c.* 113. The speech *Pro Attia* is not extant.

[3] The *centumviri* (One Hundred Men) formed the chancery-court at Rome.

[4] Marcus Ulpius Traianus, emperor A.D. 98–117. Pliny's

Cluentius surpassed himself; Marcus Fronto [1] won distinction by his other orations, but excelled himself in his speech against Pelops; Gaius Plinius [2] by his speech for Attia Viriola took away with him from the centumviral tribunal [3] more glory than when he delivered a panegyric that measured up to the matchless Emperor Trajan.[4] 4. So you, too, have done; wishing to exercise your skill, you had no fear that even the guilt I have on my conscience would be an obstacle to you. Nay, rather than this, offer prayers to heal my maladies: do not use the lure of a falsely flattering eloquence, do not burden the frailty of my still ailing soul with a weight of fictitious glory. Truly, as your life is even more beautiful than your beautiful language, you will do me greater kindness by orisons on my behalf than by orations. Farewell.

XI

SIDONIUS TO HIS FRIEND LUPUS,* GREETING

1. How fare your Nitiobroges [5] and your Vesunnici,[6] who keep up a rivalry about you that is never unchristian, one people always claiming you from the other? One of them appropriates you on the strength of your patrimonial connection, the other on the strength of your matrimonial connection; a

panegyric is extant; see also Pliny's Letters I. 20 and VI. 33.

* Not Saint Lupus, Bishop of Troyes, so often mentioned (See *Ep.* VI. 1, first note), but a rhetor of Périgueux.

[5] Their chief town was Agen.

[6] Of Périgueux.

origine, iste coniugio, melius illud, quod uterque iudicio. te tamen munere dei inter ista felicem, de quo diutius occupando possidendoque operae pretium est votiva populorum studia confligere! 2. tu vero utrisque praesentiam tuam disposite vicissimque partitus nunc Drepanium illis, modo istis restituis Anthedium. et si a te instructio rhetorica poscatur, hi Paulinum, illi Alcimum non requirunt. unde te magis miror, quem cotidie tam multiplicis bybliothecae ventilata lassat egeries, aliquid a me veterum flagitare cantilenarum. pareo quidem, licet intempestiva videatur recordatio iocorum tempore dolendi. 3. Lampridius orator modo primum mihi occisus agnoscitur, cuius interitus amorem meum summis conficeret angoribus, etiamsi non eum rebus humanis vis impacta rapuisset. hic me quondam, ut inter amicos ioca, Phoebum vocabat ipse a nobis vatis Odrysii nomine accepto.[1] quod eo congruit ante narrari, ne vocabula figurata subditum carmen obscurent. huic quodam tempore Burdigalam invisens metatoriam paginam quasi cum

[1] acceptus *Wilamowitz.*

---

[1] The sense is "though you are the subject of contention, still you are a lucky man to be so much valued by two peoples." —*W.H.S.*

[2] Pacatus Drepanius wrote a fine extant panegyric on Theodosius I in A.D. 389.

[3] A poet whom only Sidonius mentions. Cf. *Carm.* IX. 312; and *Carm.* XXII (the introductory letter), § 2.

[4] Not known for certain; cf. *Ep.* IV. 3. 7.

better reason still is that both claim you by deliberate choice. After all, how fortunate you are by God's grace in the midst of all this,[1] when it is worth while for peoples to contend in eager rivalry for the privilege of annexing and possessing you for a longer time! 2. You on your part share out your presence equitably to each in turn, bringing back Drepanius [2] to the one people and Anthedius [3] to the other; and if instruction in rhetoric is wanted from you, the one does not feel the loss of Paulinus [4] or the other of Alcimus.[5] This makes me the more surprised that you, so occupied every day with sifting out the refuse of your comprehensive library, now demand from me an example of the old doggerel. Well, I obey, though the recalling of jests seems unseasonable in a time of mourning. 3. I have just heard for the first time that Lampridius the orator has been murdered.[6] To a man who loved him as I did his death would have brought anguish without measure, even if he had not been carried off by a violent assault. In the old days, in the jocular manner of friends, he used to call me Phoebus, while he received from me the name of the Thracian bard; [7] it is fitting to mention this in advance, in order that the appended poem may not be rendered obscure by its allusive use of terms. On a certain occasion when I was paying a visit to Bordeaux I sent him a billeting-letter, making the Muse my advance-courier, as it

[5] The same as Alethius, poet and orator. For the persons here mentioned see *Hist. Littéraire de la France par les Religieux de S. Maur*, I. 419; II. 136–138, 469, 537.

[6] By his slaves. Cf. *Ep.* VIII. 9, first note.

[7] Orpheus. The Odrysae were a people of Thrace.

Musa praevia misi. puto hanc liberius offerri, quam si aliquid super decedentis occasu lugubre componens, qui non placebam per eloquentiam, per materiam displicerem.

Dilectae nimis et peculiari
Phoebus commonitorium Thaliae.

paulum depositis, alumna, plectris
sparsam stringe comam virente vitta,
et rugas tibi syrmatis profundi
succingant hederae expeditiores.
soccos ferre cave nec, ut solebat,
laxo pes natet altus in coturno;
sed tales crepidas ligare cura,
quales Harpalyce vel illa vinxit,
quae victos gladio [1] procos cecidit.
perges sic melius volante saltu,
si vestigia fasceata nudi
per summum digiti regant citatis
firmi ingressibus atque vinculorum
concurrentibus ansulis reflexa

[1] stadio *Leo.*

---

[1] Anderson in his translation had put "this will be a more generous offering." I don't think this brings out the true sense in this context, where Sidonius is speaking of the difficulty of producing a tribute, or memorial, to the dead man; he feels that he can resurrect the old poem and offer it "with less compunction," "with less constraint," "more freely" than if he wrote something new for the occasion.—*W.H.S.*

[2] The Muse who presided over comedy. Sidonius speaks in the character of Apollo.

were. I think that this can be offered you with less constraint [1] than if I composed something mournful about the ending of his life, thus adding to what was an unpleasing style the further disadvantage of an unpleasing subject.

Phoebus to his well-beloved and own particular Thalia,[2] this admonition.

1.[c] For a short space, dear pupil, put aside your lyre, bind your flowing hair with verdant fillet, and let ivy-bonds gird up the folds of your sweeping robe to a shape more expeditious [3] for travel. Wear not the sock of comedy and let not your foot, as was its wont, float about, high-perched, in the loose tragic buskin; but see that you tie on such shoes as were fastened by Harpalyce [4] or by her who with the sword slew her vanquished suitors. You [5] will move better, you will advance with flying leaps, if your sandalled [6] feet are guided by toes left bare at the extremities and gripping firmly when the pace is quickened, and if a chain of ties, working back through a running row of

[3] Anderson took *expeditiores* as an attributive adjective with *hederae*, freer ivy-bonds. But surely it is accusative with *rugas* and is to be taken proleptically "gird to a more convenient shape," *i.e.* in preparation for the journey proposed.—*W.H.S.* Cf. Horace, *Ep.* V. 25; *Sat.* I. 8. 23–24.

[4] A Thracian huntress. See Virgil, *Aen.* I. 315 ff. She who killed her vanquished suitors was in Greek story Atalanta; a fast runner, she would marry only the man who could outrace her, and dealt death to any suitor who failed to do so.

[5] Lines 12–17. This translation will have to be modified a bit.—*A.* I have modified it somewhat from the phrasing in Anderson's MS.—*W.H.S.*

[6] *fasceata.* See Vol. I of Sidonius (Loeb), pp. 42–43, note.

ad crus per cameram catena surgat.
hoc pernix habitu meum memento
Orpheum visere, qui cotidiana [1]
saxa et robora corneasque fibras
mollit dulciloqua canorus arte;
Arpinas modo quem [2] tonante lingua
ditat, nunc stilus aut Maronianus
aut quo tu Latium beas,[3] Horati,
Alcaeo melior lyristes [4] ipso,
et nunc inflat epos tragoediarum,[5]
nunc comoedia temperat iocosa,
nunc flammant satirae et tyrannicarum
declamatio controversiarum.
dic: "Phoebus venit atque post veraedos [6]
remis velivolum quatit Garumnam;
occurras iubet, ante sed parato
actutum hospitio." Leontioque,
prisco Livia quem dat e senatu,
dic: "iam nunc aderit." satis facetum et
solo nomine Rusticum videto.
sed si tecta negant ut occupata,

[1] cotidiano *coni. Luetjohann.*
[2] quam *MCFP.*
[3] beans *Leo.*
[4] lyrista es *Leo.*
[5] tragoedia atrum *Wilamowitz.*
[6] veraedos *L*: veredos.

---

[1] Cf. *Ep.* IV. 1. 4. [2] Cicero. [3] Virgil.

[4] Horace (65–8 B.C.) in his Latin odes looked on the Greek lyric poet Alcaeus (fl. *c.* 600 B.C.) as a model. Fragments only

loops, rises up the leg, vaulted curve upon curve. Speeding in such nimble garb, remember to visit my Orpheus, who every day by the tuneful utterance of his sweet-voiced art charms rocks and oaks and hearts [1] of horn; whom sometimes the man [2] of Arpinum with the thundering speech enriches, sometimes the pen of Maro [3] or that wherewith you, Horace, bless the land of Latium, you, Horace, a better lyric poet than Alcaeus' [4] self; or again the epic majesty of tragedies inspires him; again mirthful comedy tempers his tone; again he flames up in satire or in declamations denouncing tyrants. Say to him: "Phoebus comes; he has finished with the post-horses and is now smiting with his oars the waters of the sail-flown Garonne: he bids you meet him, but only when, without delay, a lodging is made ready for him." And say to Leontius,[5] whom Livia [6] has given to the world from an ancient line of senators: "He will be here at any moment." And look in on that most elegant man who is Rustic [7] only in name. But if these refuse me their shelter as

of Alcaeus survive. The objection to the reading *lyristes* (Greek λυριστής) is the false quantity *-ēs*, though it may have been acceptable on the analogy of a Latin word such as *antistĕs*. Anyhow, there are in Sidonius other false quantities equally bad or worse, such as *phĭlosophus* and *phȳsicus* and Euripĭdes. But, here Leo's reading *lyrista es*, giving a Latin form like *baptista* for βαπτιστής, may well be right.

[5] Not the Bishop of Arles (see *Ep.* VI. 3, first note), but Pontius Leontius, who had a splendid villa near Bordeaux (cf. *Carm.* XXII) and was father of Pontius Paulinus of *Ep.* VIII. 12. 5.

[6] His mother, we think, not the fort Livia of *Ep.* VIII. 3. 1.

[7] This Rusticus is the Rusticus or Rusticius of *Ep.* II. 11; not otherwise known.

perge ad limina mox episcoporum,
sancti et Gallicini manu osculata
tecti posce brevis vacationem,
ne, si destituor domo negata,
maerens ad madidas eam tabernas
et claudens geminas subinde nares
propter fumificas gemam culinas,
qua serpylliferis olet catinis [1]
bacas per geminas ruber botellus
ollarum aut nebulae vapore iuncto
fumant cum crepitantibus [2] patellis.
hic cum festa dies ciere ravos
cantus coeperit et voluptuosam
scurrarum querimoniam crepare,
tunc, tunc carmina digniora vobis
vinosi hospitis excitus Camena
plus illis ego barbarus susurrem.

4. O necessitas abiecta nascendi, vivendi misera, dura moriendi! ecce quo rerum volubilitatis humanae rota ducitur. amavi, fateor, satis hominem, licet quibusdam, tamen veniabilibus, erratis implicaretur atque virtutibus minora misceret. namque crebro levibus ex causis, sed leviter, excitabatur, quod nilominus ego studebam sententiae ceterorum

[1] catinis *Mohr*: catillis *Wilamowitz*: catenis.
[2] cum crepitantibus *codd.*: concrepitantibus *Mommsen*.

---

[1] Clearly a bishop.
[2] *baca*: What is this? The button at the end of the sausage? or the skin? or does it (the sausage) lie between two

being already booked, go next to the doors of the bishops, and kissing the hand of the holy Gallicinus,[1] beg him to spare me a tiny room, lest if I am stranded by the refusal of a home I should have to go sorrowfully to damp inns and groan again and again as I stop both nostrils by reason of the many smoky kitchens where, in dishes garnished with thyme, the red sausage exhales odours amid the twin berries,[2] or where clouds of smoke mixed with steam of pots rise up amid the clattering of plates.[3] Here, when a feast-day has begun to excite hoarse songs and to resound with the popular plaints of the buffoons, then, yes then, aroused by the muse of my tipsy host, I shall become a worse barbarian than they, and murmur strains more worthy of you.

4. How dismal the necessity of birth! how miserable the necessity of living! how hard the necessity of death! There you see the end to which the whole cycle of our mutable human fate conducts us! I confess that I loved Lampridius very much, although he was subject to certain failings, but venial failings: and mingled with his good qualities he had others not so good.[4] Often he got excited over trifling matters (though only to a trifling extent); I, however, always essayed to bring others to accept

olives on the dish? or in the midst of the twin berries, *i.e.* an olive and some other kind?—*A*.

[3] The translation is rather uncertain. I must reconsider it.—*A*. I have reconsidered it and to some extent altered it.

[4] "mingled with his good points some others did not reach the same standard." Is this right? Cf. Horace *Sat.* I. 4. 130, *mediocribus et quis|ignoscas vitiis teneor*, which Sidonius may have had in mind. Also Horace. *Sat.* I. 6. 65–67 where the use of *naevus* [wart] confirms this.—*A*.

naturam potius persuadere quam vitium; adstruebamque meliora, quatenus in pectore viri iracundia materialiter regnans, quia naevo crudelitatis fuerat infecta, praetextu saltim severitatis emacularetur. praeterea etsi consilio fragilis, fide firmissimus erat; incautissimus, quia credulus; securissimus, quia non nocens. nullus illi ita inimicus, qui posset eius extorquere maledictum; et tamen nullus sic amicus, qui posset effugere convicium. difficilis aditu, cum facilis inspectu, et portandus quidem, sed portabilis. 5. de reliquo, si orationes illius metiaris, acer rotundus, compositus excussus; si poemata, tener multimeter, argutus artifex erat. faciebat siquidem versus oppido exactos tam pedum mira quam figurarum varietate; hendecasyllabos lubricos et enodes; hexametros crepantes et cothurnatos; elegos vero nunc echoicos, nunc recurrentes, nunc per anadiplosin fine principiisque conexos. 6. huc,[1] ut arreptum suaserat opus, ethicam dictionem pro personae temporis loci qualitate variabat, idque non verbis qualibuscumque, sed grandibus pulchris elucubratis. in materia controversiali fortis et lacertosus; in satirica sollicitus et mordax; in

[1] huc *L*: hic.

---

[1] Or: "a wonderful variety of feet and of shape."—*A.* I incline to take *figurae* in the sense of "poetical turns of style." Cf. Quintilian, IX. 1. 4 and 14.—*W.H.S.*

[2] Which are the same if read backwards from end to beginning. See Sidonius himself on this, pp. 582 ff.

that this in him was a natural, rather than a moral weakness; and I added a more favourable interpretation, suggesting that, since this tendency to anger so constitutionally inherent in the man's breast had been infected by an element of cruelty, it might be excused at least on the plea of stern rectitude. Moreover, although weak in counsel, he was completely steady in fidelity; he was most incautious because trustful, and free from fear because he did no harm. No enemy was so bitterly unfriendly as to force a curse out of him; at the same time, no friend was so intimate as to escape abuse. He was difficult to approach, though easy enough to get a view of, and he had to be borne with but was not unbearable. 5. Further, if you estimate his speeches you find him vehement and smoothly rounded, quiet and energetic; if you examine his poems you find he was tender, a master of many metres, sonorous, and of finished artistry; for he composed verses perfectly constructed with a remarkable variety both of feet and of phrasing [1]—hendecasyllables gliding and smooth; hexameters resounding and majestic; elegiacs now echoic, now palindromic,[2] now with end linked with beginning by duplication. 6. Further, following the dictates of whatever work he had taken in hand, he would vary the style of his character-drawing in accordance with the nature of the person, the time, and the place, and in so doing he used, not the first words that occurred, but elevated, graceful, and carefully studied expressions. In argumentation he was vigorous and sinewy, in satire earnest [3]

[3] For *sollicitus* see § 10.

tragica saevus et flebilis; in comica urbanus multiformisque: in fescennina vernans verbis, aestuans votis; in bucolica vigilax parcus carminabundus; in georgica sic rusticans multum, quod nihil rusticus. 7. praeterea quod ad epigrammata spectat, non copia sed acumine placens, quae nec brevius disticho neque longius tetrasticho finiebantur, eademque cum non pauca piperata, mellea multa conspiceres, omnia tamen salsa cernebas. in lyricis autem Flaccum secutus nunc ferebatur in iambico citus, nunc in choriambico gravis, nunc in alcaico flexuosus, nunc in sapphico inflatus. quid plura? subtilis aptus instructus quaque mens stilum ferret eloquentissimus, prorsus ut eum iure censere post Horatianos et Pindaricos cygnos gloriae pennis evolaturum. 8. aleae aut [1] sphaerae non iuxta deditus; nam cum tesseris ad laborem occuparetur, pila tantum ad voluptatem. fatigabat libenter, quodque plus dulce, libentius fatigabatur. scribebat assidue, quamquam frequentius scripturiret. legebat etiam incessanter auctores cum reverentia antiquos, sine invidia recentes, et, quod inter homines difficillimum est, nulli difficulter ingenii laude cedebat. 9. illud sane non solum culpabile in viro

[1] aut *L*: et *T*: *om. MCFP*: at *Mommsen*: ut *Luetjohann*.

---

[1] He is thinking particularly of weddings and the like. Cf. *Carm.* XIV, in the letter, § 1; *Carm.* X. 21. *Fescennini* (*versus*) were coarse songs sung in connection with weddings, and probably at harvest-festivals also. The origin of the word is uncertain.

and mordant, in tragedy furious and pathetic, in comedy polished and versatile, in fescennines[1] blossoming with words and afire with good wishes; in pastorals alert, restrained, and melodious; in georgics full of rustic life without being at all rustic. 7. Now further, as regards epigrams, he gave pleasure not by length but by point; they were never shorter than a couplet or longer than a quatrain and while one could find not a few with some pepper in them and many that were honeyed, one detected in all of them a seasoning of salt. In his lyrics, following Horace, he sometimes moved rapidly in iambic measure, sometimes with stately dignity in the choriambic, now with supple modulation in the Alcaics, now loftily inspired in the Sapphics. In short, he was refined, felicitous, and richly equipped; and wherever his mind carried his pen, he was such a master of utterance that one justly thought he would soar on wings of glory next after the Horatian and Pindaric swans. 8. As between dicing and ball-play his interest was unequal: he engaged in dicing as a toil, but played ball solely for pleasure. He enjoyed bantering, and—what is more likeable—he enjoyed even more being bantered in return. He wrote constantly, though not as often as to satisfy his urge. He was also an incessant reader, reading the old writers with reverence and the modern ones without jealousy; and, the most difficult thing in the world, he was ready to think himself second to anyone in intellectual glory. 9.[2] There was indeed one

[2] § 9: a full explanation and translation of this difficult passage will be found in my *Quaestiones Exegeticae*, 49–51. Anderson has almost entirely followed my note there.—*W.H.S.*

fuit, sed peremptorium, quod mathematicos quondam de vitae fine consuluit, urbium cives Africanarum, quorum,[1] ut est regio, sic animus ardentior; qui constellatione percontantis inspecta pariter annum mensem diemque dixerunt, quos, ut verbo matheseos utar, climactericos esset habiturus, utpote quibus themate oblato quasi sanguinariae genituræ schema patuisset, quia videlicet amici nascentis anno, quemcumque clementem planeticorum siderum globum in diastemata zodiaca[2] prosper ortus erexerat, hunc in occasu cruentis ignibus inrubescentes seu super diametro Mercurius asyndetus seu super tetragono Saturnus retrogradus seu super centro Mars apocatastaticus exacerbassent. 10. sed de his, si qua vel[3] quoquo[4] modo sunt, quamquam sint maxume falsa ideoque fallentia, si quid plenius planiusque, rectius coram, licet et ipse arithmeticae studeas et, quae diligentia tua, Vertacum Thrasybulum Saturninum sollicitus evolvas, ut qui semper nil nisi arcanum celsumque meditere. interim ad

[1] quorum *LR*: quibus.

[2] diastemata zodiaca *vulgo*: diastemate zodiaco *FP*: diastema zodiaca *LTC*: die (e *eraso*) astemate zodiac$\overset{o}{a}$ M^1.

[3] vel *fortasse secludendum* (*Mohr*): si qua vel *L*: si qua *N*: qualia *MCFPN*^{1} qualia vel *T*: signa vel *coni. Warmington*.

[4] quoque *codd.*: quoquo L^1. cf. Additional Notes, p. 615.

---

[1] Returning to its position of the year before.

[2] Perhaps Sidonius is intentionally ambiguous in this passage. He has a lurking suspicion that there is something in astrology, but as a good Catholic he condemns it as false. In these concluding paragraphs he is not consistent.—*A*. Perhaps we can accept the reading *signa* (see critical note) and still maintain sense and ambiguity: "But on these matters, even whatever the condition as regards constellations

thing about him which was not merely blameworthy but fatal: he once consulted astrologers on the subject of his death; they were citizens of African towns, men whose mind, like their climate, is overfervid. These men, on examining the disposition of the planets which affected their inquirer, told him alike the year the month and the day which would be for him climacteric (to use the astrological term); for, when the aspect of the heavens presented itself to their eyes, clearly, they said, the diagram of a bloody nativity had been revealed: in our friend's natal year (they explained) any benevolent planetary orb that a propitious rising had lifted into the houses of the zodiac had been rendered malignant at its setting by some planet red with a bloody flame—either by Mercury asyndetic in opposition; or by Saturn retrograde, in square; or by Mars, apocatastatic,[1] in configuration. 10. But on these matters (if they have anything in them at all, though they are for the most part false and therefore deluding) any fuller or more explicit [2] discussion had better wait till we meet—although you are yourself a student of arithmetic [3] and, with characteristic diligence, painstakingly pursue the pages of Vertacus and Thrasybulus and Saturninus,[4] being a man who never spends a thought on anything but the mysterious and lofty. Meanwhile on this occasion there

(*signa*)" or "whatever the position of constellations . . ."

[3] Calculation was, of course, a vital element in astrology.

[4] Fullonius Saturninus and Iulianus Vertacus are mentioned in § 3 of the letter to Leontius prefixed to *Carm.* XXII. Thrasybulus, astrologer, lived early in the third century A.C.

praesens nil coniecturaliter gestum, nil per ambages, quandoquidem hunc nostrum temerarium futurorum sciscitatorem et diu frustra tergiversantem tempus et qualitas praedictae mortis innexuit. 11. nam domi pressus strangulatusque servorum manibus obstructo anhelitu gutture obstricto, ne dicam Lentuli Iugurthae atque Seiani, certe Numantini Scipionis exitu periit. haec in hac caede tristia minus, quod nefas ipsum cum auctore facti parricidalis diluculo inventum. nam quis ab hominum tam procul sensu, quis ita gemino obtutu eluminatus, qui exanimati cadavere inspecto non statim signa vitae colligeret extortae? 12. etenim protinus argumento fuere

[1] "Long halting between two opinions on the matter." This seems to be the meaning of *tergiversantem.—A.* I think rather the word means "trying to dodge but in vain." This seems to give rather better sense, and I have adopted it.—*W.H.S.* Sidonius now goes on to describe the murder of Lampridius. Cf. *Ep.* VIII. 9; IX. 13. 2. 4.

[2] Publius Cornelius Scipio Aemilianus Africanus, who captured Carthage in 146 B.C., was also called Numantinus after he ended the wars in Spain by capturing Numantia in 133. In 129 he was found dead in his room from an unknown cause, about which various stories were told.

[3] At least three Lentuli were put to death for political reasons in the first century B.C.; but the one alluded to here would be Publius Cornelius Lentulus Sura, who was strangled in 63 B.C. for the part he had played in the conspiracy of Catiline. Iugurtha, King of Numidia in north Africa, defied the Romans until his capture; he was strangled or starved to death in Rome in 104 B.C. L. Aelius Seianus who had such strong influence over the Emperor Tiberius was put to death in A.D. 31.

[4] It is all very obscure. Where was he (Lampridius) murdered? Was the body carried from the scene of the murder? It seems that the reference at the beginning (*terra tabo madefacta deciduo*) is still to the face (the *obrutus vultus* of the previous sentence). And therefore I think the full stop

has happened an occurrence which has nothing conjectural or ambiguous about it, for our friend, this rash enquirer into the future, who for so long had been vainly dodging [1] his doom, has been caught by the time and manner of the death foretold. 11. In his own home he was choked and strangled by the hands of his slaves, who stopped his breath by throttling, thus causing him to meet the end of Scipio Numantinus [2] at least—I will not say of Lentulus, Jugurtha, and Sejanus.[3] One relieving feature in this homicide was that the outrage itself and the author of the heinous crime were discovered at dawn. For who so bereft of human intelligence, who so blind in both eyes, as not to recognise at the first sight of the dead body the evidences of a violent murder? 12. It [4] was proved at once by the livid

after *doloris* should be a semicolon. Near the face the ground was wet with blood that had dripped down from it (from the mouth?). The raised pavement will account for the direction of the dripping. The murderers thought the body was already drained of blood. It seems odd that, after what had happened, they should have such a finicky regard for cleanliness! I wish I knew what and where the *pavimentum* was. This is by no means the only place where Sidonius leaves us guessing. If he would use fewer words and tell us more, it would be a great improvement.—*A.* I incline to the view taken by Dalton in his translation that the intention of the murderers was to lay the body on its face as if to suggest that it had fallen prone because of a seizure and violent haemorrhage—so that the pool of blood on the pavement of the room would look like the whole blood-content of the body. This seems to fit in with "*tamquam . . . exinanisset*"—they wish to make it appear that a terribly violent flux from the mouth had drained the body of all its blood. But the sense would be greatly improved, I think, if we could read *exanimasset* for *exinanisset.* Is this a possibility?—*W.H.S.*

livida cutis, oculi protuberantes et in obruto vultu non minora irae vestigia quam doloris. inventa est quidem terra tabo madefacta deciduo, quia post facinus ipsi latrones ad pavimentum conversa defuncti ora pronaverant, tamquam sanguinis eum superaestuans fluxus exinanisset.[1] sed protinus capto qui fuerat ipsius factionis fomes incentor antesignanus ceterisque complicibus oppressis seorsumque discussis criminis veritatem de pectoribus[2] invitis tormentorum terror extraxit. 13. atque utinam hunc finem, dum inconsulte fidens[3] vana consultat, non meruisset excipere! nam quisque praesumpserit interdicta secreta vetita rimari, vereor huius modi[4] catholicae fidei regulis exorbitaturum et effici dignum, in statum cuius respondeantur adversa, dum requiruntur inlicita. secuta quidem est ultio extinctum, sed magis prosunt ista victuris. nam quotiens homicida punitur, non est remedium sed solacium vindicari. 14. longiuscule me progredi amor impulit, cuius angorem silentio exhalare non valui. tu interim, si quid istic cognitu dignum, citus indica, saltim ob hoc scribens, ut animum meum tristitudine gravem lectio levet. namque confuso pectori maeror, et quidem iure, plurimus erat, cum paginis ista committerem sola.

[1] exanimasset *coni. Semple.*

[2] peccatoribus *L.*

[3] fidens *Wilamowitz*: fides. *coni. Warmington* inconsulta fides.

[4] huius modi ⟨hominem⟩ *Luetjohann.*

skin, the glaring eyes, and the traces of anger no less than of pain on his prostrate face. The floor was found to be wet with the blood that had dripped, because after the foul deed the villains themselves had turned the dead man's face flat to the pavement, as if to suggest that a sudden overwhelming haemorrhage had drained the blood from his body. But when the ringleader who fired and incited the gang had been captured, and when all his accomplices were arrested and separately examined, the terror of torture extracted the truth about the crime from their unwilling breasts. 13. I only wish that our friend had not deserved this end by seeking vain advice with such ill-advised credulity. For I fear that everyone who presumes to pry into banned and secret and prohibited mysteries will thus deviate from the rules of the Catholic faith, and by enquiring into unlawful matters he deserves to get answers that bode ill for him. True, vengeance followed his murder, but such compensations benefit rather those who survive; for when a murderer is punished the retribution may give some comfort, but it cannot undo the deed. 14. My affection has compelled me to continue rather too long: such a grief, a grief of affection, I could not have worked off in silence. In the meantime, if there is anything in your place worth knowing about, be quick and notify me: if for no other reason, write in order that the reading of the letter may relieve my mind so burdened with grief; for there was a heavy weight of sorrow, and naturally so, on my troubled heart when I committed to paper these words—I say—my only words; for at the present time I have no inclination, ab-

neque enim satis mihi aliud hoc tempore manu sermone consilio scribere loqui volvere libet. vale.

XII

SIDONIVS TRYGETIO SVO SALVTEM

1. Tantumne te Vasatium civitas non caespiti imposita sed pulveri, tantum Syrticus ager ac vagum solum et volatiles ventis altercantibus harenae sibi possident, ut te magnis flagitatum precibus, parvis separatum spatiis, multis exspectatum diebus attrahere Burdigalam non potestates, non amicitiae, non opimata vivariis ostrea queant? an temporibus hibernis viarum te dubia suspendunt et, quia solet Bigerricus turbo mobilium aggerum indicia confundere, quoddam vereris in itinere terreno pedestre naufragium? 2. ubi, quaesumus, animo tam celeriter excessit vestigiis tuis nuper subacta Calpis? ubi fixa tentoria in occiduis finibus Gaditanorum? ubi ille Trygetio meo idem qui Herculi quondam terminus peregrinandi? tantumne a te ipso ipse tu discrepas, ut totus in desidiae iura concesseris, quo peragrante secreta regionum fabulosarum prius defuit actio laboris quam fatigationis

---

* It is not likely that this Trygetius was the one sent with Pope Leo and Gennadius Avienus in A.D. 452 on an embassy to Attila.

[1] Bazas in Gironde. Cf. *Ep.* VII. 6. 7.

[2] Gibraltar.

[3] Straits of Gibraltar.

[4] "a sphere of exercise for your toil came to an end before your ardour for exertion failed."—*A*.

solutely no inclination, to use hand, speech, or thought, in writing, uttering, or pondering anything else. Farewell.

XII

SIDONIUS TO HIS FRIEND TRYGETIUS,* GREETING

1. Does the town of Bazas[1], built not on solid ground but on dust, Bazas with its Syrtes-like territory and shifting soil and its sands flying this way and that with the quarrelling winds, does Bazas hold you so firmly that neither the powers-that-be, nor friendships, nor oysters fattened in fishponds can lure you to Bordeaux, although you have been besought with earnest entreaties, and are only a short distance away, and your coming has been awaited for many days? Are you kept in two minds by the risks of the roads in the winter season, fearing a sort of landlubber's shipwreck on an overland journey because the whirlwind of Bigorre is wont to obliterate the traces of the unstable roads? 2. Where, pray, has the memory of Calpis [2] so quickly gone from your mind, Calpis lately conquered by your feet? Where has gone the memory of your camp pitched on the western bounds of Cadiz? Where the memory of those travels which my dear Trygetius ended at the same place [3] as Hercules? Are you now so unlike yourself that you have passed wholly under the dominance of sloth—you whose physical energy gave out sooner than your will for exertion,[4] as you traversed the dark recesses of those fabulous

intentio? 3. et post haec portum Alingonis tam piger calcas, ac si tibi nunc esset ad limitem Danuvinum contra incursaces Massagetas proficiscendum, vel si nunc etiam tuae navi [1] stagna Nilotidis aquae per indigenas formidata crocodillos transfretarentur.[2] et cum nec duodecim milium obiectu sic retarderis, quid, putamus, cum exercitu Marci Catonis in Leptitana Syrte fecisses? 4. sed quamlibet sola hiemalium mensium nomina tremas, tam clemens est facies caeli, tam tepida, tam suda et sic auras mage quam ventos habet, ut te non valeat enixius retinere tempus quam invitare temperies. sed si epistulam spernis evocatoriam, credo, vel versibus non reluctaberis impulsoribus blandis et desiderii mei, quantum suspicor, strenuis executoribus, quorum in te castra post biduum commovebuntur. 5. ecce Leontius meus, facile primus Aquitanorum, ecce iam parum inferior parente Paulinus ad locum quem supra dixi per Garumnae fluenta refluentia non modo tibi cum classe verum etiam cum flumine

[1] tuae navi *L*: tuae naves.
[2] transfretarentur *LN*: transfretarent.

---

[1] On the Garonne.
[2] Trygetius is wasting so much time in making up his mind whether to adventure on the journey to Bordeaux some twelve miles downstream from Langon, that one would imagine he was contemplating a journey to the Danube or the Nile. —*W.H.S.* The Massagetae were a people living on the eastern shore of the Caspian Sea.

regions. 3. And after all this you boggle at the harbour of Langon,[1] showing as little spirit as if you had now to start for the Danubian frontier against the raiding Massagetae,[2] or as if your ship were actually crossing the waters of the Nile dreaded because of native crocodiles. And indeed, if you are so delayed by an intervening space of barely twelve miles, what can we suppose you would have done had you been with the army of Marcus Cato in the desert of Leptis?[3] 4. But however much you may dread the mere names of the winter months, the aspect of the sky is so genial, so warm, so sunny, with breezes rather than winds, that the season cannot deter you more strongly than the seasoned climate invites you. If, however, you reject this letter of summons, you will not, I think, resist my verses,[4] a host of which will leave camp against you in two days' time, agents as charming as they are compelling and, I imagine, capable of actively enforcing my desire. 5. And behold! my friend Leontius,[5] easily first among the Aquitanians, and Paulinus,[6] who is now no whit inferior to his father, will traverse the back-flowing flood[7] of the Garonne and meet you at the above-mentioned place not only with a fleet

[3] M. Porcius Cato crossed this desert in north Africa with ten thousand men in thirty days, before his suicide in 46 B.C.

[4] If Trygetius can resist prose, Sidonius means to try him by the more subtle and attractive method of verse.—*W.H.S.*

[5] Not Leontius of *Ep.* VI. 3, but Pontius Leontius (cf. *Ep.* VIII. 11. *carm.* 33) of Bordeaux. Cf. *Carm.* XXII.

[6] Pontius Paulinus, son of Pontius Leontius. See Index.

[7] The tidal Garonne seems to flow backwards towards Langon upstream. See also my note in *Quaest. Exeg.*, 51.—*W.H.S.*

occurrent. hic tuas laudes modificato celeumate simul inter transtra remiges, gubernatores inter aplustria canent. hic te aedificatus culcitis torus, hic tabula calculis strata bicoloribus, hic tessera frequens eboratis resultatura pyrgorum gradibus expectat; hic, ne tibi pendulum tinguat volubilis sentina vestigium, pandi carinarum ventres abiegnarum trabium textu pulpitabuntur; hic superflexa crate paradarum sereni brumalis infida vitabis. 6. quid delicatae pigritiae tuae plus poterit impendi, quam ut te pervenisse invenias, cum venire vix sentias? quid mussitas? quid moraris? ipsae mihi tuum videntur adventum reptiles cocleae cum domibus nativis antecessurae. est praeterea tibi copiosissima penus aggeratis opipare farta [1] deliciis, modo sit eventilando par animus impendio. 7. quid multa? veni ut aut pascaris aut pascas; immo, quod gratius, ut utrumque; veni cum mediterraneo instructu ad debellandos subiugandosque istos Medulicae supellectilis epulones. hic Aturricus piscis Garumnicis mugilibus insultet; hic ad copias

[1] farta *L*: referta.

---

[1] *celeuma* (Greek κέλευμα "command") is properly the command or call of the chief oarsman to the others in their rowing.

[2] Gaming-board and pieces of two colours and dice (cf. *Ep.* I. 2. 7) suggest a game in which dice as well as pieces were used, as in backgammon; or two different games may be meant. The Romans were keen gamblers, especially during the imperial period, and usually played with three dice thrown

but with the river. Here your praises will be sung in a melodious boat-song [1] both by the rowers on the thwarts and the helmsmen at the stern. Here there await you a couch built with cushions, a gaming-board set with two-coloured pieces, and many dice [2] ready to rebound from the ivory-covered steps of the boxes. Here, to prevent the swirling bilge-water from wetting your dangling feet, a pinewood flooring will be laid across the curving belly of the hull. Here also you will be screened from any treachery on the part of the clear winter sky by a wicker awning overhead. 6. What more could be contributed to your fastidious indolence than to find you have arrived while scarce conscious of moving? Why do you hum and haw? Why do you hold back? It looks to me as if even crawling snails with their houses on their backs would get here before you. Moreover, there is for you a richly stocked larder, filled to overflowing with masses of costly delicacies, if only you felt inclined to ransack its contents.[3] 7. In a word, come here, either to be fed or to feed others, or, more pleasing still, to do both; come with your inland commissariat to beat down and subjugate the local gourmands equipped with the oysters of Médoc. Here let the fish of the Adour [4] triumph over the

from a box. *Tesserae* (dice) as a word comes from the Greek τέσσαρες (four), and was used because some oblong *tesserae* used for purposes other than dice-play were inscribed on their four long sides. The *pyrgus* (Greek πύργος, tower) was a wooden dice-box, shaped like a tower, with steps inside it.

[3] *impendium* is used to denote the contents of the larder.

[4] The Latin here refers to the river Adour, whereas in *Ep.* II. 1. 1 Aturres is the town, of the Aturenses, now called Aire (on the left bank of the Adour), in Landes, Gascony.

Lapurdensium lucustarum cedat vilium turba cancrorum. 8. tu tamen etsi ceteris eris in hoc genere pugnandi dimicaturus, si quid iudicio meo censes adquiescendum (neque enim iniustum est credere experto), senatorem nostrum, hospitem meum, conflictui huic facies exsortem; cuius si convivio tectoque succedas, dapes Cleopatricas et loca lautia putas.[1] nam quamvis super hoc studio tam ipse quam patria confligant, olim lata sententia est, quod ille transeat ceteros cives, licet et illa ceteras civitates. vale.

XIII

SIDONIVS DOMINO PAPAE NVNECHIO SALVTEM

1. Multa in te genera virtutum, papa beatissime, munere superno congesta gaudemus. siquidem agere narraris sine superbia nobilem sine invidia potentem, sine superstitione religiosum sine iactantia litteratum, sine ineptia gravem sine studio facetum, sine asperitate constantem sine popularitate communem. 2. praeterea his hoc praestantissimum

[1] putas *LFP*: putes *TC*: putas (e supra) *M*[1]: puta *Mommsen*. *Post initium sequ. sententiae deficit V*.

---

[1] *putas*: probably right, the present indicative being used for the future indicative, as often in Sidonius.

[2] Does it mean that he and the town are rivals to one another? The Latin does not look like it. Much more probable

mullets of the Garonne; here let our horde of humble crabs give way before an army of lobsters from Bayonne. 8. But a word of warning! even though you are ready to engage in this sort of contest against the rest of us, yet (if you think any deference should be paid to my judgment—and it is surely not unreasonable to trust one who knows), you will omit from the competition the senator who is my host. If you enter his home and come to his table you will think[1] the feast like Cleopatra's and the accommodation fit for a state-guest. For though in this matter of hospitality he and his native town challenge the world,[2] it has long been a settled verdict that he surpasses all other citizens, though it, too, surpasses all other cities. Farewell.

XIII

SIDONIUS TO THE LORD BISHOP NUNECHIUS,* GREETING

1. I rejoice, most blessed Bishop, that by heaven's grace there are combined in you virtues of many kinds. You are reported to carry your nobility without haughtiness and your power without obnoxiousness, to be religious without superstition, cultured without ostentation, serious without pedantry and witty without studied effort, steadfast without harshness, genial without courting popularity. 2. To these good qualities fame makes a

that he and the town vie with others, "although he as well as his native city vie with others in this kind of effort."—*A.*

* Bishop of Nantes.

bonis fama superaggerat, quod te asserit hasce tot gratias fastigatissimae caritatis arce[1] transcendere; fama, inquam, quae de laudibus tuis cum canat multa, plus reticet. nam longius constitutis actionum tuarum propositum potest assignare, non numerum. quarum relatione succensus ultro primus, ut longe inferiorem decet, ad solvenda officia procurro nec vereor garrulitatis aliquando argui, qui potui taciturnitatis hucusque culpari. 3. commendo Promotum gerulum litterarum, vobis quidem ante iam cognitum, sed nostrum nuper effectum vestris orationibus contribulem; qui cum sit gente Iudaeus, fide tamen praeelegit censeri Israelita quam sanguine, et municipatum caelestis illius civitatis affectans occidentemque litteram spiritu vivificante fastidiens, pariter huc[2] iustis praemia proposita contemplans, huc,[3] nisi faceret ad Christum de circumcisione transfugium, praevidens sese per aeterna saecula aequiterna supplicia passurum, patriam sibi maluit Ierusalem potius quam Hierusolymam computari. 4. quibus agnitis adventantem Abrahae nunc filium veriorem maternis ulnis spiritalis Sara[4] suscipiat. namque ad Agar ancillam pertinere tunc desiit, cum legalis observantiae servitutem gratiae libertate mutavit. de cetero, quae

[1] apice *Wilamowitz*.
[2] huc *L*: hinc.
[3] huc *L*: hinc.
[4] sarra *LMTCP*.

---

[1] The Jewish faith.
[2] *I.e.* the heavenly Jerusalem rather than the Jerusalem on earth.

crowning addition, declaring that you outtop all these graces by the towering eminence of your charity—aye, and fame, though it tells much about your excellences, leaves still more unsaid; for while it may present to those at a distance the purposed aim of your actions, it cannot count their number. And it is because I am fired by what I have heard of these, that taking the initiative (as becomes one who is far beneath you) I haste to pay my respects, nor do I fear some day to be accused of talkativeness when I might well have been blamed for keeping silent so long. 3. I commend to you Promotus, the bearer of my letter, who is already known to you, but has recently, through your prayers, been made a member of our tribe. A Jew by race, he has now chosen to be accounted an Israelite by faith rather than by blood. Aiming at citizenship of the Heavenly City and, by the power of the spirit that giveth life, scorning the letter that killeth, viewing, on the one hand, the rewards appointed for the just, and on the other hand, foreseeing that through never-ending ages he would suffer never-ending punishment unless he changed from the Circumcision [1] to Christ, he has chosen that the new Jerusalem rather than the old [2] should be considered his country. 4. Recognising this, let now the spiritual Sarah receive into her maternal arms as he approaches one who is now in a truer sense a son of Abraham; for he ceased to belong to the hand-maid Hagar [3] when he exchanged the servitude of the Law's observance for the freedom that Grace confers.

[3] Genesis, XVI, 1 ff. The whole paragraph is influenced by Paul's letter to the Galatians IV. 21–31.

ipsi fuerit isto causa veniendi, praesentaneo conducibilius idem poterit explicare memoratu. nobis vero propter quae supra scripsi carissimus habetur; quod ideo significo, quia is efficacissime quemque commendat, qui meras causas iustae commendationis aperuerit. memor nostri esse dignare, domine papa.

XIV

SIDONIVS DOMINO PAPAE PRINCIPIO SALVTEM

1. Iam diu nobis, papa venerabilis, etsi necdum vester vultus aspectus, tamen actus inspectus est. namque sanctorum laus diffusa meritorum stringi spatiis non est contenta finalibus. hinc est quod, quia bonae conscientiae modus non ponitur, nec bonae opinioni terminus invenitur. 2. quae loquor falsa censete, nisi professioni meae competens adstipulator accesserit, satis in illo quondam coenobio Lirinensi spectabile caput, Luporum concellita Maximorumque et parsimoniae saltibus consequi affectans Memphiticos et Palaestinos archimandritas.

---

[1] Cf. Pliny, *Ep.* II. 13. 11.

* Bishop of Soissons. Cf. *Ep.* IX. 8.

[2] This (*i.e.* what has just been mentioned) " arises from " (is explained by) " the fact that . . ."—*A.*

[3] Or " leader in " or " figure in."—*A.*

[4] The monastery founded by Honoratus. See *Ep.* VI. 1. 3; *Carm.* XVI. 104 ff.

[5] Bishop of Troyes. See *Ep.* VI. 1, first note.

For the rest, he will be able to explain to you more fittingly by personal word the reason for his coming to your neighbourhood. To me indeed he is very dear for the reasons which I have stated above. I make this plain, because the most effective recommendation of a person comes from one who has disclosed the precise reasons that justify his recommendation.[1] Deign to hold me in remembrance, my Lord Bishop.

XIV

SIDONIUS TO THE LORD BISHOP PRINCIPIUS,* GREETING

1. Venerable Bishop, although I have not yet viewed your face, I have long reviewed your conduct; for the praise of saintliness spreads abroad and is not content to be limited by any confining bounds. The explanation of this is that,[2] because the cultivation of a good conscience admits no limit, the good report that results is equally unbounded. 2. You are at liberty to think my words untrue if my declaration is not supported by a competent guarantor, in the person of one who was formerly an eminent head of[3] the Lérins community,[4] a cell-mate of men like Lupus[5] and Maximus,[6] striving by the lengths to which he carried abstinence[7] to overtake the archimandrites[8] of Memphis and of Palestine. He

[6] Abbot of Lérins; later, Bishop of Riez. Cf. *Carm.* XVI. 112, 128.

[7] " springing strides of self-denial."—*A.*

[8] In the Orthodox Eastern Church these corresponded to the abbots in the west.

is est[1] episcopus Antiolus,[2] cuius relatu, qui pater vobis, quique qualesque vos fratres, qua morum praerogativa pontificatu maximo ambo fungamini, sollicitus cognoscere studui, gaudens cognovisse me memini. 3. cui patri quondam, videlicet vos habenti, vix domus Aaron pontificis antiqui merito compararetur: quem licet primum in medio plebis heremitidis sanctificationis oleo legiferi fratris dextra perfuderit, filios eius in similis officii munia vocans, tamen ipsius super Ithamare[3] et Eleazaro felicitatem Nadab et Abiu fulminibus afflati decoloravere; quorum quamlibet interemptorum credamus abquorum quamlibet interemptorum credamus absolvendas animas, punitas tamen scimus esse personas. 4. vos vero tacturi paginam altaris nihil, ut audio, offertis ignis alieni, sed comitantibus victimis caritatis castitatisque fragrantissimum[4] incensum turibulis cordis adoletis. ad hoc quotiens iugum legis cervicibus superbientum per vincula praedicationis adstringitis, tunc deo tauros spiritaliter immolatis. quotiens conscientiae luxuriantis fetore pollutos ad suaveolentiam pudicitiae stimulis correctionis impellitis, hircorum vos obtulisse virulentiam Christus sibi computat. 5. quotiens hortanti-

[1] is est *vulgo*: scilicet *coni. Luetjohann*: is et *codd.*
[2] antiolius *M*.
[3] Ithamare *Luetjohann*: ithamar.
[4] fragrantissimum *vulgo*: flagrantissimum.

---

[1] Or Antiolius; not otherwise known.

is Bishop Antiolus;[1] from his lips, I remember, I anxiously sought to learn, and to my great joy I did learn, the name of your father, the personality and character of you and your brother, and the moral pre-eminence by reason of which you both hold a prelate's office. 3. With your father, having two such sons as you, the family of the ancient pontiff Aaron would scarcely have borne comparison; for although Aaron was anointed with the oil of consecration by the hand of his brother the law-giver amid the people in the wilderness, and though the same hand summoned his sons to the duties of a like office, yet the bliss that Ithamar and Eleazar brought him was marred by the fate of Nadab and Abihu who were scorched by shafts of lightning,[2] for, however convinced we are that after death their souls would find absolution, we know that their persons were punished. 4. But when you are about to touch the altar-slab you do not, I hear, offer any strange fire, but along with sacrifices of charity and chastity you burn most fragrant incense [3] in the censers of the heart. Moreover, as often as with the cords of preaching you fasten the yoke of the law upon the necks of the proud, you are in a spiritual sense sacrificing bulls to God. As often as, plying the goads of correction, you impel to the sweet savour of continence sinners tainted with the noisomeness of a wanton nature, Christ reckons that you have offered to him the fetid bodies of goats. 5. As often as,

[2] Leviticus VIII. 2; 12; X. 1 ff.; Numbers III. 4.

[3] What of the v. 1. *flagrantissimum*? What would it mean? Probably brightly growing.—*A*. Cf. Leviticus X. 1 ff.; Numbers III. 4.

bus vobis in quocumque conpuncto culpas suas anima poenaliter recordata suspirat, quis vos ambigat paria turturum aut binos pullos columbarum, qui duplicem substantiam utriusque hominis nostri tam numero quam gemitu assignant, mystico litasse sacrificio? quotiens vestro monitu obesum quicumque corpus aestuantemque turgidi ventris arvinam crebro ieiuniorum decoquendus igne torruerit, nulli dubium est vos tunc simulam [1] frictam [2] in quadam continentiae sartagine consecraturos. 6. quotiens aliquem mentis perfidae figmenta ponentem sanam respondere doctrinam fidem credere, viam tenere vitam sperare suadetis, quis vos dubitet in huius emendatione conversi, qui iam sit liber ab haeresi, liber ab hypocrisi, liber ab schismate, purgatissimum propositionis panem cum sinceritatis et veritatis azymis dedicaturos? 7. postremo quis nesciat, quicquid legis diebus figuraliter immolabatur in corporibus, quod totum id gratiae tempore manifeste vos offeratis in moribus? atque ideo gratias uberes deo refero, quod secundum vestrae paginae qualitatem facile agnosco antistitem suprafatum de vobis, cum magna dixerit, maiora tacuisse. qua-

[1] simulam *L*: similam.
[2] frixam *FP*.

---

[1] Cf. Leviticus I. 14; V. 11; XII. 6; XII. 8; XIV. 22, 30; XV. 14, 29; Luke II. 24. There is no example in the Vulgate of *binos* or of *paria* (which seems to mean *par*).

through exhortations, the spirit of any conscience-stricken sinner, painfully recalling his faults, heaves a sigh, who can doubt that you have acceptably offered in mystic sacrifice a pair of turtle-doves or two young pigeons,[1] which betoken by their number and their moaning the double entity [2] of which we are constituted? As often as anyone, on your admonition, seeking to reduce his grossness, grills in the fire of frequent fasting his obese body with its load of fat heaving on his swollen belly, it is clear to all that you will then be in a manner consecrating an offering of fine flour baked in a pan of self-denial.[3] 6. As often as you prevail on someone to discard the figments of a deceitful mind, to repeat sound doctrine,[4] and to believe the true faith, holding to the way and hoping for eternal life, who could doubt that in reforming this convert so that he is now free from heresy, hypocrisy, and schism, you will be dedicating the purest shewbread together with the unleavened bread of innocence and truth? [5] 7. Lastly, who could fail to know that the sacrifice which in the days of the Law was made emblematically by the bodies of victims is now in the reign of Grace, no longer in emblem but in reality, made by your character? And so I offer abundant thanks to God inasmuch as I easily see from the quality of your letter that the aforesaid bishop, while saying great things of you, omitted still greater things; hence no one could

[2] The inner and the outer man, I suppose.—*A*.

[3] Cf. Leviticus VI. 20, 21; II. 5.

[4] I suppose when catechised.—*A*.

[5] Leviticus II. 4; Exod. XL, 21; Reg. I = I Samuel XXI. 6.

propter nemo dubitaverit, qui bonus es, cum indicaris, et melior, cum legeris, esse te optimum, cum videris. 8. Megethius clericus, vestri gerulus eloquii, rebus ex sententia gestis, quia tuorum apicum detulit munera, meorum reportat obsequia; quem saltim iuvimus voto, quia re forsitan non valemus. per quem obsecro impense, ut sitim nostram frequenter litteris litteratis, ambo germani, tu frequentius, inrigetis. sed si difficultas itineris intersiti resultat optatis, vel aliquotiens pro supplicibus supplicate. maius est autem, si nobis tribuere dignemini raris intercessionibus salutem quam si crebris affatibus dignitatem. memor nostri esse dignare, domine papa.

XV

SIDONIVS DOMINO PAPAE PROSPERO SALVTEM

1. Dum laudibus summis sanctum Annianum,[1] maximum consummatissimumque pontificem, Lupo parem Germanoque non imparem, vis celebrari fideliumque desideras pectoribus infigi viri talis ac

[1] Anianum *MTCFP*.

---

[1] Cf. *Ep.* IX. 8. 1. Not the Megethius of *Ep.* VII. 3.

* Bishop of Orléans, mentioned elsewhere by Bede only.

doubt that you, who are good when described and better when read, are best of all when seen face to face. 8. The cleric Megethius,[1] bearer of your epistle, has had his business settled as desired, and since he brought me the boon of a letter from you, now he carries to you my respects in return: I have helped him at least by my good wishes; more substantial help is perhaps beyond my power. Through him I send my earnest prayer that both your brothers and yourself may often (and you yourself particularly often) refresh my thirst with draughts of your lettered letters; but if the difficulty of the route between us frustrates my desires, at least offer occasional supplications for this suppliant. It would be a greater thing if you condescended to confer on me salvation by occasional intercessions than if you chose to do me honour by frequent communications. Deign to hold me in remembrance, my Lord Bishop.

XV

SIDONIUS TO THE LORD BISHOP PROSPERUS,* GREETING

1. You were anxious that the holy Annianus,[2] that great and consummate prelate, the equal of Lupus [3] and no whit inferior to Germanus,[4] should be glorified with the highest praises, and that there should be implanted in the hearts of the faithful for ever the

[2] St. Aignan, Bishop of Orléans at the time of Attila's invasion. Gregory of Tours, *Hist. Franc.* II. 7.
[3] Bishop of Troyes. See *Ep.* VI. 1, first note.
[4] Bishop of Auxerre.

tanti mores merita virtutes, cui etiam illud non absque iustitia gloriae datur, quod te successore decessit, exegeras mihi, ut promitterem tibi Attilae bellum stilo me posteris intimaturum, quo videlicet Aurelianensis urbis obsidio oppugnatio, inruptio nec direptio et illa vulgata exauditi caelitus sacerdotis vaticinatio continebatur. 2. coeperam scribere; sed operis arrepti fasce perspecto taeduit inchoasse; propter hoc nullis auribus credidi quod primum me censore damnaveram. dabitur, ut spero, precatui tuo et meritis antistitis summi, quatenus praeconio suo sub quacumque et quidem celeri occasione famulemur. ceterum tu creditor iustus laudabiliter hoc imprudentiae temerarii debitoris indulseris, ut quod mihi insolubile videtur tibi quoque videatur inreposcibile. memor nostri esse dignare, domine papa.

---

[1] *decessit* has the two meanings—retired, and died.

[2] Attila invaded Gaul in A.D. 450; driven from Orléans by the arrival of Aëtius, he was defeated.

[3] *quo . . . continebatur* looks like an indicative in a clause where the subjunctive is expected; but the indicative here implies a statement of fact by Sidonius.

character, merits, and virtues of that great and good man (a man to whom is most rightly given the crowning glory of having handed on [1] his office to such a successor as you). Accordingly, you have urged me to promise to ply my pen in narrating for posterity the story of the war with Attila,[2] which included,[3] of course, the investment and the attack on Orléans, when the city was invaded but never plundered, and the far-famed prophesy of the priest who won the ear of heaven.[4] 2. I began the story; but when I realised the immensity of the work I had undertaken I regretted having ever started it. Hence I have never submitted to the ears of any critic a work which I had myself already judged and condemned. But I hope to satisfy both your request and the merits of the great bishop by devoting myself to a panegyric on him at the first, and indeed a very early, opportunity. For your part, like a fair-minded creditor, you will win praise if you make allowance for your rash debtor's improvidence by writing off the debt which he knows he cannot pay. Deign to hold me in remembrance, my Lord Bishop.

[4] It was alleged that in A.D. 451, when Orléans was threatened with capture by Attila and his Huns, Annianus promised or prophesied that the general Aëtius would bring help; Aëtius arrived just in time to prevent the capture.

XVI

Anderson was puzzled by certain aspects of this letter. Its import is as follows: Constantius was the earlier inspirer of the publication of Sidonius' letters Books I–VII (Ep. I .1. VII. 18), though Petronius was the instigator of Book VIII just as Firminus was of Book IX (Ep. IX. 1.) Constantius had also recently encouraged Sidonius to publish an addendum (Ep. VIII. 1). Constantius had acted as reviser of Books I–VII before publication. Sidonius now explains to

SIDONIVS CONSTANTIO SVO SALVTEM

1. Spoponderam Petronio, inlustri viro, praesens opusculum paucis me epistulis expediturum; cuius auribus non peperci, dum tuis parco. malui namque, ut illum correctionis labor, te honor editionis aspiceret perveniretque in manus vestras volumen istud alieno periculo, obsequio meo. peracta [1] promissio est; nam peritia tua si coactorum in membranas

[1] infracta *Mommsen*: perfracta *Kraemer*.

---

* See *Ep.* III. 2, first note.

[1] See *Ep.* V. 1, first note.

[2] *cuius auribus*: Notice that the emphasis is on *sound.* We moderns would say "eyes." (In *Ep.* VIII. 15. 2, *auribus* is somewhat similar, though there is a notion of a judged hearing.)—*A*.

[3] Cf. Claud. Mamertus 20. 15 ff., *ego conscriptionis periclitabor, sed tu editionis*: different, but the similarity of language is noteworthy. *Obsequium* also appears in the dedicatory epistle (to Sidonius) of Mamertus' treatise *de Statu Animae.*

[4] *in manus vestras*: Birt would give plural meaning to *vestras* (the hands of you and Petronius). But the plural

XVI

Constantius why he had asked Petronius (the instigator of Book VIII) and not Constantius, to undertake the scrutiny of this Book VIII before publication; and Sidonius wishes Constantius to believe that for him, Constantius, was reserved the honour of dedication by Sidonius all the same; so that Book VIII reaches Constantius on Petronius' responsibility (alieno periculo) and is sent with Sidonius' profound respect (obsequio meo).

SIDONIUS TO HIS FRIEND CONSTANTIUS,* GREETING

1. I had promised the illustrious Petronius [1] that I would quickly finish off the present little work in a few letters. I have not spared his ears; [2] and at the same time I spare yours; for I chose that the work of correction [3] should be his and the honour of the final issue yours, and that the volume should come into your hands [4] on another's responsibility, my own part being to make a respectful dedication. My promise has been more than fulfilled,[5] for if your skilled eye examines the lettering of the headings [6]

adjective is used so frequently in reference to one person in these Letters that he is surely wrong.

[5] *peracta promissio est*: *peracta* seems impossible, unless we assume a pun on the use of *promittere* in the sense of "let (make) grow." Kraemer's *perfracta* and Mommsen's *infracta* do not satisfy. *Proiecta* or *perrupta* would give good sense.—*A*. I think the *per* gives an intensive force in *peracta*: "my promise to Petronius has been kept to the uttermost."—*W.H.S.*

[6] *inspiciat signa titulorum*: *signa* = *litterarum signa*. Claud. Mam. 8.3.4. The idea is apparently of separate *sigillae* with the superscriptions of the respective letters.

inspiciat signa titulorum, iam copiosum te, ni fallor, pulsat exemplar; iam venitur ad margines umbilicorum, iam tempus est, ut satiricus ait, Orestem nostrum vel super terga finiri. 2. non hic ego commenticiam Terpsichoren more studii veteris adscivi nec iuxta scaturriginem fontis Aganippici per roscidas ripas et pumices muscivos [1] stilum traxi. atque utinam hic nil molle, nil fluidum, nil de triviis compitalibus mutuatum reperiretur! siquidem maturo, ut es ipse, lectori non tantum dictio exossis tenera delumbis, quantum vetuscula torosa et quasi mascula placet. sed reserventur ista potioribus; mihi sufficit, si cito ignoscas, quod sumus tardi. 3. praeterea si vir inlustris aliquid insuper ampliuscule scribi depoposcisset, in moras grandes incidissemus. nam per armariola et zothecular nostras non remanserunt digna prolatu. unde cognosce, quod, etsi tacere necdum, coepimus certe taciturire, duplici ex causa: ut si placemus, pauca lecturis incitent voluptatem; si refutamur, non

[1] muscivos *LN*: muscidos.

---

[1] *pulsat exemplar*: the meaning of *pulsat* is obscure. And does the present indicative here equal a future?—*A*.

[2] *umbilicorum*: Sometimes there were two rollers, but perhaps *umbilici* is here used for the finials of one roller.

[3] Juvenal, in Satire I, 5–6. Orestes of Greek mythology was a favourite subject and character of tragedy, for example the extant *Orestes* of Euripides.

[4] Terpischore was the Muse of choral song and dance.

[5] In Greek mythology Aganippe was daughter of the

assembled on the parchment labels, you will be appalled,[1] I doubt not, by the already bulky size of the volume. I am now reaching the edges of the rollers;[2] it is now time, as the Satirist[3] says, for my Orestes to be finished even if I write on the back of the parchment. 2. I have not admitted here a fictitious Muse[4] as in my earlier work, nor have I let my pen move through the region of Aganippe's[5] bubbling spring amid dewy banks and mossy stones. I only wish that nothing relaxing, nothing flaccid were to be found in my work, and nothing borrowed from the street corner;[6] for a reader of your experience does not care for a spineless, soft emasculate style: what attracts him is a diction somewhat old-fashioned, a diction muscular and what one might call virile. But let such qualities be left to better writers than myself; it is enough for me if you are quick to forgive me for being so slow. 3. I may say also that, if our illustrious friend had demanded ever so small an addition to what I have written, I should have encountered formidable set-backs; for there remained in all my cases and closets nothing worthy of publication. Hence you must infer that, although I have not yet begun to be silent,[7] I have at least begun to have silence in view—and for a two-fold reason, first, that if I am well received the smallness of my material may increase the reader's pleasure and, secondly, if I am scorned he may not

river-god Permessus and nymph of a spring, called by her name, on Mount Helicon (in Boeotia), sacred to the Muses.

[6] That is, commonplace. The Latin *triviis compitalibus* means "junctions of three roads which are at roadsmeets."

[7] *I.e.* because I am publishing these letters.—*A*.

excitent multa fastidium, quippe in hoc stilo, cui non urbanus lepos inest, sed pagana simplicitas. 4. unde enim nobis illud loquendi tetricum genus ac perantiquum? unde illa verba saliaria vel Sibyllina vel Sabinis abusque Curibus accita, quae magistris plerumque reticentibus promptius fetialis aliquis aut flamen aut veternosus legalium quaestionum aenigmatista patefecerit? nos opuscula sermone condidimus [1] arido exili, certe maxima ex parte vulgato, cuius hinc honor rarus, quod frequens usus, hinc difficilis gratia, quod facilis inventio est. 5. sane profiteor audenter, sicut istic nil acre, nil eloquens, ita nihil inditum non absolutum,[2] non ab exemplo. sed quid haec pluribus? dictio mea, quod mihi sufficit, placet amicis. in quibus tamen utrumque complector, sive non fallunt examine seu caritate falluntur, deumque, quod restat, in posterum quaeso, ut secuturi aut fallantur similiter aut censeant. vale.

[1] edidimus *MTCFP*.

[2] adsuetum *coni. Luetjohann*: ab solito *Wilamowitz*: obsoletum *Mommsen*.

---

[1] *quippe in hoc stilo*: is *hoc* = *eo*? and does he mean that the letters still in his *scrinia* are without polish? I don't think that the words that follow bear that out.—*A*.

[2] Sidonius here takes as examples of simple early language the chant of the very old Italian and Roman Salii ("dancers"), a guild of priests; the prophecies of the "wise-women" of the ancient Greeks and other races kept in books by the Romans; and the speech of the old Sabine town Cures, in Italy, from which, according to tradition, settlers came to join the earliest people of primitive Rome. *W.H.S.* points to Quintilian I. 6. 39–41 on the use of archaic words.

[3] The *fetiales* were in ancient Rome a college of apparently

have many pages to excite his disgust, especially in a style [1] which shows not polite elegance but rustic bluntness. 4. For where could I ever acquire the severe, archaic mode of expression? Where could I ever acquire those words employed by the Salii and the Sibylline oracles, or those brought all the way from Sabine Cures,[2] words which our school-teachers generally pass over in silence and which some member of the College of Heralds [3] would more readily expound, or some flamen, or some antiquated riddler of legal quiddities? For my part, I have composed my little works in arid bald language,[4] which for the most part is quite ordinary speech such as is rarely esteemed because in common use, and such as wins favour with difficulty because too easily come by. 5. I do indeed make bold to claim that this book, though presenting nothing spirited nor eloquent, has had nothing inserted that is not clear or that departs from precedent. But I need not say more about this: it is enough for me that my diction pleases my friends—though I include in the category of friends both those who refuse to deceive me in their criticisms and those who deceive themselves through their affection for me. It remains for me in the future only to pray God that those who come after may either criticize or be deceived in the same way. Farewell.

twenty priests whose duty as guardians of public good faith was to ask for satisfaction in disputes between Rome and any foreign power, decide in what circumstances war might begin, perform the rites when war was declared, and preside at the ratification of peace. In the times of the Roman Empire they were no longer important.

[4] Cf. Cicero, *de Oratore*, II. 159.

LIBER NONVS

I

SIDONIVS FIRMINO SVO SALVTEM

1. Exigis, domine fili, ut epistularum priorum limite irrupto stilus noster in ulteriora procurrat, numeri supradicti privilegio non contentus includi. addis et causas, quibus hic liber nonus octo superiorum voluminibus accrescat: eo quod Gaius Secundus, cuius nos orbitas sequi hoc opere pronuntias, paribus titulis opus epistulare determinet. 2. quae iubes non sunt improbabilia; quamquam et hoc ipsum, quod pie iniungis, arduum existat ac laudi quantulaecumque iam semel partae non opportunum, primum, quod opusculo prius edito praesentis augmenti sera coniunctio est; deinde, quod arbitros ante quoscumque, nisi fallimur, indecentissimum est materiae unius simplex principium, triplices epilogos inveniri. 3. pariter et nescio, qualiter fieri veniabile queat, quod coerceri nostra garrulitas nec post denuntiatum terminum sustinet: nisi quia forsitan qui modus potest[1] paginis, non potest poni ipse amicitiis. quapropter esse

[1] *om.* potest *CFM*[1]: *om. hanc epist. LNT.*

* Cf. *Ep.* IX. 16. A learned man of Arles who urged Sidonius to add this book of letters to his published series.

[1] Nine. Pliny the younger's tenth book of letters concerns the Emperor Trajan, and is excluded by Sidonius from the total of Pliny's books.

[2] *ipse* here is equivalent to *idem.* He had set a limit for his

BOOK IX

I

SIDONIUS TO HIS FRIEND FIRMINUS,* GREETING

1. My noble Son, you demand that my pen should break through the bounds set by my former letters and should advance into further regions, not content to be confined within the generous concession of the aforesaid total. You add some reasons why this ninth book should be annexed to the eight earlier ones, pointing out that Gaius Secundus, whose tracks you declare me to be following in this work, completes his collection of letters in the same [1] number of parts. 2. Your demand is laudable enough; and yet the task which your affection lays upon me is in itself a difficult one and unlikely to enhance such meagre commendation as I have already gained: first, because the present is a rather late addition to the trifling work previously published, and secondly, because, if I mistake not, any judge must regard it as highly improper that the same body of material should have one single beginning and three epilogues. 3. Moreover, I do not know how it can be found excusable that my loquacity cannot restrain itself even after its declared limit—unless perhaps it is excusable on the ground that the limit for one's pages cannot be made the limit for one's friendships.[2]

pages; but the number of his friends claiming mention could not be so limited.—*A*.

te in quadam tuendae opinionis meae quasi specula decet curiosisque facti huiusce rationem manifestare quidque [1] ad hoc sentiant optimi quique, rescripto quam frequentissimo mihi pandere. 4. porro autem si me garrire compulso ipse reticere perseveraveris, te quoque silentii nostri talione ad vicem plecti non periniurium est. itaque tu primus, tu maxime ignosce negotio quod imponis ac ministerio. nos vero, si quod exemplar manibus occurrerit, libri marginibus octavi celeriter addemus. 5. etsi Apollinaris tuus cui studium [2] in ceteris rebus est in hac certe neglegentissimus, quippe qui perexiguum lectione teneatur vel coactus vel voluntarius, quan-

[1] quidque *Luetjohann*: quidve.

[2] cū in ceteris rebus tū *PM*[2] (*in ras.*): cui anim' cū in ceteris rebus *C*: cui studi //// in cetis rebu /// *in marg. M*[1]: cui studium in ceteris rebus *F*: *om. hanc epist. LNT. pro* cui studium *coni.* frugi *Wilamowitz*: totius studii *Mohr, qui et* totus tui (*i.e.* totus tuus) *coni.*: cui nimium studii *Semple*: cui sat (*aut* satis) studii *coni. Anderson*: tuus, cum in ceteris rebus, tum est *Savaron*: tuus, cuius animus iacet et in ceteris rebus, est *Gustafsson*: plus quam animosus in ceteris rebus *Mildmay*.

---

[1] Anderson's full translation in MS runs: "Hence it behoves you, as it were, to man a watch-tower from which to observe the opinion held of me." I have altered this version somewhat in order to bring out more clearly, and express more tersely, the metaphorical turn of speech.—*W.H.S.*

[2] Son of Sidonius. With regard to the doubtful reading of the text here, Anderson, on p. 52 of his copy of Semple's *Quaest. Exeg.*, wrote, against the word *studium* there: "perhaps *sat studii* or even *satis studii*." See Additional Notes, p. 616.

[3] *quantum tamen mihi videtur etc.*: "at least so it seems to me, who am quite willing to be ranked among those fathers whose fond affection and wishes and fears are such that, when there is some merit in their sons, even if they have difficulty in

Hence it behoves you, like a sentinel, to keep a kind of watch-tower guard over my reputation,[1] explaining to the curious the reason for my action and communicating to me in letters as frequent as possible the opinion of all the best people in respect of it. 4. If, however, after compelling me to chatter on, you yourself persist in silence, it is surely not very unfair to pay you back by retaliatory silence. So you, before all others and above all others, must be indulgent to a task and service undertaken at your behest. For my part, I will promptly append to the margins of the eighth book any fresh copy that comes to hand. 5. It is true that your friend Apollinaris,[2] who shows plenty of interest in other fields, is utterly listless in this one, being very little attracted by reading, either compulsory or voluntary: at least [3]

eliciting it, they find it more difficult to be satisfied with it." Probably this is some approach to the meaning, but the passage is hard, even apart from the uncertain text at the beginning of the paragraph. I take the last bit to mean, "even when it is only with difficulty that fathers induce their sons to shew some praiseworthy trait, it is with much more difficulty that they satisfy themselves with the degree of merit attained." Am I right about *quantum tamen mihi videtur*? I think the sense of the corrupt part is moderately clear, but the exact text seems beyond reach. As Mohr says in his *praefatio*, the word *tuus* is rather surprising: *meus* might have been expected; but I suppose *tuus* is possible.—*A*. The *crux* in the rendering of this last sentence seems to me to lie in the passive *persuadeatur*. In a rough pencilled marginal note (evidently an afterthought), Anderson has reached what I believe to be the true sense—"are slow to convince themselves that such merit exists at all." The subject of *persuadeatur* is *laudabile aliquid*, and *studio, voto* and *timori* are datives dependent on *persuadeatur*—thus, "these devoted, ambitious and nervous fathers are only with difficulty convinced of any praiseworthy

tum tamen mihi videtur, qui patribus his iungi non recusaverim, quorum studio voto timori laudabile aliquid in filiis, licet difficile persuadeatur, difficilius sufficit. vale.

II

SIDONIVS DOMINO PAPAE EVPHRONIO SALVTEM

1. Albiso antistes Proculusque levites, ideo nobis morum magistri pronuntiandi, quia vestri merentur esse discipuli, litteras detulerunt, quarum me sacrosancto donastis affatu;[1] quae tamen litterae plurimum nobis honoris, plus oneris inponunt. unde et ipsarum sic benedictione laetor, quod iniunctione confundor, quippe qui ex asse turbatus vel ex parte non pareo. iubetis enim tam diversa quam nimia[2] explicarique decernitis opus, quod ab extremitate mea tam difficile conpletur quam inprudenter incipitur. 2. sed si amplitudinem in vobis pietatis expertae bene metior, plus laborastis, ut affectus vestri cordis quam nostri operis effectus publicaretur. neque[3] enim, cum Hieronymus interpres, dialecticus Augustinus, allegoricus Origenes gravidas tibi spiri-

[1] affatu *CM*[1]*T*[2]: affectu. [2] nimia *L*: minima. [3] haec *Mommsen*.

---

trait in their sons, and only with greater difficulty made to express themselves as satisfied."—*W.H.S.* It is possible that, in the corrupt part of the text, Savaron's reading is nearest the truth, and that *studium* was added only after *cum* had been wrongly altered to *cui*. See Additional Notes, p. 616.

* Cf. *Ep.* VII. 8, first note; IV. 25. 3.

that is how it appears to me, who am quite willing to be ranked with those fathers who, however eager, ambitious, and apprehensive in their sons' behalf, are slow to be convinced of any merit in their sons, and even slower to be satisfied with it. Farewell.

II

TO THE LORD BISHOP EUPHRONIUS,* GREETING

1. The priest Albiso and the deacon Proculus,[1] whom I must rank as masters of good conduct, since they are held worthy to be your disciples, have brought me a letter in which you have favoured me with your hallowed greeting. But that same letter, though it confers a great honour, imposes a still greater onus upon me; hence while rejoicing in the benediction it brings, I am dismayed by its injunction. I am so completely nonplussed that I cannot comply even partially. You demand efforts as various as they are formidable, when you order me to execute a work which, for a person of my contemptible abilities, would be as hard to complete as it would be rash to begin. 2. But if I truly gauge the full measure of the well-tried love within you, your purpose was rather to declare the affection of your heart than that such a completed work of mine should be published. When an expositor [2] like Jerome, a dialectitian like Augustine,[3] and a master of allegory like Origen [4] pro-

[1] Not he of *Ep.* IV. 23.

[2] "expositor," "exegete"; but in the present passage it may mean "translator."—*A.*

[3] Cf. *Ep.* IV. 3. 7.

[4] A.D. 185 or 186–*c.* 254.

talium sensuum spicas doctrinae salubris messe parturiant nunc[1] scilicet tibi a partibus meis arida ieiunantis linguae stipula[2] crepitabit.[3] hoc more tu et olorinis cantibus anseres ravos et modificatis lusciniarum querelis inproborum passerum fringultientes susurros iure sociaveris. 3. quid quod sic[4] quoque arroganter fieret indecenterque, si negotii praecepti pondus aggrederer, novus clericus peccator antiquus, scientia levi gravi conscientia, videlicet ut, si scriptum quocumque misissem, persona mea nec tunc abesset risui iudicantum, cum defuisset obtutui? ne, quaeso, domine papa, nimis exigas verecundiam meam qualitercumque latitantem coepti operis huiusce temeritate devenustari, quia tantus est livor derogatorum, ut materia, quam mittis, velocius sortiatur inchoata probrum quam terminata suffragium. memor nostri esse dignare, domine papa.

[1] nunc *L*: non *MTP*: num *CF*.
[2] aridae . . . stipulae *coni. Luetjohann.*

duce for you, in a harvest of health-giving doctrine, ears of grain full of spiritual meanings, it is not to be expected that from my quarter the dry stubble of a parched tongue should be allowed to crackle in your hearing. You might just as reasonably join the honking of geese with the song of swans and the soft chirping of cheeky sparrows with the melodious plaints of the nightingale. 3. Besides this, it would be a presumptuous and unseemly thing if the burden of the task you prescribe were shouldered by me, a new cleric and an old sinner, with slight knowledge and a heavy conscience; assuredly with the inevitable result that, if I sent my writing anywhere in the world, my person would not escape the ridicule of the critics, even when out of their immediate view. No, my Lord Bishop, do not, I pray, insist too strongly that my modesty, which seeks concealment as best it can, should be spoilt by the foolhardiness of beginning this work, for such is the spite of the detractors that a mere beginning on the subject you suggest would more readily bring their reproach than completion would bring their approval. Deign to hold me in remembrance, my Lord Bishop.

---

[3] crepitabunt *LN*.

[4] sic *Elmenhorst*: si *L*: *om. rell.*

III

SIDONIVS DOMINO PAPAE FAVSTO SALVTEM

1. Servat consuetudinem suam tam facundia vestra quam pietas, atque ob hoc granditer, quod diserte scribitis,[1] eloquium suspicimus,[2] quod libenter, affectum. ceterum ad praesens petita venia prius impetrataque cautissimum reor ac saluberrimum per has maxume civitates, quae multum situ segreges agunt, dum sunt gentium motibus itinera suspecta, stilo frequentiori renuntiare dilataque tantisper mutui sedulitate sermonis curam potius assumere conticescendi. quod inter obstrictas affectu mediante personas asperrimum quamquam atque acerbissimum est, non tamen causis efficitur qualibuscumque, sed plurimis certis et necessariis quaeque diversis proficiscuntur ex originibus. 2. quarum ista calculo primore numerabitur, quod custodias aggerum publicorum nequaquam tabellarius transit inrequisitus, qui etsi periculi nihil, utpote crimine vacans, plurimum sane perpeti solet difficultatis, dum secretum omne gerulorum pervigil

[1] diserte scribitis *Wouweren*: diserte (disserte *C*) scriptis *LTC*: sic diserte (disserte *F*) in scriptis.
[2] suspicimus *Wouweren*: suscipimus.

---

* Cf. *Ep.* IX. 9 especially § 6. Born perhaps in Britain, he became Abbot of the monastery at Lérins (for which see below, § 4) in A.D. 433 and Bishop of Riez (Reii) *c.* 460; and was one of the four bishops who negotiated with the Visigoth Euric in 475; he was exiled by Euric in 476 or 477 because he opposed the Arian creed, freed in 484, and lived till about 490. Duch-

III

SIDONIUS TO THE LORD BISHOP FAUSTUS,* GREETING

1. Both your eloquence and your love are still the same as ever, and so the eloquence of your letters wins my high esteem for their style, and the spontaneous pleasure with which you write wins my highest esteem for your affection. But for the present, if I may beg and obtain your leave to say so, I think it is the wisest and safest course, especially between our two cities far separated as they are, and with the roads rendered insecure by the commotions of peoples, to renounce our rather too busy pens, putting off for a little our diligent exchange of letters, and concerning ourselves rather with silence. Between persons so closely joined in mutual affection, this is a very harsh and bitter course to take, but it is necessitated not by vague circumstances but by causes [1]—many, certain, inevitable—springing from various origins. 2. The first item to be included in this reckoning is that a courier can by no means pass the guards of the public highroads without a strict scrutiny; he may indeed incur no danger, being free from guilt, but he usually experiences a great deal of difficulty, as the watchful searcher pries into every

esne, I. 284; Chaix, I. 248–249; II. 294; anon., *Hist. Litt. de la France* II. 587; Stevens, *Sid. Apoll.*, 77; Sidonius, *Carm.* XVI. The present letter may well have been written when Sidonius was in exile at Bordeaux after confinement in the fort Livia. See pp. 406, 442–443.

[1] "a nondescript medley of reasons"; or "casual reasons."—*A.*

explorator indagat. quorum si forte responsio quantulumcumque ad interrogata trepidaverit, quae non inveniuntur scripta mandata [1] creduntur; ac per hoc sustinet iniuriam plerumque qui mittitur, qui mittit invidiam, plusque in hoc tempore, quo aemulantum invicem sese pridem foedera statuta regnorum denuo per condiciones discordiosas ancipitia redduntur. 3. praeter hoc ipsa mens nostra domesticis hinc inde dispendiis saucia iacet; nam per officii imaginem vel, quod est verius, necessitatem solo patrio exactus, hoc relegatus [2] variis quaquaversum frangor angoribus quia [3] patior hic incommoda peregrini, illic damna proscripti. quocirca solvere modo litteras paulo politiores aut intempestive petor aut inpudenter aggredior, quas vel ioco lepidas vel stilo cultas alternare felicium est. porro autem quidam barbarismus est morum sermo iucundus et animus afflictus. 4. quin potius animam male sibi consciam et per horas ad recordata poenalis vitae debita contremiscentem frequentissimis tuis

[1] mendacia *coni. Warmington*: "all that is not found written in a letter is believed to be lies."

[2] relegaẗ *MTP*: relegatur *C*: relegor *FM*[1]*P*[1]:

[3] frangor angoribus quia *Wouweren*: feror angoribus quia *coni. Mohr*: fragoribus quia *codd.*: *del.* quia *Mommsen*.

---

[1] *aemulantum invicem sese . . . regnorum*: this clause is not very clear. And what is the reference—Goths and Romans? Burgundians?—*A*. Manuscripts *T* and *P* insert a note saying that Roman and Gothic Kingdoms are meant here. See also pp. 323, 360, 519 where a similar doubt arises about *regnum*.

secret of the letter-carriers, and if their answers to his questions should happen to show the least nervousness, they are believed to carry verbally in their heads the messages not committed to writing; thus the man sent often suffers ill-treatment and the sender acquires an ill name, more particularly in these days when the established treaties of kingdoms long jealous of one another[1] are made unstable by fresh conditions tending to produce discord. 3. Besides this, my mind itself is wounded and prostrated by personal troubles on every side; for I have been driven from my own soil on the pretext of some duty,[2] but more truly by compulsion, and in my banishment from it[3] I am broken[4] by diverse tortures at every turn, since I suffer here the distresses of an alien, and in my own town the losses of an outlaw. This being so, a request for a more or less elegant reply must at this time be unseasonable, while on my part it would be shameless to attempt it: the exchanging of letters graced with jests and polished in style belongs to the fortunate; indeed, to combine pleasant discourse and a mind distressed is a sort of moral barbarism. 4. Nay rather, my sin-laden soul, trembling as hour after hour it recalls the trangressions of a guilty life, craves the gracious help of those unceasing and

[2] It is quite unknown what this was.

[3] *solo patrio exactus, hoc relegatus*: what is *hoc* (if the reading is correct)? Does it go with the following *quia*, etc.? Or should we read *hic* or *huc*?—*A*. I take it to be *hoc solo relegatus*.—*W.H.S.* It could mean simply "hither."

[4] *frangor angoribus*: the text translated is Wouweren's correction, which seems a reasonable one.—*A*. It would make good sense also if we kept *fragoribus* of MSS and deleted *quia*; or read *quae* or *qualia*—"what distresses I suffer!"

illis et valentissimis orationum munerare suffragiis, precum peritus insulanarum, quas de palaestra congregationis heremitidis et de senatu Lirinensium cellulanorum in urbem quoque, cuius ecclesiae sacra superinspicis, transtulisti, nil ab abbate mutatus per sacerdotem, quippe cum novae dignitatis obtentu rigorem veteris disciplinae non relaxaveris. his igitur, ut supra dixi, precatibus efficacissimis obtine, ut portio nostra sit dominus atque ut ascripti turmis contribulium levitarum non remaneamus terreni, quibus terra non remanet inchoemusque ut a saeculi lucris, sic quoque a culpis peregrinari. 5. tertia est causa vel maxuma, exinde scribere tibi cur supersederim, quod immane suspicio dictandi istud in vobis tropologicum genus ac figuratum limatisque plurifariam verbis eminentissimum, quod vestra quam sumpsimus epistula ostendit: licet olim [1] praedicationes tuas, nunc repentinas, nunc, ratio cum poposcisset, elucubratas, raucus plosor audierim,

[1] licet olim *Luetjohann*: licet etiam *Mohr*: licet enim *MTCFP*: leceto in *L*. Cf. Additional Notes, p. 616.

---

[1] Of the islands of Lérins.

[2] See *Ep*. VI. 1. 3; VII. 17. 3; VIII. 14. 2.

[3] *portio nostra Dominus*: see Ps. cxix (cxviii Vulgate) v. 57, *portio mea Domine*. Cf. Augustine's disquisition on this (VI. p. 679 A–B). He gives *pars mea Dominus* and mentions the Vulgate reading as a *var. lect.* Does anyone read *portio mea Dominus* here or in Lament. 3. 24, where the Vulgate has *pars mea Dominus*?—*A*. Cf. Ps. xv. 5, *Dominus pars haereditatis meae*; lxxii. 26, *pars mea Dominus in aeternum*.

potent prayers of yours; for you are versed in the orisons of the island brethren,[1] and you have brought them from the training-ground of the hermit congregation and from the conclave of the monks of Lérins [2] right to the city in which you control the religious life of the church; in your episcopal office you remain an abbot still, for you have not made your new dignity a pretext for relaxing the rigour of the old discipline. By these prayers, these most effective prayers, as I have already called them, I beg you to ensure that the Lord may be my portion,[3] and that I, who have been enrolled in the company of Levites, now fellow-tribesmen,[4] may not remain earthly when not an inch of earth remains mine,[5] but that I may begin to live a foreigner from sin as I am from worldly riches. 5. The third reason, why I have forborne to write to you immediately, is one of the highest importance: I have a boundless admiration for that style of yours rich in tropes and figures and distinguished by the varied elegance of its vocabulary, as shown in the letter of yours which I have taken as an example—although long ago I applauded until I was hoarse, when I listened to your preaching sometimes extempore, sometimes, when occasion required, carefully prepared, especially at the week's festival at

portio seems to be rarely used in this sense, compared with *pars.*—*W.H.S.*

[4] *ascripti turmis contribulium levitarum*: "enrolled among the Levites (deacons)," *i.e.* ordained to the Christian ministry, I suppose. *contribulis*, used again in *Ep.* VIII. 13. 3, means "co-religionist."—*A.* Cf. Deuteronomy XVIII. 1 ff.; Numbers XVIII. 20.

[5] Sidonius had lost his property, it seems; at least he was an exile.

tunc praecipue, cum in Lugdunensis ecclesiae dedicatae festis hebdomadalibus collegarum sacrosanctorum rogatu exorareris, ut perorares. ubi te inter spiritales regulas vel forenses medioximum quiddam contionantem, quippe utrarumque doctissimum disciplinarum, pariter erectis sensibus auribusque curvatis ambiebamus, hinc parum factitantem desiderio nostro, quia iudicio satisfeceras. 6. hisce de causis temperavi stilo temperaboque, breviter locutus, ut paream, longum taciturus, ut discam. sunt de cetero tuae partes, domine papa, doctrinae salutaris singularisque [1] victuris operibus incumbere [incumbere] [2] satis. neque enim, quisquis auscultat docentem te disputantemque, plus loqui discit quam facere laudanda. nunc vero, quod restat, donate venia paginam rusticantem [3] vobis obsecundantem, cui me quoque auctore, si vestris litteris comparetur, stilus infantissimus inest. 7. sed ista quorsum stolidus allego? nam nimis deprecari ineptias ipsas [4] est ineptissimum, in quibus tu

[1] singularisque ⟨virtutis⟩ *Wilamowitz*.
[2] incumbere incumbere *L*: incumbere.
[3] rusticantem *MTCFP*: rusticanter *L*.
[4] istas ipsum *coni. Anderson*.

---

[1] *exorare* may be a strong *orare* or a strong *impetrare*.—*A*.

[2] *erectis sensibus auribusque curvatis*: notice Sidonius' itch for antithesis. What does *curvatis* mean? I have not found any parallel.—*A*. Probably bent forward, perhaps by hand, in eagerness.

[3] See *Quaest. Exeg. Sidon.* pp. 54–56.—*W.H.S.*

[4] I am sure the point of *me quoque auctore* is to stress Sidonius' parade of his humility about his style (which, in fact, he is really very proud of). So he says, " Please forgive my letter,

the dedication of the church at Lyon, when, asked by reverend colleagues, you were entreated[1] to make an address. There you delivered an oration, steering as it were, a middle course between the rules of religious and forensic usage, being yourself a master of both lores; and as we flocked around with minds uplifted and ears attentive,[2] you never did enough to gratify our wish—and why? just because you had so completely satisfied our judgment. 6. For these reasons I have restrained my pen, and I shall do so in future: I have now uttered a few words in order to obey you, but I shall be silent for a long time in order to learn. For[3] the future it is your part, my Lord Bishop, to apply yourself busily to writings destined to live, fraught with your health-giving and unrivalled instruction; for whoever hears you teaching and arguing learns to do noble deeds no less than to speak noble words. But for the present I have only this to say: grant your indulgence to my uncouth screed written at your behest, for even by my own judgment[4] its style, compared with that of your letters, is inarticulate as a babe's. 7. But what is the good of such stupid pleading? To apologise excessively for these absurdities[5] is the height of

this uncultured production, which I have sent only in deference to your command. Compared with your style of writing, it is as immature as a child's first essay at talking—and you may judge how poor my style must be, when I the author of it (who might be expected to admire and defend it) actually condemn it."—*W.H.S.*

[5] There is something to be said for Luetjohann's suggestion of *ipsum* for *ipsas*. The only objection is that the following *in quibus* seems to pre-suppose a definite reference in the antecedent. Perhaps Sidonius wrote *istas ipsum*.—*A.*

merus arbiter, si rem ex asse discingas, ridebis plurima, plura culpabis. sed et illud amplector, si pro caritate qua polles non fueris usquequaque censendi continentissimus, id est, si sententia tua quippiam super his apicibus antiquet. tunc enim certius te probasse reliqua gaudebo, si liturasse aliqua cognovero. memor nostri esse dignare, domine papa.

IV

SIDONIVS DOMINO PAPAE GRAECO SALVTEM

1. Viator noster ac tabellarius terit orbitas itineris assueti spatium viae regionumque, quod oppida nostra discriminat, saepe relegendo. quocirca nos quoque decet semel propositae sedulitatis officia sectari, quae cum reliquis commeantibus tum praecipue Amantio intercurrente geminare cum quadam mentis intentione debemus, ne forte videatur ipse plus litteras ex more deposcere quam nos ex amore dictare, domine papa; ideoque vestrorum plus mementote, quos inter praesumimus computari, quique, sicut vestris erigimur secundis, ita deprimimur adversis. 2. nam quod nuper quorumpiam

---

* See *Ep.* VI. 8, first note.

[1] See *Ep.* VII. 2. 1; 7. 1; 10(11). 1; cf. VI. 8.

absurdity. In them a consummate judge like you, if you test the case thoroughly, will find much to laugh at and much to blame. But I shall actually welcome it if, in view of that kindness which is so strong in you, you do not everywhere entirely refrain from censure—in other words, if your vote rejects some part of this letter; for if I find that you have struck out some bits I shall then feel more happily confident that you have approved the rest. Deign to hold me in remembrance, my Lord Bishop.

IV

SIDONIUS TO THE LORD BISHOP GRAECUS,* GREETING

1. Our traveller and courier wears down the track of his customary journey in his frequent comings and goings along the stretch of road and through the extensive regions that divide our respective towns; therefore it becomes us also, having planned a diligent correspondence, to maintain these mutual attentions; indeed, we ought with a fixed purpose of mind to redouble them, using both other travellers who pass to and fro, and especially our messenger Amantius,[1] lest perhaps he should think that he calls for our letters as a matter of habit rather than that we compose them as a labour of love, my Lord Bishop; and therefore I would have you more often remember us, your friends, among whom I presume to count myself, your friends who are uplifted by your good news and cast down by your bad. 2. As a matter of fact, we have been saddened by the sad

fratrum necessitate multos pertuleritis angores, flebili ad flentes relatione pervenit: sed tu, flos sacerdotum gemma pontificum, scientia fortis fortior conscientia, minas undasque mundialium sperne nimborum, quia frequenter ipse docuisti, quod ad promissa convivia patriarcharum vel ad nectar caelestium poculorum per amaritudinum terrenarum calices perveniretur. 3. velis nolis, quisque contempti mediatoris consequitur regnum, sequitur exemplum. quantumlibet nobis anxietatum pateras vitae praesentis propinet afflictio, parva toleramus, si recordamur, quid biberit ad patibulum qui invitat ad caelum. memor nostri esse dignare, domine papa.

V

SIDONIVS DOMINO PAPAE IVLIANO SALVTEM

1. Etsi plusculum forte discreta, quam communis animus optabat, sede consistimus, non tamen medii itineris obiectu quantum ad solvendum spectat officium nostra sedulitas impediretur, nisi quod per regna divisi a commercio frequentiore sermonis diversarum sortium iure revocamur; quae nunc saltim post pacis initam pactionem quia fidelibus

---

[1] Note *propino* with the accusative in the sense of "ply with," "tender to," "hold to lips of."—*A.*

* Not otherwise known.

[2] The treaty of peace between the Emperor Iulius Nepos and King Euric in A.D. 475. See Vol. I of Sidonius, Loeb, pp. xlvii–xlviii, and above pp. 322–323. In this letter the

news that reached us that you have lately suffered much anguish through the straits of some brothers. But, flower of the priesthood, jewel among pontiffs, strong in knowledge and stronger still in the purity of true conscience, I urge you to despise the threatening floods from earthly storm-clouds, since you yourself have often taught that we meet bitter cups of earthly troubles on our way to the promised banquets of the patriarchs and the draughts of heavenly nectar. 3. Whether he likes it or not, whoever gains the kingdom of our despised Mediator, follows his example. However much the affliction of this present life tenders to our lips [1] cups of anxiety, we endure but little, if we recall what was drunk on the cross by Him who invites us to Heaven. Deign to hold me in remembrance, my Lord Bishop.

V

SIDONIUS TO THE LORD BISHOP JULIANUS,* GREETING

1. Although we happen to dwell in places a little farther apart than our common friendship led us to hope for, yet, as far as concerns due maintenance of correspondence, our regularity would not have been hindered by the intervening distance, but for one thing—we live in different realms and are thus prevented from more frequent contact by the rights of conflicting governments. But now at least, on the conclusion of the peace-treaty,[2] they will be

" realms " are apparently the Visigothic Kingdom and the Roman Empire. See pp. 323, 360, 510.

animis foederabuntur, apices nostri incipient commeare crebri, quoniam cessant esse suspecti. proinde, domine papa, cum sacrosanctis fratribus vestris pariter Christo supplicaturas iungite preces, ut dignatus prosperare quae gerimus nostrique dominii[1] temperans lites arma compescens illos muneretur innocentia, nos quiete, totos securitate. memor nostri esse dignare, domine papa.

VI

SIDONIVS DOMINO PAPAE AMBROSIO SALVTEM

1. Viguit pro dilectissimo nostro (quid loquar nomen personam? tu recognosces cuncta) apud Christum tua sanctitas intercessionis effectu; de cuius facilitate iuvenali saepe nunc arbitris palam adscitis conquerebare, nunc tacitus ingemiscebas. igitur his proxime abrupto contubernio ancillae propudiosissimae, cui se totum consuetudine obscena vinctus[2] addixerat, patrimonio posteris famae subita sui correctione consuluit. 2. namque per rei familiaris damna vacuatus ut primum intellegere coepit et retractare, quantum de bonusculis avitis pater-

[1] dominii *CFPM*[1]: domini *MT*: domi xxxxxxx *L*: nostrorumque dominorum *Leo*. [2] iunctus *MTCFP*.

---

[1] Does *cessant* imply "for the time being"? The conclusion of the letter rather favours this.—*A.*

[2] "reward them (? the Goths) with harmlessness."—*A.* *dominii* is not certain; perhaps *domini* "quarrels of our lord and master" (Euric).

* This Ambrosius is not otherwise known for certain.

leagued together in loyal harmony, and our letters will begin to pass in quick succession, seeing that they cease to be under suspicion.[1] 2. Therefore, my Lord Bishop, join your prayers with those of your holy brethren in beseeching Christ that he may be pleased to prosper what we do, and that, allaying the quarrels and restraining the hostilities of our dominion, he may bless those people with guiltlessness,[2] ourselves with peace, and all with freedom from fear. Deign to hold me in remembrance, my Lord Bishop.

VI

SIDONIUS TO THE LORD BISHOP AMBROSIUS,* GREETING

1. Your Holiness, by the efficacy of your intercession, has prevailed with Christ on behalf of our dearly beloved brother (why should I mention the name or specify the person? You will recognise all the details of the case), about whose youthful pliability you used often to complain, sometimes openly before witnesses summoned, at other times sorrowing in silence. Well, he has recently broken off his association with the shameless slave-girl to whom he had surrendered himself, body and soul, in the bonds of an obscene intimacy; and suddenly reforming himself, he has taken thought for his patrimony, his descendants, and his reputation. 2. As soon as he found himself reduced to indigence by the inroads on his purse and began to understand and consider how much of the modest fortune from

nisque sumptuositas domesticae Charybdis abligurrisset, quamquam sero resipiscens, attamen tandem veluti frenos momordit excussitque cervices atque Ulixeas, ut ferunt, ceras auribus figens fugit adversum vitia surdus meretricii blandimenta naufragii puellamque, prout decuit, intactam vir laudandus in matrimonium adsumpsit, tam moribus natalibusque summatem quam facultatis principalis. 3. haec quidem gloria, si voluptates sic reliquisset, ut nec uxori coniugaretur; sed, etsi forte contingat ad bonos mores ab errore migrare, paucorum est incipere de maxumis, et eos,[1] qui diu totum indulserint sibi, protinus totum et pariter incidere. 4. quocirca vestrum est copulatis obtinere quam primum prece sedula spem liberorum; consequens erit, ut filio uno alterove susceptis (et nimis dixi) abstineat de cetero licitis, qui inlicita praesumpsit. namque et coniuges ipsi, quamquam nupti nuper, his moribus agunt, hac verecundia, vere ut agnoscas, si semel videris, plurimum esse quod differat ille

[1] et ⟨difficillimum⟩ eos *coni. Luetjohann*: ut eorum *coni. Warmington.*

---

[1] Homer, *Odyssey*, XII. 173 ff. Odysseus anointed with wax not his own ears, but those of his companions.

[2] "It is given to only a few to . . ." *paucorum est* governs the infinitive *incipere*. The next part of the sentence, *eos, qui . . . indulserint sibi, . . . incidere*, must depend on the idea of rarity which is implicit in *paucorum est*: otherwise there is an anacoluthon—unless, with Luetjohann, we insert *difficillimum* before *eos*. This is the syntactical explanation

his father and grandfather had been swallowed up by the extravagance of that domestic Charybdis, he came to his senses—a late repentance indeed, but now at long last he took the bit in his teeth, shook his shoulders clear of the yoke, and, like Ulysses in the story,[1] put wax in his ears and so, deaf to evil temptations, he fled the enticements of moral shipwreck with a mistress. Very properly, he has now become a respectable husband by marrying a girl of unblemished reputation, lofty in character and birth, and also possessed of a princely fortune. 3. It would, of course, have been truly splendid if he had renounced his life of pleasure so completely as not even to take a wife; but while one may succeed in altering course from error to virtue, it is given to few [2] to begin at the highest level, and it is rare for those who have long allowed themselves every licence to cut off all indulgence immediately and simultaneously. 4. Therefore it now behoves you by diligent prayer to gain for the wedded pair as soon as possible the prospect of having children, so that after the birth of one or two sons (and I have mentioned the extreme limit) this husband who before marriage had taken his lawless pleasures may for the future refrain from lawful pleasures. For this couple, though newly married, behave with such propriety and modesty that on observing them you can clearly realise what a world of difference there is

of what Anderson has put in his translation.—*W.H.S.* If we read *maxumis, ut eorum* . . . , then we could translate: "it is given to few to begin at the highest level, for example [*or* as in the present instance it is given] to people who have allowed themselves every licence, to cut off all indulgence . . ."

honestissimus uxorius amor figmentis inlecebrisque concubinalibus. memor nostri esse dignare, domine papa.[1]

VII

SIDONIVS DOMINO PAPAE REMIGIO SALVTEM

1. Quidam ab Arvernis Belgicam petens (persona mihi cognita est, causa ignota; nec refert), postquam Remos advenerat, scribam tuum sive bybliopolam pretio fors fuat officione demeritum copiosissimo velis nolis declamationum tuarum schedio emunxit. qui redux nobis atque oppido gloriabundus, quippe perceptis tot voluminibus, quaecumque detulerat,[2] quamquam mercari paratis, quod tamen civis (nec erat iniustum), pro munere ingessit. curae mihi e vestigio fuit hisque qui student, cum merito lecturiremus, plurima tenere, cuncta transcribere. 2. omnium assensu pronuntiatum pauca nunc posse similia dictari. etenim rarus aut nullus est, cui meditaturo par affatim assistat dispositio per causas, positio per litteras, compositio per syllabas,

[1] *Post ep. 6 deficiunt NT.*

[2] quaecumque detolerat *L*: quicquid detulerat *MFP*: quicquid q̄q̄ mercari paratis detulerat *C*.

* Saint Remi (Remy), Bishop of Reims. He was born in or near Laon *c.* A.D. 458, son of Count Emilius. In 496 he

between the honourable love of husband for wife and the illusory attractions of concubinage. Deign to hold me in remembrance, my Lord Bishop.

VII

SIDONIUS TO THE LORD BISHOP REMIGIUS,* GREETING

1. A certain man was on his way from Auvergne to Belgian Gaul (I do know him personally, but not the object of his journey; nor does it matter); after reaching Rheims, he won the favour of your amanuensis or your bookseller possibly by a gift of money or by conferring a service, and so tricked him into giving willy-nilly a very full section of your declamations. He returned here wholly exultant over his rich harvest of volumes; and although I and the town were ready to buy, nevertheless, because he was a citizen, he quite properly presented us with all he had brought as a free gift. I and all others here who have literary tastes were eager to read the books, as we well might be, and we set ourselves without delay to transcribe the whole, besides memorizing a great many passages. 2. The unanimous verdict was that few things like it can be written nowadays; for there are few or none who, when about to compose, have abundantly at command the same power of arranging subjects, the same power of allocating letters and combining syllables,[1] or the same aptness

baptised King Clovis and three thousand other Franks on Christmas Day. Chaix, II. 88.

[1] Cf. Quintilian, IX, 4, especially § 61.

ad hoc opportunitas in exemplis fides in testimoniis, proprietas in epithetis urbanitas in figuris, virtus in argumentis pondus in sensibus, flumen in verbis fulmen in clausulis. 3. structura vero fortis et firma coniunctionumque perfacetarum nexa caesuris insolubilibus sed nec hinc minus lubrica et levis [1] ac modis omnibus erotundata quaeque lectoris linguam inoffensam decenter expediat, ne salebrosas passa iuncturas per cameram palati volutata balbutiat; tota denique liquida prorsus et ductilis, veluti cum crystallinas crustas aut oncyhitinas [2] non impacto digitus ungue perlabitur, quippe si nihil eum rimosis obicibus exceptum tenax fractura remoretur. 4. quid plura? non extat ad praesens vivi hominis oratio, quam peritia tua non sine labore transgredi queat ac supervadere. unde et prope suspicor, domine papa, propter eloquium exundans atque ineffabile (venia sit dicto) te superbire. sed licet bono fulgeas ut conscientiae sic dictionis ordinatissimae,[3] nos tibi tamen minime sumus refugiendi, qui bene scripta laudamus, etsi laudanda non scribimus.

[1] *post* levis *deficit L.*
[2] onychitinas *Luetjohann*: onychintinas *aut* onichintinas.
[3] ornatissimae *coni. Anderson.*

---

[1] *coniunctionumque perfacetarum nexa caesuris insolubilibus*: Anderson's translation in MS is " the structure is strong and firm, with a chain of indivisible phrases which cut up the very neat periods." But I am not satisfied that this gives the true sense, which surely is that the structure of Remigius' composition is strong and compact, "being bound together (*nexa*) by close-fitting (indistinguishable) connections where sentences are joined together by artistically wrought transitions." Yet in spite of this tight close-fitting structure, the effect is smooth and easy —*W.H.S.*

in the instances quoted and reliability in the testimonies; the same propriety in the epithets and urbanity in the figures; the same force in the arguments and weight in the sentiments, the same flow in the words and the same vivid flash in the endings. 3. The structure is strong and compact, bound together by close-fitting connections [1] where sentence is joined to sentence by masterly transitions: nor from this does the composition fail to be easy and smooth and completely rounded, letting the reader's tongue run on gracefully without impediment and not bothered by harsh word-connections which make the voice stutter as it rolls round the arched palate; in short, the whole texture is absolutely fluent and ductile—as smooth as when the finger glides over plaques of crystal or onyx without striking the nail, because there are no gaping cracks or fissures to catch the nail and delay its progress. 4. In a word, there is no oration by any man living today which your skill could not effortlessly surpass and outstrip. For this reason I really almost suspect, my Lord Bishop, that (if you will excuse my saying so) you must feel proudly superior on account of your rich and ineffable eloquence. But although you are conspicuously blest with a good conscience, as well as with a most correct [2] style, you should by no means avoid me,[3] who praise good writings although I do not write anything worth praising. 5. So cease

[2] *dictionis ordinatissimae*: should it not be *ornatissimae*? —*A*.

[3] *nos tibi tamen minime sumus refugiendi*: in view of the earlier reference in § 1 to *mihi hisque qui student*, this present use of the 1st plural is rather ambiguous.—*A*.

5. quocirca desine in posterum nostra declinare iudicia, quae nihil mordax nihil quoque minantur increpatorium. alioquin, si distuleris nostram sterilitatem facundis fecundare colloquiis, aucupabimur nundinas involantum et ultro scrinia tua coniventibus nobis ac subornantibus effractorum manus arguta populabitur inchoabisque tunc frustra moveri spoliatus furto, si nunc rogatus non moveris officio. memor nostri esse dignare, domine papa.

VIII

SIDONIVS DOMINO PAPAE PRINCIPIO SALVTEM

1. Quamquam nobis non opinantibus, desiderantibus tamen litteras tuas reddidit gerulus antiquus, idoneus inventus, cui iure repetita credantur officia, quandoquidem prima sic detulit. igitur affatu secundo vel potius benedictione donatus ipse quoque rependo alterum salve, obsequia combinans numeris aequata, non meritis. 2. et quia, domine papa, modo vivimus ⟨animis⟩[1] iunctis abiunctisque regionibus conspectibusque mutuis frui dissociatae situ habitationis inhibemur, orate, ut optabili religiosoque decessu vitae praesentis angoribus atque onere

[1] animis *add. Luetjohann.*

---

[1] The contrast may be *spoliatus furto rogatus officio* rather than *moveri furto moveris officio*. Note that *officio* may perhaps mean "letter."—*A.*

* Bishop of Soissons. See *Ep.* VIII. 14.

[2] Megethius; cf. *Ep.* VIII. 14. 8.

henceforth to fight shy of my judgments; there is no threat of anything bitter or fault-finding in them. On the other hand, if you are slow to fertilise my barren soil with your eloquent converse I shall await the hiring-day for thieves, and the burglars' cunning hands will actually plunder your book-boxes while I who incited the theft pretend not to see: and then, when burgled, you will begin to be upset, to be helplessly upset, if now, when politely asked, you are not moved by any sense of duty.[1] Deign to hold me in remembrance, my Lord Bishop.

VIII

SIDONIUS TO THE LORD BISHOP PRINCIPIUS,* GREETING

Although I was not expecting it, I was longing for a letter from you at the moment when it was duly delivered by the same bearer [2] as before, who had proved himself worthy to be entrusted with other messages, as he brought the first so efficiently. And so, having been presented with a second communication, or rather benediction, I too in my turn repay you with a second greeting, thus making a pair of homages on each side, equal in number but not in merit. 2. And, my Lord Bishop, because we now live with hearts indeed united but in separate regions, and because we are prevented by the distance of our homes from enjoying the sight of one another, pray that when, by a happy death in the faith, we are released from the anguish and the burden of this present life, and when the holy Day

perfuncti, cum iudicii dies sanctus[1] offulserit cum resurrectione, agminibus vestris famulaturi vel sub Gabaoniticae servitutis occasione iungamur; quia secundum promissa caelestia, quae spoponderunt filios dei[2] de nationibus congregandos, si nos reos venia soletur, dum vos beatos gloria manet, etsi per actionum differentiam, non tamen per locorum distantiam dividemur. memor nostri esse dignare, domine papa.

IX

SIDONIVS DOMINO PAPAE FAVSTO SALVTEM

1. Longum tacere, vir sacratissime, nos in commune dequestus es; cognosco vestrae partis hinc studium, nostrae reatum non recognosco. namque iampridem iussus garrire non silui litteris istas antecurrentibus, quibus tamen[3] recensendis, cum Reios advenerant, qui tunc Aptae[4] fuistis, aptissime defuistis. idque votivum mihi granditer fuit ac peroptatum, ut epistula iniuncta nec negaretur scripta amicitiae nec subderetur lecta censurae. 2. ista

[1] sanctis *Wilamowitz*.
[2] fidei *MCP*.
[3] quibus tamen *Luetjohann*: quibus etiam *MFP*: quibusdam etiam *C*.
[4] Aptae *Sirmond*: apte.

---

[1] Joshua IX. 3 ff., 27.
[2] See *Ep*. IX. 3, the first note.

of Judgment dawns at the resurrection I may be joined to your company to minister to them, even on terms of serfdom like the Gibeonites;[1] for according to the heavenly promises, which have given assurance that the sons of God shall be gathered together from out the nations, if I in my guilt have the comfort of pardon, and you saints have the expectation of glory, then, separated though we shall be by the dissimilarity of our activities, we shall not be separated by a remoteness of locality. Deign to hold me in remembrance, my Lord Bishop.

IX

SIDONIUS TO THE LORD BISHOP FAUSTUS,* GREETING

1. My saintly friend, you have complained that we have long maintained a mutual silence. While I realise the keen interest you feel on your side, on my side I do not recognise any guilt; for having been long pressed to produce some chatter, I was anything but silent in a letter which preceded this one; but when that letter arrived at Riez you were away at Apt, and most aptly failed to examine it.[2] Really I could hope for nothing more agreeable to my wishes than that the letter I was enjoined to write by being written was not refused to friendship, and by failing to be read was not subjected to criticism. 2. But let us say no more about that.

[2] For want of anything better, I adopt Luetjohann's *tamen.* The next sentence seems to show that *recensendis* must have a stronger meaning than merely "read."—*A.*

omittamus. mitti paginam copiosam denuo iubes. parere properanti adsunt vota, causae absunt. nam salutatio, nisi negotium aliquod activa [1] deportet materia,[2] succincta est; quam qui porrigit verbis non necessariis, a regula Sallustiani tramitis detortus exorbitat, qui Catilinam culpat habuisse satis eloquentiae sapientiae parum.[1] unde ave dicto mox vale dicimus. orate pro nobis. 3. sed bene est, bene est, quia chartulam iam iamque [3] complicaturo res forte succurrit,[4] de qua exprobranda si diutius vel laetitia sese mea vel ira cohibuerit, ipse me accepta dignum contumelia iudicabo. venisti, magister, in manus meas (nec exulto tantum, verum insulto), venisti, et quidem talis, qualem abhinc longo iamdiu tempore desideria nostra praestolabantur. dubito sane utrum et invitus, at certe similis invito, quippe quo providente vel, si tamen hoc nimis abnuis, adquiescente sim tuis libris insalutatus hisque, quod multo est iniuriosius, territorium Arvernum cum praeterirent, non solum moenia mea, verum etiam latera radentibus. 4. an verebare, ne tuis dictis invideremus? sed dei indultu vitio nulli minus addicimur; cui si ita ut ceteris a mea parte subiaceretur, sic quoque auferret

[1] activum *coni. Mohr*: activam *coni. Luetjohann.*
[2] materiam *coni. Luetjohann.*
[3] iam iamque *vulgo*: iamque.
[4] forte succurrit *Luetjohann*: fortis accurrit.

---

[1] Sallust, *Catiline*, V. 4.
[2] *A.* accepted Luetjohann's *forte succurrit*, which is retained in our text. But *fortis accurrit* of the MSS makes good sense "a matter of pressing urgency came up" or even "came running up" (instead of the letter-carrier).

Once more you bid me send you a bulky letter. I make haste to obey you, but although the wish is present, the subject-matter is absent. For a message of greeting is necessarily short, unless some stirring material provides a topic to occupy the writer; and anyone who spins it out with unessential words breaks right away from the path prescribed by Sallust, who blames Catiline for having had "plenty of eloquence but too little wisdom."[1] So having expressed my greeting, I thereupon say "Farewell." Pray for me. 3. But I am delighted, yes, delighted that, when I was on the point of folding this sheet, by chance[2] a certain matter occurred to my mind, such a matter that, if either my joy or my anger refrains any longer from taunting you with it I shall consider myself worthy of the insult which I have received. Yes, my master, you have fallen into my hands, and I not only exult but insult you in consequence; you have fallen into my hands, and in the guise which my dearest hopes had long looked forward to. I am not indeed sure whether you were actually unwilling that this should happen, but at least you gave every appearance of unwillingness, for by your instructions or, if you absolutely deny this, at least with your acquiescence, your books left me unvisited: and, what makes it still more outrageous, in passing the territory of Auvergne they were not merely passing my city walls but actually grazing my side. 4. Were you really afraid that I might be jealous of your composition? But, by the mercy of God, there is no fault to which I am less addicted, and if I had been as subject to that fault as to all other faults, any

congrediendi aemulationem desperatio consequendi. an supercilium tamquam difficilis ac rigidi plosoris extimescebas? et quaenam [1] est cuiquam peritiae cervix tanta quive [2] hydrops, ut etiam tepida vestra non ferventissimis laudibus prosequatur? 5. an ideo me fastidiendum neglegendumque curasti, quia contemneres iuniorem? quod parum credo. an quia indoctum? quod magis fero, ita tamen, ut qui dicere ignorem, non et audire; quia et qui circensibus ludis adfuerunt, sententiam de curribus non ferunt. an aliquo casu dissidebamus, ut putaremur his quos edidissetis libellis [3] derogaturi? atqui praesule deo tenues nobis esse amicitias nec inimici fingere queunt. 6. ista quorsum? inquis. ecce iam pando, vel quid indagasse me gaudeam vel quid te celasse succenseam. legi volumina tua, quae Riochatus antistes ac monachus atque istius mundi bis peregrinus Britannis tuis pro te reportat,

[1] et quaenam *codd.*: ecquaenam *Luetjohann.*
[2] ingenive *Leo*: *fortasse* quaeve: *vix* cuive.
[3] edidissetis libellis *Luetjohann*: libellis edidissetis.

---

[1] Is *hydrops* an allusion to Claudianus Mam. *de Statu Animae* 3.7. ? —*A*. A more complete rendering here would be " Where is there such a great or inflated audacity in anyone's expert knowledge . . ."

[2] Sidonius means: ordinary spectators are admitted to watch, not to judge. So with me.

[3] *dissidebamus* . . . *putaremus* . . . *nobis*. Is it " me " or " we "? But the first person plural seems to refer to Sidonius. The ambiguous use in the last part of this paragraph is annoying.—*A*.

idea of jealous competition would have been removed by my despair of success. Or did you fear disdain as if from a churlish inflexible applauder? and what rigidity of expertise, what bloated [1] pride can be so dominant in a person as not to greet even your less ardent utterances with the warmest praises? 5. Or did you studiously treat me with disdain and neglect, because you looked down on me as your junior? I scarcely think that. Or because you thought me unlearned? I can accept that more willingly, though I must add that though I may not be able to speak, I am not also unable to listen. Even people who have attended the Circensian games do not act as judges in the races.[2] Or was I by some chance estranged,[3] so that I seemed likely to disparage the books you had produced? Yet, thanks be to God, not even my enemies can pretend that my friendship is weak. 6. "Why all this?" you ask. Listen; I now reveal what I am so glad to have discovered, or so angry that you concealed from me. I have read those works of yours which Riochatus, the priest [4] and monk, and so twice over a pilgrim and stranger in this world, is duly carrying to your dear Britons [5] on behalf of you, you the man who here and

[4] *antistes*. Cf. *Ep*. VII. 13. 1.

[5] It is possible that the Bretons of France north of the Loire are meant, but there is other evidence that Faustus was a native of Great Britain (see introductory note to *Ep*. IX. 3), and also evidence that Riochatus (who must not be confused with Riothamus, King of the Bretons—*Ep*. III. 9) was St. Riochatus of Wales (Tillemont, *Mém. Ecclés.*, XVI. 421). Cf. Nora Chadwick, *Poetry and Letters in Early Christian Gaul*, 191 ff.; Stevens, *Sid. Apoll.*, 77.

illo iam in praesentiarum fausto potius, qui non senescit quique viventibus non defuturus post sepulturam fiet per ipsa quae scripsit sibi superstes. igitur hic ipse venerabilis apud oppidum nostrum cum moraretur, donec gentium concitatarum procella defremeret, cuius immanis [1] hinc et hinc turbo tunc inhorruerat, sic reliqua dona vestra detexit, ut perurbane quae praestantiora portabat operuerit, spinas meas illustrare dissimulans tuis floribus. 7. sed post duos aut his amplius menses sic quoque a nobis cito profectum cum quipiam prodidissent de viatoribus mysticae gazae clausis involucris clam ferre thesauros, pernicibus equis insecutus abeuntem, qui facile possent itineris pridiani spatia praevertere, osculo in fauces occupati latronis insilui, humano ioco, gestu ferino, veluti si excussura quemcumque catulorum Parthi colla raptoris pede volatili [2] tigris orbata superemicet. 8. quid multa? capti hospitis genua complector iumenta sisto, frena ligo sarcinas solvo, quaesitum volumen invenio produco, lectito excerpo maxima ex magnis capita defrustans. tribuit et quoddam dictare celeranti scribarum sequacitas saltuosa [3] compendium, qui comprehendebant signis quod litteris non tenebant.

[1] immanis *Luetjohann*: imaginis.
[2] volatili *cd. Vat.* 3421: volatici *aut* volatico.
[3] *cp.* saltuatim *Ep.* IV. 3. 9 *et alibi.*

[1] The idea in *potius* must be " now " rather than " only in after ages."—*A*.

now is as fortunate [1] as his name Faustus implies, a man whom age does not touch, who will not desert the living after his burial, but through his writings alone will be immortal.[2] Well, the venerable man I have mentioned stopped in our town, until the storm of angry nations, which had surged up in an awful whirlwind on every side, should expend its fury. During that time he displayed the other gifts you were sending, but always most politely concealed the finest items in his baggage, refraining from brightening my thorns with your flowers. 7. But after two months or more, when he had hurriedly departed from me still without disclosing his secret, some of the travelling-party revealed that he was secretly carrying treasures of mystic riches in closed cases. Thereupon I chased the runaway with swift horses, easily capable of catching up on the one day's start he had had. So I headed off the brigand, threw myself at his throat with a kiss, playing a human prank with the air of a wild beast, just as if a tigress, a tigress robbed of her whelps, were hurling herself with flying feet on the neck of a Parthian to force from him one, no matter which, of the cubs he had stolen. 8. In short, I embraced the knees of my captured guest, stopped the horses, tied up their bridles, undid his baggage, and, finding the book I sought, drew it forth, read and re-read it, and made excerpts, picking out the greatest of those great chapters. I also secured some saving of time by the speed of the scribes in following my rapid dictation and denoting with signs what they did not

[2] Literally "will survive himself." Sidonius makes word-play with *antistes* and *superstes*.

quibus lacrimis sane maduerimus mutuo vicissim fletu rigati, tunc cum ab amplexu saepe repetito separaremur, longum est dixisse nec refert; quod triumphali sufficit gaudio, spoliis onustum caritatis et spiritalis compotem praedae me domum rettuli. 9. quaeris nunc, quid de manubiis meis iudicem; nollem adhuc prodere, quo diuturnius expectatione penderes; plus me enim ulciscerer, si quod sensi tacerem. sed iam nec ipse frustra superbis, utpote intellegens tibi inesse virtutem sic perorandi, ut lectori tuo seu reluctanti seu voluntario vis voluptatis excudat praeconii necessitatem. proinde accipe, quid super scriptis tuis et iniuriam passi censeamus. 10. legimus opus operosissimum multiplex, acre sublime, digestum titulis exemplisque congestum, bipertitum sub dialogi schemate, sub causarum themate quadripertitum. scripseras autem plurima ardenter plura pompose; simpliciter ista nec rustice; argute illa nec callide; gravia mature profunda sollicite, dubia constanter argumentosa disputatorie, quaedam severe quaepiam blande, cuncta moraliter lecte, potenter eloquentissime. 11. itaque per tanta te genera narrandi toto latissimae dictationis campo secutus nil in facundia ceterorum, nil in ingeniis

---

[1] *scribarum sequacitas saltuosa*: "through the talent of the scribes who followed my rapid dictation with leaps and bounds, compressing by symbols what they could not get hold of by letters."

compass by letters.[1] It would be tedious and also unnecessary to tell you of the tears we shed and how we wet each other's cheeks with mutual weeping as with oft-repeated embraces we parted; but what affords ample reason for triumphant joy is this—that I returned home laden with spoils of charity and in possession of spiritual booty. 9. Now you ask what I think of my plunder. I should have liked not to tell you, in order to prolong your suspense; for by keeping silence about the opinion I have formed, I should gain an ample revenge. But already you yourself must be feeling a justifiable pride, knowing that you have in you such pre-eminent power of eloquence that the sheer force of enjoyment wrings from the reader, whether reluctantly or willingly, an overmastering need to praise. So here is what I think of your writings even after the bad treatment I received from you. 10. I read a work laborious and many-sided, vigorous and lofty, well divided by headings, well provided with examples, bipartite in the plan of its dialogue, quadripartite in the presentation of the subject-matter. Much you have written ardently, much more with grandeur; some parts are simple without being uncouth, others are subtle without being crafty; weighty matters are treated maturely, deep things with earnest care, doubtful points resolutely, debatable points controversially; some things are handled sternly, others winningly, all is morally exquisite and powerfully eloquent. 11. Thus having followed you through all these different kinds of discourses ranging over the whole field of composition at its widest, I have been hard put to it to find anything so exquisite in

facile perspexi iuxta politum. quae me vera sentire satis approbas, cum nec offensus aliter iudico. denique absentis oratio, quantum opinamur, plus nequit crescere, nisi forsitan aliquid his addat coram loquentis auctoris vox manus, motus pudor. artifex (12.) igitur [1] his animi litterarumque dotibus praeditus mulierem pulchram sed illam deuternomio astipulante nubentem, domine papa, tibi iugasti; quam tu adhuc iuvenis inter hostiles conspicatus catervas, atque illic in acie contrariae partis adamatam, nil per obstantes repulsus proeliatores, desiderii brachio vincente rapuisti, philosophiam scilicet, quae violenter e numero sacrilegarum artium exempta raso capillo superfluae religionis ac supercilio scientiae saecularis amputatisque pervetustarum vestium rugis, id est tristis dialecticae flexibus falsa morum et illicita velantibus, mystico amplexu iam defaecata tecum membra coniunxit. 13. haec ab annis vestra iamdudum pedisequa primoribus, haec tuo lateri comes in-

[1] motus pudor artifex. igitur *Mohr.*

---

[1] *pudor*: "shy or modest demeanour," cf. IX. 14. 9 and VIII. 6. 6.

[2] Deuteronomy XXI. 11–13.

[3] *raso capillo*, etc. Dalton represents the shaving, etc. as done by Faustus. This is against both the Latin and passage of Deuteronomy.—*A*. Sidonius has something of the contemporary Church's distrust of philosophy, which it regarded as a product of paganism and therefore inimical to the faith. But he regards Faustus as an instance of a Christian scholar who had used philosophy in the service of the Church, and he therefore represents him as a man who, under the provisions of the Mosaic Law as set out in Deuteronomy XXI. 11–13, has taken a fancy to a beautiful captive and wishes to marry

the eloquence or the talents of other writers. That these sentiments of mine are true you can feel quite sure, since even the affront I have suffered does not make me think otherwise. In short, your oratory, read in your absence, could not, in my opinion, be improved upon unless perhaps the author delivered it in one's presence and added something to the effect by his use of voice, gesture, movements, and modest demeanour.[1] 12. An artist then endowed with all these intellectual and literary excellences, you have joined to yourself a beautiful woman, but who married you in the ritual prescribed by Deuteronomy,[2] my Lord Bishop. You had seen her, while still in your youth, among the hordes of the enemy, and there in the midst of the hostile ranks you fell in love with her and, defying the attempts of the opposing warriors to drive you back, you carried her off with the conquering arm of desire. Her name was Philosophy; rescued by force from the crowd of blasphemous sciences, she shaved off the locks [3] that betokened false religion, shaved off the disdainful eyebrows of worldly knowledge, cut away the folds of her old former raiment—and by folds I mean the twists and turns of sinister dialectic screening wrong and unlawful behaviour: and then, when cleansed in every part, she united herself with you in a mystic embrace. 13. She has long been your attendant, even from your early years: she is your

her. The ritual of her preparation for marriage to an Israelite (the shaving of her head, the cutting of her nails, the change of raiment) are adapted (very cumbrously, in my opinion) to the process of making pagan Philosophy suitable to be the spiritual bride of a Christian bishop.—*W.H.S.*

separabilis, sive in palaestris exerceris urbanis sive in abstrusis macerare solitudinibus, haec Athenaei consors, haec monasterii, tecum mundanas abdicat, tecum supernas praedicat disciplinas. huic copulatum te matrimonio qui lacessiverit, sentiet ecclesiae Christi Platonis Academiam militare teque nobilius philosophari; 14. primum ineffabilem dei patris asserere cum sancti spiritus aeternitate sapientiam; tum praeterea non caesariem pascere neque pallio aut clava velut sophisticis insignibus gloriari aut affectare de vestium discretione superbiam, nitore pompam, squalore iactantiam neque te satis hoc aemulari, quod per gymnasia pingantur Areopagitica vel prytanea curva cervice Speusippus [1] Aratus panda, Zenon fronte contracta Epicurus cute distenta, Diogenes barba comante Socrates coma

[1] Speusippus *Savaron*: zeuzippus *aut* zeutip(p)us *codd.*

---

[1] No doubt an educational institution in the likeness of Hadrian's at Rome. Cf. *Ep.* IX. 14. 2.

[2] *sentiet ecclesiae Christi Platonis Academiam militare*: Anderson's translation here runs " he will realize that Plato's Academy wars against the Church of Christ." There can be no doubt that *ecclesiae Christi* is *dativus commodi* and that the whole point of the passage is missed if we do not make it plain that the weapons of the enemy are now, by Faustus' special talent, being used to support the Christian faith. Cf. § 15 *init.—Stoicos, Cynicos, Peripateticos haeresiarchas propriis armis, propriis quoque concuti machinamentis.* In view of this, I have altered the translation.—*W.H.S.*

[3] The hill west of the northern edge of the Acropolis at Athens.

inseparable companion whether you are exercising yourself in the hard school of the city or wearing yourself out in hidden solitudes; she is your partner in the Athenaeum [1] and in the monastery; with you she renounces worldly studies, and with you she proclaims heavenly doctrine. If anyone assails you now that you are wed to this spiritual bride he will learn that Plato's Academy is now enlisted in the cause of Christ's church [2] and that you practise philosophy in a nobler sense. 14. He will learn that in the first place you affirm the inexpressible wisdom of God the Father together with the everlastingness of the Holy Spirit; secondly, he will learn that you do not let your hair grow long nor flaunt a gown or a club as badges of the professional philosopher; nor do you affect a proud superiority by a difference of dress, using splendid apparel for dignity and an unkempt appearance for ostentation. You do not burn with envy at the thought of those paintings all over the gymnasia of the Areopagus [3] and in the prytanea showing Speusippus with his head bowed forward, Aratus with his head bent back, Zenon with knitted brow, Epicurus with unwrinkled skin, Diogenes with long beard,[4] Socrates

[4] Speusippus of Athens, born *c.* 407 B.C., nephew and successor of Plato at the Academy; Aratus of Soli, didactic poet, born *c.* 315 B.C., author of two extant Greek astronomical poems; Zenon of Elea, fifth century B.C., proposer of famous arithmetical paradoxes—or perhaps the later Stoic Zenon of Citium (see note on p. 545—hardly the Stoic Zenon of Tarsus), or the Epicurean Zenon of Sidon, first century B.C.; Epicurus of Samos born 342 or 341 B.C., famous in logic, physics, and ethics; Diogenes of Sinope, born *c.* 412 B.C., ascetic. "Zeuxippus" for Speusippus would name a man otherwise unknown.

cadente,[1] Aristoteles brachio exerto[2] Xenocrates crure collecto, Heraclitus fletu oculis clausis Democritus risu labris apertis, Chrysippus digitis propter numerorum indicia constrictis, Euclides propter mensurarum spatia laxatis, Cleanthes propter utrumque corrosis. 15. quin potius experietur, quisque conflixerit, Stoicos Cynicos Peripateticos haeresiarchas propriis armis, propriis quoque concuti machinamentis. nam sectatores eorum, Christiano dogmati ac sensui si repugnaverint, mox te magistro ligati vernaculis implicaturis in retia sua praecipites implagabuntur, syllogismis tuae propositionis uncatis volubilem tergiversantum linguam inhamantibus, dum spiris categoricis lubricas quaestiones tu potius innodas acrium more medicorum, qui remedium contra venena, cum ratio compellit, et de serpente conficiunt. 16. sed hoc temporibus istis sub tuae tantum vel contemplatione conscientiae vel virtute doctrinae. nam quis aequali vestigia tua gressu sequatur, cui datum est soli loqui melius quam didiceris, vivere melius quam loquaris? quo-

[1] cadente *cod. Laur.* xlv. 26 *et alii*: candente *MCFP*.
[2] extento *C*.

---

[1] Xenocrates of Chalcedon, born in 396 B.C., head of the Academy at Athens 339–314 B.C.; Heraclitus of Ephesus *c.* 540–475 B.C., physical and metaphysical philosopher; Democritus of Abdera, born *c.* 465 B.C., the physical philosopher who developed the atomic theory; Chrysippus of Soli and then Athens *c.* 280–206 B.C., pupil of Cleanthes (see below); Euclid, third century B.C.; Cleanthes of Assos, born *c.* 301

with trailing hair, Aristotle with out-thrust arm; Xenocrates with gathered leg, Heraclitus with eyes closed through weeping, Democritus with lips wide open with laughter, Chrysippus with fingers bent to denote counting, Euclid with fingers extended because of the size of his measurements, Cleanthes[1] with fingers gnawed for both reasons. 15. Far otherwise: whoever disputes with you will find those protagonists of heresy, the Stoics, Cynics, and Peripatetics,[2] shattered with their own arms and their own engines; for their followers, if they resist the doctrine and spirit of Christianity, will under your teaching be caught in their own familiar entanglements and fall headlong into their own toils; the barbed syllogism of your argument will hook the glib tongues of the casuists, and it is *you* who will tie up *their* slippery questions in categorical clews, after the manner of clever physicians, who, when compelled by reasoned thought, prepare antidotes for poison even from a serpent. 16. But in these days you are the only one who has either spiritual vision or the consummate learning to accomplish this. Who could follow your lead and keep pace with you, for to you alone has been granted the power to speak better than you have learned and to live better than you speak? For this reason all good men in

B.C., Stoic philosopher. A single finger-joint could mean a number in counting.

[2] Stoic philosophy was derived from the school founded, by Zenon of Citium, in Athens *c.* 300 B.C.; Cynic from the principles of Diogenes of Sinope; Peripatetic from the name Peripatos (a covered "walking-place" in a gymnasium, not connected with activities in the open air) of the school (also called Lyceum) founded by Aristotle.

circa merito te beatissimum boni omnes idque supra omnes tua tempestate concelebrabunt, cuius ita dictis vita factisque dupliciter inclaruit, ut, quando quidem tuos annos iam dextra numeraverit, saeculo praedicatus tuo, desiderandus alieno, utraque laudabilis actione, decedas te relicturus externis, tua proximis. memor nostri esse dignare, domine papa.

X

SIDONIVS DOMINO PAPAE APRVNCVLO SALVTEM

1. Reddidit[1] tibi epistulas meas quem mihi tuas offerre par fuerat; nam frater noster Caelestius nuper ad te reversus de Biterrensi quoddam mihi super statu Iniuriosi nostri vinculum cessionis elicuit. quod quidem scripsi non minus tua verecundia fractus quam voluntate: namque nos ultro vestro

[1] reddidit *vulgo*: reddidi.

---

[1] I don't think *tua tempestate* can go with *omnes* in the sense *tuae tempestatis*. It is really contrasted with what follows.—*A*.

[2] In large counts, fingers of the right hand were used, in one method, for hundreds and thousands; but Sidonius must refer to the method by which Romans counted up from the thumb of the left hand, ten for each finger, and then from the little finger of the right hand; thus when the thumb of the right hand is reached, a hundred has been counted. Sidonius hopes Faustus will live to be a hundred years old.

[3] *utraque laudabilis actione*: i.e. *dictis . . . factisque* mentioned earlier in the sentence.—*A*.

[4] Perhaps—" you will leave yourself (*i.e.* the inspiration of

your own times will justly call you blessed, yes, blessed above all men,[1] for your life has won such renown on the double count of your writings and your good deeds that, when you have reached the years that are counted on the right hand,[2] you will depart this life acclaimed by your own age and coveted by generations to come, thus winning glory on two scores,[3] since you will bequeath your possessions to your immediate flock but your real self to the world at large.[4] Deign to hold me in remembrance, my Lord Bishop.

X

SIDONIUS TO THE LORD BISHOP APRUNCULUS,* GREETING

1. My letter has been delivered to you by the messenger who ought rightly to have brought me one from you, for our brother Caelestius, who lately returned to you from Béziers, extracted from me a bond of cession [5] defining the standing of our friend Iniuriosus. As a matter of fact, I was induced to write it no less from respect for your modesty than from my own inclination; for it was only right that I

your life and work) to outsiders, to the world at large, while you leave your property to your next-of-kin."

* Bishop of Langres who succeeded Sidonius in Clermont after taking refuge there under suspicion by the Burgundian King Gundobad of friendly dealings with the Franks. Gregory of Tours, *Hist. Franc.*, II. 23; Duchesne, II. 185.

[5] *nam frater noster Caelestius, etc.*: What he gave to Caelestius appears to have been a *promise* to give a dimissional letter. So strange is Iniuriosus as a man's name that one suspects that Sidonius, annoyed, substituted it for another—perhaps Innocentius.

pudori quasi quibusdam pedibus obsequii decuit occurrere. 2. quocirca me quoque volente posside indultum, sed liberaliter (nec enim, ut suspicor, plus aliquid hoc genere solacii vel ipse quaesisti), quem litteris istis non commendatoriis minus quam refusoriis iam placatus insinuo; sic tamen, ut tibi assistat, tibi pareat, te sequatur atque ut, si permanserit tecum, neutri nostrum iudicetur famulus, si forte discesserit, quaeratur utrique fugitivus. memor nostri esse dignare, domine papa.

XI

SIDONIVS DOMINO PAPAE LVPO SALVTEM

1. Propter libellum, quem non ad vos magis quam per vos missum putastis, epistulam vestram non ad me magis quam in me scriptam recepi. ad exprobrata respondeo pro aequitate causae, non pro aequalitate facundiae. quamquam quis nunc ego aut quantus, qui agere praesumam, vobis im-

---

[1] Sidonius is, or pretends to be, rather resentful over the attempt to rob him of one of his clergy. *vel ipse* will suggest "even you, you thief. You have had the cheek to steal one of my men. I don't think that even you wanted me to do more than authorize his leaving me." I should think that Iniuriosus was not in full priestly orders. I think Dalton (both in his translation and in his note) misunderstands this letter. —*A*.

* See *Ep*. VI. 1, first note.

[2] *libellum*: *i.e.* the first eight books of the Letters? If *libro* in § 5 is the same as *libellus* here, then the *liber* or *libellus* sent to Lupus may be assumed to have contained Books VI–

should come forward, with swift strides of obedience, to meet your diffident approach. 2. So, by my wish as well as your own, take possession of the man I have now resigned to you; but be a generous master too (for I imagine that even you did not seek anything more from me than this kind of assistance).[1] Having got over my annoyance, I introduce him to you in this letter, which is no less commendatory than dismissory—but on the understanding that he will assist you, obey you, and follow you, and that if he remains with you neither of us will regard him as our servant; but that, if he should leave you, we will both go seeking the runaway. Deign to hold me in remembrance, my Lord Bishop.

XI

SIDONIUS TO THE LORD BISHOP LUPUS,* GREETING

1. On account of the little book [2] which you considered to have been sent *through* you rather than *to* you, I have received your letter written rather *against* me than *to* me. I answer your reproaches as one who has an equitable cause but not an equal gift of words. Yet who am I, and what do I amount to, that I should presume to represent myself as

VIII. But would Book VI, which opens with a letter to Lupus, be sent in this casual way? Of course, however, *Ep.* VI. 1 in its original form might have been sent to Lupus as it professes to have been.—*A.* It may be that Sidonius sent his *liber* to Lupus for reading and passing on to another person; and perhaps Lupus had felt hurt by this request and had written accordingly.

putantibus innocentem? quocirca delicto huic, quantulumcumque est, inter principia confestim supplico ignosci, diffidentiae tantum, non et superbiae fassus errorem. 2. nam cum mihi rigor censurae tuae in litteris aeque ut [1] moribus sit ambifariam contremescendus, fateor tamen in voluminis [2] ipsius operisque reseratu illam mihi fuisse plus oneri [3] quam praetenditis caritatem. nec citra iustum ista conicio, quandoquidem mortalium mentibus vis haec naturalitus inest, ut, si quid perperam fiat, minus indulgeant plus amici. 3. scripseram librum, sicut pronuntiatis, plenum onustumque vario causarum temporum personarumque congestu: facturus rem videbar impudentissimam, si tantum mihi cuncta placuissent, ut nulla tibi displicitura confiderem; huc item, quisquis iudicii eventus foret, vidi partibus meis nequaquam pietatis ex solido constare rationem, si non saltim vobis esset anterius allatum volumen, etsi non videretur oblatum; sub hoc scilicet temperamento, ut, si forte placuissem, non vos arrogantia praeterisse, si secus, non vos improbitas expetisse iudicaretur. 4. nec sane multo labore me credidi deprecaturum vitatas causas

[1] ut ⟨in⟩ *edit. Baret.*
[2] velaminis *coni. Anderson.*
[3] oneri *vulg.*: oneris.

innocent when you reproach me? So I hasten at the outset to beg your pardon for this misdemeanour, however trivial it is, but the only mistake I admit is one of diffidence, not of pride as well. 2. The strictness of your criticism in the two spheres of literature and morals is to me a matter of fear and trembling, but I confess that, in the publication of the volume and work, the affection which you allege for me weighed on me more heavily than anything else.[1] And I think this is perfectly reasonable, since in the human mind it is a natural tendency for a man's closest friends to be the least forgiving when he perpetrates a piece of bad workmanship. 3. Now, I had written a book, as you state, crammed and loaded with a motley assemblage of topics, times, and persons. I thought I should be guilty of gross shamelessness if I were so pleased by it all as to feel sure that nothing would displease you. And besides, I realised that, whatever the outcome of your judgment, on my side my dutiful regard for you must be entirely discounted if the book were not, at least, brought to you first, even if this seemed something different from presenting it to you.[2] In this compromise either contingency was provided for: if I happened to give you pleasure I should not be judged to have arrogantly ignored you; and if I failed to give pleasure I should not be thought to have sought your favour out of sheer impudence. 4. And indeed I did not believe I would have all this trouble in asking to be forgiven for avoiding

[1] Perhaps we should read *oneris* with the MSS.

[2] *allatum volumen . . . oblatum*: Notice the pun between *allatum* and *oblatum*. Cf. in § 8, *collatus, antelatus*.—*A.*

erubescendi. pariter illud nosse vos noveram, quod auctores in operibus edendis pudor potius quam constantia decet quodque tetricis puncta censoribus tardius procacitas recitatoris quam trepidatio excudit. alioquin, si quis est ille qui cum fiduciae praerogativa thematis ante inauditi operam [1] pervulgat, incipit expectationi publicae, quamvis solverit multa, plura redhibere. praeterea quicquid super huiusce rescripti tenore censueris, malui factum confiteri simpliciter quam trebaciter diffiteri. 5. dixisset alius: "neminem tibi praetuli, nullas ad ullum peculiares litteras dedi: quem praelatum suspicabare, unius epistulae forma contentus abscessit, atque ea quidem nihil super praesenti negotio deferente: tu, qui te querer is omissum, tribus loquacissimis paginis fatigatus potius in nausiam concitaris, dum frequenter insulsae lectionis verbis inanibus immoraris. adde, quia etiam in hoc, quod forsitan non notasti, reverentiae tuae meritorumque ratio servata est, quod sicut tu antistitum ceterorum cathedris, prior est tuus in libro titulus.

[1] opera *Luetjohann*.

---

[1] What is the sense of *constantia* here? Does it mean "assurance"?—*A*.

[2] Notice the use of *recitator* for an author publishing his work.

[3] *si quis est ille qui*: does this mean "if he is anybody, somebody"? I do not think so.—*A*.

[4] What is the meaning of *forma* here? Is the idea that a

what might bring a blush to my face. Besides, I knew that you knew how modesty better becomes an author than self-assurance [1] on the occasion of publishing his works, and that from austere critics favourable votes are less readily drawn by brashness on the part of an author [2] than by nervousness. And another point—a writer [3] who self-confidently publishes a work on an entirely new theme thereby (no matter how much he has paid to satisfy public expectation) begins to be in arrears. Further, whatever you think about the tenor of this reply, I preferred to confess frankly what I had done rather than to prevaricate and deny it. 5. Another person would have said "I did not give anyone precedence over you, nor did I write anyone an individual letter. The man you suspected me of preferring to you went on his way contented with the formality of a single letter,[4] and that letter said not a word about the present business; on the other hand, you, who complain of being passed over, have instead been bored with three most garrulous letters, yes, bored and nauseated as three times over you immerse yourself in the empty verbiage of such stupid matter. Add to this another point, perhaps not noticed by you, in which I have shown due consideration for your venerable character and high merits: just as you hold the first place among the enthroned bishops, so your name forms the first superscription in one of

letter addressed to him at some time and incorporated in the collection of letters had contented him, and at the present time he had got nothing? Why *abscessit*? Could it mean "retired from the picture," "faded out, never to reappear in the correspondence," "retired into the background"?—*A*.

illius nomen vix semel tantum et sibi adscripta pagina sonat; tuo praeter tibi deputatas frequenter illustrantur alienae. 6. illud his iunge, quod, si quid ibi vel causaliter[1] placet, tu per consilium meum lectitas, ille quandoque per beneficium tuum, qui munusculi mei incassum pressus invidia necdum ad facultatem legendi, ut suspicor, venit, cum iamdiu ipse perveneris ad copiam transferendi. aio,[2] tamquam non sit authographas[3] membranas arbitraturus, si tamen, quod[4] ante percurreras,[5] vel exemplar acceperit; neque enim in his, quae tractaveris, ulla culpabitur aut distinctionum raritas aut frequentia barbarismorum. nempe ad extremum palam videtur etiam tibi transmissa proprietas, cui usus absque temporis fixi praeescriptione transmissus est quique supradicto tamdiu potes uti libello, ut eum non amplius zothecula tua quam

[1] casualiter *PM*[1].

[2] addo *Mommsen*.

[3] autholographas *Gustafsson recte?*: autographas *Savaron*: holographas *Sirmond*: autolographas *CP*: autulographas *F*: autolografas *M*.

[4] si tamen quod *codd.*: si, tamen quod *Mohr* (*praef.* xl): si a me quod *Mommsen*.

[5] ante percurreras *coni. Luetjohann*: a te percursum *coni. Gustafsson*: a te percurras *CM*: ante percurras *FPM*[1].

---

[1] *prior est tuus in libro titulus*: *i.e. Ep.* 1 of Book VI. For the question whether *liber* here means "the first super-

my books.[1] The name of the other man is scarcely once mentioned even in the epistle devoted to himself, whereas your name (not to speak of letters directed to yourself) often lends distinction to letters I send to other men. 6. Note also that if anything in the book pleases you, at least in its subject-matter,[2] it is by my contrivance that you can read and re-read it; but it is by your favour that the other man will some day be able to do so—and I suspect that,[3] helplessly inarticulate with jealousy, he still awaits a chance of *reading* my little gift, whereas you have long ago had the opportunity of *transcribing* it. I say ' transcribing '; but really he would regard it as a genuine original if he received a copy transcribed and revised by you;[4] for no writing that has been through your hands will ever be chargeable with a deficiency of punctuation or an accumulation of barbarisms. Lastly, I declare, it seems obvious [5] that the right of ownership has actually passed to you, since the use of the property has been conveyed to you without any prescribed limit of time, and so you are able to enjoy the little book long enough for your memory to absorb it as completely as your book-cabinet contains

scription in one of my books," or whether it is equal to *libellus* of § 1, see above.—*A*.

[2] Keep *causaliter* and not *casualiter*: I agree with Mohr, even if there is no parallel for this use of the word. *vel* with *casualiter* would seem inexplicable—neither " even " nor " at least " (both meanings common in Sidonius) gives sense. —*A*.

[3] Anderson made a valiant effort. But the translation from here down to " revised by you "; is Semple's.

[4] The text and meaning are very uncertain.

[5] *palam videtur*: " seems obvious "?—*A*.

memoria concludat." 7. haec et his plura fors aliquis. ego vero cuncta praetereo et malo precari veniam quam reatum, si hoc esse creditur, deprecari. praesentum quoque neglegentiam litterarum nunc nec excuso, primum quod, etsi cupiam, parum cultius scribere queo, dein quod libellari opere confecto animus tandem feriaturus iam quae propalare dissimulat excolere detractat. 8. at tamen, cum satis tibi et quidem merito (quidnam enim simile?) in omnibus cedam, quippe qui in alio genere virtutum iam per quinquennia decem non aequaevis sacerdotibus tantum verum et antiquis, quotiens collatus, antelatus quoque [1] sis, noveris volo, quamvis astra questibus quatias atque maiorum cineres favillasque in testimonium laesae caritatis implores, pedem me conflictui tuo, si mutuo super amore certandum est, non retracturum, quia cum in ceteris rebus tum foedissimum perquam est in dilectione superari. quae velis nolis certa professio conviciis tuis illis cuncta sane blandimentorum mella vincentibus non praeter aequum reponderatur. 9. ecce habes litteras tam garrulas ferme quam requirebas; quamquam sunt

[1] antelatus quoque *Mohr*: antelatus que.

---

[1] *animus tandem feriaturus, etc.*: is this one of Sidonius' attempts to elicit a request that he *should* publish?—*A.*

[2] *alio* has the sense of *omni alio.*—*A.*

it." 7. This and more than this might be urged by someone; but I for my part forgo all such pleas and prefer to ask for pardon rather than to make excuses for my guilt, if my action is regarded in that light. Another thing which I do not try to excuse is the slipshod style of the present letter; first, because I cannot write in a moderately finished style even if I wished to do so; and secondly, because after the completion of a work in book-form my mind wants to take a holiday[1] and declines to polish what it does not at once intend to publish. 8. Nevertheless, there is one thing I want you to know: in all other matters I entirely and rightly give precedence to your inimitable self, for in every other kind of excellence[2] for fifty years you have, on comparison, surpassed not only contemporary priests but those of former times;[3] but, though you shake the stars with your protestations and invoke your ancestors' ashes as a witness to the outrage against friendship, I will hold my own against you without retreating one single foot, if there is to be a contest on the subject of our mutual affection; for, as in other fields, so particularly in the field of affection it is most shameful to be worsted. This declaration, which (whether you approve of it or disapprove) is true, counters not unfairly those reproaches of yours—and though I call them reproaches, they surpassed in fact the quintessence of honeyed charm. 9. Well, there you have a letter almost as full of chatter as you demand—though all my letters,

[3] *aequaevis sacerdotibus*: if *sacerdos* here means "bishop" this is a useful indication of the date of the letter.—*A*. That is, since Lupus was made bishop in 427 or 426 A.D., this letter was written in 477 or 476 A.D. Duchesne, II. 449.

omnes, si quae uspiam tamen sunt, loquacissimae. namque in audentiam sermocinandi quem non ipse compellas? qui omnium (de me enim taceo) litteratorum, licet occuli affectent, sic ingenia producis, ut solet aquam terrae visceribus absconditam per atomos bibulas radius extrahere solaris? cuius lucis[1] aculeo non sola penetratur aut harena subtilis aut humus fossilis, sed si saxei montis oppressu fontium conditorum vena celetur, aperit arcanum liquentis elementi secretorum caelestium natura violentior. ita si quos, vir sacrosancte, studiosorum senseris aut quietos aut verecundos aut in obscuro iacentis famae recessu delitescentes, hos eloquii tui claritas artifice confabulatu, dum compellit,[2] et publicat. 10. sed quorsum ⟨plusculum⟩[3] quam moris est? redeamus ad causam, super cuius abundante blateratu, quia pareo, precor, ut errata confessum veniae clementis indultu placatus impertias, licet, quae laetitia tua sancta quaeque communio, copiosius hilarere, si meae culpae defensio potius tibi scripta feratur quam satisfactio. memor nostri esse dignare, domine papa.

[1] *seclud.* lucis *Luetjohann.*
[2] compellit M^1: compellat.
[3] quorsum ⟨plusculum⟩ *coni. Mohr.* Cf. Additional Notes, p. 617.

---

[1] *si quae uspiam tamen sunt*: another hint about publication? Or does he mean "all my letters existing anywhere are garrulous"?—*A.*

if indeed there are any now in existence anywhere,[1] are very talkative. For whom could you not tempt to make the venture of writing? Never to mention myself, you bring to light the talents of all men of letters, however much they seek obscurity—just as the sunbeam is wont, by means of its thirsty particles, to draw out the water hidden in the bowels of the earth; and this shaft of sunlight penetrates not only fine sand or surface soil, but, if there is any hidden trickle from springs buried under the mass of a rocky mountain, the stronger natural force emanating from the secret places of heaven reveals the mystery of the fluid element. Thus when you, my saintly friend, find any men of literary tastes inactive or shy or hidden in some obscure retreat where their fame languishes, your brilliant eloquence with its skilful admonition urges them on[2] and thereby brings them to public notice. 10. But why continue a little longer than usual? Let us return to the subject, and since my blathering at such length about it is done in obedience to you, I pray you to relent and to meet my confession of error with the indulgence of a merciful pardon—though, in view of your sanctified sense of humour and geniality, you may be more richly entertained if the letter now delivered to you turns out to be a defence of my sin rather than amends for it. Deign to hold me in remembrance, my Lord Bishop.[3]

[2] *dum compellat*: which *compello* is this? It looks as though it ought to be *compellit*, and there is MS support. I translate *compellit*.—*A*.

[3] Here Anderson wrote in a footnote: "This letter was the last to be translated. 29 May, 1948."

XII

SIDONIVS ORESIO SVO SALVTEM

1. Venit in nostras a te profecta pagina manus, quae trahit multam similitudinem de sale Hispano in iugis caeso Tarraconensibus. nam recensenti lucida et salsa est, nec tamen propter hoc ipsum mellea minus. sed [1] sermo dulcis et [2] propositionibus acer: [3] sic enim oblectat eloquio quod turbat imperio, quippe qui parum metiens, quid ordinis agam, carmina a nobis nunc nova petat. primum ab exordio religiosae professionis huic principaliter exercitio renuntiavi, quia nimirum facilitati posset accommodari, si me occupasset levitas versuum, quem respicere coeperat gravitas actionum. 2. tum praeterea constat omnem operam, si longa intercapedine quiescat, aegre resumi. quisnam enim ignoret cunctis aut artificibus aut artibus maximum decus usu venire, cumque studia consueta non frequentantur,[4] brachia in corporibus, ingenia pigrescere in artibus? unde est et illud, quod sero correptus aut raro plus arcus manui, iugo bos, equus freno rebellat. insuper desidiae nostrae verecundia

[1] minus sed *C*: min' si *M*: mins (u superscr.) *M*[1]: minus *FP*.
[2] et *codd.*: e *Mommsen*.
[3] acet *Wilamowitz*.
[4] frequententur *coni. Luetjohann*.

---

* Not otherwise known.
[1] Cf. Gellius II, 22. 7—a large mountain in Spain made of pure salt; all that one takes from it is replaced by nature.
[2] Cf. Pliny, *N.H.*, XXXI. 80—salt in Spain cut or mined

XII

SIDONIUS TO HIS FRIEND ORESIUS,* GREETING

1. There has come into my hands a letter from you which bears much likeness to Spanish salt cut on the hills of Tarraconensis;[1] for the reader finds it luminous and salty;[2] but none the less honeyed on that account. But its sweet language is also sharp in its content, for while it delights by its style, it disturbs by its injunction, because, without considering my clerical position, it now begs for new poems from me. But in the first place, I especially renounced this exercise of verse-writing from the very beginning of my religious profession because undoubtedly it might be a concession to weakness if I occupied myself with the levity of verse-writing when seriousness of action had become my duty. 2. Again, it is well known that every activity, if suspended for a long interval, is resumed only with difficulty. Who could fail to know that to all arts and artists the highest distinction accrues by practice and that, when the accustomed exercise is not frequently repeated, the arms in our bodies and our talents in the arts lose their aptitude? Hence it is that a bow when used late or infrequently is less responsive to the hand, and similarly an ox to the yoke and a horse to the bridle. Moreover, my modesty joins with my indolence in influencing my

in almost transparent blocks or lumps and valued by doctors above all other kinds of salt. Hence Anderson translated *lucida* " luminous," " glistening," " sparkling."

comes ad hoc sententiam inclinat, ut me, postquam in silentio decurri tres olympiadas, tam pudeat novum poema conficere quam pigeat. 3. huc[1] item nefas etiam difficilia factu tibi negari, cuius affectum tanto minus decipi decet, quanto constantius nil repulsam veretur. tenebimus igitur quippiam medium et sicut epigrammata recentia modo nulla dictabo, ita litteras, si quae iacebunt versu refertae, scilicet ante praesentis officii necessitatem, mittam tibi, petens, ne tu sis eatenus iustitiae praevaricator, ut me opineris numquam ab huiusmodi conscriptione temperaturum. neque enim suffragio tuo minus augear, si forte digneris iam modestum potius quam facetum ⟨me⟩[2] existimare. vale.

XIII

SIDONIVS TONANTIO SVO SALVTEM

1. Est quidem, fateor, versibus meis sententia tua tam plausibilis olim, tam favorabilis, ut poetarum me quibusque lectissimis comparandum putes, certe compluribus anteponendum. crederem tibi, si non, ut multum sapis, ita quoque multum me amares. hinc est, quod de laudibus meis caritas tua mentiri

[1] hoc *FP*. [2] me *add. Mohr.*

[1] Twelve years. For the date when Sidonius became bishop see pp. 4–5.

mind to such a degree that, having gone through three Olympiads[1] in silence, I am as much ashamed as disinclined to compose a new poem. 3. To this I must add a further point: it would be outrageous that things even difficult of achievement should be denied to you—to you whose friendship is all the less deserving of disappointment because of the steadfastness with which it refuses to fear a rebuff. So I shall keep a sort of middle course; I shall not now write any new poems, but if there happen to be any letters lying about containing verses—written, of course, before the constraint imposed by my present profession—I will send them to you, begging you at the same time not so far to pervert justice as to imagine that I shall *never* abstain from this kind of composition. For I should be no less complimented by your approval if you thought fit to regard me now as modest rather than accomplished. Farewell.

XIII

SIDONIUS TO HIS FRIEND TONANTIUS,* GREETING

1. Your opinion of my verses is sometimes, I must confess, so laudatory and so prone to partiality that you judge me comparable with the choicest poets and indeed preferable to a good many of them. I should believe you were it not that, though you have great discrimination, you also have a great affection for me. Hence it comes that your affection may exaggerate

* Son of Tonantius Ferreolus (for whom see *Ep.* VII. 12, first note); cf. *Ep.* IX. 15. 1; *Carm.* XXIV. 34.

potest nec potest fallere. 2. praeter hoc poscis, ut Horatiana incude formatos Asclepiadeos tibi quospiam, quibus inter bibendum pronuntiandis exerceare, transmittam. pareo iniunctis, licet, si umquam, modo maxime prosario loquendi genere districtus occupatusque. denique probabis circa nos plurima ex parte metrorum studia refrigescere; non enim promptum est unum eundemque probe facere aliquid et raro.

Iam dudum teretes hendecasyllabos
attrito calamis pollice lusimus,
quos cantare magis pro choriambicis
excusso poteras mobilius pede;
sed tu per Calabri tramitis aggerem
vis ut nostra dehinc cursitet orbita,
qua Flaccus lyricos Pindaricum ad melos
frenis flexit equos plectripotentibus,
dum metro quatitur chorda Glyconio,
nec non Alcaico vel Pherecratio
iuncto Lesbiaco sive anapaestico,
vernans per varii carminis eglogas
verborum violis multicoloribus.
istud, da veniam, fingere vatibus

---

[1] The poem which Sidonius gives below is written in the same kind of Asclepiad metre as is Horace's first ode.

[2] *attrito . . . pollice* probably does not refer to "thrumming."—*A*.

[3] A "choriambic" is a foot consisting of two shorts between two longs: – ⏑ ⏑ –.

my achievements and yet not deceive me. 2. Besides this, you ask me to send you some Asclepiads [1] shaped on the Horatian anvil, in order that you may be diverted in reciting them over your wine. I yield to your demand, although, at this time of all times, I am deeply occupied and engrossed in prose composition. Lastly, you will find it true of me that, in very large degree, the study of metrical composition is waning; for it is not easy for one and the same man both to do a thing well and to do it seldom.

"Long have I with pen-worn hand [2] lightly essayed the smooth hendecasyllable: these you might have sung rather than choriambics,[3] flinging out your foot with greater freedom, but it is your will that henceforth my wheel should follow the course of the Calabrian road [4] along which, with reins mighty in music, Flaccus [5] guided his lyric steeds towards [6] Pindaric melody, while his lyre vibrates with the Glyconic measure and the Alcaic and the Pherecratian, with the Sapphic added or the anapaestic; [7] and in all this series of varied song [8] he flowers with words as with violets of many hues. But you must pardon me; there is one thing difficult for the old

[4] Calabria: vaguely for the south-east of Italy. See p. 593, n. 7. In Roman times it was the "heel," now it is the "toe" of Italy.

[5] Horace, 65 B.C.–8 B.C. He was born at Venusia (Venosa to-day).

[6] Perhaps "to the accompaniment of," but this is less likely.—*A.* The poetry of Pindar (518–438 B.C.) was and is renowned for its noble and joyful grandeur, and sometimes great sublimity, of thought and diction.

[7] All these metres were used by Horace in his odes.

[8] Should we print *eclogas*?—*A.*

priscis difficile est, difficile et mihi,
ut diversa sonans os epigrammata
nil crebras titubet propter epistulas,
quas cantu ac modulis luxuriantibus
lascivire vetat mascula dictio.
istud vix Leo, rex Castalii chori,
vix, hunc qui sequitur, Lampridius queat,
declamans gemini pondere sub stili
coram discipulis Burdigalensibus.
hoc me teque decet? parce, precor, iocis;
quaeso, pollicitam servet ad extimum
oratoris opus cura modestiam,
quo nil deterius, si fuerit simul
in primis rigidus, mollis in ultimis.

3. Quin immo quotiens epulo mensae lautioris hilarabere, religiosis, quod magis approbo, narrationibus vaca; his proferendis confabulatio frequens,

---

[1] Does it mean "to contrive"? so that *istud fingere . . . ut* means "to contrive this—viz. that . . ."—*A.*

[2] A Catholic, but a minister of King Euric of the Visigoths. See *Ep.* IV. 22, first note.

[3] Castalia was the name of a fountain rising on Mount Parnassus in Greece and sacred to Apollo and the Muses.

[4] Cf. *Ep.* VIII. 9.

[5] Prose and verse.

[6] *hoc me teque decet*: I think I have got near the meaning here. Sidonius has devoted himself to serious letter-writing; so the duty of Tonantius and himself is clear. "Tonantius must abstain from such jests as begging Sidonius to relax; and Sidonius must preserve in all that he now writes the modest rôle to which he has limited himself: he must not turn 'soft.'"—*A.* Should not this phrase be printed as a question? "This is almost too much for champions like Leo and Lampridius—is it something, then, that is becoming to

poets and difficult also for me—to contrive [1] that the lips, in uttering poems which are so different, should not falter through having written great numbers of prose-letters, whose manly diction forbids them to unbend in song and sportive measures. This could scarce be achieved by Leo,[2] king of Castalia's [3] choir, or by his close follower, Lampridius,[4] as he holds forth, in the massive grandeur of both styles,[5] before his pupils of Bordeaux. Is this what becomes you and me? [6] Refrain, I pray, from jesting; and please let your prose-writer's efforts [7] preserve to the end of his work the restraint he had promised: for nothing is worse than the orator who in the early stages begins with stern dignity and in the end collapses into disarray."

3. But rather,[8] when you are making merry at a specially sumptuous feast, please take my advice and occupy yourself with religious tales; let the conversation be constantly devoted to telling [9] them and

lesser writers like you and me? enough of such jesting!"—*W.H.S.* The text and the translation have been changed accordingly.

[7] *cura*: to be taken, I think, in the literary sense, "literary labour."—*A*.

[8] *quin immo*: *i.e.* "but really I would have you . . .": "but rather than this sort of thing, do what is more to my liking and . . . occupy yourself with . . ."—*A*.

[9] *redicendis*: impossible, I think; but the emendations proposed are not convincing. Perhaps *rediscendis*. In the margin of his Luetjohann edition Arnold suggests *perdiscendis* (his own conjecture?), which would give good sense but is palaeographically improbable. Perhaps for *his redicendis* we might have *hisce discendis*.—*A*. "Telling and re-telling"?

his rediscendis[1] sollicitus auditus inserviat. certe si saluberrimis avocamentis, ut qui adhuc iuvenis, tepidius[2] inflecteris, a Platonico Madaurensi saltim formulas mutuare convivialium quaestionum, quoque reddaris instructior, has solve propositas, has propone solvendas hisque te studiis, et dum otiaris, exerce. 4. sed quia mentio conviviorum semel incidit tuque sic carmen nobis vel ad aliam causam personamque compositum sedulo exposcis, ut me eius edendi diutius habere non possis haesitatorem, suscipe libens quod temporibus Augusti Maioriani, cum rogatu cuiusdam sodalis ad cenam conveniremus, in Petri librum magistri epistularum subito prolatum subitus effudi, meis quoque contubernalibus, dum rex convivii circa ordinandum moras nectit oxygarum, Domnulo, Severiano atque Lampridio paria pangentibus (iactanter hoc dixi, immo

[1] rediscendis *Anderson*: perdiscendis *coni. Arnold?*: recipiendis *Wilamowitz, Leo*: retinendis *coni. Luetjohann*: redicendis.

[2] tepidus *F*: trepidius *C*.

---

[1] Apuleius of Madaura in Africa.

[2] A.D. 457–461.

[3] *conveniremus.* The imperfect is a rather odd tense here. —*A.* This dinner-party may have taken place in A.D. 459—Stevens, *Sid. Apoll.*, 51.

[4] Not Petrus of *Ep.* VII. 11(10). 2, but secretary (*magister epistolarum*) of the Emperor Majorian. He died in A.D. 473 or 474. See *Ep.* IX. 15. *carm.* 40; *Carm.* V. 568–571; IX. 307–308; III. 5. Apparently he helped to reconcile the Emperor to Sidonius and arranged conditions of surrender for the

let the listeners be earnestly bent on learning them. But if, being still a young man, you are only faintly attracted by such salutary diversions, at least borrow from the Platonist [1] of Madaura his patterns of convivial problems, and (to improve your education) solve these when propounded, and propound these to be solved; and busy yourself with such pursuits even in your free time. 4. But as convivial parties have been mentioned, and as you urgently demand from me even one written for another occasion and another person, and as your insistence is such as to permit no further hesitation on my part, be pleased to receive one which goes back to the time of the Emperor Majorian.[2] We were assembling [3] for dinner at the invitation of a friend when a book by Petrus [4] the Imperial Secretary was suddenly produced, whereupon I with similar suddenness wrote this effusion [5] about it, during the interval in which the master of the feast [6] was tarrying over the preparation of the relishes. My cronies Domnulus,[7] Severianus,[8] and Lampridius [9] composed similar pieces (this is a boastful way to put it; "better

Gallo-Romans when they were besieged. See Vol. I of Sidonius (Loeb), p. xxxvii.

[5] *subitus effudi*: "wrote this effusion *about* it." I think this is the meaning. The four of them could scarcely have written their verses *on* the book at the same time.—*A.*

[6] *dum rex convivii etc.*: I think this simply means "before the first course was ready to be served."—*A.*

[7] See *Ep.* IV. 25.

[8] Cf. *Ep.* IX. 15. 1, *carm.* 37; *Carm.* IX. 315. A rhetorician and poet to whom might be ascribed an extant series of rhetorical precepts attributed to a Iulius Severianus (*Rhet. Min.* ed. Holm, pp. 350–370).

[9] See above, line 21 and *Ep.* VIII. 9.

meliora); quos undique urbium ascitos imperator in unam civitatem, invitator in unam cenam forte contraxerat. 5. id morae tantum, dum genera metrorum sorte partimur. placuit namque pro caritate collegii, licet omnibus eadem scribendi materia existeret, non uno tamen epigrammata singulorum genere proferri, ne quispiam nostrum, qui ceteris dixisset exilius, verecundia primum, post morderetur invidia. etenim citius agnoscitur in quocumque recitante, si quo ceteri metro canat, an eo quoque scribat ingenio. tu vero tunc opportunius subiecta laudabis, cum totus otio indulseris. non enim iustum est, ut censor incipias cum severitate discutere quod non potuit amicus cum serietate dictare.

Age, convocata pubes,
locus hora, mensa causa
iubet ut volumen istud,
quod et aure et ore discis,
studiis in astra tollas.
Petrus est tibi legendus,

---

[1] *imperator . . . invitator*: Anderson took both words as referring to Majorian and therefore the banquet as being not the one just mentioned but the dinner described in *Ep.* I. 11. But, in view of the phrase *rogatu cuiusdam sodalis ad cenam conveniremus*, I take the sense to be that the Emperor's order had accidentally brought the companions to the same city, and the friend's invitation had brought the lot of them together to the same function.—*W.H.S.*

[2] Arles, where Sidonius was with Majorian *c.* A.D. 461.

[3] "Anacreontic" verses, a very rare metre in Latin.

pieces," I ought to have said); they happened to have been brought together by the Emperor,[1] who from widely scattered cities had summoned them to one city;[2] and now a common host had united us all at his board. 5. The only thing that delayed the start was the choosing of our metres by lot; for although the subject-matter was the same for all, yet, as was proper for devoted colleagues, we resolved that the poems of the several competitors should not be in the same metrical form, so that none of us whose piece might be poorer than the others should be stung first with shame and later with envy. For in any case where a reciter of his poetry, no matter who, composes in the same metre as his rivals, it can more easily be discerned whether he also writes with the same talent. But you will more seasonably take a favourable view of the appended verses[3] when you have given yourself up entirely to relaxation; it is not fair that you should become a critic and proceed to examine with severity something that your friend had not the chance of composing as a serious effort.

"Come, assembled youth, the place, the hour, the table, and the occasion bid you raise to the skies with your acclamations this book which you learn by the ear and by the lips.[4] Petrus is to be read to

[4] *et aure et ore discis*: why *aure* et *ore*? does it mean by hearing it read and by reciting it yourselves?—*A*. I am sure that Sidonius uses the two words *partly* because of the jingle and *partly* because the process of learning is twofold—first by the hearing of the ear, and then by the recital of the voice. —*W.H.S.*

in utraque disciplina
satis institutus auctor.
celebremus ergo, fratres,
pia festa litterarum.
peragat diem cadentem
dape, poculis, choreis
genialis apparatus.
Rutilum toreuma bysso
rutilasque ferte blattas,
recoquente quas aeno
Meliboea fucat unda,
opulentet ut meraco
bibulum colore vellus.
peregrina det supellex
Ctesiphontis ac Niphatis
iuga texta beluasque
rapidas vacante panno,
acuit quibus furorem
bene ficta plaga cocco
iaculoque ceu forante
cruor incruentus exit;
ubi torvus et per artem
resupina flexus ora
it equo reditque telo
simulacra bestiarum
fugiens fugansque Parthus.
Nive pulchriora lina
gerat orbis atque lauris
hederisque pampinisque
viridantibus tegatur.
cytisos, crocos, amellos,
casias, ligustra, calthas
calathi ferant capaces,

you, a master right well schooled in both disciplines.[1] So, my brethren, let us celebrate (as in duty bound) a festival of letters. Let the jovial entertainment conclude the fading day with viands, cups, and dances.

"Bring the couch red with fine linen, bring the gleaming purple which the Meliboean[2] dye stains in the twice-boiling cauldron, to enrich the absorbent fleece with the purest tint. Let foreign furnishings show in embroidery the hills of Ctesiphon and Niphates[3] and beasts rushing over the roomy cloth,[4] their rage wetted by a wound well counterfeited in scarlet, and, at the seeming thrust of a javelin, blood that is no blood issues: where the Parthian, wild-eyed and cunningly leaning over with face turned backwards, makes his horse go and his arrow return, flying from or putting to flight the pictured beasts. Let the round table show linen fairer than snow and be covered with laurel and ivy and vine-shoots fresh and verdant. Let cytisus, crocus, starwort, casia, privet, and marigolds be brought in ample baskets

[1] Prose and verse.

[2] Meliboea was a seaside town (now Kastri) in Thessaly at the foot of Mount Ossa.

[3] Of Sassania (Parthia, Persia) and Armenia where Niphates was the name of a mountain.

[4] Semple in *Quaest. Exeg.* 58–59 gives a different explanation. See Additional Notes, p. 617.

redolentibusque sertis
abacum torosque pingant.
manus uncta suco amomi
domet hispidos capillos
Arabumque messe pinguis
petat alta tecta fumus.
veniente nocte nec non
numerosus erigatur
laquearibus coruscis
camerae in superna lychnus:
oleumque nescientes
adipesque glutinosos
utero tumente fundant
opobalsamum lucernae.
  Geruli caput plicantes
anaglyptico metallo
epulas superbiores
umeris ferant onustis.
paterae, scyphi, lebetes
socient Falerna nardo
tripodasque cantharosque
rosa sutilis coronet.
iuvat ire per corollas
alabastra ventilantes;
iuvat et vago rotatu
dare fracta membra ludo,
simulare vel trementes
pede, veste, voce Bacchas.
bimari remittat urbe
thymelen palenque doctas
tepidas ad officinas
citharistrias Corinthus,
digiti quibus canentes

and colour the side-board and couches with fragrant garlands. Let a hand smeared with oil of amomum smooth your ruffled hair, and let a smoke rich with the products of Araby soar to the lofty roof. Yes, and when night draws nigh, let many a light be raised to the top of the vaulted chamber to make the panelled ceiling flash; and let lamps innocent of oil and greasy fat shower balm from their capacious bowl.

"Let attendants, their heads bent by the chased metal, bring in lordly dishes on their laden shoulders. Let bowls, goblets, and basins join Falernian with nard,[1] and let roses stitched together wreathe tripods [2] and tankards. It is a joy to pass through lines of garlands, waving scent-bottles as we go; it is a joy to surrender our languid limbs to frolic in aimless circling and to counterfeit even Bacchanals with foot and dress and voice all a quiver. From her town between the two seas let Corinth send harping-girls who have learned stage singing and dancing at the warm training-school,[3] and whose musical

[1] I think the poet does not mean mixed or spiced wines: he simply means that at the symposium the wine and the perfume were used by the guests at the same time.—*W.H.S.*

[2] Tripods were used as stands for *crateres.*

[3] On *tepidas* see Additional Notes, p. 618. *officina* is a workshop. The Greek word *thymele* means a platform where the chorus-leader stood in the middle of the orchestra. On the other hand the Greek word *pălē,* "wrestling-place," is a puzzle. Cf. *Carm.* IX. 188, where it certainly means wrestling. In XXIII. 302 it is associated with clowns, musicians and tight-rope walkers. In this letter it may simply mean gymnastics.

pariter sonante lingua
vice pectinis fatigent
animata fila pulsu.
  Date et aera fistulata,
Satyris amica nudis;
date ravulos choraulas,
quibus antra per palati
crepulis reflanda buccis
gemit aura tibialis.
date carminata socco,
date dicta sub cothurno,
date quicquid advocati,
date quicquid et poetae
vario strepunt in actu:
Petrus haec et illa transit.
opus editum tenemus,
bimetra quod arte texens
iter asperum viasque
labyrinthicas cucurrit.
sed in omnibus laborans
et ab omnibus probatus
rapit hinc et inde palmam,
per et ora docta fertur.
procul hinc et Hippocrenen
Aganippicosque fontes
et Apollinem canorum
comitantibus Camenis
abigamus et Minervam
quasi praesulem canendi;
removete ficta fatu:
deus ista praestat unus.
  Stupuit virum loquentem
diadematis potestas,

fingers replacing the quill shall ply the strings that wake to life at their touch, while their tongues sound in harmony.

"Give us also the brass-bound syrinx,[1] friend of the naked satyrs; give us the reedy notes of pipe-players in whom the breath that is to fill the pipe comes humming through the cavern of the palate,[2] to be forced out by the noisy puffed cheeks. Give us the ditties of comedy and the utterances of tragedy;[3] give us all that the advocates, all that the poets, shout with diverse gestures: Petrus surpasses all of them alike. We have here a work from his hands; he has wrought it skilfully in the two rhythms of prose and verse, and has essayed a rough course with labyrinthine ways; but toiling in all things, by all men is he approved; both in prose and in verse he bears away the palm, and his name is on the lips of all the learned. Far hence let us banish Hippocrene and the fount of Aganippe,[4] tuneful Apollo with his attendant Muses, Minerva, too, reputed patron of music. Away with all things fabled by fiction. This achievement is due to one 'god' only.[5] This man's power of speech has struck with amazement the sovereign that wears the diadem,

[1] *aera fistulata*: "brass furnished with tubes," *i.e.* reed tubes bound together with brass.—*A*.

[2] *antra per palati*, etc.: *i.e.* the breath comes from the lungs and fills the mouth, and the swelling cheeks discharge it into the instrument.—*A*.

[3] The *soccus* was worn by actors in comedy, the *cothurnus* in tragedy. See *Ep.* VIII. 11. *carm.* 7–8.

[4] Aganippe and Hippocrene were both fountains, sacred to Apollo and the Muses, on Mount Helicon in Greece.

[5] Petrus is meant.

toga, miles, ordo equester
populusque Romularis;
et adhuc sophos volutant
fora, templa, rura, castra.
super haec fragorem alumno
Padus atque civitatum
dat amor Ligusticarum.
similis favor resultat
Rhodanitidas per urbes,
imitabiturque Gallos
feritas Hibericorum.
nec in hoc moratus axe
cito ad arva perget euri
aquilonibusque et austris
zephyrisque perferetur.

6. Ecce, dum quaero quid cantes, ipse cantavi. tales enim nugas in imo scrinii fundo muribus perforatas post annos circiter viginti profero in lucem, quales pari tempore absentans, cum domum rediit, Ulixes invenire potuisset. proinde peto, ut praesentibus ludicris libenter ignoscas. illud vero nec verecunde nec impudenter iniungo, ut quod ipse de familiaris mei integro libro pronuntiavi, hoc tu quasi sollicitatus exempli necessitate de meo sentias.[1] vale.

[1] ⟨schedio⟩ sentias *aut* sentias ⟨schedio⟩ *coni. Anderson*: de meo sentias *om. C.*

civilians, soldiers, the knighthood, and the populace of Romulus' race; and still the market-places and the temples, the countryside and the camps re-echo their huzzahs: the river Po also and the towns of Liguria sound the praise of the son they love. Like applause echoes through the cities near the Rhône, and the wild men of Spain will follow the example of the Gauls. Nor shall his name tarry in this clime; soon it will advance to the lands of the East, and the breezes of North, South, and West will likewise waft it on."

6. Lo and behold! In seeking something [1] for you to sing, I have myself sung; for I now bring to light about twenty years after they were written some trifling verses which have been lying at the bottom of a book-case, nibbled full of holes by the mice—the sort of stuff that Ulysses might have found on his return home after an absence of like duration. So I beg that you will readily forgive these absurdities; but one thing I do insist on without either modesty or impudence—you must be moved by the compulsion of my example to have the same opinion of my book as I have expressed about my friend's whole book.[2] Farewell.

[1] This looks as if Anderson read *quod* which indeed is what one would expect here (cf. IX. 15. 1 *si quod et ipse decantes mittam*). But the MSS have *quid*: "while I am asking (seeking) what you are to sing," or "what you are singing."

[2] *integro libro . . . de meo sentias*: I think that *schedio* may have dropped out before, or after, *sentias*. I feel that some contrast to *integro libro* has dropped out.—*A*. There is no need to add anything if we take *integro libro* as "(my friend's) book as a whole."

XIV

SIDONIVS BVRGVNDIONI SVO SALVTEM

1. Dupliciter excrucior, quod nostrum uterque lecto tenetur. nihil enim est durius, quam [1] cum praesentes amici dividuntur communione languoris; quippe si accidat, ut nec intra unum conclave decumbant, nulla sunt verba, nulla solacia, nulla denique mutui oratus vicissitudo: ita singulis maeror ingens, isque plus de altero; nam parum possis quamquam et infirmus periclitante quem diligas tibi timere. 2. sed deus mihi, fili amantissime, pro te paventi validissimum scrupulum excussit, quia pristinas incipis vires recuperare. diceris enim iam velle consurgere, quodque plus opto, iam posse. me certe taliter consulis et sollicitudine prope praecoqua quaestiunculis litterarum iam quasi ex asse vegetus exerces, audire plus ambiens etsi adhuc aeger Socraten de moribus quam Hippocratem de corporibus disputantem; dignus omnino, quem plausibilibus Roma foveret ulnis, quoque recitante crepitantis Athenaei subsellia cuneata quaterentur. 3. quod procul dubio consequebare, si pacis locique condicio permitteret, ut illic sena-

[1] quam *om. C., add.* M^1.

---

* Not otherwise known.

[1] *nihil . . . durius quam cum etc.*: *quam* is omitted by *C* and *M*; it might be omitted. Somewhat similar (if MSS are correct) is Pliny, *Ep.* II. 12. 4, *quid publice minus aut congruens aut decorum quam notatum a senatu in senatu sedere*: here *quam* is inserted by the editors, but is not in the MSS.—*A*.

[2] *quippe si accidat*: or does *quippe* mean "nay"? It seems almost as if it were "but."—*A*.

XIV

SIDONIUS TO HIS FRIEND BURGUNDIO,* GREETING

1. It is a double affliction to me that each of us is confined to bed. There is nothing more distressing than [1] when two friends not sundered by distance are in fact separated by their common illness; for if it happens [2] that they are not even laid up in the same room, there can be no conversation, no attempt at comfort, above all no reciprocity of prayers for one another; so each of them carries a heavy weight of grief, but more on his friend's account; for a patient, however ill, cannot feel anxious about himself when a dear friend is in danger. 2. But now in my concern for you, my loving son,[3] God has removed my heaviest anxiety, since you are beginning to recover your former strength. It is said that you now have the wish to get up, and (what I desire still more) that you now have the strength to do so. You certainly show signs of this when you consult me, and when, with an interest almost too forward, you ply me with literary problems as if completely restored—desiring, though still convalescent, to hear Socrates discussing morals more than Hippocrates discussing bodies. Right worthy are you to have Rome gathering you into her approving arms and to have the blocks of seats in the Athenaeum [4] shaken with clamorous applause as you recite. 3. And this triumph you would undoubtedly have been achieving, if peaceful conditions and

[3] Not of course his real son. [4] Cf. *Ep.* IX. 9. 13.

toriae iuventutis contubernio mixtus erudirere. cuius te gloriae pariter ac famae capacem de orationis tuae qualitate coniecto, in qua te decentissime nuper pronuntiante[1] quae quidem scripseras extemporaliter admirabantur benivoli, mirabantur[2] superbi, morabantur[3] periti. sed ne impudenter verecundiam tuam laudibus nimiis ultro premamus, praeconia tua iustius de te quam tibi scribimus. hoc potius, unde est causa sermonis, intromittamus.

4. igitur interrogas per pugillatorem, quos recurrentes asseram versus, ut celer explicem, sed sub exemplo. hi nimirum sunt recurrentes, qui metro stante neque litteris loco motis ut ab exordio ad terminum, sic a fine releguntur ad summum. sic est illud antiquum:

Roma tibi subito motibus ibit amor.[4]

et[5] illud:

sole medere pede,[6] ede perede melos.[5]

[1] pronuntiantem *Luetjohann*: pronunciante *MFP*: pronunciante te *C*.
[2] mirabantur *vulgo*: mirabuntur.
[3] morabantur *vulgo*: morabuntur.
[4] amor et. si bene te tua laus taxat sua laute tenebis *C*.
[5] et . . . melos *seclud. Luetjohann.*
[6] pedes *F*.

---

[1] Verses which are palindromic ("running the same backwards") were supposed to have been invented by Sotades of the third century B.C. The first one, a pentameter, given below by Sidonius was preceded by a palindromic hexameter, and both were imagined as spoken to a holy man by the animal on which he was riding on a pilgrimage to Rome, the animal being Satan, changed by the man into a beast: *Signa te signa; temere me tangis et angis;|Roma tibi subito motibus ibit*

possibility of travel allowed you to improve yourself by associating there in Rome with young men of senatorial rank. That you are capable of gaining such glory and fame I infer from the quality of that recent oration of yours, in which you declaimed with the utmost grace words which you had actually written ex tempore; and so you won the admiration of the well-disposed, the astonishment of the proud, and the delaying applause of the experts. But lest I should embarrass your modesty with shameless excess of praise, it behoves me to make you the subject rather than the recipient of my eulogies. So let me introduce the matter which is the cause of my writing. 4. Well, you write to ask me through the letter-carrier in an immediate reply to explain, with an example, what kind of verses I entitle "palindromic."[1] There is no doubt that those are palindromic which with no change in the metre or dislocation of the letters can be just as well read backwards from end to beginning as from beginning to end. Such is the old example:

Roma tibi subito motibus ibit amor.

This also:

sole medere pede, ede perede melos.

amor—"cross yourself, cross yourself; rashly do you touch me and torture me; suddenly through my movements will Rome, your heart's desire, come to you." The origin of the other line (which Luetjohann would omit) given by Sidonius is unknown: *sole* = you alone (*or* O Solus); *medere* = cure you!; *pede* = by or in the foot; *ede perede melos*: utter, utter in full, a song. *pedes* (for *pede*) in *F* makes some sense: "cure your verses' feet!" But *medeor* properly takes a dative.

5. nec non habentur pro recurrentibus, qui pedum lege servata etsi non per singulos apices, per singula tamen verba replicantur, ut est unum distichon meum (qualia reor equidem legi multa multorum), quod de rivulo lusi, qui repentino procellarum pastus illapsu publicumque aggerem confragoso diluvio supergressus subdita viae culta inundaverat, quamquam depositurus insanam mox abundantiam, quippe quam pluviis appendicibus intumescentem nil superna venae perennis pondera inflarent. 6. igitur istic (nam viator adveneram), dum magis ripam quam vadum quaero, tali iocatus epigrammate per turbulenti terga torrentis his saltem pedibus incessi:

Praecipiti modo quod decurrit tramite flumen
tempore consumptum iam cito deficiet.

Hoc si recurras, ita legitur:

Deficiet cito iam consumptum tempore flumen
tramite decurrit quod modo praecipiti.[1]

En habes versus, quorum syllabatim mirere[2] rationem. ceterum pompam, quam non habent, non docebunt. sufficienter indicasse me suspicor

[1] praecipiti et. Musa michi causas memora quo numine leso *C* (*ex Verg. Aen.* I. 8).
[2] rimere *coni. Luetjohann*: metiere *Wilamowitz.*

5. Another class of verses regarded as palindromic consists of those which are reversed, not letter by letter but word by word. To this class belongs a certain couplet of mine (though I fancy that many similar lines by many authors are in circulation). It is a sportive trifle about a brook which, swollen by a sudden onset of stormy weather and overflowing the high road in a turbulent rush of water, had inundated the fields at a lower level; but it was at once to lose this enormous volume, which was merely swollen by the extra rainstorm, not flooded by any weight of water from a perennial source at the head-stream. 6. Well, I had come upon this scene in the course of a journey; and while trying to find the bank, let alone the ford, I amused myself by composing the following epigram: and so on these feet, if not on my own, I advanced over the back of the raging torrent.

Praecipiti modo quod decurrit tramite flumen
tempore consumptum iam cito deficiet.

(The stream which now rushes down in headlong course will be exhausted as time passes and quickly spend itself.)

If you take it the other way round, it reads thus:

Deficiet cito iam consumptum tempore flumen
tramite decurrit quod modo praecipiti.

There you have the verses; you can marvel at their design syllable by syllable, but they will not give a lesson in grandeur for they have none. I imagine I have given you a sufficient idea of the thing you

quod tu requirendum existimasti. 7. simile quiddam facis et ipse, si proposita restituas eque diverso quae repeteris expedias. namque imminet[1] tibi thematis celeberrimi votiva redhibitio, laus videlicet peroranda, quam meditaris,[2] Caesaris Iulii. quae materia tam grandis est, ut studentum si quis fuerit ille copiosissimus, nihil amplius in ipsa debeat cavere, quam ne quid minus dicat. nam si omittantur quae de titulis dictatoris invicti scripta Patavinis sunt voluminibus, quis opera Suetonii, quis Iuventii[3] Martialis historiam quisve ad extremum Balbi ephemeridem fando adaequaverit? 8. sed tuis ceris haec reservamus. officii magis est nostri auditoribus scamna componere, praeparare aures fragoribus intonaturis,[4] dumque virtutes tu dicis alienas, nos tuas dicere. neque vereare me quospiam iudices Catonianos advocaturum, qui modo invidiam, modo ignorantiam suam factae severitatis velamine tegant.

[1] imminet *Wilamowitz*: eminet.
[2] quam meditaris *Anderson*: quam edixeras *Wilamowitz*: cum edideris *coni. Warmington*: quam edideras *FP*: quam ididas *M*: quae dederas *C*.
[3] vivencii *F*.
[4] intonaturos C^2: intonaturas *ed. Savaron.*

---

[1] *quam edideras*: we must read *quam meditaris*: *meditaris* became *editaris* and was corrupted to *edideras*, which makes nonsense because clearly a *forthcoming* effort of Burgundio's is referred to.—*A*. I fully agree.—*W.H.S.*

[2] Titus Livius, 59 B.C.–A.D. 17, was born at Patavium (Padua). That part of his history which dealt with Julius Caesar the " invincible dictator " is lost.

thought fit to enquire about. 7. You on your part will do a similar service if you requite the foregoing and send me something which I ask of you in return. An ideal chance will shortly be yours of repaying me by means of your exercise on an illustrious theme, I mean the laudatory declamation on Julius Caesar which you are composing.[1] The subject is so colossal that even the most eloquent of students must guard against one thing particularly—the danger of not rising to the occasion. For if we leave out of account all that is recorded of the invincible dictator's glories in the books of Livy,[2] what author's style could match the works of Suetonius,[3] the history of Iuventius [4] Martialis, and lastly the journal of Balbus? [5] 8. But I leave this to you and your writing-tablets; my duty lies rather in assembling the benches for your audience, in preparing their ears for the thunderous applause that will greet you, and in proclaiming *your* virtues while you proclaim the virtues of Caesar. And you must have no fear that I will summon judges of Catonian sternness [6] who will conceal perhaps their jealousy, perhaps their ignorance, under a veil of artificial severity. It is

[3] Of C. Suetonius Tranquillus almost the only surviving work is *Lives of Caesars*, written during the first part of the second century after Christ.

[4] Or possibly Viventius. Nothing is known about this Martialis.

[5] L. Cornelius Balbus, of the first century B.C., was friend and then secretary of Julius Caesar and wrote a diary (not extant) of events in his own life and Caesar's—Suetonius, *Caes.* 81. "Caesar's" eighth book of the *Bellum Gallicum*, probably written by Hirtius, was dedicated to Balbus.

[6] Cato "of Utica" was a stern opponent of Caesar.

quamquam imperitis venia debetur; ceterum quisquis ita malus est, ut intellegat bene scripta nec tamen laudet, hunc boni intellegunt nec tamen laudant.

9. proinde curas tuas hoc metu absolvo: faventes[1] audient[2] cuncti, cuncti foventes, gaudiisque, quae facies recreaturis,[3] una fruemur. nam plerique laudabunt facundiam tuam, plurimi ingenium, toti pudorem. non enim minus laudi[4] feretur aduescentem vel, quod est pulchrius, paene adhuc puerum de palaestra publici examinis tam morum referre suffragia quam litterarum. vale.

XV

SIDONIVS GELASIO SVO SALVTEM

1. Probas (neque deprecor) me deliquisse; deliqui, quippe qui necdum nomine tuo ullas operi meo litteras iunxerim. sed tamen scribis tum quod erraverim veniabile fore, si quod et ipse decantes mittam ab exemplo, quia scilicet Tonantio meo ad parem causam futuras usui litteras bimetras miserim. praeter hoc quereris paginam meam, si resolvatur in lusum, solis hendecasyllabis frequentari. qua de re

[1] fatentes *C*.

[2] audient *ed. Sirmond.*: audiunt.

[3] recreaturis *C*: recreatur$\overset{u}{i}$s M^1: recreaturus *FP*: recreatus *Wilamowitz*: recitaturus *vulgo*. *Vix* remeaturis?

[4] laude *aut* laudibus *coni. Luetjohann.*

* Cf. *Ep.* IX. 16. 3. Not otherwise known.

[1] Cf. *Ep.* IX. 13.

[2] In which the trochee (– ⏑, pp. 590–591) is prominent.

indeed true that allowances must be made for the unacademic; but anyone who is so mean as to refuse praise to good writing when he recognises it, is recognised by good men for what he is—a character undeserving of their praise. 9. So I free your anxious heart from fear of such a misfortune; all will listen to you with approval and admiration, and we shall enjoy together the refreshing joys which you will bring. Many will praise your eloquence, most will praise your talent, all will praise your modesty; I say your modesty, for it will be considered no less to your honour that a young man or, more creditable still, one scarcely more than a boy, should carry off from the competition of a public examination the highest marks for character as well as for literary excellence. Farewell.

XV

SIDONIUS TO HIS FRIEND GELASIUS,* GREETING

1. You prove (and I do not demur) that I have misbehaved; I *have* misbehaved, in not yet having included in my work a letter addressed to you. Nevertheless, you write that my delinquency will be pardoned if only I follow precedent and send something in verse for you also to recite, because, to be sure, I have sent to my friend Tonantius [1] a letter in prose and verse for a similar purpose. You also complain that, when a letter of mine launches into the freedom of light verse, it is entirely filled by hendecasyllables.[2] You therefore demand a

trochaica garrulitate suspensa senariolos aliquos plus requiris. servio iniunctis; tu modo placidus excipias, sive oden [1] hanc ipsam mavis vocare sive eglogam. nam metrum diu infrequentatum durius texitur.

Iubes, amice, nostra per volumina
modis resultet incitatioribus
ferox iambus, ut [2] trochaeus hactenus,
pigrasque bigas et quaterna tempora
spondeus addat, ut moram volucripes
habeat parumper insitam [3] trimetria,
resonetque mixtus ille pes celerrimus,
bene nuncupatus quondam ab arte pyrricha,
loco locandus undecumque in ultimo;
spondam [4] daturus et subinde versui,
modo in priore parte, nunc [5] in extima
anapaestus, ipse quamquam et absolutius
pronuntietur, cum secuta tertia
geminae brevique longa adhaeret syllaba.[6]

[1] oden *Luetjohann*: odem *CF*: odē *M*: od$\overset{a}{e}$ P^1.
[2] ut *ed. Elmenhorst.*: et.
[3] insitam *vulgo*: insita.
[4] pondus *coni. Anderson*: pompam *Warmington.*
[5] non *aut* numquam *coni. Semple.*
[6] geminaeque adhaeret longa syllaba et brevi *coni. Warmington.*

---

[1] The metrical units here mentioned are as follows, if we use – for a long syllable, ◡ for short: iambus ◡ –; trochee – ◡ (not its resolution ◡◡◡ = tribrach); spondee – – ; pyrrhic ◡ ◡; anapaest ◡ ◡ –. The iambic line was a trimeter because it was envisaged as ◡ – ◡ – uttered three times.

[2] *spondam daturus . . . anapaestus*: I don't know what this means. Does he allude to the literal meaning of *ana-*

suspension of my trochaic garrulity in favour of some trifle in six-footed lines. I bow to your command—only you must give an indulgent reception to my piece, whether you choose to call it an ode or an eclogue; for composition in a metre long disused is harder work.

It is your will, my friend, that the spirited iambus [1] with its more vigorous strains should echo through my works as did the trochee heretofore; that the spondee should add its slow-moving pair of feet with its four time-units, thus for a moment inserting a check in the swift-footed trimeter; that, mingled with the rest, should resound that swiftest of feet well named of old from the art of pyrrhic dancing—a foot which must in every case be put in the final place; and the anapaest also, to give from time to time a frame to the iambic verse,[2] now in the first half, now in the last, though the anapaest is more readily pronounceable when the third syllable in the sequence (that is, the long syllable) clings closely to the syllable which has a twin and is short.

paestus (striking or struck backward), and is he speaking of dactyl or anapaest as the same three syllables in reversed order? I don't think Semple's explanation in *Quaest. Exeg.* pp. 60–61 will do—nor his emendation of *nunc* to *non*.—*A.* If we keep *nunc*, the meaning of the passage is this—"the anapaest, if used in an iambic line, provides a rim, a frame, at the beginning of the line or in the second half of the line—but unquestionably this alien foot in the iambic line is more easily spoken, is spoken with less entanglement, if it is included in one word and not syllabically divided between two words. —*W.H.S.* See Additional Notes, p. 619.

Quae temperare vix valet gregarius
poeta, ut ipse cernis esse Sollium;
mihi pecten errat [1] nec per ora concava
vaga lingua flexum competenter explicat
epos. sed istud aptius paraverit
Leo Leonis aut secutus orbitas
cantu in Latino, cum prior sit Attico
Consentiorum qui superstes est patri,
fide, voce, metris ad fluenta Pegasi
cecinisse dictus omniforme canticum,
quotiensque verba Graia carminaverit,
tenuisse celsa iunctus astra Pindaro
montemque victor isse per biverticem
nullis [2] secundus inter antra [3] Delphica.
at uterque vatum si lyrae poeticae
Latiare carmen aptet absque Dorico,
Venusina, Flacce, plectra ineptus exeras
Iapygisque verna cygnus Aufidi
Atacem tonare [4] cum suis oloribus
cana et canora colla victus ingemas.

[1] mihi pecten errat *Luetjohann*: mi in pectine errat *aut sim.*

[2] nulli *vulgo.*

[3] antra *Luetjohann*: astra.

[4] sonare *Leo.*

---

[1] Lit. " cannot properly straighten out, unravel, the tangle of my utterance." *epos* may perhaps mean " epic song," but I think this unlikely.—*A.*

[2] See *Ep.* IX. 13 for persons mentioned in this poem.

[3] *qui superstes est patri*: that one of the two Consentii who perpetuates his father's glory, or " in whom his father lives on."

[4] See p. 407, n. 6.

To mix these metres duly is scarcely in the power of such an ordinary poet as you yourself know Sollius to be; my quill strays uncertainly, and my tongue floundering in the chamber of my mouth has no skill to articulate the modulations of poetry.[1] Indeed, the poem you ask for would more fitly be composed by Leo, or by that other poet who has followed Leo's [2] tracks in Latin song, but is his superior in Greek, Consentius, who perpetuates his father's glory; [3] of him, it is said that he has sung by the waters of Pegasus,[4] with harmony of lyre and voice and metre, an ode that ranged through every form,[5] and that, whenever he made Greek words into song, he held the starry heights in Pindar's company and passed victorious over the twin-peaked mountain amid the caves of Delphi, second to none. But should either of these bards adapt to his poetic lyre a Latin song forsaking Greek, then, Flaccus, you would bring out your Venusine quill in a futile effort,[6] and you a native swan of Calabrian Aufidus, with your aged tuneful neck now humbled in defeat, would lament that Atax with its swans can bring forth tones of thunder.[7]

[5] *omniforme canticum*: " an ode that ranged through every form " or " sang every kind of song."—*A*.

[6] *plectra ineptus exeras*: " bring out your quill in a futile effort " or " you would be foolish to bring out " (as Purser takes it).—*A*.

[7] Venusia (Venosa to-day) was Horace's birthplace on the borders of Apulia; Iapygia was a name for Calabria, the S.E. of Italy; and the river Aufidus is the Ofanto. The Atax is a small river, now the Aude, in Gallia Narbonensis. Sidonius tiresomely prolongs the metaphorical contrast between Horace, the swan of Apulia, and his own contemporary swans of Southern Gaul.

Nec ista sola sunt perita pectora,
licet et peritis haec peritiora sint:
Severianus ista rhetor altius,
Afer vaferque Domnulus politius,
scholasticusque sub rotundioribus
Petrus Camenis dictitasset acrius,
epistularis usquequaque nec stilus
virum vetaret, ut stupenda pangeret.
potuisset ista semper efficacius
humo atque gente cretus in Ligustide
Proculus melodis insonare pulsibus
limans faceta quaeque sic poemata,
Venetam lacessat ut favore Mantuam
Homericaeque par et ipse gloriae,
rotas Maronis arte sectans [1] compari.
Ego corde et ore iure despicabilis
quid inter hosce te rogante garriam,
loquacitatis impudentiam probans [2]
animique vota destituta [3] litteris?
sed quid negabo nec pudore territus?
amor timere nescit: inde parui.

2. Ignosce desueta repetenti atque ob impleta quae iusseras nihil amplius quam raritatis indulgentiam praestolaturo. ceterum mihi si similia

[1] artexate *C*: artet axe *ed. Elmenhorst.* sectans Maronis arte compari rotas *coni. Warmington.*
[2] approbans *Leo.*
[3] destituta *Sirmond*: destentuta *CF*: *sim. indicant alii.*

---

[1] Mommsen takes *Afer* as a proper name. Mohr disagrees and thinks it an adjective.—*A.* Clearly Sidonius has used *Afer* merely to get the word-play with *vafer*. I would incline to Mohr's opinion.—*W.H.S.* Perhaps Aper (*Ep.* IV. 21; V. 14).

"Nor are these two the only skilled minds, albeit they are more skilled than the skilled. Severianus the rhetor would have written these lines more sublimely, 'African '[1] and astute Domnulus more elegantly; the learned[2] Petrus, with his more polished Muse,[3] would have written with greater force, nor would his constant letter-writing have prevented such a man from composing wondrous verse. Proculus,[4] sprung from Ligurian soil and race, could with more masterly effect have made these verses ring with tuneful lyre-throbs—he who gives all his poems such a graceful finish that he challenges Venetian Mantua[5] by the plaudits he wins, matching even the glory of Homer as he follows Virgil's chariot with a skill no less than equal.

"But why should I, in talent and tongue so worthy of contempt, why should I babble in such company at your request, exposing thereby the shamelessness of my garrulity, exposing my heart's ambitions to be so destitute of literary skill? Well, what shall I refuse if not even shame deters me? Love knows no fear; that is why I have obeyed you."

2. Forgive this reversion to a form of composition I am no longer used to. The utmost I shall expect for carrying out your orders is the indulgence due to an exercise rarely practised. But if you give me

[2] *scholasticus*: "the savant" or "the learned."—*A*.

[3] *sub rotundioribus . . . Camenis*: "with his more polished, more finished Muse." But Purser takes it "in more ample strains."—*A*.

[4] Not he of *Ep*. IV. 23.

[5] Near Mantua was Andes (Pietola? to-day), Virgil's birthplace. On the text of l. 49 see Additional Notes, p. 622.

post iusseris,[1] quo queam fieri magis obsequens, sic curabis [2] ad vicem carminis aut dictare [3] quae cantem aut saltare [4] quae rideam. vale.

XVI

SIDONIVS FIRMINO SVO SALVTEM

1. Si recordaris, domine fili, hoc mihi iniunxeras, ut hic nonus libellus peculiariter tibi dicatus [5] ceteris octo copularetur, quos ad Constantium scripsi, virum singularis ingenii, consilii salutaris, certe in tractatibus publicis ceteros eloquentes, seu diversa sive paria decernat, praestantioris facundiae dotibus antecellentem. sponsio impleta est, non quidem exacte, sed vel instanter. 2. nam peragratis forte dioecesibus [6] cum domum veni, si quod

[1] iusseris *codd.*: iniunxeris *Wilamowitz.*

[2] si curabis *aut* sic curabis *codd.*: scilicet curabis *coni. Luetjohann*: ipse curabis *Wilamowitz*: sis curabis *Engelbrecht.*

[3] (si curabis, *etc.*) dicta *Mommsen.*

[4] salta *Mommsen.*

[5] dicatus *Luetjohann*: dictatus.

[6] diocesibus *MCFP.*

---

[1] *curabis ad vicem carminis*, etc.: "you must, in return for my poem, either write something for me to recite or perform some dance to make me laugh." This seems to be the meaning. But *in formatae vicem* of *Ep.* VII. 2. 1 seems to be a different use, and all other instances I have noted of *ad vicem* are used absolutely—"turn and turn about."—*A.* I wonder whether the last sentence could mean "you must see to it that, in return for my poem, you either compose a poem for me to sing or with appropriate gesture recite it for me to laugh at." Cf. Ovid, *Tristia* II. 519–520, *et mea sunt populo*

similar orders in future, then, to make me more inclined to oblige you, you must make it your business, in return for my poem, either to write something for me to sing or perform one of your dances for me to laugh at.[1] Farewell.

XVI

SIDONIUS TO HIS FRIEND FIRMINUS,* GREETING

1. If you remember, my Lord and Son, you had urged that this ninth book specially dedicated to you should be added to the other eight, which I had inscribed to Constantius,[2] that man of unique talent and wholesome judgment, who in his public discourses[3] certainly excels all other speakers—whether he agrees with or differs from them—by virtue of his pre-eminent eloquence. My promise is now fulfilled, not indeed perfectly, but at least promptly.[4] 2. For when I got home after a diocesan visitation,[5] I copied out hastily and under pressure,

saltata poemata saepe,|saepe oculos etiam detinuere tuos.—*W.H.S.*

* See *Ep.* IX. 1, first note.

[2] See *Ep.* I. 1; III. 2; VII. 18; VIII. 16.

[3] *in tractatibus publicis*: Dalton gives "discussion of public affairs." But *tractatibus* need not mean "affairs" in Sidonius.—*A.*

[4] *non quidem exacte sed vel instanter*: In Sidonius *exacte* means "with the perfection of good taste."—*W.H.S.* *Instanter* is rather difficult, but I think "zealously" is pretty near.—*A.*

[5] *peragratis . . . dioecesibus*: properly "after a tour of the parishes." *dioecesis* sometimes means "parish."—*A.*

schedium temere iacens chartulis putribus ac veternosis continebatur, raptim coactimque translator festinus exscripsi, tempore hiberno nil retardatus, quin actutum iussa complerem, licet antiquarium moraretur insiccabilis gelu pagina et calamo durior gutta, quam iudicasses imprimentibus digitis non fluere sed frangi. sic quoque tamen compotem officii prius agere curavi, quam duodecimum nostrum, quem Numae mensem vos nuncupatis, Favonius flatu teporo pluviisque natalibus maritaret. 3. restat, ut te arbitro non reposcamur res omnino discrepantissimas, maturitatem celeritatemque. nam quotiens liber quispiam scribi cito iubetur, non tantum honorem spectat auctor a merito quantum ab obsequio. de reliquo, quia tibi nuper ad Gelasium virum sat benignissimum missos iambicos [1] placuisse pronuntias, per hos te quoque Mytilenaei oppidi vernulas munerabor.

Iam per alternum pelagus loquendi
egit audacem mea cymba cursum
nec bipertito timuit fluento
flectere clavum.

[1] iambos *coni. Luetjohann.*

---

[1] *translator*: this is the noun for *transferre* which is used for "to transcribe."—*A.*

[2] Does this imply a papyrus wrapper?—*A.*

[3] *Favonius . . . pluviisque natalibus*: *i.e.* rains from the region of his birth—the west.—*A.* Maybe "life-giving rains."

[4] *mensem*: February, the twelfth month if the year is taken to begin in March. Cf. *Ep.* II. 14. 2.

[5] Traditional King of ancient Rome who was said to have

working in a fury of transcription,[1] all the bits of writing that lay about at random in crumbling worn-out papers:[2] nor did I let the wintry season hinder me from at once carrying out your orders, although the amanuensis was delayed by the cold which prevented the page from drying and by the ink-drops freezing harder than the pen, so that you might have thought them to be not flowing but breaking into pieces when his fingers pressed the nib. But even so, I strove to fulfil my obligation before the west wind with its warm breath and native[3] rains should arrive to fertilise the month that we reckon the twelfth[4] and you call Numa's[5] month. 3. It remains for you, in judging my work, not to require of me two entirely incompatible things, finish and speed; for whenever the writing of a book is demanded at short notice the author looks for credit more on the ground of obedience than of merit. As a conclusion, since you assure me that you enjoyed the iambics I sent to my very kind friend Gelasius,[6] I will reward you in your turn with these humble natives[7] of the town of Mytilene.

"Now my ship has driven its bold course over the twin seas of utterance,[8] nor has it feared to guide its helm through the two sundered streams.

added two months (to a Roman year of ten months), January and February.

[6] Cf. *Ep.* IX. 15.

[7] *Mytilenaei oppidi vernulas*: *i.e.* Sapphic verses, Sappho having been a native of Mytilene in the island Lesbos.

[8] Prose and verse.

Solvit antemnas, legit alta vela,
palmulam ponit manus, atque transtris
litori iunctis petit osculandam
saltus harenam.

Mussitans quamquam chorus invidorum
prodat hirritu rabiem canino,
nil palam sane loquitur pavetque
publica puncta.

Verberant puppim, quatiunt carinam,
ventilant spondas laterum rotundas,
arborem circa volitant sinistrae
sibila linguae.

Nos tamen rectam comite arte proram,
nil tumescentes veriti procellas,
sistimus portu, geminae potiti
fronde coronae,

Quam mihi indulsit populus Quirini,
blattifer vel quam tribuit senatus,
quam peritorum dedit ordo consors
iudiciorum,

Cum meis poni statuam perennem
Nerva Traianus titulis videret,
inter auctores utriusque fixam
bybliothecae;

Quamque post, visus prope, post bilustre
tempus accepi, capiens honorem,

---

[1] Prose and verse again.
[2] The Romans.

"Now my hand loosens the yards, furls the tall sails, and lays down the oars, and I leap from the thwarts alongside the shore, eager to kiss the land.

"Though the muttering chorus of my detractors betrays its rage by dog-like snarling, they utter not a single word aloud, fearing the voice of public favour accorded me.

"Malignant hissing tongues lash the stern and shake the keel; they sway the rounded framework of the sides and flit around the mast.

"But I, fearing not at all the swelling storms, have guided my prow with the skill that never leaves me, and now bring her to rest in the harbour, having gained the leafage of a double crown.[1]

"One crown was bestowed on me by Quirinus' people [2] and by the purple-clad senate, and by the learned company of judges unanimously,

"When Nerva Trajan [3] saw my statue,[4] with all my honours inscribed, set up for all time, firmly fixed amidst the writers of the two libraries.[5]

"The second crown was that which ten [6] years later I was awarded when received into the Presence,[7]

[3] Nerva was Emperor A.D. 96–98. But Sidonius here means Nerva's adopted son Trajan the next emperor A.D. 98–117, who completed a famous Forum at Rome.

[4] In bronze, set up in the reign of Avitus (Emperor in A.D. 455–456) after his son-in-law Sidonius had spoken in his honour a panegyric (*Carm.* VII.). Cf. *Carm.* VIII. 7–10.

[5] One devoted to Greek literature, the other to Latin.

[6] In fact, twelve.

[7] I recall a phrase in *Ep.* VIII. 9, in *carm.* 17, *nos istic positos semelque visos*, "only once admitted into the King's presence." So here, "admitted to the presence (of the Emperor Anthemius)," or, "seen near at hand in Rome, not at a distance in Gaul."—*W.H.S.*

qui patrum ac plebis simul unus olim
iura gubernat.

Praeter heroos ioca multa multis
texui pannis; elegos frequenter
subditos senis pedibus rotavi
commate bino.

Nunc per undenas equitare suetus
syllabas lusi celer atque metro
Sapphico creber cecini, citato
rarus iambo.

Nec recordari queo, quanta quondam
scripserim primo iuvenis calore;
unde pars maior utinam taceri
possit [1] et abdi!

Nam senectutis propiore meta
quicquid extremis sociamur annis,
plus pudet, si quid leve lusit aetas,
nunc reminisci.

Quod perhorrescens ad epistularum
transtuli cultum genus omne curae,
ne reus cantu petulantiore
sim reus actu;

Neu puter solvi per amoena dicta,
schema si chartis phalerasque iungam,
clerici ne quid maculet rigorem
fama poetae.

on the occasion when I took up that office [1] which, since of old, singly controls the rights of senate and people alike.

"Besides my hexameter verses I have fashioned many sportive poems in many patterns: oft have I turned off two-limbed [2] pentameters placed under hexameters.

"Yet again, I have amused myself, a practised rider, by cantering through the eleven syllables, and many a time I have sung in the Sapphic measure, but rarely in the swift iambic.

"Nor can I recall how many things I wrote in the first fervour of youth; I only wish that most of them might be buried in silence!

"For as the bourn of old age draws nearer, the closer I get to my last years, the more I am ashamed to remember now the flippant frolics of my youth.

"Appalled by this memory, I have transferred my study in all its forms to the cultivation of letter-writing, lest, guilty as I was of wanton song, I should be guilty also of wanton deed;

"And lest I should be thought a voluptuary demoralised by prettiness of language if I added to my pages tropes and trappings, so that my fame as a poet might not cast a slur on my strictness as a cleric.

[1] Office of Prefect of the City, *i.e.* Rome, conferred on Sidonius in A.D. 468 by Anthemius, Emperor A.D. 467–472. The holder of this office was "President" of the Senate. Stevens, *Sid. Apoll.*, 100 ff. Chaix, I. 16–17.

[2] The pentameter was metrically divided into halves.

---

[1] posset *Luetjohann.*

Denique ad quodvis epigramma posthac
non ferar pronus, teneroque metro
vel gravi nullum cito cogar exhinc
promere carmen:

Persecutorum nisi quaestiones
forsitan dicam meritosque caelum
martyras mortis pretio parasse
praemia vitae.

E quibus primum mihi psallat hymnus
qui Tolosatem tenuit cathedram,
de gradu summo Capitoliorum
praecipitatum;

Quem negatorem Iovis ac Minervae
et crucis Christi bona confitentem
vinxit ad tauri latus iniugati
plebs furibunda,

Vt per abruptum bove concitato
spargeret cursus lacerum cadaver
cautibus tinctis calida soluti
pulte cerebri.

Post Saturninum volo plectra cantent,
quos patronorum reliquos probavi
anxio duros mihi per labores
auxiliatos,

Singulos quos nunc pia nuncupatim
non valent versu cohibere verba;
quos tamen chordae nequeunt sonare,
corda sonabunt.

"Lastly I shall not henceforth plunge headlong into the writing of a trivial poem, nor from this time on shall I be easily induced to produce a poem in either light or weighty measure—

"Unless perhaps I tell of the inquisitions of the persecutors[1] and how the martyrs, earning a place in heaven, won the reward of life at the cost of death.

"Of these may he[2] be the first theme of my hymn who held the bishop's throne at Toulouse and was flung headlong from the topmost step of the Capitol;[3]

"Who for denying Jove and Minerva[4] and confessing the blessings of Christ's cross was tied by the maddened mob to the side of a bull that had not known the yoke,

"That, the beast being driven wildly down the steep, its rushing course might scatter asunder his torn body, staining the rocks with the warm pulp of his mangled brain.

"After Saturninus I would have my quill sound the praises of the other patrons whom I have found to be helpers in my hard struggles when my heart was troubled.

"These my grateful words cannot now fit by name within the limits of verse; but though my harp cannot sound their names, my heart shall ever sound their praise."

[1] Anderson wrote "trials of the persecuted"; but here *persecutorum* must be genitive plural of *persecutor*.

[2] Saint Saturninus, the first Bishop of Toulouse, martyred in the second half of the third century (Gregory of Tours, *Hist. Franc.* I. 28; *Acta Sanctorum*, Nov. 29).

[3] At Toulouse, not at Rome.

[4] Taken as typical heathen gods.

4. Redeamus in fine[1] ad oratorium stilum materiam praesentem proposito semel ordine terminaturi, ne, si epilogis musicis opus prosarium clauserimus, secundum regulas Flacci, ubi amphora coepit institui, urceus potius exisse videatur. vale.

[1] fine *Luetjohann*: finem.

4. In conclusion, let me return to prose style and so bring my present material to an end according to the plan [1] which I determined at the outset, lest, if I round off my prose with a poetic epilogue, it might look like what Horace has in his manual—the wine jar that was to have been moulded turning out to be a pitcher instead.[2] Farewell.

[1] *Ordine* may refer to word-order. But I do not think so here, where " plan " is much more suitable.—*A.*

[2] Horace, *Ars Poetica*, 21–22 *amphora coepit|institui: currente rota cur urceus exit?*

ADDITIONAL NOTES ON THE TEXT

III. 2. 3: *valles lapsuum adsiduitate derasas.* "Valleys scraped down by frequent landslides" gives such good and graphic sense (better perhaps than even *derosas* would) that one may be surprised that this reading of the MSS could be doubted. But in preceding antithetic phrases the epithets are *putres, tribulosas, asperos, lubricos,* and *salebrosos,* all adjectives and all apparently containing an element of meaning which refers to the feelings of travellers. Not so the participle *derasas.* Changes such as *taediosas* (proposed by Wilamowitz) or *desperatas* or *dolosas* or *onerosas* or *molestas* suggest themselves but none except possibly *desperatas* is worth pressing. To take *lapsuum adsiduitate* as "frequency of falls" of travellers seems out of the question. If *derasas* is right, it indicates probably that the Romans thought rather of the sides of a valley than its hollow.

III. 3. 7: Anderson accepted either the conjecture of Engelbrecht or that of Luetjohann. But it seems to me needless to reject the reading *quam villis* of the MSS. A more literal rendering than the one given now on page 19 would be "as if it would involve less revelation of identity to have abandoned a man beheaded than to be recognised while still topped with one's tufts of hair." *Villus* is normally used of the shaggy hair of some animals.

IV. 10. 2: *qui parum cultior est*: here *qui* codd. *L T*: *qua C F*: *ali*[a]*q ex pte* in marg. F^1: *quo P*: *quo*[in] M^1. Then *cultior est LMTCP*: *cultiorē F*. Luetjohann suggests [*qui*] *parum cultiorem*. Perhaps simply *qua* (*CF*) *parum cultior est* "where it is too little polished."

IV. 20. 1: 1. *frequenter arma et armatum et armatos inspicere* is supported by the writers of MSS *VCF* (and by the " correctors " M^1 P^1).
2. *frequenter arma et armatum et animatos inspicere* is supported by the writers of *MP* (and the " corrector " T^2).
3. *frequenter arma et armatos inspicere* is supported by the writers of *LNT* (and by the " corrector " R^2, the writer of *R* having put senseless *frequenter arma et armatu et armatus inspicere*).

Of these readings 1 and 3 have roughly equal support, 3 having the testimony of the best MS. Sidonius may indeed have written all three things *arma et armatum et armatos* " arms and armour and armed men "; but this has only partial support in the MSS; " arms and armour " have not obviously got each a separate word in Latin; and the expression itself suggests that in *et armatum* and *et armatos* (or possibly in *arma*) some repetition has occurred in copying. Hence the guess *et animatos* of some MSS—unless this is a miscopying of *armatos*. Now *arma et armatos* looks quite natural, " arms and men in arms." But what produced *armatum* in the tradition? Quite likely the cause was that Sidonius actually wrote in this sentence *arma et armatum* only—" arms and armour." *Armatus* (4th declension masculine) was properly a word for " arms and armour " (Livy XXXIII. 3. 10; XXXVII. 40. 13; XLI. 55. 10; Curtius, III, 2. 5; Fronto, 206 p. 19 Naber), but occurs also in the sense of " (armed) soldiery " (Livy XXVI. 5. 3; XXXVII. 41. 3). Now in all instances (Burke cites two only) this word is in the ablative case *armatu* (a fact not mentioned by Burke); *armatu* is what the original writer of MS. *R* put here without sense. So, we may argue, after Sidonius had written the accusative *armatum* contrary to custom, it was, in the transmission of his letters, expanded by the intrusion of *et armatos* either as an explanation of *et armatum* in the sense of " and armed soldiers," or as an addition intended to take the place of an apparently past participle passive masculine singular *armatum* " an armed man." I would myself suggest that, if we treat as an intrusion not *et armatos* but *arma* or *arma et* (intruded by dittography), then we have a not un-Sidonian expression *frequenter et armatum et armatos inspicere* without any tautology, " to gaze on both arms and armed men " from which the first *et* could be

omitted. However, maybe we ought to accept Burke's rejection of *et armatos* and to read *frequenter arma et armatum inspicere*.

V. 2. 1: Wilamowitz wished to interchange the positions of *musica* and *metrica* so as to read *metrica ponderat. . . . musica modulatur*. This looks a tempting alteration, but Anderson seems to have been right in keeping the order shown in the MSS. If we were to read *musica moderatur . . . metrica modulatur*, we would get a Sidonian word-play besides the antithesis. But we need not father on Sidonius more of such artifices than we know him to have been prone to.

V. 8. 3: *quos nostra iudicia saeculi culpa fortunatos putant* needs further consideration. *nostra iudicia saecula loca* (codd. *MTCFP*) is indeed possible—" our judgments, the passing ages, the various places "; not so *nostra iudicia saeculi loca* (cod. *L*). Sidonius has just before mentioned *aurea saecla*, where the plural is poetic for the singular, " golden age." It is likely that Sidonius would go on to contrast the present age, " our " age, in the normal manner of " moralising," but not by suggesting in prose a plural *nostra saecula* " our ages." *nostri iudicia saeculi⟨et⟩loca* is doubtfully acceptable; *nostra iudicia saeculi culpa* (thus Leo, as in our text here) is possible; *nostra* (or *nostri*) *iudicia saeculi loci* (" according to the age and locality ") is also possible. Although no MS has *nostri*, I favour reading either *quos nostra iudicia saeculi loco fortunatos putant* " whom our judgments regard as fortunate in wordly degree " (*saeculi loco*); or *quos nostri iudicia saeculi loco fortunatos putant* " whom the judgments of our age regard as fortunate by mere circumstance " (or " position " or " rank ").

VI. 12. 8: *Arelatenses . . . exsolvat.* Sidonius' meaning is clear, but how he expressed it is not certain. It is perhaps rash to alter, as Luetjohann did, the two plurals (if they are wrong, the errors were caused partly by assimilation to *gratias*, in copying). Several times we find in Latin that a person of *Avennio* was called *Avenniensis*; but the form used later

was *Avennicus,* as indeed cod. *F* of Sidonius has here. Only once elsewhere do we find anything similar to *Avenniocus* of other Sidonian MSS, namely in Gregory of Tours, *Hist. Franc.,* IV. 42, where we have *in Avennioco* (with variant readings *Avenioco* and *Avennico*) *terreturio.* If we accept such slender support, all we need to do in this passage of Sidonius is to add punctuation and to fill out the syntax thus: *Arelatenses Reienses* (sc. *exsolvant*), *Avenniocus Arausionensis quoque et Albensis* (sc. *exsolvat* or *exsolvant*), *Valentinaeque . . . possessor exsolvat.* I punctuate accordingly on p. 282 and modify Anderson's translation. If we prefer to emend, I suggest reading *Avennionis* and putting this name, as the first of three genitives singular of cities, after *Albensis.* We would thus have a not un-Sidonian sequence—a pair of nominatives plural, a pair of nominatives singular, and a pair of genitives singular to which is added, as if in afterthought introduced by the words *nec non et,* a third.

VII. 6. 2: *istius aeris lupus.* Mohr and Anderson accepted the conjecture *aetatis* of M^1. I thought of emending to *aeri is* or *aevi* or *aedis* ("the House," meaning the Church) or *arcis* or *generis* (on the assumption that an abbreviation for *gen* was miscopied). But *aeris* of the original writers of the available MSS might well be sound. Both pagans and Christians imagined our air to be inhabited by spirits and powers perceived mentally. Thus Varro, according to Augustine, *de Civitate Dei,* VII 6, spoke of *aeriae animae,* perceived by the mind only, existing between the orbit of the moon and the clouds and winds of the earth; Chalcidius, *Comment. in Timonem Plat.* 134 says *quae potestates aetherii sunt aeriique daemones*; Servius *ad Aen.* IV. 201 says that *potestates* are *terrenae* or *aeriae* or *aetheriae;* and Paulinus of Nola, *Carm.* XV 49 has *aerios proceres vincens in corpore nostro;* cf. also Augustine, *de Civ. Dei,* VIII. 16; Martianus Capella, VIII. 910; Cassianus, *Collationes,* XV. 8; and also XVIII. 16. 2 (*aerii hostis insidias*). Further, in translating the passage where Paul writes τὰς ἀρχὰς . . . τὰς ἐξουσίας . . . τοὺς κοσμοκράτορας τοῦ σκότου τούτου, in the Epistle to the Ephesians, VI. 12, whereas the Vulgate has, for τοῦ σκότου τούτου, *tenebrarum harum,* the codices of the Old Latin version have

aeris huius. Lastly, Augustine again in *de Civitate Dei* XIV. 3 speaks of the Devil as in *carceribus caliginosi huius aeris aeterno supplicio destinatus.* From this evidence it is clear that the Christians thought of *aer* as a region, haunted by maleficent spirits and powers, between the earth and heaven but belonging to the earth. So in Sidonius' letter here we might ignore *aetatis* and any other conjecture, and keep the reading *aeris.* Sidonius clearly refers to Euric, and might represent him as a personified but spiritual wolf or power in this earth's air—"a wolf of this our worldly clime." But Semple insists that the image of an air-borne wolf raiding the *ecclesiasticas caulas* is too bizarre even for Sidonius; and I am inclined to agree.

VII. 7. 1: *si tamen* ⟨. . . .⟩ *aut cataplus arriserit.* If we omit *aut* or accept *ante* with Gustafsson, we can keep *tamen* or change it to *tandem* without assuming a lacuna in the text. But if *tamen aut* before *cataplus* is right, a lacuna there must be. It could be filled by *sors* (thus Semple suggests) or by *fatum,* which might, more easily than *sors,* drop out before *aut* (either word could be substituted for *tamen,* again getting rid of the lacuna). But it looks as if a word connected with land-trade could come well here, instead of *tamen.* Did Sidonius write here *trāmen* or *trahamen*? It is a word which does not occur but could be deduced from *traharii* of *Ep.* VI. 1. 3. (page 248). The meaning would be "sledge-traffic," "land-transport." I admit that in VI. 8. 1 also we have (again connected with Amantius) *cataplus* mentioned, without any alternative, in an undisputed passage. So I do not stress my suggestion, and would prefer to accept Gustafsson's *si tamen ante.*

VII. 9. 1: *quam videor* looks troublesome. But it simply introduces a (mock-) modest colloquial understatement like the common interjection of *opinor* "I think," "I believe," when *I* with everyone else know. (In *Ep.* III. 1. 2 Sidonius uses the expression '*praepositus videor*' even of his office as bishop.) If we change it, the following suggestions go in descending order of improbability: *rideor* "I am laughed at" or "People smile at" (or "ridear" "I might be laughed at"); but (deus

bone!) this is hardly in Sidonius' character and certainly not in keeping with the address itself, which he quotes in full later in this letter; *rideo* "I laugh" and *rubeo* "I blush" are likelier. More probable would be *confiteor* or *fateor* "I confess"; or I would accept *qua* (of the good cod. *L*) *videor* "in which I seem to have adopted a conversational tone". This agrees with a statement made by Sidonius himself about the nature of the address, though the address itself does not strike us as conversational; *sermocinari* is not properly a transitive verb, but *quam*, if not taken with *sermocinatus*, could go with any of my suggestions except *rideor* or *ridear*. But I retain *videor*.

VIII. 6. 5: *consuli proximis proximus eram.* Everybody from ancient scribes to modern scholars inclusive wants to have a try at this one. The reading of *L* (accepted by Luetjohann) *consulis proximae* (sc. *turmae*) *proximus eram* means "I was the very nearest of the consul's troop" (of census-officers) "which was the nearest to him". The following is possible: *consuli proximae proximus eram* so that with *adhaerebam sellae curuli* . . . the sentence means "I stuck close to the curule chair . . . and, mingled with the troop of cloaked census-officers which was nearest to the consul, I was nearest of all". This would mean that *L*, the best MS, is wrong by only one letter. The original reading of *MP consuli proxime proximus* "I was most nearly the nearest to the consul" seems rather forced, but might be Sidonian. The text of Sirmond has *proxime consuli proximis eram.*

VIII. 6. 11: *et quidem solus.* Translating this doubtful passage Anderson put "and you're the only man that does so" which I did not like because *solus* (if right) would seem to mean "alone," "without human companions." So I have substituted an ambiguous rendering. *Equis idem solis* "and also with horses alone" has occurred to me. If *solus* is wrong, I suggest *etsi quidem* (so cod. *L*) *Scoticis* "although indeed they are Scottish hounds." The same sense would be implied by *et his quidem* (so Mommsen) *Scoticis* or *et sic quidem Scoticis.* Such dogs were brought to Rome in iron cages and let loose among the wild animals in the circus (Symmachus *Ep.* II. 77).

They were, not "Scotties" nor probably Scottish mastiffs, but rather Irish wolf-hounds.

VIII. 11. 10: *si qua vel quoquo modo sunt*. In the Latin on p. 568 I give the text as it is in Luetjohann and in Mohr, but discuss it further here. The MSS have:

si qua vel quoquo L^1
si qua vel quoque L
si qua quoque N
qualia vel quoque T
qualia quoque N^1*MCFP*

From cod. *R* this part of Sidonius is missing. Several points arise, in which it does not matter whether we take *si qua* to be *si quă* "if any" or *si quā* "if in any way." (i) *vel* has the authority of the best MS *L* and of *T*; but Mohr would delete it. (ii) *quoquo* is based simply on an alteration by L^1 of *quoque* in *L*; *quoque* (which must be *quōque* because *quŏque* cannot by any means make sense) is what all the MSS have and what their archtype must presumably have had. I feel that if Sidonius had written *quoquo* it would never have been altered in copying even by writers such as he of cod *L* whose Latinity was "vulgar" rather than "good." Although *quoque* will not make sense here, *quōque* will in the uncommon meaning of *quocumque* or *quoquo*, as elsewhere in Sidonius (*Ep.* IV. 11. 22 *quisque doles*; VII. 9. 5 *quisque coeperat*; the present letter VIII. 11. 13. *quisque praesumpserit*; IX. 4. 3. *quisque consequitur*; and other examples, all in the nominative singular). (iii) The second point indicated above suggests that not only *vel* but also either (and preferably) *si qua* or (less reasonably) *quoque modo* should be deleted, on the ground that *vel* could originally be a scribe's intrusion meaning "or alternatively." *si qua* is not supported by MSS other than *L* and *N*, the favoured reading in MSS being *qualia*. But *qualia* cannot stand for *qualiacumque* as *quōque* can for *quoquo* or *quocumque*, though Sirmond seems to have thought so, reading *qualia, quoque modo sint*. I think we must reject *qualia* and return to *si qua*. So I suggest either: (iv) Accept *si qua vel quoque modo sunt* of *L* and translate: "these matters, if there is anything in them or whatever the fashion of them is,

. . ." or: (v) read *signa vel quoque modo sunt* "these matters, whatever even the position of constellations is" (the import of the Latin could be purposely vague here). Omission of *vel* would get rid of all awkwardness here except that, if *signa* is admitted as right, *falsa* and *fallentia* should really apply to *signa* but in fact apply to astrology in general. Later in the text of this doubtful sentence I accept *rectius coram* of *LNT* in place of *rectius cohaeret* of *MCPV*. Sirmond accepts *cohaeret*, omitting *rectius*. But in Pliny, *Ep*. VIII. 22. 4 we have *sed melius coram*, which seems conclusive.

IX. 1. 5: *studium* of cod. *F*. With others I have come to suspect this word, which seems to me to have been intruded. *P* has *cū in ceteris rebus tū*, as also has M^2 (codd. *L N* and *T* omit the whole Epistle; *R* and *V* are lacking here). This prompts us to read: *etsi Apollinaris tuus cum in ceteris rebus tum est in hac re certe neglegentissimus*' . . . —"Although your friend Apollinaris is, as in other matters, so also in this one surely, a listless fellow, . . ." This is an emotional and sweeping statement such as anyone might make of anyone, though we must not overlook the possibility that Sidonius was so influenced by his predecessor in correspondence Cicero as to write of Apollinaris as Cicero did of his own son. In any case, I suggest that, in the transmission of the text, *cū* (= *cum*) was altered in error to *cui*; then, to make some sense of *cui*, a word *studium* (*F*: *studi* //// M^1 in a margin) or *animus* (*cui anim' cū* cod. *C*) was added. No change of *cui* to *qui* can make sense.

The corruption dealt with in this note and the omission of this whole letter IX. 1 by some codd. may have arisen like other deliberate omissions (but for a different reason) at a very early stage in the transmission of Sidonius' published letters, from deliberate suppression, on the part of the Visigoths in the first instance, with whom Apollinaris was in high favour.

IX. 3. 5: *licet olim*. I would be prepared to keep *licet enim* and to translate: "for it is true I listened long ago to your preaching, sometimes extempore, sometimes . . . carefully prepared, and became hoarse with applause; but I did so especially when . . ."

IX. 11. 10: *quorsum quam moris est* codd. *MCP*. This might be taken as *Quorsum*? *Quam moris est*! "Whither tends all this? How true to my custom!" But *F* has *quorsum quod morarum est* (and M^1 put something similar); this might be right (or *morae* instead of *morarum*)—"whither tends what involves delays?" Yet it looks like a conjecture. *Quorsum*? *quid morarum* Wouweren: *quorsum ista, quid morarum* Sirmond. Possible is: *Quorsum? Quam morae est*! "Whither tends all this? How it delays us!"

IX. 13. 2nd *carm.* 23 *vacante panno.* In lines 20–27 Sidonius describes a hunting-scene woven into a tapestry. In the Latin text we may rule out such possibilities as *volante* and *volente* and other verbs, even *patente* and other possibilities which have occurred to me, such as *cavo ante* (cloth "which was an empty hollow before"), as being little better than *vacante,* and *sequente* (cloth "which follows" as a complete whole on the completion of the various figures); we should reject Wouweren's tempting *vocante* ("inviting," "provoking") and the feasible alternative *vagante* ("wandering," with scene shifting as the eye moves), and maintain the manuscripts' reading *vacante.* Then what is meant by *vacante* as applied to *panno* "cloth"?—"roomy" thinks Anderson; "motionless" Chaix with Savaron; "empty" Semple (*Quaest. Exeg.* 58–59) in the sense of not having in fact the real things depicted on it. It is true that Sidonius in his description suggests the illusory nature of the scene. Thus there is *cruor* but not real blood, wounds well imitated in scarlet, animals that are merely images, ranges of hills that are simply woven. Yet the cloth is at the same time not "empty," but full. Some "oxymoron" or some double meaning is involved, I believe. The cloth is "empty" of real things; it is also, compared with the scene shown on it, "invisible" (*latente* is possible here), and appears to have no entity or function of its own. There is no single English word which could well cover all the senses. I suggest that we translate "while the cloth takes a holiday"—this gets one of the meanings of *vacare.*

ADDITIONAL NOTES ON THE TEXT

IX. 13, the second *carm.*, 68–71:

> *bimari remittat urbe*
> *thymelen palenque doctas*
> *tepidas ad officinas*
> *citharistrias Corinthus. . . .*

Instead of *tepidas* in line 70 Anderson was strongly in favour of the conjecture *lepidas* "elegant." But the MSS can, I suggest, be defended for alternative reasons. (i) *officina* is properly any workshop, here a training-school; *tepidus* properly means "fairly warm" or "lukewarm" or (mentally) "languid." Here Sidonius perhaps transfers the idea of a warm workshop or forge and of the heat of the workers' bodies therein to a training school, but puts the word *tepidas* to imply moderately fervent or energetic, perhaps because the people attending it are to be women engaged in activities less violent than a forge or some other "workshop" might suggest; whereas *calidas* (which could fit into the line equally well) "hot," "warm," would apply to real forges or the like for the more violent work of men. (ii) But I believe *tepidas* is used here as Catullus in that magnificently powerful poem LXIII, 65–66 "*mihi ianuae frequentes, mihi limina tepida;* | *mihi floridis corollis redimita domus erat.*" "I had doorways that were warm" that is, with visitors (cf. our "house-warming"). So here in Sidonius *tepidas* would mean simply well-visited. Dalton (Vol. II, p. 252) compares Sidonius, *Carm.* XXIII. 131–132 (see Loeb Sidonius, Vol. I; Anderson, in *Classical Quarterly*, XXVIII, 21–22; Semple, *Quaest. Exeg.*, 115–116) where we have:

> hic cum senipedem stilum polibat
> Zmyrnaeae vice doctus officinae . . .

Now Anderson there adopts, as does Loyen also in the first volume of the Budé Sidonius, the reading *vice* of cod. *C*, and translates "When he (sc. Homer) skilfully embellished the six-footed style after the manner of Smyrna's school . . ." Dalton on the other hand, in his note on the present passage in the Letters and citing the passage in *Carm.* XXIII mentions *incude doctus* (*doctas* in Dalton is a misprint) where *incude* is the reading of *F*. Now this word *incūde* is there unmetrical because *incŭde* is required. But it could be right—Sidonius is

fond of *incus* "anvil" and may have erred, shortening the sound *ū* to *ŭ*. If so, then the translation there might be "when, taught by" (or "at") "the anvil of Smyrna's workshop, he embellished . . ." In section 2 of the present letter IX. 13 Sidonius speaks of poetry "shaped on the Horatian anvil" (cf. Ep. VII. 17. 1 "the anvils of my old workshop" cf. IV. 1. 3; IV. 8. 5). But I feel that, in *Carm.* XXIII, *incude* is an intelligent though unmetrical guess in *F* as a correction for *cute* (*cute* is accepted by Luetjohann and by Mohr) of other MSS. *cute* means "in skin" which seems senseless here ("*ego te intus et in cute novi*" of Persius, III. 30 "I know you inside and out" is of no apparent help here). In place of it I would suggest not *inclyta* or *inclita* (Sidonius' spelling elsewhere) "renowned things," which I once thought of, but *cata* "clever things." However, *doctus* can take a genitive of what one is learned in; and one can be learned as regards an *officina*. But this leaves *vice* and *cute* unaccounted for. If Sidonius had written *bene doctus* it would not have been altered; nor would *puto doctus*.

IX. 15. *carm.* 10 ff.:

spondam daturus et subinde versui,
modo in priore parte, nunc in extima
anapaestus, ipse quamquam et absolutius
pronuntietur, cum secuta tertia
geminae brevique longa adhaeret syllaba.

Anderson was puzzled by this passage. In line 10 the reading *spondam* of the MSS and Semple's explanation of the word must I feel be accepted, though I have suggested emending it to *pompam* ("dignity," "majesty," "ceremonial effect") as preferable to Anderson's conjecture *pondus* ("weight"); if *spondam* is wrong, it might have arisen under the influence of the word *spondeus* which begins line 5. Attention should also be given to the MSS' reading *nunc* before *in extima* in line 11. Sidonius, a competent metrist, is dealing here in the normal way with iambi (iambic feet or metres) and other feet [1] as

[1] Sidonius' list of feet possible in an iambic line is not complete—thus he does not mention the dactyl – ◡ ◡, which in places could come instead of an iambus.

units—see his correct statement in lines 8 and 9 that a pyrrhic foot ⏑ ⏑ must come, whenever it is used, at the end of an iambic line, in place of the last iambus ⏑ – in the line. In some other places in an iambic line two short syllables could come by using a regular alternative ⏑ ⏑ for –; but this would not be a pyrrhic foot in place of a whole iambus-foot. I exclude from consideration any groupings of shorts and longs other than such as are substitutes for whole iambus-feet.

We have then Sidonius implying, if our text is right, that an iambic line of six feet may have an anapaest "now in the former part, now in the last (lines 11–12)." This is quite true of such iambic poetry in Greek comedy (Greek tragedy was more restricted) and most Latin iambic poetry, as is clear from old Latin comedy and tragedy, from Cicero in his translations from Greek tragedy, Publilius Syrus in his "sayings," Phaedrus in his fables, Seneca in his tragedies, Petronius in *Sat.* 89, and later writers such as Avienus in *Ora Maritima*; we find not only that an anapaest could come anywhere in the first part of any line, but also that the fifth foot was almost by rule a spondee – – (with no regular option of an iambus ⏑ – as in Greek), and that the first long syllable of this spondee was often resolved into two shorts ⏑ ⏑, producing an anapaest for the fifth foot; that is, in agreement with Sidonius' words, in the latter part of the line. So one may reasonably decide that Sidonius was thinking partly of this second regular place in Latin iambics, though he chose not to give an example in his poem; and he may even have approved of Horace's *Epodes* II. 35 which for special effect has an anapaest for both the first foot and the fifth, as has also Seneca, *Hercules Furens*, 1140 (cf. *Oed.* 796—anapaest in the third and also in the fifth foot). But as I shall indicate, I doubt whether Sidonius did have this in mind, because his fifth foot is always an iambus ⏑ – except in the text of lines 14 and 49 which I call in question (see also the next Additional Note). In this respect his iambics are like Catullus' and some of Horace's and other examples (see next paragraph) rather than those of most Latin composers.

Another point is that the rhythm of line 14, as also that of line 49 (see the next Additional Note), like iambic lines of old Latin, Cicero, Publilius Syrus, Horace, Phaedrus, Petronius,

Avienus and so on, is not as it stands in accordance with the so-called "Porson's law of the final cretic" (– ∪ –) in Greek iambic verse of tragedy (not comedy). This "law" rules that, if the last three syllables – ∪ – or – ∪ ∪ of an iambic line extend over a whole word or whole words, then the syllable preceding this word or words should be short, unless the three-syllabled word-unit is so closely connected, in syntax and meaning, with an immediately preceding monosyllable as to form with that syllable the equivalent of a four-syllabled word. Now, although old Latin poets and others in their freer, more primitive senarii, ignore if they even knew this rule, a different effect is produced by Catullus in his few iambics (IV; XXII, LII) and by iambic lines such as "Virgil's" *Priap.* (*Catalept.*) II; *Catalept.* VI. X; and Sidonius' iambic lines, of which this poem gives the only ones he published, are of this rarer kind of trimeters—neat, clear cut so to speak, rather rapid and with regular run in metre, avoiding spondees. They tend to jump along nimbly. Their exceptional and artificial preference for freer iambic feet automatically "obeys" the final cretic "law."

Look now at Sidonius' poem more closely. Only lines 14 and 49 as they stand read like the older and typical Latin iambic lines. As regards the anapaest ∪ ∪ –, Sidonius of course knew that, in Greek iambics, whereas an anapaest was allowed in place of the first iambic of any iambic line, an anapaest could not, except in comedy and the like, appear anywhere else in a Greek iambic line unless it was necessary so as to allow the admission of some proper name such as Hērmĭŏnē which would otherwise be excluded. Now all the anapaests in Sidonius' poem are substitutes for the first iambus. So it may be argued that he supports and illustrates in this poem no more than the permitted use, according to Greek method in tragedy, of one whole anapaest instead of one whole iambus at the beginning only of any iambic line; and, as Semple reasonably interprets, says that even here the best effect is produced if the long syllable of the anapaest "clings" (*adhaeret*, line 14) in pronunciation to its preceding two shorts by not sharing the anapaest with more than one word. The word *anapaestus* itself in line 12 is an example of this best method; the other examples of this best method are in lines 6, 7, 14, 24, 25, 30, 31, 33, 43, 45, 47, and 53; whereas the

anapaest in lines 8, 17, 18, 23, 29, 36, and 50 is shared with more than one word.

Are we then to alter the text of lines 11–14? I am inclined to believe so. The words *nunc in extima* (line 11) "now in the last part" are not illustrated in this poem. *extima* means "outermost" and implies "furthermost" and should refer here to the end of the line where an anapaest for an iambus was allowed neither in Greek nor in Latin iambic lines; even if *extima* means here simply "further part" in contrast with "former part," anapaest for iambus was not allowed except in comedy, at the end of Greek iambic lines, though it was in Latin. Yet *extima* looks right. It is perhaps *nunc* that is wrong. I thought of *nunquam* or *numquam*; and this or *non* was suggested by Semple long ago; so that Sidonius reasonably advised using in an iambic line an anapaest in the first part only (*modo* in this sense), never (*nunquam*) in the latter part; and illustrates this procedure in this poem itself where every anapaest used comes as the first foot of a line. The error *nunc*, if it is an error, in the transmission of the text could well have arisen through the common habit of the Romans in iambic lines (see below), and the influence of *modo* taken in the sense of "now" ("at one time ...") which could cause some abbreviation of *-quam* in *nunquam,* so producing *nunc.* If Sidonius had really meant to put "now in the former part, now in the latter," he could easily have written *nunc . . . nunc,* though *modo . . . nunc* means the same. It is remotely possible that *extima* "outermost" refers to the first foot of the line; and that we might read *nonne* ("only in the former part, in the outermost portion of it [i.e. the former part], don't you agree?") or *et hic* ("and here") instead of *nunc.*

Lastly, in view of the endings of all the other lines of the poem except line 49, I suggest in line 14 *geminaeque ahhaeret longa syllaba et brevi* "clings closely to a syllable which is both a twin and short."

IX. 15. *carm.* 49: *rotas Maronis arte sectans compari.* The reading here perhaps need not be questioned despite *artexate* of *C.* But like 14 it has a spondee for the fifth foot and conforms to the typical Latin "senarian" method rather than the Catullan style (see the preceding Additional Note).

Now, this effect could be avoided by a change of no more than the order of words so as to read:

sectans rotas Maronis arte compari

or, keeping the caesura in the same place as in all the other lines of this poem:

sectans Maronis arte compari rotas

or even:

Maronis arte compari sectans rotas

though, as indicated already, Sidonius seems to avoid a long syllable as fourth from the end of any line.

But I have another possible objection to *arte sectans.* This objection is the participle in *sectans* in line 49 coming after *Homericaeque* in line 48, where the reading seems indisputable. One should not prefix " and " to any participial clause unless more than one such clause is involved. Here in line 49 another subjunctive like that in *lacessat* in line 47 seems to be wanted. So, if it is simply *arte sectans* which is wrong, one might suggest instead the subjunctive *stringat* (" such . . . that he grazes ") *arte* or *signet* (" marks ") *arte;* not *Maronis arte sectet* or *M. sectet arte* (see below). Sidonius would have been quite capable of publishing *artet* (" presses in," " confines," " pushes against ") *arte*, with shocking word-play. But to suggest this provides another case (see p. 611) of that doubtful logic whereby one reasons that, because any person did something at some former time, he or she did it now also. *rotas Maronis arte sectet compari* (with the same rhythm as *arte sectans compari*) or *rotas M. sectet arte compari* looks possible. But, although Sidonius uses the past participle of the deponent verb *sector* as a passive (*Ep.* V. 2. 1 *sectatae philosophiae* where Luetjohann's suggestion *secretae* is needless; VII. 9. 9 *sectatae anachoreseos*, where *secretae*, not there suggested by Luetjohann, would fit well), it would be rash to assume as correct *sectet* as if from *secto*, in spite of a passive *sectari* in Varro, *R. Rust.* II. 9. 6. I keep *arte sectans* with Anderson.

E. H. W.

INDEX OF NAMES

Ep. = Epistles (Letters). C. = Carmina (Poems). Roman figures in small type refer to pages of the introduction in Volume I.

INDEX OF NAMES

INDEX OF NAMES

INDEX OF NAMES

INDEX OF NAMES

INDEX OF NAMES

INDEX OF NAMES

INDEX OF NAMES

INDEX OF NAMES

Printed in Great Britain
by Richard Clay (The Chaucer Press), Ltd.,
Bungay, Suffolk

THE LOEB CLASSICAL LIBRARY

VOLUMES ALREADY PUBLISHED

Latin Authors

AMMIANUS MARCELLINUS. Translated by J. C. Rolfe. 3 Vols.

APULEIUS: THE GOLDEN ASS (METAMORPHOSES). W. Adlington (1566). Revised by S. Gaselee.

ST. AUGUSTINE: CITY OF GOD. 7 Vols. Vol. I. G. E. McCracken. Vols. II and VII. W. M. Green. Vol. III. D. Wiesen. Vol. IV. P. Levine. Vol. V. E. M. Sanford and W. M. Green. Vol. VI. W. C. Greene.

ST. AUGUSTINE, CONFESSIONS OF. W. Watts (1631). 2 Vols.

ST. AUGUSTINE, SELECT LETTERS. J. H. Baxter.

AUSONIUS. H. G. Evelyn White. 2 Vols.

BEDE. J. E. King. 2 Vols.

BOETHIUS: TRACTS and DE CONSOLATIONE PHILOSOPHIAE. Rev. H. F. Stewart and E. K. Rand. Revised by S. J. Tester.

CAESAR: ALEXANDRIAN, AFRICAN and SPANISH WARS. A. G. Way.

CAESAR: CIVIL WARS. A. G. Peskett.

CAESAR: GALLIC WAR. H. J. Edwards.

CATO: DE RE RUSTICA. VARRO: DE RE RUSTICA. H. B. Ash and W. D. Hooper.

CATULLUS. F. W. Cornish. TIBULLUS. J. B. Postgate. PERVIGILIUM VENERIS. J. W. Mackail.

CELSUS: DE MEDICINA. W. G. Spencer. 3 Vols.

CICERO: BRUTUS and ORATOR. G. L. Hendrickson and H. M. Hubbell.

[CICERO]: AD HERENNIUM. H. Caplan.

CICERO: DE ORATORE, etc. 2 Vols. Vol. I. DE ORATORE, Books I and II. E. W. Sutton and H. Rackham. Vol. II. DE ORATORE, Book III. DE FATO; PARADOXA STOICORUM; DE PARTITIONE ORATORIA. H. Rackham.

CICERO: DE FINIBUS. H. Rackham.

CICERO: DE INVENTIONE, etc. H. M. Hubbell.

CICERO: DE NATURA DEORUM and ACADEMICA. H. Rackham.

CICERO: DE OFFICIIS. Walter Miller.

CICERO: DE REPUBLICA and DE LEGIBUS. Clinton W. Keyes.

CICERO: DE SENECTUTE, DE AMICITIA, DE DIVINATIONE. W. A. Falconer.

CICERO: IN CATILINAM, PRO FLACCO, PRO MURENA, PRO SULLA. New version by C. Macdonald.

CICERO: LETTERS TO ATTICUS. E. O. Winstedt. 3 Vols.

CICERO: LETTERS TO HIS FRIENDS. W. Glynn Williams, M. Cary, M. Henderson. 4 Vols.

CICERO: PHILIPPICS. W. C. A. Ker.

CICERO: PRO ARCHIA, POST REDITUM, DE DOMO, DE HARUSPICUM RESPONSIS, PRO PLANCIO. N. H. Watts.

CICERO: PRO CAECINA, PRO LEGE MANILIA, PRO CLUENTIO, PRO RABIRIO. H. Grose Hodge.

CICERO: PRO CAELIO, DE PROVINCIIS CONSULARIBUS, PRO BALBO. R. Gardner.

CICERO: PRO MILONE, IN PISONEM, PRO SCAURO, PRO FONTEIO, PRO RABIRIO POSTUMO, PRO MARCELLO, PRO LIGARIO, PRO REGE DEIOTARO. N. H. Watts.

CICERO: PRO QUINCTIO, PRO ROSCIO AMERINO, PRO ROSCIO COMOEDO, CONTRA RULLUM. J. H. Freese.

CICERO: PRO SESTIO, IN VATINIUM. R. Gardner.

CICERO: TUSCULAN DISPUTATIONS. J. E. King.

CICERO: VERRINE ORATIONS. L. H. G. Greenwood. 2 Vols.

CLAUDIAN. M. Platnauer. 2 Vols.

COLUMELLA: DE RE RUSTICA. DE ARBORIBUS. H. B. Ash, E. S. Forster and E. Heffner. 3 Vols.

CURTIUS, Q.: HISTORY OF ALEXANDER. J. C. Rolfe. 2 Vols.

FLORUS. E. S. Forster.

FRONTINUS: STRATAGEMS and AQUEDUCTS. C. E. Bennett and M. B. McElwain.

FRONTO: CORRESPONDENCE. C. R. Haines. 2 Vols.

GELLIUS. J. C. Rolfe. 3 Vols.

HORACE: ODES and EPODES. C. E. Bennett.

HORACE: SATIRES, EPISTLES, ARS POETICA. H. R. Fairclough.

JEROME: SELECTED LETTERS. F. A. Wright.

JUVENAL and PERSIUS. G. G. Ramsay.

LIVY. B. O. Foster, F. G. Moore, Evan T. Sage, and A. C. Schlesinger and R. M. Geer (General Index). 14 Vols.

LUCAN. J. D. Duff.

LUCRETIUS. W. H. D. Rouse. Revised by M. F. Smith.

MANILIUS. G. P. Goold.

MARTIAL. W. C. A. Ker. 2 Vols. Revised by E. H. Warmington.

MINOR LATIN POETS: from PUBLILIUS SYRUS to RUTILIUS NAMATIANUS, including GRATTIUS, CALPURNIUS SICULUS, NEMESIANUS, AVIANUS and others, with "Aetna" and the "Phoenix." J. Wight Duff and Arnold M. Duff. 2 Vols.

MINUCIUS FELIX. Cf. TERTULLIAN.

NEPOS CORNELIUS. J. C. Rolfe.

OVID: THE ART OF LOVE and OTHER POEMS. J. H. Mosley. Revised by G. P. Goold.

OVID: FASTI. Sir James G. Frazer

OVID: HEROIDES and AMORES. Grant Showerman. Revised by G. P. Goold

OVID: METAMORPHOSES. F. J. Miller. 2 Vols. Revised by G. P. Goold.

OVID: TRISTIA and EX PONTO. A. L. Wheeler.

PERSIUS. Cf. JUVENAL.

PERVIGILIUM VENERIS. Cf. CATULLUS.

PETRONIUS. M. Heseltine. SENECA: APOCOLOCYNTOSIS. W. H. D. Rouse. Revised by E. H. Warmington.

PHAEDRUS and BABRIUS (Greek). B. E. Perry.

PLAUTUS. Paul Nixon. 5 Vols.

PLINY: LETTERS, PANEGYRICUS. Betty Radice. 2 Vols.

PLINY: NATURAL HISTORY. 10 Vols. Vols. I–V and IX. H. Rackham. VI.–VIII. W. H. S. Jones. X. D. E. Eichholz.

PROPERTIUS. H. E. Butler.

PRUDENTIUS. H. J. Thomson. 2 Vols.

QUINTILIAN. H. E. Butler. 4 Vols.

REMAINS OF OLD LATIN. E. H. Warmington. 4 Vols. Vol. I. (ENNIUS AND CAECILIUS) Vol. II. (LIVIUS, NAEVIUS PACUVIUS, ACCIUS) Vol. III. (LUCILIUS and LAWS OF XII TABLES) Vol. IV. (ARCHAIC INSCRIPTIONS)

RES GESTAE DIVI AUGUSTI. Cf. VELLEIUS PATERCULUS.

SALLUST. J. C. Rolfe.

SCRIPTORES HISTORIAE AUGUSTAE. D. Magie. 3 Vols.

SENECA, THE ELDER: CONTROVERSIAE, SUASORIAE. M. Winterbottom. 2 Vols.

SENECA: APOCOLOCYNTOSIS. Cf. PETRONIUS.

SENECA: EPISTULAE MORALES. R. M. Gummere. 3 Vols.

SENECA: MORAL ESSAYS. J. W. Basore. 3 Vols.

SENECA: TRAGEDIES. F. J. Miller. 2 Vols.

SENECA: NATURALES QUAESTIONES. T. H. Corcoran. 2 Vols.

SIDONIUS: POEMS and LETTERS. W. B. Anderson. 2 Vols.

SILIUS ITALICUS. J. D. Duff. 2 Vols.

STATIUS. J. H. Mozley. 2 Vols.

SUETONIUS. J. C. Rolfe. 2 Vols.

TACITUS: DIALOGUS. Sir Wm. Peterson. AGRICOLA and GERMANIA. Maurice Hutton. Revised by M. Winterbottom, R. M. Ogilvie, E. H. Warmington.

TACITUS: HISTORIES and ANNALS. C. H. Moore and J. Jackson. 4 Vols.

TERENCE. John Sargeaunt. 2 Vols.

TERTULLIAN: APOLOGIA and DE SPECTACULIS. T. R. Glover. MINUCIUS FELIX. G. H. Rendall.

TIBULLUS. Cf. CATULLUS.

VALERIUS FLACCUS. J. H. Mozley.

VARRO: DE LINGUA LATINA. R. G. Kent. 2 Vols.

VELLEIUS PATERCULUS and RES GESTAE DIVI AUGUSTI. F. W. Shipley.

VIRGIL. H. R. Fairclough. 2 Vols.

VITRUVIUS: DE ARCHITECTURA. F. Granger. 2 Vols.

Greek Authors

ACHILLES TATIUS. S. Gaselee.

AELIAN: ON THE NATURE OF ANIMALS. A. F. Scholfield. 3 Vols.

AENEAS TACTICUS. ASCLEPIODOTUS and ONASANDER. The Illinois Greek Club.

AESCHINES. C. D. Adams.

AESCHYLUS. H. Weir Smyth. 2 Vols.

ALCIPHRON, AELIAN, PHILOSTRATUS: LETTERS. A. R. Benner and F. H. Fobes.

ANDOCIDES, ANTIPHON. Cf. MINOR ATTIC ORATORS.

APOLLODORUS. Sir James G. Frazer. 2 Vols.

APOLLONIUS RHODIUS. R. C. Seaton.

APOSTOLIC FATHERS. Kirsopp Lake. 2 Vols.

APPIAN: ROMAN HISTORY. Horace White. 4 Vols.

ARATUS. Cf. CALLIMACHUS.

ARISTIDES: ORATIONS. C. A. Behr. Vol. I.

ARISTOPHANES. Benjamin Bickley Rogers. 3 Vols. Verse trans.

ARISTOTLE: ART OF RHETORIC. J. H. Freese.

ARISTOTLE: ATHENIAN CONSTITUTION, EUDEMIAN ETHICS, VICES AND VIRTUES. H. Rackham.

ARISTOTLE: GENERATION OF ANIMALS. A. L. Peck.

ARISTOTLE: HISTORIA ANIMALIUM. A. L. Peck. Vols. I.–II.

ARISTOTLE: METAPHYSICS. H. Tredennick. 2 Vols.

ARISTOTLE: METEOROLOGICA. H. D. P. Lee.

ARISTOTLE: MINOR WORKS. W. S. Hett. On Colours, On Things Heard, On Physiognomies, On Plants, On Marvellous Things Heard, Mechanical Problems, On Indivisible Lines, On Situations and Names of Winds, On Melissus, Xenophanes, and Gorgias.

ARISTOTLE: NICOMACHEAN ETHICS. H. Rackham.

Aristotle: Oeconomica and Magna Moralia. G. C. Armstrong (with Metaphysics, Vol. II).

Aristotle: On the Heavens. W. K. C. Guthrie.

Aristotle: On the Soul, Parva Naturalia, On Breath. W. S. Hett.

Aristotle: Categories, On Interpretation, Prior Analytics. H. P. Cooke and H. Tredennick.

Aristotle: Posterior Analytics, Topics. H. Tredennick and E. S. Forster.

Aristotle: On Sophistical Refutations.
On Coming to be and Passing Away, On the Cosmos. E. S. Forster and D. J. Furley.

Aristotle: Parts of Animals. A. L. Peck; Motion and Progression of Animals. E. S. Forster.

Aristotle: Physics. Rev. P. Wicksteed and F. M. Cornford. 2 Vols.

Aristotle: Poetics and Longinus. W. Hamilton Fyfe; Demetrius on Style. W. Rhys Roberts.

Aristotle: Politics. H. Rackham.

Aristotle: Problems. W. S. Hett. 2 Vols.

Aristotle: Rhetorica Ad Alexandrum (with Problems. Vol. II). H. Rackham.

Arrian: History of Alexander and Indica. Rev. E. Iliffe Robson. 2 Vols. New version P. Brunt.

Athenaeus: Deipnosophistae. C. B. Gulick. 7 Vols.

Babrius and Phaedrus (Latin). B. E. Perry.

St. Basil: Letters. R. J. Deferrari. 4 Vols.

Callimachus: Fragments. C. A. Trypanis. Musaeus: Hero and Leander. T. Gelzer and C. Whitman.

Callimachus, Hymns and Epigrams, and Lycophron. A. W. Mair; Aratus. G. R. Mair.

Clement of Alexandria. Rev. G. W. Butterworth.

Colluthus. Cf. Oppian.

Daphnis and Chloe. Thornley's Translation revised by J. M. Edmonds: and Parthenius. S. Gaselee.

Demosthenes I.: Olynthiacs, Philippics and Minor Orations I.–XVII. and XX. J. H. Vince.

Demosthenes II.: De Corona and De Falsa Legatione. C. A. Vince and J. H. Vince.

Demosthenes III.: Meidias, Androtion, Aristocrates, Timocrates and Aristogeiton I. and II. J. H. Vince.

Demosthenes IV.–VI: Private Orations and In Neaeram. A. T. Murray.

Demosthenes VII: Funeral Speech, Erotic Essay, Exordia and Letters. N. W. and N. J. DeWitt.

Dio Cassius: Roman History. E. Cary. 9 Vols.

Dio Chrysostom. J. W. Cohoon and H. Lamar Crosby. 5 Vols.

Diodorus Siculus. 12 Vols. Vols. I.–VI. C. H. Oldfather. Vol. VII. C. L. Sherman. Vol. VIII. C. B. Welles. Vols. IX. and X. R. M. Geer. Vol. XI. F. Walton. Vol. XII. F. Walton. General Index. R. M. Geer.

Diogenes Laertius. R. D. Hicks. 2 Vols. New Introduction by H. S. Long.

Dionysius of Halicarnassus: Roman Antiquities. Spelman's translation revised by E. Cary. 7 Vols.

Dionysius of Halicarnassus: Critical Essays. S. Usher. 2 Vols. Vol. I.

Epictetus. W. A. Oldfather. 2 Vols.

Euripides. A. S. Way. 4 Vols. Verse trans.

Eusebius: Ecclesiastical History. Kirsopp Lake and J. E. L. Oulton. 2 Vols.

Galen: On the Natural Faculties. A. J. Brock.

Greek Anthology. W. R. Paton. 5 Vols.

Greek Bucolic Poets (Theocritus, Bion, Moschus). J. M. Edmonds.

Greek Elegy and Iambus with the Anacreontea. J. M. Edmonds. 2 Vols.

Greek Lyric. D. A. Campbell. 4 Vols. Vol. I.

Greek Mathematical Works. Ivor Thomas. 2 Vols.

Herodes. Cf. Theophrastus: Characters.

Herodian. C. R. Whittaker. 2 Vols.

Herodotus. A. D. Godley. 4 Vols.

Hesiod and The Homeric Hymns. H. G. Evelyn White.

Hippocrates and the Fragments of Heracleitus. W. H. S. Jones and E. T. Withington. 4 Vols.

Homer: Iliad. A. T. Murray. 2 Vols.

Homer: Odyssey. A. T. Murray. 2 Vols.

Isaeus. E. W. Forster.

Isocrates. George Norlin and LaRue Van Hook. 3 Vols.

[St. John Damascene]: Barlaam and Ioasaph. Rev. G. R. Woodward, Harold Mattingly and D. M. Lang.

Josephus. 10 Vols. Vols. I.–IV. H. Thackeray. Vol. V. H. Thackeray and R. Marcus. Vols. VI.–VII. R. Marcus. Vol. VIII. R. Marcus and Allen Wikgren. Vols. IX.–X. L. H. Feldman.

Julian. Wilmer Cave Wright. 3 Vols.

Libanius. A. F. Norman. 3 Vols. Vols. I.–II.

Lucian. 8 Vols. Vols. I.–V. A. M. Harmon. Vol. VI. K. Kilburn. Vols. VII.–VIII. M. D. Macleod.

Lycophron. Cf. Callimachus.

Lyra Graeca, J. M. Edmonds. 2 Vols.

Lysias. W. R. M. Lamb.

Manetho. W. G. Waddell.

Marcus Aurelius. C. R. Haines.

Menander. W. G. Arnott. 3 Vols. Vol. I.

Minor Attic Orators (Antiphon, Andocides, Lycurgus, Demades, Dinarchus, Hyperides). K. J. Maidment and J. O. Burtt. 2 Vols.

Musaeus: Hero and Leander. Cf. Callimachus.

Nonnos: Dionysiaca. W. H. D. Rouse. 3 Vols.

Oppian, Colluthus, Tryphiodorus. A. W. Mair.

Papyri. Non-Literary Selections. A. S. Hunt and C. C. Edgar. 2 Vols. Literary Selections (Poetry). D. L. Page.

Parthenius. Cf. Daphnis and Chloe.

Pausanias: Description of Greece. W. H. S. Jones. 4 Vols. and Companion Vol. arranged by R. E. Wycherley.

Philo. 10 Vols. Vols. I.–V. F. H. Colson and Rev. G. H. Whitaker. Vols. VI.–IX. F. H. Colson. Vol. X. F. H. Colson and the Rev. J. W. Earp.

Philo: two supplementary Vols. (*Translation only.*) Ralph Marcus.

Philostratus: The Life of Apollonius of Tyana. F. C. Conybeare. 2 Vols.

Philostratus: Imagines; Callistratus: Descriptions. A. Fairbanks.

Philostratus and Eunapius: Lives of the Sophists. Wilmer Cave Wright.

Pindar. Sir J. E. Sandys.

Plato: Charmides, Alcibiades, Hipparchus, The Lovers, Theages, Minos and Epinomis. W. R. M. Lamb.

Plato: Cratylus, Parmenides, Greater Hippias, Lesser Hippias. H. N. Fowler.

Plato: Euthyphro, Apology, Crito, Phaedo, Phaedrus, H. N. Fowler.

Plato: Laches, Protagoras, Meno, Euthydemus. W. R. M. Lamb.

Plato: Laws. Rev. R. G. Bury. 2 Vols.

Plato: Lysis, Symposium, Gorgias. W. R. M. Lamb.

Plato: Republic. Paul Shorey. 2 Vols.

Plato: Statesman, Philebus. H. N. Fowler; Ion. W. R. M. Lamb.

Plato: Theaetetus and Sophist. H. N. Fowler.

Plato: Timaeus, Critias, Clitopho, Menexenus, Epistulae. Rev. R. G. Bury.

Plotinus: A. H. Armstrong. 7 Vols. Vols. I.–V.

Plutarch: Moralia. 16 Vols. Vols I.–V. F. C. Babbitt. Vol. VI. W. C. Helmbold. Vols. VII. and XIV. P. H. De Lacy and B. Einarson. Vol. VIII. P. A. Clement and H. B. Hoffleit. Vol. IX. E. L. Minar, Jr., F. H. Sandbach, W. C. Helmbold. Vol. X. H. N. Fowler. Vol. XI. L. Pearson and F. H. Sandbach. Vol. XII. H. Cherniss and W. C. Helmbold. Vol. XIII 1–2. H. Cherniss. Vol. XV. F. H. Sandbach.

Plutarch: The Parallel Lives. B. Perrin. 11 Vols.

Polybius. W. R. Paton. 6 Vols.

Procopius. H. B. Dewing. 7 Vols.

Ptolemy: Tetrabiblos. F. E. Robbins.

Quintus Smyrnaeus. A. S. Way. Verse trans.

Sextus Empiricus. Rev. R. G. Bury. 4 Vols.

Sophocles. F. Storr. 2 Vols. Verse trans.

Strabo: Geography. Horace L. Jones. 8 Vols.

Theocritus. Cf. Greek Bucolic Poets.

Theophrastus: Characters. J. M. Edmonds. Herodes, etc. A. D. Knox.

Theophrastus: Enquiry into Plants. Sir Arthur Hort, Bart. 2 Vols.

Theophrastus: De Causis Plantarum. G. K. K. Link and B. Einarson. 3 Vols. Vol. I.

Thucydides. C. F. Smith. 4 Vols.

Tryphiodorus. Cf. Oppian.

Xenophon: Cyropaedia. Walter Miller. 2 Vols.

Xenophon: Hellencia. C. L. Brownson. 2 Vols.

Xenophon: Anabasis. C. L. Brownson.

Xenophon: Memorabilia and Oeconomicus. E. C. Marchant. Symposium and Apology. O. J. Todd.

Xenophon: Scripta Minora. E. C. Marchant. Constitution of the athenians. G. W. Bowersock.